Emmet Connor

Red Pandemic:
The Global Marxist Cult

OMNIA VERITAS®

Emmet Connor

Emmet Connor is an Irish author and Youtuber. His work focuses on subjects including patriotism, ideology, indoctrination, globalism, current affairs, and geopolitics. In his first book – *Red Pandemic: The Global Marxist Cult* – Connor exposes the source of all the crazy revolutionary activism in the world today – the ideology of Marxism – highlighting its unrivaled toxic impact on world affairs and humanity in general.

RED PANDEMIC:
The Global Marxist Cult

Published by
OMNIA VERITAS LTD
ⓄMNIA VERITAS.
www.omnia-veritas.com

© Omnia Veritas Limited – Emmet Connor – 2024

This work is dedicated to the hundreds of millions of people (and counting) who've had to endure 'revolutionary', 'progressive', or 'activist' irritation, inconvenience, judgement, ostracisation, harassment, intimidation, property damage, assault, torture, rape, forced suicide, murder and genocide throughout the history of Marxism; and to all genuine lovers of truth, freedom, and justice, whomever you are, and wherever you may be in this infected world.

"(religion) Marxism is the sigh of the oppressed creature, the heart of a heartless world, and the soul of our soulless conditions. It is the opium of the people"

KarlMarx

"My people are destroyed for lack of knowledge"

Hosea 4:6

"When there's no more room in hell, the dead will walk the Earth"

Peter Washington, Dawn of the Dead, 1978

Red Pandemic: The Global Marxist Cult—Table of Contents

PREFACE

We can see that the world has been undergoing profound, extraordinary changes in recent times. We have also seen that these colossal changes are not merely circumstantial, or the result of some sort of organic societal evolution, or other factors beyond humanity's control; but changes that have been encouraged and supported by certain motivated movements, organisations, and individuals.

In 2020 we saw the Covid Pandemic became a universally live-changing event; a situation that impacted virtually the population of the whole world. The Black Lives Matter protests and riots of the same year dominated the headlines in the Western world, creating repercussions in many countries, though most intensely (and predictably) in the U.S. We've seen the Climate alarmist movement gain even more momentum; we've been told that 'going green' is so crucial, that if it's not achieved, will lead to inevitable global catastrophe unless immediate action is taken. This seemingly applies even in countries whose CO2 output is comparatively infinitesimal in the global scheme of things, such as Ireland.

We have seen massive changes being pushed in matters of sex, sexuality, gender, and relationships; and not just involving adults, but, bizarrely, adolescents and children. There has been an intensification of the LGBTQ movement, and the proliferation of 'trans rights' organisations. The so-called *Pride* marches have been a regular feature on the streets of many of the world's cities.

We have also seen a disturbing emphasis on the issue of paedophilia from some quarters; and not a hardening on the issue (as any reasonable person would subscribe to) but actually a softening; a 'normalisation'. It's strange that something which has been previously regarded by many as a mental illness or just downright evil, is now being suggested by some as being basically just another form of sexual orientation.

Mass migration has been a very divisive and impactful issue worldwide; in Europe in particular. However, it has not been a two-way street: it is overwhelmingly the mass movement of people mostly from third-world areas in to generally more prosperous, stable, and civilised Western countries. This was sometimes packaged as being a reasonable, natural organic movement of large amounts of people from one area to another, yet it is encouraged, promoted, co-ordinated, and justified by the establishment at a national level (and also by international conglomerate organisations such as the United Nations and the European Union). It has also been packaged as a movement of refugees from war-torn areas, but this is clearly untrue for the majority of the masses, considering the sheer numbers and (non-war-torn) countries of origin in question; others reasonably retort that these are economic migrants, coming for a better life in the West. There has also been an increase in anti-white rhetoric. At first glance, it's most apparent in the U.S., thanks to the English-speaking West's interest in American affairs, but this racist rhetoric is also present in other parts of the world in varying degrees.

Some countries are undergoing changes more drastically than others. Ireland, a country that is relatively geographically-isolated compared to the rest of Europe–and previously regarded as being Christian Catholic and traditional to a degree–has seen change at an alarming rate: between 2015 and 2018, there were noticeable constitutional referenda to change the law on gay marriage and abortion; and the changes are still coming. Considering the speed at which that country is being transformed, it's almost as if it's being forced to 'catch-up' with others, as it was not becoming 'progressive' quickly enough..

Looking at world events, we could merely say that not everyone agrees with these changes, but this is a massive understatement. Indeed, there's a growing movement of individuals from all over the world who are objecting to–or actively opposing–this global 'revolution'. In fact, once we put all the distractions to one side, we can see that what's transpiring is nothing less than conflict: between those who welcome these colossal changes—this 'revolution'—and those who do not.

That most primary question of "why?" must be asked: why are these changes happening? And why are they happening now in this time, and in relatively quick succession? Why so much revolutionary activist mentality? Why so many divisions between different groups and in society in general? Why are so many of these groups claiming oppression of some kind? Why do we hear all this talk of social justice?

Why is it that, often, whenever you want to express an opinion that is not 'politically correct' in public, you expect immediate contradiction, almost by default? Why is it that, eventually, even the mere thought of expressing an idea like this can often make one uncomfortable? Why does political correctness now seem to be a cornerstone of society that our behaviours must comply with? Why can non-compliance often result in dire consequences for those who contradict this status quo?

Why are we seeing an intensification of the phenomenon of virtue-signalling? Why is this behaviour the go-to behaviour of anyone in a position of influence in our world? Why are we observing it to a nauseating degree and frequency? Are those who engage in virtue-signalling actually exceptional human beings (as they would like us to believe), or are there other reasons why they are behaving like this?

Why is it that the state apparatus' in Western countries insist that we engage in pathological altruism, and try to save the world at the expense of our owns countries and populations? Why have they been constantly re-injecting this message in to the psyche of the masses? Why are we told that Western countries have an obligation to accept a never-ending stream of migrants, even though our governments cannot even manage our countries with population levels as they are?

Why is it that countries like Sweden and Germany—who are at a much more advanced and catastrophic stage of migration saturation – have still been obliged to import them, despite these countries now being in dire straits? Why does this suicidal behaviour continue regardless of the obvious results? Why this extreme dominance of emotions over logic?

Why is it that the Mainstream Media in western countries constantly show us how wonderful 'multiculturalism' is and regularly feature foreigners who have 'integrated' into our societies; yet the almost systematic assault, rape and murder of indigenous Europeans daily by migrants hardly makes the news?

Conversely, why is it that the killing or shooting of gang members, dangerous junkies and other criminals are now held-aloft by the mainstream-media as horrific crimes against humanity, if they are not white? Why is it that we are regularly reminded of the suffering of non-white people in Africa or the Middle East, yet government-approved discrimination and violence towards white people in South Africa is ignored? Why are we being told in Western countries to care for and respect other groups, but this attitude is not generally reciprocated? Why these double standards? Where does this blatant, racist, disregard for white people come from? Why, if you raise these points, will you be contradictorily (and bizarrely) labelled a racist?

Why, despite the numerous, genuine on-going problems and evils in our world, are we being incessantly told that racism is one of the worst, if not the worst?

Why is it that when criminal George Floyd is killed in the U.S. by a white police officer, it's cause for the whole world to take a knee? Who (or what) is making the decision which incidents the world should be made aware of and get upset over? Why, in a world where there is a death every few seconds, are some being emphasised in this way?

Why are our governments and institutions spending time, energy, and resources on bizarre, perverted initiatives such as the 'sexual education' of our young? Why their almost predatorial and forceful attitude when doing this? Why do we hear things like 'queer theory', and 'heteronormativity'? Why the recent phenomenon of males and females saying that they are 'gender non-binary', believing that they are neither male nor female? Where are all the experts explaining that this is impossible? Why is there a forceful insistence by some governments that children, who want to have 'sexual re-assignment' surgeries, should not have to consult their parents before having their bodies altered, their genitalia butchered, and ending up sterile? Why are we being told that we must call a person who is clearly male a "she"? Or a person who is clearly female a "he"? Why must we call others by the pronouns "they" or "them? Why are parents and teachers getting in trouble for calling the young by the (apparently) wrong term?

Why are subjects that should be emphasised more in schools such as history, national culture, and indigenous languages, now marginalised or neglected entirely in favour of more 'progressive' subjects? Why are our children being encouraged to become publicly active quasi-political revolutionaries and involve themselves in issues such as climate change, when they are barely old enough to tie their own shoelaces? Why are we being told that young boys need to be educated not to rape girls, to combat something called "Rape Culture"? Why do we see the weird, inappropriate practice of "Drag-Queen Story Time"? What is this supposed to achieve? What knowledge, qualifications, or life-skills do drag-queens possess that is of benefit to our children exactly? Does trying to appear like a woman (if you are a man) require knowledge or skill? Of all the brilliant men and women in the world who could be presented as role models to our children, why these odd, unremarkable characters?

Why is it that open criticism and state-approved marginalisation of Christianity is permitted, but criticism of other religious denominations is not allowed? Why is it that furthermore, as is the case with Islam, a non-Christian denomination can be actively promoted and supported by the state? Why this double standard, particularly in a time where the notion of equality is sacrosanct? Why have we seen white, non-Muslim political figures all across the West speaking and acting in fake 'solidarity' with Islam and Muslims? Why is it that any criticism of Judaism or Jews is considered condemnable and 'anti-Semitic', yet criticism of Christianity and Christians is not only permitted, but encouraged and fashionable? Why this bias?

Why is it that we constantly hear terms like "equality", "diversity", "multiculturalism", "compassion", and "solidarity"; and they are always emphasised as being positive? Why are they continuously being chanted like the mutterings of a cult? Why do we hear an almost never-ending list of terms, conversely, that are used as slurs, such as: "homophobe; misogynist; xenophobe; Islamophobe; transphobe; racist; climate change denier; anti-vaxxer; conspiracy theorist; fascist; Nazi" etc.? Why do we hear terms like "vaccine hesitancy" spring up when the Covid vaccine appeared on the scene?

Why do we hear all this talk of "hate-speech"? Why do we hear people using the word "hate" when referring to criticism? Why is it being used to dismiss criticism out of hand? And what kind of criticism is it being used to dismiss/neutralise exactly? All kinds, or only certain kinds?

Why do we hear all these people talking about being 'oppressed', or talking about the 'oppression' of others? Why all the emphasis on identity politics? Why do we often hear so many organisations, politicians, and media talk about the 'far-right'? Why do we hear other terms to describe certain concepts, such as 'victim blaming' and 'slut shaming'? Why do we hear things like 'toxic masculinity' but not 'toxic femininity'? Why do we hear things like 'man-splaining' but not 'woman-splaining'? Why do we hear things like 'white privilege' or 'male privilege', but not 'black privilege' or 'Asian privilege'; or 'female privilege'? Is it because only white males have all the 'privilege'? Are white males privileged, but Black or Asian people or women are not? Or is there another reason why we are hearing these unequal, double-standards in terms? Why do we hear terms like 'Critical Race Theory', 'Cultural Relativism', and 'Moral Relativism'? Where are all these relatively new terms coming from?

Why does it seem, in the last few decades, like the world is filling up with revolutionary activists? Why are many of them associated with universities somehow, or are students themselves? In the U.S. during the Black Lives Matter unrest, why is it that these student activists are so fanatical to the point where they will get themselves hurt or run over by vehicles? What has them so willing to get themselves maimed or killed? Why are these activists, many of them kids, so completely possessed with this revolutionary energy and detached from reality? Why do they seem so intensely brainwashed? Why is it that the U.S. was plunged in to such violent unrest on such a large scale over the death of one person, when people die there all the time? (as they tend to do in other countries also). Why is it that ordinary, everyday people are forced to get out on to the streets and deal with these 'revolutionary' mobs? Why are these people forced to do the job that the police/state forces are (in many cases) refusing to do, to stop these aggressive mobs from destroying their homes and businesses? Why do these 'revolutionaries' attack these ordinary, everyday people as if they are the problem, when it fact, they themselves are the problem? How can they have it so completely backwards?

Why is it that the worldwide patriot movement – which is opposed to international totalitarianism/'globalism' – is harassed by these 'revolutionary' or 'rebel' groups, who, by default, are serving the system they say they are opposed to? How is it that they (seemingly contradictorily) now serve and protect the system? Again, how can they have things so upside down? Why the inversion?

Why are all these 'revolutionary' activists basically identical, as if they all rolled-off the same production line at a factory? Why do the ones in Canada seemingly think the same as the ones in Australia? Why do the ones in the U.S. use the same terminology and catch-phrases as the ones in Ireland? Why do the ones in New Zealand act the same as the ones in Sweden? Whether you are in Toronto or Tokyo, Perth or Portland, London or Los Angeles, Stockholm or Stanley, Dublin or Dubai, Cape Town or Canberra, Amsterdam or Aberdeen, Seattle or Seville, Paris or Prague, Moscow or Monaco, Rome or Reykjavik, San Paulo or San Francisco, Santiago or San Jose, Edmonton or Edinburgh, Berlin or Beijing, Buenos Aires or Bangkok, New York or New Delhi, Chicago or Shanghai, Washington or Wellington, Helsinki or Hell's Kitchen—why are these people all virtually identical in their attitudes, behaviour, and speech?

How can this be, despite all the varieties of locations, languages, and cultures? Why are they so un-diverse? Why do they all have the same views, and promote the same agendas? Why do they all call people who don't agree with them "racists", "fascists", and "Nazis" etc. and with the same level of animosity?

Why is it that the mainstream media in Ireland is behaving the same way, more or less, as it is in other western countries? Why are the mainstream media in the UK, Canada, Australia, France, Spain, Italy, Germany, Sweden etc. behaving in a very similar fashion, albeit with slight variations? Why are they all more-or-less singing from the same hymn sheet?

Why is it that a person can happily tweet/post/publish the most degenerate, dumb things as long as they conform with political correctness, yet if they criticise 'PC culture' with venom, these opinions may be suppressed? Why is it that some are banned online, while others are not? Who decides what is right and what is wrong in this case, and what is their reasoning? Why are some opinions permitted, yet others are suppressed, and what types of opinions are they?

Why is it that there is a state-sponsored emphasis on 'mental health' in society right now, yet we have the enormous, global, mental health problem of indoctrination coming from the same system? Why do we have this problem of rampant, mass-psychopathy in the world right now which the overwhelming majority of 'experts' never address?

Why do all of these 'politically correct' terms/concepts/agendas seem to dominate the political, social, cultural, educational, and media discourse in recent decades, and with an alarming rise of saturation in those areas? Why is it that we cannot even look at a newspaper, or turn on the TV or radio without being constantly reminded of them? These things we apparently must focus on—climate change, social justice, inequality, racism etc. - are they serious issues we should be genuinely concerned about, or are we being told to focus on them for other reasons? Why are all these issues and behaviours manifesting globally and almost simultaneously, as if co-ordinated?

Why does it seem like we are living in this zombie apocalypse, where we have brain-less millions who are unable to form their own opinions and who all think, speak, and act the same way? Why are we experiencing this pandemic of crazy, co-ordinated, civilisation-destroying behaviour, as if we are dealing with a massive global cult?

Introduction

> "Thus heaven I've forfeited, I know it full well. My soul, once true to God, is chosen for hell"
>
> Karl Marx, *Pale Maiden*, 1837[1]

Only one core problem...

The cause of all those changes and problems listed is a global ideological infection called Marxism.

The main problem in your country is not the government or political class, the organs of the state, the police, the United Nations, the European Union, the multinational corporations, the 'Elites', capitalism, the bankers and the international banking system, the 'bourgeoisie', the NGOs/non-profits, George Soros, the main-stream Media, migrants, Muslims, Zionists, the Freemasons, Illuminati etc. etc. The core, root problem in your country (and most others) is that it has an infection of Marxism. You will struggle to find any problematic issue in the world today that is not connected to, influenced by, or originating from, this ideology. Throughout society and the world, the Marxist 'red thread' is there. This core problem in your country exists because the indigenous/normally resident people have (or have had historically) a suicidal lack of hostility towards this toxic, foreign ideology. This is the foundational problem, and all the other listed major problems we are experiencing right now stem from this one.

The word to emphasise here is hostility. As history shows us, any other attitude is inadequate to protect a nation from the damaging effects of this ideology. Any sort of tolerance or compromise towards it is only seen as a sign of weakness, and you will be over-run regardless; any tolerance for its presence is fully taken advantage of. Tolerance for it is, in fact, suicidal for a people and nation. We can see, when we examine society today, that not only is there a lack of hostility towards this anti-sovereignty, internationalist ideology, but a disturbing fascination with it. It has become entrenched in our countries to the point where it has become part of the furniture, so to speak. Due to this entrenchment, politely asking it to leave

---

[1] Marx, M. "Pale Maiden", 1837 ("Young Marx—Writings from Karl Marx before Rheinsche Zeitung", 1975).

simply won't do. Without an extremely tough stance on the subject, removing it in the first place is impossible. Furthermore, without this strong stance, re-infection will re-occur as the ideology will inevitably find the weakest point(s) in society (i.e. certain individuals and groups) and use those to re-assert itself. This has happened many times before in the history of our struggle with this ideology.

"Best of luck…"

To any (reasonably) free people trying to prevent this internationalist 'globalist' machine from destroying their country, I say this: best of luck trying to stop it without first sufficiently dealing with the Marxist infection in your land. Once it's acknowledged and understood by a sufficient number, it needs to be tackled head-on.

Trying to get some real traction with a pro-sovereignty/patriotic/nationalist (call it whatever you like) movement in your land – without first dealing with the Marxism problem – will be extremely difficult. Perhaps no matter how much energy/enthusiasm you give it, you would be merely spinning your wheels.

Perhaps freedom could still be achieved without first dealing with the Marxist infection, but this would be inefficient and would be more time-consuming a process than it needs to be; and is it not true that time is of the essence?

The purpose of this book is not to examine the monotonous dogmatic ins and outs of (official) Marxist theory and all the various interpretations; it would take volumes and would only result in one conclusion anyway—it doesn't deserve this type of analysis. It would be like sifting through a stinking landfill with your bare hands for years looking for trinkets. Besides, what difference would that make? It would have zero effect on those who are already indoctrinated, and for those who are not, it would be like "preaching to the queer" (I'm aware no one actually says that). Having said all that, I am confident that the message of this book will provide tremendous value, clarity, and enjoyment to those with the correct attitude. Those who are able to understand this work, will. It's obviously not aimed at the indoctrinated types, since they already have their minds made-up (or made up for them, to be more precise); it's aimed towards those who are keen to put a stop to this global pandemic of madness.

As you progress through this work, it will become clear why we should be focusing on Marxism specifically. Whatever particular causes you yourself like to champion, having a deep understanding of this issue will benefit you (and those who benefit from your efforts). Or if you simply want to protect those close to you, this work will provide you with the antidote in case they become 'exposed' to this pathogen.

It has often been said in recent years, due to Covid, that the world has never experienced anything like this; that this is an unprecedented time. Indeed. These times are also unique for another reason; one less-obvious: never before in history have we seen such a global pandemic of psychotic, civilisation-destroying behaviour.

A key ingredient

Marxism is not the only problem in our world, or the origin of every single problem, but it's a big problem. It is itself, as we will see, the origin of many problems (some of which were mentioned in the preface). If we have to focus on just one thing in order to produce the biggest effect, we should focus on this. By comparison, discussing other things in order to improve our overall situation is simply a waste of time.

Since this subject can be, in terms of logic, a tangled ball of string in some ways, we must de-tangle something before we move on. We must address the "this or that" psychological tendencies we have when deciding what stance to take on big subjects like this. When the proposition is put "Marxism is a serious problem, and we should focus mainly on this!", the responses may come back such as "There's more to blame than just Marxism!" and "Marxism is not the origin of the problem!". This is true in a sense, and some of that will be addressed later; but we must prioritise. Besides, these types of attitudes are unconstructive since they don't allow a consensus to be formed (which you absolutely need in order to deal with the problem of Marxism).

So, because of this tendency in some (and those who the reader might interact with), we need to re-state the point: this book is not suggesting that Marxism is the only ingredient used in the internationalist 'globalist' machine, or that it's the origin of all the world's chaos. It is, however, highlighting that Marxism is a key, universal ingredient that allows the internationalist globalist machine to function at a ground level in our societies.

All pushing in the same direction

Additionally, it's not good to have too many divergent or antagonistic, contradictory opinions; you really need everyone pushing in one direction. Too many conflicting ideas/solutions just negate any possible impact of any one idea/solution, and no progress is achieved. Therefore, to make progress in sorting out this mess we're in, there needs to be a massive consensus.

Imagine a few hard-working men trying to move a large boulder off a road in days gone past, with no help from an animal (e.g. an Ox), or helpful tools. It doesn't matter how many men there are or how strong they are—if they all push in alternate or opposite directions, it's a big waste of time and energy. If they push together in the one direction, however, that is a different matter. This is efficiency of force, due to them combining their effort. There are efficient and inefficient ways of doing things, and our collective quest to have some freedom from this globalist monster is no different. If we all want a better, freer, saner world, we must work together on this issue, to be efficient, and have consensus.

Consider also, that we are in a world full of Marxist deception/propaganda and demoralisation, which is always trying to exploit any weaknesses in its opposition, by capitalising on any dis-unity within it. Therefore, our message must be clear and united—No to Marxism, No exceptions. Once we get control of this problem, we will be able to see some improvements in our collective situation.

The importance of maintaining focus

We need to focus on this problem and maintain it permanently, while not getting distracted with other issues. The Marxist indoctrination is always trying to get us to focus (and assign blame) elsewhere: the religious institutions (i.e. the Catholic Church); the banking system/capitalism; the 'U.S. Empire'; the bourgeoisie/elites, or the multinational corporations etc. In addition, we are constantly being divided-and-conquered by the various Marxism-supported initiatives or 'sub-agendas' (some of which were mentioned in the preface). So, all this divergence and lack of focus is not conducive to building a resistance to this big internationalistic system we are up against. In fact, Marxism is good at taking any opposing energies and diffusing or deflecting them, to the point where there is no cohesive opposition to it at all.

Another reason why we should focus on the Marxist ideology (and its adherents), is that this is a problem that we can address and highlight relatively easily in our countries. It also happens that Marxism is the first line of defence being used by the internationalist globalist machine to stop any genuine resistance from developing in society. If the big 'globalist' monster has an exploitable chink in the armour, this is it...

A key ingredient of control

Marxism is a key ingredient for global control and a massive causal factor of all the world's chaos, because of the elements that make up this ideology; the concepts of equality, 'revolution', internationalism (and One-World Government), and the oppressor v oppressed formula, to name a few. These have been its core elements from the beginning, but there are others too.

It's important to note that it's the combination of these elements that makes the mixture of Marxist ideological indoctrination so potent. The Oppressor v Oppressed formula in particular (and its many manifestations), combines very well with the other elements of 'revolution' and equality.

The dramatic, cynical, oversimplification of how society operates championed by Karl Marx (1818–1883) and Friedrich Engels (1820–1895)—the 'class struggle' of the 'oppressor' "bourgeoisie" rich capitalists vs the 'oppressed' "proletariat" poor workers—was an oversimplification featured in *The Communist Manifesto* (1848) that echoed in to eternity.[2] This oversimplification—being fawned-over since by 'intellectuals' and others the world over—has now morphed in to this monster that is destroying civilisation; the ramifications of which will take the world to ever-more dark places if nothing is done to stop it. To be clear, we're not merely talking about what is called "Cultural Marxism" or the *Frankfurt School*. As we will see, any form of Marxism (from any point in its history) is a problem for society; including socialism or democratic socialism, and the multitude of other manifestations/labels, regardless of how benign they seem to be, or how many people like them.

All traces have to go

So, all traces of Marxism must go. If you want to re-gain control of your country by stopping this globalist totalitarian monster, you and your fellow countrymen must completely reject and hate Marxism in all its forms. We need a strong, zero-tolerance stance on it due to the overall situation we are in: because of how the individual human mind works, and because of the highly contaminated social landscape in our countries at present. Hence the word "hate": having this emotional punch to it will help to generate the required mentality in the general population. The more people feel and express hostility towards Marxism, and the more the ideology is regarded as toxic, the better. Then, you will give yourselves a fighting chance…

Understanding the effects of this parasitic ideology on our world—and striving to be 'immune' from it—is a massive undertaking. It has an insidious nature, and it expresses this using a variety of methods. It's an ever-present, transforming threat that has a long, proud tradition of adaptation and subversion. There are several 'strains', and it's still adapting, even today. In recent times, it has adapted to subvert the patriotic/nationalist movements world-wide. Therefore, the more united a population is in its hostility towards it, the better.

---

[2] Marx and Engels, *The Communist Manifesto* (1848).

Can't a society just be, and stay, immune?

Without this unified, hostile, almost allergic rejection, does the average person have the ability to stay immune from this? Is this why it has been so effective at proliferating and entrenching itself in our societies, despite its horrific résumé? Can't a society just be immune without being vigilant? Essentially, can a society have anything less than a zero-tolerance stance against the ideology and remain unaffected overall? These are big, important questions.

Considering the modus operandi of Marxism (past and present), perhaps many people would struggle to encounter this ideology without being led astray; being "sucked-in to the cult" as it were. This is not to dismiss the discernment of so many just for the sake of it; this is just illustrating how good Marxism is at wriggling its way into society/people's minds, and making a home for itself there, like any good parasite would. It infects those who are not psychologically immune, and then spreads from one 'vulnerable' person to another.

The many ways in which this ideology can distort a person's perceptions and start dictating their emotional responses could make it very difficult for someone to be unaffected, especially if they were in a pro-Marxist environment (e.g. an infected University).

For some, trying to stay immune in a setting like that would be like walking a tightrope psychologically, trying to stay on the straight and narrow. For some, they may have to choose between conforming or being ostracized, or simply deciding to exit that environment asap!

Exposure to this ideology can be risky for anyone, but especially the young. We can clearly see how the indoctrination policy of this cult targets the unsuspecting public at younger and younger ages. In recent times, they have been using the insane climate change movement to turn teen and pre-teen kids into little revolutionaries. This is no accident: the younger a person is, the more susceptible they are to being indoctrinated, especially by an emotionally manipulative ideology like Marxism. Life-experience, emotional control, and general maturity can help to keep a person immune, and these are things that young people generally just don't have to a sufficient degree. They need guidance and protection from those who are more mature to avoid these pitfalls, and that's where parents and teachers (are supposed to) come in. Of course, if these 'adults' are indoctrinated themselves, then the kids have no chance...In other cases, parents simply being ignorant of Marxism is enough to create a disaster.

This ideology can be pumped into the soft heads of students at any age. There are several other mediums through which it can reach people's minds, and 'education'/academia is just one of them. However, it's perhaps the most effective since it can mask itself as 'education' to hide its true face—indoctrination.

Priorities...

Let's prioritise and put things into a rational perspective, from a nation-management point of view. Considering the damage being done to western countries thanks to internationalist/Marxist attitudes, is it not a bit silly to focus on domestic issues while forgetting the bigger picture? In Ireland's case, for example, focusing on such things as housing prices/renting costs, crime, the state of the health service, mental health, vulture funds, or homelessness is irrelevant if the country is being progressively driven towards a cliff due to the Marxist ideology being in the driving seat. Is it good prioritisation to focus on those things in our foreground, while the various consequences of a serious Marxist infection (and the various 'sub-agendas' it supports) are tearing-up the fabric of society in the background?

For example, mass immigration into a country (which is due to the Marxist infection being present in the first place) will destroy everything, and those domestic issues already present will be exacerbated in the extreme (e.g. housing availability and cost, the health service, the economy, schooling etc.). By us prioritising those domestic issues and trying to fix them in a society of ever-changing racial demographics and increasing population levels (due to Marxism being in control), we are simply wasting our time! Priorities. It must be noted too that the various Marxist movements in a given country just love to involve themselves in these types of domestic issues, as part of their virtue-signalling DNA; blissfully unaware that the ideology they subscribe to will ensure these issues never get resolved! Naivety to the max.

Why we should say #Notomarxism

> "You can't give shit leftists an inch, if you give them an inch, they will use it to destroy you!"

> Argentinian President Javier Milei during TV interview[3]

If patriotism/nationalism/national sovereignty (choose your label) is the idea of a country having a sovereign right to decide its own future, then this is a rational ideological response to the internationalist totalitarianism being forced upon our countries today. These 'right-wing' stances generally allow a country to have more freedom to refuse to participate in the internationalist's plans. This is because they advocate that a country should

---

[3] *Milei, J., "Javier Milei: you can't give sh*t l3ftards an inch! "* , YouTube.

have a reasonable degree of separation from the rest of the world (aka independence). This should be obvious to all!

Conversely, an internationalist ideology – like Marxism – results in a country having less ability to decide its own future. Why? It's because Marxism (in general) advocates that a country should be 'equal' to other countries and should not/does not have a degree of separation from the rest of the world. In essence, countries should show 'unity' or 'solidarity' with other countries, and each would be moulded according to the ideology/cult. Think of the naive "who needs borders anyway?" mentality. In addition, subscribing to this ideology (even partially) is enough to ensure that your country is swept away by the internationalist ideological red wave; and this is exactly what's transpiring across the globe at this time. The cult, in general, wants a 'socialist' federation of the world.

If a country is infected with Marxism to a significant degree, this simply means that a significant portion of the population is psychologically contaminated by the ideology. This leads to a lack of will, belief (and consensus!) that this country should have independence and even identify as a separate, distinct entity at all! These indoctrinated types tend to like the idea of the country being part of the international collective, and that it should give its sovereignty to organisations like the European Union and the United Nations. All because Marxism is an internationalist ideology. Of course, Marxist apologists might retort that not all forms of Marxism are internationalist, but this is irrelevant. Marxism inevitably leads to a country joining the international cult movement, being swept away in the 'revolution', and losing control of its affairs.

Marxism is the most dangerous, almost universal, core ideology in the world today. It's truly global and has destroyed wherever it has taken hold throughout its history. It's extremely toxic for a country. Marxism (or its outgrowth socialism) is not an alternative economic or political system, or a system of 'philosophy' or analysis. It is a cult-like ideology that does the opposite of what it claims—it serves the true bourgeoisie 'elites' internationalist types, not opposes them; it suppresses the proletariat 'working classes', not liberates them; it doesn't make a country and its people strong—it makes them weak.

Marxism is a country's internal drain on its sovereign, patriotic energy. It is the anti-thesis to true, healthy, natural freedom and patriotism, sabotaging a country from the inside-out. Patriotism is the antidote to the globalist internationalism, and Marxism is the poison that neutralises the antidote, by keeping it occupied—occupied long enough for the global machine to enforce its agenda on a given country.

Just look at how Marxist cult members all across the globe have been trying to suppress the non-Marxist/patriotic resistance to 'globalism' in recent times—that's all the evidence you need really. Never mind what they think they are, or what they claim to be—what do their actions tells us? It tells us they are essentially traitors, in national terms.

Marxism is international totalitarian control. It is not the opposite to things like the international banking system, it compliments it nicely; it is not an opponent to the world control system, it is a critically important aspect of it; it is not the anti-thesis to oligarchical imperialistic rule, it serves it.

This ideology is the focus of this book, because it's the common red thread throughout the world: it's the red elephant in the LGBTQIXYZ+ rainbow-coloured dildo-shaped gay disco VIP area of a room we are all in.

Marxism is the root ideology of the various anti-civilisation agendas active in our societies: whether we examine the anti-white Marxist movement in South Africa, or the legalisation of abortion in Ireland, or the Black Lives Matter riots in the U.S. or London, or the mass immigration problem in Western countries, or the economic woes of socialistic countries, or the climate change sub-agenda globally—Marxism is the society-level ideology at the heart of it all. Without the millions of adherents to this red cult worldwide, those destructive, society-destroying movements would not exist.

There are other ideologies at play behind Marxism, that stretch right back into human history, but this one in particular is the key to combating the chaos. The concept of revolution is still as effective today as it was in the run-up to the *French Revolution* (1787–1799), as an incendiary, psychologically manipulative tool. (The catchphrase back then was "Liberté! Égalité, Fraternité!", which equals "Liberty, Equality, Fraternity (Solidarity)!").[4] As for the potency of the ideology—you would struggle to come up with a more efficient form of brainwashing if you tried! It's a fantastic system, and (at first) difficult to identify and neutralize in a population.

Marxism is the core ingredient in the stew of globalist totalitarianism (mmm, totalitarian stew!). To be more precise, if this global totalitarianism is an alchemical potion, then Marxism is the binder that holds all the other ingredients together. Without this binder, the potion will not work. So what, then, is the equation for freedom? The golden formula, the skeleton key, the magic bullet is this: the less Marxism you have in your country, the

---

[4] "Unity and Indivisibility of the Republic. Liberty, Equality, Fraternity or Death", Wikipedia.

better chance you have to stop this globalist monster. Conversely, the higher the level of contamination, the more you will struggle to stop it.

Drawing that line in the sand...

If we remove the Marxist indoctrination factor in greater society, and we just had the political class and some other globalist fanatics trying to enforce their will on us, they would be vastly outnumbered (much more than they are now)! In addition, since the majority would be rational, anti-globalist, anti-Marxist people, this minority of traitors would stick-out like sore thumbs. As would their views, agendas etc. It would be much easier to keep an eye on them and ensure that they are powerless. To put it another way, it would be easy to draw that clear line in the sand.

Unfortunately, though, it's not that simple, and this is where the Marxist ideology comes in. It's the factor that sways things in the globalists' favour.

Not only can it foster a pro-globalism mindset in the population in general, it actually turns people in to mini globalists. Since numbers matter, we need to incrementally reduce the amount of people in society with that mindset.

This is a book of "hate", right?

No doubt, the brainwashed ones would describe this as a book of hate. "This is hate speech!" and "it's a horrible book of evil fascist, racist, evil, worthless, evil, crappy, horrible evil, evil!" (insert list of Marxist 'insults' here). When we know what Marxism really is, what it has already done, and what it continues to do to our world, this becomes amusing; it should make us giggle at the hypocrisy of such childish, obnoxious virtue-signalling pseudo-logic.

This is like a paedophile criticising a father for shouting at one of his kids. Or like a rapist trying to shame a man for not chivalrously holding a door open for a lady. Or like a superficial, narcissistic female scolding a friend for taking too many selfies. Psychotic. Hypocritical. Double. Standards.

Like red moths to a 'Nazi' flame

Ever noticed how, when someone publicly express views that contradict the 'PC' (politically correct/Marxist) narratives, they attract the bitchy parasite behaviour of the Marxist drones? They are compelled to fly into the person, like moths flying into the proverbial lightbulb. They are programmed, through Marxian indoctrination, to swarm (consciously or subconsciously) any source of light (truth). They swarm to try to block or diffuse the light. Those of us who speak the truth, who speak-out against the behaviour of the cult: we are the light, we are the truth, and we will inevitably attract these little red Marxist moths. "This is a fascist Nazi racist lightbulb! Let's get it!"(insert moth-hitting-bulb SFX and soy-induced tantrum screams). "This lightbulb is hateful!... it's emanating racist, hateful light!" (etc. etc. ad nauseam)

When we criticize the cult/ideology (or its initiatives and effects) we come under fire—we present a threat that needs to be dealt-with and silenced asap. As this is an ideological battleground, your voice must be drowned out with more Marxist rhetoric, allowing them to dominate. This can involve you being contradicted, 'debated' or even shouted down. Petty, bitchy harassment of their political/ideological opponents is a Marxist tradition; the use of 'ridicule'. Any threat is countered by collectivist, pack-like retaliation from cult members. This is extremely important to stifle any dissenting opinions to the cult's/ideology's various sub-agendas/initiatives, often the moment they appear in public discourse.

This retaliation is often childish in nature and can be anything ranging from simple ad hominem attacks to those of a more elaborate variety. It can be abuse over the target's appearance, how they speak/their accent, social/family life, mocking their children/family/partners etc.; or it can include such things as disinformation, smearing, professional character assassination, attempts to get people fired (or otherwise affecting their employability or income), or just plain old lying. For Marxists, the ends justify the means. It's the usual hypocrisy from this cult of 'compassion', 'humanitarianism', 'tolerance' and 'human rights'.

Regular re-application is required

This anti-Marxism message must be repeated, until everyone (who is capable) gets it. The warnings have either been suppressed or gone unheeded. Regardless of what's been said or written before, too many people still fall for the con and become indoctrinated, which is why this message needs to be repeated regularly, till it becomes second nature for a society to react this way. In world history, whenever this anti-Marxist message was scribed on a wall, once the graffiti was forgotten about (or, in fact, the minute you take your eyes off it!), along comes a zombified Marxist minion to dutifully slop-on the red paint... The anti-Marxist message needs regular re-application it seems. The philosopher George Santayana (1863–1952) once said "Those who cannot remember the past are condemned to repeat it"[5]; a relevant variant is — "Those who cannot understand the past are condemned to repeat it".

An error that is committed in recent times, is that some don't believe that the horrors of the past few centuries can be repeated in their time. This is a

---

[5] Santayana, G., *Life of Reason, Reason in Common Sense* (1905), P. 284.

very dangerous presumption to make. If history is not understood, they can and they will, in one way or another. Naivety will be the end for us all. This is a reasonable attitude to have in general, but especially when we are all dealing with a dangerous ideology with the horrific track record of Marxism. It's an ideology that is not merely part of our history, or that has waned somehow, but an ideology that is becoming more powerful than at any point previously.

Magic Anti-Red Sunglasses

Marxism is an ideological programme for brainwashing people. Therefore, this is a psychological issue, as much as it is political, geo-political etc. We cannot dismiss the former; it's of central importance. Focusing only on politics/geo-politics, is just not good enough. We need to be smarter and deeper than that; and approach this problem with a fresh, new mindset.

In order to be the best freedom advocates/patriots/nationalists/sovereigns/anti-globalist individuals we can be, we need to combat Marxist indoctrination; and therefore, we need to fully understand what we are all dealing with here; how the whole process works. Ideally, we should strive to better understand the programme, the programmed, and the programmers. We need to look at this issue on a broad societal level, while also carefully examining the affected individuals contained therein. With a new perspective and the required knowledge, we can easily identify who is indoctrinated and who isn't, and to what degree. Crucially, we can also identify when someone is at risk of being indoctrinated, based on an analysis of their personality, environment, background, age etc. With practice, we can do all these things in a matter of seconds. Essentially, we will be able to see who is infected and who isn't, and how much of a problem they will be for the rest of us.

In the movie *They Live* (1988)[6] the central character discovers that the elites who rule society are actually aliens disguised as humans (two words: David Icke). And how did he do this? By putting on these amazing sunglasses—glasses that show you what the being you are looking at really is underneath their disguise. This is what we must collectively do in our respective societies: put on our anti-Marxism glasses.

---

[6] *They Live* (1988).

Section I—Definitions

"Communism is a disease of the intellect. It promises universal brotherhood, peace and prosperity to lure humanitarians and idealists into participating in a conspiracy which gains power through deceit and deception and stays in power with brute force. Communism promises Utopia. It has delivered mass starvation, poverty, and police state terror to its own people and promoted worldwide strife and hatred by pitting race against race, class against class, and religion against religion. Treason, terror, torture, and Moscow-directed wars of "national liberation" spread communist "brotherhood, peace and social justice around the world"[1]

John A. Stormer, *None Dare Call It Treason* (1964)

Introduction

Since Marxism is a slippery customer, it's prudent we go through some definitions in this section; even the word "Marxism" itself is problematic in that it can diverge opinions (to the benefit of the cult/ideology). In the next section we'll also go through some of the relevant background and elements of the ideology. We should always endeavour not to get sucked-in to the pseudo-intellectual babble around this ideology, but some elements do need to be examined. This is to prepare the reader for the later sections, where we look at how the Marxist infection is destroying civilisation today. Looking at definitions in this section, remember our previous perceptions of what Marxism is may be based on definitions, interpretations and analysis that have come from the system, which is itself riddled with Marxism/Marxists (particularly 'education').

In Section III ("Our History of Global Infection") we'll look at the geographical spread of the ideology/infection, plus a general rundown of its presence throughout history. Further on, in "The Red Steps to Utopia" section, we'll look at the merits of Marxist theory in economic terms (aka socialism), so we don't get bogged-down in this section. It's a common misinterpretation that Marxism is mostly about sociology, economics, and politics but it isn't. This is just a smokescreen that gives it legitimacy, to

---

[1] Stormer, J., *None Dare Call It Treason* (1964), P. 16.

hide its true nature, as we will see.

Theory v Reality

The Theory v Reality problem is a tool we can use to understand why some people defend Marxism, despite its malevolent nature, history, and effects. Many Marxist apologists (casuals or fanatics) who try to convince us that we're wrong about the ideology, fail to understand that it shouldn't be defended. Likewise, they fail to understand (somewhat ironically) that it's in our collective interests not to do so (on the contrary, as this book states, the ideology should be actively criticised, suppressed and eliminated). But why is this the case? Why are these people so completely mistaken? How can someone have it so backwards? Is it simply because they have a distorted perception of its nature?

The problem, for some, is that the reality and results of Marxism do not match what they think Marxism is and what it results in. They are caught up in the theoretical, hypothetical, academic analysis of what some dead guys (or their fans) have said. Certainly, Marxist indoctrination plays the key role here. We shall refer to this concept throughout as the Theory v Reality problem.

Definitions

It's important we devote a bit of time to definitions because there are several distorted perceptions of various concepts related to this subject, which could be problematic for some readers. Problematic not just in terms of understanding it for yourself, but also problematic when trying to analyse the cult/ideology in the world around us and, more importantly, actively exposing it. There are literally piles of definitions and interpretations of Marxism, so we'll be covering a selection of those that are common and/or relevant. It will also be beneficial to readers who are totally new to this subject, who may be unfamiliar with the various terms. They will be brief, and many/most will be expanded upon more in later sections.

Before we list the definitions, it must be noted that even the various labels/names associated with Marxism can confuse. They do a real good job of distracting people away from the basic truth—it is a dangerous, subversive ideology that we should give our full attention to, and these various labels help to prevent the general population from coming to this conclusion. It's quite fitting that even these various labels for Marxism can induce confusion, which assists one of the core attributes of the ideology—subversion. This attribute itself often involves obfuscation: to intentionally hide the true meaning of something.

So, how can we solve a problem if it can't be clearly identified first? How can we show others it even exists in the first place, if we can't all agree on what it should be called?!? (never mind convince them of the seriousness of the issue, and its negative effects etc.). While we are doing definitions....

What is an Ideology?

Let's cut to the chase on this one first: an ideology is a belief-system; a way of looking at the world around us; a way of perceiving reality; a certain way of perceiving ourselves, others, life etc. But are ideologies bad? This depends on whether they are positive or negative. We can judge this based on the effect(s) that they have. Sounds straight-forward, right? So we don't go too deep just yet, here's a definition from *Dictionary.com*:

"*1*. The body of doctrine, myth, belief, etc., that guides an individual, social movement, institution, class, or large group". This definition will do. So when we say "Marxism is an ideology" we're saying that it's a belief(s) held by a group. Funny, the second definition is this one: "2. such a body of doctrine, myth, etc., with reference to some political and social plan, as that of fascism, along with the devices for putting it into operation".[2] The use of the word "fascism" here is amusing. There's no escape is there? Even online-dictionaries are biased in favour of Marxism, and its old foe is mentioned here instead. (fascism and Marxism are not the same. There are some general similarities, but they are not the same ideology. This point is expanded upon later).

What is a Marxist?

There is some confusion with labelling here. You will see/hear other terms like "socialist" or communist" or even "liberal" being used (sometimes the term "Neo-con" is used in the U.S.). Don't let these confuse you and leave any pre-conceived ideas aside; let's build this from the ground up.

Since we are focusing on the ideology itself (and its cult-member adherents) in the modern world, the label of "Marxist" is perfectly accurate. In the interests of consensus and efficiency (as outlined earlier) and keeping things simple while solving this problem, we should all just call them "Marxists".

A Marxist 'cult member' is someone who – wittingly or unwittingly – is advocating/supporting any strain of Marxist ideology (listed later), and are, therefore, contributing to the overall ideological infection of Marxism in our world. Due to their beliefs, they are giving the ideology energy, and therefore support it to one degree or another (whether they realise this or

---

[2] https://www.dictionary.com/browse/ideology

not). Their beliefs help the infection to proliferate. The more people like this in the world, the more influential/powerful the ideology becomes, the more people who can potentially be influenced, and the more influential/powerful the ideology becomes etc. ad infinitum. Hence, ideological "pandemic".

These people can come in all shapes and sizes, and they can be only mildly infected/indoctrinated or severely infected/indoctrinated, and all the levels in between. This is not a black and white thing; it's nuanced; a sliding scale of fanaticism and indoctrination. They may be an outright advocate, or an apologist. They may be an avid apologist, or an unenthusiastic apologist (some can be an apologist without even realising it, or even knowing what Marxism is). They may be politically knowledgeable and active, or not. They can be young or old, rich or poor, educated or not, and of any nationality, ethnicity, or religious creed. They can be a shopkeeper, policeman, teacher, doctor, carpenter, actor, student, your girlfriend/boyfriend, family member, long-lost cousin, co-worker, neighbour etc. The cult/ideology does not discriminate in this regard. It's not fussy.

The term "Marxist" does not only include those who like/advocate/support the traditional, surface-level interpretation of Marxism—meaning those who see Marxism as a form of revolution against the system, or as an alternative political or economic system (aka "socialism"). It also includes those who like/advocate/support the more modern sociological aspects of Marxism, more commonly known as "Cultural Marxism" (which is where, arguably, Marxism-based theories really impact society and do the real damage). These types are often erroneously labelled "liberals" (more on this later).

Though all those types of people are connected, being Marxist adherents, does this mean they are all identical? Of course not. If we regard this as being one, big, international cult or quasi-religion, then not all of them are "true believers"; some are just following the crowd somewhat. And neither is it true that all those people are degenerate, evil, nihilistic, unethical, destructive etc. They are all, however, mistaken (to one degree or another), whichever aspect of Marxism they subscribe to. Since Marxism has many different varieties/interpretations, they can be mistaken in many different ways (as many as they like! It's a free buffet of mistaken beliefs!).

It's Marxist tradition to discombobulate ideological and political enemies by using confusing or distracting terms, even to describe themselves. They may not use the term "Marxist" but other terms including (but not limited to): The Left, Progressives, Anti-racists, Radicals, Revolutionaries, Anti-Fascists, Anti-Fascist Partisans, Partisans; or other terms like Social Justice

Activists, Black Lives Matter Activists, Feminists/Radical Feminists; or other combinations of the words "Radical", "Activist", "Progressive", "Revolutionary", "Left", "Socialist" etc. Other terms like "Workers" or "League" or "Party" or "Anti-Fascist" will especially feature when labelling clubs, organisations, unions etc. The reality, of course, is that it's just one big movement. The result of the cult/ideology having such a variety of labels has helped keep this truth sufficiently hidden, until now…

What is Marxism?

This is a very important one. It's basically any form of crazy 'revolutionary' activism.

Some who have merely looked at the book and its title will be put-off or stumped due this word "Marxism". The word "Marxism" means any variation of: socialism, communism, Cultural-Marxism, Neo-Marxism, Classical Marxism (itself containing Orthodox Marxism and Revisionist Marxism), Libertarian Marxism, social democracy (related to revisionist Marxism and considered a "capitalism-friendly" strain by some), democratic socialism, Fabian socialism, western-Marxism, Leninism, Marxism-Leninism, Maoism, Castroism, Guevarism, Hoxhaism, Euro-communism, Titoism, Khrushchevism, Ho Chi Minh-ism (aka Ho Chi Minh Thought), Juche communism, Goulash communism, Trotskyism, Luxemburgism, Anarcho-communism, libertarian socialism, progressivism, political correctness etc. etc. ad nauseam.

(Anarchism deserves a mention here too; it's a movement contaminated with Marxism/Marxists. While it can be argued that 'pure' anarchism is, in theory, the idea of having a society without rulers (which kinda sounds nice), it also happens to greatly serve Marxism by wanting the structures of civilisation to be broken down in order to achieve that. 'Pure' anarchism is utopian in that it envisages a vastly different, better society without rulers. Many variations of anarchism are just destructive and nihilistic for the sake of it).

These are all connected, being different interpretations/variations of the same core ideology; some are truer to the original ideas of Karl Marx and Friedrich Engels than others (which is irrelevant; they are all part of the problem). Others have roots further back in history, as socialistic ideas did not begin with those two men of course; in fact, they plagiarised many concepts.

Some of them are strains spawned by early strains. Marxism-Leninism, for example—itself being a fusion/interpretation of the ideas of Karl Marx and Vladimir Lenin (1870–1924)—spawned several strains. Overall, they all boil down to the same thing in the end; they are all just different shades of the same shite as we say in Ireland. Fans of one particular variety may insist that they're different from the rest, and that any criticisms you have of Marxism, socialism, or communism don't apply to their particular brand (little conundrums like these are listed in the "Excuses (Marxist) People Make" section").

Let's keep in mind here, that all these different labels, are just one person's interpretation or ideas based on another person's interpretation or ideas. Some of the strains, are ideas based on ideas of the ideas of someone else's ideas about someone else's ideas (no, not really).

In logical terms, if the original, foundational ideas are flawed, this is like building a shoddy wall, one layer on top of another: the first layer of 'brick' is ice cream bars, the second is B.L.T. sandwiches, the third is rotten bananas, the fourth is small, lunchbox-sized bags of vomit etc. Best of luck trying to get that wall to stand, particularly on a hot summer's day!

Think of all the countless different 'genders' that some of the brainwashed nuts come up with today: just because there are loads of labels being used doesn't increase the legitimacy of the foundational erroneous concept (i.e. that there is anything more than 'male' and 'female')! It's the same with Marxism: they can come up with a million names for it if they want to, it doesn't change the fact that it's ideological poison.

Some of the strains are re-interpretations of the same core ideology (e.g. The Frankfurt School's "Cultural Marxism"); or various methods by which to spread that ideology (i.e. Fabian Socialism). Some may also represent different phases of the same process by which Marxism takes hold of a country: this process starts with slight infection all the way through to the domination of Marxism in that country (e.g. "political correctness" is a sign of a mild infection).

What impression does all this labelling give us? That there is a lot of experimentation going on, as if civilisation itself – and those of us within it – should be experimented upon. It has been said that insanity is making the same mistakes repeatedly and expecting different results. Considering its résumé of constant failure, what does that make Marxism? If Marxist theories had any real value, they would not need to be modified constantly and then re-attempted, ad infinitum. The massive control-freak egos traditionally dominant in this cult eternally attempt to convince us otherwise.

It is possible, considering the cult's modus operandi, that Marxists have (consciously or subconsciously) invented/used terms like "Stalinism", "Leninism", and "Maoism" as ways of distracting us from the underlying truth (that the ideology itself has always been the underlying problem).

Since this compartmentalisation of terms protects the cult/ideology, by hiding this truth from us, it's a serious issue. It prevents us from attacking and suppressing it.

Marxism, Socialism, Communism—what's the difference?

Some basic interpretations first:

"Marxism" is the core, source ideology and foundation for all the other variations; the common (red) thread running through them all. It's not only about what authors like Marx and Engels said in their writings. It's the ideological driver of all the Marxian revolutionary sentiment.

"Socialism" is the political, economic, and sociological method for putting Marxist theories into practice; of building a society according to Marxian principles. According to some interpretations, socialism is the phase a society goes through in its hypothetical 'transition' from capitalism to communism.

"Communism" is the 'utopian' egalitarian society envisaged by Marx and his disciples once socialism was fully implemented and capitalism was completely replaced. Of course, according to Marxism in general, a 'revolution' of some kind is required to bring about these changes and achieve this 'utopia'. 'Communism' is the ultimate goal of Marxism.

In the Communist Manifesto (1848), Marx and Engels refer to this 'new' revolutionary movement and its adherents as "communism" and "communists". [3] It's also accurate, in some ways, to call Marxists "communists", but since the words "communist" and "communism" are mostly equated to certain regimes throughout history, and this hypothetical future 'utopia', it's not as beneficial for us to use those terms instead (plus other reasons, as we'll see). Besides, Marx himself is the main origin for the ideology.

To keep our collective focus on the problem (the cult/ideology in general), it's more efficient to use the terms "Marxism" and "Marxists" (regardless of whether or not they are genuine disciples of Marx). They are the superior choice.

What is Socialism?

Socialism, officially, is a revolutionary, anti-establishment, alternative political, sociological, and economic system. Its aim is to create a 'socialist' society in which the means of production, distribution and exchange are owned by the community ('the people') as a whole, rather than private

---

[3] Marx and Engels, *The Communist Manifesto* (1848).

individuals. In practice, this means a central leadership and government ownership of these means of production, distribution, and exchange (in the name of 'the people'). In some interpretations (e.g. Classical Marxism), socialism is a transitional phase between capitalism and communism, so a socialist society would then, in theory, 'progress' on towards its final destination of communism.

Socialism was presented as being an improvement to previous systems in terms of ethics, especially for the working-class 'proletariat' who generally formed the population's majority. It's the idea that there should be collective public ownership of the 'means of production', resources, land etc to benefit this majority, as opposed to private ownership/control of those things by the rich 'bourgeoisie' few. Marx believed that the new, industrial capitalist system that emerged in the 19th century, thanks to the advancements in industrial technologies, was creating an intolerable situation where the rich capitalist business owners were able to exploit the workers (on an industrial scale). This critically important 'class struggle' concept was an early manifestation of the oppressor vs oppressed principle (one of the core, ever-present pillars of the ideology).

It must be noted at this point that socialism has never been proven to be an effective, functioning system that works in practice (though Marxist propaganda insists otherwise). We will be looking at socialism in a following section ("Red Steps to Utopia", under the sub-heading "The Destruction of the Capitalist System").

What is Democratic Socialism?

Officially, democratic socialism seeks to establish a democratic society with a socialist-style mode of production. It simply means that socialism is in place in a country via the democratic system, as opposed to a military coup, dictatorship, or invasion by outside forces. Of course, it doesn't matter how this system is implemented, the destructive end results – its social and economic impacts – are the same. So still socialism, but the illusion of democracy is upheld, as this type of socialism allows 'unbiased' elections (in theory). Democracy, where Marxism is involved, really means 'democracy'—a situation where, apparently, 'the people' get to choose who their leaders are and how society is structured; but in practice, Marxism dominates.

So, the question is—if Marxists are in control, will any real anti-Marxist opposition be allowed? Obviously not. We can see this process in action all across the word today in 'democratic' countries that have a significant Marxist infection (e.g. western countries in general).

Communism

Communism (the 'goal' of socialism) is the aim of creating a society based on Marxist principles: an egalitarian ('equal') society without social classes, where private property ownership and rights of inheritance, religion, and the capitalist system (including money itself) are all abolished. A 'utopia'.

Again, this is all just theory, and cult members will say that, historically, communism (as envisaged by Marx and Engels et al) has never actually been achieved. If we regard this as being true, then the various now-infamous "Communist" regimes throughout the 20th century were not "Communist".

This is an extremely problematic, irrelevant, erroneous argument which allows the ideology of Marxism to survive in the present, by constantly 'getting off the hook' (this is expanded on in the "Excuses (Marxist) People Make" section).

These 'communist' regimes were highly repressive towards the inhabitants in their respective countries, hence communism having a reputation for being ultra-totalitarian in nature. This involved a centralisation of power, a one-party state, and the inevitable abolition of democracy, freedom etc. Mass murder of civilians and war were also typical results of these countries being at a high level of infection (since the infection seeks to spread, naturally). Examples are featured in the historical section.

The term "communism lite" means a 'soft' totalitarian dictatorship. If "communism" is overt totalitarian control by the state, then communism lite is more covert. So not the hard, boot-in-the-face version, but a more 'nice' and subtle variety. The same system of control overall, and same results, but different methods. A somewhat related term is "creeping socialism": a gradual, incremental, relatively slow takeover, as opposed to a sudden or instant takeover (i.e. a military invasion by "socialist" or "communist" forces).

Official interpretations

A definition of "Marxism" from *Dictionary.com*: "The system of economic and political thought developed by Karl Marx, along with Friedrich Engels, especially the doctrine that the state throughout history has been a device for the exploitation of the masses by a dominant class, that class struggle has been the main agency of historical change, and that the capitalist system, containing from the first the seeds of its own decay, will inevitably, after the period of the dictatorship of the proletariat, be superseded by a socialist order and a classless society".[4]

---

[4] https://www.dictionary.com/browse/Marxism

Funny, there is no mention of it being an ideology there… Does this mean I'm wrong? What about another. This time, we'll use *Merriam-webster.com:* "The political, economic, and social principles and policies advocated by Marx especially: a theory and practice of socialism, including the labor theory of value, dialectical materialism, the class struggle, and dictatorship of the proletariat until the establishment of a classless society."[5] Ok, no mention of ideology yet… Perhaps we'll pack it in and quit right now? Nah, I think not.

Looking at the definitions, what impression do they give us so far? They both essentially say that Marxism is concepts of a political, economic, and sociological nature, devised by a guy called Karl and another guy called Friedrich. There is this fancy term called "dialectical materialism", and this aggressive concept of a "dictatorship of the proletariat" that's giving off these revenge vibes. That's roughly the impression we are getting here. It's suggesting big change, with an almost incendiary tone.

So why am I insisting that this is an ideology? Here's the definitions of "ideology" from earlier, but let's substitute the word "Marxism" in place of "fascism": "1. The body of doctrine, myth, belief, etc., that guides an individual, social movement, institution, class, or large group. 2. such a body of doctrine, myth, etc., with reference to some political and social plan, as that of Marxism, along with the devices for putting it into operation".

Now if we look at what's going on in the world today, which word looks more appropriate in that slot? Is Marxism the body of doctrine/myth/belief that is guiding individuals/social movements/institutions/classes/large groups? Yes, absolutely—that is more obvious than ever.

Does Marxism have somewhat of a political and social plan, and are there devices for putting it into operation? Yes, undeniably; most organs of the state worldwide are devoted to its cause. As we will see, according to these definitions of what an ideology is, Marxism fits the bill very well.

As for those definitions of what Marxism is (according to *Dictionary.com* and *Merriam-webster.com),* they are reflective of the official, 'politically correct', everyday perception of what Marxism is. The truth is that Marxism is an ideology that goes far beyond the political, financial, or sociological. It affects individuals and society in many ways previously not examined. Besides, a big red bloody ideological mess like this cannot be fully encapsulated in a couple of sentences within a simple definition,

---

[5] https://www.merriam-webster.com/dictionary/Marxism

unfortunately.

In addition, it's not just about what Marx or Engels thought or said, or what was in The Communist Manifesto and *Das Kapital* (Marx, 1867),[6] or what any other Marxist/Marxist apologist (past or present) has said; nor is it merely about the various so-called Communist regimes, The Frankfurt School, or democratic socialism etc. It's much bigger than all that! Most of the definitions or official articles you will find online describing what Marxism is will be tainted by Marxism itself. Biased is not the word.

"Cult"

The word "cult" From the Latin "cultus" which means "worship", and the word "colere" meaning "cultivate". From *Dictionary.com* (edited down to relevant parts. Underlined for emphasis): "an instance of great veneration of a person, ideal, or thing, especially as manifested by a body of admirers; a group or sect bound together by veneration of the same thing, person, ideal, etc.; a group having a sacred ideology and a set of rites centering around their sacred symbols; a religion or sect considered to be false, unorthodox, or extremist".[7]

Looking at the Marxist collective in general, do they show great veneration for certain historical personalities and hold them aloft as quasi-prophets (Marx, Lenin, Trotsky, Guevera, Mao etc.)? Yes.

Do they use certain universal sacred symbols and imagery (clenched fist; the colour red; hammer and sickle; the red star)? Yes.

Are they joined by collective worship of certain ideals (revolution, equality, solidarity, 'compassion', internationalism, class struggle/the oppressor vs oppressed principle etc.)? Yes. Are they extremist/fanatical and regard themselves as different (and superior) to those outside the cult? Yes.

Another definition of "cult" from *merriam-webster.com* (edited to relevant parts): "a religion regarded as unorthodox or spurious. Also: its body of adherents. The voodoo cult. A satanic cult; a great devotion to a person, idea, object, movement, or work (such as a film or book); a usually small group of people characterized by such devotion".[8]

We can use these definitions and combine them with our general perceptions of what cults are. Is Marxism a religion regarded as unorthodox or spurious (meaning "outwardly similar or corresponding to something

---

[6] Marx, K. *Das Kapital* (1867).

[7] https://www.dictionary.com/browse/cult

[8] https://www.merriam-webster.com/dictionary/cult

without having its genuine qualities" and "of a deceitful nature or quality")? Does the idea of 'utopia' (and the promise of it) match the "deceitful nature" part? As in, Marxism promises utopia, so it falls into the category of a "spurious" religion (aka a cult).

Is Marxism a "great devotion to a person (Marx et al), idea (socialism/communism), or work, such as a book" (The Communist Manifesto, Das Kapital, the *Little Red Book* (Mao Zedong, 1964) etc?[9] Could we call all the various strains/interpretations of Marxism "sects"?

What are the attributes of a cult? A cult is often a group that has a superiority complex. It may also have a strong sense of fraternity or 'love' amongst its members that does not apply to those outside it (whatever they may claim). A group that has delusions of grandeur, which appeals to the delusions of grandeur of the individuals that are attracted to (and compose) it. A group that feels it's 'fighting' for some sort of important, unresolved issue that the world must be made aware of, or some other lofty purpose! Therefore, it's often 'revolutionary' in nature—it wants to influence or change the world, by forcing it to change.

In cults, they may tell you that you're special and may fill your head with lofty notions—that you are going to change/save the world; that you understand things that others don't (particularly those outside the cult). It's a very effective brainwashing method because it utilises/stimulates the ego, and we all have egos! In addition, many people would indeed like to feel special and/or powerful on some level of their being.

Cults can have chants or mantras, such as "power to the people", "one race, human race!", "homes for people, not for profits!" or "Nazi scum off our streets!". Plus, there's the oft-used Marxist terms, "equality", "diversity", "solidarity" etc. It's like a religious chant, A trance…Red (as opposed to black) magic. The terms and catchphrases the cult uses world-wide are a type of incantation, to invoke the 'spirit' of revolution.

Cult members can be from all walks of life: rich/poor, black/white/Asian, tall/short, male/female/other/non-binary/tertiary/hermaphrodite trans bi gay queer/you like to try shoving the thick end of a champagne bottle up your ass once a week to prove you're not homophobic. The members come in all shapes and sizes because this is an ideology that brainwashes.

All you need is a brain capable of being brainwashed; there are no other requirements, and the ideology (clearly) is not fussy about what brain it infects. In a pseudo-spiritual sense, they are all one within the cult.

---

[9] Zedong, M. *The Little Red Book* (1964).

Trotskyism

Trotskyism is another strain of Marxism, named so after a 'man' called Lev Davidovich Bronstein or Leon Trotsky (1879–1940) as he chose to be called. Trotsky was one of the chief protagonists of the Russian Revolution in 1917, along with Vladimir Lenin. Trotskyism is commonly attached to the concept of "permanent revolution" and the idea that socialism should be an international affair not merely national. Adherents of this particular strain are Trotskyites (or colloquially referred to as "Trots" in Britain).

Marxism-Leninism

This strain is a fusion of ideas from two different characters – Karl Marx and Vladimir Lenin – and the two different interpretations of Marxism that are named after them: Marxism and Leninism. It combines Marx's idea of a centralised economy (and the ownership of the resources and means of production by 'the people'), with Lenin's idea of a "proletarian vanguard" (Marxist cult member leadership group). This ideological monstrosity was helped into existence by a biological monstrosity known as Joseph Stalin (1878–1953), who came to power in Lenin's wake. This strain often receives the brunt of the criticism over the totalitarian reputation of 'communism'.

It's an important term because it's problematic in understanding the nature of Marxist infection worldwide. Why? Because the catastrophic and downright evil consequences of Marxism taking hold in a country are often attributed to this 'Marxist-Leninist' strain of Marxism.

This then allows cult members to detach themselves from these regimes, claiming it has nothing to do with "true" Marxism/communism etc.

Essentially Marxism-Leninism is what you get when you combine the ideas of two disturbed personalities. It's difficult to know which one of these characters deserves more blame for establishing the ideology in the world: though Marx himself was earlier in the process, Lenin's contribution led to the creation of the Soviet Union (and all that entailed), in addition to the subsequent emulations by the likes of Mao Zedong (1893–1976) and his Red China (which led to events such as the Korean War (1950–1953), the Vietnam War (1954–1975), and numerous other manifestations). If the Soviet Union never existed, the ideology may not have spread globally as it did.

'Centrist' Marxism

This is a descriptive term generally used to denote a type of Marxism that falls between two types of strategy typically used by the cult: Revolution—the assault and destruction of the existing established system, to then replace it with a Marxist one. And Reformism—infusing the existing established system with Marxism to turn it Marxist. The latter is often more insidious and arguably a much more difficult strategy to counter. Centrist Marxism isn't any less destructive than other strains/interpretations. Centrist in this context does not mean "moderate" of course since Marxism can't quality as being moderate in any form.

Western-Marxism

This is linked to "Neo-Marxism". Just another name for yet another strain or interpretation of Marxist ideas, that started to move away from the bloody-workers-revolution format/strategy to a more 'civilised' and eventually academic one. The period after WW1 and the Russian Revolution marked a new phase in Marxism, with cult members such as the Italian Antonio Gramsci (1891–1937), German Karl Korsch (1886–1961), and Hungarian Gyorgy Lukacs (1885–1971) coming to the force, espousing their own interpretations. Later, an infamous crypto-Marxist group called the Frankfurt School would appear on the scene to do the same thing, proliferating the ideological infection further.

Putting the "cult" in "culture": Cultural Marxism

This is an often-coined term given to the legacy of the "Western-Marxists" of the Frankfurt School, or other individuals/groups who had/have a distinctly Marxian influence on western countries. The term can be used when someone is describing the initiatives/concepts promulgated by these types of individuals/groups and their effects, such as what's called multiculturalism, political-correctness, and critical theory etc.

Marxists/apologists claim (predictably) that this apparent agenda to destroy western countries is a conspiracy theory. Others try to discredit or dismiss this term "Cultural Marxism", saying that it's not accurate etc. None of that matters—it's very real regardless of what it's called. We could call it "social group Marxism" or "group conflict Marxism" or "social classes-struggle Marxism", but they don't sound as cool, do they? We can't call it "Social Marxism" because earlier incarnations of Marxism had a social element too.

"Cultural Marxism" takes the oppressor v oppressed formula of class struggle and applies it to other groups in society. So instead of it being about rich vs poor (as in traditional Marxism), it's now about man v woman (feminism), black v white ('racism'), straight v gay/bisexual (gay rights), 'trans' v non-trans (trans rights), 'cis gender' v 'gender non-binary' (??? rights), animals v humans (veganism), humans v the planet (climate change) etc. This has the eternal, omnipresent Marxian effect of creating conflict between different groups so they will destroy each other (divide and conquer).

'PC' and 'Hate Speech'

As it exists today, this is another important aspect of Marxian totalitarianism. It's a mechanism for keeping the public under control, particularly those who have opinions that challenge the status quo (which Marxism has created). Put simply, if you express an opinion that is not approved by the system, you (and your opinion) will be targeted for suppression.

"Politically correct" (PC) or "Political correctness" is also a very effective way for the Marxist cult to keep tabs on its political opponents, by controlling the use of language in society. This allows these potential political opponents to be identified literally the minute they open their mouths. It's also a form of subtle psychological terrorism since it can make a person afraid (consciously or subconsciously) to express any opinions that do not conform to the Marxist programme. This can create stress in the minds of the cult's potential opponents in society and stifle the generation of morale in any anti-Marxist movements that may develop.

This one is a classic! Nowadays 'hate speech' is essentially any opinion that is not Marxist in nature; it often means just telling the truth. It embodies the ideology very well—virtue-signalling and the trademark hypocritical double-standards, all contained in just two words! Magnificent, isn't it? The ideology is allergic to truth; it cannot function in its presence, so it must be destroyed. Ergo, the linguistic propaganda payload "hate speech".

It's a way of controlling public discourse, by labelling any non-Marxist opinions as being bad/negative/evil. A way of programming and convincing the sleeping masses (who may be neither pro or anti-Marxism) that non-Marxist opinions are bad (and by suggestion, that Marxist opinions are good). It does this by emotionally controlling their perception of those opinions.

Obviously, the introduction of 'hate-speech' laws in a country is the creation of pro-Marxism laws, and therefore a clear sign that the cult/ideology is becoming dominant within that country.

We've heard cult members comment on 'the far-right', speaking words to the effect of "we don't agree with the politics of hate"; this is like an arsonist saying "check your fire alarms regularly". To them, anything 'right-wing' or nationalistic is the politics of hate, which implies that Marxism is the politics of love (!). Being pro-genocide, pro-racial conflict, anti-culture, and pro-One World Government is 'love', is it? Oh, I see, now

I understand (face palm). In a sense, Marxism is indeed about love: love for the ideology, for revolution; love for the cult/cult members (by cult members); love for the ego, delusion, conflict, anarchy, degeneracy, imbalance etc. The "politics of hate" phrase is typical virtue-signalling Marxist wolf-in-sheep's-clothing deception. It's a classic, and people fall for it all the time.

Cultural or Moral Relativism

These are concepts we can trace back to another manifestation of Marxism called Postmodernism. 'Relativism' comes from the idea of subjectivity: that reality is open to individual interpretation, as it's not necessarily set in stone. (Postmodernism is examined more in its own section). From Wikipedia: "Cultural relativism is the idea that a person's beliefs and practices should be understood based on that person's own culture. Proponents of cultural relativism also tend to argue that the norms and values of one culture should not be evaluated using the norms and values of another".[10]

Cultural Relativism is the Marxism-inspired idea that all cultures are equal and should be considered so. It insists, most importantly, that we should not decide that some cultures/cultural practices are superior to others (particularly if we deem Western culture(s) to be superior to non-Western ones in any way). In addition, the cult/ideology is opposed to hierarchies, so it cannot allow anyone to think this way. Obviously, we can see that concepts like these are used to indoctrinate the masses in to accepting Marxian sub-agendas such as 'multiculturalism' and mass migration.

From Wikipedia: "Moral relativism or ethical relativism (often reformulated as relativist ethics or relativist morality) is a term used to describe several philosophical positions concerned with the differences in moral judgments across different peoples and their own particular cultures".[11] So "Moral Relativism" is another concocted term to stop people passing judgement on any behaviour in cultures or groups different to their own.

For example, if a person in a western country expresses judgment against Female Genital Mutilation that takes place in their country, their objections can be dismissed using these terms of Cultural and Moral relativism. They may be confronted with things like: "it's not wrong, you just think it's wrong, because your culture is different to theirs!". This is absolute

---

[10] https://en.wikipedia.org/wiki/Cultural_relativism

[11] https://en.wikipedia.org/wiki/Moral_relativism

nonsense—female genital mutilation is wrong.

Interestingly, in other instances (when it suits them), the cult will often insist that all cultures are the same and equal (e.g. in 'multiculturalism'), but in instances like this (FGM) they will highlight that they are different, and these differences just need to be accepted. Some cherry-picking is evident here.

Of course, this acceptance of the differences in cultures is not a two-way street: Western countries must accept any of these 'cultural differences' and adapt their behaviour/attitudes accordingly, yet non-Westerners migrating to Western countries are not required to adapt their behaviour/attitudes (because this would be bowing to the whims of 'racists', right?). Cherry-picking and double standards are continuously recurring themes within the ideology. The former is interlinked with propaganda—the selective, creative use of information/intel.

"Champagne Socialist"

A common theme throughout the ideology's history is that people from privileged backgrounds ally themselves to socialist causes, claiming to be 'champions of the poor' etc. As pointed out earlier, people from all walks of life have become sucked into the Marxist cult, not just the poor or the privileged. That aside, there has been a significant presence of these 'bourgeois' types.

Are these people true humanitarians, who really care about the less fortunate? Are they truly empathetic, or are they just romanticising poverty and depravity? Do they genuinely believe Marxism is benevolent? Or are they perhaps aware that it, in fact, keeps the masses under control?

In understanding the ideology, there may be a perception in some that capitalism and socialism/communism are polar opposites, and if you participate in/advocate one you must be surely rejecting the other one hundred percent. In practice, this suggests that a person cannot be rich and serve/support/encourage Marxism.

This is clearly not true when we look at the global membership of the cult. The world of politics, for example, is brimming with hypocritical characters who espouse Marxist concepts yet are happy to become filthy rich (usually while engaging in traitorous behaviour and other criminal enterprises). That also goes for the endless conveyor belt of celebrities and media mouthpieces who constantly ideologically whore themselves out to promote Marxist causes in public, all year round (more on this later). The ideology itself doesn't care whether you are rich or not, just that you help it spread.

This apparent contradiction has indeed been a cornerstone of the ideology since it first reared its ugly head. In fact, when examining the various movements around the world pushing Marxist concepts, often the instigators are from relatively privileged backgrounds; Marx and Engels included. So no, Marxism is not a movement of 'the poor' or 'the workers' solely populated by the 'lowly' working classes.

"Useful Idiot"

This term implies two parties—the manipulator, and the manipulated. It's often coined to describe those who are being used to further a cause (i.e. ideological/political), while not being fully (or perhaps even partially) aware of this fact. It perfectly describes those on the naiver end of the spectrum who are helping to spread the Marxist infection, wittingly or unwittingly, even to their own detriment.

What's an "SJW"?

Acronym for Social Justice Warrior—a person who thinks they are behaving for the benefit of society; a hero of the down-trodden, the 'oppressed'. The SJW culture only exists because of Marxism, so an SJW could be classed as a useful idiot of the ideology.

All those protestors who hit the streets in cities and towns across the world in this era, with their clenched fists, banners, and megaphones, supporting Marxist sub-agendas, fit this category.

Amusingly, the Wikipedia page for Social Justice Warrior has an obvious Marxist bias in its 'definition': "Social Justice Warrior" (SJW) is a pejorative term and internet meme mostly used for an individual who promotes socially progressive, left-wing or liberal views, including feminism, civil rights, gay and transgender rights, identity politics, political correctness and multiculturalism. The accusation that somebody is an SJW carries implications that they are pursuing personal validation rather than any deep-seated conviction and engaging in disingenuous arguments".[12] Welcome to hell folks. Note how "liberal" is used, yet "Marxism/Marxist" is nowhere to been. As mentioned, the ideology is trying to control the narrative, via controlling perceptions.

"Woke"

"You are an infection, the definition of weakness. Everything that is wrong with the world, is because of fucking you. The world's not buying your bullshit your fucking pedalling. This guy's the fucking enemy.

---

[12] https://en.wikipedia.org/wiki/Social_justice_warrior

You wanna look at the enemy to our world, it's that motherfucker right there"[13]

UFC fighter Sean Strickland responds to 'woke'
journalist at press conference, Jan 2024

From the *macmillan dictionary* website: "Woke—aware of social and political issues relating to race, gender, class etc".[14]

The use of the term "woke" is an attempt by the cult/ideology to market itself as being a form of higher-intelligence and awareness. It suggests that supporting the ideology (and its sub-agendas) is a sign of a person with a superior sense of ethics, particularly on social issues (which is the exact opposite of the truth; an inversion). By extension, it suggests that being a cult member is actually a form of higher consciousness or 'awakening' (there is a link with 'spirituality' and the 'new age' movement here of course). If you're 'woke' you are a 'spiritually evolved' cult member, basically (rolls eyes).

It's just another example of the cult/ideology trying to control how it's perceived, via propagandised language. This term too is used as a pejorative term by non-cult members, while simultaneously being an indirect source of pride for some sections of the cult.

What's a "Fundamentalist Ideologue"?

This is a fanatic, basically. Someone who has tunnel-vision about whatever ideology they subscribe to, who is intolerant of other views, and may express themselves with religious fervour when defending their 'faith'.

Not everyone infected with Marxism (to one degree or another) is a fundamentalist ideologue, but there are many in the cult who are; many different levels of fanaticism within it.

The fact, though, that not all involved are full-blown fanatics is irrelevant when it comes to the overall impact of the cult on society, because the fundamentalist ideologues who are in positions of dominance/influence will dictate how the movement behaves overall. In addition, each infected/indoctrinated person who supports any aspect of the ideology (regardless of their indoctrination level), is giving the ideology their support/energy somewhat. Each contribution like this, big or small, increases the overall power of the cult/ideology.

---

[13] MMAWeekly.com, "Sean Strickland SLAYS Reporter 'You are an INFECTION'", 18 January 2024.

[14] https://www.macmillandictionary.com/dictionary/british/woke_2

Cognitive Dissonance

Cognitive dissonance is a state of mind that's absolutely relevant to the subject of Marxist indoctrination. Someone can slip into this mental state when they are simultaneously holding conflicting beliefs in their mind, and this can result in 'psychological conflict'. From the *psychologytoday.com* website: "Cognitive dissonance is a term for the state of discomfort felt when two or more modes of thought contradict each other. The clashing cognitions may include ideas, beliefs, or the knowledge that one has behaved in a certain way".[15]

Perhaps if a person is only mildly indoctrinated and/or young, they can slip into this state quite easily, since the brain-cement (the ideology in the brain wiring) is not completely 'set', so to speak. Conversely, perhaps for someone who has been indoctrinated for quite some time and who is older, it's much less likely to happen. For some, they may lose that 'neural plasticity' more over time. Hence "You can't teach an old dog new tricks". Pride and/or fear may also be an issue in this case, and obviously a person consciously using their free will to dig their heels in and be stubborn is quite a powerful thing.

In other words, when you are dealing with someone who is fully brainwashed, they won't have any doubt at all that they're right and that you're wrong (if you disagree with them). These people are what I affectionately call 'write-offs' (like a destroyed crashed car). A ruined personality, likely beyond salvage—the indoctrination has done its job on them. They are finished as an authentic human being. A non-individual. Unfortunately, the world is filling-up with them due to the infection...

To view this concept of Cognitive Dissonance from an optimistic perspective, when dealing with cult members, perhaps a person who shows signs of this (when we try to talk sense into them) is not beyond saving?

Maybe this applies to young people in particular, because of that neural plasticity factor? Future studies and experimentation on the indoctrinated ones will answer these (and other) questions.

"Don't you mean "Liberalism"?

"When we get ready to take the United States, we will not take it under the label of communism; we will not take it under the label of socialism. These labels are unpleasant to the American people and have been speared too much. We will take the United States under the labels which we have made

---

[15] "Cognitive Dissonance". https://www.psychologytoday.com/us/basics/cognitive-dissonance

very lovable; we will take it under "liberalism", under "progressivism", under "democracy". But, take it we will"[16]

Speech by millionaire cult member Alexander Trachtenberg, member of the CPUSA's Central Control Committee, at the Communist Parties National Convention, Madison Square Garden, 1944 (as recounted by whistleblower Bella Dodd in a lecture at Fordham University in 1953)

No. A Marxist infection and the resulting consequences are often attributed to liberalism. This is a common misdiagnosis. It can often occur when some of the effects of 'Cultural Marxism' are becoming obvious in society, such as: the constant emphasis on 'equality' (which many erroneously think is something to do with genuine humanitarianism); the effects of mass migration/multiculturalism and 'diversity'; the prevalence of the LGBTQ movement and feminism etc. To some, these effects (amongst others) can make it seem like 'liberalism' is the cause, but in fact it's Marxism. If a person/society does not understand the ideology and isn't able to identify where and how it's making an impact, they will often come to this erroneous conclusion.

This incorrect labelling may be due to a variety of reasons, but it's primarily due to this lack of knowledge/understanding (which, to be fair, is very common). One may use this incorrect label of "liberalism" when they're trying to explain the above social changes using only the inadequate official, superficial definition of what Marxism is (i.e. not a malevolent, subversive ideology, but a benevolent revolutionary political and socioeconomic school of thought etc.).

In other words, in that person's mind they may think "Well, Marxism/socialism is about economic equality and how society as a whole is structured politically etc., and not so much about modern civil rights and the freedom to choose our own beliefs, sexual behaviour etc., so these societal changes we are seeing here are due to liberalism, not Marxism". And that's the conclusion that they make. Others then copy them. (Again, if we don't know what Marxism actually is (in truth), how will we know what to blame it for? How will we be able to distinguish it from other things (such as liberalism)? How will we be able to see the effects it produces? Labels are important! Wrong labels = incorrect identification).

Linked to the problem of only knowing the official interpretation for Marxism, is another factor: if someone is not even aware of the Frankfurt School and "Cultural Marxism", they may be unable to identify Marxism

---

[16] "Bella Dodd Explains Communism Ducks",
https://www.YouTube.com/watch?v=VLHNz2YMnRY

as being responsible for these societal changes. They don't understand the snaky subversive nature of Marxism, hence, "liberalism" seems like a fitting label. They can't see how Marxism could be responsible for those societal changes because liberalism is an officially acknowledged, openly discussed thing in mainstream education/society, whereas Marxist subversive influence is not.

In addition, the term "liberalism" can also be used by witting disinformation agents (cult members) in order to divert attention and blame away from Marxism (a tactic mentioned earlier).

Liberalism and Marxism are very different (different strains/interpretations of what these things are aside). Liberalism can be described as a political philosophy, whereas Marxism (in truth) is a revolutionary movement that aims to change society by forcing it to change. True, liberalism may have been considered revolutionary for its time, but Marxism has an enduring revolutionary aspect which is never satisfied.

Liberalism emphasises certain ideas associated with personal freedom, such as: property ownership; the right to choose a religion/to be non-religious; and on a societal level, things like peace, democracy, free speech, equality under law, limited government, tolerance and other civil rights. This would be the general definition for 'classical' liberalism.

The last ones—"tolerance" and "civil rights"—may be where the confusion is for some. Doesn't Marxism advocate for tolerance and civil rights? No, it just seems to, in order to achieve 'equality'. Doesn't Marxism advocate for democracy? No, but it's happy to use the democratic system to achieve political dominance. Marxism for the most part is opposed to the idea of property rights. It's also, as we've seen in recent times, opposed to the idea of free speech once it's sufficiently dominant. In economic terms, liberalism supports the idea of the free market, whereas Marxism is anti-capitalism altogether.

A key difference between Marxism and liberalism is that the former (as we'll see) uses 'revolution' to attack the foundational pillars of western civilisation – capitalism, Christianity, and culture – in addition to other related components (i.e. the traditional family unit).

Another is that liberalism advocates freedom for the individual, whereas Marxism wants to force equality and change on society; and you are only allowed freedom provided you conform to Marxism. Creating an 'equal' society requires the application of totalitarian control, since equality is a man-made, artificial concept (i.e. it does not reflect how society works in practice).

On that point, liberalism is not ruthless and militant in its attitude, so does not actively pursue the suppression of political opposition. Nor does liberalism have a long heritage of professional, systematic subversion, with a worldwide network of organisations trying to force the world to conform to its ideology(!). (Again, this point is unseen by someone unaware of the subversive nature of Marxism). Finally, liberalism is the idea of a person having freedom from totalitarian/governmental control, whereas Marxism (as the world is now finding out, but the cult members are oblivious too) is actually pro-totalitarianism.

Most importantly of all, being a very pertinent point for this work: liberalism cannot explain the level of systemic, co-ordinated indoctrination we are seeing in the world. It does not explain how we are dealing with a massive, global cult that exemplifies fanaticism! If that's not clear to the reader by this point, it will be as we progress through it.

Is Marxism hiding behind liberalism? As in, is the destructive nature of the ideology camouflaging itself using the mask of social liberalism? Marxism feigns benevolence, so liberalism provides this pleasant veneer. In other words, Marxism can appear to be in favour of 'freedom for the individual' etc., but it only does this because it knows that these 'freedoms' only result in destructive effects. Abortion fits into this category. The Marxian sub-agenda of feminism promotes/supports it under the guise of wanting what's best for women in the name of 'equality', but what Marxism really wants is the destruction of the family unit, population reduction, the encouragement of 'radical' feminism, the destruction of masculinity etc., as they all help to destroy civilisation.

One of the smoking guns to show us that it's Marxism and not liberalism, is when these apparently 'humanitarian' or 'civil rights' movements are very over-the-top and seem to be intentionally causing destruction. This shows us that the idea that the movement in question is actually helping anyone is just a smokescreen; the real intention is destruction. A very clear example of this was the Marxist Black Lives Matter movement in the U.S. in 2020. It pretended to be about civil rights, but just ends up being destructive and calls for the complete overhaul of society. Some would mistakenly call that OTT liberalism or call them "Liberals". This is wrong! It's the ideology doing what it does best: it finds a cause and gathers the useful dupes in order to further its own agenda; then, the chaos and destruction ensues.

It starts off with a catalytic event (death of George Floyd), and they then claim their response is all about justice, human rights, equality, etc. (and some will attribute that to 'liberalism'); but soon you have people talking about the destruction of the evil oppressive capitalistic fascist police state, business owners and private property being attacked/destroyed, and calls to destroy and restructure the whole country etc! That's Marxism, not liberalism!

We must be aware of the application of Marxist tactics here. Marxist deceivers will happily throw this term "liberalism" into the mix to prevent the masses catching-on to who the real enemy is. We see this happening all the time online in the multitude of discussions, even in conservative/right-wing/nationalist/patriotic circles. Wittingly or unwittingly, cult members don't want us talking about Marxists/Marxism, and identifying them/it as the problem, since it's the beginning of the end for them…

As stated, this incorrect labelling is a serious problem. We need to keep in mind that this word "liberalism" can be used in public discourse for several reasons including clumsiness, habit, a lack of understanding/awareness of the cult/ideology, or deliberate use of that term by cult members for the aforementioned reasons. Remember, they don't call themselves Marxists, and with good reason (because it's advantageous for them). For the same reason, they don't want us calling them that.

Bolshevik

This term described the members of a Russian political faction that was created at the start of the 20th century, during Vladimir Lenin's time. Bolshevik just means the "majority" in Russian (bolshinstvo), and it emerged from a split with the Mensheviks ("minority"); both of these groups were essentially factions of the Social Democratic Labour Party— a Marxist party in Russia at that time.[17] The Bolsheviks rose to infamy by being the driving force of the two transformative revolutions in Russia in 1917. Bolshevism is the term used to describe this mobs modus operandi.

So, is it accurate to call Marxists all over the world today "Bolsheviks"? No. Nor is it constructive/practical, since Marxists just love to distance themselves from what happened in those big 'socialist' disaster states like Russia post-1917.

So yes, there's a connection between the Bolsheviks, Bolshevism and Marxism; but Marxism is more to the core of the issue. What we are focusing on here is the core, ubiquitous ideology, not a group, movement, regime etc.

Evil terms

[17] "Bolshevism",
https://www.oxfordreference.com/display/10.1093/oi/authority.20110803095516209

Here's some definitions of terms for things that cult members don't like. The cult's propaganda over the decades has done a really good job at distorting how non-Marxist concepts are perceived (no surprise there!). In fact, in this book we consider that Marxism has ensured a consistently distorted perception of these concepts in much of the modern world, including concepts which might be to our benefit (i.e. 'right'-leaning ideologies such as 'nationalism'). One step at a time though… Also, for the reader's benefit, we need to be clear in what these terms mean. We may be expanding on (some of) these terms in later sections, but for now, it's prudent to give them at least a mention.

What is "Right-wing"?

Not Marxist. This includes having political or social views that may be considered nationalistic, conservative, or traditional. We explore the left v right political dichotomy later. Suffice to say for now, that 'left' and 'right' are not equal! The 'left' are the real troublemakers in the world today, not the 'right' (as the cult would like us to believe, of course). The 'left' are the ones mostly in the driving seat, not the 'right', and we are all headed towards the cliff.

What's "Nationalism" and "Patriotism"?

Nationalism is the idea that a country can have independence and sovereignty as a nation, and that it can be a distinct, separate entity from other countries. As in, it can govern itself, without having to relinquish its control to a foreign entity. For example, a European country not being controlled by the European Union, and therefore deciding its own fate. Due to the confusion that Marxism inspires, some may feel that one can be nationalistic yet also be 'left-wing' on certain things (e.g. a Marxist 'Republican' movement, that claims to be nationalist while also being socialist/Marxist; more on this later).

We would need to examine this on a person-by-person basis to understand what exactly this interpretation means. All that matters though is how much this person supports Marxism. The rest is just labelling and discussion.

What is patriotism? The mindset of an individual/group who wants sovereignty for their folk, their country. A patriot is also someone who is proud of their national identity (culture, traditions etc.) and wants to preserve it, who wants what's 'best' for their country/people, and who cares about the conditions therein. Unfortunately, not everyone's perception of what's 'best' is correct; it really depends on whether someone has a conscience or not. Of course, if someone is an indoctrinated cult member, with a distorted perception of right and wrong (a sub-standard conscience), their perception of what's best for a country/group/individual is going to be inferior to that of someone who isn't indoctrinated.

This is a massively important central issue throughout our struggle with the cult/ideology—the importance of what is ethically 'right' becoming manifest in our reality.

The Marxist interpretation of those things

Later, we'll do a more in-depth analysis of the various Marxist terms (and 'insults'). For now, here's the short version: Marxist propaganda has been trying to convince us all throughout its history that certain things are downright evil. Anything that opposes the cult/ideology is 'evil', basically. Surely this is familiar to you all, thanks to the recent pathetic behaviour of cult members around the world.

According to the cult, if you are 'right-wing' this means you are not a Marxist and are therefore evil. You are fascist, authoritarian, potentially murderous and genocidal etc. Naturally 'left-wing' means humanitarianism, peace, love, compassion etc. Basically, if you are 'right-wing' you are bad, and if you are 'left-wing' you are a fantastic human being. So 'left' is good, and 'right' is bad. Anyone who the cult doesn't like is labelled 'right' ('bad'), or even worse — 'far-right' ('very bad'). So essentially, it's a very childish way for the cult to call their enemies bad. That's all it is! Nothing intellectually complex here: just playground-style psychologically elementary name calling, with a dollop of childishness and virtue-signalling, plus a large economy bag of ego. It's very sad that a large chunk of the world's population seems to have fallen for this word-play con. Juvenile bullshit.

If you are a 'nationalist' this means you are not a Marxist and you are just like the Nazis who wanted to take over the world so you want to take over the world too because you are a Nazi and you're gonna invade Poland and start World War three and gas 666 million Jews (and breathe and relax). Which is all evil!! Evil, evil, eeeeeviiiiiiillllll!

If you are a 'nationalist' (according to Marxists) it means you think your country and people are so great, that you will inevitably want to start attacking other countries etc. Ergo, "nationalism" = evil. Obviously, the millions of sane, intelligent, good-natured human beings across the world who may call themselves "nationalists", "patriots" or by another label (and who refuse to conform to 'globalism'/Marxism) are not intending to be militaristic, globe-trotting murderers as the cult is insinuating! They just want to be left alone in peace!

Section II—Overview and Relevant Bits

"Capital is an international force. To vanquish it, an international workers' alliance, an international workers' brotherhood, is needed. We are opposed to national enmity and discord, to national exclusiveness. We are internationalists"[1]

Lenin, "Letter to the Workers and Peasants of the Ukraine", 1919

"Marxism is internationalism. Our aim is not to erect new frontiers but to dissolve all frontiers in a socialist federation of the world"[2]

Article on *socialist.net* (*Socialist Appeal*)
by Alan Woods, July 2001

Things it's for or against

Keeping in mind the various strains of Marxian thought, here's the stance of the internationalist cult on various issues in general (we are examining the ideology here, not the particular opinions of any individual or group).

Marxism is for: Revolution and changing society according to its will; 'open' or non-existent borders, since countries shouldn't even exist anyway, and, by extension, countries/regions being part of big international organisations (e.g. The UN, the EU); 'equality'; dividing people in to groups; collectivism and uniformity; 'Multiculturalism'/multi-ethnic societies; socialist-style government and that 'the people' should have 'collective ownership' of a country's property, resources, infrastructure, utilities etc. (aka 'communal ownership'); having a 'progressive' stance on social issues and 'civil rights' causes, including feminism, LGBTQ issues, abortion etc.; degeneracy (in health, relationships, social behaviour, drug use, law and order etc.).; free speech (when it's not in control/in its

---

[1] Lenin, V.I., "Letter to the Workers and Peasants of the Ukraine", 28 December 1919.

[2] Woods, A., "Marxism versus feminism — The class struggle and the emancipation of women", 18 July 2001. https://socialist.net/marxism-feminism-class-struggle-emancipation-women/

ascension to dominance).

Marxism is against: having borders/separation from other countries; capitalism, free market, wealth, profits, private property and rights of inheritance; anything considered right-wing, fascist etc., including anything considered 'racist', xenophobic etc.; 'conspiracy theorists' and anything the system considers a 'conspiracy theory'; nationalism, national identity and culture (the idea of a country having sovereignty, pride in its unique identity, ethnically or otherwise); free speech (or to be more precise, any non-Marxist points of view) when it's in control; religion (in general, but particularly Christianity); racial homogeneity (a country/its population remaining predominantly one racial group. This only applies to traditionally/predominantly white countries); any perceived criticism or mistreatment of any person/creature belonging to an 'oppressed' group (including women, non-white people, those in LGBTQ categories, certain animals etc.); privatisation of services (as opposed to state ownership/nationalisation); hierarchies; American 'imperialism'/foreign policy.

The promise of 'Utopia'

Marxism promises to deliver 'utopia' once there is the required 'revolution', which is a massive psychological carrot to dangle in front of people. It's the promise of a better world in a hypothetical distance future. Some forms of the ideology ostensibly push for 'reformism', which is still a type of revolution anyway: it's deliberate change of the established order in a society to make it more Marxist. Whatever method the cult/ideology chooses, this utopia is always just around the corner, like a mirage in the desert.

Has there ever truly been a 'utopia' in the world? Do we tend to like the idea of utopia as human beings? Absolutely, it sounds very nice. And it's because of this tendency that the idea of utopia creates an opportunity for emotional manipulation in the minds of anyone exposed to the ideology. Cult members feel that they're ushering-in a beautiful revolution, that in the end, what's left is a quasi-utopian society (provided the revolution is successful and complete). This noble quest can give a person 'purpose' in their lives. As the great Bolshevik Marxist prophet Leon Trotsky once wrote: "Life is not an easy matter…You cannot live through it without falling into frustration and cynicism unless you have before you a great idea which raises you above personal misery, above weakness, above all kinds of perfidy and baseness". That's very true, but it doesn't give a person the right to be a degenerate Marxist cult member of course.[3]

Destruction to create Utopia

> "A Marxist begins with his prime truth that all evils are caused by the exploitation of the proletariat by the capitalists. From this he logically proceeds to the revolution to end capitalism into a new social order of the dictatorship of the proletariat, and...(then) the political paradise of communism"

Saul Alinsky, Reveille for Radicals (1946)[4]

> "The revolution is not an apple that falls when it is ripe. You have to make it fall"[5]

Argentinian cult member Ernesto "Che" Guevara

The concept of destroying the structure of society, to create an injustice-free, egalitarian Communist utopia has always been at the core of Marxist revolution, though the exact methods by which this would be achieved (according to the cult's prophets) have evolved over time.

Karl Marx and Friedrich Engels predicted that the workers would rise-up and overthrow their capitalist overlords in a bloody revolution and establish a dictatorship of the proletariat. In the Communist Manifesto they wrote: "The Communists disdain to conceal their views and aims. They openly declare that their ends can be attained only by the forcible overthrow of all existing social conditions. Let the ruling classes tremble at a Communistic revolution. The proletarians have nothing to lose but their chains. They have a world to win. Working Men of All Countries, Unite!".[6]

Later, one of the chief protagonists of the Russian Revolution of 1917 - Vladimir Lenin - realised that the proletariat workers wouldn't just 'rise-up' without receiving some 'guidance'.

He then came up with the idea of a 'proletarian vanguard' (also known as a 'revolutionary vanguard' and other names), which meant that a group of dedicated Marxist cult members would lead the way towards revolution.

They would then (inevitably) govern thereafter once the previous

---

[3] Trotsky, L., *Diary in Exile* (1935). https://libquotes.com/leon-trotsky/quote/lbq4f3f

[4] Alinsky, S., *Reveille for Radicals* (1946). https://libquotes.com/saul-alinsky/quote/lbt7s4h

[5] Che Guevara speaks: Selected Speeches and Writings (1967). https://libquotes.com/che-guevara/quote/lbi9v5x

[6] Marx and Engels, *The Communist Manifesto* (1948), section 4, paragraph 11.

establishment was overthrown and destroyed. This idea started to make an appearance in his 1902 pamphlet "What is to be Done? Burning Questions of Our Movement". In it Lenin asserted that a political party needed to be created to embody this revolutionary movement. It could then 'influence'/indoctrinate the proletariat class to participate in the revolution.

He wrote: "Everyone agrees that it is necessary to develop the political consciousness of the working class. The question is, how that is to be done and what is required to do it".[7] He talked about the idea of "going among the workers" and that "Class political consciousness can be brought to the workers only from without, that is from outside the sphere of relations between workers and employers".[8]

He spoke of subversion (underlined for emphasis): "We must "go among all classes of the population" as theoreticians, as propagandists, as agitators, and as organisers",[9] and "The principal thing, of course, is propaganda and agitation among all strata of the people".[10] Finally: "We must take upon ourselves the task of organising an all-round political struggle under the leadership of our Party in such a manner as to make it possible for all oppositional strata to render their fullest support to the struggle and to our Party. We must train our Social-Democratic practical workers to become political leaders, able to guide all the manifestations of this all-round struggle".[11]

On 14 November 1917, in his Speech on the Agrarian Question he said: "A party is the vanguard of a class, and its duty is to lead the masses and not merely to reflect the average political level of the masses".[12]

So essentially, after all those speeches and grandstanding, and all that upheaval and bloodshed, you are just left with a single-party regime who are accountable to no-one, and who are going to run the place in to the ground with civilisation-wrecking Marxist theories.

In his 2008 book *The World on Fire: 1919 and the Battle with Bolshevism,* historian Anthony Read wrote: "Bolshevism was founded on a lie, setting

---

[7] Lenin, V. I. "What is to be Done? Burning Questions of Our Movement", 1902, P. 48.

[8] Ibid. P. 48.

[9] Ibid. P. 50.

[10] Ibid. P. 50.

[11] Ibid. P. 52–53.

[12] Lenin, V.I., "Speech on the Agrarian Question", 14 November 1917.

a precedent that was to be followed for the next ninety years. Lenin had no time for democracy, no confidence in the masses and no scruples about the use of violence. He wanted a small, tightly organised, and strictly disciplined party of hard-line professional revolutionaries, who would do exactly as they were told".[13]

So Lenin, as a major Marxist figure, started to promote this idea that the 'proletariat' had to be 'guided' (pushed) towards revolution. A departure somewhat from the ideas of Marx and Engels that it would be a natural, evolutionary process (remember "ideas based on ideas based on ideas").

Lenin's ideas about revolution and the proletariat class evolved over time. He had originally thought that the workers would rise-up spontaneously, as Marx and Engels did; but by the time of his 1920 pamphlet "Left-Wing" Communism: An Infantile Disorder. A Popular Exposition of Marxist Strategy and Tactics" he realised that his earlier opinions of how the proletariat class would behave were too 'optimistic' (as in, they weren't behaving like a Marxist would want).[14] And here we have the idea that these workers were just too under the spell of the bourgeois capitalist system to want revolution. Well, how fucking convenient!

Later in the ideology's evolution, cult members developed the idea that the masses didn't want to rise-up or fully-embrace socialism because they were too wedded to, and influenced by, the perceived pillars of the west: capitalism, Christianity, and culture. Therefore, in order for the masses to accept socialism (and eventually communism), first Western Civilisation had to be destroyed. These ideas were then expanded-upon by the likes of Herbert Marcuse (1898–1979) and Theodore Adorno (1903–1969) of *The Frankfurt School*.

This destructive 'critical' nature of Marxism explains much of the anti-civilisation behaviour we are experiencing in the world today. This nature is evident in Marxism's product of socialism. Socialism helps to achieve the destruction of western civilisation by attacking capitalism and offering an unviable 'alternative' to it; an alternative that could lead to a more 'just' (utopian) society. It should also be noted that 'socialist' movements are not merely anti-capitalistic—they are generally anti-Christianity and anti-culture too.

"The end justifies the means"

---

[13] Read, A. *The World on Fire: 1919 and the Battle with Bolshevism* (2008). P. 5.

[14] Lenin "Left-Wing" Communism: An Infantile Disorder. A Popular Exposition of Marxist Strategy and Tactics", 1920.

"To do evil a human being must first of all believe that what he's doing is good, or else that it's a well-considered act in conformity with natural law. Fortunately, it is in the nature of the human being to seek a justification for his actions... Ideology—that is what gives the evildoing its long-sought justification and gives the evildoer the necessary steadfastness and determination"[15]

Aleksandr Solzhenitsyn, *The Gulag Archipelago:*
An Experiment in Literary Investigation (1973)

The idea that "the end justifies the means" is another major aspect of Marxism that's interlinked with its proclivity towards destruction to create 'utopia'. This essentially means that whatever suffering, death, and depravity is experienced while all this destruction is taking place is not only completely justifiable, but actually positive! It's the inversion of what's ethical/moral (according to any sane, rational person), so what was previously considered bad behaviour, is now actually good. If you ever wondered why, daily, Marxists all over the world of all stripes can commit the unforgivable crimes that they do against their fellow countrymen/women (wittingly or unwittingly), this is why. They are being done 'for the greater good'.

What we must understand about the cult's members is that most are believers in the ostensibly benevolent, Marxian (socialist/communist) utopian fantasy, but not perceivers of the actual malevolent effect of the ideology in the real world (the theory v reality problem). For some, they are unable to process reality from a conscious, pragmatic, ethical point of view. These types may be simply indoctrinated and are perhaps lacking somewhat as human beings regardless.

For others, they can see that it's destructive, but they don't care and may in fact enjoy the destruction. These types are sadistic psychotics. Marxism caters for many types of damaged person, and its destructive nature gives destructive personality types the excuse they need...to destroy. We can see this process in action when observing these 'righteous' riots involving Marxist groups throughout history.

The idea of having a revolution to destroy the existing order and replace it with a utopian society—or indeed 'reforming' society to make it more 'utopian'—is a major, central aspect of the ideology. The chaos we are experiencing in our societies now, exists because of this misguided erroneous principle. The cult/ideology thinks it's taking us towards heaven,

---

[15] Solzhenitsyn, A., *The Gulag Archipelago: An Experiment in Literary Investigation* (1973).

but, in fact, it's dragging us all to hell (not necessarily in a 'religious after-life' sense, but a literal shit-hole existence here on Earth, in this life).

To summarise here—Marxism is going to destroy or transform everything that's good or that functions, so it can then re-build society based on a bunch of faulty theories. In other words, it's going to destroy everything for no good reason, as it has always done.

Some shit Karl and Freddy said

Between them Marx and Engels produced many written works, the most famous being The Communist Manifesto in 1848 (Marx's most famous other writing would be Das Kapital or "Capital" in 1867). Overall, their opinions on how the emergent capitalism was shaping their world were generally negative, and their opinions on the motives of businessmen, landowners, the rich (the "bourgeoisie") were cynical to say the least. That cynicism is the origin of the cult's hatred for capitalism, and anything associated with it including profits, land ownership, business hierarchies, and any perceived 'exploitation' therein etc. The idea that a person might be grateful for having the ability to earn some money and support themselves and their families (or indeed, to simply survive) was not emphasised overall.

Marx and Engels thought it unethical that one person could profit from another person's labour in the manner that the capitalists of their time did. Marx would later add to this notion by promoting erroneous concepts such as the 'labour theory of value' and the ridiculous theory of 'alienation' in his book Capital (which is regarded as a work of genius by many). It's because of shit like this, we see the "profits are evil!" mentality emanating from cult members.

According to them, due to the shortcomings of capitalism and the "naked, shameless, direct, brutal exploitation"[16] within it, this system – and the bourgeoisie business/landowners who lorded over it – were destined to be violently overthrown by the working classes ("the proletariat") whom the capitalists had been (apparently) preying upon.

This negative, oversimplifying, incendiary concept of dividing society in to two distinct classes—Oppressor (rich) v Oppressed (poor)—was the seed which has grown into this juggernaut of chaos now destroying civilisation; it's the shoddy foundation upon which all Marxist 'revolutions' and institutions are built.

It must be noted that in Marxism the 'middle-classes' have been

---

[16] Marx and Engels, *The Communist Manifesto* (1848). P. 16.

traditionally regarded as connected to the 'bourgeoisie' class, which inevitably made them a target; anyone with wealth, basically. (Obviously, the definition of what 'middle-class' is has changed over time).

We will be analysing and utilising this 'Oppressor v Oppressed' concept in-depth throughout. For now, it suffices to say that this concept has given countless people in the last couple of centuries an outlet for their feelings of disenfranchisement, and an excuse to 'revolt' and destroy: "We are the poor, innocent oppressed, and we are taking revenge against the oppressor!".

Hegel

Components of the theoretical work of Marx and Engels were influenced by the work of German philosopher G.W.F. Hegel (1770–1831). The Hegelian Dialect, for example, has been quite rightly identified as part of the DNA of Marxism. This dialect was described using the triad of terms thesis, antithesis, and synthesis, though not by Hegel himself (the description came from another German philosopher by the name of Heinrich Moritz Chalybaus (1796–1862)). Hegel used the terms abstract, negative and concrete (another interpretation of this is Problem-Reaction-Solution) Dialectical manipulation, essentially, is when a 'choice' is presented to a subject (individual or group) with an ulterior motive, and the party presenting this 'choice' desires a certain outcome. The oppressor v oppressed principle is based on this—it encourages you to 'pick a side', through emotional manipulation (explained elsewhere). Other familiar concepts were evident in Hegel's work too: "The Catholics had been in the position of oppressors, and the Protestants of the oppressed".[17]

Though heavily influenced by the largely philosophical work of Hegel, Marx's and Engel's work retained less of the philosophical, placing more emphasis on a materialistic perspective of how society is structured and the dynamics between these components (labour, class, economics etc.). It's interesting that for Marx, civilisation was mostly based around materialistic things including money (probably because he never really worked or generated wealth in his life and had a complex about this).

Their work combined the dialectical element and the idea of 'class struggle' with their opinions on history, society, and economics. Their primarily materialistic analysis of those subjects (and the subject of nature) led to the eventual creation of 'Dialectical Materialism' and 'Historical Materialism'

---

[17] Hegel, G.W.F., *The German Constitution* (1802). https://libquotes.com/georg-wilhelm-friedrich-hegel/quote/lbr3v8e

as sort of sub-ideologies within Marxism.

We can also say that Marx and Engels reinterpreted Hegel's ideas in a less-idealistic manner; their work became more 'scientific'. This is a very significant point, and in part explains the nature of the ideology: lacking in true human qualities (including genuine empathy); lacking appreciation for naturally occurring uniqueness, inequality, and diversity; excessively 'logical' on certain issues, such as religiosity etc.

Another influential concept of Hegel's was the master-slave relationship. This laid the foundations for the oppressor v oppressed principle in Marxism.

We can see the Marxian DNA when Hegel wrote: "The master is in possession of a surplus of what is physically necessary; the servant lacks it, and indeed in such a way that the surplus and the lack of it are not accidental aspects but the indifference of necessary needs".[18]

We can swap "master" for "oppressor" or "bourgeoisie", and "servant" for "oppressed" or "proletariat". In addition, that quote relates to the "labour theory of value' that Marx used in his work Das Kapital—the idea that the 'master' unfairly keeps the 'surplus' value of a worker's labour.

'Oppressor' v 'Oppressed'

This is an original aspect of Marxism that still exists today, as the foundation for most Marxist sub-movements and agendas. Originally, 'oppressor' v 'oppressed' were terms used to describe the wealthy capitalist/business-owner class (the bourgeoisie) and the poor working class (proletariat). We can also say: the user v the used; the controller v the controlled; the dominant v the dominated; or master and slave.

Crucially, this formula plays off people's emotions, by using any feelings of resentment or disenfranchisement they might feel towards others, life etc. It draws-out and encourages the victim mentality, using it to manipulate the person in to actively participating-in (or at least supporting) 'revolutionary' (Marxist) action. The end result is destruction, via chaos. A large portion of the world's population has been experiencing this process for many decades now, with many not even knowing it exists.

We have all, during the courses of our lives, felt disenfranchised or victimised at some point; it's just a psychological tendency that human beings have; but it must be kept in check! However, sometimes, we may be justified in feeling that way (if we have genuinely been mistreated

---

[18] Hegel, G.W.F., *System of Ethical Life and First Philosophy of Spirit* (1802).

somehow), but sometimes we jump to convenient conclusions, and we need to get a hold of ourselves; some people, clearly, just don't have the required constitution to do this. Until we get a handle on this tendency in our lives, with time and maturity, it can be a real balancing act deciding whether we are justified in feeling victimised. All it takes is a nudge in the wrong direction (at the right time) for a person to decide to choose victimhood as their 'default' mindset, in a sense.

It's for this reason that many fall in to the psychological/emotional trap of the Marxist oppressor v oppressed indoctrination. (It should be common knowledge that people mistreating each other has been a natural feature of existence for humanity—trying to somehow prevent this from happening on a societal level can itself be interpreted as 'utopian', revolutionary behaviour).

The ideology feeds on this mechanism by providing a convenient outlet for our emotions. If we don't understand this mechanism within ourselves, and are unable to control it, absorbing the ideology can then make us emotionally charged, in addition to being potentially dumb and irrational. In this 'lower frequency' mental state, we are then more predictable, more easily manipulated, and therefore easier to control.

Looking at the global Marxist activist, 'revolutionary' cult movement, are these people not the perfect example of this? If we had to pick one term to describe them, words like "controlled" and "predictable" would be just as appropriate as "Marxist" or "cult member" or anything else.

This element of emotional manipulation has always been a feature of Marxism. Whether we are picturing a mob of disgruntled factory workers somewhere in Europe in the 1800s, who are in a frenzy at the factory gates; or the aggressive mobs during the Black Lives Matter riots in 2020, assaulting shop owners or stopping traffic and damaging cars; it's the same mechanism at work. You simply: inject some Marxism into people's minds (via government initiatives, academia, media, community groups etc.); tell them what they want to hear ("you're oppressed!") and stroke their ego's; tell them who the enemy is; sit back and watch the carnage!

The beginning of the Communist Manifesto clearly shows the emphasis on the division between groups in society; encapsulated in the core, destructive, pervasive concept of Oppressor v Oppressed (underlined for emphasis): "The history of all hitherto existing society is the history of class struggles. Freeman and slave, patrician and plebeian, lord and serf, guild-master and journeyman, in a word, oppressor and oppressed, stood in constant opposition to one another, carried on an uninterrupted, now hidden, now open fight, a fight that each time ended, either in a revolutionary reconstitution of society at large, or in the common ruin of the contending classes".[19]

In addition to dividing society into groups/classes, it also suggests conflict, and that either there will be revolution, or all groups will be annihilated. One of the catchphrases of the French Revolution was "La Liberté ou la mort!", Liberty or Death. Now, imagine how many impressionable minds have read that passage in the past century or so? Right there at the start of the Manifesto. Can you imagine? Even the laziest reader would have absorbed it, even though the whole thing is only 68 pages.

Marxists also teach that historical forces are a cause of oppression, having been forced upon them without their consent, thus leading them toward the need for complete societal revolution to throw off these forces. From the preface of the 1883 German edition, written by Engels: "this struggle, however, has now reached a stage where the exploited and oppressed class can no longer emancipate itself from the class which exploits and oppresses it, without at the same time forever freeing the whole of society from exploitation, oppression, class struggles".[20] Talk about drinking your own Kool-aid! This suggests that the whole of society needs to 'liberated', and that the revolution needs to be total.

Think of the Marxist cult members ('activists') today—are they still repeating these concepts like parrots constantly? Yes, nauseatingly so. Again, this is why the whole lot must go in the trash. The basic principles that have been part of this from the beginning are the problem, not simply any particular interpretation or faction.

Again, we must avoid getting sucked-in to the pseudo-intellectual babble around Marxism, particularly the non-useful parts. These are all just men with opinions, theories. There's nothing necessarily wrong with that, but the problems start when brainwashed cult members want to construct society around these opinions. If the theories are faulty (or if they are useful but are incorrectly interpreted), they may become harmful. Particularly if their application in society needs to be forced (i.e. trying to enforce the artificial concepts of uniformity and equality).

The centralisation of power

Collectivisation is one of the ideology's fundamental principles. Marxism (through its vehicle socialism) insists that if a society is to be transformed in to a more 'just', egalitarian one, then more power and wealth must be

---

[19] Marx and Engels, *The Communist Manifesto* (1848), P. 14.

[20] Engels, F., *The Communist Manifesto* (1848), preface to 1883 German edition, P. 6.

given to 'the people' (i.e. people who aren't wealthy and/or have no 'freedom' or 'power'). This is the path to 'equality'. The concept of 'communism', in a sense, is the community of these relatively 'dis-empowered' types that could be formed in to one collective (according to the ideology).

The theory is that a government system can be created to make manifest this ideal, with a collective ownership/direction coming from 'the people'. Inevitably, in practice, someone/some group needs to actually run the show. Obviously, 'the people' – as a whole population of millions of individuals – can't run a country; any other thinking is just ridiculous collectivist nonsense. It's just not how reality works. If society is a ship, then someone controls the rudder.

Wherever and whenever Marxism has gained enough momentum to take control of a country, this results in a Marxist one-party system of control (or similar system). Even if it doesn't fit this exact format, the ideology is still in the driving seat. Control of the economy, nationalisation of industries and infrastructure, confiscation of land and resources etc. usually follows. Any personal, individual lust for power aside (amongst the cult members involved), the ideology itself, in a sense, demands control of these things.

So historically, though Marxism was supposed to be about giving 'power to the people', it inevitably resulted in this centralisation of power, usually in the hands of violent Marxist thugs/criminals/terrorists of one type or another, who (shockingly!) lacked the required skills to manage a country once they acquired control of it. Why? It's because they are not qualified to do so; the only knowledge they have of economies and business is flawed Marxist perceptions and theories about them. Participating in a destructive revolution doesn't contradictorily, as if by magic, imbue one with constructive abilities!

Cult members may disagree that this is not real communism, insisting that a one-party totalitarian government is not what was envisaged by Marx and Engels (and their faithful disciples), that it should be a government composed of 'the people'. Who cares what they may or may not have envisaged! In practice, when Marxist revolutionaries take power, they end up in control, naturally. Whenever there is a power vacuum, someone will always step in to that void: this is how its always worked, way before Marxism arrived on the scene.

If you destroy the established order, a power vacuum is created. And when society is in a state of chaos, this is when the brutish psychos enter the picture..

The story of power and control in the world goes back millennia, to the dawn of man. We have always had psychopathic control freaks in society, long before Marxism appeared. However, since it manifested, it has provided a convenient vehicle for these types to get their hands on the reins of power. When we talk about the many Marxist regimes throughout history—Lenin and Trotsky (then Stalin) in Russia, Mao Zedong in China, Fidel Castro (1926–2016) in Cuba, Nicolae Ceausescu (1918–1989) in Romania, Pol Pot (1925–1998) in Cambodia, Robert Mugabe (1924–2019) in Zimbabwe, and the many other regimes in Africa and South America—all of them (to one degree or another) have the same pattern.

The pattern is: Marxism convinces enough people that Marxism is the answer, which means a destruction of all (non-Marxist) opposition by the leading Marxist group involved. This dominance then leads to a situation where the psycho leader of this group will be able to rule a whole country. (It's also true that not all these revolutions were one hundred percent grass-roots movements, and there were no external parties involved. For example, the Bolsheviks being financed and encouraged by parties outside Russia; the rise of Mao and the birth of Red China being supported by similar parties etc.).

Any sort of centralisation of power poses this inherent risk, of course, but it depends on who's holding the reins, doesn't it? Certainly, having a bunch of ultra-partisan fanatics with destructive tendencies in charge is bad news, particularly for anyone not part of the gang/cult. Since Marxism has been operating in our world consistently for quite some time now, we must always be vigilant, because power and control is the name of the game.

On a global scale, when we are looking for signs of these things, any big international organisations who are trying to consolidate power should be viewed with suspicion (using our special anti-Marxist glasses). Obviously, when an entity like the United Nations – a big global intergovernmental conglomerate organisation with 193 member countries – starts talking about having 'unity' or 'solidarity', we should see this as being a massive commie red flag. The ideology is present here and you–and your country - better watch-the-fuck-out.

Of course, trying to create an 'equal' society requires coercion, since equality is an artificial, Marxist concept. We are currently seeing this coercion manifesting across the globe, through the enforcement of control over our lives. 'Equality' is Marxist code for uniformity and conformity (which leads to the passivity and control of the masses). It has nothing to do with benevolence or charity of any kind, or 'humanitarianism'. Tens of millions of people worldwide – who are cult members whether they realise it or not – are controlled with this simple, virtue-signalling deception.

('Equality' is expanded upon later).

Conspiracy and subversion: a Marxist tradition

"Communism is frequently described as a philosophy—but it is not a philosophy in which intellectually honest men can believe for long. It is a conspiracy in which hate-driven men participate. Lenin confirmed this. In his important and authoritative work What is to be Done?, written in 1902 he set forth his views on the structure on the Communist Party, and said: "Conspiracy is so essential a condition of an organisation of this kind that all other conditions...must be made to conform with it." in other words, the philosophy of communism must be bent and twisted as needed to fit the conspiratorial needs of the situation"[21]

John A. Stormer, *None Dare Call It Treason* (1964)

"It is necessary to agree to any and every sacrifice, and even – if need be – to resort to all sorts of stratagems, manoeuvres and illegal methods, to evasion and subterfuges in order to penetrate the trade unions, to remain in them, and to carry on Communist work in them at all costs"[22]

Vladimir Lenin, *V.I. Lenin Selected Works* (1938)

Let's look at this from a rational point of view: is the very notion of 'conspiracy' ridiculous? Or is it just a made-up thing that should make us giggle? Is this something that is the domain of hysterical paranoid types, or is it something we should take seriously? In recent times, the term "Conspiracy Theorist" has played a role in how the concept of a 'conspiracy' is now perceived.

The concept of a conspiracy is contained in criminal law. From Wikipedia: "In criminal law, a conspiracy is an agreement between two or more persons to commit a crime at some time in the future".[23] From the *Legal Information Institute* website: "An agreement between two or more people to commit an illegal act, along with an intent to achieve the agreement's goal. Most U.S. jurisdictions also require an overt act toward furthering the agreement".[24] It must be noted that treason is a crime, and that's what Marxist subversion and activism is: treason. This is a point often missed in the fog of war, thanks to the ideology's effect on people's perceptions (on topics such as nation, law, ethics etc.).

---

[21] Stormer, John A., *None Dare Call It Treason* (1964), P. 16.

[22] Lenin, V.I., Selected Works, vol. 10, (p. 95), 1938.

[23] https://en.wikipedia.org/wiki/Criminal_conspiracy

[24] "Conspiracy". https://www.law.cornell.edu/wex/conspiracy

Conspiracy and subversion are at the heart of Marxism. Originally, it was a movement to go against the system, and the early proponents were conspiratorial and subversive in their mindset. To have their meetings and develop a movement, it was a necessity. So, this was a feature of the cult's activities all long. The early socialist movement in Germany contains an example: Marx and Engels suggested that this group should form an alliance with the Liberal Democrats. This would allow them to gain power from the Conservatives who were in power at that time. Once this was achieved, the plan was to turn on their 'allies'.[25]

The Fabian Society was founded on the principle of subversive 'reformist' socialism (expanded later). The *Third International* or *Comintern* was a professional, Soviet state-funded, international subversive organisation. The subsequent attempts by (some) Americans to rid their country of the Marxist rot highlighted the conspiratorial and subversive issues ("McCarthyism"). All the various Marxism-inspired revolutions and regimes in the ideology's history have involved conspiracy and subversion. We are expanding on these elements/groups elsewhere. This should all make it obvious why the term 'conspiracy theorist' is a valuable defensive tool for the cult/ideology.

A (Red) Trojan Horse

"Comrades, you will remember the ancient tale of the capture of Troy…The attacking army was unable to achieve victory until, with the aid of the famous Trojan Horse, it managed to penetrate to the very heart of the enemy camp. We revolutionary workers should not be shy about using the same tactics with regard to our fascist foe"[26]

George Dimitrov, Comintern General Secretary, August 1935

A fitting metaphor for the ideology – and its impact on society – is the Trojan Horse from Greek mythology, and an incident that apparently took place during the *Trojan War* (circa 13th and 12th centuries BC).

The story goes that the ancient city of Troy was under attack by the Greeks, who – after a decade-long siege – devised a cunning plan to bypass the cities defences: they constructed a huge wooden horse large enough to contain some soldiers and left it outside the city gates. A thoughtful peace offering, it seemed.

---

[25] Marx and Engels, "Address of the Central Committee to the Communist League," March 1850 (*MESW*, vol. 1, pp. 175-85).

[26] Dimitrov, G., "The Fascist Offensive and the Tasks of the Communist International in the Struggle of the Working Class against Fascism", 2 August 1935.

As the Greeks appeared to have given-up and sailed away, the Trojans then brought the horse inside the city, totally unaware that it harboured a hidden cargo of enemy warriors inside its unassuming belly. When the time was right, the men emerged from the horse and opened the city gates. This then allowed the Greek army to enter and take the city, since they had returned to the area under cover of darkness. The incident was decisive and brought an end to the war.[27]

The common modus operandi of the ideology is a similar type of sneaky, penetrative attack on any given society. It is wheeled-in as something benign: a gift, a saviour, a solution to any problems (real or perceived). It becomes part of the environment, part of the furniture. It's not seen for what it is and is then forgotten about. Unbeknownst to the target society, it's a parasite that burrows its way into the heart of a nation, effectively rotting the host organism from the inside out. After gestation, it then eats away at the society like a cancer, devouring those organs of the organism that are essential for its health: healthy relationships, family, tradition, cultural identity, patriotism, sovereignty, physical and psychological health, constructive forms of religiosity and spirituality etc. It can infect and destroy many societies in the world, hence the term "pandemic". In a computer system, a Trojan is a type of malicious virus; society is the "system" in this case.

The Red Trojan Horse principle is crucial in understanding the effectiveness of the ideology's subversion of any given society. This concept is present throughout.

---

[27] https://www.britannica.com/topic/Trojan-horse

Section III — Our History Of Global Infection

"We are invincible, because the world proletarian revolution is invincible"

Vladimir Lenin, "Letter to American Workers", August 1918[1]

Introduction

The Marxist infection is global and has been for quite some time. Historically, it has had an easily identifiable presence, in one form or another, in: Europe and Russia, Asia, Africa, the Middle East, the U.S., and Central and South America. Needless to say, it still has a presence in those locations, regardless of the status or official political stance of countries in those areas today (since an ideology resides in the minds of the population, not merely in a country's political sphere). It also has had a presence in other countries/regions outside these zones, such as Canada and Australasia, albeit not as identifiably at first glance. Australia and New Zealand, for example – while not making the list of countries normally regarded as being Marxist historically– are significant points of infection for 'Fabian socialism' and 'Cultural Marxism'. The same applies to Canada—it's obvious even to the layman that this country is riddled with 'Cultural Marxism' or 'progressiveness' today.

Ideologies have no borders

As we incorporate some geographical matters in this section, let's keep in mind this is not just about countries. This is about ideology, mentality, indoctrination, beliefs etc. The ideology has been present almost all over the globe to one degree or another, in one form or another, for more than two centuries; and it disregards man-made borders (as pandemics do). I raise this point because of how this issue can be perceived by some, particularly when they hear the words "socialism" or "communism". Some (older generations in particular) may identify this issue to certain countries, for example, the more-commonly referred to "Communist" regimes: USSR, China, North Korea, Cuba, Vietnam, Cambodia etc; or the less well-known instances in Africa, South America, India, Romania, Albania etc; or whatever other examples a person might think of when they hear the words

---

[1] Lenin, V.I., "Letter To American Workers", 20 August 1918.

"Marxism", "socialism", or "communism".

An ideology can exist in disparate types of individuals, locations, cultures etc. It can be omnipresent and thrive regardless of unfavourable changes in its surrounding environment. It can exist in someone's mind wherever they may be located, or whatever the demographics may be.

Events in the commie historical calendar

Here's a selection of notable events in the history of Marxism. This will give the reader some scope as to what we are dealing with here; a more panoramic point of view.

Even though The Communist Manifesto can be regarded as a milestone in the development of Marxism and revolution, similar revolutionary thought goes back further than this. In fact, since we are dealing with the ideology of Marxism (and its core/related concepts, including 'socialism'), "Marxism" encompasses more than just the work of Marx and Friedrich Engels, and it predates it quite considerably.

We won't go right back into history because this would be too time-consuming and is counter-productive for our purposes. Having said that, the Athenian philosopher Plato includes ideas like a quasi-utopian 'just' society in *Republic* (circa 375BC).[2]

Alexander "The Great" of Macedon, himself a pupil of Aristotle, wanted to create a utopia of sorts.[3] Sir Thomas More authored *Utopia* in 1516.[4] The French philosopher Jean Janques-Rosseau (1712–1778) wrote *Discourse on Equality* (1755) and the *The Social Contract* (1762).[5]

Getting back to Karl Marx's era, he was influenced by the proto-Marxists of his time, including French socialists Charles Fourier (1772–1837), Rousseau, and Pierre-Joseph Proudhon (1809–1865). He attended *Trier High School,* the *University of Bonn,* and later the *University of Berlin;* educated by those who were themselves influenced by The French Revolution.[6]

Also, Marx was born in 1818 at a time of great revolutionary change in Europe, not long after the *Napoleonic Wars* (1801–1815) and the

---

[2] Plato, *Republic* (circa 375BC).

[3] https://www.britannica.com/biography/Alexander-the-Great

[4] More, T. *Utopia* (1516).

[5] https://www.britannica.com/biography/Jean-Jacques-Rousseau

[6] https://en.wikipedia.org/wiki/Karl_Marx#Influences

subsequent *Council of Vienna* (1814–1815). The ideas of Hegel heavily influenced academic thought at that time (particularly after his death in 1831). Naturally, Marx himself was an SJW (social justice warrior) who was 'radicalised' during his 'education' just like Vladimir Lenin and the millions of Marxist cult members since.

On this modern-age 'revolution' and its longevity, the British author Nesta Webster (1876–1960) had this to say in her 1921 book *World Revolution: The Plot Against Civilisation* (underlined for emphasis): "The truth is that for the last one hundred and forty-five years the fire of revolution has smouldered steadily beneath the ancient structure of civilisation, and already at moments has burst out into flame threatening to destroy to its very foundations that social edifice which eighteen centuries have been spent in constructing. The crisis of today is then no development of modern times, but a mere continuation of the immense movement that began in the middle of the eighteenth century. In a word, it is all one and the same revolution—the revolution that found its first expression in France in 1789. Both in its nature and its aims it differs entirely from former revolutions which had for their origin some localized or temporary cause. The revolution through which we are now passing is not local but universal, it is not political but social, and its causes must be sought not in popular discontent, but in a deep-laid conspiracy that uses the people to their own undoing".[7]

Webster wrote this when the cult/ideology was really starting to proliferate in the post-WW1 era. No doubt that the cult's activities in Russia and across Europe at that time inspired her.

The French Revolution

"To punish the oppressors of humanity is clemency; to forgive them is cruelty"[8]

Maximillien Robespierre, *Principles of Political Morality*, 1794

What has this historical event got to do with Marxism? In addition to having international notoriety as a revolutionary milestone, it deserves a mention since certain aspects of it echoed through the subsequent history of the ideology. It's also very significant due to being a major source of inspiration for the early figureheads of the Communist movement in the decades to follow.

---

[7] Wester, N., *World Revolution: The Plot Against Civilisation* (1921)

[8] Robespierre, M. "On the Principles of Political Morality" (1794).

Some relevant aspects of this revolution included: mob violence; theft of private property; massacre of Catholic priests and nuns; and of course, catchy catchphrases. The slogan "Unity et Indivisibilite de la République. Liberté, Égalité, Fraternité ou la Mort", meaning "Liberty, Equality, Fraternity or Death". Like the Marxist language of today: Solidarity (unity and indivisibility), equality, collectivism/'love'/brotherhood (fraternity) and having to conform or face death (mort). The "Conjuration des Égaux" (Conspiracy of Equals), which took place during the revolution in 1796, was one of several attempted coups to replace the governing Directory committee ('le Directoire'). This group wanted a type of socialist, egalitarian republic.[9]

The French Revolution led to the Napoleonic Wars, which made Napoleon himself a sort of proto-Marxian anti-monarchy, pro-'Republic' dictator. He came to power after a period of 'revolution' and the instability it causes— a common theme with Marxist dictators throughout the ideology's history.

1800s

The 19th century saw much revolutionary upheaval, as the age of traditional imperial, oligarchical and state-connected religious systems began to be replaced with democracy and liberalism. The Napoleonic Wars, springing from the aftermath of The French Revolution (and little Napoleon's big ego) set the tone for this change. The Congress of Vienna restructured Europe after the defeat of Napoleon.[10]

The *Communist League* is established on 1 June 1847. It was formed when two other organisations – The *League of the Just* and the *Communist Correspondence Committee* – were merged.[11] The Communist Manifesto was written by Marx and Engels for this group. The year 1848 marked a key year of revolutionary upheaval throughout Europe, but these revolutions had varying degrees of success. [12] In 1850, a socialist newspaper called *The Red Republican* was published in Britain. It later continued under the name *The Friend of the People*.[13]

The First International (1864–1876) was an organisation created to unite a

---

[9] https://www.britannica.com/event/French-Revolution

[10] https://www.britannica.com/event/Napoleonic-Wars

[11] https://www.history.com/this-day-in-history/marx-publishes-manifesto

[12] https://en.wikipedia.org/wiki/Revolutions_of_1848

[13] https://en.wikipedia.org/wiki/The_Red_Republican

variety of Marxist groups around the world.[14] Marx produces the first volume of the other famous work Das Kapital in 1867 (with two more volumes arriving in 1885 and 1894).[15] In April in 1870, Vladimir Ilich Ulyanov (aka V.I. Lenin) emerges from the womb of hell.[16]

In 1871, after the defeat of France by Germanic forces in the *Franco-Prussian War* (1870–1871), a group referred-to as *The Communards* created *The Paris Commune*.[17]

This group saw an opportunity to attempt a proletarian revolution, set against the backdrop of war (another recurring theme with these 'revolutions'); the commune lasted from March to May of that year. This was one of the only examples of socialism-inspired 'revolution' that Marx himself got to witness. He commented: "If the Commune should be destroyed, the struggle would only be postponed. The principles of the Commune are eternal and indestructible; they will present themselves again and again until the working class is liberated".[18] The miserable evil bastard was right when he said "eternal"—we are still dealing with this eternal shit today (incorrect, however, when he said "indestructible").

On Tuesday 5 September 1882, the first U.S. *Labor Day*–organised by the *Central Labor Union* - is held in New York City.[19] The Second International chose the first day of May as the "International Worker's Day" in 1889, and most countries in the world hold it on this date, hence "May Day".[20] (Incidentally this date marks *Walpurgisnacht* in German folklore, and the foundational date of the now infamous Bavarian Illuminati in 1776).[21] In March 1883, Karl Marx goes (back) to hell.[22] In January 1884, less than a year later, as one demonic monstrosity has left the Earth, another

---

[14] https://www.britannica.com/topic/First-International

[15] https://www.britannica.com/money/Das-Kapital

[16] https://www.britannica.com/biography/Vladimir-Lenin

[17] https://www.britannica.com/event/Commune-of-Paris-1871

[18] Marx, K. "The Record of a Speech on the Paris Commune", 1871.

[19] "History of Labor Day". https://www.dol.gov/general/laborday/history

[20] Chase, E. "The Brief Origins of May Day", 1993.
https://archive.iww.org/history/library/misc/origins_of_mayday/

[21] https://www.britannica.com/topic/Walpurgis-Night

[22] https://www.britannica.com/biography/Karl-Marx

takes its place in the form of The Fabian Society.[23]

During 1886, Lenin's brother and father died when he was just fifteen. Vladimir's brother, Alexander, being an activist troublemaker himself, was part of a plot to kill Tsar Alexander Romanov III (1845–1894). He was hung for his part in this conspiracy, and the execution took place in May of that year.[24] Lenin was apparently uninterested in politics at this point and was not 'radicalised' by it (he would take revenge many years later on Alexander's son, Tsar Nicholas Romanov II, and his family following the 1917 Bolshevik revolution). The *Second International* is formed in 1889 (dissolving in 1916).[25]

1900s

In June 1908, a demonstration took place in Tokyo, Japan called the *Red Flag Incident*. This event was a display of solidarity from Japanese cult members towards the release of their 'anarchist' comrade Koken Yamaguchi (1883–1920). The state managed to crack down on this cult gathering, arresting several attendees.[26]

Shortly after, there was the *High Treason Incident* in 1910. It centred around the cult's plot to kill the Japanese Emperor Meiji (1852–1912), and several of them were executed.[27] (It's a common historical theme that laws are created by the state to deal with such activities by cult members, and those involved with the High Treason incident were prosecuted under the Japanese Criminal Code of 1908; which the cult itself had essentially provoked).

It's untrue, as some believe, that Japan has managed to stay relatively unscathed by the infection. In fact, the *Japanese Communist Party* (JCP) has a membership of around 250,000 today and is the country's oldest party.[28] The key early figures of that group included Hitoshi Yamakawa (1880–1958) who was arrested over the Red Flag Incident, and Fukumoto Kazuo (1894–1983) who became infected/indoctrinated while studying in

---

[23] https://www.britannica.com/topic/Fabian-Society

[24] https://www.britannica.com/biography/Vladimir-Lenin

[25] https://www.britannica.com/topic/Second-International

[26] https://en.wikipedia.org/wiki/Red_Flag_Incident

[27] Mackie and Yamaizumi, "Introduction: Japan and the High Treason Incident", 2013.https://ro.uow.edu.au/lhapapers/832/

[28] "What is the JCP? A Profile of the Japanese Communist Party", 1 November 2022.

https://www.jcp.or.jp/english/what-jcp.html

Europe in 1922.[29]

Skipping ahead chronologically, Japan's history contains a symbolic, brutal act of anti-communism. On 12 October 1960, on live television, 17-year-old student Otaya Yamaguchi (1943–1960) killed the chairman of the *Japan Socialist Party* Inejirō Asanuma (1898–1960) with a samurai sword.[30] This is the equivalent of an Irish person 'taking-out' the leader of Ireland's most overtly Marxist party - *Sinn Fein* President Mary Lou McDonald - with a pint of Guinness.

Russia

In 1905, an attempt at revolution in Russia fails (a dress rehearsal for the 1917 shenanigans).[31] The *February Revolution* of 1917 and the *October Revolution* of 1917 by Vladimir Lenin's Bolshevik's, starts a major revolutionary period in Russia, which lasted until 1923, when the *Soviet Union* was established. The revolution marked the end of monarchical rule by the House of Romanov, and Tsar Nicholas II (1868–1918).[32] On the clandestine orders of Lenin, the Tsar and his family were lured to a basement by the Bolsheviks, who then shot them. Always take out the relations/descendants of your target, or they will take revenge someday (as Lenin did).[33]

A brutish police force called the *Cheka* are formed in December 1917. The full name in Russian translated to "All-Russian Extraordinary Commission for Combating Counter-revolution and Sabotage" (in other words "silence/kill anyone who opposes the cult"). Active until 1922, they were the first in a series of Soviet secret police forces. Under the command of Felix Dzerzhinsky (1877–1926), this group was responsible for ensuring any political opposition to the Bolsheviks was crushed, in addition to murdering anyone guilty of 'anti-social thinking' (i.e. anyone who disagreed with them).[34]

---

[29] https://en.wikipedia.org/wiki/Fukumoto_Kazuo; https://en.wikipedia.org/wiki/Hitoshi_Yamakawa

[30] https://en.wikipedia.org/wiki/Otoya_Yamaguchi

[31] https://www.britannica.com/event/Russian-Revolution-of-1905

[32] https://www.britannica.com/event/Russian-Revolution

[33] Remnick, D., "Historian says Lenin Ordered Tsar's death", 20 November 1990. https://www.washingtonpost.com/archive/politics/1990/11/21/historian-says-lenin-ordered-/

[34] "The Cheka". https://alphahistory.com/russianrevolution/cheka/

The Revolution of 1917 involved various factions in a struggle for control. It eventually led to large-scale conflict and several groups were involved, including the Marxist pro-Lenin Bolshevik *Red Army,* and the *White Army* which was itself composed of various political stances including pro-democractic, pro-capitalistic, pro-monarchy. A third group – composed of a mixture of non-Bolshevik socialists and non-partisan militias etc. – fought both sides. Unfortunately for Russia (and humanity), the Bolsheviks were victorious. The Red Army—led by the 'intellectual' psychopath Leon Trotsky—then inflicted a 'Red Terror' on the Russian people. This eventually led to the deaths of millions and was subsequently covered-up by the Marxism-infected writers of history.[35]

The Bolshevik invasion of Poland - the *Polish-Soviet War*–takes place in 1920. Lenin and Stalin believed that Poland separated the Russian revolution from the European one, and that Christian Poland was in the way; therefore, it needed to be liquidated.[36]

This post-Russian Revolution period included a little-discussed yet significant event—the invasion of the Soviet Union by U.S. military forces (1918–1920). President Woodrow Wilson (1856–1924) sent troops to achieve various objectives, including containing the Bolshevik regime. The failed mission, and the general interference of the U.S. and its allies (and their siding with the White army against the Bolsheviks in the Russian civil war) catalysed Lenin's adversarial attitudes towards the capitalist behemoth.[37]

The Comintern

The *Third International* or *Communist International* (or "Comintern") existed between 1919–1943. This is a critically important group in the history of Marxist subversion around the world. Lenin, in his arrogance, was not content with trying out his Marxist theories on only Russia (and thereby running it into the ground); he wanted to export this madness internationally. The Comintern was created for this purpose. Amongst other duties, it was responsible for establishing (and controlling) various Communist parties around the globe. These parties would then act as local branches/divisions of the Comintern in their respective countries. (As this

---

[35] https://www.britannica.com/event/Russian-Revolution

[36] Centek, J., "Polish-Soviet War 1920–1921", 8 October 2014.

https://encyclopedia.1914-1918-online.net/article/polish-soviet_war_1920-1921

[37] Hoslter, Roderick A., "The American Intervention in North Russia, 1918–1919".

https://armyhistory.org/the-american-intervention-in-north-russia-1918-1919/

organisation was established in 1919, this obviously doesn't apply to any Marxist party/group established before this date; however, these groups were still established by cult members, of course).[38]

The Comintern was a pioneering, professional, state-funded entity with an unambiguous mandate: to essentially export the 'revolution' – the ideology – and infect other countries from within, using all means necessary including subversion. It also spawned a myriad of other international organisations. Later we will see Marxist groups listed country by country, continent by continent, including which parties were established and/or controlled by them (first national groups, then international groups).

The Banana Massacre

An interesting example of another Marxist 'protest' which happened in Columbia in 1928. It involved workers of the *United Fruit Company* and a strike ostensibly over working conditions. The *Columbian Liberal Party* and *Columbian Socialist Party* – in addition to members of the soon to emerge *Columbian Communist Party* – were involved (cult member Mariá Cano was imprisoned in the aftermath). The U.S. was aware of developments and exerted some diplomatic pressure to ensure that the situation was resolved, apparently threatening to invade if it was not.

Having identified that the protest had an ideological component to it, the Colombian government then called in the army to deal with the protestors.[39]

As in all instances where the cult feels they have been wronged/refused, there were claims that up to 2,000 people were killed, that bodies were buried in mass graves, that children were shot etc. It exemplifies the Marxist tactic of making useful idiots out of workers in order to advance the ideology.

Stalin's Russia

"Comrade Stalin, having become Secretary-General, has unlimited authority concentrated in his hands, and I am not sure whether he will always be capable of using that authority with sufficient caution"[40]

---

[38] "The Communist International (1919–1943), Organisational History".

https://www.marxists.org/history/usa/eam/ci/comintern.html

[39] https://www.britannica.com/event/Banana-Massacre

[40] Lenin, V.I., "Letter to the Congress", 1922.
https://www.marxists.org/archive/lenin/works/1922/dec/testamnt/congress.htm

Vladimir "Mr. Understatement" Lenin, "Letter to the Congress", 1922

A man of steel is born

In 1878, in a land sandwiched between Europe, the Middle East, and Asia, between the Black and the Caspian Seas, another Marxist credit to humanity is born. Ioseb Dzhugashvili emerges from the womb of hell in the town of Gori, Georgia, in the Russian Empire. As a young man, while attending a Russian Orthodox seminary, Ioseb started reading the works of influential revolutionary writers such as Marx and Nikolay Chernyshevsky (1828–1889). He leaves around the age of twenty to become a Marxist activist. Later he becomes involved with industrial workers movements to foment unrest and aligns himself with the Bolsheviks. He eventually meets Vladimir Lenin in 1905, who gives him the task of raising funds for the revolution. He then engages in a range of criminal activities including bank robbery, extortion, assault, theft, and even running brothels ("the end justifies the means").

After many name changes throughout his life (in order to avoid the authorities in Tsarist Russia), he would eventually take the name of Joseph Stalin in his thirties ("Stalin", Russian for "man of steel"). He would remain a supporter of Lenin, kept close to him, and bided his time in his lust for power. At about five feet four inches (162 centimetres), he definitely had 'small man syndrome'.[41]

Leader of Red Russia

In 1924, upon the death of Lenin, Stalin – now the General Secretary of the Communist Party – manoeuvres himself into the position of de facto leader of the Soviet Union, marking the beginning of what would become arguably the most despotic tyranny ever. One of his first aims was to neutralise political rivals, including Leon Trotsky (whom he exiled, then had assassinated in Mexico in 1940).[42]

In 1929, Stalin has his first big bright idea, which manifests via the usual insane Marxist obsessions with class struggle, private property, workers, agriculture, and any perceived modicum of wealth. He identifies the Kulaks – land-owning farmers – as being a class fit for extermination. They are then wiped-out en masse.

With the Kulaks ruthlessly removed from the equation, Stalin then forces collectivisation on the peasant class, using his thugs to force them to work

---

[41] https://www.britannica.com/biography/Joseph-Stalin

[42] https://www.britannica.com/biography/Leon-Trotsky/Exile-and-assassination

on large agricultural zones now owned by the state. The produce is then confiscated and used elsewhere. Inevitably, the system fails and millions die.[43] The situation was hidden from the western world, thanks to lying piece of trash cult members like journalist Walter Duranty (1884–1957). Instead, he reported on the great successes of the Communist experiments and was awarded the Pulitzer Prize on several occasions for his 'work'. Duranty was a New York Times correspondent, serving as the chief of the paper's Moscow bureau.[44]

The Holodomor

Under Stalin's direction, the Soviet Union commits a horrific crime against the Ukrainian people in 1932 and 1933. This was a genocide, by forced famine, which came to be known as the *Holodomor*.[45] Estimates of the death toll vary, and due to the fact that the Marxist cult either continuously covers-up or lies about its crimes, there is no broad consensus on the figures. It seems reasonable to place the estimate between the five and ten million mark.

The crime of the Ukrainians was that they resisted collectivisation. The cult also saw to it that the starving masses couldn't get their hands on any grain from the collective farms. The "Law of Three Spikelets" was introduced— those caught stealing grain would either be shot or incarcerated for ten years.[46] On 16 November 1933, the *Union of Soviet Socialists Republics* (U.S.S.R.) is recognised internationally.[47]

The Gulag

The regime also included the use of a brutal, forced labour prison camp system spread out across Russia, referred to as the *Gulag* ("The word is Russian, from G(lavnoe) u(pravlenie ispravitel'no-trudovykh) lag(ereĭ)

---

[43] https://www.britannica.com/topic/kulak

[44] "New York Times Statement About 1932 Pulitzer Prize Awarded to Walter Duranty".

https://www.nytco.com/company/prizes-awards/new-york-times-statement-about-1932-pulitzer-prize-awarded-to-walter-duranty/

[45] https://www.britannica.com/event/Holodomor

[46] https://en.wikipedia.org/wiki/Law_of_Spikelets

[47] "Recognition of the Soviet Union, 1933". https://history.state.gov/milestones/1921-1936/ussr

'Chief Administration for Corrective Labour Camps').[48] Millions were worked to death at the camps, died of illness or starvation, or were executed (some in transit). Many camps were in isolated, inhospitable parts of the country, dissuading (most of) those who contemplated escape. This Gulag system was the brainchild of V.I. Lenin, built for the purpose of intimidating or imprisoning any enemies of the cult, but it was Stalin who really tested its capacity. Other psycho cult members active during Stalin's era would try to emulate this system, such as Enver Hoxha (1908–1985) in Albania, and Mao Zedong in China.

This style of forced labour camp prison system is still in use today— China's *Laogai* network. It's host to happy tenants of all kinds, including political dissidents (e.g. critics of the Chinese Communist Party—the permanent ruling party of China). Over 1,000 of these prisons exist, and according to the *Laogai Research Foundation* had between 500,000 and 2,000,000 prisoners in 2008.[49]

Red China

In 1917, a 24-year-old Mao Zedong (aka Mao Tse Tung) starts to read Marxist literature, including the Communist Manifesto. He received more brainwashing while at *Beijing University* and was a founding member of the *Chinese Communist Party* (CCP) in 1921. In 1927 he is given the token title of "Commander in Chief of the Red Army" by the CCP leadership.

This small group (more akin to a militia) then travels the countryside spreading the ideological infection, by stirring-up revolutionary fervour in the unsuspecting peasants: indoctrinating them, encouraging hatred for the landowners, gaining support, recruiting new members etc. These were the small beginnings that would decide China's destiny. (Intentionally targeting the uneducated, the 'oppressed' is a common tactic).[50]

China had been undergoing major upheaval at the beginning of the 20th century: transitioning from its imperial past and rulership of the *Qing Dynasty* (1644–1912); the formation of the *Republic of China* (1912–1949); the factional warfare of the *Warlord Era* (1916–1928 approx); the invasion of Japan and the subsequent conflict (1937–1945); and finally the *Chinese Civil war* (1945–1949), which would ultimately decide the permanent fate

---

[48] "Gulag", Oxford Reference.
https://www.oxfordreference.com/display/10.1093/oi/authority.20110803095912832

[49] https://en.wikipedia.org/wiki/Laogai

[50] https://www.britannica.com/biography/Mao-Zedong

of the country, creating the China of today.[51]

Cult members in the Soviet Union were keenly interested in capitalising on the unrest during this period. They were involved in the creation of the CCP – via the Comintern and the Communist Party of the Soviet Union's *Far Eastern Bureau* – using figures like Li Dazhao (1888–1927) and Chen Duxiu (1879–1942). Mao would eventually manoeuvre his way to the top of the CCP.[52]

China's proximity to the well-entrenched cult members in the Soviet Union meant that it was always going to become highly infected. Despite all the warring factions in China in those first few unstable decades of the 20th century, it was the influence and support of the Soviet cult members that allowed the Chinese cult members to emerge atop. It's a good example of how the ideology proliferates itself.

In 1949, after decades of conflict and following the defeat of the nationalist *Kuomintang* forces led by Chiang Kai Shek, the *People's Republic of China* is announced by Mao. At last, cult members were now militarily in control of China, and the nationalist forces withdrew to the island of Taiwan (aka *Republic of China*).[53]

This Marxist takeover of the country created a second major global point of origin/infection for the ideology (in addition to the U.S.S.R.). It meant China would be a staunch supporter of Marxist takeovers in other nearby countries including Korea, Cambodia, Vietnam etc., in addition to areas further afield, such as Africa. Red China would also have violent border disputes with India. The infection in that country marked not only a significant point in China's history, but also world history, as it's now arguably the main point of infection on the planet. A situation with potentially catastrophic consequences...

Mao's Great leadership

The rulership of Mao led to the most horrific period of Chinese history via decades of despotic rule. One such example was the *Great Leap Forward* (late 1950s to early 1960s). This 'great' leap involved the application of

---

[51] "Timeline of China's Modern History", 30 April 2012.
https://www.chipublib.org/timeline-of-chinas-modern-history/

[52] Jianyi, L., "The Origins of the Chinese Communist Party and the role played by Soviet Russia and the Comintern", March 2000.
https://etheses.whiterose.ac.uk/9813/1/341813.pdf

[53] "The Chinese Revolution of 1949". https://history.state.gov/milestones/1945-1952/chinese-rev

Marxist collectivism to the infrastructure of China, to mould it according to the desires of Mao and the Chinese Communist Party.

It involved putting a heavy emphasis on industrial production, forcing the Chinese to work in slave-labour collectivist agricultural systems, and the governmental appropriation of resources and agricultural produce (aka theft of private property).[54]

Cult members operating across the country – eager to please Mao – put the plans in to action, stealing farm produce from the masses who were reliant on this for food. Mao ruled by fear, so rather than inform him about actual farm produce quantities, his faithful commissars resorted to stealing some, giving Mao the impression they were in abundance. In addition, the population was forced to participate in Mao's industrialisation plans (including focusing on steel production), rather than being left to farm the land. Steel is not edible of course (hard on the teeth; a bit 'ow-ey').

Another bird-brained idea from Mao was the "Four Pests" campaign. This involved targeting certain rodents, flies, mosquitos, and sparrows (who were blamed for: the plague, malaria, and eating grain seeds respectively). The Chinese mobilised in solidarity to kill the sparrows en masse, believing this would help rice crop yields. Idiots.

In reality, it did the exact opposite since Sparrows eat insects too. As a result, the bugs – including plant-decimating caterpillars and locusts – had a field day (pun), cleaning out the crops across the country. At least the Chinese achieved some solidarity, right?[55] These events triggered a period of mass starvation called the *Great Chinese Famine,* which resulted in the deaths of approximately 30 million.[56]

These foolish initiatives were examples of what happens when theories/ideas meet reality; if they are forced, they disturb the natural equilibrium that exists in society and nature. Destruction of life is the result (another common pattern with the ideology). The killing of the sparrows, besides being incredibly dumb and short-sighted, is also almost amusing since it fits the looney modus operandi of the ideology—destroy/kill stuff to make life better! In fact, it's surprising that Mao didn't order the masses to start killing the rice seeds with samurai swords to make them grow faster. Or start viciously karate-chopping iron ore to make steel. Racist Asian

---

[54] https://www.britannica.com/event/Great-Leap-Forward

[55] https://en.wikipedia.org/wiki/Four_Pests_campaign

[56] Brown, Clayton D. "China's Great Leap Forward", 2012.

https://www.asianstudies.org/publications/eaa/archives/chinas-great-leap-forward/

stereotyping aside, what they did was wong.

Flowers and Cultural Revolution

The *Hundred Flowers Campaign* of the late 1950s was an attempt to consolidate the cult's control over the country. Mao achieved this by deviously suggesting that criticism of the regime was not only acceptable, but desirable.

This flushing-out of dissenters worked when a cult member named Wang Shiwei (1906–1947) spoke out. He was brutally tortured and executed, serving as an example to any others who defied the leadership.[57] Mao was nothing if not a sneaky snaky cunt.

Another was the *Great Proletarian Cultural Revolution* (or the *Cultural Revolution*) from the mid-1960s to the mid-1970s. The regime brainwashed the younger generations to purge the country of the older (and non-indoctrinated) generations (take note!). An organisation called the *Red Guards* were given carte blanche to terrorise, assault and kill. Anyone not part of the cult was fair game. Vandalism or destruction of anything cultural or historical was encouraged. This 'cleansing' process also included the purge of Mao's political rivals within the Communist Party.[58] Remember, this is brainwashed Chinese people killing each other in their droves, even killing other cult members; for nothing!

Mao the man

Mao was one of the most brutal leaders in the cult's history. A heartless, manipulative, sadistic psycho, and fanatic. Definitely one of my nominees for the "worst piece of human trash ever" award, right up there with his inspiration—Stalin. He knew how to create wholesale death and terror; a genuine disciple of the Marxist maxim "the end justifies the means".

Mao's rulership was known for the tactic of neutralising political opponents before they materialised, using labour camps, torture, and the murder of the country's 'intelligentsia' ('educated' people). In terms of the regime's body count, the highest death-toll estimate of seventy million plus comes from a book by authors Jung Chang and Jon Halliday entitled *Mao: The Unknown Story* (2006). This estimate was more or less supported by

---

[57] King, G. "The Silence that Preceded China's Great Leap into Famine", 26 September 2012. https://www.smithsonianmag.com/history/the-silence-that-preceded-chinas-great-leap-into-famine-51898077/

[58] Lamb, S. "Introduction to the Cultural Revolution", December 2005.

https://spice.fsi.stanford.edu/docs/introduction_to_the_cultural_revolution

Professor R.J. Rummel (1932–2014)—a specialist in estimating the deaths caused by Communism (expanded upon later). (Apparently, according to Chang and Halliday, the cult received some financing from opium. Step right up and get your commie smack folks!).[59]

Obviously, the cult will downplay death tolls where "Communist" regimes are concerned. It's all P.R. damage-control. Trying to get an honest, accurate estimate of how many actually died is almost impossible, since the cult just loves to lie and sweep things under the carpet. The Chinese Communist Party is not going to allow a real investigation obviously.

Mao's rule would also lead to the creation of yet another interpretation/strain of the ideology—Maoism. In 1964, he produced a collection of his jabberings and speeches in the *Little Red Book*. Billions of copies were published, and the youth in particular were targeted, naturally.[60] These generations, brainwashed as vulnerable kids, would carry the ideology forward in the following decades, helping create the China of the future. Mao survived until his eighty-second year. Outstanding, right? Arguably the worst mass murdering nutcases ever, he should've been burnt alive using a few hundred copies of his book as the firewood.

The Indochina Wars

This was a series of conflicts across Asia – fomented by the cult – beginning in the post-WW2 period in 1946, and lasting until approximately 1991 (the most famous being the *Vietnam War, 1955–1975*).[61] These conflicts were spread over the territories of several countries in the region including Cambodia, Laos, Thailand, and Vietnam. The parties to the conflict were generally divided along Marxist and anti-Marxist lines. The ideology was key in convincing prospective cult members that achieving independence from the waning colonial powers (i.e. France) was desirable. Some of these conflicts (e.g. Cambodian-Vietnamese War) also illustrate how different factions of the cult will sometimes eliminate each other.

Essentially, all the conflict in that region was the result of the Marxist rot developing in those countries, with the support of the larger previously infected entities to the north (Russia and China). For example, in Vietnam's case, Mao was allied to Vietnamese cult member Ho Chi Minh (1890–1969) in North Vietnam.[62] The conflict there at one point pitted the French-

---

[59] Chang And Halliday, *Mao: The Unknown Story* (2006).

[60] https://en.wikipedia.org/wiki/Quotations_from_Chairman_Mao_Tse-tung

[61] https://www.britannica.com/event/Indochina-wars

[62] https://www.britannica.com/biography/Ho-Chi-Minh

backed Vietnamese National Army against Ho Chi Minh's Communist forces. Minh fought the VNA for many years, until roughly 1954. That was the first Indochina war and it ended with a Geneva Accord. The French and the Chinese made a deal, and Vietnam was divided in to two. Though gaining control of the north, obviously the cult/ideology were not satisfied with this and sought control of the south; the result is the Vietnam War. The rest is history.

The Korean War

A conflict resulting from the infection taking hold in what is now North Korea. It lasted from 1950 to 1953, and resulted in the division of Korea in to north and south (a division which lasts until this day): in the north is the *Democratic People's Republic of Korea,* and in the south is the *Republic of Korea.*[63] This conflict was not unrelated to the Indochina Wars, since the Marxist rot spread across the whole of Asia, more or less. Just like the Indochina Wars/Vietnam War, the parties to the conflict were divided along Marxist and anti-Marxist lines, with Red China and the U.S.S.R assisting the infection in the north.

North Korea was then ruled over by the Kim Dynasty (a lineage of cult members). It even led to their own interpretation of the ideology called *Juche Communism*[64] (China and North Korea have the same system: officially, it's a multi-party system, but in reality, a single party rules permanently. Does this not make the use of "Democratic" in the title amusing?).

In South Korea, a prominent anti-Marxist called Syngman Rhee (1875–1965) was at the helm. He had to deal with a severe problem of Marxist activism and subversion during his term as president of the *First Republic* (1948–1960). This led to the *April Revolution* of 1960 which eventually toppled him from power. Traitorous cult members within South Korea (in the universities in particular) were the driving force behind the constant unrest.[65]

The *Second Korean War* took place from 1966 to 1969. This was an attempt by the cult in North Korea to take South Korea as the bulk of U.S. forces

---

[63] https://www.britannica.com/event/Korean-War

[64] "A Brief Introduction and Assessment of the Juche Ideology", November 1980.

https://digitalarchive.wilsoncenter.org/document/brief-introduction-and-assessment-juche-ideology

[65] "First Republic of South Korea".
https://countries.fandom.com/wiki/First_Republic_of_South_Korea

were tied-up in Vietnam, with some of their resources being redeployed there. This was a relatively small-scale conflict when compared to other incursions by the cult in Asia. It proved to be unsuccessful, and the infection did not spread to the south of the country.[66] It's an example of how the ideology, regardless of the disagreements between different factions of the cult, is always trying to find ways to spread.

Today, North Korea has "Juche" as the officially state ideology, which is merely the Kim dynasty's interpretation of Marxism fused with their interpretation of nationalism. Juche means "self-reliance". [67] The constitution was amended in 2009 to remove the traditional terms and passages normally associated with the Marxist ideology, such as the word "communism". But why bother? Perhaps it was done to prevent any sleeping North Koreans from realising they live in a communistic prison state? Or also could be because outward appearances are important to the regime's leader—Kim Jong Un (aka Fatboy Kim). (Not his personal appearance, obviously).

Ceausescu's Romania

Another Marxist fiasco, this time in Count Dracul's neck of the woods (pun?) in Eastern Europe, in a place once called the Kingdom of Romania. This shit show was run by another cultish nut called Nicolae Ceausescu, who would go down in infamy (and a hail of bullets).[68] Things, as usual, started to change when the Marxist rot appeared on the scene in the early part of the 20th century. There were several cult groups involved here, the most significant of which was the *Romanian Communist Party (Partidul Comunist Roman)* or PCR. It was established in 1921 and was under the control of the Comintern, though was not prominent for many years.[69]

Of course, Romania was part of the Axis powers in WW2, with Ion Antonesu at the helm. He was removed from power and executed in 1944. At this point, Romania would progressively fall under the cult's control. The PCR would now be able to expand openly and unmolested (because no-one wants to be molested by Nazis). King Michael was forced to abdicate in December 1947, under pressure from the cult (he later claimed they threatened to kill one thousand students, whom they had in custody, if

[66] Lerner, M. "The Second Korean War".
https://digitalarchive.wilsoncenter.org/essays/second-korean-war

[67] https://en.wikipedia.org/wiki/Juche

[68] https://www.britannica.com/biography/Nicolae-Ceausescu

[69] https://dbpedia.org/page/Romanian_Communist_Party`

he would not comply). The Kingdom of Romania would now become the *Socialist Republic of Romania,* and a satellite state of the Soviet Union. There was much restructuring of the government over the following years.

The cult members engaged in the forceful suppression of political opponents (non-cult members) with the help of the *Securitate*—a state secret police force who were established in 1948, modelled on the Russian NKVD. The Securitate had an extensive network of spies and rats in the Romanian population, to monitor any dissent against the regime. It was one of the biggest groups of its kind (relative to the size of the population it was terrorising): Romania had a population of twenty-two million by the mid-1980s, and apparently the Securitate had approximately 500,000 informers ratting-out their countrymen. The Securitate was noted for its brutality, and many Romanians have attested to this.[70]

From the early 1940s to the early 1950s, at Pitesti Prison, the cult members tried to 'liberate' anti-Marxists from their apparent 'brainwashing'. Many of these prisoners included Christians, who were predictably targeted because this new Communist Romania was to enforce state atheism. They were tortured and 'baptised' by the cult members using urine and faeces.[71] Predictably, the cult also enforced collectivisation in agriculture, with consequences for those who defied the revolution; any anti-Marxist resistance groups, religious elements or peasants were dealt with using torture, imprisonment, murder, and forced relocations or exile.

Keeping up with the Ceausescus

The year 1965 was a turning point for the PCR, as the General Secretary Gheorghiu-Dej died. Though there was a 'collective leadership' at first, Nicolae Ceausescu – as it often happens with fanatic cult members – started to manoeuvre himself into the top job. After a power struggle, he emerged as leader, and announced that Romania was now a Socialist Republic (rather than a 'People's Democracy'). He then started to project the image to the Romanian people of a 'nationalistic' Communist leader, independent from Moscow. This gained him some popular support, and membership of the PCR increased considerably.[72]

Eventually, Ceausescu turned in to an extreme control freak, with a tight

---

[70] https://balkaninsight.com/2019/12/25/keys-mikes-spies-how-the-securitate-stole-romanias-privacy/

[71] Mihai, HRH King., "What was done to Romania between 1945 and 1947 has been done since 1989" (Romanian article), 23 August 2000.

[72] https://www.britannica.com/biography/Nicolae-Ceausescu

grip over the Romanian people. He would be aided in his quest by his wife Elena (1919–1989)—another dedicated cult member. During their reign, the Ceausescu's lived a life of extreme opulence. Their palace in Primaverii, Bucharest, featured carved ornate wooden walls, silk carpets, a cinema, and a gold-encrusted bathroom.[73] Very elitist, very 'bourgeois' methinks. So, while most of the Romanian people were forced to ration and live a life of extreme oppression and destitution, the higher-ranking cult members did just the opposite. This is not untypical of when the cult takes over a country, but in Romania's case, Ceausescu and his wife took it to a whole new level.

The level of ego emanating from this man was unreal. In 1974, he appointed himself President of the Socialist Republic; this was in addition to him being the General Secretary of the PCR. He insisted on receiving a multitude of honours and titles both home and abroad, eventually making himself essentially president for life.

The decisions the new el presidente made from the 1970s onwards caused the cracks to appear, and austerity policies and rationing became the developing theme in the 1980s.[74] This was due, in part, to Ceausescu's insistence on reducing international debt, in addition to simply blowing cash. His needless, cash-wasting decisions included *Sistematizarea* (Systematization)—a massive socialist-style reconstruction of the urban and rural landscape; this involved the demolition of cities, towns and villages, and the construction of uniform and ugly high-density tower clocks (blocks of 'flats'). In the spirit of socialism, these would be more 'efficient' and 'equal' for the happy comrades living inside. An earthquake in 1977 and the resultant damage provided Ceausescu with an excuse to bulldoze cultural and historical structures.

Despite Romania's access to large amounts of oil – and their ability to therefore refine petroleum on a large scale – they had to ration petroleum (!). Even basic utilities such as electricity were becoming scarce, and there were severe levels of pollution (again, too much emphasis on industrialisation!). The masses were told by the regime that having to ration food was good to combat obesity (face palm). Romania had the lowest standard of living in Europe. What a wasteful fucking mess. [74]

The end

The Romanians had enough by 1989. Anti-Communist sentiment was growing, being directed at the Ceausescu's and the PCR. This was no doubt

---

[73] Euronews, "See Nicolae Ceausescu's gold bathroom", 20 June 2016. https://www.YouTube.com/watch?v=M4XLXzUmZHw

[74] https://www.britannica.com/place/Romania/Communist-Romania

accelerated by the increasing levels of oppression they had to endure at the hands of the Securitate. Ceausescu, sensing the growing discontent (and rather than do the noble thing and drop a plugged-in toaster in to his evening bubble bath), pushed his goons to extend their network of informants and upgrade their surveillance techniques. What a cunt.

Despite the state's effort to insulate the Romanian public from information not approved by the cult, awareness of the discontent was starting to diffuse throughout the masses. Protests and strikes were organised. Ironically, one of the catalysts of this new revolution to depose the regime was a strike involving workers from Trucks Brasov. As these particular proletarians were being hostile to the cult, they were swiftly dealt with. Several more protests and riots followed, resulting in the police and Securitate forces becoming even more heavy-handed. Many protestors were shot at the Timisoara protests on 17 December. [74]

Unsurprisingly, due to the brainwashing, Ceausescu was incredulous at the unrest, and gave an incredible, delusional speech at the Central Committee Building on 21 December (available on YouTube!).[75] He was jeered by the huge crowd. The military eventually sided with the protestors, and Ceausescu was overthrown. He and his wife Elena were quickly tried and executed on 25 December. What a festive gift to the Romanian people! The commie spell had finally been broken, thank Jesus!

Ceausescu was one of the few cult leaders in history to have received his comeuppance; most of them tend to escape punishment via a relatively pleasant death. The most fascinating thing about his end, was that he was still defiant and protesting almost right up to the point he was executed, as he sang the Communist anthem "Internationale". An example of how the indoctrinated can't understand what they are, even when they are about to die.[76]

Communist Albania

"No force, no torture, no intrigue can eradicate Marxism-Leninism from the minds and hearts of men"[77]

Enver Hoxha, *Eurocommunism is anti-Communism* (1980)

---

[75] "Nicolae Ceausescu Last Speech".
https://www.YouTube.com/watch?v=TcRWiz1PhKU

[76] TVR (Romanian Public Broadcaster), "Trial and Execution".
https://artsandculture.google.com/story/HQVhRMp6MAUA8A?hl=en

[77] Hoxha, E., "Eurocommunism is anti-Communism", 1980.
https://www.marxists.org/reference/archive/hoxha/works/euroco/env2-1.htm

"The world socialist system.. has become today the decisive factor in the development of the world history. It exerts a tremendous influence on the world; it has become a great attractive and revolutionizing force… (it) is showing with every passing day its indisputable superiority over the capitalist system. It has become the shield of all the progressive forces of the world, the impregnable bulwark of freedom and peace, democracy and socialism"[78]

Enver Hoxha, 20th Party Anniversary Address (1961)

Another monstrous infection took hold just down the road in the Balkans, on the coast of the Adriatic Sea, in the form of the *People's Socialist Republic of Albania*. It existed from 1946 to 1992.[79] The Marxist psycho-in-chief was Enver Hoxha (pronounced "hoe-ja". J for "Jennifer"). This guy receives five commie stars for fanaticism.

The only thing stopping him from creating a large death toll was the limits to his power and influence, due to the relatively isolated location of Albania, and its size/population (as compared to other Communist countries of the era). Indeed, if there was a big red button to start WW3, this guy would've fucked that button many times over given the chance. He personified the ideology's tendency to manifest evermore extreme versions of itself, as he would eventually consider other forms of communism too 'soft', even traitorous to the cause! Amusingly, at one point Hoxha even referred to Mao Zedong (arguably the worst commie scumbag ever) as a "capitalist pig", to give you an idea of how extreme this guy was.[80]

The beginnings of the infection

Aided by other cult members in the already-infected neighbouring 'country' of Yugoslavia, he helped found the *Communist Party of Albania* in 1941 (later re-named the *Party of Labour of Albania* (or PLA) in 1948); the catalyst for this was the German invasion of Yugoslavia in the same year. The cult leader in Yugoslavia was Josip Broz (aka "Tito"), and his assistance in spreading the infection to Albania was encouraged by the Soviet Comintern.

Hoxha was also the leader of the *National Liberation Movement* (there's that word again)—a Marxist group which opposed Nazi occupation of

---

[78] Hoxha, E., 20th Party Anniversary Address, 1961.
https://en.wikiquote.org/wiki/Enver_Hoxha

[79] https://www.britannica.com/topic/history-of-Albania/Socialist-Albania

[80] https://www.britannica.com/biography/Enver-Hoxha

Albania during WW2.[81] Though Albania joined the worldwide commie party relatively later than in other European countries (in terms of when they got themselves a bona fide Marxist party), Hoxha ensured they caught-up reeeaal fast. The initial actions of the cult predictably included the elimination of any opponents, many being conveniently labelled 'Nazi collaborators' or 'enemies of the people'. Another predictable move was the attack on religion. An early, typical statement by cult members – on the Central Committee of the PLA – included the notion that they should "struggle against the attempt by fascism to split up the Albanian people by means of religion".[82] Right (rolls eyes), that old commie chestnut.

Just as in the establishment of the Socialist Federal Republic of Yugoslavia before it next door, sham elections were organised in Albania to give the illusion that its creation was the choice of 'the people'.

Hoxhaism is the interpretation/strain of the ideology named after Enver Hoxha.[83]

It's characterized as a variant which is 'anti-revisionist' in nature, and loyal to the interpretations of Joseph "Little Bastard" Stalin. To put it another way, Hoxha subscribed to the hardcore version.

The regime

This was a particularly brutal and repressive regime, even by the cult's standards. Those directly executed by it and 'political prisoners' (who had various fates) were in the tens of thousands. Many also died trying to escape—either by swimming to Greece (via the island of Corfu), or by hiking over the mountains to Yugoslavia. Poor, desperate bastards. Revolution or death. Albania's population is relatively small—it was approx. 1.2 million in 1946, rising to almost 3.3 million in 1991.[84]

The state goon squad/not-so-secret police force in this instance was the infamous *Sigurimi*. They monitored, terrorised, tortured, and 'disappeared' Albanians throughout Hoxha's reign. The regime included the usual things, such as the ensured dominance of the ideology, enforced by the state through intimidation, coercion, violence, and murder.

It also engaged in surveillance of the population; forced 're-education' of

---

[81] https://en.wikipedia.org/wiki/National_Liberation_Movement_(Albania)

[82] Tonnes, B., "Albania: An Atheist State". https://biblicalstudies.org.uk/pdf/rcl/03-1_3_04.pdf

[83] "Hoxhaism". https://en.prolewiki.org/wiki/Hoxhaism

[84] https://www.statista.com/statistics/1076307/population-albania-since-1800/

dissenters; the diverting of resources to build military infrastructure, contributing to the starvation of the population; the construction of 'socialist-style' cramped accommodation; resource and food rationing; and the use of Gulag-style labour camps, where prisoners were sent to work in the mines (the Spac labour camp being one of the most notorious). Many 'went missing' or were tortured to death, then buried en masse in secret graves, with the use of black plastic bags.[85]

Albanians were not allowed to travel – unless on official business – and were arrested if they tried to leave; the movements of foreign visitors to the country were controlled and monitored. During this virtual imprisonment, the cult members – including Hoxha himself – enjoyed a relatively bourgeois existence in the wealthy Ish-Blloku district of Tirana. It was encircled by a wall to separate it from surrounding areas (and therefore the general population which it preyed upon). In addition, the regime banned private ownership of cars (unless you were a party member). An 'anti-bourgeois' bourgeois cult?

Anti-religion and freedom of expression

In the purest tradition of the cult, Hoxha was extremely anti-religious, and atheism was enforced by the state apparatus, with religious practice being effectively banned in 1967. In a speech of the same year, he confidently declared that Albania was the "first atheist state of the world". Similar to what Mao encouraged in Red China during the Cultural Revolution there, Hoxha encouraged the destruction of mosques and churches across the country by (cultish) youth organisations.[86]

Of course, since Albania had to endure its version of a 'cultural revolution', naturally the arts needed to extol the brilliance of Marxism. Speaking in an interview with *NBC Left Field* in 2018, a prominent Albanian artist by the name of Maks Velo spoke of his harassment by Hoxha's regime.[87] He was being monitored by cult members in 1978, who then approached him. Velo wasn't producing the kind of pro-Marxist work that was expected of

---

[85] Abrahams, F., "Communist-Era Disappearances Still Haunt Albania", 17 March 2021. https://www.hrw.org/news/2021/03/17/communist-era-disappearances-still-haunt-albania

[86] Bezati, V., "How Albania Became the World's First Atheist Country", 28 August 2019. https://balkaninsight.com/2019/08/28/how-albania-became-the-worlds-first-atheist-country/

[87] "What if Your Loved Ones' Betrayal Landed You in Prison? | NBC Left Field", July 2018.

https://www.YouTube.com/watch?v=OHfg2mog2sk

artists—his was considered 'hostile' to the regime. As punishment, he was sent off to prison camp, receiving a ten-year sentence. The hangable scumbags at the Sigurimi then unsuccessfully tried to recruit him as an informant on his fellow countrymen. The cult eliminates any perceived dissent by trying to control all forms of expression.

The Sigurimi

A group as fanatical and cruel as its state police counterparts in Romania (Securitate), East Germany (Stasi), Hungary (AVH), or the U.S.S.R.. (KGB), the Sigurimi ruined the lives of generations of Albanians. They were somewhat different to those other groups as their powers were relatively unrestricted—any actions committed were acceptable if they were supportive of the regime. Another difference – owing to Albania's small population/area – was that they could actually deliver on their intentions to monitor (and control) the whole population (whereas their counterparts listed above had to instead project the illusion they had this ability, through indoctrination, propaganda, fear etc.).[88][89]

The organisation was split into different departments, dealing with everything from censorship to counterespionage to public records to interrogations etc. They even investigated fellow cult members in the PLA ranks to purge any ideologically disloyal party members. Those targeted included, for example, those with pro-Soviet, pro-Yugoslavia, or pro-China sympathies. This included Central Committee and Politburo members.

In addition to conventional phone-taps, they used bugs to monitor the conversations of the general public, even in their own homes. Thousands of these devices were placed all over the country, sometimes planted in shoes, bags, ties, furniture, vases, jewellery, and even smoking pipes (everywhere but Hoxha's asshole basically). Conversations were then recorded in Sigurimi HQ, the House of Leaves building. These scumbags encouraged Albanians to rat out their own friends and relatives, using coercion in some cases. In short, they were trying to create a cult society of rats. This form of control capitalizes on a tendency many people have to criticize or bitch about others when it's not justified. The ideology brings out the evil in people, encouraging them to destroy each other.

---

[88] https://www.wikiwand.com/en/Sigurimi

[89] Gjoka, B. "Declassified Documents Show Power of Albania's Communist Secret Police", 16 November 2021.

https://balkaninsight.com/2021/11/26/declassified-documents-show-power-of-albanias-communist-secret-police/

This is all pretty amazing stuff when you consider this cracker from Hoxha: "A country where a man is afraid to criticise another one is no socialist country".[90] Obviously Hoxha didn't tolerate any real criticism of himself. At the First Congress of the Communist Party in November 1948, Hoxha referred to the Sigurimi as the "loving weapon" of the party. P.s.y.c.h.o! By the end of Communist Albania, too many Albanians had been terrorised by them. So many lives ruined.

Legacy

On 11 April 1985, Hoxha departed this realm for the fires of hell, to be lovingly raped by Marx et al (his lifelong fantasy probably). With the worldwide collapse of communism beginning in 1988, perhaps somewhat in the spirit of the (insane) defiance of Hoxha, the regime in Albania 'hung-on' a bit longer than in other non-Soviet countries. Another factor was that since the regime still tightly-controlled the flow of information – including news from the outside world – the Albanians were not even aware of the collapse of the Berlin Wall! The PLA eventually allowed free elections and opposition parties in December 1990. Hoxha's statue in Tirana was toppled in 1991.[91]

Unfortunately, since many cult members managed to remain present in Albanian politics after the regime's fall (and their attempts to keep the truth buried), the process of finding and identifying all the victims has been severely curtailed. Attempts to access the information amassed by the Sigurimi has been a topic of political discussion.

In 2008, the Socialist Party of Albania obstructed such attempts in the Albanian parliament (not surprising since the Socialist Party of Albania is a continuation of the PLA, which ruled during Hoxha's one-party state). Things may be changing—the *Balkaninsight* website reported in June 2023 that an investigation was being planned regarding victims of the Spac labour camp.[92]

Almost unbelievably, as another brazen insult to the Albanian people, a group called the *Communist Party of Albania* still exists there and have been allowed to participate in elections. They also go by the name

---

[90] https://www.azquotes.com/quote/770880

[91] Cavendish, R., "Death of Enver Hoxha", 4 April 2010. https://www.historytoday.com/archive/months-past/death-enver-hoxha

[92] Erebara, G., "Albania to Start Searching for Remains of Communist Camp Victims", 2 June 2023. https://balkaninsight.com/2023/06/02/albania-to-start-searching-for-remains-of-communist-camp-victims/

"Volunteers of Enver".[93] These pricks should be buried alive in huge, durable, black plastic bags, in honour of the victims of Hoxha! Like other post-communism lands, Albania is still recovering from being ravaged by the cult/ideology. It was – and still is – one of Europe's poorest countries.[94]

Hungarian Revolution

On 4 November 1956, Soviet forces invade the Hungarian People's Republic, bringing the *Hungarian Revolution* to an end.[95] The disgruntled Hungarians had been unhappy living under the country's sole party – the *Hungarian Working People's Party* – which was under the direct control of the Kremlin.

Inspired by Nikita Khruschev's speech earlier in the year, which denounced Stalin's regime, the protests started in earnest, demanding democracy and freedom from Soviet oppression. The leader of the rebellion was life-long cult member Imre Nagy (1896–1958). Nagy had intentions to allow multi-party elections, and even to remove Hungary from the Warsaw Pact.[96] The bulk of the conflict lasted only twelve days, before the rebels were defeated by the far superior Soviet Army.

In the aftermath, Nagy was executed, and thousands were tried and jailed; there was also a mass execution. It led to the creation of the *Hungarian Socialist Workers Party,* who ruled as the sole party until the fall of communism in 1989.

The Soviets would subsequently claim that what began as an honest, reasonable protest was then high-jacked by fascist, western-backed forces. The Soviets only invaded at the request of the 'genuine patriots' (i.e. pro-Soviet Marxist cult members), whom they joined with to crush this counter-revolution. Oh… so fascism and western imperialism was to blame, right? (rolls eyes). (As an aside, in recent times, note how Russian President Vladimir Putin has claimed Ukraine is full of 'Nazis'….).

The great wall of communism

"It is worth acknowledging that the demise of the Soviet Union was the

---

[93] https://en.wikipedia.org/wiki/Communist_Party_of_Albania_(1991)

[94] https://worldpopulationreview.com/country-rankings/poorest-countries-in-europe

[95] "Soviets put a brutal end to Hungarian revolution", 24 November 2009. https://www.history.com/this-day-in-history/soviets-put-brutal-end-to-hungarian-revolution

[96] https://www.britannica.com/event/Hungarian-Revolution-1956

greatest geopolitical catastrophe of the century"[97]

Russian President Vladimir Putin,
speech in the Russian parliament, 25 April 2005

In 1961, construction begins on the infamous *Berlin Wall*, which divided Germany in to the ostensibly democratic 'West Germany' (*Federal Republic of Germany*) and the Communist 'East Germany' (*German Democratic Republic*).[98]

Eventually appearing owing to the division of Berlin at the end of WW2, the wall was a symbolic, physical manifestation of the ideology's divisive, controlling nature. It served the dual function of keeping out non-Marxists, while preventing those in East Germany from leaving as they pleased. It composed part of what was called the *Iron Curtain*—a physical and ideological barrier that effectively imprisoned everyone East of it in the "Eastern Bloc", separating them from the 'free' West.

As a physical barrier this 'curtain' stretched almost entirely across Europe – from the German Coast in the North to Yugoslavia in the South – measuring roughly 7,000 kilometres in length. Videos online showing people trying to escape through the barbed wire illustrates the desperation better than words ever could. The wall fell in November 1989, symbolising the end of the Cold War and freeing peoples east of it from the economic stagnation and ideological oppression.

The Sino-Soviet split

An ideological difference of opinions within the cult, between members in the Soviet Union and China. In the post-Stalin U.S.S.R., the premier Nikitia Khruschev publicly denounced many aspects of Uncle Joe's regime in a speech he gave in 1956 (he didn't actually refer to him as Uncle Joe; they weren't related). This marked what was to be called the 'De-Stalinization' process of the Soviet Union. This departure from the previous approach/system (termed Stalinism), caused a ripple effect in the worldwide cult; most immediately causing the leader of Red China – Mao Zedong – to label this as 'revisionism'.[99]

In this context, revisionism meant a departure from traditional Marxist

---

[97] Associated Press, "Putin: Soviet Collapse a 'genuine 'tragedy'", 25 April 2005. https://www.nbcnews.com/id/wbna7632057

[98] https://www.britannica.com/topic/Berlin-Wall

[99] https://www.britannica.com/topic/20th-century-international-relations-2085155/The-Sino-Soviet-split

principles; a kind of 'softening' on certain issues (particularly on the idea of Communist nations having peaceful relations with non-Communist ones, where they could both co-exist). This development had a knock-on effect on other Communist countries and led to the development of new strains/interpretations of the ideology (listed elsewhere).

The speech Khruschev gave in 1956 was entitled "On the Cult of Personality and its Consequences".[100] The ideology/cult itself is the cult of Marx. Interestingly, the alternate title for this book you are reading was "The Cult of Cunts and its Cuntish Consequences".

The Prague Spring

In 1968, internal attempts were made to reform the *Czechoslovak Socialist Republic;* a satellite state of the Soviet Union at the time. This period of political reforms, along with the mass protests that took place in the country, are known as the *Prague Spring.*[101] The catalyst for this uprising was the then leader of the *Czechoslovak Communist Party* Alexander Dubcek. As with the Hungarian Revolution of 1956, the Czechoslovaks wanted a liberalisation of their society: freedom of speech, movement, decentralisation of the economy etc. As before, the fanatics in the Kremlin were not having any of this, and the invasion of Czechoslovakia takes place on the night of 20 August.

Unlike the Hungarian Revolution, there was no combat between the residents and the invaders. There was, however, a mass exodus, with over a quarter of a million fleeing (I wonder why people would be fleeing from the heroic, glorious Red Army??). On 25 August 1968, eight people held an anti-invasion protest in Red Square, Moscow.[102] Obviously, it was seen as treasonous by the Soviet government, and was suppressed with extreme prejudice. Some protestors were sent to the brutal Gulag prison camps in Siberia, others to psychiatric hospitals. When the cult/ideology is in full control, protests are not allowed.

Democratic Kampuchea and the Khmer Rouge

"Am I violent? No. As far as my conscience and mission was concerned,

---

[100] Khruschev, N. "Speech to 20th Congress of the C.P.S.U.", 1956.https://www.marxists.org/archive/khrushchev/1956/02/24.htm

[101] https://www.britannica.com/event/Prague-Spring

[102] Kramer, M. "The August 1968 Red Square Protest and Its Legacy", 24 August 2018. https://www.wilsoncenter.org/blog-post/the-august-1968-red-square-protest-and-its-legacy

there was no problem"

The final interview of Saloth Sar (aka Pol Pot), 1979[103]

Another absolute monstrosity, even by Marxist standards, took place in what is now called Cambodia in South-East Asia. For a time, this country was a one-party 'Marxist-Leninist' state called *Democratic Kampuchea*, that existed between 1975 and 1979. It was ruled over by the *Communist Party of Kampuchea* (aka the *Khmer Rouge*).[104] This group appeared on the scene as the Marxist rot spread across Asia in the post-WW2, post-colonialism era. Its allies at various times included Mao Zedong's China, the Viet Cong, North Korea, and the *Pathet Lao* (*Lao People's Liberation Army*) in neighbouring Laos.

The name "Khmer Rouge" means "Red Khmers": "Rouge" is "Red" en Français of course, and the "Khmer" people were the dominant ethnic group in that area. So, another cult group basically.

The leadership of the Khmer Rouge consisted of Cambodian cult members, many of whom were exposed to Marxism while receiving 'educations' in France. The psycho at the helm in this instance was a Cambodian by the name of Saloth Sar (who later renamed himself Pol Pot).[105] Mr. Pot came from a relatively wealthy agricultural background, and eventually ended up with somewhat of a champagne socialist education. He learned about historical figures like Maximillian Robespierre (1758–1794) of the French Revolution) and became a fan of Uncle Joe Stalin. After receiving his brainwashing in Paris as a student, he returned to Cambodia in 1953 to do what cult members usually do: infect their home country.

When the Khmer Rouge took control, Pol Pot had the capital Phnom Penh emptied, forcing people out into the rural areas, which were divided into zones. He wanted everyone to be peasants, so they could all be treated equally (here we go again…).[106] Wealthy people who tried to bring their possessions with them were denied. The regime featured the usual Marxist authoritarianism; forced 'equality'; forced labour; collectivisation; liquidation of many of the wealthy (i.e. middle class or higher),

[103] "The last interview with Pol Pot (English Subtitles)".
https://www.YouTube.com/watch?v=CQ9_BMshyiw

[104] "Khmer Rouge". https://www.britannica.com/topic/Khmer-Rouge

[105] "Pol Pot", 21 August 2018. https://www.history.com/topics/cold-war/pol-pot

[106] Deth, S.U., "The Rise and Fall of Democratic Kampuchea", 2009.

https://www.asianstudies.org/publications/eaa/archives/the-rise-and-fall-of-democratic-kampuchea/

intellectuals, and political dissenters etc. Predictably, when the fucked-up system the regime enforced didn't work, Pol Pot didn't accept blame. Instead, he blamed political enemies and infiltrators for ruining everything. Former Khmer Rouge members were themselves killed in the interrogation centres. Pound-for-pound it has one of the highest body counts – relative to population levels – of any Marxist cult regime. Estimates for the death toll vary between 1.5 to 3 million.[107] It was another manifestation of the ideology, resulting from the instability and conflict it generated in Asia as a whole.

As the prelude to this fiasco, the *Cambodian Civil War* ran concurrently to the Vietnam War from 1968–1975. It was between the Khmer Rouge and their Marxist allies (Viet Cong and North Vietnam etc.), and the Kingdom of Cambodia and their allies (South Vietnam, U.S. etc.).[108] Unfortunately, the cult prevailed and the Khmer Rouge took control. Since Marxist forces often retreated across the border to Cambodia and Laos during the Vietnam War, U.S. action across the border was inevitable, officially or unofficially. Though their forces forayed into Cambodia (half-heartedly) with *Operation Menu* (1969–1970) and *Operation Freedom Deal* (1970–1973), unfortunately, the Khmer Rouge were not properly dealt with. Naturally, the cult used these military actions to generate sympathy for their 'cause', both regionally and internationally. Commies playing victim by complaining that someone is trying to stop them. Trying to blame the U.S. as being the bad guy in the equation. Typical.

The political pressure generated by cult members internationally— including the 'peace' movement on American soil—contributed to U.S. withdrawal from the region, and the resultant dwindling public support meant that a more effective full-scale invasion of Cambodia would never happen, of course.

The infection remained and the Cambodians would be left at the mercy of the cult, who not only slaughtered millions of their own civilians but the Vietnamese along the border too. So, all those brainwashed hippie morons and students at American 'peace' protests had blood on their hands… just like all the Marxist traitors in the U.S. at that time.

The Khmer Rouge regime was eventually toppled by the Vietnamese in 1978 in the *Cambodian-Vietnamese War*, in the years following the

---

[107] "Cambodia". https://cla.umn.edu/chgs/holocaust-genocide-education/resource-guides/cambodia

[108] https://www.britannica.com/place/Cambodia/Civil-war

withdrawal of U.S. forces from the region.[109] The conflict between these two groups continued long after the former were removed from power, with hostilities continuing until 1989 when the Vietnamese withdrew from the country. Interestingly (and tellingly), the U.N. actually recognised Democratic Kampuchea as the legitimate government during the Vietnamese occupation (!).

That situation shows the ideology's ability to spawn different regimes that will then compete for control of the region and eliminate each other. It's also a lesson in what horrors may transpire when you don't fully intervene and eliminate cult regimes.

Rhodesia/Zimbabwe

Another Marxist horror show, this time in Zimbabwe, Southeast Africa. This land had the typically complex attributes of many post-colonial African nations, including division within the non-white population (the Shona and Ndebele peoples). Formally controlled by the *British South Africa Company*, it eventually declared its independence as Rhodesia in 1965, and was Zimbabwe Rhodesia in 1979.[110] For much of this period, the white minority government was in control, albeit of an internationally unrecognised country. This situation was the result of the British policy of only granting independence to its African colonies provided there was majority rule. In other words, the white minority were shit out of luck.

The white minority was then largely left to deal with the rising murderous tide of black Marxism on their own, receiving some support from neighbouring South Africa. This conflict constituted the *Rhodesian Bush War* or *Zimbabwe War of Liberation* ('Liberation' to be Marxist; we can also call it the "Marxist takeover of Rhodesia").[111] The war pitted two main Marxist factions—Z.A.N.L.A. (*Zimbabwe African National Liberation Army*) and Z.I.P.R.A. (*Zimbabwe People's Revolutionary Army*)—against the white minority. ZANLA was the military wing of ZANU (*Zimbabwe African National Union*); ZIPRA was the military wing of ZAPU (*Zimbabwe African Peoples Union*).

Both ZANU AND ZAPU formed a coalition called the *Patriotic Front*. The Marxist factions were supported by *FRELIMO* (from neighbouring Mozambique) and the *African National Council* (from neighbouring South

---

[109] "Vietnam-Cambodia War | Overview, Background & History".
https://study.com/learn/lesson/vietnam-cambodia-war-causes-effects.html

[110] https://www.britannica.com/place/Zimbabwe

[111] "Bush War". https://www.rhodesianstudycircle.org.uk/bush-war/

Africa), as well as *FROLIZI* (*Front for the Liberation of Zimbabwe*). Mercenaries such as the American *Crippled Eagles* fought for the Rhodesian Security Forces.

ZANLA launched their campaign from Mozambique, situated to the East of Zimbabwe. They were composed mostly of the Shona ethnic group and were supplied by Red China. ZIPRA, consisting mostly of Ndebele, were based in Zambia (North/North-West of Zimbabwe). This group had the Soviets as their sponsor. Cuba's Fidel Castro also offered support.

So essentially, it was several cult groups on the one side, and the Rhodesian Security Forces (plus allies) on the other. The Marxist factions sometimes fought each other. The conflict lasted approximately fifteen years from 1964 to 1979, ending in a stalemate. The British got involved at the end of the war as mediator between all parties involved, resulting in the *Lancaster House Agreement*.[112]

This eventually led to black majority rule, with the Marxist *ZANU-PF* party winning the first election held in the now internationally recognised Zimbabwe. So, it wasn't really a 'stalemate'—the cult was victorious. As a result, a man named Robert Mugabe became the country's first leader, in the role of Prime Minister.

Enter Mugabe

Robert Gabriel Mugabe was another university 'educated' African man who would take his country's destiny by the scruff of the neck and drag it towards a delightful Marxist utopia. This idiot attended the *University of Fort Hare* in South Africa on a scholarship in 1949. It was here that Mugabe became initially infected, contracting it from cult members there. He joined the *African National Congress* and was exposed to the ideas of 'African Nationalism'. He later showed an interest in the writings of Comrades Marx and Engels. After obtaining a BA degree in history and English literature, he returned to Southern Rhodesia in 1952.[113]

He then began his teaching career at various locations (poor kids!), and eventually ended up in Ghana in 1958. It was there that he received his second dose of Marxism, when he attended the *Kwame Nkrumah Ideological Institute* in Ghana. Kwame Nkrumah (1909–1972) was another university 'educated' cult member who became the first President of Ghana in 1960. Nkrumah created a one-party state, and proceeded to run his

---

[112] https://en.wikipedia.org/wiki/Lancaster_House_Agreement

[113] https://www.britannica.com/biography/Robert-Mugabe

country in to the ground by enforcing 'African socialism'.[114]

Mugabe began his involvement in politics during the 1960s, and was incarcerated in 1964 due to his activities, spending the next ten years in prison, being released in 1974. He fled to Mozambique, where he spent a few years in exile as the Rhodesian Bush War raged on. After the conflict, once he assumed power, Mugabe went on to create a one-party dictatorship and the inevitable persecution of the Ndebele minority began.

His policies led to new government controls on the economy and state-run enterprises; and the confiscation (without compensation of course) of properties owned by white farmers. This land grab followed the 'anti-colonialism'/'anti-capitalism' Marxist formula, in the name of 'equality'. Nobody considered that the white farmers were the best people to run the farms (due to experience and know-how n' stuff), and food production ground to a halt, leading to widespread starvation. Millions fled. The short-sighted, clumsy fanaticism of Marxism strikes again.

(Another example of this idiotic and typically Marxist tunnel-vision happened during the Rhodesian Bush War, when the Marxist forces based across the border in Zambia were perplexed that they had cut themselves off from the water supply coming from Zimbabwe—a water supply built and maintained by those evil, oppressive, non-Marxist, colonist whites).

Later, the *Zimbabwe National Army* would conduct the *Gukurahundi* massacres, against mostly the Ndebele minority (1982 to 1987 approx).[115] Besides the ethnic genocidal element to this, the Ndebele were typically ZAPU supporters; labels of parties and domestic politics aside, this was political suppression of those in opposition to the Marxist government (typical of the cult when in power). Reasonable estimates for the massacres varied, ranging from eight to twenty thousand. Another example of the mask slipping—the cult/ideology didn't care about black/Africans rights in this instance.

Once known as the "Jewel of Africa" Mugabe's reign turned Zimbabwe in to a relative hellhole. It never crossed the minds of those who fought for the cult or otherwise supported it that it was unwise to destroy the infrastructure that the white minority had built. It really is a mind-boggling level of stupidity since they literally fought to the death for about fifteen years with this goal in mind. It's another good example of what happens

---

[114] https://en.wikipedia.org/wiki/Kwame_Nkrumah_Ideological_Institute

[115] Boddy-Evans, A. "What Was Gukurahundi in Zimbabwe?", 12 Feb 2019. https://www.thoughtco.com/what-is-gukurahundi-43923

when the organic order of the infrastructure is replaced by Marxist theories.

Perestroika

During the second half of the 1980s, towards the end of the U.S.S.R. era, the Soviet administration made an apparent effort to modify how it conducted its affairs. This involved changes in a variety of areas. The ostensible goal was not to abandon socialism, but to include aspects of 'liberal economics'. The term "Perestroika" was made famous by the Soviet premier Mikhail Gorbachev (1931–2022) and means "reconstruction" or "restructuring".[116]

Another term used was "Glasnost" meaning "openness" or "transparency" (sounds lovely, right?). This, I believe, was an attempt by the cult to try to hide its intentions, by pretending that 'communism' was softening; essentially becoming more benevolent and reflective of Western culture. This subject is dealt with in *The Perestroika Deception: Memoranda to the Central Intelligence Agency* (1998), by a high-profile KGB defector named Anatoliy Golitsyn.

To put all this in context, the Russian regime of today has an image in some quarters of being much 'nicer' than previous regimes, but we shouldn't make assumptions. It's clear that Putin's Russia has alliances with China and North Korea et al, which is disturbing. At time of writing, Russian forces are currently in Ukraine. I pray that by the time you read this, it hasn't essentially annexed the country. This would mean the 'Communist' alliance has taken another step west, and another piece on the chessboard...

Summary for historical section

Some might feel that these 'Communist' regimes of the past don't have any parallels in the societies of today; that it was a bygone era. This is wrong—there are many similarities. There might be differences in the cult's/ideology's methods, but what's important is its level of ideological influence/dominance overall.

Some things happening in recent times are reminiscent of those regimes: the control of movement within a country, and the ability to leave/enter a country only under certain conditions (i.e. you are willing to be injected with something (Covid); the state deciding which types of foods, services, and jobs are 'essential' (Covid lockdowns); harassment/punishment by state policing services if you openly criticize the cult/cult members ('hate-speech' enforcement), and/or the protection of cult members by the state; the creation of 'politically correct' brainwashed rat societies, and the use of

---

[116] https://www.britannica.com/topic/perestroika-Soviet-government-policy

technology to monitor the general public.

Also: the mainstream media constantly pumping out propaganda, and the censorship of anything that contradicts it; the cult's control of education systems and the indoctrination of the young using various methods; the attempts to gain more influence over the young by 'legally' separating them from their parents; the control of speech/language in society; the control of the arts/culture/entertainment, and the Marxification of it; the attack on religion and spirituality, particularly Christianity; the attempts at enforcing equality; the promotion/use of socialism as an economic system; the constant re-emphasise on the apparent imperialism of the United States/NATO countries (as a form of distraction and propaganda etc. etc.).

The ideology itself, as a whole, is to blame

Every single occurrence of the infection was not included; that was just a brief overview. They have been examined elsewhere and would require books and books. Let's keep in mind a key point here: if 'revolutionary' Marxism didn't exist – or at least, if it was treated like the toxic ideology that it is – then all those regimes/incidents would not have happened.

All that intimidation, torture, theft, terror, violence, starvation, and death would not have affected all those tens of millions or destroyed all those lands. I'm including the negative impacts of any strain of the ideology, whether it be the consequences of economic catastrophe created by socialism, or invasion/warfare by Marxist forces etc.

Modern day cult members all over the world will constantly try to distance themselves from this history of events. They can identify as any type of 'leftist', socialist, Marxist, Trotskyist etc., and claim they are separate from all of that. Don't let them get off the hook! Shout it at them, shove it into their ears, and ram it down their throats. It isn't a waste of time just because they won't listen or understand, because other non-cult members will hear you and join in.

In many cases, we're not trying to convince, we are trying to criticise and suppress. It's absolutely your/our right to vent at them in this way, for stupidly supporting this ideology. This is their ideology/cult.

This is what they're trying to impose on us today. This is their cause, wittingly or unwittingly, and what they are proud of. This is their Marxist legacy, and we will hold the mirror up to them.

Different strains (for different folks)

"Beginning with the revolutionary Marx, a political group with concrete ideas establishes itself. Basing itself on the giants, Marx and Engels, and developing through successive steps with personalities like Lenin, Stalin, Mao Tse-tung and the new Soviet and Chinese rulers, it establishes a body of doctrine and, let us say, examples to follow"[117]

Fanatical Argentinian cult member Ernesto "Che" Guevara,
Notes on the Cuban Revolution (1960)

Let's take a look at the Marxist 'strains'—various interpretations, 'brands', or sects of the cult—that have spawned globally at various points in the ideology's history. Focus on the idea that the ideological infection has been present in all these situations (in one form or another to one degree or another), whatever label these groups put on themselves, or whatever they are now called. The ideology itself played the pivotal role, so don't be confused or deceived by anyone telling you any different. What's important here is where the ideological infection has been present, not the differences between each system, regime, group etc., which others (especially cult members) like to focus on.

Following is a table of some of the various strains, showing: the variant name, its namesake, place of origin, and the approximate time period of origin and/or existence.[118]

Variant/Strain	Namesake	Origin	Time period
Fabian Socialism	Fabian Society	U.K.	1884 onwards
Leninism	Vladimir Lenin	Russia	pre/post 1917
Luxemburgism	Rosa Luxemburg	Germany	pre-1919
Marxism-Leninism	Karl Marx, V.I. Lenin (Stalin)	Russia	pre/post 1924
Trotskyism	Leon Trotksy	Russia	1927 onwards
Stalinism	Joseph Stalin	Russia	1927 onwards
Maoism	Mao Ze Dong	China	1920s onwards
Titoism	Josip Broz (aka	Yugoslavia	1945– 1980

---

[117] Guevara, E., *Notes on the Cuban Revolution* (1960). https://libquotes.com/che-guevara/quote/lbd0b8u

[118] https://en.wikipedia.org/wiki/List_of_communist_ideologies

"Tito")

Castroism	Fidel Castro	Cuba	1959–2008
Guevarism	Ernest "Che" Guevara	N/A	1960s
Hoxhaism	Enver Hoxha	Albania	1978 onwards
Ho Chi Minh thought	Ho Chi Minh	Vietnam	1991 onwards

Continental tables

How can we try to quantify an ideological infection that exists in people's minds? Is this even possible? Well unless we are going to sit down with each person on Earth one-at-a-time and interview them, how are we going to know who is infected, and to what degree? Maybe in the future we could take a *Star Trek* approach to this with an automated system of some sort, involving certain probing questions etc. A person sits in a chair and bam!— gets their infection results immediately. Or a gadget like a speed gun, that you just point at someone, and it gives you the info, telling you how much of a brainwashed nutcase some is.

Unfortunately, we have no such luxuries. Yet we know that this cult is global. Well…how global? This section is only designed give the reader a general idea of the geographical and historical spread of the ideology. As this is not a historical book, trying to document the entire history of Marxism is not part of the brief, nor necessary (however, it may whet the appetite for further study).

In the following tables, therefore, there's a selection of Marxist political groups in every country to show a clear presence chronologically, from roughly their appearance up until the present day. This shows that 'communism' did not merely exist and peak in the 20th century (a most erroneous perception); it's alive and well today and stronger than ever! In fact, no other movement in history compares to it, in terms of scale and structure.

In addition, using political groups is an easy way of showing a clear Marxist organisational presence in each country, and (in many cases) the involvement of subversive international groups (e.g. the Soviet's Comintern). Of course, political groups (however important they may be) are just the more obviously visible part of the whole international cult movement.

When looking at a particular country in this context, obviously the kind of individuals who are starting-up Marxist groups/organisations are not armchair Marxists (i.e. not sitting at home reading the cult's literature and keeping their ideas to themselves, or merely influencing/infecting those around them, which is bad enough!). They are joining with other infected people and intending to infect the rest of the population in their country. Therefore, first focusing on these groups is a good starting point for our purposes, in understanding the ideology's global reach.

Also, the presence (or lack thereof) of Marxist organisations may show the level of tolerance that population has to Marxism/Marxists: a vehemently anti-Marxist society will not allow these individuals to organise and proceed with their contamination/destruction of the country (uncommon in today's world); conversely, a naive society will allow them to organise, gain momentum, grow in strength, get in to government etc. (common, unfortunately). It's probably not surprising to the reader (as the tables will show) that almost every part of the Earth has been infected at some point in time in this Marxian age. The 'point of infection' of a country, is when Marxist ideas initially appear there (e.g. individuals in a society writing or spouting Marxism).

As mentioned, it seems like the cult/ideology likes to strike when countries are in a state of transition, instability, and weakness; in other words, very favourable conditions for a takeover (e.g. Europe post-WW1). Often it creates those favourable conditions itself (expanded elsewhere). To echo a point made elsewhere, Marxism swooped in to replace traditional imperialism; we can clearly see this process where Africa is concerned. The 'independence' movements of many countries were often created by Marxism. The names of groups listed – and the time period – will reflect this.

Delayed fuse and external influence

The impact of a Marxist infection usually has a delayed fuse. If, for example, a Marxist organisation (e.g. a socialist/communist political party, or union etc.) is founded in a South American country in the year 1920, it may take years, often decades, for the infection to spread nationally sufficiently to start exerting any real influence in its affairs. There are many variables that affect this process in any given country, including its level of political stability and how susceptible/vulnerable a population is for a Marxist takeover. In addition, a country's progress towards a major infection may be expedited by the influence of other countries that are at a later, more advanced stage of infection. This manifests as the bigger country helping the 'revolution' by offering assistance/aid whether it be advisory and diplomatic, personnel, financial, military training and hardware etc. Examples of this process would be the U.S.S.R. or Red China creating/supporting/influencing the multitude of Marxist uprisings in Africa and South America in the 20th century.

A stubborn infection

Once infection of a country sets in, if not stopped, it then starts proliferating, then gains control, and starts the process of inevitably ruining the country with socialism (amongst other things). Often, there is a 'right-wing' pushback, when the general public have come to their senses; once the spell has worn off, and the promise the Marxist's made to them about a socialist utopia does not materialize, they then start to wake up to what (and who!) the problem is. Whatever regime is then put in place, if it's sufficiently anti-Marxism, can then keep the infection at bay.

Unfortunately, this period may not last indefinitely, and sooner or later, the infection re-emerges. This is precisely what happened in Spain in the period between the formation of the pro-Marxism *Spanish Republic* in 1931; the rulership of anti-Marxist Generalissimo Francisco Franco from the end of the Spanish Civil War in 1939 until his death in 1975; and the inevitable re-emergence of Marxism at that point. Another example is what happened before, during, and after the regime of Augusto Pinochet in Chile for most of the 1970s and 1980s.

Another is the story of socialism and *Bela Kun* in Hungary from 1919 right up until the final period of the Soviet Union in 1989: it was the *Hungarian Socialist Republic* briefly in 1919, then after some upheaval in the interwar period, and being allied to the *Axis Powers* in WW2, it was under complete control by the Soviets for decades. Another obvious example is Italy before, during, after Mussolini's reign. There are many other examples and variations of this pattern of infection, disinfection, and re-infection. Parties/groups can be banned in a country by a particular regime and perhaps even forced underground (it may be dormant or active illegally, during this period), only to then re-emerge at a later point. We see this frequently with Marxist groups throughout history.

And here is a point of paramount importance for this subject (and dare I say it, for humanity): once non-cult members are in a position of dominance, if the will to keep the infection suppressed is not strong enough in a given society, it inevitably re-emerges. We need to break this cycle, once and for all...

Often, as history shows, when countries emerge from a catastrophic period of outright Marxist infection (i.e. having a socialist government, who inevitably ruins the place), it then falls in to military dictatorship. This happened on several occasions in South America. A famous example is the

Presidency of democratically elected cult member Chilean Marxist Salvador Allende (1908–1973).

After a few years of destroying the place, he was replaced by a military junta, with Augusto Pinochet emerging as leader. Whether or not this is a bad thing depends on the stance the new regime has towards Marxism/the cult (Pinochet was staunchly anti-Communist).

What's included in the tables

The chief aim of this section is to show the ideology's presence/influence/dominance in these countries/states, either historically or presently. Though these tables took considerable time to put together, this is not an exhaustive list; there are innumerable short-lived groups or failed groups which are not included.

Also not included are the innumerable youth wings of each of these groups (many of which are actively influencing the youth of today). Included are some of the Marxist 'revolutionary' or 'liberation' terrorist guerilla groups active all over the globe during the 20th century. Also included are some 'Green' parties and some Feminist parties since these movements wouldn't exist without Marxism.

Not included are Anarchist groups, though many (if not all, on some level) may be contaminated with Marxism to a degree (at an ideological level/in terms of personnel/both). Also, if they are actively involved in attacking 'the system', they may be (wittingly or unwittingly) serving Marxism. So we could consider groups of this kind part of the overall world Marxist structure of organisations infected with the ideology.

Included are some parties labelling themselves as 'Liberal' or 'Progressive', as they can be contaminated too. Indeed, there is a significant presence of Marxism/Marxists in these types of groups, and they may be (wittingly or unwittingly) serving Marxism with ideas of 'Social Justice', equality etc. Whether the party/members officially identify with the ideology or not, they may still be contributing with their Marxist mentality/approach. The Marxist rot is happy to proliferate while hiding behind those labels. This is a very serious, common, and complex tangled mess that we must untangle somewhat. We do this by understanding the ideology and identifying who espouses it as being Marxist, regardless of what they call themselves, or what groups they belong to. Not included are the many labour/workers' organisations/federations or trade unions, or other types of organisations that have been used as 'Communist front organisation' that may be/have been present in a country.

Does it matter if a Marxist party is in power or not?

What we are dealing with here is a quasi-clandestine network of global ideological influence; it's both overt and covert simultaneously. It's sufficiently hidden to keep the masses unawares.

Regardless of whether a Marxist party is in power, or if it's even part of government/parliament, it can still exert influence on a country's affairs. This is possible through having connections with other ideologically contaminated entities (universities, labour and/or trade unions, NGOs etc). In Ireland, for example, Marxist political groups like *Solidarity-People Before Profit* operate in the fringe and will never be 'in government', but they do contribute in other ways towards the Marxification of Ireland overall. Groups like this also act as 'opposition' to the main (officially non-Marxist) parties in general political discourse.

Again, we are talking about the ideology of Marxism and all its variations. Therefore, it can be present in groups who identify as being 'conservative' or 'right-wing' too due to the Marxist tactics of "ideological subversion" or what's called Entryism—the infiltration of opposing groups (the former is outlined in the Various Groups and Incarnations section).

Can a non-Marxist group still be somewhat contaminated or pro-Marxist?

Yes, this is possible. To add another layer of complexity to our perceptions here, it's possible that groups (who are officially not Marxist) may appear to be relatively unscathed by direct subversion/entryism, yet these individuals/groups may already be contaminated with a Marxist/socialist mentality. This is due to the members being contaminated themselves (perhaps even totally unaware they are sabotaging their groups efforts overall).

This can apply regardless of an individual's/group's official position on things (e.g. if they are officially 'nationalist' or 'patriotic'); whether they are rich capitalists; or even if they are officially 'anti-Communist' in some cases. Just because a group is marketing itself as 'patriotic' or 'nationalist', doesn't mean it isn't peddling Marxism of one form of another, consciously or unconsciously. It really depends on the mentality and vigilance of the personalities directing the course of the group. This is what makes dealing with the Marxist infection so complex: things are not what they appear on the surface, and unfortunately many in society take things at face value (to our collective detriment).

So even though the following tables generally only list the outright socialist and communist groups, that doesn't mean there is no Marxist contamination in the 'centre' or 'right-wing' parties in any given country. Listing all incidences of this would take quite a while I suspect…

In the Republic of Ireland, two of the largest parties – *Fianna Fáil* and *Fine Gael* – are not regarded as Marxist organisations (officially, they are 'centre to centre-right' and 'centre-right' respectively; meaningless labels) but they are also riddled with Marxist thought, and Marxists posing as non-Marxists, or 'internationalists'/'globalists'. Another major party *Sinn Fein* – a pseudo-patriotic Marxist party – have often been considered 'opposition'. There is no opposition to internationalist Marxism in the Irish government! As mentioned earlier, unfortunately, all that's needed is for groups to appear different to make the masses believe there is some variety in the system, or that they have a choice when it's time to step up to the commie red star-shaped ballot box.

The names of these groups

We really must give the cult full (Karl) marks when it comes to marketing. The virtue-signalling nature of the ideology is evident even in the names it creates for itself. Many of the party/group names attempt to promote them as being benevolent humanitarians, saviours, 'radicals', warriors etc.

In addition to the more predictable terms of "Socialist", "Workers", "Communist", "Revolutionary", "Peoples", or "Labour" being used, we will see other terms: terms like "Workers", "Working People", "Labourer". (Of course, "People's" is a suggestive way of saying "We support you! The little, powerless, low-status, poor oppressed person!". Obviously, there are always many people like that, in any given society, so using these terms tends to sucker-in a significant chunk of the population). "Democratic" is an important – and ironic – one, since Marxism manipulates the democratic system, in order to bring in its own (where no dissenting (non-Marxist) voices are allowed).

To the average person in the street, terms like "Progressive" suggest a constructive change, or a benevolent movement forward; that this group intends to improve things somehow. Many "Progressive" parties are members of the *Progressive International* (which even a novice can see is a clearly Marxist organisation).[119] So yes, "progressive". Progressive in a Marxist direction. Progress for Marxism.

This ties-in with the point made earlier about Marxist groups/orgs labelling themselves absolutely anything except "Marxist". We may see names of groups including the words "Social Democratic" and "Republican". Other key terms include Liberation, Freedom, Struggle, Unity, Solidarity, Radical, Independence, Justice, Revolution. Oh, and did I mention "People"?! (I know, I already did). We can't forget that!! "People" this and "People" that

---

[119] "Who We Are". https://progressive.international/about/en

times thousand (ironic for an anti-humanity ideology). Are these all not manipulative, misleading terms, when we accept that the ideology is actually malevolent (as opposed to being benevolent, which is how it markets itself)? The Trojan Horse factor is evident here—it's emotional manipulation using language.

In some parts of the tables, where fully-infected Marxist one-party states/countries are mentioned, they are called: (insert country names) _____ Socialist Republic, Democratic Republic of _____, Federal Republic of _____, United Republic of _____, People's Republic of _____, People's Democratic Republic of _____, Democratic Socialist Republic of _____, People's Revolutionary Republic of _____ etc. etc.

Imagine, a world full of fully Marxist countries, how dull! Of course, even if a state/country has changed its name (from one of the above listed), this doesn't mean that this place is now Marxism-free. Despite the damage that Marxist infection does to countries, some will still, amazingly, have an affection for it (indeed, this is the case for the whole world).

Patriotic nationalist Marxist parties?

Some groups use words like "patriotic" and "nationalist" in their titles. This is the 'right-wing' paint job hiding the Marxist engine under the hood. They've used terms like these to great effect in countries that were (up until a given point in time) controlled by a foreign power/empire.

The term "nationalist" is a good choice, because it can unite the masses in that country as a group, making them think they are part-taking in something beneficial for themselves. Unfortunately, in this instance, they have just been suckered-in to participating-in/supporting a Marxist takeover of their own country (which inevitably leads to its destruction/their destruction). Their country – as has happened to so many in the 20th century worldwide – will then transition from being under oligarchical imperial control, to being under the control of the Marxist ideology/cult (example: the Republic of Ireland).

Almost the whole continent of Africa, in general, transformed from being under a certain level of Imperial control, to being under the influence of Marxism. This pattern was repeated time and time again there, when countries became independent of the various oligarchical European empires, including Britain, France, Netherlands, Portugal, Spain, and Italy. Indeed, many countries seemed to become increasingly under the grip of Marxism once the colonial power in question granted the country its independence. Obviously, a power vacuum was created when the colonial powers decided to withdraw from these places; a vacuum that Marxism always intended to fill.

As mentioned, Marxism itself was responsible for triggering the calls for 'independence' in the first place. To summarise this point (with our new Anti-Marxist perspective) when the Marxist movements in these countries used the term "nationalism" for their own ends, it didn't mean "freedom and independence to be free", it meant "freedom and independence to become Marxist" (and lose your freedom and independence). Big difference.

Technical notes for the tables

"Unknown": Sometimes you will see a group's active period listed as, for example, "1928-unknown". When I say "unknown" this does not mean that the information is nowhere to be found; but rather that I haven't been able to find it quickly enough. It's also a distinct possibility that I have not bothered my arse to do so. It means "not known to me" basically. Also, disturbingly, note how many groups still exist today (e.g. "1928—present").

Comintern parties: Most groups/parties established by/connected to the Comintern will be emphasised with "(Com)".

Geolocation: feel free to look at a world map while you read these tables, to get a sense of the coverage of the ideology.

North America and Greenland

The story of Marxism in the U.S. is a long one and has been covered sufficiently elsewhere. Though the ideology found its way into that country during the 19th century (just like most other places), it wasn't till the post WW1 period that the country was directly targeted for ideological subversion by Vladimir Lenin's regime. A massive subject unto itself, there have been many books written about it.

The U.S. is severely infected; a five-minute glance at the state of current affairs there confirms this. The scale of the socialist movement is reflected somewhat in the sheer number of parties in the table below, stretching back to the mid-19th century. The history of the labour and union movements in the U.S., in addition to other relevant areas of society (academia, media etc.), all point to a high level of infection. Canada – being part of the British commonwealth – was always going to become highly infected, due to its proximity and similarity to the U.S., and its ties to British society and politics.

Mexico, being the main land bridge to the U.S. for Central and South America, was destined to succumb to an infection. Note the groups in Hawaii, way out there in the Pacific. Even Greenland, way up there in the north Atlantic, hasn't remained untouched. Interesting that it achieved home rule from Denmark in 1979, around the same time that the Marxist parties were established. Many countries have followed this pattern.

Location	Notable groups
Canada	*Socialist Labor Party* (1898–2005);
	Socialist Party of British Columbia (1901–1905);
	Socialist Party of Canada (1904–1925);
	Canadian Labour Party (1917–1942);
	Communist Party of Canada (1921-present); (Com)
	Socialist Party of Canada (1931-present);
	Co-operative Commonwealth Federation (1932–1962);
	New Democratic Party (1961-present);
	Party of Socialist Democracy (1963–2002);
	Communist Party of Quebec (1965-present);
	Communist Party of Canada—Marxist-Leninist (1970-present);
	Revolutionary Communist Party of Canada (2000-present);
	Quebec Solidarity (2006-present)
Greenland	*Community for the People* (1976-present);
	Forward (1977-present);
	Labour Party (1979–1983)
	Greenland achieved home rule from Denmark in 1979.
Mexico	*Mexican Communist Party* (1917–1981);
	Bolshevik Communist Party (1963-unknown);
	Revolutionary Party of the Proletariat (1964-unknown);
	United Socialist Party of Mexico (1981–1987);
	Socialist Mexican Party (1987–1989);
	Communist Party of Mexico (1994-present)
U.S.A.	*Socialist Labor Party* (1876-present); (Com)

Social Democratic Party of America (1898–1901);

Socialist Party of America (*SPA.* 1901–1972);

Socialist Propaganda League of America (1915-unknown);

World Socialist Party of the U.S. (1916-present);

Communist Party USA (1919-present);

Workers World Party (1959-present);

Progressive Labor Party (1962-present);

Freedom Socialist Party (1966-present);

Marxist-Leninist Party USA (1967–1993);

Social Democrats (1972-present);

Communist Workers' Party (1973–1985);

Socialist Party of the United States of America (1973-present);

Revolutionary Communist Party (1975-present);

Democratic Socialists of America (a non-profit org. spawned by the *SPA.* 1982-present);

American Party of Labor (2008-present)

U.S. state of Hawaii:

Democratic Party of Hawaii (1900-present);

Communist Party of Hawaii (1937–1958);

Green Party of Hawaii (1992 approx.-present)

Latin America and the Caribbean

Latin America and the Caribbean have been riddled since the 19th century, thereby following a typical infection pattern. Since this region has an extensive colonial imperial past, and the resultant legacy, meant it was easy for the ideology to dig-in here (i.e. the exploits of the Spanish and Portuguese in this region in centuries past, plus the French, Dutch and British, to a lesser extent). It's different, however, to Africa, since the countries within this region achieved independence from the foreign empires much earlier in general than their African counterparts.

Latin America's proximity to the U.S. meant Lenin and the Comintern were very keen to start ideological fires on its geographical doorstep. In general, the 1920s onwards saw the infection gathering pace, plunging these regions in to 'revolutionary' chaos. The false promises of socialism to the less fortunate, as usual, was the carrot dangled in front of the less wealthy, and so the flames grew. Sadly, as a consequence, civil war, assassinations, military coups, and economic destitution was to be the story of Latin America for most of the 20th century, and beyond.

The ideology played a role in: the leadership of Juan Peron in Argentina; the 'progressive' impact of Jorge Gaitan in Colombia and his assassination, followed by a decade of unrest—La Violencia; the story of Jacobo Arbenz in Guatemala; the collaboration of Fidel Castro and Che Guevara, and the Cuban Missile Crisis (almost bringing the world to atomic war); the anti-Marxist regime of Alfredo Stroessner in Paraguay; the US-backed Contras opposing the Sandinista Junta in Nicaragua; the presidency of cult member Salvador Allende in Chile, followed by the regime of Augusto Pinochet; a massive, multi-national, cross-border effort to combat the infection across Latin America called Operation Condor; the Rebel Zapatista Autonomous zones in Mexico; the Bolivarian Revolution and Hugo Chavez in Venezuela; and so many more examples.

South America is also quite notable for the number of Marxist terrorist groups—aka 'freedom fighters' or 'revolutionary' groups—and the resultant drama during the 20th century. Including all of these would require an extra table.

South and Central America

Location   **Notable groups**

Argentina   *Radical Civic Union* (1891-present);

Socialist Party (1896-present);

Communist Party of Argentina (1918-present);

Workers' Party (1964-present);

Revolutionary Communist Party (1968-present);

Intransigent Party (1972-present);

Movement for Socialism (1982–2003);

Socialist Workers' Party (1988-present);

Communist Party—Extraordinary Congress (1996-present);

Free of the South Movement (2006-present);

Project South (2007-present)

Belize	*United Black Association for Development* (1969–1974); *Belize People's Front* (2012-present)
Bolivia	*Revolutionary Workers' Party* (1935-present); *Revolutionary Left Party* (1940–1979); *Communist Party of Bolivia* (1950-present); *Revolutionary Party of the Nationalist Left* (1963–1985/unknown); *Revolutionary Left Front* (1978-present); *Socialist Party-1* (1978–2003); *Movement Toward Socialism* (1995-present); *Movement Without Fear* (1999-present)
Brazil	*Brazilian Communist Party* (1922-present); *Communist Party of Brazil—Marxist-Leninist* (1922-present); (Com) *Brazilian Socialist Party* (1947-present); *Workers' Party* (1980-present); *Green Party* (1986-present); *Citizenship* (1992-present); *Unified Workers' Socialist Party* (1994-present); *Workers' Cause Party* (1995-present); *Popular Unity* (2016-present)
Chile	*Democrat Party* (1887–1941); *Socialist Workers' Party* (1912–1922); *Communist Party of Chile* (1922-present); (Com) *Socialist Party of Chile* (1933-present); *Workers' Socialist Party* (1940–1944); *Humanist Party* (1984-present); *Party for Democracy* (1987-present); *Revolutionary Workers' Party* (1999–2018);

Green Ecologist Party (2008-present);

Equality Party (2009-present);

Progressive Party (2010-present);

Democratic Revolution (2012-present);

Patriotic Union (2015-present);

Broad Front (2017-present);

Social Green Regionalist Federation (2017-present)

Colombia   *Colombian Liberal Party* (1848-present);

Colombian Socialist Party (1860–1936);

Columbian Communist Party (1930-present); (Com)

Revolutionary Armed Forces of Colombia—People's Army (1964–2017 approx.);*

National Liberation Army (1964-present);*

Communist Party of Colombia—Marxist-Leninist (1965/2009-present);

Revolutionary Independent Labour Movement (1970-present);

Marxist-Leninist League of Colombia (1971–1982);

Marxist-Leninist-Maoist Tendency (1974–1982);

Workers' Revolutionary Party of Colombia (1982–1991);

Revolutionary Communist Group of Colombia (1982-present);

Patriotic Union (1985-present);

Clandestine Colombian Communist Party (2000–2017);

Green Alliance (2005-present);

Alternative Democratic Pole (2005-present);

Common Alternative Revolutionary Force (2017-present)

* Infamous Marxist terrorist groups, known as *ELN* and *FARC/FARC-EP*

Costa Rica   *Popular Vanguard Party* (1943-present);

National Liberation Party (1951-present);

Costa Rican People's Party (1984–2006);

Democratic Force (1996–2010);

Citizens' Action Party (2000-present);

Broad Front (2004-present);

Workers' Party (2012-present)

Ecuador   *Communist Party of Ecuador* (1925-present);

Ecuadorian Socialist Party (1926-present);

Marxist-Leninist Communist Party (1964-present);

Democratic People's Movement (1978–2014);

Pachakutik Plurinational Unity Movement-New Country (1995-present);

Workers' Party of Ecuador (1996-present);

Patriotic Society Party (2002-present);

PAIS Alliance (2006-present);

Popular Unity Movement (2014-present)

El Salvador *Communist Party of El Salvador* (1930–1995);

Farabundo Marti Liberation People's Forces (1970–1995);*

National Resistance (1975–1992);

Revolutionary Party of the Central American Workers (1975–1995);

Farabundo Martí National Liberation Front (1980-present)

* Marxist terrorist group, known as the FPL

Guatemala *Revolutionary Action Party* (1945–1954);

Guatemalan Party of Labour (1949–1998);

Socialist Party (1951–1952);

Guatemalan National Revolutionary Unity (1982–1998);

National Unity of Hope (2002-present);

	Encounter for Guatemala (2007–2020); *Winaq* (2007-present); *New Republic Movement* (2009–2015)
Guyana	*Political Affairs Committee* (1946–1950); *British Guiana Labour Party* (1946–1950); *People's Progressive Party—Civic* (1950-present)
Honduras	*Revolutionary Democratic Party of Honduras* (1948–1955); *Communist Party of Honduras* (1954–1990); *Honduran Revolutionary Party* (1961–1993); *Party for the Transformation of Honduras* (1967–1992); *Movement for Socialism* (1976–1978); *Socialist Party of Honduras* (1978–1983); *Revolutionary Popular Forces Lorenzo Zelaya* (1980–1990); *Patriotic Renewal Party* (1990–1992); *Democratic Unification Party* (1992-present); *Frente Amplio* (2012-present)
Nicaragua	*Nicaraguan Socialist Party* (1944-present); *Sandinista National Liberation Front* (1961-present); *Marxist-Leninist Party of Nicaragua* (1967-present); *Communist Party of Nicaragua* (1967-present); *Marxist Revolutionary League* (1971-present); *Revolutionary Unity Movement* (1988-present); *Sandinista Renovation Movement* (1995-present); *Ecologist Green Party of Nicaragua* (2003-present)
Panama	*Labour Party* (1927–1930); *People's Party of Panama* (1930–1991); *Workers' Party* (1934-present);

November 29 National Liberation Movement (1970-present);

Socialist Workers Front—Marxist-Leninist (1973–1980);

Democratic Revolutionary Party (1979-present);

Communist Party of Panama Marxist-Leninist (1980-present);

Broad Front for Democracy (2013-present)

Paraguay   *Socialist Party* (1860–1936);

Paraguayan Communist Party (1928-present);

Revolutionary Febrerista Party (1951-present);

Workers' Party (1989-present);

Party for a Country of Solidarity (2000-present);

Progressive Democratic Party (2007-present)

Peru   *Peruvian Communist Party* (1928-present);

Revolutionary Vanguard (1965–1984);

Communist Party of Peru—Shining Path (1969-present);

Communist Party of Peru—Red Fatherland (1970-present);

Revolutionary Communist Party (1974–1977);

Revolutionary Socialist Party (1976-present);

Workers' Revolutionary Party (1978-present);

Communist Party of Peru—Marxist-Leninist (2001-present);

Socialist Party (2005-present);

Free Peru National Political Party (2007-present);

Broad Front for Justice, Life and Liberty (2013-present)

Suriname   *Communist Party of Suriname* (1973-unknown);

Progressive Workers' and Farmers' Union (1977-present);

National Democratic Party (1987-present)

Suriname was granted independence from the Netherlands relatively recently, in 1975, hence the later years of infection as compared to most other countries listed.

Uruguay   *Socialist Party of Uruguay* (1910-present);

Communist Party of Uruguay (1920-present);

Oriental Revolutionary Movement (1961-present);

Tupamaros National Liberation Movement (1967–1972); *

Broad Front (1971-present);

March 26 Movement (1971–2013);

Workers' Party (1984-present);

Movement of Popular Participation (1989-present);

Uruguay Assembly (1994-present);

New Space (1994-present);

Anti-Imperialist Unitary Commission (2008-present);

Popular Unity (2013-present);

Ecologist Radical Intransigent Party (2013-present)

* A Marxist terrorist organisation, known as the *Tupamaros*

Venezuela   *Venezuelan Revolutionary Party* (1926–1931);

Communist Party of Venezuela (1931-present);

Democratic Action (1941-present);

People's Electoral Movement (on the island of *Aruba*. 1967–2007);

Red Flag Party (1970-present);

Radical Cause (1971-present);

Movement for Socialism (1971-present);

Revolutionary Movement Tupamaro (1992-present);

A New Era (1999-present);

For Social Democracy (2002–2012);

Venezuelan Popular Unity (2004-present);

Ecological Movement of Venezuela (2005-present);

United Socialist Party of Venezuela (2007-present);

Republican Bicentennial Vanguard (2007-present);

Popular Will (2009-present)

Caribbean and Bermuda

Location	Notable groups
Bahamas	*Labour Party* (1962–1987);
	Vanguard Nationalist and Socialist Party (1971–1987)
Barbados	*Barbados Labour Party* (1938-present);
	Democratic Labour Party (1955-present);
	People's Progressive Movement (1956–1966);
	Workers' Party of Barbados (1985–1986);
	Clement Payne Movement (1988-present);
	People's Empowerment Party (2006-present)
Bermuda	*Progressive Labour Party* (1963-present)
Cuba	*People's Party* (1900–1902);
	Socialist Workers Party (1904–1906);
	Popular Socialist Party (1925–1961);
	United Party of the Cuban Socialist Revolution (1962–1965);
	Communist Party of Cuba (1965-present);
	Democratic Social-Revolutionary Party of Cuba (based in Miami. 1992-present)
Dominica	*Dominica Labour Party* (1955-present);
	People's Party of Dominica (2015-present)

Dominican Republic	*Dominican Revolutionary Party* (1939-present);
	Dominican Communist Party (1944–1996);
	Dominican Workers' Party (1979–2019);
	Broad Front (1992-present);
	Green Socialist Party (2009-present);
	Country Alliance (2011-present);
	Modern Revolutionary Party (2014-present)
Grenada	*Grenada United Labour Party* (1950-present);
	National Democratic Congress (1987-present)
Haiti	*Haitian Communist Party* (1934–1936);
	Haitian Socialist Party (1946-unknown);
	Popular Socialist Party (1946–1948);
	Unified Party of Haitian Communists (1968–1971);
	Struggling People's Organisation (1991-present);
	Fwon Lespwa (1995–2009);
	New Haitian Communist Party—Marxist-Leninist (2000-present);
	Fusion of Haitian Social Democrats (2005-present);
	Inite (2009-present)
Jamaica	*People's National Party* (1938-present);
	Communist Party of Jamaica (1975-present);
	Workers Party of Jamaica (1978–1992)
Puerto Rico	*Socialist Party* (1899–1956);
	Puerto Rican Communist Party (1934–1991);
	Puerto Rican Independence Party (1946-present);
	Puerto Rican Socialist Party (1959-1993);
	Puerto Ricans for Puerto Rico Party (2003-

present);

Working People's Party (2010-present)

Puerto Rico is an unincorporated territory of the U.S.

Saint Kitts and Nevis	*Saint Kitts and Nevis Labour Party* (1932-present)
Saint Lucia	*Saint Lucia Labour Party* (1949-present)
Trinidad and Tobago	*Trinidad Labour Party* (1934–1957);
	Workers and Farmers Party (1966-unknown);
	National Union of Freedom Fighters (1972–1974);*
	United Labour Front (1976–1986);
	Communist Party of Trinidad and Tobago (1979-unknown);
	Movement for Social Justice (2009-present);
	Patriotic Front (2019-present)

* Marxist terrorist group, known as the *NUFF*

Europe

Well...this is where it all started really. Europe has endured an infection its length and breath, from Norway to Malta, and from Iceland to Moldova. The infection point is much earlier than in other continents overall.

The ideology played a role in: the post-Russian Revolution/post-WW1 period, when the cult attempted to gain control of countries all across the continent; the establishment of the Soviet Union and the creation of the Iron Curtain, dividing Europe in two until the collapse of the Berlin Wall; the rise of fascism in Italy under Benito Mussolini, and the Italian Civil War; the Spanish Civil War and the regime of Francisco Franco; the rise of Adolf Hitler, National Socialist Germany, and the outbreak of WW2; the activities of the Marxist terrorist group ETA of the Basque Country, and the Breton Revolutionary Army in Brittany, France; the decades-long brutal conflict in Northern Ireland, which involved several Marxist organisations; the economic stagnation or ruination of countries due to their membership of the U.S.S.R, such as the Polish People's Republic; the spread of the ideology in the Balkans, with the Socialist Federal Republic of Yugoslavia as the centrepiece; the brutal regimes of Nicolae Ceausescu in Romania, and Enver Hoxha in Albania; the many anti-Communist uprisings and civil wars, including those in Czechoslovakia, Georgia, Greece, and Finland; the Pan-Europa movement, the Treaty of Rome, the European Economic Community and the formation of the European Union; the activities of the many traitorous, cruel Marxist secret/state 'police' and 'security' forces used by the cult across Europe, including the KGB in Russia and the Stasi in East Germany (and others mentioned); the German Chancellorship of former Communist Youth member Angela Merkel, which set the precedent for state-approved mass migration in to Europe; and many, many other instances.

Location	Notable groups
Albania	*Party of Labour of Albania* (1941–1991);* (Com)
	National Liberation Movement (1942–1945);
	Socialist Party of Albania (1991-present);
	Communist Party of Albania (1991-present)
	* Albania was the *People's Socialist Republic of Albania* – between 1946 and 1992 – a one-party Marxist state. The *Party of Labour of Albania* was the ruling party during this period.
Andorra	*Social Democratic Party* (2000-present);
	Greens of Andorra (2003-present)
Austria	*Socialist Party of Austria* (1889-present);
	Communist Party of Austria (1918-present) (Com)
Belarus	*Communist Party of Byelorussia* (1918–1991);* (Com)
	Belarusian Left Party—"A Just World" (1991-present);
	Belarusian Green Party (1994-present);
	Communist Party of Belarus (1996-present)
	* Belarus was part of the *U.S.S.R*, and this party was the local branch of the *Communist Party of the Soviet Union (CPSU/KPSS)*

Belgium	*Communist Party of Belgium* (1921–1989);
	Workers' Party of Belgium (1979-present);
	Communist Party of Belgium (1989-present)

Bulgaria	*Bulgarian Socialdemocratic Party* (1891–1894);
	Bulgarian Social Democratic Workers Party (1903–1919);
	Bulgarian Communist Party (1919–1990); (Com) *
	Party of Bulgarian Social Democrats (1989-present);
	Bulgarian Socialist Party (1990-present);
	Communist Party of Bulgaria (1996-present)

* Bulgaria was the *People's Republic of Bulgaria* between 1946 and 1990—a one-party Marxist state. The *Bulgarian Communist Party* was the ruling party during this period.

Czechoslovakia	*Communist Party of Czechoslovakia* (KSC. 1921-1992) (Com)*
(1918–1993)	Czech Republic

Czech Social Democratic Party (1878-present);

Communist Party of Bohemia and Moravia (1990-present);

Green Party (1990-present);

Socialist Alternative Future (1990-present);

Party of Democratic Socialism (1997–2020)

Slovakia

Communist Party of Slovakia (1939–1990);

Green Party (1989-present);

Party of the Democratic Left (1990–2004);

Communist Party of Slovakia (1992-present);

Union of the Workers of Slovakia (1994-present);

Dawn (2005-present);

Slovak Green Party (2006-present);

Progressive Slovakia (2017-present)

* Czechoslovakia was called the *Czechoslovak Socialist Republic* – from 1948 to 1990 – a one-party Marxist state. The *KSC* was the ruling party during this period.

Denmark   *Communist Party of Denmark* (1919-present);

Socialist People's Party (1959-present);

Left Socialists (1967–2013);

Communist Party of Denmark—Marxist-Leninists (1978–2006);

Socialist Workers Politics (1979-present);

Red-Green Alliance (1989-present);

Communist Party in Denmark (1990-present);

Workers' Communist Party (2000-present)

Estonia   *Estonian Radical Socialist Party* (1917–1919);

Social Travaillist Party (1917–1919);

Communist Party of Estonia (1920–1990); *(Com)

Estonian Left Party (1990–2008);

Estonian United Left Party (2008-present)

* Estonia was part of the *U.S.S.R,* and this party was the local branch of the *Communist Party of the Soviet Union* (*CPSU/KPSS*)

Faroe Islands   *Advancement for the Islands—Marxist-Leninist* (1968-unknown);

(Kingdom of Denmark)   *Faroese Communist Party* (1975–1993)

Finland   *Social Democratic Party of Finland* (1899-present);

Communist Party of Finland (1918–1992); (Com)

Socialist Workers' Party of Finland (1920–1923);

Socialist Unity Party (1946–1955);

Socialist Workers' Party (1973–1990);

Communist Party of Finland (1984-present);

Green League (1987-present);

Communist Workers' Party-For Peace and Socialism (1988-present);

Left Alliance (1990-present);

Feminist Party (2016-present)

France

Federation of the Socialist Workers of France (1879–1902);

French Workers' Party (1880–1902);

Revolutionary Socialist Workers' Party (1890–1901);

Socialist Party of France (1902–1905);

French Section of the Workers' International (1905–1969); (Com)

Republican-Socialist Party (1911–1934);

French Socialist Party (1919–1935);

French Communist Party (1920-present); (Com)

Communist Union (1939-present);

Socialist Party (1969-present)

As the following are overseas departments/regions of France, in some case the parties listed above have a presence there (or local branches), in addition to the following groups:

French Guiana (north coast of South America)

Guianese Socialist Party (1956-present);

Decolonization and Social Emancipation Movement (1991-present);

Alternative Libertaire Guyane (2004-present)

Guadeloupe (groups of islands in Eastern Caribbean)

Guadeloupe Communist Party (1958-present);

New Jewel Movement (1973–1983);

Progressive Democratic Party of Guadeloupe (1991-present)

Martinique (island in Eastern Caribbean)

Martinican Communist Party (1957-present);

Martinican Independence Movement (1978-present);

Build the Martinique Country (1998-present)

Réunion (island off East coast of Africa, near Madagascar):

Communist Party of Réunion (1959-present);

Marxist-Leninist Communist Organisation of Réunion (1975-unknown)

Georgia

Social Democratic Party of Georgia (1890–1950);

Mesami Dasi (1892-1920);

Communist Party of Georgia (1920–1991);*

Communist Party of Georgia (1992-present);

Unified Communist Party of Georgia (1994-present);

New Communist Party of Georgia (2001-present);

Social Democrats for the Development of Georgia (2013-present)

* Georgia was part of the *U.S.S.R*, and this party was the local branch of the *Communist Party of the Soviet Union* (*CPSU/KPSS*)

Germany

Communist League (1848–1852);

General German Workers' Association (1863–1875);

Social Democratic Workers' Party of Germany (1869–1875);

Social Democratic Party of Germany (1875-present);

Spartacus League (1914–1919); (Com)

Communist Party of Germany (1918–1946/1956);

(Com)

East German Communist Party (1946–1989);*

Socialist Unity Party of West Berlin (1962–1991);

German Communist Party (1968-present);

Party of Democratic Socialism (1989–2007);

Alliance 90/The Greens (1993-present)

* Also known as the *Socialist Unity Party of Germany*, it ruled the Marxist *German Democratic Republic* (or *East Germany)* until the Berlin Wall came down.

Gibraltar (British Overseas Territory)	*Gibraltar Socialist Party* (1978-present)

Greece

Communist Party of Greece (1918-present);

Socialist Party of Greece (1920–1953);

Socialist Workers' Party of Greece (1971-present);

Panhellenic Socialist Movement (1974-present);

Coalition of the Radical Left—Progressive Alliance (2004-present);

Movement of Democratic Socialists (2015-present)

Hungary

Social Democratic Party of Hungary (1890–1948);

Hungarian Communist Party (1918–1948); (Com)

Hungarian Working People's Party (MDP. 1948–1956); *

Hungarian Socialist Workers' Party (MSzMP. 1956–1989); *

Hungarian Socialist Party (1989-present);

Hungarian Workers' Party (1989-present)

* Hungary was called the *Hungarian People's Republic* – from 1949 to 1989 – a one-party Marxist state. The *MDP* and (its successor) the *MSzMP* were the ruling parties during this period.

Iceland	*Social Democratic Party* (1916–2000);
	Communist Party of Iceland (1930–1938);
	People's Unity Party—Socialist Party (1938–1968);
	People's Alliance (1968–1998);
	Icelandic Socialist Party (2017-present)
Ireland	Republic of Ireland:
	Irish Socialist Republican Party (1896–1904);
	Socialist Party of Ireland (1904–1923); (Com)
	Sinn Féin (1905-present);
	Labour Party (1912-present);
	Irish Worker League (1923–1933 approx); (Com)
	Communist Party of Ireland (1933-present);
	Republican Congress (1934–1936);
	Communist Party of Ireland—Marxist-Leninist (1965–2003);
	Workers' Party (1970-present);
	Socialist Workers Network (1971-present);
	Irish Republican Socialist Party (1974-present);
	Green Party (1981-present);
	Socialist Party (1996-present);
	People Before Profit (2005-present);
	United Left Alliance (2010–2013);
	United Left (2013–2015);
	Solidarity (2014-present);
	Social Democrats (2015-present);
	RISE ("Revolutionary Internationalist Socialist Environmentalist"). (2019-present)
	Northern Ireland:
	Belfast Labour Party (1892–1924);

Sinn Féin (1905/1970-present);

Socialist Party of Northern Ireland (1935–1940);

Communist Party of Northern Ireland (1941–1970);

Official Irish Republican Army/Official IRA (1969–1972/1998 approx);*

Irish National Liberation Army/INLA (1974–1998/2009 approx.)*

* The *Official Irish Republican Army* or *Official IRA,* and the *Irish National Liberation Army* (INLA) were Marxist terrorist groups.

Italy
Italian Socialist Party (1892–1944);

Communist Party of Italy * (1921–1926); (Com)

Italian Communist Party (1943–1991);

Democratic Party of the Left (1991–1998);

Communist Refoundation Party (1991-present);

Italian Socialists (1994–1998);

Italian Democratic Socialists (1998–2007);

Party of Italian Communists (1998–2014);

Italian Socialist Party (2007-present);

Communist Party of Italy (2014–2016);

Italian Communist Party (2016-present)

Latvia
Communist Party of Latvia (1904–1991);* (Com)

Latvian Social Democratic Workers' Party (1918-present);

Socialist Party of Latvia (1994-present);

Social Democratic Party (2009-present)

* Latvia was part of the *U.S.S.R,* and this party was the local branch of the *Communist Party of the Soviet Union* (*CPSU/KPSS*)

Liechtenstein
Free List (1985-present)

Liechtenstein is a 25km/15.5m long principality with a population of 40,000.

Lithuania	*Social Democratic Party of Lithuania* (1896-present);

Social Democratic Party of Lithuania (1896-present);

Communist Party of Lithuania (1918–1991);* (Com)

Democratic Labour Party of Lithuania (1989–2001);

Socialist Party of Lithuania (1994–2009);

Socialist People's Front (2009-present);

Lithuanian Green Party (2011-present):

Social Democratic Labour Party of Lithuania (2018-present)

* Lithuania was part of the *U.S.S.R,* and this party was the local branch of the *Communist Party of the Soviet Union (CPSU/KPSS)*

Luxembourg   *Luxembourg Socialist Worker's Party* (1902-present);

Communist Party of Luxembourg (1921-present);

Radical Socialist Party (1925–1932);

Social Democratic Party (1971–1984);

The Greens (1983-present);

The Left (1999-present)

Luxemburg has a population of approximately 660,000.

Malta   *Labour Party* (1920-present);

Communist Party of Malta (1969-present)

Malta has a population of approximately 540,000 people.

Moldova   *Communist Party of Moldavia* (1940–1991);*

Socialist Party of Moldova (1992-present);

Party of Socialists of the Republic of Moldova (1997-present)

* Moldova was part of the *U.S.S.R,* and this party was

the local branch of the *Communist Party of the Soviet Union* (*CPSU/KPSS*)

Netherlands *Social Democratic League* (1881–1900);

Social Democratic Workers' Party (1894–1946);

Communist Party of Netherlands (1909–1991); (Com)

Labour Party (1946-present);

Pacifist Socialist Party (1957–1991);

Green Left (1989-present)

Norway *Labour Party* (1887-present)*; (Com**)**

Communist Party of Norway (1923-present);

Socialist Left Party (1975-present);

Society Party (1985-present);

Green Party (1988-present);

Red Party (2007-present)

Poland *International Social Revolutionary Party* (1882–1886);

Polish Socialist Party (1892–1948);

Social Democracy of the Kingdom of Poland (1893–1918);

Communist Party of Poland (1918–1938); (Com)

Polish Workers' Party (1942–1948);

Polish United Workers' Party (1948–1990);*

Social Democracy of the Republic of Poland (1990–1999);

Labour Union (1992-present);

Democratic Left Alliance (1999-present);

Polish Left (2008-present)

* This party ruled the *Polish People's Republic* – a Marxist one-party state – from 1948 to 1989.

Portugal	*Portuguese Socialist Party* (1875–1933);
	Portuguese Communist Party * (1921-present); (Com)
	Portuguese Workers' Communist Party (1970-present);
	Socialist Party (1973-present);
	Workers' Party of Socialist Unity (1976-present);
	Left Bloc (1999-present);
	Socialist Alternative Movement (2000);
	Ecologist Party (2004-present);
	Portuguese Labour Party (2009-present)
Romania	*Social Democratic Party of Romania* (1910–1916);
	Socialist Party of Romania (1918–1920);
	Romanian Communist Party (PCR. 1921–1989); * (Com)
	Romanian Social Democratic Party (1927–1948);
	Social Democratic Party (2001-present);
	Romanian Socialist Party (2003-present);
	Communist Party of Romania (2010-present)

* The *PCR* was also known as the *Romanian Workers' Party* for a time. Its most famous General Secretary was *Nicolae Ceausescu*, who ruled Romania as dictator until 1989. Romania was the *Socialist Republic of Romania* between 1947 and 1989—a one-party Marxist state.

Russia	*People's Will* (1879–1884);
	Emancipation of Labour (1883–1903);
	S.B.O.R.K. (1895–1900); #
	General Jewish Labour Bund (1897–1921);
	Russian Social Democratic Labour Party (*RSDLP*, 1898–1912);
	Socialist Revolutionary Party (1902–1921);
	Menshevik faction of *RSDLP* (1912-21 in Russia, and

until 1965 outside Russia);

Communist Party of the Soviet Union (from *Bolshevik* faction of *RSDLP.'*17—'91); *

Communist Party of the Russian Soviet Federative Socialist Republic (1990–1991);

Communist Party of the Russian Federation (1993-present);

All-Russian Social-Political Movement (aka *Spiritual Legacy*)(1995–2003);

United Socialist Party of Russia (2003–2008)

* Ruling Party of the *Union of Soviet Socialist Republics* or *U.S.S.R;* this party controlled the local branches in other Soviet countries (highlighted elsewhere)

SBORK: St. Petersburg League of Struggle for the Emancipation of the Working Class

San Marino   *Sammarinese Communist Party* (1921–1990)

Spain   *Spanish Socialist Workers' Party* (*PSOE.* 1879-present);

Spanish Communist Party (1920–1921); (Com)

Communist Party of Spain (1921-present);

Workers' Party of Marxist Unification (1935–1980);

Communist Party of the Balearic Islands (Mallorca, 1977-present);

Progressive Federation (1984–1988);

Communist Party of the Peoples of Spain (1984-present);

Animalist Party Against Mistreatment of Animals (:)))(2003-present);

United We Can (2016-present);

Communist Party of the Workers of Spain (2019-present)

Canary Islands:

Canary Islands Independence Movement (1964–1979 approx);

Communist Cells (1969–1984);

Socialist Party of the Canaries (Canarian branch of the PSOE. 1970s-present);

Communist Party of the Canary Islands (1973–1991);

Party of Communist Unification in the Canaries (1975–2012);

Canarian People's Union (1979–1986);

Canarian Assembly (1982–1987);

Canarian United Left (1986/1993-present);

Azarug (1992-present);

Socialist Canarian Party (1995-unknown);

Canarian Nationalist Alternative (2006-present);

Inekaren (2008-present)

Sweden   *Swedish Social Democratic Party* (1889-present);

Left Party (1917-present); (Com)

Communist Party of Sweden (1924–1926);

Socialist Party (1929–1948);

Communist Party (1970-present);

Communist Party of Sweden (1977–1995);

Green Party (1981-present);

Feminist Initiative (2005-present)

Switzerland   *Social Democratic Party of Switzerland* (1888-present);

Communist Party of Switzerland (1918 approx.-1940); (Com)

Swiss Party of Labour (1944-present);

Communist Party of Switzerland—Marxist-Leninist (1969–1987);

Green Party of Switzerland (1983-present);

	Solidarity (1992-present); *Alternative Left* (2010–2018)
Turkey	*Communist Party of Turkey* (1920–1988); (Com) *Workers' Party of Turkey* (1961–1987); *United Communist Party of Turkey* (1987–1991); *Socialist Unity Party* (1991–1995); *Workers' Party* (1992–2015), then became *Patriotic Party* (2015-present); *Communist Party of Turkey* (1993-present); *People's Liberation Party* (2005-present); *People's Democratic Party* (2012-present); *People's Communist Party of Turkey* (2014–2017); *Workers' Party of Turkey* (2017-present)
Ukraine	*Communist Party of Ukraine* (1918–1991);* (Com) *Social Democratic Party of Ukraine* (1990–1994); *Socialist Party of Ukraine* (1991-present); *Peasant Party of Ukraine* (1992-present); *Communist Party of Ukraine* (1993-present); *Progressive Socialist Party of Ukraine* (1996-present); *Communist Party of Workers and Peasants* (2001–2015) * Ukraine was part of the *U.S.S.R,* and this party was the local branch of the *Communist Party of the Soviet Union (CPSU/KPSS)*
U.K.	*Communist League* (1847–1852); *International Workingmen's Association* (*IWA* or *First International* (1864—'76);* *Social Democratic Federation* (*SDF.* 1881–1911); *Fabian Society* (1884-present);

Socialist League (Spawned by the *SDF*. 1885–1901);

Labour Party (1900-present);

Socialist Labour Party (1903–1980);

Socialist Party of Great Britain (1904-present);

British Socialist Party (1911–1920);

Socialist Propaganda League (1911–1951); (Com)

Communist Party of Great Britain (1920–1991); (Com)

Welsh Communist Party (1920-present);

Communist Party of Britain (1988-present);

Democratic Left (1991–1998);

Communist Party of Scotland (1992—present);

Socialist Party (1997-present);

Scottish Socialist Party (1998-present)

*Based in London until 1873, and then New York from 1873 to 1876

Yugoslavia (1918–1992)

League of Communists of Yugoslavia (*SKJ/CKJ*. 1919–1990). (Com)

Bosnia and Herzegovina:

League of Communists of Bosnia and Herzegovina (1943–1990); *

Social Democratic Party of Bosnia and Herzegovina (1992-present);

Socialist Party (1993-present);

Workers' Communist Party of Bosnia and Herzegovina (2000-present);

Greens of Bosnia and Herzegovina (2004-present);

Communist Party (2012-present)

Croatia:

League of Communists of Croatia (1937–1990); *

Social Democratic Party of Croatia (1990-present);

Independent Democratic Serb Party (1997-present);

Socialist Labour Party of Croatia (1997-present);

Croatian Labourists—Labour Party (2010-present);

Workers' Front (2014-present);

New Left (2016-present);

Zagreb is OURS! (2017-present);

We Can! Political Platform (2019-present)

Macedonia (aka North Macedonia):

League of Communists of Macedonia (1943–1991); *

Communist Party of Macedonia (1992-present);

Union of Tito's Left Forces (2005-present);

The Left (2015-present)

Montenegro:

League of Communists of Montenegro (1943–1991); *

Democratic Party of Socialists of Montenegro (1991-present);

Socialist People's Party of Montenegro (1998-present)

Serbia:

League of Communists of Serbia (1945–1990); *

Socialist Alliance of Working People of Yugoslavia (1945–1990);

Socialist Party of Serbia (1990-present);

Communist Party (2010-present)

Slovenia:

League of Communists of Slovenia (1937–1990);*

Social Democrats (1993-present);

Initiative for Democratic Socialism (2014–2017);

The Left (2017-present)

* The *League of Communists of Yugoslavia* (*SKJ/CKJ*) had overall control of the 6 constituent republics of Yugoslavia. The symbol * denotes the local branch of the *SKJ/CKJ*

Africa

> "...the evil system of colonialism and imperialism arose and throve with the enslavement of Negroes and the trade in Negroes, and it will surely come to its end with the complete emancipation of the Black people"[120]

> Leader of Communist China Mao Zedong, "Statement Supporting the American Negroes in Their Just Struggle Against Racial Discrimination by U.S. Imperialism", 8 August 1963

> "We, in Africa, have no more need of being 'converted' to socialism than we have of being 'taught' democracy. Both are rooted in our past, in the traditional society which produced us"121

> Julius Nyerere, *Uhuru na Umoja (Freedom and Unity): Essays on Socialism* (1969)

> "The traditional African society was founded on principles of egalitarianism.. Any meaningful humanism must begin from egalitarianism. Hence, socialism. Hence scientific socialism"[122]

> Kwame Nkrumah, *African Socialism Revisited* (1967)

Africa is the epitome of a place which transitioned from foreign imperial rule to Marxist rule and self-destruction. Several European powers had a presence there including Britain, France, Belgium, Portugal, Italy and the Netherlands. The perception from some quarters that Marxism (via its product socialism) was necessary for Africa post-Colonialism was a very serious, fatal error. It has wrecked that continent; the aftermath of which Marxist propaganda has, predictably, blamed on Africa's colonial past, or modern western 'imperialism'.

It is true, however, considering how the ideology picks unstable targets, that Africa was, in general, highly vulnerable at this point in its history. In fact, it was a sitting duck. Not surprisingly, African academics who espoused the benefits of socialism were a factor; Julius Nyerere (1922–1999) for example, who was the first president of Zambia.

No doubt there were some egomaniacal imperial individuals of European

---

[120] Zedong, M. "Statement Supporting the American Negroes In Their Just Struggle Against Racial Discrimination by U.S. Imperialism", 8 August 1963.
https://www.marxists.org/subject/china/peking-review/1966/PR1966-33h.htm

[121] Nyerere, J., *Uhuru na Umoja (Freedom and Unity): Essays on Socialism* (1969).
https://www.juliusnyerere.org/resources/quotes

[122] Nkrumah, *K., African Socialism Revisited* (1967).

https://www.marxists.org/subject/africa/nkrumah/1967/african-socialism-revisited.htm

stock—such as the infamous British elitist Cecil Rhodes (1853–1902), and this is often mentioned in Marxism-infected PC culture (as 'colonial' imperialism is an evil they often remind us of). What is not highlighted, is that in post-colonial Africa, there have been many horrific African regimes run by Africans, catalysed by an almost continent-wide Marxist infection. The figures involved in those regimes were worse than Rhodes.

In fact, many of the leaders of African countries post-'independence' were Marxist activists, terrorists and dictators of African stock: Nelson Mandela (1918–2013), Robert Mugabe, Julius Nyerere, and Ghana's first PM and President Kwame Nkrumah to name a few. Cecil Rhodes died in 1902! The fact that cult members today will constantly remind us of characters in that era – while conveniently ignoring the many African cult members since then that have oppressed their own people and helped wrecked the continent – is both typical and amusing.

Of course, the white v non-white ethnic division present in some parts of Africa–with the minority whites having control of the government, infrastructure etc. - was an obvious point of entry for the cult/ideology. It could exploit this division easily, the whites being the 'oppressors'.

This particular localised brand of the ideology – African Socialism – emerged during the 1950s and 60s. This led to an almost unquantifiable amount of instability and hardship across the continent. [123] Another significant term spawned from the cult/ideology is "Pan-Africanism".[124] Another is "Ujamaa"—a term used by cult member Julius Nyerere to describe his version of socialism in Tanzania. He wrote Ujamaa: Essays on Socialism in 1969.

In a letter to the *Tanjanyika Standard* in July 1943, Nyerere said "the African is by nature a socialistic being".[125] Not all Africans bought the con—voices on the other side of the argument include George Ayittey (1945–2022) who's writing include *Africa Unchained: the blueprint for development* (2004), and *Defeating Dictators: Fighting Tyrants in Africa and Around the World* (2011).[126]

The innumerable Marxist revolutions that happened on that continent, of course, followed the usual pattern: killing the 'oppressor class' (white people); killing Christians; destroying the symbols of western culture and

---

[123] https://www.britannica.com/money/topic/African-socialism

[124] https://www.britannica.com/topic/Pan-Africanism

[125] https://en.wikipedia.org/wiki/Julius_Nyerere

[126] https://en.wikipedia.org/wiki/George_Ayittey

civilisation (including the infrastructure that the whites had built-up in Africa); taking land off the whites to redistribute it to the black majority in the name of 'equality', which led to famine (since the whites had the agricultural expertise/experience). This was all done in the name of 'justice' and 'equality' and was justified by Africa's apparently oppressed history.

Marxist Propaganda Hiding What Happened In Africa

A primary cause of Africa's economic stagnation is the Marxist infection, specifically the implementation of socialism throughout the continent. In a typical manoeuvre by the ideology, it distracts us from its own culpability by blaming its enemies (in this case capitalism, imperialism and white people).

By blaming the current state of Africa on such things, the cult/ideology can protect its 'reputation' while simultaneously promoting it's anti-white, anti-European, anti-bourgeoisie, and 'anti-racist' 'message'. The chaos caused by the ideology is evident even today—we can see how its legacy has essentially caused the breakdown of civilisation in South Africa in recent decades.

Across the continent, the infection resulted in: the "Suppression of Communism Act" in 1950 which banned the *Communist Party of South Africa*; the twenty-four year dictatorship of Julius Nyerere in Tanzania; the rise to power of the *African National Council* (made famous by notable cult member and convicted terrorist Nelson Mandela); the ending of Apartheid in South Africa (a major contributory factor to the state of the country today); Kwame Nkrumah's reign as President of Ghana; Patrice Lumumba in the then Republic of Congo; the rise to power of dictator Robert Mugabe in Zimbabwe; the *Ethiopian Civil War* (1974–1991), the *Derg* as the Ethiopian Vanguard, and the *Ethiopian Red Terror* (1976–1978); the *Portuguese Colonial War* (1961–1974) in Guinea-Bissau, Angola and Mozambique, and the subsequent dominance of the Marxist *FRELIMO*; the *March Revolution* in Mali in 1991; the *Angolan Civil War* (1975–2002)—a conflict with a massive death toll and population displacement; the state-approved racist discrimination (and murdering) of white South African farmers (as a Marxist tradition in Africa); and many, many other events.

So many of the 'nationalist' and 'liberation' movements across the continent, which spurned so many on to fight against the 'evil, oppressive imperial forces', were merely Marxist movements, that's all; it was merely a new form of imperialism coming in to take over. In addition, the distorted perception of what's happened there (thanks to the ideology's impact) has no doubt contributed towards a distorted perception of 'racism' in western countries which is peddled and eternally perpetuated by the cult/ideology today. What happened in Africa due to Marxism has caused a ripple-effect across the West, including in U.S. racial tensions.

Nelson Mandela was revered as a quasi-messiah in the latter part of his life, post-incarceration, due to the extreme level of Marxian virtue-signalling on display across the world. He received innumerable awards and honours, including the Nobel Peace Prize and the Lenin Peace Prize (hilarious. This is like receiving a "being nice" award from the devil).[127] His term as President of South Africa from 1994 to 1999 was symbolic of the cult's success on the continent. Many of the cult's terrorist groups operated in Africa, receiving foreign support from the larger Marxist entities including Red China, the U.S.S.R., and Fidel Castro's Cuba. The rise to power of *FRELIMO (Mozambique Liberation Front)* was a good example of how Marxist groups can masquerade as 'nationalist', but then reveal their true (red) colours once they are in power. Shortly after Mozambique achieved independence from Portugal in 1975, they decided to go down the commie road, turning the country in to a one-party Marxist state.[128]

Location	Notable groups
Angola	*Party of the United Struggle for Africans in Angola* (1953–1956);
	Angolan Communist Party (1955–1956);
	People's Movement for the Liberation of Angola (*MPLA*. 1956-present);*
	National Union for the Total Independence of Angola (1966-present);
	Social Democratic Party (1988-present);
	Liberal Socialist Party (1993-present)
	* Angola was a Marxist one-party state called *People's Republic of Angola* from 1975–1992; *MPLA* was the ruling party during this period.
Algeria	*Algerian Communist Party* (1920/1936-1962);

---

[127]

https://en.wikipedia.org/wiki/Nelson_Mandela#Orders,_decorations,_monuments,_and_honours

[128] https://www.britannica.com/topic/Frelimo

Socialist Forces Front (1963-present);

Socialist Workers' Party (1989-present);

Workers' Party (1990-present);

Algerian Party for Democracy and Socialism (1993-present)

Benin   *Socialist Revolution Party of Benin* (1959-unknown);

People's Revolutionary Party of Benin (*PRPB*. 1975–1990);*

Communist Party of Benin (1977-present);

Social Democratic Party (1990-present);

Union for Homeland and Labour (1997-present)

* Benin was a Marxist one-party state called *People's Republic of Benin* from 1975–1990; *PRPB* was the ruling party during this period.

Botswana   *Botswana People's Party* (1960-present);

Botswana National Front (1965-present);

MELS Movement of Botswana (1984-present);

International Socialists Botswana (unknown);

Botswana Congress Party (1998-present)

Burkina Faso   *African Independence Party* (1963–1999);

Voltaic Revolutionary Communist Party (1978-present);

Marxist-Leninist Group (1983–1984);

Burkinabe Communist Group (1983–1991);

Union of Burkinabe Communists (1984–1989);

Organization for Popular Democracy—Labour Movement (1989–1996);

Burkinabe Socialist Party (1992–2001);

African Independence Party (1999–2011);

Union for Rebirth—Sankarist Party (2000-present);

Party for Democracy and Progress (2001-present);

Unified Socialist Party (2001-present);

Party for Democracy and Socialism (2002–2012);

Convergence for Social Democracy (2002-present);

Sankarist Democratic Front (2004-present);

Party of Independence, Labour and Justice (2011-present)

Burundi	*Free Socialist Party of Burundi* (1961-unknown);
	Burundi Workers' Party (1979–1986);
	Front for Democracy (1986-present);
	Pan Africanist Socialist Movement—Inkinzo (unknown)
Cape Verde	*African Party for the Independence of Guinea and Cape Verde* (1956-present);
	African Party of Independence of Cape Verde (1981-present);
	Labour and Solidarity Party (1998-present)
	Cape Verde achieved independence from Portugal in 1975
Central African Republic	*Movement for the Social Evolution of Black Africa* (1949–1979);
	Movement for the Liberation of the Central African People (1978-present);
	Central African Democratic Rally (1987-present);
	Social Democratic Party (1991-present);
	Patriotic Front for Progress (1991-present);
	National Convergence — Kwa na Kwa (2009-present)
Congo	*Congolese Progressive Party* (1945-unknown);
	African Solidarity Party (1959–1965);
	Unified Lumumbist Party (1964-present);

Congolese Party of Labour (PCT. 1969-present);*

Union for Democracy and Social Progress (1982-present)

* Congo was a Marxist one-party state called *People's Republic of Congo* from 1969–1992; *PCT* was the ruling party during this period.

Chad   *Chadian Progressive Party* (1947–1975);

Independent Socialist Party of Chad (1950–1956);

Independent Socialist Party of Chad—1955 split (1955-unknown);

Chadian Action for Unity and Socialism (1981-present);

National Union for Democracy and Renewal (1992-present);

Renewed African Socialist Movement (2006-approx.-present)

Comoros   *Convention for the Renewal of the Comoros* (2002-present)

Djibouti   *Party of Popular Movement* (1958–1974 approx.);

People's Rally for Progress (1979-present);

Front for the Restoration of Unity and Democracy (1991-present);

Social Democratic People's Party (2002-present)

Equatorial Guinea   *IPGE* (1958 approx-1970);

United National Workers' Party (1970–1979);

Convergence for Social Democracy (1990-present)

Eritrea   *Eritrean Liberation Front* (1961-present);

Eritrean Democratic Working People's Party (1968–1982);

People's Front for Democracy and Justice (1994-present)

Eswatini	*Swaziland Progressive Party* (1959 approx-1973);
	Ngwane National Liberatory Congress (1963–1973);
	People's United Democratic Movement (1983-present);
	Swaziland Communist Party (1994-present);
	Communist Party of Swaziland (2011-present);
	Swazi Democratic Party (2011-present)
Ethiopia	*All-Ethiopia Socialist Movement* (1968-present);
	Ethiopian People's Revolutionary Party (1972-present);
	Ethiopian Marxist-Leninist Revolutionary Organization (1974–1979);
	Tigray People's Liberation Front (1975-present);
	Ethiopian Oppressed People's Revolutionary Struggle (1975–1978);
	Revolutionary Flame (1976–1979);
	Union of Ethiopian Marxist-Leninist Organizations (1977–1979);
	Commission for Organizing the Party of the Working People of Ethiopia (1979–1984);
	Marxist-Leninist League of Tigray (1983–1991);
	Workers' Party of Ethiopia (*WPE.* 1984–1991);*
	Ethiopian People's Revolutionary Democratic Front (1988–2019);
	Somali Democratic Party (1998–2019);
	United Ethiopian Democratic Forces (2005–2008)
	* Ethiopia was a Marxist one-party state called *People's Democratic Republic of Ethiopia* from 1987–1991; *WPE* was the ruling party during this period.
Gabon	*Gabonese National Unity Party* (1958-unknown);
	Gabonese Progress Party (1990-present);

Gabonese Socialist Party (1991-present);

African Forum for Reconstruction (1992-present)

Gambia   *Gambia Socialist Revolutionary Party* (1980–1981);

People's Democratic Organisa. for Independence and Socialism (1986-present)

Ghana   *Convention People's Party* (1949-present);

People's National Party (1979–1981);

People's Convention Party (1992–1996);

Democratic People's Party (1992-present);

National Democratic Congress (1992-present);

People's National Convention (1992-present)

Guinea   *Socialist Party of Guinea* (1946-unknown);

Democratic Party of Guinea-African Democratic Rally (1947-present);

Socialist Democracy of Guinea (1954–1958);

Rally of the Guinean People (1965 approx-present);

All-African People's Revolutionary Party (1968-present)

Guinea-Bissau   *African Party for the Independence of Guinea and Cape Verde* (1956-present);

Revolutionary Armed Forces of the People (1964–1973);

Socialist Party of Guinea-Bissau (1994-present);

Workers' Party (2002-present);

United People's Alliance (2004);

Democratic Socialist Party (2004-present);

Movement for Democratic Alternation (2018-present)

Ivory Coast   *Revolutionary Communist Party of Ivory Coast* (1965 approx-unknown);

Ivorian Popular Front (1982-present);

Ivorian Party of Workers (1990-present);

People's Socialist Union (1996-present. London-based)

Ivory Coast achieved independence from France in 1960

Kenya	*Kenya People's Union* (1966–1969);

Communist Party of Kenya (1992-present);

Mazingira Green Party of Kenya (1997 approx-present) |

Liberia	*African Revolutionary Party* (1861–1936);

Communist Party of Liberia (1878–1936);

United People's Party (1985 approx-present) |

Libya	*Libyan Communist Party* (1945–1952);

Libyan Arab Socialist Ba'ath Party (1950s–1980s approx);

Libyan Revolutionary Command Council (1969–1977);

Arab Socialist Union (1971–1977);

Libyan Popular National Movement (2012-present) |

Lesotho	*Basutoland Congress Party* (1952-present);

Communist Party of Lesotho (1962-present);

Lesotho Congress for Democracy (1997-present);

Democratic Congress (2011-present) |

Madagascar	*Communist Party of the Region of Madagascar* (1936–1938);

Malagasy Communist Party (1958-unknown);

Party of the Independence Congress of Madagascar (1958-present);

Movement for the Progress of Madagascar (1972-present);

Association for the Rebirth of Madagascar (1976- |

present)

Mali	*Sudanese Union—African Democratic Rally* (1945–2010);
	Malian Party of Labour (1965-present);
	Democratic Union of the Malian People (1975–1991);
	Alliance for Democracy in Mali (1990-present);
	African Solidarity for Democracy and Independence (1996-present);
	Rally for Mali (2001-present)
Malawi	*Socialist League of Malawi* (1964–1991);
	Alliance for Democracy (1993-present)
Mauritania	*Union of the Forces of Progress* (1991-present);
	Socialist Democratic Unionist Party (1994-present);
	People's Progressive Alliance (2002-present);
	Rally of Democratic Forces (2002-present);
	Alliance for Justice and Democracy (2007-present)
Mauritius	*Labour Party* (1936-present);
	Independent Forward Bloc (1958–1976 approx);
	All Mauritius Hindu Congress (1964–1967);
	Mauritian Militant Movement (1969-present);
	Mauritian Militant Movement—MMMSP (1973–1980approx);
	Mauritian Socialist Party (1979–1983);
	Lalit (1981-present);
	Militant Socialist Movement (1983-present);
	Mauritian Militant Socialist Movement (1995–2008);
	Fraternal Greens (2002-present);
	Liberator Movement (2014-present);
	Militant Platform (2018-present)

Morocco	*Moroccan Communist Party* (1943–1964);
	Party of Liberation and Socialism (1968–1974);
	Forward (1970–1974 approx);
	March 23 Movement (1970–1983 approx);
	Party of Progress and Socialism (1974-present);
	Action Party (1974-present);
	Socialist Union of Popular Forces (1975-present);
	Socialist Democratic Vanguard Party (1991-present);
	Democratic Way (1995-present);
	Front of Democratic Forces (1997-present);
	National Ittihadi Congress Party (2001-present);
	Labour Party (2005–2013);
	Unified Socialist Party (2005-present);
	Socialist Party (2006–2013)
	Western Sahara
	Polisario Front (1973-present)
Mozambique	*Mozambique Liberation Front—FRELIMO* (1962-present);*
	Communist Party of Mozambique (1995-unknown);
	Party of Greens of Mozambique (1997-present)
	* Mozambique was a Marxist one-party state called *People's Republic of Mozambique* from 1975–1990; *FRELIMO* was the ruling party during this period.
Namibia	*South West Africa National Union* (1959-present);
	South West Africa People's Organisation (1960-present);
	Communist Party of Namibia (1981–1989);
	Workers Revolutionary Party (1989-present);
	Congress of Democrats (1999-present);
	All People's Party (2008-present);

	Namibian Economic Freedom Fighters (2014-present);
	Affirmative Repositioning (2014-present)
Niger	*Union of Popular Forces for Democracy and Progress* (1956-present);
	Nigerien Party for Democracy and Socialism (1990-present);
	Party for Socialism and Democracy in Niger (1992-present)
Nigeria	*Northern Elements Progressive Union* (1950–1964);
	Communist Party of Nigeria and the Cameroons (1951-unknown);
	Action Group (1951–1966);
	Communist Party of Nigeria (1960–1966 approx.);
	Socialist Workers and Farmers Party of Nigeria (1963-present);
	Nigerian Communist Party (unknown-1966 approx.);
	People's Redemption Party (1978-present);
	Unity Party of Nigeria (1978-unknown);
	Democratic Socialist Movement (1986-present);
	Social Democratic Party of Nigeria (1989 approx.-present);
	Socialist Party of Nigeria (2013-present);
	Young Progressives Party (2017-present)
Rwanda	*Rwandan Socialist Party* (1991-present);
	Social Democratic Party (1991-present);
	Democratic Green Party of Rwanda (2009-present)
Sao Tomé and Principe	*Movement for the Liberation of Sao Tome and Principe* (1960-present);
	Sao Taoméan Workers Party (2002-unknown)

The population of these archipelagos is just under

234,000.

Senegal	*Independent Socialist Republican Party* (1919-unknown);
	Senegalese Socialist Party (1934–1938);
	Senegalese Democratic Union (1946–1956);
	Senegalese Party of Socialist Action (1957–1958);
	African Independence Party (1957-present);
	Socialist Party of Senegal (1958-present);
	Senegalese Communist Party (1965-unknown);
	Committee for the Initiative for Permanent Revolutionary Action (1970 approx);
	Movement of Young Marxist-Leninists (1970-unknown);
	Democratic League-Movement for the Labour Party (mid-1970s-present);
	Socialist Workers Organisation (1973–1991);
	And-Jef Revolutionary Movement for New Democracy (1974–1991);
	Communist Workers League (1977-unknown);
	Party of Independence and Labour (1981-present);
	And-Jef/African Party for Democracy and Socialism (1991–2014);
	Movement of Leftwing Radicals (2004-present);
	Socialists United for Renaissance of Senegal (2004-present)
Seychelles	*Seychelles People's Progressive Front* (1978–2009);
	Parti Lepep — United Seycheles (2009-present)
Sierra Leone	*All People's Congress* (1962-present);
	Revolutionary United Front (1991–2002)

Somalia	*Work and Socialism Party* (1960–1969);
	Supreme Revolutionary Council (1969–1976);
	Somali Revolutionary Socialist Party (*SRSP.* 1976–1991);*
	Somalia Green Party (1990-present);
	Somali Social Unity Party (2004-present);
	Somali Labour Party (2011-present);
	Cosmopolitan Democratic Party (2015-present);
	Wadajir Party (2016-present)

* Somalia was a Marxist one-party state called *Somali Democratic Republic* from 1969–1991; *SRSP* was the ruling party from 1976–1991.

Somaliland

For Justice and Development (2001-present)

South Africa	*South African Labour Party* (1910–1958);
	African National Congress (1912-present);
	South African Communist Party (1921-present);
	Workers Party of South Africa (1935-unknown);
	Pan-Africanist Congress of Azania (1959-present);
	Black People's Convention (1972-unknown);
	Azanian People's Organisation (1978-present);
	Workers and Socialist Party (1979-present);
	Workers International Vanguard Party (1985-present);
	Keep Left (1987-present);
	Workers Organisation for Socialist Action (1990-unknown);
	Ecopeace Party (1995-present);
	Socialist Party of Azania (1998-present);
	Green Party of South Africa (1999-present);

African People's Convention (2007-present);

Women Forward (2008-present);

Economic Freedom Fighters (2013-present);

United Congress (2013-present);

Black First Land First (2015-present);

National People's Ambassadors (2015-present);

Bolsheviks Party of South Africa (2016 approx.-present);

African Content Movement (2018-present);

Good (2018-present);

Socialist Revolutionary Workers Party (2019-present);

Land Party (2019-present)

South Sudan   *Communist Party of South Sudan* (2011-present)

South Sudan only recently became independent of Sudan in 2011, hence only one group

Sudan   *Sudanese Communist Party* (1946-present);

Anti-Imperialist Front (1952–1958 approx.);

Sudanese Communist Party-Revolutionary Leadership (1965-unknown);

Workers Forces (1967-unknown);

Sudanese Socialist Union (1971–1985);

Sudanese People's Socialist Front (1984-unknown);

Sudanese Movement of Revolutionary Committees (1985–1987 approx.)

Tanzania   *Tanganyika African Association* (1929–1954);

Tanganyika African National Union (1954–1977);

Chama Cha Mapinduzi (1977-present);

Alliance for Change and Transparency (2014-present)
Zanzibar

Afro-Shirazi Party (1957–1977);

Umma Party (1963-unknown)

Togo   *Socialist Revolution Party of Benin* (1959-unknown);

Communist Party of Togo (1980-unknown);

Democratic Convention of African Peoples (1980s-unknown);

Pan-African Socialist Party (1991 approx.-unknown);

Workers' Party (1998-present);

Lets Save Togo Collective (2012-present)

Tunisia   *Tunisian Communist Party* (1934–1993);

Socialist Destourian Party (1964–1988);

Popular Unity Movement (1973-present);

Movement of Socialist Democrats (1978-present);

Popular Unity Party (1981-present);

Democratic Patriots Unified Party (1981-present);

Workers' Party (1986-present);

Union Democratic Union (1988-present);

Ettajdid Movement (1993–2012);

Green Tunisia Party (2004-present);

Socialist Party (2006-present);

Democratic Current (2011-present);

Social Democratic Path (2012-present)

Uganda   *Uganda National Congress* (1952–1960 onwards);

Uganda People's Congress (1960-present);

National Resistance Movement (1986-present);

People's Progressive Party (2004-present)

Zambia   *United National Independence Party* (1959-present);

Movement for Multi-party Democracy (1990-present);

Revolutionary Socialist Party (1991–1998);

Patriotic Front (2001-present)

Zimbabwe   *Rhodesia Labour Party* (1923–1950s approx);

Southern Rhodesia Communist Party (1941-unknown);

Zimbabwe African National Union—Patriotic Front (1953-present);

Zimbabwe African People's Union (1961-present);

People's Democratic Party (2015-present);

Movement for Democratic Change (2018-present)

Middle East (and west Asia)

| Location | Notable groups |

Armenia   *Communist Party of Armenia (CPA.* 1920–1991);* (Com)

Armenian Communist Party (1991-present);

Democratic Party of Armenia (1991-present);

People's Party of Armenia (1998-present);

Renewed Communist Party of Armenia (2002–2003);

United Communist Party of Armenia (2003-present);

Citizen's Decision (2018-present)

* Armenia was part of the *U.S.S.R,* and this party was the local branch of the *Communist Party of the Soviet Union (CPSU/KPSS)*

Azerbaijan   *Communist Party of Azerbaijan (CPA.* 1920–1991);*

United Communist Party of Azerbaijan (1993-present);

Communist Party of Azerbaijan—CPA-2 (1996-present)

* Azerbaijan was part of the *U.S.S.R,* and this party was the local branch of the *Communist Party of the Soviet Union (CPSU/KPSS)*

Bahrain — *Arab Socialist Ba'ath Party* (1947–1966);

National Liberation Front—Bahrain (1955-present);

Popular Front for the Liberation of Bahrain (1974–2001);

National Democratic Assembly (1991-present);

Progressive Democratic Tribune (2001-present)

Cyprus — *Progressive Party of Working People* (1926-present);

(Rep of. and — *Movement for Social Democracy* (1969-present);

Northern) — *New Cyprus Party* (1989-present);

United Cyprus Party (2003-present);

Cyprus Social Ecology Movement (2009-present);

ERAS — Committee for a Radical Left Rally (2011–2014);

Coalition of the Radical Left—Progressive Alliance (2012-present)

Egypt — *Egyptian Socialist Party* (1921–1923);

Arab Socialist Union (1962–1978);

Egyptian Communist Party (1975-present);

Arab Democratic Nasserist Party (1984-present);

Revolutionary Socialists (1995-present);

Socialist People's Alliance Party (2011-present);

Workers and Peasants Party (2012-present);

Revolutionary Democratic Coalition (2012–2015);

Bread and Freedom Party (2013-present)

Iran — *Social Democratic Party* (1904–1910);

Communist Party of Persia (1917–1921);

Socialist Party (1921–1926);

Revolutionary Republican Party of Iran (1925-unknown);

Tudeh Party of Iran (1941-present);

Iran Party (1941-present);

Comrades Party (1942–1944);

League of Iranian Socialists (1960–1980 approx.);

Labour Party of Iran (based in Germany. 1965-present);

Laborers' Party of Iran (based in Sweden. 1979-present);

Communist Party of Iran (1983-present);

Worker-communist Party of Iran (based in Germany. 1991-present);

Green Party of Iran (1999-present);

Communist Party of Iran—Marxist-Leninist-Maoist (2001-present)

Iraq   *Iraqi Communist Party* (1934-present);

Forward (1942–1944);

Arab Toilers' Movement (1962–1964);

Iraqi Arab Socialist Union (1964–1968);

Arab Unity Party (1967–1971);

Kurdistan Socialist Democratic Party (1976-present);

Kurdistan Toilers' Party (1985-present);

Worker-Communist Party of Iraq (1993-present);

Kurdistan Communist Party/Iraq (1993-present);

Green Party of Iraq (2003-present);

Left Worker-communist Party of Iraq (2004-present);

People's Union (2005–2010)

Israel   *Maki* (1948–1973);

Israeli Communist Party (1965-present);

Israeli Labor Party (1968-present);

Moked (1973–1977);

Democratic Front for Peace and Equality (1977-present);

Da'am Workers Party (1995-present)

As Israel was formed in 1948, see "Palestine" below for pre-1948 groups.

Jordan	*Jordanian Communist Party* (1948-present);
	Jordanian Democratic People's Party (1989-present);
	Jordanian Communist Toilers Party (1997-present)
Kuwait	*Kuwaiti Progressive Movement* (1975-present)
Lebanon	*Lebanese Communist Party* (1924-present);
	Syrian-Lebanese Communist Party (1924–1964);
	Progressive Socialist Party (1949-present);
	Socialist Lebanon (1965–1970);
	Toilers League (1968-present);
	Communist Action Organisation in Lebanon (1970-present);
	Palestinian Communist Workers Party (1978–1991)
Oman	*Popular Front for the Liberation of Oman* (1974–1992)
	Oman is an absolute monarchy; no political parties are allowed
Palestine	*Socialist Workers Party* (1919–1921 approx.);
	Palestinian Communist Party (1922–1923);
	Palestine Communist Party (1923–1982);
	Popular Front for the Liberation of Palestine (1967-present);
	Democratic Front for the Liberation of Palestine (1968-present);
	Palestinian People's Party (1982-present)
Qatar	N/A
	Qatar is a de-facto absolute monarchy (officially transitioning to being a constitutional monarchy). Previously, no political parties were allowed.
Saudi Arabia	*Arabian Peninsula People's Union* (1959–1990 approx);
	Arab Socialist Action Party—Arabian Peninsula (1972–1990);
	Communist Party in Saudi Arabia (1975-unknown)

Saudi Arabia is an absolute monarchy; no political parties are allowed

Syria	*Syrian Communist Party* (1924–1986);
	Arab Socialist Movement (1950-1960s);
	Socialist Unionist Party (1962-present);
	Arab Revolutionary Workers Party (1966-present);
	Arab Communist Party (1968-unknown);
	Communist Action Party (1976-present);
	Syrian Communist Party—Unified (1986-present);
	Syrian Communist Party—Bakdash (1986-present);
	People's Will Party (2012-present)
United Arab Emirates	N/A
	UAE is a federal monarchy; no political parties
Yemen	*Yemeni Socialist Party* (1978-present)
	South Yemen (southern and eastern province of Yemen, plus island of Socotra)
	South Yemen was a Marxist one-party state called *People's Democratic Republic of Yemen* from 1967–1990

Asia

This continent has been absolutely ravaged by the infection, causing much division and conflict throughout the 20th century which persists to this day. It's also home to one of the biggest strongholds for the infection right now—the *People's Republic of China*. In addition, Asia contains some of the most populous countries in the world, with China and India both hovering around the 1.4 billion mark. Indonesia is 273 million, and Pakistan is 220 million.[129]

Actually, the population of China is estimated to be over 1.4 billion (1,445,327,346). This is particularly disturbing, since if we say that only half of that population are indoctrinated cult members, this is 722,663,673 people (almost the current population of Europe). If it's only one quarter, that's 361,331,836.5 (higher than the present U.S. population of almost 340

---

[129] https://www.worldometers.info/world-population/population-by-country/

million).

Not surprisingly, due to its British colonial past, India has a long history of fascination with the ideology too, and it has (as the table will show), a considerable number of cults groups. Included are some of the Middle Eastern countries bordering Asia, such as Afghanistan, Kazakhstan, Kyrgystan, Tajikistan, Turkmenistan, and Uzbekistan; most of which spent most of the 20th century as part of the Soviet Union (that goes for Mongolia too).

In Asia the ideology had a role to play in: the *Chinese Civil War* and the formation of Red China; the *Second Sino-Japanese War;* Siam and its transition to becoming Thailand, and the conflict and power struggles that continued to recent years; the *Communist Party of Malaya,* the *Malayan General Labour Union* and the infiltration of trade unions in Singapore; the *Soviet-Afghan War* (1979-89) during the Cold War; the *Korean War;* the Indochina Wars, including the *Vietnam War*; the *Pathet Lao* and the establishment of another one-party Marxist state—*Lao People's Democratic Republic* (aka Laos); the invasion and annexation of Tibet by Red China called the *Peaceful Liberation of Tibet* (giggles. 1950–1951); the presidency of Sukarno in Indonesia, the *Gerakan 30 September Movement,* and an anti-Marxist purge called *Pembunuhan;* the *Khmer Rouge* and Pol Pot's regime in Cambodia; the formation of the *Wa state* in Burma; the *Communist Party of Nepal* and the *Nepali Civil War* (1996–2006); Velupillai Prabhakaran (1954–2009) and the *Tamil Tigers* in Sri Lanka; China's repression of any non-conformers within its borders, its expansionism, and its plans to be the world's number one power this century.

Location	Notable groups
Afghanistan	*Progressive Youth Organization* (1965–1972);
	People's Democratic Party of Afghanistan (PDPA. 1965–1992);*
	Progressive Democratic Party of Afghanistan (1966-present);
	Afghanistan Liberation Organization (1973-present);
	Liberation Organization of the People of Afghanistan (1977–1989);
	Watan Party of Afghanistan (1997-present);
	Republican Party of Afghanistan (1999-present);

National United Party of Afghanistan (2003-present);

Solidarity Party of Afghanistan (2004-present);

Communist Party of Afghanistan—Maoist (2004-present)

* Afghanistan was a Marxist one-party state called *Democratic Republic of Afghanistan* from 1978–1992; *PDPA* was the ruling party during this period.

Bangladesh

Communist Party of Bangladesh (1968-present);

Bangladesh Communist Party—Leninist (1971–1980);

National Socialist Party of Bangladesh (1972-present);

Bangladesh Krishak Sramik Awami League (1975);

Socialist Party of Bangladesh (1980-present);

Workers Party of Bangladesh (1980-present);

National Socialist Party (2002-present);

Revolutionary Workers Party of Bangladesh (2004-present)

Bangladesh became a 'sovereign' nation in 1971

Bhutan

Bhutan Peoples' Party (1990-present. In exile in Nepal);

Bhutan Communist Party—Marxist-Leninist (2003-present);

Bhutan Kuen-Nyan Party (2013-present);

Party of the Common People of Bhutan (2013–2018)

Brunei

Brunei Peoples' Party (1956–1962)

Burma/Myanmar

Communist Party of Burma (1939-present);

Burma Socialist Party (1945–1964);

Red Flag Communist Party (1946–1978);

Burma Workers Party (1950–1962);

Union Revolutionary Council (1962–1974);

Burma Socialist Programme Party (1962–1988);

National Unity Party (1988-present);

United Wa State Party (1989-present);

People's Party of Myanmar Farmers and Workers (2014-

present);

Confederate Farmers Party (2015-present)

Cambodia	*United Issarak Front* (1950–1954);
	Cambodian People's Party (1951-present);
	Communist Party of Kampuchea (1951–1981);*
	People's Group (1954–1972);
	Party of Democratic Kampuchea (1981–1993);
	Cambodian National Unity Party (1992–1997)

* ruling party of *Democratic Kampuchea* (Marxist one-party state. Existed 1975–1979)

China (aka People's Republic of China)

Chinese Communist Party (*CCP*. 1921-present);*

Minor Parties:

China Zhi Gong Party (1925-present);

Chinese Peasants' and Workers' Democratic Union (1927-present);

China Democratic League (1941-present);

Jiusan Society (1945-present);

National Democratic Construction Association (1945-present);

China Association for Promoting Democracy (1945-present);

China Democratic Socialist Party (1946–2020);

Taiwan Democratic Self-Government League (1947-present);

Revolutionary Committee of the Chinese Kuomintang (1948-present)

Other parties:

Communist Party of China (1976–1978);

Maoist Communist Party of China (2008-present);

Zhi Xian Party (2013)

* The CCP is the ruling party in the *People's Republic of China*. It controls all minor parties via the *United Front*—an organisation that also includes other groups under the control

of the *CCP*

Hong Kong:

Revolutionary Communist Party of China (1948-present);

Hong Kong Federation of Trade Unions (1948-present);

April Fifth Action (1988-present);

Communist Party of Hong Kong (1997-present);**

Socialist Action (2010-present);

People Power (2011-present);

Land Justice League (2011-present)

** Hong Kong's territorial status changed in 1997, being transferred to China by the United Kingdom

East Timor   *Revolutionary Front for an Independent East Timor* (1974-present);

Socialist Party of Timor (1990-present)

India   *Indian National Congress* (1885-present);

Communist Party of India (1925-present);

Congress Socialist Party (1934–1948);

Revolutionary Communist Party (1934-present);

All India Forward Bloc (1939-present);

Revolutionary Socialist Party (1940-present);

Bolshevik-Leninist Party of India, Ceylon and Burma (1942–1947);

Kisan Mazdoor Praja Party (1951–1952);

Praja Socialist Party (1952–1972);

Mizo National Front (1961-present);

Communist Party of India—Marxist (1964-present);

Communist Party of India—Marxist-Leninist (1969–1972);

Communist Party of India—Marxist-Leninist Liberation (1974-present);

Marxist Communist Party of India (1983–2005);

Communist Party of India—Marxist-Leninist Red Flag (1988–2005);

Sikkim Democratic Front (1993-present);

National People's Party (1997-present);

People's Democratic Front (2001-present);

Janata Dal—United (2003-present);

Communist Party of India—Maoist (2004-present);

Manithaneya Makkal Katchi (2009-present);

Sikkim Revolutionary Front (2013-present);

Janta Congress Chhattisgarh (2016-present);

Apna Dal Sonelal (2016-present);

All India Women's Empowerment Party (2017-present);

Jannayak Janta Party (2018-present);

Progressive Socialist Party—Lohia (2018-present)

Indonesia   *Communist Party of Indonesia* (1914–1966);

Peasants Front of Indonesia (1945-65);

Indonesian Marhaen People's Union (1945–1955);

Socialist Party of Indonesia (1945);

Socialist People's Party (1945);

Socialist Party of Indonesia (1948–1960);

Murba Party (1948–1973);

Labour Party (1949–1956);

Acoma Party (1952–1965);

People's Democratic Party (1996-present);

New Indonesia Party of Struggle (2002-present);

Indonesian Green Party (2012-present);

Indonesian Solidarity Party (2014-present)

Japan   *Social Democratic Party* (1901);

Japan Socialist Party (1906–1907);

Japanese Communist Party (1922-present); (Com)

Japan Labour-Farmer Party (1926–1928);

Socialist Masses Party (1932–1940);

Japan Proletarian Party (1937);

Japan Socialist Party (1945–1996);

Social Democratic Party (1996-present);

New Socialist Party of Japan (1996-present);

Greens Japan (2008-present)

Kazakhstan   *Communist Party of Kazakhstan* (*QKP.* 1936–1991);*

Socialist Party of Kazakhstan (1991-present);

Communist Party of Kazakhstan (1991–2015);

*Rukhaniyat Party (*1995–2013);

Socialist Resistance of Kazakhstan (2002-present);

Communist People's Party of Kazakhstan (2004-present);

Nationwide Social Democratic Party (2006-present)

* Kazakhstan was part of the *U.S.S.R,* and this party was the local branch of the *Communist Party of the Soviet Union* (*CPSU/KPSS*)

Kyrgyzstan   *Communist Party of Kirghizia* (*CPK.* 1924–1991);*

Fatherland Socialist Party (1992-present);

Party of Communists Kyrgyzstan (1992-present);

Social Democratic Party of Kyrgyzstan (1993-present);

Communist Party of Kyrgyzstan (1999-present)

* Kyrgyzstan was part of the *U.S.S.R,* and this party was the local branch of the *Communist Party of the Soviet Union* (*CPSU/KPSS*)

Laos   *Lao Nation* (1950–1975);

Lao People's Revolutionary Party (*LPRP.* 1955-present);

Lao Front for National Construction (LFNC. 1979-present)

Laos is a one-party state, and the *LPRP* is the ruling party. The

LFNC is subservient to the *LPRP*, as a national organising body.

Malaysia	*Malayan Communist Party* (1930–1989);
	Kesatuan Melayu Muda (1938-1945);
	Malaysian People's Party (1955-present);
	Democratic Action Party (1965-present);
	Communist Party of Malaya—Revolutionary Faction (1970–1983);
	North Kalimantan Communist Party (1971–1990);
	Communist Party of Malaya—Marxist-Leninist (1974–1983);
	National Trust Party (1978-present);
	Malaysian Communist Party (1983–1987);
	Socialist Party of Malaysia (1998-present)
Maldives	*National Unity Party* (2013-present);
	Maldives Socialist Communist Movement (2016-present);
	Maldives Labour and Social Democratic Party (2019-present)
Mongolia	*Mongolian People's Party* (MPP. 1920-present); (Com) *
	Mongolian Social Democratic Party (1990-present);
	Mongolian Green Party (1990-present);
	Mongolian Democratic New Socialist Party (1992-present)
	* Mongolia was a Marxist one-party state called *Mongolian People's Republic* from 1924–1992; *MPP* was the ruling party during this period.
Nepal	*Communist Party of Nepal* (1949–1962);
	Nepali Congress (1950-present);
	Nepal Workers and Peasants Party (1975-present);
	Communist Party of Nepal—Unified Marxist-Leninist (1991–2018);
	National People's Front (1999-present);
	Sanghiya Loktantrik Rastriya Manch (2007-present);

Communist Party of Nepal (2013-present);

Federal Socialist Forum (2015–2019);

New Force Party (2016–2019);

Nepal Federal Socialist Party (2016-present);

Nepal Communist Party (2018-present);

Socialist Party Nepal (2019–2020);

People's Socialist Party (2020-present)

Pakistan   *Pakistan Socialist Party* (1948–1958);

Communist Party of Pakistan (1948-present);

East Pakistan Communist Party—Marxist-Leninist (1966–1978);

Pakistan People's Party (1967-present);

Awami National Party (1986-present);

Labour Party Pakistan (1986–2012);

Pakistan People's Movement (1989-present);

Communist Mazdoor Kissan Party (1995–2015);

Awami Workers Party (2012-present);

Barabri Party (2018-present)

Philippines   *Communist Party of the Philippines* (1930-present);

Labour Party Philippines (1963-present);

Communist Party of the Philippines (1968-present);

Philippine Democratic Socialist Party (1973-present);

Democratic Party—People's Power (1983-present);

Akbayan Citizens Action Party (1998-present);

Bayan Muna (1999-present);

Ang Ladlad LGBT Party Inc (2003-present);

Patriotic Coalition of the People (2009-present);

Party of the Laboring Masses (2009-present)

Singapore   *South Seas Communist Party* (1925–1930);

Communist Party of Malaya (1930–1989);

Labour Party (1948–1960);

Labour Front (1954–1960);

Liberal Socialist Party (1956–1963);

Workers' Party of Singapore (1957-present);

Singapore Peoples Alliance (1958–1965);

Socialist Front (1961–1988);

Democratic Progressive Party (1973-present);

Socialist Front (2010–2011);

People's Power Party (2015-present)

Sri Lanka   *Lanka Equal Society Party* (1935-present);

Communist Party of Sri Lanka (1943-present);

Ceylon Communist Party—Maoist (1964-present);

People's Liberation Front (1965-present);

Communist Party of Sri Lanka—Marxist-Leninist (1972-present);

New Equal Society Party (1977-present);

United Socialist Party (1989-present);

Democratic Left Front (1999-present);

United People's Freedom Alliance (2004–2019);

Socialist Party of Sri Lanka (2006-present);

Frontline Socialist Party (2012-present);

Sri Lanka People's Freedom Alliance (2019-present)

Taiwan   *Taiwanese Communist Party* (1928–1931);

(Republic of China)   *Labor Party* (1989-present);

Green Party Taiwan (1996-present);

Taiwan Solidarity Union (2001-present);

Taiwan Communist Party (2008–2020);

Taiwan Democratic Communist Party (2009–2020);

Communist Party of the Republic of China (2009–2018);

Social Democratic Party (2015-present);

Taiwan Statebuilding Party (2016-present)

Tajikistan   *Communist Party of Tajikistan* (1918-present);*

Socialist Party of Tajikistan (1996-present)

* Tajikistan was part of the *U.S.S.R*, and this party was the local branch of the *Communist Party of the Soviet Union* (*CPSU/KPSS*)

Thailand   *South Seas Communist Party* (1925–1930);

Communist Party of Thailand (1942–1990 approx);

Socialist Party of Thailand (1974–1976);

New Force Party (1974–1988)

Turkmenistan   *Communist Party of the Turkmen Soviet Socialist Republic* (1924–1991);*

Communist Party of Turkmenistan (1998–2002)

* Turkmenistan was part of the *U.S.S.R*, and this party was the local branch of the *Communist Party of the Soviet Union* (*CPSU/KPSS*)

The country declared independence from the *U.S.S.R.* in 1990. Since independence, it has been a one-party state, until recently

Uzbekistan   *Communist Party of Uzbekistan* (1925–1991);*

Justice Social Democratic Party (1995-present);

Ecological Party of Uzbekistan (2008-present)

* Uzbekistan was part of the *U.S.S.R*, and this party was the local branch of the *Communist Party of the Soviet Union* (CPSU/KPSS).

The country declared independence from the U.S.S.R. in 1991. Since independence, it has been a one-party state, until recently

Vietnam	*South Seas Communist Party* (1925–1930);
	New Vietnam Revolutionary Party (1925–1930);
	Vietnamese Revolutionary Youth League (1925–1929);
	Indochinese Communist League (1929–1930);
	Communist Party of Annam (1929–1930);
	Communist Party of Indochina (1929–1930);
	Communist Party of Vietnam (CPV. 1930-present);*
	Indochinese Communist Party (1930–1945);
	Ho Chi Minh Communist Youth Union (1931-present);
	International Communist League (1932–1946);
	Democratic Party of Vietnam (1944–1988);
	Socialist Party of Vietnam (1946–1988);
	Vietnamese Fatherland Front (1977-present)

* The *Communist Party of Vietnam (CPV)* is the ruling party; Vietnam is a one-party state

Australasia

Location	Notable groups
Australia	*Australian Labor Party* (1901-present);
	Socialist Labor Party (1901-1940/1970s);
	Communist Party of Australia (1920–1991); (Com)
	Australian Fabian Society (1947-present)
Fiji	*Fiji Labour Party* (1985-present)
New Caledonia	*Kanak and Socialist National Liberation Front* (1984-present)
New Zealand	*New Zealand Socialist Party* (1901–1913);
	Independent Political Labour League (1904–1919);
	United Labour Party (1912–1916);

Communist Party of New Zealand (1921–1994);

Socialist Unity Party (1966–1990)

International organisations

Here are some notable international organisations. EP = European Parliament group. (Com) = Created/controlled by the Comintern:

Period	Organisation
1847–1852	*Communist League*
1864–1876	*First International or International Workingmen's Association* (IWA)
1889–1916	*Second International*
1904-present	*World Socialist Movement* (WSM)
1919–1943	*Third International* (aka the Comintern)
1920–1937	*Red International of Labour Unions, or "Profintern"* (Com) *
1920–1930s	*Communist Women's International* (Com)
1921–1923	*International Working Union of Socialist Parties* (IWUSP)
1922–1938	*International Red Aid* (MOPR) (Com)
1922–1933	*Workers International Relief* (WIR)
1923–1939	*Peasant International or Krestintern* (Com)
1923–1940	*Labour and Socialist International* (LSI)
1927–1936	*League Against Imperialism and Colonial Oppression* (Com)
1932-unknown	*International Revolutionary Marxist Centre or the London Bureau*

1938-several	*Fourth International* (FI) (suffered several splits)
1947–1956	*Information Bureau of the Communist and Workers' Parties (aka the Cominform)*
1951-present	*Socialist International* (SI)
1973-present	*Party of European Socialists* (PES)
1974-present	*Committee for a Workers' International* (CWI)
1979-present	*Permanent Conference of Political Parties Latin America Caribbean* (COPPPAL)
1984-unknown	*Revolutionary Internationalist Movement* (RIM) (Marxism-Leninism-Maoism)
1886-present	*SAMAK — Joint Committee of the Nordic Social Democratic Labour Movement*
1989-present	*League for the Fifth International* (L5I)
1990-present	*Sao Paulo Forum* (FSP)
1990-present	*Workers International to Rebuild the Fourth International* (WIRFI)
1992–2014	*International Communist Seminar* (ICS)
1992-present	*International Marxist Tendency* (IMT)
1993-present	*Union of Communist Parties—Communist Party of the Soviet Union* (UPC-CPSU)
1994-present	*International Conference of Marxist-Leninist Parties and Organisations* (ICMLPO)
1995-present	*European United Left/Nordic Green Left* (GUE) EP
1995-unknown	*International Workers' Unity—Fourth International*

1998-present	*International Conference of Marxist-Leninist Parties and Organisations* (ICMLPO)
1998-present	*International Meeting of Communist and Workers' Parties* (IMCWP)
2000-present	*European Anti-Capitalist Left* (EACL)
2001-present	*Global Greens* (GG)
2004-present	*Bolivarian Alliance for the Peoples of Our America* (ALBA)
2004-present	*Nordic Green Left Alliance* (NGLA)
2004-present	*Party of the European Left* (PEL) EP
2004-present	*European Green Party* (EGP)
2010-present	*International Coordination of Revolutionary Parties and Organizations* (ICOR)
2012-present	*Progressive Alliance* (PA)
2013-present	*Initiative of Communist and Workers' Parties*
2018-present	*Progressive International* (PI) #
2019-present	*Committee for a Workers' International* (CWI)
2020-present	*International Socialist Alternative* (ISA)

The Slogan of this organisation is "Internationalism or Extinction". A perhaps unintentional subtle threat, hidden in plain sight ("communism or death!").

* The Profintern was created to recruit/control cult members via the Labour unions movements [130]

The death toll of Marxism

One of the most horrific consequences of the global Marxist infection has

---

[130] https://en.wikipedia.org/wiki/Profintern

been the death toll. This is a topic sufficiently examined elsewhere but must be briefly included here. Usually, this point is raised when taking about the catastrophic effects that ensue when the cult controls a country, including forced collectivisation and egalitarianism in industry, agriculture etc.; and then there's deaths through other means (murder, warfare, ethnic cleansing, mass political/partisan executions etc.).

Is the ideology the biggest killer of all time? Has anything in the history of the world killed more people in one century than Marxism? Pound-for-pound, in terms of impact, has anything been worse? Though the ideology is relatively new in the world, it indeed has no equal in terms of body count. More than religions/religious wars, or other political ideologies etc. Perhaps more than many of those combined. How many did the Roman Empire kill? The Ottaman or British Empire? In the 13th century, the Mongol Empire of Gengis Khan and the Mongol Invasions which spread across large swathes of land in Eurasia, apparently killed 30 million upwards. The total death toll estimates for the Napoleonic Wars range from 3.5 million to 6 million. In the 20th century: the *Influenza Pandemic* or *Spanish Flu* of 1918 has an average estimate of 50 million, and upper estimate of 100 million. The Second World War is put at 60 to 85 million; the first was around 15–20 million. (all war figures are inclusive of civilian deaths).[131] [132] [133]

When the subject of the death toll of socialism/communism is raised, cult members will typically often try to wiggle off the hook by claiming 'Red Scare' propaganda, or will try diverting attention towards their old enemy – the Catholic Church – mentioning the Crusades (1095–1291 approx) or the Spanish Inquisition (1478–1834 approx). Though it's impossible to get reliable figures, the Crusades are generally estimated to have killed a few million[132]; three being the upper figure (interestingly, the outlandish figure of nine million was suggested by a Scottish cult member and anti-Jesus fanatic John M. Robertson (1856–1933)).[134] The Spanish Inquisition was more of a torture fest, but realistic estimates are only in the thousands.

---

[131] "Selected Death Tolls for Wars, Massacres and Atrocities Before the 20th Century".

http://necrometrics.com/pre1700a.htm#Mongol

[132] "List of wars by death toll".

https://military-history.fandom.com/wiki/List_of_wars_by_death_toll

[133] https://www.britannica.com/event/influenza-pandemic-of-1918-1919

[134] https://en.wikipedia.org/wiki/J._M._Robertson

Obviously, in the modern age, technology allows one to rack up the body count somewhat. The cult will also point to American 'imperialism'. As mentioned elsewhere, many of the high-profile conflicts that the U.S. have been involved in during the 20th century (Korea, Vietnam etc.) would not have happened if Marxism did not exist. The death tolls in those instances should be attributed to the cult/ideology, not the U.S. As for the several incursions of the U.S. military in to the Middle East in the modern era since *Operation Desert Storm* (1990–1991), rough estimates put fatalities (from the actual conflicts) easily under two million. [132]

It's obvious why the cult often emphasises these death tolls—it's a deflection away from the cult's body count (that many have been suckered-in by unfortunately). The buponic plague pandemic – or *Black Death* – of the late 14th century seems to be the only contender to the cult's overall death toll; no reliable figures, but it apparently wiped-out up to 200 million (though a February 2022 New York Times article highlighted how previous estimates for the death toll are being questioned)[135]. Now that's a pandemic! Imagine how many masks and vaccines you would need for that.

Le Petit Livre Noir

A French book entitled *Le Livre noir du communisme: Crimes, terreur, répression* or *The Black Book of Communism: Crimes, Terror, Repression*, was published in 1997. Put together by a group of European academics - headed by French professor Stephane Courtois–it documented the history of crimes against humanity committed by the various Communist regimes. Often with these regimes, the forced collectivisation and centralisation of power, including control of the means to produce food, created an almost unbelievable level of suffering, horror, and death.

A very useful term here is "Democide". It was coined by the late author, Professor and Political Scientist R.J. Rummel (1932–2014) in his book *Death by Government: Genocide and Mass Murder since 1900* (1997). It was used to describe "the intentional killing of an unarmed or disarmed person by government agents acting in their authoritative capacity and pursuant to government policy or high command".[136] According to The Black Book of Communism, the unofficial estimation of deaths caused via democide by Communist regimes amounted to almost 100 million. Rummel's estimate was higher.

---

[135] https://www.britannica.com/event/Black-Death

[136] Rummel, R.J., *Death by Government: Genocide and Mass Murder since 1900* (1997).

On the *WND* website 15 Dec 2004, Rummel's pertinent words were featured: "Of all religions, secular and otherwise, that of Marxism has been by far the bloodiest—bloodier than the Catholic Inquisition, the various Catholic crusades, and the Thirty Years War between Catholics and Protestants. In practice, Marxism has meant bloody terrorism, deadly purges, lethal prison camps and murderous forced labor, fatal deportations, man-made famines, extrajudicial executions and fraudulent show trials, outright mass murder and genocide. In total, Marxist regimes murdered nearly 110 million people from 1917 to 1987. For perspective on this incredible toll, note that all domestic and foreign wars during the 20th century killed around 35 million. That is, when Marxists control states, Marxism is more deadly then (*sic*) all the wars of the 20th century, including World Wars I and II, and the Korean and Vietnam Wars. And what did Marxism, this greatest of human social experiments, achieve for its poor citizens, at this most bloody cost in lives? Nothing positive. It left in its wake an economic, environmental, social and cultural disaster".[137]

Page four of The Black Book of Communism lists the methods by which these regimes killed their victims in their respective countries, in addition to the estimates (formatted to save space): "These crimes tend to fit a recognizable pattern even if the practices vary to some extent by regime. The pattern includes execution by various means, such as firing squads, hanging, drowning, battering, and, in certain cases, gassing, poisoning, or "car accidents"; destruction of the population by starvation, through man-made famine, the withholding of food, or both;

deportation, through which death can occur in transit (either through physical exhaustion or through confinement in an enclosed space), at one's place of residence or through forced labor (exhaustion, illness, hunger, cold). Periods described as times of "civil war" are more complex—it is not always easy to distinguish between events caused by fighting between rulers and rebels and events that can properly be described only as a massacre of the civilian population. Nevertheless, we have to start somewhere.

The following rough approximation, based on unofficial estimates, gives some sense of the scale and gravity of these crimes: U.S.S.R.: 20 million deaths; China: 65 million deaths; Vietnam: 1 million deaths; North Korea: 2 million deaths; Cambodia: 2 million deaths; Eastern Europe: 1 million deaths; Latin America: 150,000 deaths; Africa: 1.7 million deaths; Afghanistan: 1.5 million deaths; The international Communist movement

---

[137] Rummel, R.J. "The Killing Machine that is Marxism", 15 December 2004. https://www.wnd.com/2004/12/28036/

and Communist parties not in power: about 10,000 deaths. The total approaches 100 million people killed".[138] Even if we cut that number in half, that's still absolutely horrific for an ideology that's supposed to be the liberator of humanity!

The cult's response to the book was that it was obviously anti-Communist propaganda, which is as typical as it is delusional. There will always be a never-ending queue of cult members – academics or not – who will attempt to minimise these atrocities (this was evident looking at how the book was received at the time). The fact that anyone would try to criticize a book that documents Communist atrocities exposes them as cult members. Courtois' introduction also clearly touched a nerve by suggesting that their beloved communism was as bad as their dreaded foe – Nazism – and this they could not tolerate. Interestingly, Courtois was once a cult member himself – a Maoist – but 'woke-up' and admirably went down this road instead.[139]

On this topic it must be added (though it's impossible to quantify) that the actual figures for the ideology are higher than what's above. Take abortion, for example—in the modern age, the ideology's sub-agenda of feminism has helped to normalise and popularise it, leading to wholesale killing of the unborn. Therefore, abortion is murder resulting from the ideology, but that's not included in the above conventional discourse about the death toll of 'communism' (abortion/abortion figures are discussed later). Keep in mind, this book you're reading is about the Marxist ideology in its entirety, not just about 'Communist' regimes and their resultant death tolls (as Le Livre noir du communisme was). 'Socialist' or 'Communist' regimes are just one kind of manifestation of the ideology.

There's also the problematic sterility issue in western populations – which the cult/ideology exacerbates – via the transgender/gender-nonbinary sub-agenda, and the animal rights/veganism sub-agenda. Combined, they help to create societies full of individuals who cannot create life. In addition to the cult/ideology killing what already lives, we also must hold it accountable for how it prevents life from beginning in the first place. This is why Marxism is far, far worse than any other form of ideology, warfare, imperialism, or plague as listed earlier! Marxism is a plague of its own unique type.

To say that the ideology is anti-life is a gargantuan understatement. The ideology is both simultaneously anti-life and a creator of conflict and death.

---

[138] Courtois (et al), *The Black Book of Communism* (1999), P. 4.

[139] https://fr.wikipedia.org/wiki/Stephane_Courtois

In a sense, it doesn't just manifest death, it is death.

How many lives destroyed

Marxism has destroyed/ended an unquantifiable number of lives. Nobody can know the answer to this; unless we had the ability to time travel and interview the whole population of the world the past couple of centuries.

We must also include not just those who fought against communism, but those who fought for it—remember, we are dealing with an aggressive, dangerous, violent cult that has destroyed (and continues to destroy) the lives of whoever gets sucked in to joining it... An example of this would be all those Marxists who got themselves beaten, maimed, incarcerated, tortured, accidentally killed or executed throughout the 20th century in the multitude of Marxist 'protests', 'rebellions' and wars (e.g. being shot by state forces during these events, or executed after them). In most of these cases, these people voluntary got themselves in to trouble through their own gullibility, egoism, and ignorance. This process was clear to see in many situations around the world, where the cult was trying to take control yet failed, or was in control but was removed from power; I refer to the various 'right-wing' regimes—Pinochet in Chile, Franco in Spain, Mussolini in Italy, Hitler in Germany, Salazer in Portugal etc.

"Capitalism is much worse!"

Another typical cult member response to all this is that capitalism has killed more than Marxism. This mentality is partially inspired by V.I. Lenin's *"Imperialism: The Highest State of Capitalism"* (1917). The governments of capitalistic countries don't engage in mass scale Democide—the destruction of a country's people! Where in the 20th century can it apply that capitalism has killed more people than Marxism?!

In terms of warfare, in a modern context, cult members will refer to what's happened/is happening in the Middle East as being due to the supposed imperial nature of capitalism (Lenin would be proud). They will talk about the Gulf War, the Iraq War, and U.S. support of Israel etc. They may link all these events to capitalism and project blame there, and not blame the actions of certain powerful groups. To use U.S.-led invasions of the Middle East as an example, by this logic, the actions of the Bush family in the U.S., along with the pro-Israel lobby and military industrial complex are not blamed; instead, the whole economic system of capitalism is blamed! How ludicrous!

Marxists fail to acknowledge that capitalism functions in many countries around the world, and no international military action is required to maintain its functioning (despite Mr. Lenin's opinions to the contrary); just ask Switzerland! As an economic system it would exist and function just fine without the Gulf Wars, Vietnam War, the establishment of Israel, multinational corporations, or any other examples of the apparent imperial nature of capitalism that cult members may raise! By the same token, in a historical context, the actions of the European empires around the globe are used by Marxists to attack capitalism and advocate socialism (as the solution).

Let's be rational here—any crimes against humanity or unjustifiable behaviour by those groups historically anywhere (ever) is nothing to do with capitalism today. As in, no, we should not replace capitalism with the Marxist system of socialism because of what happened in the past! Any truly greedy, inhumane behaviour by those Imperial forces was the result of decisions made by elitist types in their respective countries, not the entire global capitalist system.

Imperial armies throughout history (European or otherwise) were controlled by a relatively small (and identifiable) group of individuals, not by a comparatively nebulous thing such as capitalism! Of course, the cult's perception that any sort of profiteering is inherently evil is at the heart of this, and ipso facto, everyone benefiting from it are evil too (rolls eyes). Does this mean that a modern filthy-rich business owner is just as evil as some inbred Oligarchical freak who sat on the throne of an Imperial country in centuries past? Or some British elitist nut like a Cecil Rhodes?

All things considered it's completely ludicrous to say that capitalism has killed more people than the ideology. There is no contest here at all if we are comparing them in terms of economics prosperity or death toll. This is just another deflection. In addition, economically prosperous countries don't, under normal circumstances, have a shortage of food or health services (unlike Marxist regimes), which tends to lead to death/early death.

Finally, cult members have sometimes accused capitalism of having an unquantifiable, high death toll due to people being overworked, stressed, slave-like conditions and/or oppression, or simply dying too young (due to being exploited by the oppressive bourgeois class etc). I have a three word fully comprehensive rebuttal: communist labour camp.

Population replacement as genocide

Some might not see how the ideology's genocidal track-record is applicable to modern times, especially for Western countries, but it is since modern agendas labelled 'depopulation' or 'population replacement' are forms of genocide are they not? (in the end, they amount to the same thing—a lack of certain people/groups). Modern forms of genocide are enabled by the cult's/ideology's presence in the affected regions.

The more widespread and entrenched the ideology is globally, the more lands/peoples there are participating in internationalist, racial, genocidal, society-transforming initiatives such as 'multicultural' (aka anti-white) mass immigration. This genocidal anti-white agenda is a prime example of how the ideology creates destruction and death—death of a race in this case. (We look at 'mass immigration' in a separate section).

Section IV — The Red Steps To Utopia

"A map of the world that does not include Utopia is not worth even glancing at, for it leaves out the one country at which Humanity is always landing. And when Humanity lands there, it looks out, and, seeing a better country, sets sail. Progress is the realisation of Utopias"[1]

Author and playwright Oscar Wilde,
"The Soul of Man under Socialism", 1891

Introduction

In this section we'll go over the main objectives of the ideology, and the methods by which it plans to bring about its 'utopia'. We'll start by going over some historical artefacts such as the Ten Planks of the Communist Manifesto and the interesting observations of Willard Cleon Skousen's "Current Communist Goals". Then we focus on the "three C's"—the three main areas in Western society that the ideology targets: capitalism, Christianity, and culture. In addition to the destruction of the family unit.

Markey Marx's n' freaky Freddy's terrible ten red planks

From the Communist Manifesto, "Chapter II—Proletarians and Communists", page 26: "These measures will, of course, be different in different countries. Nevertheless, in most advanced countries, the following will be pretty generally applicable.

1. Abolition of private property and the application of all rents of land to public purposes; 2. A heavy progressive or graduated income tax; 3. Abolition of all rights of inheritance; 4. Confiscation of the property of all emigrants and rebels; 5. Centralization of credit in the hands of the state, by means of a national bank with state capital and an exclusive monopoly; 6. Centralization of the means of communications and transportation in the

---

[1] Wilde, O. "The Soul of Man Under Socialism", 1891, P. 3.

https://web.seducoahuila.gob.mx/biblioweb/upload/the_soul_of_man_under_socialism.pdf

hands of the state; 7. Extension of factories and instruments of production owned by the state, the bringing into cultivation of waste lands, and the improvement of the soil generally in accordance with a common plan; 8. Equal liability of all to labor. Establishment of industrial armies, especially for agriculture; 9. Combination of agriculture with manufacturing industries, gradual abolition of the distinction between town and country, by a more equitable distribution of population over the country; 10. Free education for all children in public schools. Abolition of children's factory labour in its present form. Combination of education with industrial production".[2]

Communist goals for taking over America

> "The West, with its imperialist ogres, has become a centre of darkness and slavery. The task is to destroy this centre, to the joy and relief of the workers"[3]

Joseph Stalin, *Zhizn Narsional' nosti*, No. 6, 1918

During the 1940s and 1950s, American patriots, dealing with a serious, decades-old infection, took steps to protect their country from Communist infiltration and subversion. This resulted in governmental investigations to deal with the problem, exemplified by the efforts of Senator Joseph McCarthy (1908–1957). Though efforts like this—later termed "McCarthyism"[4]—failed to stop the Marxist infiltration and rot from spreading overall, some Americans still publicly (and bravely) expressed anti-Communist sentiment. This period has been analysed extensively by other authors, so we won't be delving in to it here. That being said, there is an absolute gem of analysis from that period which is useful for our purposes.

On Thursday 10 January 1963, Florida Congressman Albert S. Herlong Jr., spoke in the House of Representatives. At the request of Patricia Nordman – a constituent and prominent anti-Communist voice – he included in the congressional record a list of "Current Communist Goals".[5] This list was compiled by the American author Willard Cleon Skousen in his 1954 book

---

[2] Marx and Engels. *The Communist Manifesto* (1848). P. 26.

[3] Suvorov, V., *Icebreaker* (1988).
https://ia801301.us.archive.org/10/items/IcebreakerWhoStartedTheSecondWorldWar/SuvorovVikto r-Icebreaker.WhoStartedTheSecondWorldWar.pdf

[4] https://www.britannica.com/event/McCarthyism

[5] Congressional Record—Appendix, pp. A34-A35, "Current Communist Goals", 10 Jan 1963. https://cultureshield.com/PDF/45_Goals.pdf

The Naked Communist.

Although the *Communist Party USA* (CPUSA) was not directly mentioned in the statement, it's implied as it was a key organisation. It's an excellent analysis of the modus operandi of the cult/ideology. As we go through the list, ask yourself if this goal has been achieved in your country (if it's relevant). Many of them have already been achieved in western countries, and others are (arguably) obsolete due to the Cold War being defunct (e.g. those that refer to atomic war).

In Skousen's book, "Chapter 12 — The Future Task" page 259, the list reads:[6]

"1. U.S. acceptance of coexistence as the only alternative to atomic war.

2. U.S. willingness to capitulate in preference to engaging in atomic war.

3. Develop the illusion that total disarmament [by] the United States would be a demonstration of moral strength.

4. Permit free trade between all nations regardless of Communist affiliation and regardless of whether or not items could be used for war.

5. Extension of long-term loans to Russia and Soviet satellites.

6. Provide American aid to all nations regardless of Communist domination.

7. Grant recognition of Red China. Admission of Red China to the U.N.

8. Set up East and West Germany as separate states in spite of Khrushchev's promise in 1955 to settle the German question by free elections under supervision of the U.N.

9. Prolong the conferences to ban atomic tests because the United States has agreed to suspend tests as long as negotiations are in progress.

10. Allow all Soviet satellites individual representation in the U.N.

11. Promote the U.N. as the only hope for mankind. If its charter is rewritten, demand that it be set up as a one-world government with its own independent armed forces.

12. Resist any attempt to outlaw the Communist Party.

13. Do away with all loyalty oaths.

14. Continue giving Russia access to the U.S. Patent Office.

---

[6] Skousen, W.C., *The Naked Communist* (1954). P. 259.

15. Capture one or both of the political parties in the United States.

16. Use technical decisions of the courts to weaken basic American institutions by claiming their activities violate civil rights.

17. Get control of the schools. Use them as transmission belts for socialism and current Communist propaganda. Soften the curriculum. Get control of teachers' associations. Put the party line in textbooks.

18. Gain control of all student newspapers.

19. Use student riots to foment public protests against programs or organizations which are under Communist attack.

20. Infiltrate the press. Get control of book-review assignments, editorial writing, policy-making positions.

21. Gain control of key positions in radio, TV, and motion pictures.

22. Continue discrediting American culture by degrading all forms of artistic expression.

23. Control art critics and directors of art museums. "Our plan is to promote ugliness, repulsive, meaningless art."

24. Eliminate all laws governing obscenity by calling them "censorship" and a violation of free speech and free press.

25. Break down cultural standards of morality by promoting pornography and obscenity in books, magazines, motion pictures, radio, and TV.

26. Present homosexuality, degeneracy and promiscuity as "normal, natural, healthy."

27. Infiltrate the churches and replace revealed religion with "social" religion. Discredit the Bible and emphasize the need for intellectual maturity, which does not need a "religious crutch."

28. Eliminate prayer or any phase of religious expression in the schools on the ground that it violates the principle of "separation of church and state."

29. Discredit the American Constitution by calling it inadequate, old-fashioned, out of step with modern needs, a hindrance to cooperation between nations on a worldwide basis.

30. Discredit the American Founding Fathers. Present them as selfish aristocrats who had no concern for the "common man."

31. Belittle all forms of American (insert your country here) culture and discourage the teaching of American (same here) history on the ground that it was only a minor part of the "big picture." Give more emphasis to

Russian history since the Communists took over.

32. Support any socialist movement to give centralized control over any part of the culture—education, social agencies, welfare programs, mental health clinics, etc.

33. Eliminate all laws or procedures which interfere with the operation of the Communist apparatus.

34. Eliminate the House Committee on Un-American Activities.

35. Discredit and eventually dismantle the FBI.

36. Infiltrate and gain control of more unions.

37. Infiltrate and gain control of big business.

38. Transfer some of the powers of arrest from the police to social agencies. Treat all behavioral problems as psychiatric disorders which no one but psychiatrists can understand [or treat].

39. Dominate the psychiatric profession and use mental health laws as a means of gaining coercive control over those who oppose Communist goals.

40. Discredit the family as an institution. Encourage promiscuity and easy divorce.

41. Emphasize the need to raise children away from the negative influence of parents. Attribute prejudices, mental blocks and retarding of children to suppressive influence of parents.

42. Create the impression that violence and insurrection are legitimate aspects of the American tradition; that students and special-interest groups should rise up and use ["]united force["] to solve economic, political or social problems.

43. Overthrow all colonial governments before native populations are ready for self-government.

44. Internationalize the Panama Canal.

45. Repeal the Connolly reservation so the United States cannot prevent the World Court from seizing jurisdiction [over domestic problems. Give the World Court jurisdiction] over nations and individuals alike".

The destruction of the capitalist system

"In a higher phase of communist society, after the enslaving subordination of the individual to the division of labor, after labor has become not only a means of life but life's prime want, after the productive forces have also increased with the all-around development of the individual, and all the springs of co-operative wealth flow more abundantly—only then can the narrow horizon of bourgeois right be crossed in its entirety and society inscribe on its banners: From each according to his ability, to each according to his needs!"[7]

Karl Marx, "Critique of the Gotha Programme", 1875, part 1

Of the three aforementioned main pillars of western civilisation – capitalism, Christianity, and culture – perhaps capitalism is the one that is most frequently and openly attacked by the cult. Indeed, I'm sure you've noticed how critical cult members are of it (and dramatically, nauseatingly so), and how it gets the blame for everything (excluding, of course, issues that are solely blamed on religion, racism, the 'far-right', nationalism, fascism etc.).

And as already mentioned, Marxism – as an ideology – presents itself as being some sort of political, sociological, and economic alternative to how things are already structured. A benevolent, rebellious antithesis to the established order, right? Therefore, its many adherents believe that the Marxian 'scientific' system of socialism is the answer to society's – and indeed the world's – perceived ills. In fact, Socialism is not merely presented as being an alternative to capitalism, but superior to it. Is this actually true? Does it have any merit at all, or is this just more Marxist propaganda? In this section, we'll look at some of the impacts of socialism. Of course, fully analysing the ins-and-outs of Marxian socialist thought is not only outside the book's scope, but a waste of time. We are sifting through enough trash.

It can save us from the evils of Capitalism

There is a perception from some quarters that Marxism has tremendous value because it gave us socialism, which is (amongst other things) an alternative economic system, we are told. It has been proven many, many times that implementing Marxist theories (via socialism) is guaranteed to destroy your country, especially economically. This is because these theories, while attractive and valuable to some, are mistaken when it comes to human nature and what motivates people to work, to survive, and indeed, to excel.

It's the authors position that the perception of Marxism (via socialism) being an alternative economic system is just a smokescreen—another

---

[7] Karl Marx, "Critique of the Gotha Programme", 1875, part 1.

https://www.marxists.org/archive/marx/works/1875/gotha/

distraction. As stated, the ideology's real purpose is to destroy western civilisation in order to re-build it in its image. The economic argument is just used as the carrot, which is dangled in front of the unsuspecting masses, as the bait, to make people accept the ideology as a whole: "If we have this revolution, it will make our lives better! We'll get more free things and have more money for no reason!" etc. It's a Trojan Horse which is covered in a myriad of 'facts' convincing the unsuspecting reader of the evils of capitalism, and why socialism is the answer. As the reader reads, the demons inside sharpen their blades.

What Socialism really is

Before we go on, what is 'socialism'? As mentioned, it's a theoretical system that involves the application of Marxist principles. A system that can then be applied to a society's various sectors, including the economy (resources, trade, industrial, commercial etc.), and obviously government too. The principles include things like egalitarianism/equality/'social justice', collectivism/solidarity, the 'communal ownership of the means of production and distribution', a government that serves 'the people' (a 'dictatorship of the proletariat'), the equal distribution of wealth, class struggle/oppressor v oppressed, the opposition to hierarchies etc. It's presented as a seemingly more benign system compared to the established order. In a sense, socialism supposedly represents the idea of a more ethical distribution of resources and wealth.

One of the most famous catchphrases associated with communism and Karl Marx is "From each according to his ability, to each according to his needs".[8] Marx had the idea that in this 'utopian' society the masses would have access to free goods and services, according to what they required. This would be possible due to the abundance of resources that a society built around socialism would supposedly have access to. The irony of concepts like this is that socialism produces the exact opposite—scarcity. Communism (according to most definitions) is the end state of a society that successfully transitions from being a capitalist country, through the socialism stage, and then on to the final stage (communism). A society without the 'evils' of classes, money, religion, ownership of private property, profits etc. A 'utopia'.

The communal ownership of property, resources etc.

---

[8] Marx was not the originator of the phrase, but it's in his "Critique of the Gotha Program", 1875.

https://www.marxists.org/archive/marx/works/1875/gotha/index.htm

The cult's defining obsessions with collectivism and egalitarianism leaves the ideology/cult blind to certain realities in society, such as the importance and necessity of hierarchies. If socialism is "a society in which the means of production, distribution and exchange are owned by the community as a whole, rather than private individuals" (who want those evil profits!), how would that work? Who would make the decisions? How can decisions be made unless there's a hierarchy/chain of command? Again, in practice, someone needs to take the reins.

The community trying to own/run those things as a community (whether represented by a 'proletarian vanguard' or not) is just a Marxist fantasy. We are not all equal, and we are all not equally capable of making decisions. There are naturally occurring dynamics and equilibria that can develop in a society when it comes to things like leadership, infrastructure, resources, property, personal/professional achievement and ambition, business, production etc. The history of Marxism illustrates the catastrophic consequences of interfering with these dynamics.

Marxism and the Anti-Capitalism narrative

Should we trust the cult's opinion of capitalism? If you asked one person for an unbiased opinion of another person – whom you know they hate – could you trust that opinion? No, you would have to take their attitude towards them (aka bias) into consideration, right? Would you trust an ideology which has been openly hostile towards capitalism since its birth when it comes to analysis of the capitalist system?

In other words, if we have this global Marxist cult – with millions of brainwashed anti-capitalist mouthpieces all over the world in our respective countries – is our environment now not saturated with Marxian anti-capitalistic opinions?

Here's an ironic aspect of the ideology's presence in today's societies, particularly the relatively prosperous western countries: these societies all contain significant amounts of these brainwashed cult members who (in general) say they hate the idea of profits, private property, big business, and financial inequality etc. Yet the ability to make profits or have private ownership of businesses/property, or the ability to have large industry and businesses, are what ensures a successful economy and country. They are key aspects of economics that allows civilisation to run. (Even the existence of (evil!) economic inequality is part and parcel of a healthy economy since it's reflective of the fact that people just aren't equal by nature).

It's ironic because the lives/pleasures/freedoms that these cult members enjoy during their time in prosperous countries (western or otherwise), including the freedom of speech (and therefore to criticise), only exist because the ideology has not completely contaminated that country.

So, they are constantly promoting an ideology that would ruin their lives/pleasures/freedoms, and that of their loved ones, friends etc. Of course, they are totally unaware of what they are doing. It's contradictory, because the anti-capitalism brainwashing makes people in capitalistic countries have anti-capitalistic attitudes while simultaneously being unconsciously happy to live in a capitalistic system (and all the benefits that this provides them!). It's an ungrateful, disrespectful, short-sighted attitude.

It's a very amusing element of Marxist brainwashing when we see defiant cult members trying to 'go it alone' and be 'separate from the system' in various demonstrations, often promoting socialism. It's extremely naive, detached from reality. (During the BLM-inspired unrest in Portland during 2021, after cult members amusingly attempted to set up their little 'independent' Marxist community, I believe I saw media coverage of them trying to grow vegetables to sustain themselves, in an urban area with very little soil. There's nothing like having to do the work yourself to appreciate/respect the work that goes into producing something).

Zooming out to a society-wide perspective, on a more serious note, these anti-capitalistic attitudes must surely be having an impact on a country's affairs. One can only speculate as to how much these bizarre and contradictory attitudes affect a country's level of prosperity and overall performance economically. Though this is impossible to quantify, to me it's another reason why the ideology needs to be cut-out of society—it will help a country to achieve higher levels of prosperity.

Should we 'replace' Capitalism?

If capitalism is considered one of the cornerstones of Western civilisation, and socialism has never had any success as an economic system (more on this later), is it wise to substitute the former for the latter? Would there be any calls to replace the capitalist system with anything else if it were not for the ideology? We must keep in mind, that Marxism has been trying to convince us since the beginning that capitalism is the problem; and we have been exposed to incrementally intensifying propaganda to this end.

This is in addition to the fact that the cult/ideology has been trying to sabotage the system from without and within during all that period, via: the cult's manipulation of the trade union movement; the infiltration of big business; the progressive income tax/punishment of wealth; the attempts to steal profits from industries via the carbon tax; the encouragement and expansion of the welfare state (which bleeds a country economically); the funnelling of funds in to the money-wasting Marxist NGO/non-profit complex; sending foreign aid for humanitarian reasons; and the cult's facilitation of mass immigration etc.

Mark and Engels believed that capitalism had the seeds to its own destruction contained within it, and when any negative situations have arisen in that system since the cult arrived on the scene (crises, depressions, crashes, financial bailouts etc.), these are viewed as 'evidence' that the predictions were correct; making Marx and his disciples seem like prophets (besides, as others have pointed out, those types of events may have been actually manufactured, and not necessarily par for the course in a capitalistic system).

Notice how in general, as a movement, they aren't interested in attempting to resolve any perceived issues within capitalism; they merely insist that it must be destroyed, replaced, or transformed severely. Isn't that odd? Is it more intelligent/efficient to completely destroy and replace a whole system (that society is currently built around) than it is to just repair/modify it? I don't think so. The cult/ideology doesn't want to build, improve or repair; just destroy.

"It will work this time…"

Here's an important recurring theme: there will always be a new wave of indoctrinated cult members who think they will be the ones to make it work. They're the special ones who can take the flawed theories of socialism and somehow create prosperity. Socialism can't be 'fixed' or modified, so that it works. Again, the principles of Marxism themselves are flawed, and it doesn't matter what variant is tried, it will result in failure. Where the newest generation of Marxists are concerned, the level of intelligence (for the cult's standards), experience, or talent they possess is irrelevant. To use a disgusting analogy – it doesn't matter how good a cook you are and how many delicious deserts you've made – if the ingredients you use are literally dirty rotten bags of shit, then the whole cake is going to stink.

Putting Socialism in the trash

We need to put socialism in the trash, repeatedly, as this is crucial for stopping the Marxist infection from proliferating itself further. This is crucial, and one of my highest recommendations.

Socialism—and the quasi-utopian society it will eventually lead to (according to cult members)—is the ever-appealing carrot that is dangled in front of the masses (particularly potential cult members). It promises a better society, a better way of life, and more prosperity for 'the people' etc. Socialism is the carrot that acts as a wedge that is used to open a society up (in any given country) to this 'revolution' ideology. Once this wedge is in place, and people generally think that Marxism/socialism is benign, that then opens the gap wider for allowing total Marxism in (and all that entails). It's the Trojan Horse principle in action. This especially applies to the young and impressionable. They're constantly being targeted by the cult, being told socialism is cool, particularly through the Universities.

For these reasons, we must target/destroy socialism as a concept and put it in the trash where it belongs. This massively reduces the marketability – and therefore the potency – of Marxism as an ideology overall, by diminishing its perceived benefits.

Marxism is all about fakery and deception, and socialism – being presented as some sort of superior alternative to capitalism – is a bad joke you've heard a million times. The cult/ideology attacks capitalism because they know that it gives western countries a certain degree of strength, stability, quality of life etc., in addition to a sense of separation from non-western countries. Since the ideology wants to destroy then rebuild civilisation in its image, capitalism becomes one of the main pillars that must be destroyed first. Only an idiot who's detached from reality would suggest that a bunch of prolifically failing theories – that have done nothing but cause hardship, instability, chaos, and death – should replace an entire system at the backbone of civilisation!

A more ethical system than Capitalism?

The things that Marxists accuses capitalism of being – oppressive, enslaving, violent, inefficient, authoritarian, inhumane etc. – are even more pronounced in a socialist system. Anything bad that capitalism does, socialism does it worse. As an example, the cult/ideology in general (varying interpretations/strains aside) tries to convince us that capitalism is an inherently oppressive system; insinuating that socialism is not. Three words for you: Pot. Kettle. Black. More virtue-signalling, double-standards and propaganda.

Who, in a civilised, stable, western country nowadays, can really state that they are (or have been) genuinely, horrifically oppressed due to living under a capitalist system? Conversely, how many have told us their stories of genuine oppression while living in a country with the cult at the helm? capitalism allows for some freedom to make money, own property etc. These freedoms don't exist in a socialist system; in theory, there would be collective ownership of the land, resources, means of production by the people etc., but in practice it never works out that way.

Of course, the cult will continuously try to sidestep this criticism by claiming that the real socialism or communism has never been tried or existed, and then we get stuck in that same cycle again where they can continuously promote their alternative system (the "Theory v Reality" problem again). Whatever issues arise in a capitalistic system, the cult/ideology will continuously draw attention to them in order to promote the Marxist alternative. Perhaps these issues would be experienced regardless of what system we use. The difference is that in a capitalist system, we have much more freedom to avoid the pitfalls.

"We need Socialism!"

Cult members insinuate that we need to hang on to Marxist thought because of the perceived flaws and evils of capitalism. Of course, if enough people agree with this, and Marxist thought isn't being viewed as toxic, then it will obviously not be removed from society. This, in turn, leads to all the other issues described in this book.

In addition, some of the problems that are perceived to be the result of capitalism are actually due to the fact we live in a highly controlled, internationalist, globalised world (which is inherently antagonistic to prosperity on a national level). A major step in changing this situation would be by removing Marxism from our societies as much as possible.

We don't need any form of Marxism to resolve any issues within a nation! Any issues therein that are associated with the capitalist system could be resolved by having patriotic, sovereign, nationalist governments in place. There would be no need to let Marxism back in the door.

This is why we must focus on the ideological makeup of a nation—it's more important than economics. If you have an internationalist, pro-Globalism government in your country, you will always have persistent issues (economic or otherwise). Keeping in mind, that economics don't matter if the country is tearing itself apart due to the other effects of the cult/ideology mentioned elsewhere (Ireland, for example, is sinking as a nation due to mass immigration; itself due to EU membership. Many would cite economic reasons for staying in the EU, which is poor prioritisation in this case). Essentially, the benefits of the ideology are nil, but the damage it causes is catastrophic. Therefore, it should be given no quarter.

Socialism will destroy your country economically

Is it not obvious that an ideology that promotes hatred for profits, private ownership of businesses and private properties (and the means of production etc.), is going to wreck an economy? Of course, we should judge the merits of socialism based on its effects in the real world, not on any theoretical or hypothetical applications of it. Therefore, the impact of socialism (past or present) is overwhelmingly negative.

Cult members will obviously try to either obscure this from us, by suppressing any emphasis on that fact; or they will, predictably, emphasise the apparent benefits. An example of this is when Marxist voices highlight the existence of 'successful' socialist countries.

The American 'progressive' politician Bernie Sanders famously made some vacuous claims about the success of socialism, particularly in Scandinavian countries: "When I talk about democratic socialist, I'm not looking at Venezuela. I'm not looking at Cuba. I'm looking at countries like Denmark and Sweden",[9] citing their welfare state policies etc. We can see how that's worked for them. Sanders is an avid cult member who has frequented Moscow, and is known for having anti-American views on various issues, including U.S. foreign policy, gun control etc.

Implementing socialism to a country's economy only results in its destruction. The only way it can stay afloat, is if they are either living off the benefits of wealth accumulated when they were not being socialist, or if they receive financial assistance from the outside. The former applies to Sweden, which generated its wealth when it was capitalistic, before cult members started to direct its affairs. Essentially, it was only successful as a country temporarily due to the previous progress it made. They started to lean towards socialism after WW2. It could only function because of GDP gains they made when they had a more capitalistic free market approach.

The latter applies to many countries in the history of Marxism, who would then receive aid from other countries (including capitalist ones (!). Lenin's Russia received foreign aid, and he was eventually forced to start allowing limited private enterprise. This allowed the industrial machinery to function normally again.[10] [11]

Castro's Cuba needed financial sponsorship from the Soviet Union to stay afloat (not surprising really, as I believe, at one point, the psychotic Che Guevera (1928–1967) was in charge of economics. A great choice since he studied medicine at university).[12]

---

[9] MSNBC, "Hillary Clinton—Bernie Sanders Town Hall Part 1 | MSNBC", 19 February 2016. https://www.YouTube.com/watch?v=w1cuTmJh8xM

[10] "Revelations from the Russian Archives". https://www.loc.gov/exhibits/archives/sovi.html

[11] https://www.britannica.com/money/New-Economic-Policy-Soviet-history

[12] Anderson, J. "Soviet aid to Cuba: $11 million a day", 18 June 1983. https://www.upi.com/Archives/1983/06/18/Soviet-aid-to-Cuba-11-million-a-day/2328424756800/

An example of a highly contaminated country lightening-up their attitude towards economics is China. In the period from 1979, perhaps motivated by the economic powerhouse of the relatively non-Marxist (then British colony) of Hong Kong, the Chinese Communist Party decided to allow the adoption of capitalistic principles, allowing China to modernise and become what it is today.[13]

In 1989, the (soon-to-be-ex) Soviet Republic of Estonia helped to start the snowball effect that caused the U.S.S.R. to collapse. The Estonians realised that the development of their economy was limited due its membership of the 'union'. There were many reasons why member countries wanted to be released from the grip of Moscow during the Soviet era; economic freedom and prosperity was one of them.[14]

Other Soviet era countries, while not being part of the U.S.S.R. as member state Soviet republics, were considered satellite states. These included Poland, East Germany, Romania, Hungary, Bulgaria, Albania and Czechoslovakia. They all went through severe adaptation periods post-communism, with some taking decades to recover from the effects of centralisation.

Socialism wrecked Latin America. From earlier examples such as the Argentina of Juan Peron in the 1940s and 1950s, to Cuba, Chile, Columbia, and numerous others.

A more recent high-profile example is the Venezuela of Hugo Sanchez et al, even with all the oil they have. India, post-independence from Britain, decided to go down the socialist road, with disastrous results. Even Britain itself–under the leadership of cult member Clement Atlee - decided on some experimentation after WW2, which led to economic ruination.

Socialism is theft

As the acquisition of 'unjustifiable' wealth – via profits – by private individuals and business owners is immoral according to Marxist dogma, the gains of such businesses must be confiscated, ostensibly for the 'greater good'. This is why the cult/ideology peddles the idea that profits are evil. It's one of the many things they get wrong—profits are not evil; they allow

---

[13] Coase and Wang, "How China Became Capitalist", January/February 2013. https://www.cato.org/policy-report/january/february-2013/how-china-became-capitalist

[14] The Collapse of The Soviet Union - A Documentary Film (2006).

https://www.YouTube.com/watch?v=OYD6ouVHXbo

a country's economy to function.

This mentality encourages destruction, violence, and theft of private property in the name of 'justice' and 'equality'. It also allows those who don't have wealth to vent their emotions on those who do; their personal insecurities manifest in murderous sentiment and action. The history of the cult illustrates what this looks like when put in to practice—the imprisonment and/or murder of anyone who isn't part of the poor/proletariat class. This often goes together with the elimination of the 'intelligentsia', who may become dissenters or political opponents if not suppressed/eliminated.

Here are planks one to five of the Communist Manifesto: Abolition of private property and the application of all rents of land to public purposes; A heavy progressive or graduated income tax; Abolition of all rights of inheritance; Confiscation of the property of all emigrants and rebels; Centralization of credit in the hands of the state, by means of a national bank with State capital and an exclusive monopoly.[15]

Planks one to four—confiscation of property, taxation, and "abolition of all rights of inheritance"—are all forms of theft. Plank five is centralised financial control/dominance in the name of "the people". While it's not stealing directly, it does help to prevent the acquisition of wealth by those not allied to the government (which may be Marxist; so basically any wealth or power that does not belong to the cult must not be allowed to gather). A contemporary example of Marxian theft, hidden in plain sight, is the carbon tax, via the climate change movement.

DiLorenzo's problems with socialism

> "To be a modern day advocate of socialism is to completely ignore all sound economic logic, more than a century of history, and the words of honest socialist intellectuals like Heilbroner who were finally forced to confront reality after ignoring it for most of their adult lives"[16]
>
> Thomas DiLorenzo author and Professor of Economics,
> *The Problem With Socialism* (2016)

Let's go into more detail as to why socialism is destructive. My favourite analyst in this area is Thomas DiLorenzo. DiLorenzo is an author and professor of economics at *Loyola University Maryland*, in Baltimore, Maryland, USA. He is also considered to be of the Austrian School discipline of economics (i.e. "laissez-faire" or minimal government

---

[15] Marx, Engels. *The Communist Manifesto* (1848). P. 26.

[16] Di. Lorenzo, T., *The Problem with Socialism* (2016), P. 28.

intervention).[17] His presentations at the *Mises Institute* in Alabama are easily found online. His written works have covered a variety of topics, but the most relevant to this book include *The Problem With Socialism* and *How Capitalism saved American* (2004). An article he wrote entitled "Why Socialism Causes Pollution" is also relevant.

I would highly recommend The Problem with Socialism for those want a comprehensive summary of the impact of the ideology economically in the real world. The book also highlights the negative impacts of socialism in various other ways, including politically, socially, environmentally etc.

It's very useful for our purposes to list the main points that Lorenzo outlines in his work. I will, where applicable, tie them in to the 'bigger picture' of course (as this is not just about economics or socialism). What we are doing in this sub-section is highlighting socialism as a product of the ideology— a physical manifestation of it as applied to government, economics, infrastructure, utilities, education, health etc.

DiLorenzo once mentioned that, in the earlier part of the 20th century, socialism was generally defined as the government ownership of the means of production (on behalf of 'the people'), but the definition would later include the welfare state (and its institutions) and the progressive income tax. This was highlighted by the work of Economist Friedrich von Hayek (1899–1992) in the *Road to Serfdom* (1944).[18]

Since Marxism is all about control through the enforcement of (artificial) egalitarianism, these are just various methods to achieve this objective. The three central problems of socialism. Though he didn't originate these concepts, DiLorenzo's work refers to the three main problems with having a socialist system, and why it inevitably results in failure to one degree or another, regardless of how it's implemented:

The Incentive Problem

In an egalitarian socialist system, there is no incentive to be ambitious, succeed, or prosper fiscally or otherwise. If the state denies the general public the freedom to create/produce via their own methods, this causes a serious problem. Without the incentive of being able to gain wealth, through the exploits of our own labour (or even to earn a living at all!), why should anyone bother to excel in entrepreneurial endeavours and business etc.? Success is actually punished in a socialist system, so there's no

---

[17] https://en.wikipedia.org/wiki/Thomas_DiLorenzo

[18] Hayek, F., *The Road to Serfdom* (1944).

incentive to succeed.

The cult will retort that, in a more socialist society, people wouldn't be so 'selfish' and would do those things out of the goodness of their own hearts, for the benefit of their comrades, for free (rolls eyes. Typical virtue-signalling and patronising). Whatever; even if that was practical/possible, that's just not the reality of what motivates people. Their insistence that making profits for personal (private) benefit is somehow immoral (according to Marxist dogma) makes them blind to this fact.

The incentive problem is part of the explanation why all the various Marxist cult regimes in history had to use coercion (including intimidation, violence, murder etc.) to force people to work and get other things done; things which a person wouldn't want to do in those situations if they were not forced. An example of that is the slave labour on the collectivist farms of the Soviet Union, China, Cambodia, North Korea, Albania etc.

The Knowledge Problem

When a centralised state (with a bunch of Marxist cult members at the helm), starts to centralise power on behalf of 'the people', it leads to another problem. The individuals involved with this centralised state (and all their individual talents) cannot replace the multitude of skills, talents, knowledge, professions etc. that the masses provide (in a capitalist system), in the form of business owners, entrepreneurs, service providers, and the multitude of specialists across all sectors. This is a concept that Friedrich Von Hayek highlighted in his 1945 article "The Use of Knowledge in Society".[19]

DiLorenzo expands on this, highlighting that even something as simple as the production of a slice of pizza (itself composed of many ingredients) involves several industries and processes, each involving specialised skills, technology, and equipment. Obviously, many individuals and companies are involved in that whole process (agriculture, logistics, marketing etc.), who interact with each other in order to allow you to have your slice of pizza. "The lesson here is that what makes the economic world – indeed, human civilisation itself as we know it – possible is the international division of labor and knowledge in which we all specialize in something in the marketplace, earn money doing it, and use that money to buy things from other "specialists".[20]

---

[19] Hayek, F., "The Use of Knowledge in Society, September 1945.
https://www.cato.org/sites/cato.org/files/articles/hayek-use-knowledge-society.pdf

[20] Di. Lorenzo, T., *The Problem with Socialism* (2016), P. 24.

He goes on to say that the whole process occurs spontaneously without the need of any government planning. The key word there being "spontaneously", meaning this is all naturally occurring within society, and that it functions regardless.

This ties into that tendency the ideology has to interfere with (and potentially ruin) things that are working perfectly fine (whether that be infrastructure, economics, nature, social interactions etc.)! Any instances where cult members gain power inevitably results in increasing levels of destructive interference. Of course, their usual built-in arrogance (combined with the tunnel-vision indoctrination), reinforces their belief that they already have everything it takes to run things, including the knowledge, which is absolute nonsense!

The Calculation Problem

The "Calculation Problem" involves the fact that private property and market prices need to exist in order to have rational, efficient economic calculation. In a socialist system, since the government owns all the resources (and land), there would be no trade, and no prices for resources, capital goods etc. This in turn means there is no way to calculate prices for goods and services. Financial analysts (in a market economy) can use market prices to determine if a project/initiative is financially reasonable or profitable, for example. In short, having a socialist system (that doesn't include private property and market prices etc.) removes the foundational elements from an economy, leading to chaos.

The work of Economist Ludwig von Mises (1881–1973) highlighted this issue in *Socialism: An Economic and Sociological Analysis* (1922). He noted the relationships between the players in a free-market economy— entrepreneurs, promoters, speculators (and the consumers), and the fact that they have personal stakes in their investments, who allocate the capital in a market economy.

As DiLorenzo points out: "Their indispensable tool is market prices, which guide them to invest in a rational, profitable way, meeting consumer demand". He added that under socialism "where government owns all the means of production "capital" markets are non-existent, and resources are allocated by bureaucrats to meet "plans" that might have no basis in economic reality.".

Also, consumer demand was a factor here: "In a capitalist economy, entrepreneurs have to meet consumer demand or go bankrupt...This incentive, however, is totally absent from a socialist economy".[21]

Again, like the "knowledge problem" (if we zoom-out for a moment), this is a case of the ideology interfering with the organic, functioning processes that take place within society. As DiLorenzo once said: "if the prices are arbitrarily dictated by government, and they don't reflect scarcity or supply and demand in general, then you're just doing everything random. It's like trying to drive around a strange city without street signs and find where you're going. It's an impossibility".[22] (Google maps or GPS tech aside).

The "public choice" problem

Another problem linked to the state's control of society (with the cult at the helm), is the lack of power held by the general public. Friedrich Von Hayek highlighted this problem. Since all the freedom to be successful or to acquire power and wealth as an individual is forbidden, then the only avenue open to someone seeking those things is to be become part of the cult's state apparatus. You can't decide to gather wealth or to excel as an entrepreneur, business owner or businessman/woman etc. since those are not options.

This is evident when looking at all those willing commissars, activists, operatives, organisers, soldiers, and politicians who were busy working for the system throughout the cult's history. For a modern example, we can look at North Koreans. Look at the number of pathetic servants to the regime there, many of whom might have had, at one point of their lives, dreams to be something else.

Destructionism

This is a fundamental aspect of socialism highlighted by Ludwig Von Mises in *Socialism: an Economic and Sociological Analysis* (1922): "In fact, Socialism is not in the least what it pretends to be. It is not the pioneer of a better and finer world, but the spoiler of what thousands of years of civilisation have created. It does not build; it destroys. For destruction is the essence of it. It produces nothing, it only consumes what the social order based on private ownership in the means of production has created".[23] In other words, socialism is not a generator of wealth and prosperity, but its destroyer; a parasite even. The inevitable will result for any country that structures its economy around socialist policies, includes the emptying of

---

[21] Ibid. P. 27.

[22] Misesmedia, "Ten Things You Should Know About Socialism | Thomas J. DiLorenzo 20 July 2018. https://www.YouTube.com/watch?v=hTvQBhYoJms

[23] Von Mises, L. *Socialism* (1922), P. 458.

the coffers and dwindling GDP figures.

Then comes the attempts to put various, temporary financial band-aids over the issues—more taxes, printing more money etc., which lead to even more instability and problems. It's a recurring theme in the history of socialism that once they start to crash, they try to print themselves out of trouble, leading to catastrophic levels of inflation, and rising costs of living etc. This chaotic situation is compounded by the tendency of socialist government/policies to give away things for 'free' (e.g. welfare, services, foreign aid, housing etc.), in order to appease the general public's building frustrations.

The Anti-Capitalism mentality

Getting away from economics briefly and back to the indoctrination issue, DiLorenzo utilised a good point about anti-capitalist sentiment, and envy. He highlights Ludwig von Mises's 1956 book *The Anti-Capitalist Mentality* here. Mises attributed this mentality to several things, including the fact that some people are wealthier and more successful in society, and that this creates envy and hatred in those who are not.

In his book, Mises also made the point that, in a free-market economy where a person's own level of success is (in theory) not limited, they are responsible for their own success or failure. The less successful may then express hatred for the capitalist system, making it an easy scapegoat for them. This mentality also ties-in with the 'oppressed/victim' aspect of the ideology—it's much easier to blame someone/something else for your failures than accept responsibility for it yourself.

Clearly, this is a factor in today's world. All you have to do is spend five seconds listening to the venomous vitriol coming out of the mouths of cult members towards anyone they regard as 'bourgeois' (unless, of course, that bourgeois type is doing some Marxist virtue-signalling, champagne socialist-style. Then they are forgiven! Indeed, some of these types may feel guilt for being wealthy; a sentiment which the ideology/cult helps to manifest). Of course, this all ties-in with the 'free stuff' mentality in adherents of socialism—it's a sense of entitlement that compliments the aforementioned envy quite well. People should get free things as a form of 'revenge' against the bourgeoisie, this logic says.

On this scapegoating, Mises wrote "...it is quite another thing under capitalism. Here everybody's station in life depends on his own doing... The sway of the principle, "to each according to his accomplishments", does not allow of any excuse for personal shortcomings".[24] Since this 'free stuff' mentality exists, it then gives politicians an opportunity for psychological manipulation by offering people things like free healthcare, free education etc.

DiLorenzo makes a great point on this scapegoating (underlined for emphasis): "Perhaps the most popular scapegoats of all are "greedy capitalists" who are often accused of doing well financially by some nefarious, unscrupulous, or illegal means. There are of course people like this, but it is not a general characteristic of markets. There are sinners in all walks of life, not just the business world; and in a market economy (as opposed to a socialist, government-monopoly economy, where bribes are often a fact of life), no one wants to do business with dishonest people, so the market penalizes the cheaters, and products with bad reputations don't get purchased".[25]

This bitchy, begrudging anti-capitalist mentality is a loser's opinion, and can be traced back to Karl Marx himself. A bitter, miserable, relatively spoilt and useless man who couldn't be successful, so insisted the world needed to change and not he.

Things can't be 'free'

Marxist voices often push this idea of free stuff, but can things actually be 'free'? Since when does anything that is worth anything cost nothing? (don't be a smart-ass and say "love" or "peace" etc.:). The truth is that nothing (that costs something) can be given away for free without consequences for the economy. The costs are felt somewhere.

On the subject of government-run enterprises versus privately-run enterprises, DiLorenzo wrote: "We are told that when the government provides a service it is free, but of course nothing is free, because someone has to pay all the government employees, their overheads, and everything else that government does, buys, or appropriates. That "someone" is of course the taxpayers. Whenever socialist-minded politicians speak of "free" services, what they really mean is that the service will be hidden in taxes".[26]

This also applies to government-run healthcare and education systems etc.: everything and everyone involved in those systems either costs money or receives a wage/payment. The utilities (e.g. electricity, water), building

---

[24] Von Mises, L. *The Anti-Capitalist Mentality* (1956), P.11-12.

[25] Ibid. P. 39.

[26] Ibid. P. 46.

maintenance, equipment, raw materials, and resources etc.

The result of all this is added pressure on these 'free' services, since they are free, and that's just the domestic population—let's keep in mind that the cult is a fanatical proponent of mass immigration, which tends to add even more. The result is severe delays and reduction in availability of services for the normally resident population.[27]

Things being "free" and being spoilt go together

Though cult members come in all shapes and sizes, socialism is certainly very popular with the younger generations of today. Perhaps this 'free stuff' mentality is linked-in with the fact that Marxism and being spoilt often goes hand-in-glove. In fact, the ideology is keen to encourage things such as superficiality, selfishness, ego, and materialism in the youth of today—things which encourage the spoilt brat mentality.

There's a correlation here between this problem and the sense of entitlement which leads people to believe that we can have things for 'free' (i.e. when someone else is paying for them). Not all individuals in the younger generations are spoilt or indoctrinated of course, but nonetheless—these combined reasons must be a factor in why the more spoilt ones among them are suckers for socialism. Is it because they think material things just fall from the sky?

Indeed, though the ideology has a history of affecting all types of people, it has been long recognised that those from more 'privileged' backgrounds are often the most avid proponents of socialism. There's a correlation between this and the indoctrination of young, privileged kids today—their own ignorant perception of where physical, material things come leaves them with a mind that thinks that things (services etc.) can be given away for free.

In addition to all of that, having a spoilt personality often leads a person to lacking appreciation and respect for how things are produced and organised in society. Therefore, they are happy to insist that the resources/wealth or products/services others produce (through their own toil) should be given away for nothing, with no reward. In short, learning how to do things/earn things for oneself can instil some humility—a virtue sorely missing in cult members in general by default.

Another factor is the anti-capitalistic indoctrination mentioned earlier which comes from the ideology. We can add this on top of all the previous factors where indoctrinated young people are concerned: they will have so

---

[27] Ibid. P. 47.

much stupid animosity towards capitalism, money, wealth, private property etc., that they will be happy to see any/all those things given away for free, regardless who owns them; particularly if it will (apparently) lead to 'equality' and a 'better' (Marxist) world. It's a utopian giveaway! They view this process as being fair and righteous, humanitarian even; especially if it somehow benefits the 'oppressed'.

Welfare harming the proletarians

Speaking of 'free' stuff, in The Problem with Socialism DiLorenzo states that welfare payments actually harm the poor, rather than benefits them. Before we continue—I totally understand that there are a variety of people in the world who can't or won't work for a variety of reasons, and who may be receiving financial support from the state. There is no need for anyone to take this personally, and (wittingly or unwittingly) using that energy to then justify socialism (!).

The point to remember here is that in a healthier, more prosperous, balanced society, individuals would be financially self-sufficient and prosperous if they had the choice. Socialism (quite counter-intuitively to some perhaps) doesn't benefit 'the people'; it denies them prosperity.

One of the main points put forward by this book is that society would be greatly improved if Marxism was greatly suppressed (while always aiming to eradicate it completely). This would have a positive impact in many areas, including the levels of enthusiasm, productivity, ambition, opportunity, and personal confidence etc. This, in turn, would have a multitude of positive knock-on effects. In other words, there would be no need for the welfare state as it exists today in a healthier Marxism-free society!

On a side note, we had the Covid payments during the Covaids scamdemic. So the worldwide Marxist cult is pivotal in causing the Covid deception in the first place (Communist China, our contaminated governments, open borders, cult members in the mainstream media across the world etc.), then starts doing things like: denying people the right to work and earn money by denying them travel to/from work unless they are 'essential' workers; denying them the right to open their businesses, leading to their bankruptcy; forcing them to accept state payments to survive via the Covid payment; calling those who resist government pressure to get vaccines "conspiracy theorists"; saying that any protests/riots about all this are fuelled by "misguided far-right" thinking individuals etc. Obviously, denying people the right to go to work or run their own business, and encouraging/forcing them to take Covid payments, are all attacks on capitalism and on an individual's financial independence from the state.

Really though, this is just another example of the damaging effects of the ideology on the human psyche, including the reduction of personal sovereignty. In fact, if we accept that socialism is just the implementation of destructive Marxian revolutionary principles to the fabric of society, it's not only destructive for the individuals within it but destructive for the "evil" capitalistic system itself.

Though this following point from DiLorenzo is focusing on the impact of the welfare state on a capitalistic society, it also reinforces the points I made above—that the ideology is increasing its power and control while simultaneously attacking its old foe capitalism: "The welfare state has done an excellent job of crippling an important cornerstone of an enterprising, free market, capitalist society: the incentive to work. Instead, it has created a dependent class that it serves (with programs), and from whom it benefits (justifying government programs and jobs)".[28]

The welfare state and the destruction of the family

DiLorenzo raises a very important point that links the welfare state with other sub-agendas coming from the ideology. Essentially, the introduction of welfare payments for single-parent families has helped the cult's attack on the traditional nuclear family unit (though DiLorenzo doesn't say that was necessarily the intended goal, but rather a consequence): "Between 1960 and 2000, out-of-wedlock births increased by more than 400 percent, and a big driver of that, especially in black communities, was that single parenthood brings government benefits. In 1950, before the "war on poverty", about 88 percent of white families and 77 percent of black families in the United States consisted of husband-and-wife households.

By 1980 the proportion of black families with husband-and-wife households had declined to 59 percent; among white families it was 85 percent. And the numbers continue to get worse. In 1960, 73 percent of kids lived in a traditional two-parent family. In 2013, the number was 46 percent".[29]

He also wrote that welfare payments can essentially replace the income coming from a husband/partner with a job. He also raises the issue of stigma and its effect on the whole situation—that in addition to the absence of the stigma of receiving welfare payments from the state (as opposed to working), the stigma of having children out of wedlock ('illegitimacy') is also now gone. These are all Marxian attacks on what is traditional via

---

[28] Ibid. P. 47.

[29] Ibid. P. 91.

socialism—the benefit system encourages the breakdown of society through the breakdown of the traditional family unit.

DiLorenzo added the points that children coming from single-parent families are more likely to have a variety of issues, including "behavioural or emotional problems", having children out of wedlock themselves, getting involved in crime etc. Dependency on welfare "has a"domino effect" that not only harms society but also destroys people's lives".[30] The ideology destroys.

The relationship between mother-only families and the ideology

In terms of indoctrination and the spread of the ideology, the single-parent welfare payments are also destructive in other more insidious ways. They encourage children to be born out of wedlock, and the main result overall is kids are being raised with the woman as the primary parent (most single-parent families are of this type). This situation also helps to feminise society overall, as women are obviously unable to provide the male dynamic that a man can provide.

This is especially significant in societies that are riddled with the ideology since males are generally better suited to protecting their children from the effects of Marxist indoctrination. This is related to the often-highlighted 'attack on masculinity'. The more a society lacks in masculinity, the more susceptible those in it are prone to Marxist indoctrination (since it relies heavily on emotional manipulation, via the oppressor v oppressed principle). I raise this point because if it's true, then this single-parent phenomenon is created by the ideology, supported by it, and it ultimately helps to create a society that is pro-Marxism in the long run. Its short-term initiatives feed its long-term goals.

To illustrate this point, we can see how the single-female-parent-family issue dovetails nicely with other Marxist sub-agendas such as the 'women's liberation' movement, and the things that it promotes including: female promiscuity, non-monogamous relationships, sex out of wedlock, the attack on the institution of marriage, the attack on masculinity etc.

Again, this is not an attack on individuals! Obviously, there are many fantastic single mothers out there doing a great job with their kid(s). It's true that not all single-parent families (male or female) are the same, or that those involved have the same personalities/intentions, or that every situation has the same impact on the development of children (or, therefore, that every situation has the same impact on society etc.). These things need

---

[30] Ibid. P.92.

not be stated. However, single-parent families are not ideal for anyone involved or society, and the ideology benefits greatly from this in several ways.

Conversely, what is more ideal to create strong, healthy, happy, prosperous societies, is the emphasis on more traditional values including the nuclear family unit. The fact that such things give a society strength and stability is precisely the reason why the ideology seeks to destroy them. (We examine the traditional family unit later).

Government-run businesses v privately run businesses

On the issue of government-run v privately-run enterprises, DiLorenzo explains how there is no negative consequences or 'punishments' for government businesses if they are making bad financial decisions (unlike with private companies). They can just request more funding to pay their staff more, dip into the tax revenue coffers etc. The result of this is that government-run enterprises are generally far inferior to privately-run enterprises. Basically, there is no incentive (or "pressure") for government-run enterprises to perform well. Privately-run enterprises who don't do a good job (of providing products or services to consumers), will not make profits and will go under. This doesn't apply to government-run enterprises, who will receive budgets regardless of how they perform(!). In fact, if they blow money, they will often receive more: "No such mechanism exists in government enterprises, for there are no profit-and-loss statements, in an accounting sense, there are only budgets". Indeed.[31]

Having a socialist healthcare system

DiLorenzo points out that the socialist healthcare systems in places like the U.K. (the *National Health Service*), and Canada (*Medicare*), are inferior to other types of systems, because they are nationalised and under the control of the government (note: we can include the Irish *Health Service Executive* (HSE) too). They typically have: a lower quality of service, longer waiting times in general (to see specialists, to get life-saving ops), lower life expectancy, less specialist medical equipment available, higher mortality rates, "brain drain" (skilled employees going abroad for better employment opportunities). Some might retort "sure, it's not perfect, but it's free, right?". In this context, surely having something good is better than having something "free".

"Free" = rationing

Having a 'free' service, though it sounds nice, humane, and appealing at

---

[31] Ibid. P. 94.

first glance (particularly to the patients/customers), inevitably leads to imbalances in the system, which in turn creates a cycle of knock-on effects; the end product of which is typically rationing (which is typical of the ideology). DiLorenzo explains that since the perception exists that the service is "free", it has a myriad of negative effects, and that "declaring anything to be a "free" good or service will cause an explosion of demand, which in turn will ratchet up the costs of providing the good or service". Other effects include the reckless wasting of time and resources etc.[32]

The next stage in the cycle, is the response of the (cult members in) government to the obvious rising expense of this "free" service: "To cover-up these costs, socialist governments typically impose price ceilings on everything from doctors' visits and salaries to hospital room rates and technology. A price ceiling is a government-imposed price that is below the existing price".[33]

This links to the imposition of artificial government-prices for things, that don't reflect the reality of the situation, including their actual value (mentioned earlier in the 'calculation problem).

DiLorenzo says that the effect of these imposed price ceilings is "to stimulate the demand for healthcare services even more", and since supply cannot catch up with the demand, it then leads to shortages "in everything from doctors to MRI machines"; in addition to the "brain-drain" factor— the exodus of skilled personnel abroad where they can receive better salaries for their work. And then comes the inevitable: "Governments always respond to the shortages that their policies created by imposing some kind of rationing.".

Lorenzo noted that elderly patients tend to feel the impact of this rationing the most. He outlines how the NHS denies older patients vital services such as cancer screening if they are above a certain age threshold (65). He adds: "some Commentators have charged the British National Health Service with practising "Euthanasia". Even if euthanasia was not the intent of the British Government, it has been the effect of healthcare socialism in that country".[34] A very interesting point. Considering the ideology's track-record when it comes to death, nothing should surprise us. It also endeavours to replace the older generations with younger generations who can be moulded more easily (to support/join the cult/ideology). In addition, the ideology/cult supports the mass immigration/'population replacement'

---

[32] Ibid. P. 95.

[33] Ibid. P. 96.

[34] Ibid. 101.

sub-agenda in western countries, which this practice (of neglecting the elderly) supports. This essentially accelerates the process, as younger generations of migrants are brought in to the country in question while older generations of locals are essentially allowed to die off.

Nationalised 'health' service and Covid

Another problem with having a government-controlled health system has manifested during the Covid fiasco. The British NHS, Irish HSE (and their counterparts in other countries) will obviously both follow government and 'expert' or 'specialist' instructions on how to deal with the Covid plandemic—no questions asked, no dissenting voices (not near the top of the leadership structures anyway). And many (if not all) of the staff directing and controlling these organisations are cult members themselves, having come through the Marxian education system. Organisations like this are an integral part of the control system, more than ready to inject millions of people in their respective countries, without pausing to ask if they should.

Socialist education systems

Obviously, control of the education systems is an important strategic objective for the cult, and it always has been (the first part of plank ten of the Communist Manifesto is "Free education for all children in public schools"). It allows the creation of generations of subservient, state-obeying drones who will be infected with the ideology. We can see this clearly nowadays with the 'teaching' of degenerate sex and sexuality 'education', in addition to the promotion of feminism, climate change, 'diversity' programming etc. They will try to stuff in as much crap as a child's vulnerable mind can handle, basically. In a socialistic government-controlled education system, DiLorenzo explained, public schools are financially dependent upon – and therefore controlled by – the state. The state can then dictate what they teach, and how they teach it. To put it another way—they don't have the ability to depart from the government plans and not teach Marxist crap.

In addition, DiLorenzo explains how these institutions have similar issues to other government-run enterprises or services: "A private school has to compete for students…(otherwise).. it loses money, and it could eventually go out of business. A government-run school enjoys a virtual monopoly, especially among the poor, who can't afford a private school; and as with all monopolies, the convenience of administrators and employees comes before the needs of the customers, because the customers will always be there. They have no choice".[35]

Government-run schools can actually get more money for doing a mediocre or even sub-standard job, because the claim of "we need more funding/staff" can always be made (unlike in private schools). DiLorenzo noted how increased spending doesn't necessarily improve education levels. So, he stated, they are essentially pumping up their costs, for not "making the grade" themselves!

On this issue, he writes: "One would be hard-pressed to find any private enterprise that had declining production, performance or sales, after massive infusions of capital. Only in monopolistic, socialistic enterprises like the public schools does one find the absurdity of paying more for the service and getting nothing in return".[36] He added that private schools need to "spend their money efficiently" because they are trying to make a profit; whereas public schools tend to spend more to justify budget increases.

The progressive income tax

> "The theory of the Communists may be summed up in the single sentence: Abolition of private property"[37]

> Marx and Engels, *The Communist Manifesto* (1848)

A Progressive Income Tax is listed in the Communist Manifesto (plank two), and is, amongst other things, a form of theft; in addition to being an attempt to enforce equality. Most people within this system are literally forced to pay taxes or there will be consequences for them, including imprisonment (or the threat thereof). DiLorenzo wrote that this is a "discriminatory income tax" that "penalises productivity by taxing higher incomes at progressively higher tax rates" because it's "their denial of the reality of human inequality". A fantastic point! It's quite incredible how this tax has existed in (most) of our societies for over a century now (in one form or another), with the majority unaware of its ideological origins. It's simply accepted as a normal part of life.[38]

Though we're told that this progressive income tax is fair and reasonable, it isn't. Again, the indoctrination convinces the masses otherwise, and that the higher earners (aka 'bourgeois oppressors') deserve to be penalised. As DiLorenzo explains: "The ideal of a "progressive" income tax is to create

---

[35] Ibid. 173, 174.

[36] Ibid. P. 175-176.

[37] Marx and Engels, *The Communist Manifesto* (1848). P. 22.

[38] DiLorenzo, T., *The Problem with Socialism*, P. 123.

greater "equality" by treating people unequally".[39] He adds that it is the exact opposite of "the fundamental principle of fairness in a society, which is equality under the law. A progressive income tax is a policy of inequality under the law". It's part of the destabilisation of capitalist societies, he explains, and that the exploitation of envy is a great way of doing that.

The progressive income tax is enforced based on the ever-present idea that the proletariat/working classes are being exploited by the bourgeoisie/wealthy class.[40] This tax also works against the principle of "human capital development" (that DiLorenzo mentions)—the idea that increased productivity in a capitalist economy is rewarded with higher wages because "employers will compete for their services".[41] This creates an incentive for people to develop their skill sets as employees etc.; in short, "Capitalism encourages upward mobility".[42] The progressive income tax actively works against this positive feature of capitalism, by penalising higher earners (ipso facto, it's an attack on capitalism).

A centralised banking system

> "Central banking is one of the major planks of the Communist Manifesto. We talk about America being a capitalistic country, but yet at the same time we have a central bank"[43]

> The late American film producer Aaron Russo
> on the Federal Reserve system, 2009

Is there such thing as a "commie bank", or it that an oxymoron? Though the central banking system may be viewed as capitalistic, it in fact originated from the ideology, which is something that's overlooked. Plank number five of the Communist Manifesto is "Centralization of credit in the hands of the state, by means of a national bank with state capital and an exclusive monopoly.". This means that when the *Federal Reserve* was established in 1913 (after the now infamous meeting on Jekyl Island by the banking tycoons in 1910), the fifth plank of the Communist Manifesto was achieved.

DiLorenzo wrote that there was a functioning economy in the U.S. up until

---

[39] Ibid. P. 124.

[40] Ibid. P. 124.

[41] Ibid. P. 124.

[42] Ibid. P. 125.

[43] TruthTube1111, "Alex Jones Interviews Aaron Russo (Full Length)", 8 June 2011. https://www.YouTube.com/watch?v=N3NA17CCboA

this point, with competitions between various banks: "The Fed, like all central banks, is essentially a socialistic central-planning agency that claims to "stabilize" and "fine tune" the economy. No such central planning agency existed for much of American history…There was some regulation of branch banking…but for the most part, the United States enjoyed a free-market capital system, with no army of central planners.".[44]

He also highlighted the erroneous perception that the Fed stabilises the economy, and that it actually created the various boom-and-bust cycles including the "2000 stock market bubble (and bust) and the housing bubble that exploded into the Great Recession of 2008.". Its policies during the 1920s "generated a stock market bubble followed by the famous crash of October 1929".[45] The existence (and power) of a central bank in a country leads to these types of issues.

Just like the other socialistic elements mentioned in this section (healthcare, education, land, and resource management etc.), the issues caused by them are due to the centralisation—a central control that creates restriction and instability within the system. There's a lack of freedom within this system for true prosperity to develop, resulting from free-market competition. Of course, this socialisation of banks is international, not just in the U.S.

As a closing point for this subject: note how the issues listed above, caused by these communistic centralised systems, are blamed on capitalism by cult members? How many times have you heard them blame financial crashes etc. on their old foe, as they cry for 'an alternative system'?

They exclaim so because they believe that capitalism has within it the seeds of its own destruction, blissfully unaware that since Marxism appeared on the scene in the 19th century, capitalism has rarely been allowed to function unmolested by it. Essentially, they see what they expect – and want – to see but are blind to everything else (including the truth of the matter). Due to the indoctrination, many can't see that capitalism has elevated so many from poverty in the modern era.

The destruction of the church and religion

> "Socialism is precisely the religion that must overwhelm Christianity"46

---

[44] Ibid. P. 162.

[45] Ibid. P. 163.

[46] *Selections from the Prison Notebooks* (1999), (written 1929–1935). https://abahlali.org/files/gramsci.pdf

Antonio Gramsci, Prison Notebooks, 1929–1935

"We Communists are like Judas. It is our bloody work to crucify Christ. But this sinful work is at the same time our calling: only through death on the cross does Christ become God, and this is necessary to be able to save the world. We Communists then take the sins of the world upon us, in order to be able thereby to save the world"47

Gyorgy Lukacs in Communist Hungary 1919

"Communism is that stage of historical development which makes all existing religions superfluous and supersedes them"48

Friedrich Engels, The Communist Question of Faith, 1847

"Religion is the sigh of the oppressed creature, the heart of the heartless world, and the soul of soulless conditions. It is the opium of the people"49

Karl Marx, "Critique of Hegel's Philosophy of Right", 1844

Marxism is as anti-Christian as it is anti-capitalist. Why is this? Yes, it's because Marxism wants to destroy western civilisation, and Christianity (like capitalism) has traditionally been regarded as one of its pillars. But are there other reasons? Indeed, the anti-religious aspect of the ideology was a feature right from the start.

Moses Kiessel Marx Mordechai Levi (aka Karl Marx) himself was a disturbing guy and a Satanist. He was undeniably, bitterly, and fanatically anti-God, and wrote several pieces expressing his views, which almost seems odd since he descended from a long line of Jewish rabbis.

In his poem "Human Pride" (pre-1837) he wrote: "Words I teach all mixed up into a devilish muddle. Thus, anyone may think just what he chooses to think. With disdain I will throw my gauntlet full in the face of the world, and see the collapse of this pygmy giant whose fall will not stifle my ardor. Then will I wander godlike and victorious through the ruins of the world.

---

47 Lopez, D., "The Conversion of Georg Lukács".
https://www.jacobinmag.com/2019/01/lukacs-hungary-marx-philosophy-consciousness

48 (48) Engels, F., "Draft of a Communist Confession of Faith", 9 June 1847.

https://www.marxists.org/archive/marx/works/1847/06/09.htm

49 Marx, K. "Critique of Hegel's Philosophy of Right", 1844.
https://www.marxists.org/archive/marx/works/download/Marx_Critique_of_Hegels_Philosophy_of_Right.pdf

And, giving my words an active force, I will feel equal to the Creator".[50] Hmm, sounds like an insane, bitter guy with a massive ego problem, who fancies himself as a God, determined to ruin the Earth…Interesting that the first two sentences suggest his works are just manipulative gibberish, and the reader may choose their own interpretation (post-modernistic thought; explored later) and be delusional. Indeed. That perfectly sums up the cult/ideology today. So, he was a prophet, after all. In addition, the title "Human Pride", relates to the ego—a primary psychological driver of the cult.

An excerpt from another poem of his called "The Fiddler" (pre-1837): "Till heart's bewitched, till senses reel: With Satan I have struck my deal. He chalks the signs, beats time for me, I play the death march fast and free".[51] A pact with Satan, eh? I'd say he was great to have a beer with. There are many examples of such writing. Let's keep in mind that this guy is world-renowned in many circles, regarded as some sort of genius, and the god(ahem)father of sociology etc. So we are worshipping Satanists now? Moses Hess was apparently responsible for introducing Marx and Engels to Satanism.

Interesting to note, judging from Marx's writings, he was not an atheist (as the cult/ideology advertises itself to be)—he clearly believed in, yet hated God, choosing to side with Satan. Whether or not anyone believes in God or the Devil is irrelevant here—if the ideology/cult has Satanic, destructive origins (and it does), this concerns us all. Know thy enemy human.

Marx would eventually focus on the economic and sociological side of things, and his work ostensibly became all about labour, class struggle etc. In addition, Marx was a fan of Charles Darwin (1809–1882), who published *On the Origin of Species by Means of Natural Selection* in 1859 (11 years after the Commie Manifesto). Marx liked Darwin's theory because it denies a creation took place (another defiance of God). It legitimised a 'scientific' approach and atheism in a popular book. Perhaps Marxism and Darwinism were the most impactful factors contributing to atheism in this age. In correspondence with the German socialist Ferdinand Lasalle, Marx wrote that Darwin's work "is most important and suits my purpose in that it provides a basis in natural science for the historical class struggle".[52] Of course, Darwin's theory of evolution is 'scientific' in the

---

[50] Marx, K. "Human Pride" (early works of KarlMarx book of verse, pre-1837).

[51] Marx. K. *"Wild Songs"*, *"The Fiddler"*, (early works of Karl Marx: book of verse, pre-1837).

[52] Marx and Engels, *Selected Correspondence 1846–1895* (1975), Vol. 41: 246–47.

way that the ideology is—theoretical, based on assumptions, and not reflective of reality, yet also largely accepted by the intellectual establishment as legitimate and brilliant.

This is a large subject, but the main point is that Marxism is outwardly anti-religion (in a sense), and specifically anti-Christianity. Overall, the ideology is also hostile towards other types of spiritual beliefs (unless it's advantageous for it to act otherwise). Modern examples include China's treatment of Buddhists in Tibet, the Falun Gong, and the Uyghurs Muslims in Xinjiang.[53]

The ideology has a long history of not merely criticism or condemnation for religious or spiritual practices, but an almost unbelievable level of viciousness, resulting in everything from assault to torture to mutilation to vicious raping to mass liquidation of practitioners. This extreme anti-Christian violence has been a feature of all major Marxian revolutions since the French Revolution. The cult's notions of 'diversity' and 'equality', typically, are not applied where Christianity is concerned.

Despite the above, however, certain interpretations of spirituality seem to dovetail nicely with the ideology. For example, any types of spiritual practices that are all about false interpretations of 'love' and 'compassion', the whole 'we are all one' concept (unity, solidarity, equality), or making hedonism or happiness the centre of your existence; anything that's mostly about being emotional rather than rational basically. The ideology pairs nicely with fake alternatives to genuine, benevolent spirituality or religiosity. The New Age movement contains many examples of these fake alternatives, or pseudo-spirituality essentially.

It should be stated here that this author is not Christian nor affiliated with any religion, yet is the perfect non-Christian ally for Christians. This is stated so the reader does not assume the author's protective stance towards Christianity comes from personal bias. No, my reasoning is far more lucid and strategic than that. I take a protective stance because it's in all of our interests to do so, whether you are Christian or religious or not; or whether or not you consider yourself a spiritual person of any sort. If you are non-Christian, you must understand and follow my lead, and Christians need to understand this too. This allows for a powerful alliance.

Those of us who are opposed to the ideology (and internationalism/'globalism', one-world government etc.) should resist the

---

[53] Cook, S. "Falun Gong: Religious Freedom in China", 2017.

https://freedomhouse.org/report/2017/battle-china-spirit-falun-gong-religious-freedom

attack on Christianity across the world, whether we are Christian or not. We should do this because it's part of the Marxian agenda to achieve global dominance. If we engage in open mockery of Christianity or Christians, we are effectively behaving how the cult/ideology wants us to behave. Likewise, if we stand back and allow Christianity to be systematically removed from our countries/cultures by the cult, we are complicit in this particular sub-agenda. The reasons will become apparent as we go along. You must put any personal biases aside to do what's right.

Specifically anti-Christian

The ideology/cult is specifically anti-Christian. It will attack Christianity and Christians at every opportunity, as it always has done, using various methods. Though historically there was blatant Marxist slaughter of this religious group, there isn't outright murder in Western countries today; yet the anti-Christian mentality is evident. Christianity's influence is increasingly marginalised and suppressed.

The cult (in general) claims to be atheist, and that religion is bad for humanity etc., which seems to explain its stance on Christianity; yet they don't treat other religions the same way. In fact, not only does the cult not attack Judaism/Jews or Islam/Muslims, they will criticize you for doing so and unleash their dreaded insults, such as "antisemitic" and "islamophobe". So essentially this means attacking Christianity/Christians is ok, but attacking other religious groups is not permitted.

Doesn't that seem strange? Isn't this a blatant double-standard? Even a rookie should figure this one out very quickly. All we have to do is pay attention to the Marxist-ridden pop-culture for five minutes to see it in action, including in the anti-Christian media produced by the cult, via the 'entertainment' industry. It is now open season on Christianity, but again, the same treatment is not permitted for other denominations.

Comparing Christianity and Islam

In addition, in order to justify the anti-Christianity stance, they will constantly bring up examples of evil behaviour inspired by Christianity (i.e. the Inquisition, The Crusades), yet have nothing to say about the bloody (sometimes imperial) history of Islamic Jihad. You could argue that they are simply not aware of the violent history of Islam, but if they are aware of the Crusades – a related conflict primarily between Christians and Muslims – there's no excuse really.

Besides, they would probably blame any Islamic Jihad sentiment on U.S./NATO 'imperialism' (I have seen some cult members make stupid points like this!), even though Jihad was around long before Christopher

Columbus even 'discovered' the Americas in 1492! Muhammad died around 632AD, and Jihad was in full swing during his lifetime. The U.S. Declaration of Independence was in 1776! We are not criticising Islam/Muslims here, just highlighting the double-standards.

When it comes to Christianity, the cult will highlight any perceived weakness/negative points, such as paedophilia/raping minors, crime and corruption, that it's oppressive, and has been responsible for so many wars, executions, slaughter etc. Even though we could say those things about Islam in equal measure, this is not highlighted. The history of Islam – in the time of their prophet Muhammed – is the history of conquest, forced conversion, and slaughter of the Kafir (non-Muslim 'infidels' or 'non-believers').

In addition, there is no such thing as Christian torture, mutilation, murder, extremism, and terrorism in the world today, but we can't say the same about Islam. This too, is conveniently ignored, while the cult tries to minimise or cover-up incidences of Islamic extremism in western countries. It's just the usual cherry-picking, double standards bullshit that is typical of the cult. It's also traitorous since they are basically siding with those who are not of their own nationality or race; using them to advance itself.

Christian beliefs are silly, but Muslim or Jewish beliefs are not?

The Marxist mob love to mock Christianity and Christians, with their praying and rituals, and their belief in God or adulation of Jesus Christ, stating that this is superstitious mumbo-jumbo; but if some Muslims are performing Salah (prayer) or talking about the Qur'an or Allah, all of a sudden, "oh it's so wonderful, it's so diverse! I mean, I don't share your beliefs, but I respect them" etc. etc. blah blah; more "arse-licking" (as we say in Ireland).

Same goes for the other Abrahamic religion—Judaism. If one was to publicly suggest that the 'chosen' people were not, in fact, special or deserving of special treatment, or you stated that you thought Brit Milah (circumcision of baby boys) was barbaric, you are hit with the 'antisemitic' label. The cult doesn't treat all religions the same, and it considers Christianity – and the Roman Catholic Church in particular – the enemy.

The cult will act 'atheistic' and say that Ireland is now so much more progressive after the separation of Church and state but won't have any problem at all when Muslims inevitably start dominating political affairs, and prioritise Islam and Muslims or non-Muslims in western countries.

Obviously, the cult supports the Islamification of the West, particularly in Europe. This itself could be construed as an attack on Christianity, since

Islam will inevitably start to dominate the religious landscape (thanks to a rapidly increasing population). True, this doesn't appear to contradict the idea that their ideology is atheist—they are programmed to support Muslims (they think) because of humanitarian reasons (equality, diversity, compassion etc.).

The ideology's programming is the driving force here. It would be interesting to quiz some cult members about whether or not they respect a Muslim's religious beliefs more than a Christian's (especially Catholics). If not, why not? Of course, thanks to the indoctrination and 'PC' culture created by the Marxist rot, if you raise these points, you are an 'Islamophobe'. It's true that these ignoramus cult members don't really have any knowledge and are only aware of history from a pro-Marxian perspective; but still, things like these are more obvious double-standards; another (commie) Red flag. The anti-Christianity bias is evident.

Paedophilia as a propaganda weapon

Another example of the double-standards is on the issue of paedophilia. In the cult's attack on the Catholic Church and the Vatican, the issue of paedophilia is highlighted time-and-time again. This then allows the propaganda to equate Christianity/Christians with paedophilia. If we are going to equate paedophilia with Christianity based on the instances of it where the Catholic Church is concerned, then we should equate it to Judaism and Islam too, since there has been plenty of instances involving those religious groups, past and present.

Again, the ideology doesn't care about people, including children—it only cares about perpetuating itself. So, in this instance, feigned concern for the well-being of children is used to achieve one of the ideology's/cult's goals (the destruction of Christianity).

Why it needs to destroy Christianity

The most important reason why the ideology attacks Christianity (without going in too deep or esoteric for now), is because it's an ideological opponent, with a well-entrenched belief set. The global spread of the infection has always been hampered somewhat by the presence of this belief system.

In general, genuine Christianity – Catholicism in particular – has been opposed to many of the degenerate, civilisation-destroying things that the ideology/cult promotes, while also being in favour of healthy, civilisation-building things that the ideology/cult is opposed to (listed further along). Essentially, Christianity and Marxism have an antagonistic relationship, and they cannot co-exist.

Why it attacks Catholicism

Roman Catholicism and the Vatican have traditionally been a high-priority target for the cult/ideology. Christianity is the most popular religion globally, making up about 30% of the world's population or 2.36 billion (the total world population figure at time of writing is 7.88 billion).[54]

Though there are many denominations of Christianity, the overwhelming majority are Catholics, with approximately 1.3 billion adherents.[55] This makes the Catholic church, headquartered in the Vatican, the largest, most influential and powerful Christian organisation on the planet. Though the Church and Vatican itself has been bent out of shape in many ways, for several reasons (a large subject of research and discussion covered by other authors), Christianity still remains highly influential, retaining adherents in the Americas, Europe, sub-Saharan Africa, Russia and Australasia.

This well-entrenched, global presence of Christianity poses a major strategic problem for Marxism, simply due to the number of adherents involved (and therefore its global influence). For illustration purposes, the population of Christians in the world, at 2.3 billion, is higher than the population of China. Even if we presume every single person in that country of roughly 1.4 billion is fully brainwashed by the ideology (which isn't true), we can see that Christianity represents a problem.

Though Christians are spread-out across the globe, so are Marxist cult members (whether of Chinese persuasion or not). In a sense, this is a global religious turf-war, with team God/Yahweh/Allah on one side, and team Lucifer/Satan on the other. Speaking of figures, one can only speculate how many people there are in the world who can be categorised as Marxist cult members...

Christianity/religiosity opposes the ideology

Now we can get in to more detail about how Christianity (and other religions in general) opposes the ideology. Traditionally, Christianity is in favour of things like marriage (and therefore the traditional family unit), while also being against contraception, abortion, gay marriage etc. These are all positive stances to have in any given society, as they help to encourage a culture where men and women come together and have

---

[54] Hackett and McClenon. "Christians remain world's largest religious group, but they are declining in Europe", 5 April 2017. https://www.pewresearch.org/fact-tank/2017/04/05/christians-remain-worlds-largest-religious-group-but-they-are-declining-in-europe/

[55] https://en.wikipedia.org/wiki/List_of_religious_populations

meaningful monogamous child-bearing relationships. It's good for the integrity of nations, peoples, and cultures, not to mention long-term life satisfaction for individuals!

The ideology, of course, has been promoting the opposite of those things via its various sub-agendas including feminism and women's 'liberation' (which in turn has ensured large uptake of contraception and abortion), and the LGBTQ movement which tries to push the idea that non-heterosexual relationships are equal to heterosexual ones (which they obviously aren't in a parenting context); in addition to other sub-agendas, such as even blurring the lines between 'male' and 'female' altogether(!).

So basically, the religious influence is promoting higher birthrates, and encouraging personal maturity and duty (by encouraging monogamous, child-bearing relationships and marriage); while Marxism is promoting everything else but that. Even in this one area – which involves birthrates and stable family environments – it's clear there's no contest between Christianity and Marxism when it comes to which one is bad for civilisation.

On another level, we can see how the cult/ideology is opposed to God/the creator/nature in general, with its various sub-agendas. Veganism contradicts the idea that God/the creator gave us dominion over other life forms, and that it's more than acceptable for us to use animals for agricultural purposes, since that's why they are here.

Obviously, supporting abortion and contraception is about as anti-life/creation as you can get—it directly prevents human life from being created as part of 'God's plan'. (Incidentally, they are both also symbolic acts in that they place someone's personal gratification and ego above God's 'will' (what's best for humanity), which is a form of Satanism—the religion of the ego, of self-worship).

And then there's the fact that religion and spirituality can encourage non-materialistic thinking. Of course, since Marxism is based upon soul-less materialism, the spiritual aspects of Christianity poses problems for the ideology too; including the belief that morality/ethics are not something that we can just invent as human beings—they are a built-in component of life, of the creation.

In addition, the idea that humanity is the result of a creation, and not just a 'scientific' materialistic atheistic accident (aka evolution, entropy etc.), is something else in conflict with Marxian dogma. The idea that something divine (if we are receptive to it) can guide our lives and our actions is yet another problem for the ideology.

Lastly, many religions (Christianity included) have traditionally suggested that what we do in our lives here on Earth – using our own free will – matters and that we will be judged afterwards; also, that we are being watched by the creator. Naturally, this insinuates that there's a universal, objective standard of morality that a person must conform to somewhat.

Note how this was a widely held belief across the world before Marxism emerged, particularly in the West, and such sentiments obviously vanish in societies that become 'atheist' thanks to the ideological infection. Obviously, being 'free' from the worry of this judgement, a human may choose a path of degeneracy, or become a traitor to humankind in one way or another. Cult members, wittingly or unwittingly, often fit this bill by default. Marxism, if you will, removes the incentive to be a good person according to traditional moral standards, which are part of 'God's plan'.

Christianity contains moral standards

This one is crucial. As stated throughout, the ideology distorts people's perceptions of many things, including the perception of objective, universal, actual right and wrong (aka 'good and evil'). Looking at the psychotic, immoral behaviour of the cult throughout the world, we can see the effects of this distortion. The ideology comes with a pre-packaged unethical set of fucked-up beliefs, contained within the indoctrination. It goes without saying that they contradict the belief set that Christianity provides. (And before we continue—of course a person can have a conscience without being Christian/religious, spiritual etc., but that's not the issue here!).

Religion often comes with certain interpretations of right and wrong, certain standards and rules for how to behave. Marxism needs to impose its own rules of behaviour on you (including how you think, speak, feel, what you should believe etc.), therefore, it needs to eliminate any competing ideologies that are trying to do the same job. A person can only have one belief system driving their thoughts, words, actions, and beliefs at a time. We can compare this to swapping one operating system (OS) for another on a computer system (e.g. Windows or Mac to Linux, or vice-versa).

So, do cult members believe in morality/ethics, the idea of 'right' and 'wrong'? I have seen/heard cult members mock Christianity/Christians on the subject of objective morality. The general Christian interpretation is that there's an objective, universal, God-given system in place, being part of creation itself; a notion which the cult members feel is ridiculous and 'irrational'. Other cult members simply seem to not believe in the idea of objective morality, Christianity aside.

Yet, the cult's fanaticism and activism are based on their belief that they know the difference between right and wrong! Not only that, but they believe they even have the right to impose this on society. This is contradictory in the sense that who is to know what right and wrong is? According to whom? On who's authority? Other cult members? Marxist 'experts'? Perhaps their benchmark is that wrong is being committed when someone cries 'oppression'?

Atheism and the anti-white agenda

Interestingly, one of the many various sub-agendas that Marxism supports is the racist anti-white sub-agenda. In fact, many of the ideology's other sub-agendas support this one: feminism, abortion, multiculturalism/diversity programming etc. all help to lower birthrates primarily in western countries; themselves primarily Caucasian (we are looking at mass immigration and multiculturalism in more detail elsewhere).

Before Marxism came along, the majority of white populations around the world were Christians of some kind. Since Marxism entered the picture and started making a significant cultural impact (during the 20th century), there has been a massive increase in atheism among these populations. This atheism has been a major factor in the dominance of the ideology, which itself has led to the many destructive, civilisation/race destroying consequences we are experiencing today in western (predominantly white, Christian) countries. This is no coincidence.

Knowing how the ideology operates, it would be foolish for it to allow this opposing ideology of Christianity to exist and having to compete with it for influence over the masses. It's much more tactically efficient to remove its influence from the equation entirely. And that's precisely what it has been doing. Unfortunately, due to lack of understanding/consciousness, millions upon millions of people in the world (cult members or not) have been assisting the ideology in this removal during their lives, thereby empowering the cult/ideology and precipitating their own destruction.

Being murderous towards Christians

"The leading Bolsheviks who took over Russia were not Russians. They hated Russians. They hated Christians. Driven by ethnic hatred they tortured and slaughtered millions of Russians without a shred of human remorse. It cannot be overstated. Bolshevism committed the greatest human slaughter of all time. The fact that most of the world is ignorant and uncaring about this enormous crime is proof that the global media is in the hands of the perpetrators"

Aleksandr Solzhenitsyn, *The Gulag Archipelago*, 1973[56]

Isn't it odd that they always seem to directly attack Christianity? If these revolutions are supposed to be about making society better, more egalitarian etc., then why make it such a priority to kill Christians? It's a big commie red flag when we observe this aspect of Marxist revolutions. We can see that it's not just about economics or politics—there is a religious/anti-religious element to its agenda.

From the time of the French Revolution, the revolutionaries have always blatantly made a violent beeline for Christians to effectively genocide them by any available means (the clergy and Christian population in general). In addition to Christianity being an ideological opponent to Marxism, it has been a physical, military opponent at times. Since the Marxists were always keen to liquidate Christians at every opportunity, it was prudent for them to physically fight back when possible, or to at least side with a protective ally: photos from the Spanish Civil War, for example, shows armed men of the cloth fighting with Spanish nationalists against the international cult. On other occasions, cult members have instigated violence by attacking the church via politics, encouraging the separation of church and state: in Mexico during the 1920s and 1930s, President Calles' (cult member) actions led to the *Cristero War* (1926–1929).[57]

Other examples of cult assaults on Christianity: a well-known feature of the French Revolution was the vicious attack on not just private property belonging to the church, but the slaughter of the clergy;[58] soon after the Bolsheviks took power in Russia, a civil war broke out, with Trotsky's Red Army on one side, and the Christian White Army on the other. The persecution and murder of Christians by the Bolsheviks was commonplace;[59] during the Spanish Civil War, the Catholic Church and Francisco Franco's nationalist forces fought against the domestic and international Marxist forces;[60] In Soviet Ukraine between 1932 and 1933, millions of Christians were starved to death by Joseph Stalin's regime in the *Holodomor* (mentioned earlier). There are countless other examples.

This is as much a clash between 'atheism' and Christianity as anything else, and the cult has been trying to eradicate Christianity and Christians. And

---

[56] Solzhenitsyn, A. *The Gulag Archipelago* (1973).

[57] https://www.britannica.com/biography/Plutarco-Elias-Calles

[58] https://www.britannica.com/event/French-Revolution

[59] https://www.britannica.com/event/Russian-Civil-War

[60] https://www.britannica.com/event/Spanish-Civil-War

we are not just talking merely oppression or execution here—we are talking about horrifically inhumane torture and mutilation, with an almost Satanic element (i.e. bloody, unnatural abominations).

The work of Richard Wurmbrand (1909–2001) details such things. Being a Lutheran priest and critic of the cult, Wurmbrand was imprisoned for 14 years in Communist Romania in the post-WW2 period.

He authored several pieces including *Marx & Satan* (1976), which documented brutal crimes committed against Christians by cult members; including one instance of 'crucifixion'.[61] A tremendous amount of hatred is evident here. Why? The more fanatical cult members will insist that this genocide improves things, that it's part of the wonderful 'cleansing' effect of Marxist revolution. They will also repeat the notion that Christianity is an inherently murderous ideology itself, so what goes around comes around, in a sense. An eye for an eye, right?

Marxism as a quasi-religion

The irony of the cult's attitude towards religious adherents is lost on them. They will mock religious people, regarding them as irrational; that their beliefs are not backed up by science, truth/reality. But by these standards, their ideology is also an irrational quasi-religious belief system.

The cult's ideas – on everything from social dynamics to economics to biology to science to revolution itself – are just as unscientific and detached from reality as they accuse traditional religious beliefs of being. They will accuse religious adherents of thinking they have the truth, yet cult members are the same. They believe they have a superior belief system that makes them ethically superior to others (whether they openly admit it or not), which is exactly what they accuse religious adherents of (particularly Christians).

They also mock how these adherents may respect or even blindly follow their respective priests, pastors etc., stating that this is due to being blinded by their authority. Meanwhile, their ideology has its priest-class too: the innumerable cult members around the globe posing as teachers/professors in schools, colleges, and universities, for example. It's their position as authority figures – speaking to rooms full of vulnerable, naive young minds – which leads to the blind faith fanaticism of the cult!

Others – friends, partners, family members – may be the ones to 'initiate them' into the cult, if that authority is there, provided they blindly believe what they are being told. Those influencers may even be held aloft as a

---

[61] Wurmbrand, R. "Hour of the Time/Marx & Satan" (1976).

wondrous human being by this new inductee, though they have essentially infected them with the ideology (and therefore have potentially ruined their lives for them)! Imagine admiring someone who has ruined your life while you are not aware of this fact...

Prophets and martyrs

The cult mocks the worship of religious idols, perplexed as to why someone would venerate a dead person who said or did some stuff. It's obviously stupid to worship someone like Jesus Christ, right? Yet, in all the Communist regimes in history, we can see the veneration of the Communist prophets Marx, Lenin, Mao etc. Even Leon Trotsky (Lev Bronstein) has been venerated by the Trotskyite sub-cult. Venerating a Jesus (who wasn't a murderous thug that created mass death around him) is sad and backward, but venerating a murdering psychopath like Bronstein isn't? We've seen the worship of Che Guevera – the Marxist Jesus – who's face has graced a million cheap t-shirts and graffiti-covered walls (another murdering fanatic).

The cult also loves to worship other long-dead 'revolutionary' types like Rosa Luxemburg and Antonio Gramsci, or even hip, influential intellectuals like Noam Chomsky, Herbert Marcuse or Christopher Hitchens (1949–2011). Even today, we see the idol-worship of fanatical cult members Chinese Premier Xi Jinping and North Korean 'leader' Kim Jong Un. The cult just loves to worship its own idols, and always has.

It wants to be a religion

The cult mocks Christians for wanting to believe in something bigger (a higher power etc.), and be united with other Christians, yet they themselves have 'religious' beliefs and want to be part of something bigger too. If the world "religion" comes from the Latin "religare" or "religio", which means to 'bind' or 'union' (solidarity!), then cult members themselves are in a union and want the world to join this union, bound together ("One race, human race!"; one of their protest slogans).

Is this because (many) human beings do want to belong to something bigger? They want to feel connected to others who want to feel the same thing. I don't see any problem with that. If the only affect is benevolent, then why not? Interesting that the ideology allows for this type of religiosity/connectedness too, except it's not about a higher power or divinity, it's about believing in an egalitarian, one world 'utopia', and being connected with others who believe the same thing. It's about being joined in this belief of a better, more ethical world (from a Marxian point of view). Obviously, the Marxian interpretations of these ideas are not beautiful; they are ugly and misguided (and dangerous!).

Ten planks and ten commandments

Interestingly, the ideology has its version of the Ten Commandments—the ten planks of the Communist Manifesto. In addition, the ideology/cult also openly acts in defiance of these commandments, which are: You shall have no other gods before me; You shall make no idols; You shall not take the name of the Lord your God in vain; Keep the Sabbath day holy; Honor your father and your mother; You shall not murder; You shall not commit adultery; You shall not steal; You shall not bear false witness against your neighbour; You shall not covet.[62]

In defiance of those, the ideology/cult: ostensibly encourages atheism, yet promotes what we can call Satanism or Luciferianism (anti-God/anti-creator/anti-nature, and the self/ego); encourages the worship of idols (including Marxist idols); has a history of openly citing religion as a major evil; has always tried to separate children from their parents and encourages children to defy them; as ideologies go, is the biggest killer of all time pound-for-pound; has tried to destroy marriage, monogamy, and normal relationships; encourages theft in many forms in the name of 'social justice' and 'equality'; encourages people to rat on each other through slander and deception (particularly if they question the ideology), and turns people in to traitors against the human race; encourages covetousness, envy, and jealousy, particularly of anything/anyone successful, wealthy etc.

Once again, this shows the evil, Satanic tactic of inversion—it turns things upside down, in defiance of what is good.

Hypocrisy and Paedophilia

Since Marxism needs to destroy religion, and Christianity in particular, it has sought to exploit any weaknesses (perceived or otherwise) to achieve its goal. This is the typical modus operandi of the ideology in tactical terms. When it comes to the Catholic Church in particular, one issue the ideology uses to its advantage is paedophilia. It's used in a similar fashion to how the feminist sub-agenda uses the issue of rape and amplifies it, to make it seem like all men are rapists/potential rapists, or that it's a more frequently occurring act than it is in reality. In a word: propaganda. When we look at the number of men in the world, obviously a negligible amount of them have engaged in rape. This is the case with priests engaging in paedophilia throughout the course of Christianity. As we are analysing Marxian tactics—what better way to attack your enemy than to have them viewed

---

[62] "Ten Commandments List". https://www.bibleinfo.com/en/topics/ten-commandments-list

as being disgusting, evil, willing to abuse children etc?

The church paedophilia issue is linked to the subject of the cult's infiltration of the Catholic Church, covered by other authors. In addition, Freemasonry is linked to Marxism, and though that topic is outside the scope of this book, it can be stated here that the 'God' of both is Lucifer. The Masonic infiltration of the church is outlined in several works, including *The Permanent Instruction of the Alta Vendita* (John Vennari, 1999) and *Freemasonry and the Vatican: a Struggle for Recognition* (Leon De Poncins, 2000). This was an agenda to inject the Church with 'liberal', degenerative, and anti-Christian ideas and practices. Catholics will be aware of bizarre changes of direction and departures from traditional practices in the Church, such as the Second Vatican Council (1962–1965). There seems to be a clear correlation between this infiltration and the paedophilia issue.

Leaving that aside for a moment, even if it were true that paedophilia is a cornerstone of organised religion, it's hypocritical of the cult to highlight this, as if they are opposed to sexual degeneracy! Just look at what influence they're having on society today with regards to sex, sexuality, and relationships, including promoting/normalising: homosexuality (for heterosexuals); polyamory (having more than one partner); promiscuity (especially in females); gender 'non-binary' (which itself amounts to child abuse via self-mutilation) etc. All these things, while achieving certain objectives in themselves, have also just been 'progressive' stepping stones towards more sinister things. The cult/ideology is now going to actively promote and support paedophilia, while defending paedophiles and labelling those who oppose the agenda as being "homophobic" or "uncompassionate" or other bizarre, irrational nonsense. Tellingly, a former civil servant and the founder of Antifa in Ireland Pat Corcoran was caught with thousands of child pornographic images in 2009. He appeared in court but did not go to prison.[63]

As stated, the cult/ideology is not highlighting any problem (perceived or otherwise) with paedophilia in the Catholic Church due to 'compassion' for children! It's done because it will help destroy the Church, by destroying its public image. It's just their tried-and-trusted method of hypocritical virtue-signalling to achieve certain tactical objectives. They have decided to latch-on to (and constantly highlight) the most controversial and sickening thing that the general public attaches to the Catholic Church in

---

[63] "Former civil servant caught with 7,000 child porn images avoids jail", 14 November 2013. https://www.independent.ie/irish-news/courts/former-civil-servant-caught-with-7000-child-porn-images-avoids-jail/29755182.html

their minds—paedophilia. Then it's repeated by cult members constantly, till eventually, through conditioning, it's the first thing you think of when someone says "Catholic Church" (like what just happened this moment as some readers read those two words).

The destruction of culture and national identity

"Revolutionary culture is a powerful revolutionary weapon for the broad masses of the people. It prepares the ground ideologically before the revolution comes and is an important, indeed essential, fighting front in the general revolutionary front during the revolution"[64]

Mao Zedong, "On New Democracy", Selected Works, Vol. II, (1940)

"Every record has been destroyed or falsified, every book rewritten, every picture has been repainted, every statue and street building has been renamed, every date has been altered. And the process is continuing day by day and minute by minute. History has stopped. Nothing exists except an endless present in which the Party is always right"[65]

George Orwell, 1984 (1949)

The destruction of culture and national identity is another major strategic objective for the cult, making it an anti-culture cult. This is a large subject deserving of a separate, deep analysis, but must be listed here in brief. This too, just like the assault on capitalism and Christianity, has been a feature of the ideology's behaviour throughout its history. From the Black book of Communism: "Communism has committed a multitude of crimes not only against individual human beings but also against world civilization and national cultures. Stalin demolished... dozens of churches in Moscow; Nicolae Ceausescu destroyed the historical heart of Bucharest to give free reign to his megalomania; Pol Pot dismantled the Phnom Penh cathedral stone by stone and allowed the jungle to take over the temples of Angkor Wat; and during Mao's Cultural Revolution, priceless treasures were smashed or burned by the Red Guards".[66]

This Marxian attack on indigenous culture connects with several of the ideology's other objectives including: the mass-immigration/multiculturalism sub-agenda through the destruction of National identity; the enforcement of equality on a cultural level (the "all cultures are equal" myth); the obliteration of a people's understanding of

---

[64] Zedong, M, "On New Democracy", Selected Works, Vol. II, (1940). https://www.marxists.org/reference/archive/mao/works/red-book/ch32.htm

[65] George Orwell, G. (Eric Blair), 1984 (1949).

[66] Courtois et al, The Black Book of Communism, P. 3.

their own history in order to replace it with historical narratives approved by the cult/ideology; the suppression of art since this can be a form of political expression (and therefore a potential source of dissent against the cult/ideology); the creation of dull, uniform, lifeless societies to literally drain the humanity out of people by removing any semblance of beauty from their surroundings (in buildings, housing, infrastructure etc); and the destruction of western civilisation in general.

Another interlinked objective of the cult is the erosion of any genuine sovereign, patriotic, nationalistic sentiment which inspires/enables a country's population to resist the cult/ideology on an international level. This is perhaps the most crucial effect of the destruction of culture/national identity. 'Culture/national', in this case, includes the burial of memories of any genuinely patriotic nationalistic rebellious activity in the past. With mass-immigration/multiculturalism/diversity, obviously, the established indigenous culture and religious beliefs of any given country must take a backseat to those of the incoming migrants.

This is why, for example, you will see the Marxist-ridden establishments in western European countries simultaneously allowing the destruction of Christianity (and all that entails) while simultaneously accommodating (or prioritising) Islam. This is symbolised in the construction of mosques, combined with the physical and ideological attacks on Christianity including the physical destruction and desecration of Christian property, monuments, artefacts etc.

The destruction of Christian buildings

The Marxian attack on western culture also connects with the aforementioned destruction of religion, since religion (specifically Christianity) has become a major part of western culture too. This is exemplified by the vandalism and destruction of church property in western countries.

An article on the *Catholic News Agency* website on 4 May 2021 highlighted this issue, which included the opinions of the president of the *Observatoire du Patrimoine Religieux* Edouard de Lamaze. Lamaze apparently said that one religious building on average is disappearing every two weeks in France.[67] The article stated, according to Lamaze, that although there were several reasons why these buildings were disappearing – including demolition, accidental fire, transformation, and collapse – "about two

---

[67] Tadie, S, "Why France is losing one religious building every two weeks", 4 May 2021. https://www.catholicnewsagency.com/news/247514/why-france-is-losing-one-religious-building-every-two-weeks

thirds of fires in religious buildings are due to arson". I'm sure that many of the 'accidental' fires only appear to be accidental. The article also includes criminal intelligence figures from French authorities, which indicated that "877 attacks on Catholic places of worship were recorded across the country in 2018" alone. Perhaps the most high-profile fire was the Notre Dame Cathedral in April 2019.[68]

Hatred breeds neglect and destructive acts. No prizes for guessing who and what is breeding the hate. The spirit of Maximilien Robespierre lives on it seems.

Why they destroy culture and national identity

When the cult takes over, it's important to destroy any connections with the past. This must be done in order to destroy any notions that the group/nation/people is/are unique and different from others. This in turn then makes the group more willing to accept being a part of the international cult, since the same process happens in other infected countries too. It's forced egalitarianism and uniformity, on a cultural level. Obviously, according to Marxist dogma in general (different interpretations aside), the notion of national separation from other groups/countries is not only undesirable, but downright evil (and fascist, racist, ____phobic, white supremacist etc.)!

Since each country will have its own history, statues/monuments, artefacts, art, music, languages etc., that may be unique to that country, these must all either be destroyed, co-opted, or re-interpreted from a Marxian perspective. For maximum efficacy, from the cult's perspective, this must be done internationally and simultaneously (as has been happening for decades now worldwide). An example of a famous historical event In Ireland, the *Easter Rising* of 1916 falls into this category—it's now interpreted by many in the Marxism-infected mainstream through a Marxian lens (i.e. revolution against the empire is good). That can be applied to other historical rebellions too.

The underlying truth that rebellions of this nature were about Ireland having true sovereignty—which includes freedom to be truly Irish and different from other countries, and free from foreign ideologies (!)—is obviously not emphasised (since this can potentially cultivate the idea of nationalism: Marxism's eternal enemy). Again, it's the ideology cherry-picking the elements it needs to further its own agenda.

---

[68] Gray, Shamsian. "Haunting photos of the Notre-Dame Cathedral's charred remains show what's left on the inside", 17 April 2019.

Physical items – such as statues – can be destroyed, replaced, defaced etc. Immaterial things, such as language, are dealt with differently: changes in the culture—via changes in attitudes (through Marxist influence)—achieve the desired results.

The Irish language

The complete destruction of the Irish (Gaelic) language in Ireland will be another casualty of Marxist infection, though the occupation of Ireland by the British Empire initiated the process. Though Irish is still officially a compulsory subject in general, the Department of Education has been bringing in progressive changes in recent years. It's allowing exemptions for certain students.

This will inevitably lead to more and more exemptions, especially as the racial demographics of Irish schools will continue to change thanks to mass migration (which the ideology/cult is responsible for). Predictably, non-Irish parents and children will have no interest in speaking Irish. Eventually, as the numbers of non-Irish students in schools increase, it will be considered completely unviable for it to be taught at all.

The feeling that "it isn't practical" has been (and will be) enthusiastically pushed by the Marxist mainstream in the country. Is Irish practical for everyday use? Unless a person is living in or near one of the Irish speaking "Gaeltacht" areas in Ireland, no, it isn't. It's not practical or necessary; but that's not the issue here. The Irish Gaelic language is one of the things that makes Irish people (and Ireland) relatively unique in the global scheme of things, where western countries are concerned. The Scottish and Welsh, plus the Isle of Man (Manx) and parts of England (Cornish) have their dialects and Celtic influences too. The roots of these languages stretch back many thousands of years. Naturally, this uniqueness must be stamped out if egalitarianism and uniformity is to be achieved. A January 2024 article on the *rte.ie* website entitled "Should Irish still be a compulsory subject in schools?" stated that the "future of how we teach the Irish language in schools is under scrutiny". Adding that almost "60,000 schoolchildren received an exemption from the subject between 2022 and 2023, according to the Department of Education".[69]

From G.A.A. To G.A.Y.

Another unique aspect of Irish culture is Gaelic sports, including Gaelic

---

[69] Upfront, "Should Irish still be a compulsory subject in schools?", 10 January 2024. https://www.rte.ie/news/upfront/2024/0108/1425307-should-irish-still-be-a-compulsory-subject-in-schools/

football, Hurling, and Camogie. These are still as popular as ever within Ireland, and even have clubs in other countries (the U.S. in particular). The *Gaelic Athletic Association* is the prominent organisation for these sports. Traditionally, it has mainly been nationalistic, conservative, and Catholic.

Since Gaelic sports are as much a part of Irish culture as the Irish language, this has placed the G.A.A. in a central position of influence. Not surprisingly, this organisation is progressively succumbing to the Marxist rot, having been firmly within the crosshairs for decades.

In recent years, there have been calls for more 'diversity' and 'inclusion' of the LGBTQ groups in the G.A.A. and Gaelic sports. The organisation took part (for the first time) in the Dublin Pride parade on 29 June 2019.[70] In the same year, the *Gender Diversity Working Group* (giggles) was established as part of the G.A.A., along with other similar organisations such as the *Ladies Gaelic Football Association* (L.G.F.A.). Its chairperson is Gearóid Ó Maoilmhichíl, who is also the GAA's National Children's Officer (another person in a position of influence over children who is assisting the ideology). It was reported in the Irish media in late 2020 that an LGBTQ-friendly club would be registered with the G.A.A.[71] The name chosen was Na Gaeil Aeracha, which translates as "Rainbow Gaels" (pronounced "Gayles"); they are clearly trying to put the "gay" in "Gael".

Mecca Park

This piece could be in the "destruction of religion/Christianity" section, but since it involves the G.A.A. it's placed here. The headquarters for the Gaelic Athletic Association – and primary venue for Gaelic sports in Ireland – is Croke Park. It's the largest sports stadium in the country with a capacity of over 82,000. This iconic sports ground has been synonymous with Gaelic sports since 1891 and is therefore a symbol of Irish culture. As with the G.A.A. itself, Croke Park was always going to become a target for the cult sooner or later. A very symbolic and blatant Marxian manoeuvre was pulled here on Fri 31 July 2020; and not in a function room somewhere at the venue, but right there in the middle of the playing field.

According to the MarxiStMedia in Ireland, around 200 Muslims attended

---

[70] "GAA to take part in Dublin LGBTQ+ Pride Festival", 24 May 2019.

https://www.gaa.ie/hurling/news/gaa-to-take-part-in-dublin-lgbtq-pride-festival

[71] "The Rainbow Gaels: The first of its kind", November 2020.

https://www.rte.ie/gaeilge/2020/1123/1179874-the-rainbow-gaels-the-first-of-its-kind/

this "historic" prayer service to mark the festival of *Eid al-Adha*.[72] Of course, the event was upheld as a wonderful display of 'unity' and 'diversity' etc. by Irish cult members. Symbolic of the Islamification of western countries including Ireland, this event showed the G.A.A.'s willingness to conform to the 'progressiveness' destroying the country. Apparently, the person who came up with the idea (to approach the G.A.A.) was Dr. Shaykh Umar Al-Qadri, a prominent member of the Muslim community in Ireland, and chair of the *Irish Muslim Peace & Integration Council*. He is not significant; if it wasn't him, it would be someone else. The important point here is that such things would not (and should not) happen if the country was not institutionally Marxist (and therefore more patriot/nationalistic).

Desecration and destruction of monuments

Does it not seem bizarre, that during the Black Lives Matter riots in the U.S. and U.K., monuments were attacked? What on earth has the death of George Floyd got to do with statues? Naturally, if we listen to the brainwashed ones, this is all about the evil culture of institutional racism against non-whites, right? So this is about racism is it? (rolls eyes). No, it isn't, that's just the excuse. As stated, property damage/vandalism is part of the cult's classy heritage. The chief goal of Marxism is to destroy western civilisation first before it can build its utopia; the destruction or replacement of the established culture is therefore crucial. This is why they attack any symbols of it, including monuments.

During the Marxist BLM 'protests', riots and chaos etc., there began a trend of pulling-down or vandalising statues in the UK, U.S. and elsewhere. The statues targeted by cult members were of anyone who was remotely connected with 'white institutional oppression' etc. In London, a statue of Winston Churchill (1874–1965) was targeted. In Oxford, a statue of Cecil Rhodes. In Washington DC, the statue of Albert Pike (1809–1891). Others included statues of Christopher Columbus (1451–1506), slave-trader Edward Colston (1636–1721), and King Leopold II of Belgium (1835–1909). Ostensibly it was being done because these people are evil and pulling the statues down is for the good of society, right? Or is there some ulterior motive?

There's a U.K. website called *toppletheracists.org*.[73] The header on the

---

[72] Ní Aodha, G, "Muslims pray at Croke Park for the first time in celebration of Eid al-Adha", 31 July 2020. https://www.thejournal.ie/eid-celebrations-in-croke-park-5164698-Jul2020/

[73] https://www.toppletheracists.org/

homepage: "A crowdsourced map of UK statues and monuments that celebrate slavery and racism". Statues that celebrate slavery and racism? What? This group's initiatives included removing statues, renaming buildings, and the removal of plaques and signs from around the U.K. including (at time of writing): a statue of a kneeling African holding a sundial in Cheshire; the renaming of Gladstone Hall at the University of Liverpool (named after William Gladstone); The Black Boy pub sign in East Retford, Nottinghamshire; the renaming of Colston Hall in Bristol (names after Edward Colston); the statue of Robert Milligan in East London; and a blue plaque in the name of Edward Codrington in Brighton.

How should we feel about these statues getting defaced, damaged, removed, or pulled down? Were these men not rotten individuals? Churchill was a war criminal, apparently with elitist royal blood (his mother was the daughter of Queen Victoria and Nathan Meyer Rotschild). He was a key player in triggering and extending WW2, and approved the firebombing and incineration of several hundred thousand German civilians during that conflict; Cecil Rhodes was an arrogant imperialist, who wanted Britain to rule the world. The Round Table was created as part of his legacy (containing groups such as the Royal Institute of International Affairs, and the Council on Foreign Relations etc.); Albert Pike was a Confederate general during the American Civil War and a leading Freemason. He was the author of *Morals and Dogma* (1871) – a highly-influential Masonic book – and simultaneously held the three posts of world, national and state leader of Freemasonry.

Now, should we be upset that statues of men like these are attacked? To each their own, but me personally—no, I'm not upset by this, context aside. However, we must understand, as stated earlier, that the ideology demands these things are done in order to dominate/annihilate the landscape. So, we should all be very concerned when we see these things happen before our eyes. For the reason above, the cult should not be allowed to do these things! It's another form of virtue-signalling combined with violent, destructive behaviour, and most importantly—it fuels the cult and the ideology. The statues (or the individuals they honour) are not a problem in the present, the Marxist cult is!

Of course, if anyone obstructs cult members in their destructive behaviour, predictably, they are branded as condoning the lives, actions, or ideologies of the statued men. Nice try nutjobs! A typical, ingrained attempt at manipulative mind-control tactics. Again, the idiots pulling down the statues themselves are in no position to judge others! I clearly would stop them toppling the statues, while also not particularly respecting those whom the statues represent, and I'm sure many others would be of the same mindset. I would have them surrounded and arrested immediately.

Double standards

Again, we see those Marxian double-standards: they will deface or pull-down statues of your Cecil Rhodes or Winston Churchill types, yet obviously any statues of pro-Marxism figures will be unscathed. Cult members obviously would not tear down the sculpture of the Marxist Martin Luther King Jr. (1929–1968) in Washington DC; or the bronze statue of Communist, anti-white A.N.C. terrorist Nelson Mandela in Parliament Square, London. This is another example of the anti-white racism and double standards of the Marxist mob, combined with their obvious tendency to attack whoever was/is not part of their cult.

When we look at the mobs pulling down these monuments, let's remember that those people existed in the past; but these Marxists are causing destruction in the now. They only need an excuse; their egos and SJW activist indoctrination does the rest. It might seem like they have a conscience and a sense of justice, but this is only on the surface. This is part of the cult's manipulative virtue-signalling—they try to sucker you in to agreeing with them; they convince you that they have noble intentions. They want to get you to say "Oh yeah, you're right. Rhodes was an imperialist scumbag!" or "Albert Pike was a slavery-condoning Masonic bastard!" etc., and you seem reasonable to agree with them, on the surface level. The truth is, however, you are encouraging their appetite for destructive 'activism', which will never be satisfied.

Of course, when they start destroying things you don't agree with, then the penny drops, and it's too late—the red monster already has momentum! When they start insisting that the black tarmac on the roads is racist and needs to be painted LGBTQ rainbow colours or commie red (!), or that the colour of milk is racist (not making this one up), you will regret not challenging them earlier in the process. And it's your own fault! Never give brats their own way!

We should not miss the forest for the trees here. We must not get distracted by time-wasting debates, while the cult keeps marching forward. If we are talking about the destruction of statues, we are talking about statues of dead people, right? I'm not too concerned with dead people or what they did/believed—I'm concerned with the present. The cult will use any virtue-signalling reasons they can to justify destroying things that they don't approve of, so we must not be distracted by them. Remember, this is all about the dominance of the cult/ideology. An excellent and blatant example of this occurred in Germany..

Meanwhile...In Germany...

In June 2020 a statue of commie big dog Vladimir Lenin was erected in the western German city of Gelsenkirchen. [74] The brainwashed idiots responsible was the *Marxist-Leninist Party of Germany* (MLPD).[75] There was some resistance to its installation by other groups. This happened during the craze of statue-toppling that swept across the west. Coincidence, right? A statement made by the MLPD representative Commissar Gabi Fechtner referred to this: "The time for monuments to racists, anti-semites, fascists, anti-communists and other relics of the past has clearly passed". Lenin, by comparison, was "an ahead-of-his-time thinker of world-historical importance, an early fighter for freedom and democracy". That says it all. Welcome to hell folks…

As mentioned, Lenin's activities were highly significant in the proliferation and evolution of the ideology. If it wasn't for him, perhaps this book wouldn't need to exist. The destructive impact of Lenin's activities on humanity is simply incalculable; his legacy is the epitome of suffering, starvation, enslavement, and death. When compared to the characters mentioned earlier – in terms of crimes against humanity – he is right at the top of the charts.

The comments of the cult member above are beyond ludicrous. I'm no fan of these three, but it can't be argued that Churchill, Rhodes or Pike created more suffering on this planet than Lenin (due to the scope, toxicity, and death-toll of the cult/ideology)! Impossible, even if we combine their tallies! (note: the author is aware of the apparent connections between Masonic lodges, secret societies and all four men etc.).

This commie erection event was an obvious statement by the cult that they're taking over—pulling down the statues they dislike, and erecting others they like. They are marking their territory, right there, obvious, out in the open! Hidden in plain sight! The same article stated that in the same month, the Hamburg statue of the first chancellor of Germany Otto von Bismarck (1815–1898) was vandalised with (commie) red paint. The crypto-Communist Angela Merkel was the Chancellor at the time.

Digging up dead bodies

Here's two more bits of evidence that this statue business is all about the cult's dominance. The bitterness towards their enemies is palpable and is seen in their actions. One of their most hated 'fascist' figures is

---

[74] "Controversial Lenin statue unveiled in Germany", 20 June 2020.
https://www.dw.com/en/controversial-lenin-statue-unveiled-in-germanys-gelsenkirchen/a-53880002

[75] https://www.mlpd.de/english

Generalissimo Francisco Franco. Franco gave the cult no quarter in Spain right up until his death, treating them how they deserved to be treated for decades (after defeating them in all-out war). Obviously, this triggers their eternal bitterness. His statues have been systematically removed over the decades, the last one in Morocco was removed in February 2021, to the delight of the local PSOE Socialist party.[76]

In Spain in 2019, his remains were exhumed from the grand mausoleum at the Valley of the Fallen and moved to the state cemetery in Mingorrubio.[77] The Prime Minister of Spain – Socialist Pedro Sanchez – was involved. Not surprisingly, protests of this Marxian manoeuvre were not permitted by the government (they were designated 'far-right' extremists, I'm sure). Sanchez described the act as "a tribute to all victims of hate". Moving dead bodies around because their original resting place offends the cult! These 'people' are beyond pathetic! Tellingly, Sanchez was also quoted as saying "The Spain of today is a complete opposite of the one the Franco regime represented". Indeed.

Shek in Taiwan

Another example is found in Taiwan. As reported in September 2021, the left-wing ruling government had plans to remove a statue of the nationalist leader and dictator Chiang Kai Shek.[78]

Similar to Franco, Shek kept Taiwan Marxism-free until his death, suppressing the cult from 1949–1975. Franco did same from 1939 until his death in 1975 (similarly, they both fought a civil war against the cult, but Shek lost his, and the nationalist forces fled to Taiwan in 1949, as mainland China succumbed to the red fog).

The initiative is being carried out by the *Democratic Progressive Party* and its leader President Tsai Ing-wen who have been at the helm since 2016. Taiwan needs a Shek character today considering what the CCP-controlled

---

[76] "Last public statue of Spanish dictator Franco is removed", 23 Feb 2021.

https://www.theguardian.com/world/2021/feb/23/last-public-statue-of-spanish-dictator-franco-is-removed

[77] Booker, B, "Spain Moves Dictator Francisco Franco's Remains, After Months Of Legal Battles", 24 October 2019.

https://www.npr.org/2019/10/24/773022042/spain-moves-dictator-francisco-francos-remains-after-months-of-legal-battles?t=1632821666327

[78] Hale, E, "Taiwan axes symbols of authoritarian past in push to rebrand", 26 September 2021. https://asia.nikkei.com/Politics/Taiwan-axes-symbols-of-authoritarian-past-in-push-to-rebrand

People's Republic of China is up to nowadays!

This is not just mere pettiness and fanaticism, no. They are trying to bury historical traces of the anti-Marxist movements to prevent us from taking inspiration from them, thereby ensuring the cult's dominance into the future. Statues serve as reminders, and once they are removed, they are soon forgotten (along with what they represent) by all but the older generations—and that's the whole point. The aim is that the younger generations only know Marxism and Marxist idols. Obviously, when it gets to this point completely, all hope is lost…

The destruction of the traditional family

> "The state should compete with private individuals–especially with par-
> ents- in providing happy homes for children, so that every child may
> have a refuge from the tyranny or neglect of its natural custodians"79

George Bernard Shaw, *A Manifesto, Fabian Tracts No. 2.*, 1884

A 5 December 2023 article in the Irish Times reported that more Marxian 'referendums' are imminent in Ireland; possibly being held on the Marxian feminist date of 8 March 2024—International Women's Day.

The official purpose of these referendums is "to remove the constitutional reference to the role of women in the home; and expand the concept of the family within the constitution".[80] They apparently want to also introduce the term "durable relationships" (to further erode the concept of families being built around a marriage).

I remind the reader that these nutcases are conducting this bullshit in a country plagued with a myriad of other genuine, serious issues. (as an aside, there was a 'children's rights' constitutional referendum in 2012 in Ireland pushed by cult members, which essentially increased government interference in family affairs. Their successful manoeuvre was marketed, via virtue-signalling, as "child protection").[81]

Destroying the traditional nuclear family unit results in several beneficial

---

[79] *Shaw, G.B., "A Manifesto. Fabian Tracts No. 2", 1884.*
https://oll.libertyfund.org/page/shaw-s-fabian-manifesto-1884

[80] Horgan-Jones, J, "Referendums on women in the home and the concept of the family to be held next March", 5 Dec 2023.
https://www.irishtimes.com/politics/2023/12/05/referendums-on-women-in-the-home-and-the-concept-of-the-family-to-be-held-next-march/

[81] https://en.wikipedia.org/wiki/Thirty-first_Amendment_of_the_Constitution_of_Ireland

effects for the ideology, including:

(a) Controlling individuals' minds at the youngest ages possible. Since the cult/ideology aims to gain total control of society, the best way to achieve this is by indoctrinating individuals at the youngest ages possible. Obviously, those who only know the ideology – and are fully-indoctrinated from the outset – can't resist it.

By removing parents from the equation and replacing them with state-approved 'educators' (teachers), welfare advisors, social care workers etc. (who are indoctrinated themselves), the young are directly moulded in the ideology's image, and can begin serving the glorious revolution as early as possible. Tragic.

This degree of control creates generations of individuals who are completely subservient to – and dependent upon – the state. This has been a feature of cult regimes, past and present. The education systems are central in creating new generations of brainwashed cult members, from kindergarten to university.

(b) Removing any psychological protection that parents can provide from any predatory initiatives being pushed by the system (i.e. any form of Marxist activism). This is in addition to protecting them from all of the various toxic sources of influence spewing the ideology (media/entertainment, online media, social media, music industry etc.), and contaminated individuals (e.g. celebrities, activists), groups (N.G.O.'s/non-profits, community, or political groups etc.). The ideology also seeks to replace the potentially 'troublesome' (non-Marxian) views of parents with those of cult members. The cult/ideology itself – via the system and state – becomes the loving, guiding 'parent'.

The destruction of the family unit sub-agenda uses the oppressor v oppressed formula in the most bizarre, despicable way, which is coming to light even more in recent times. The cult – via the transgenderism/'non-binary' sub-agenda – has been trying to convince the masses that the 'compassionate' state is better suited to parenting children than the parents themselves! Undoubtedly, children are being 'oppressed' by their parents with regards to their sexual identity, so the 'heroic' predatory state must intervene. An Irish Independent article on 2 June 2020 reported on plans to allow children under the age of sixteen to legally 'change their gender'.[82] Naturally, the Irish gender-bender-in-Chief Leo Varadkar was involved,

---

[82] "Fine Gael seeking law change to let under-16s legally change gender", June 2020.

https://www.independent.ie/irish-news/fine-gael-seeking-law-change-to-let-under-16s-legally-change-gender/39252644.html being a member of his Fine Gael party's LGBTQ committee.

(c) Reducing/removing the possibility of any punishment and discipline from a young person's life. Such things are indispensable when raising children. This is crucial, since being a cult member and being spoilt go together. The more spoilt brats we have in society, the more weak-minded egomaniacal control-freaks we have, and the stronger the cult/ideology becomes. A general absence of this kind of parenting creates generations of individuals who are hard-wired to be primarily driven by what they want/feel, and who throw tantrums when they don't get their own way. Looking at how cult members behave, isn't this familiar? This point is linked to the next.

(d) Removing the beneficial influence of a healthy, natural masculine and feminine balance that a male and female parental partnership can provide. The traditional family unit potentially holds the best balance of this from a parenting point of view to the children's benefit, with a heterosexual male and heterosexual female in their respective roles. The cult/ideology will promote and normalise any and every type of relationship/parenting/family set-up but this one, offering false/inferior alternatives to hide this fundamental truth (e.g. gay parents adopting children or using artificial forms of conception or surrogacy; men 'being pregnant'; polyamorous additional partner 'couples' etc.).

(e) Creating a situation where young people will start to look at society/the world population/the Marxist cult as their 'family'. Families can provide a sense of unity and a bond with others that often becomes the foundations of a person's life; therefore, they must be removed from the equation. Families (including traditional nuclear families), by definition, can be simultaneously both little collectives unto themselves, while also being distinctly different and separate from other families to a certain degree, relations aside (and those other families are themselves similar collectives etc.).

It's the "separation" bit that doesn't sit well with the ideology; it simply won't do! The ideology's goal is to make humanity one big collective. There can be no "different" and "separate", there is only the all, the "people", unity, equality, solidarity etc. It's the whole "we are all one!" bullshit pushed by the New Age Movement.

(f) Removing heterosexual males as the head of the traditional family unit from their position of authority/influence within it. This helps to eliminate any sort of aggressive, combative, resistant energy from the equation that might oppose the cult/ideology (including any 'toxic masculinity'). In addition, men are removed from their traditional roles as protectors and breadwinners for the family. This is embodied in the (Marxian) feminist maxim that women don't need men to be successful parents.

As mentioned, single parents can do a relatively good job of course and every situation is different, but it's not ideal for anyone involved or society as a whole (in addition to benefiting the ideology itself). The late British historian, journalist, and author Paul Johnson (1928–2023) once said "The most socially subversive institution of our time is the one-parent family".[83] Of course, by removing men from these roles, this somehow creates 'equality', while simultaneously combating that dreaded foe of feminism— the 'patriarchy'.

(g) The removal of another thing that is traditional, cultural (and therefore connects with the past). The family unit holds a place in the traditional trio of elements for a healthy, prosperous society: family, nation, and religion. In transforming society in its image, the cult/ideology needs to remove connections with the societies of the past. Anything traditional must go!

(h) Controlling the sexual behaviour of the young. The cult/ideology aims to replace parents when it comes to educating (programming) the young about sex, sexuality, and relationships (expanded on further along).

Other sub-agendas it ties-in to

The destruction of the family unit sub-agenda is promoted by the Marxism-infused system using anti-traditionalist indoctrination (via the 'transmission belts of culture'—education, media, entertainment industry). Of course, the overall goal is to minimise the amount of stable, traditional families. It's woven-in with several other sub-agendas and concepts originating from/promoted by the ideology:

—the 'egalitarian' women's 'liberation' movement (feminism) has brainwashed/enticed women away from traditional roles as mothers and homemakers, and into the proletarian collective of the workforce (and to therefore start paying taxes). This sub-agenda combined with the Marxian education systems creates a situation where the state has more control over the psychological development of children. This was a momentous development for society during the 20th century, and indeed, the fate of the human race—women spending more time working and less time in their children's company than at any point in history.

Obviously, abortion plays a key role in discouraging/preventing women

---

[83] Quoted in the Sunday Correspondent, 24 December 1989.

https://libquotes.com/paul-johnson/quote/lbd3o0d

from having children and starting families in the first place; and it obviously wouldn't have the status it does now without the feminist movement (abortion itself is part of another agenda to create separation between sex/sexuality and procreation; that sex is just for pleasure (aka hedonism).

—the LGBTQ/transgenderism/non-binary sub-agenda attempts to destroy normal sexual development (biologically and psychologically) in the young, preventing them from being able to start families later in life (due to mental/relationship/identity issues, or physiological damage—including sterility—caused by gender 'reassignment' surgery/removing sexual organs, hormones, puberty blockers etc.).

—the anti-Christianity sub-agenda is connected here because Christianity (Roman Catholicism in particular) has traditionally played a role in encouraging marriage—the institution upon which the traditional family unit has been based for ages now. The popularisation and normalisation of divorce (thanks, in part, to feminism) obviously plays a role too—it helps to trivialise the concept of marriage.

—the destruction of the traditional family connects to the mass immigration sub-agenda (aka the anti-white, miscegenation agenda), since these sub-agendas (in addition to those listed above) are being forced on primarily western, mostly Caucasian countries. They all combine to reduce the amount of white people therein.

The beneficial influence of a natural masculine and feminine balance (continued)

The traditional family unit is based on the ages-old natural male and female parental partnership. To attack this, the cult/ideology has been trying to push the erroneous idea that all forms of sexuality are equal and should be treated as such; even when it comes to parenting issues. This also includes the notion that all sexual orientations are of equal value to society, meaning that the sexuality of a gay man is of equal value to that of a heterosexual man; no, it isn't! When it comes to having children, heterosexual men obviously contribute more; the same can be said of heterosexual women (compared to lesbian women).

On the critically important issue of procreation, heterosexual relationships are far superior to other relationship types because they can produce children naturally (artificial forms of procreation, which can be expensive for some, aside). There is no competition between heterosexual and homosexual relationships in this department. Zero! Only in a world this f*cked-up, does someone need to point these things out! This is not a personal attack on anyone, it's just biology. The cult has created terms like 'heteronormativity' to help in obfuscating this truth, attempting to make all sexuality/sexual orientations seem equal; the term suggests that heterosexuality is just what we perceive as being normal. Nice try. It's another Marxian sleight-of-hand, designed to distort our perception of reality.

The differences in biology (and therefore psychology) between heterosexual and homosexual parents is also important when it comes to actual parenting. Obviously gay parents would have to use artificial forms of conception and surrogacy, but what I'm focusing on here is what happens after the child's birth. The ideal combination is a man and woman, as nature/creation intended, if the intention is to have regular, heterosexual children.

I raise this point again because, for example, in the instance that, say, a gay male couple have a girl—what on earth would they know about being female?!? The same applies if they have a boy who doesn't turn out to be gay—what would they know about being a heterosexual male? The same for lesbian couples—what would they know about being a male? Or a straight female? Again, unless they have a gay female child, are they really going to be able to parent correctly and relate to their 'offspring'?

Of course, they might decide to (criminally) 'encourage' their child to be gay, in order to relate to them better. They certainly aren't going to discourage their child from expressing any gay tendencies (in the instance that the child is straight and may/may not have gender identity issues during their development). There are plenty of testimonies online of people who were 'encouraged' in this way, and later ended up with detrimental identity issues later in life—catastrophic in some cases.

Not all gay parents in all situations would be bad parents, of course, and the idea that all heterosexual parents are automatically great parents in all situations is false—we all know there are rotten, stupid parents out there!

Being a good parent is about personality/attitude, dedication, responsibility, patience, intelligence, love, using discipline etc.; and anyone, regardless of their gender/sexual orientation, can offer those things. However, heterosexual parents have the advantage overall, as they can relate to their children better. Plus having a father and a mother allows both parents to offer different types of input (under normal circumstances), from different points of view to each child—the masculine and the feminine; and both these parents are physically different from each other. You don't get this with same-sex couples either.

Besides, isn't it a factor too that gay parents are likely to raise children that are more 'liberal' (aka more inclined to grow up as cult members)? That means that even when it comes to how we raise our children, the ideology is trying to impose its will. Bottom line—all types of parental couples in this instance are not equal. The cult's propaganda tries to tell us otherwise.

Relationship retards

In addition to attacking the traditional family using direct means, the ideology also does it indirectly. It supports degeneracy which itself helps to destroy it, particularly when it comes to human relationships. It supports: excessive hedonism; promiscuity (the "sex is for pleasure, not for procreation" mindset); superficiality; self-centred irresponsible attitudes ("my body, my choice"); polyamory and other weird types of 'relationships'; androgyny, gender-nonbinary and transgenderism; the social media ego-driven culture (including the dopamine and serotonin manipulation/dependency that occurs) etc. And as mentioned, since the very young are now being targeted with this, they will be saturated with this crap from childhood to adolescence and beyond.

An environment full of these toxic elements helps to create individuals who end up being relationship retards—those who are unable to have functioning, stable, meaningful adult relationships. The more time a person spends in degenerate mindsets like the above, the less time they spend learning to have stable relationships that a family could be built around. This all obviously decreases the number of stable families in the general population, creating weak societies/nations, which serves the ideology. The apt term "retarded" essentially means "less advanced in mental, physical, or social development than is usual for one's age".

Interestingly, where in our lives can we possibly learn how to have these types of relationships? At home. We first learn from our own parents. If this example isn't there, we better get some positive influence from somewhere. So, imagine what state future generations of the youth will be in if the traditional family unit is further removed from society, in addition to growing up in this type of toxic environment? Prediction: generations of relationship retards. Many amongst the recent 21st century generations— who are becoming contaminated and influenced at ever-younger ages— may never learn how to have meaningful relationships.

Starting families for patriotic, religious, or ethnic reasons

The ideology neutralises any sense of duty within a population to start families for the good of their nation, religious group, or race, due to its opposition to—or outright denial of—such things. According to its dogma, countries shouldn't exist, religion is delusion, and race is a social construct; therefore, the idea of starting families and having children for these reasons is just ridiculous, right? The ideology/cult (in general) promotes these fallacies as part of its anti-traditional family sub-agenda, and its anti-nation sub-agenda (plus others). These are the types of subtle, in-direct attacks which helps the ideology achieve this particular sub-agenda (destruction of the traditional family).

The idea of starting families for the above reasons may sound like an alien idea in modern, ideologically infected societies, yet this has been a feature of countless cultures throughout history since the dawn of man! Of course, these reasons shouldn't be the only reasons to starting families, but it's a positive thing when they are in the picture; the indoctrination sees to it that they are not. Again, this sub-agenda primarily applies to western countries that have been traditionally predominantly white and Christian. The ideology has had the most impact in these countries on this issue.

Controlling individuals through sexual programming

Another huge issue, covered by other researchers and authors. Since the ultimate aim of the cult/ideology is complete dominance and destruction of anything good, it seeks ever more efficient ways of doing so. Therefore, controlling people through their sexual behaviour is desirable. Of course, it has traditionally been the responsibility of parents to educate their children about sexuality. Hence, this is another reason why the cult/ideology needs to remove their influence.

This initiative is prevalent in the various sub-agendas being pushed by the cult via 'the system' (media, entertainment, education, government etc.). The education system is the most effective at this, since children are face-to-face with their indoctrinators and can't 'switch them off' like a TV or phone, or escape.

Indeed, there is a struggle of influence happening right now in the world between cult members determined to infect the young via 'education', and the parents trying to protect their children from 'teaching material' they know to be inappropriate or downright evil. Obviously, none of this applies if the parents are not hostile to Marxism, or worse—cult members themselves—in which case there is no struggle (and their children's fate is often more or less sealed).

In our societies, thanks to the infection, we have seen: the over-emphasis on sexuality (aka "hyper-sexualisation"); the trans/non-binary nonsense; drag queen story time in schools; making kids write gay love letters; 'radical' sex education and promotion of anal sex; relationship programming; the normalisation of abortion; the promotion of feminism which warps the minds of females and males; and the normalisation/ encouragement of homo/bi-sexuality. All have a sexual element to them or are related to sex. Panels of cult members ('experts') in each infected country will explain to us what children should be learning in school.

Controlling the sexual programming/behaviour of the young helps to create generations of young people who grow up to be hedonistic, mentally unstable, superficial, relationship retards, who are either unable or unwillingly to start families. In addition, they won't have the will to resist the cult/ideology, even if they somehow had the urge to. Taking control of the sexual programming of the young can help to achieve all this.

At a national level, these various initiatives are pushed via the education systems. In Ireland, the Irish Times reported in July 2023 that "sex education classes" were becoming mandatory for senior cycle secondary (high school) students.[84] The initiative is called "Social Personal and Health Education", where students are going to be brainwashed for one hour per week. The primary school counterpart is "Relationships and Sexuality Education (RSE)".

On an international level, the sub-institutions of the (Marxist) United Nations (e.g. UNESCO) play a central role in dictating these initiatives, and the subservient governments of member 'states' (countries) are 'obliged' to comply. Global templates have been created on how children should be 'educated', particularly when it comes to sex 'education'. Very weird, paedo-esque stuff...

From the foreword of the 138-page UNESCO document "International Technical Guidance on Sexuality Education" (2018): "too many young people still make the transition from childhood to adulthood receiving inaccurate, incomplete or judgement-laden information affecting their physical, social and emotional development... This represents the failure of society's duty bearers to fulfil their obligations to an entire generation".[85] I see, so the UN has to step in. Activism requires creating a problem out of thin air that needs to be 'fixed', which is what they've done here. Note how 'duty bearers' is a sly dig at parents.

On page 71, in the "Sexual Behaviour and Sexual Response" section, the "learning objectives" for 5 to 8-year-olds includes them understanding "that people show love and care for other people in different ways, including kissing, hugging, touching, and sometimes through sexual

---

[84] O'Brien, C, "Sex education classes to be mandatory for Leaving Cert students", 12 July 2023. https://www.irishtimes.com/ireland/education/2023/07/12/sex-education-classes-to-be-mandatory-for-leaving-cert-students/

[85] "International technical guidance on sexuality education: an evidence-informed approach", UNESCO 2018. https://unesdoc.unesco.org/ark:/48223/pf0000260770

behaviour".[86] It's a wonder that humanity has procreated to this point without the UN's wise input!

I must say, it's an amusing and disturbing read—approaching human interactions, relationships, and sexuality from an ultra-analytical, structured, almost robotic point of view. (robot voice) "At this age of development you will touch your genitals."… "At that age you will choose your default gender status for today… beep bop boop".

Children (according to the UN etc.) are 'suffering' due to the inability of the parents to parent. Therefore, in this sub-agenda, the children are the 'oppressed' ones, the parents are the 'oppressors', and weirdo, paedo-enabling cult members need to come to the rescue. Children of the world unite!

---

[86] Ibid. P. 71.

Section V—Various Groups And Incarnations

"There are some of our own people who still think that the Communists are the left wing of the Socialist movement. They are not. The Socialist movement was a movement for freedom in its widest sense. From the point of view of freedom, Communists are on the extreme right"[1]

Fabian Society member and British Prime Minister Clement Atlee, speech in Glasgow, 1949

Introduction

The perceptions of many have been distorted in to accepting internationalism, with the ultimate purpose of dragging them towards global totalitarian enslavement. This has been referred-to as the One-World Government agenda, with which Marxism is inextricably linked. This is about the ideology's ambitions of global dominance.

It's true that Marxism is a leopard that never changes its spots; but it's also a serpent…a snake that—once it becomes easily recognised for what it is—will then shed its old, worn skin, replacing it with a new, beautiful, shiny layer. As it slithers around the world unmolested, time passes; its prior appearance becomes forgotten—along with its predatory nature. This cycle of constant rejuvenation and re-invention is perhaps the primary, most-used defence that this stubborn ideology has, and, of course, it can be either overt or covert in its methods. We can't go over the whole history, but we must cover a few items.

Fabian Socialism

"For the right moment you must wait, as Fabius did most patiently…but when the time comes you must strike hard or your waiting will be in vain, and fruitless"2

---

[1] Clement Attlee, speech in Glasgow (10 April 1949), quoted in *The Times* (11 April 1949), P. 4. https://en.wikiquote.org/wiki/Communism

[2] https://fabians.org.uk/about-us/our-history/

Fabian pamphlet

"We have the guidance of an expert—George Bernard Shaw of the Fabian Society who called Lenin, the "greatest Fabian of them all." He formulated and described the Fabian methodology: it used "methods of stealth, intrigue, subversion, and the deception of never calling socialism by its right name"[3]

Stormer, John, *None Dare Call It Treason*,1964

"Patriotism is, fundamentally, a conviction that a particular country is the best in the world because you were born in it"[4]

G.B. Shaw, *The World*, 1893

The *Fabian Society* or Fabian Socialists (FS) is a crucial sub-topic for a student of Marxist subversion and the 'New World Order'. This is because this organisation clearly shows the connection between quasi-secret societies, subversive socialism, and the world of politics. The FS created—and subsequently controlled—the *British Labour Party*. In addition, this group shows a clear link between those structures and academia—they created a University to further their goals called the *London School of Economics*.[5]

The Fabians aimed to bring about socialism using subversive means, via the democratic system ('democratic socialism'), education, community groups etc.[6] The concepts of *Communitarianism* (expanded later), and aspects of "Third Way" politics (a 'fusion' of left and right ideas) can be connected with Fabianism. The FS also clearly shows us the 'champagne socialist' principle in action on an organisational level too—a bunch of elitists claiming to be champions of the poor, while serving the tyrannical internationalist agenda (wittingly or unwittingly). Since many of the Fabians were 'bourgeoisie' themselves, they didn't focus on the traditional class-struggle aspect of traditional Marxist theory (as the Leninists did); otherwise, they'd have to designate themselves the enemy.

Basic info

Originally, this was a London-based outfit formed from a previous organisation called *The Fellowship of the New Life*. It's now an extremely

---

[3] Stormer, J, *None Dare Call It Treason* (1964), P. 26.

[4] Shaw, G.B., *The World* (1893). https://en.wikiquote.org/wiki/George_Bernard_Shaw

[5] https://www.britannica.com/topic/Fabian-Society

[6] Diniejko, Litt, "The Fabian Society in Late Victorian Britain", 16 September 2013. https://victorianweb.org/history/fabian.html

powerful international organization with a presence in the UK, Canada (*Douglas-Coldwell Foundation*, then *League for Social Reconstruction*), Australia (*Australian Fabian Society*), and New Zealand (*New Zealand Fabian Society*), and in Sicily, Italy of all places (*Societa Fabiana Siciliana*). Current membership of the U.K. Fabian Society is in excess of 7000 members.[7]

The society was founded on 4 January 1884 (almost 10 months after the death of Karlie Karl Marx). The founding members were middle-class 'radicals' attracted by socialist ideas: Frank Podmore, Edward R. Pease, William Clarke, Hubert Bland, Pervical Chubb, Frederick Keddell, H.H. Champion, Edith Nesbit, and Rosamund Dale Owen. Hubert Bland later recruited George Bernard Shaw (1856–1950), who was also his friend and fellow journalist. All new members were required to sign a constitution-like document called "The Basis" (1887). This programme included proposals such as "the use of the existing institutions, party and parliamentary machinery for the realization of social reforms", to achieve "the elimination of privately owned land and the establishment of community ownership of the means of production".[6]

The Fabians

The prominent members and leadership of the FS were: Irish playwright, author, and Nobel laureate G.B. Shaw; married couple Sidney (1859–1947) and Beatrice Webb (1858–1943); Graham Wallas, and Sidney Olivier. Sidney Webb was an economist, political scientist, and author. He married Beatrice Potter in 1892 (Potter was the daughter of Richard Potter—a wealthy financier in British and Canadian rail). Wallas was a social psychologist and educationalist. Sidney Olivier was a well-connected civil servant and later served as Governor of Jamaica and Secretary of State for India.

Other members of the Fabian Society included: the famous author Herbert George Wells; philosopher and mathematician Bertrand Russell; economist John Maynard Keynes; Eleanor Marx (daughter of Karlie Karl); historian and professor Arnold Toynbee; theosophist and women's rights activist Annie Besant; women's rights activist and organiser of the UK Suffragette movement Emmeline Pankhurst; Freemason and politician Clement Atlee; editor of the *New Age* magazine and Freemason Alfred Richard Orage; and *Brave New World* author Aldous Huxley (brother of notable eugenicist Julian Huxley).

---

[7] "Membership". https://fabians.org.uk/membership/

G.B.'s pearls of wisdom

Perhaps the most famous Fabian is George Bernard ("G.B.") Shaw. Here are some absolutely cracking quotes of his. This first one is from *The Intelligent Woman's Guide to Socialism and Capitalism* (1928): "Socialism means equality of income or nothing. Under socialism you would not be allowed to be poor. You would be forcibly fed, clothed, lodged, taught, and employed whether you liked it or not. If it were discovered that you had not character and industry enough to be worth all this trouble, you might possibly be executed in a kindly manner; but whilst you were permitted to live you would have to live well. In the ultimate 'nanny state', with no free will or right to choose, you are owned by the elites and discarded when you are no longer any use".[8]

This one is from a filmed speech on 5 March 1931 (available on YouTube): "I don't want to punish anybody, but there are an extraordinary number of people whom I want to kill. Not in any unkind or personal spirit, you must all know half a dozen people at least who are no use in this world it would be a good thing to make everybody come before a properly-appointed board... and say every five or every seven years just put them there and say: "Sir, or Madam, now will you be kind enough to justify your existence?. If you can't justify your existence, if you're not pulling your weight in the social vote, if you're not producing as much as you consume, or perhaps a little more, then, clearly, we cannot use the big organization of our society for the purpose of keeping you alive, because your life does not benefit us and it can't be of very much use to yourself".[9]

He was quoted as saying this in an issue of Dublin newspaper the *Evening Herald* on 3 February 1948: "I am a Communist, but not a member of the Communist Party. Stalin is a first-rate Fabian. I am one of the founders of Fabianism and as such very friendly to Russia".[10]

The genocidal/democidal track-record of the cult's regimes in the 20th century takes on a different meaning when we consider eugenics (breeding to produce certain results). The fact that Shaw was a fan of the Soviet

---

[8] Shaw, G.B., *The Intelligent Woman's Guide to Socialism and Capitalism* (1928). https://ia904704.us.archive.org/33/items/in.ernet.dli.2015.276240/2015.276240.The-Intelligent.pdf

[9] "George Bernard Shaw: There are an extraordinary number of people whom I want to kill", 27 June 2020. https://www.YouTube.com/watch?v=Ymi3umIo-sM

[10] Shaw, G.B., Evening Herald newspapers, 3 February 1948.

https://quotepark.com/quotes/2066840-george-bernard-shaw-i-am-a-communist-but-not-a-member-of-the-communis/

regime and Stalin is not surprising. In a lecture at the *Eugenics Education Society* in 1910 Shaw stated: "We should find ourselves committed to killing a great many people whom we now leave living…A part of eugenic politics would finally land us in an extensive use of the lethal chamber. A great many people would have to be put out of existence simply because it wastes other people's time to look after them ".[11]

An excerpt from None Dare call it Treason by John A. Stormer (1928–2018) (underlined for emphasis): "Shaw described himself as a "communist" but differed with Marx over how the revolution would be accomplished and by whom. He spelled out these differences in 1901 in his *Who I am, What I think* when he wrote: 'Marx's 'Capital' is not a treatise on socialism; it is a jeremiad against the bourgeoisie (middle class). It was supposed to be written for the working class; but the working man respects the bourgeoisie and wants to be a bourgeoisie; Marx never got hold of him for a moment. It was the revolting sons of the bourgeoisie itself, like myself, that painted the flag red. The middle and upper classes are the revolutionary element in society: the proletariat is the conservative element'".[12]

Interesting and revealing. As mentioned, Marx and Engels themselves were from privileged backgrounds.

War of the Wells

"This new and complete Revolution we contemplate can be defined in a very few words. It is outright world-socialism, scientifically planned and directed…and sedulous expansion of the educational organisation to the ever-growing demands of the new order"[13]

H.G. Wells, *New World Order,* 1940

The world-famous English author H.G. Wells (1866–1946) was a member of the Fabian Society from 1903–1908. Wells was a Darwinist and life-long advocate of socialism and eugenics. He believed that collectivism should become the new "opiate of the masses", the new religion. At one point he even attempted to gain control of the society's leadership (from Shaw and Webb) with some newer members.

Amongst his many works, Wells authored: *Will Socialism Destroy the Home?* (1907), *The War and Socialism* (1915), *The Open Conspiracy*

---

[11] Rose, E. "Eugenics Rises Again", 14 November 2019.

https://medium.com/@finnishrose/eugenics-rises-again-1f5421aba5ba

[12] Shaw, G.B., "Who I Am, and What I Think", 11 May 1901.

[13] Wells, H.G., *New World Order* (1940).

(1928), and *New World Order* (1940).[14] In New World Order he wrote: "Countless people, from maharajas to millionaires and from pukkha sahibs to pretty ladies, will hate the new world order...and will die protesting against it. When we attempt to estimate its promise we have to bear in mind the distress of a generation or so of malcontents".

Also: "The reorganisation of the world has at first to be mainly the work of a "movement" or a Party or a religion or cult, whatever we choose to call it. We may call it the New Liberalism or the New Radicalism or what not. It will not be a close-knit organisation, toeing the Party line and so forth. It may be very loose-knit and many faceted".[15] Considering the nature of the cult/ideology today, is this vision not almost prophetic?

Modern members and speakers

In modern times, some of the famous members and event speakers include: former leader of the British Labour Party Jeremy Corbyn; former UK Prime Minister and British Labour Party leader Tony Blair; British Labour Party MP and Mayor of London Sadiq Khan; former UK Prime Minister and Labour Party leader Gordon Brown; British Labour Party politician and president of *Policy Network* Peter Mandelson. Other notable FS members—who were also members of the British parliament—include Robin Cook, Jack Straw, David Blunkett, and Clare Short.[16]

Fabians have also been at the highest levels of Australian politics for decades. By the time Julia Gillard took office in 2010, seven Australian Prime Ministers in a row were FS members: Gough Whitlam (1972 to 1975); Robert Hawke (1983 to 1991); Paul Keating (1991 to 1996); Kevin Rudd (2007 to 2010); and then Gillard herself (2010 to 2013). Other Fabians who became top politicians include John Cain, Neville Wran and Jim Cairns, and Australian Labour Party members Bob Carr and Kelving Thompson.[17] Interestingly, Jim Cairns was heavily involved with the *World Peace Council* (a creation of Joseph Stalin's), in addition to being a notable anti-Vietnam war activist.[18]

---

[14] https://www.britannica.com/biography/H-G-Wells

[15] Wells, H.G. *New World Order* (1940), P.111.
http://www.telelib.com/authors/W/WellsHerbertGeorge/prose/newworldorder/newworldorder008.html

[16] https://en.wikipedia.org/wiki/Category:Members_of_the_Fabian_Society

[17] McGrath, A, *Wolves in Sheep's clothing* (2012), P. 20.

[18] https://en.wikipedia.org/wiki/Jim_Cairns

A Fabian New World Order

In a speech in Washington DC on 21 April 2008 then British (Fabian) PM Tony Blair said: "The transatlantic partnership was never just the foundation of our security. It was the foundation of our way of life. It was forged in experience of the most bitter and anguished kind. Out of it came a new Europe, a new world order, a new consensus as to how life should be lived".[19]

On 2 April 2009, during a G20 summit in London, then British (Fabian) PM Gordon Brown said: "I think a New World Order is emerging, and with it the foundations of a new and progressive era of international co-operation...we will together manage the process of globalisation, to secure responsibility from all and fairness to all...we will build a more sustainable more open and fairer global society".[20] "Fairer" = egalitarianism, social justice etc. Also "responsibility from all and fairness to all" is the Fabian version of "from each according to his ability to each according to his needs" (thanks Karl). New World Order, anyone?

Chronology of FS events and achievements

In 2012, the Australian author Dr. Amy McGrath (1921–2019) published a book entitled *Wolves in Sheep's Clothing*. The book is a collection of excerpts from the work of other authors on the subject of communism etc. It includes pieces linking extra-governmental organisations like the United Nations, the Club of Rome, the Council on Foreign Relations, and the Bilderberg Group etc. As suggested by McGrath, these organisations have worked together to promote the One World Government agenda, through lower-level agendas including Agenda 21 and its "sustainable development" goals. Agenda 21 is ostensibly about how to restructure the world and human behaviour for the benefit of the planet. In reality, it's all about control of the masses (how and where they live, what they eat, how they travel, what possessions they can have and how much etc.).

As listed throughout Dr. McGrath's book, here's a chronological overview of some Fabian achievements since the society was established on the 4 January 1884. They: created the *Independent Labour Party* (ILP). It was founded in January 1893 through the merging of over 70 local Fabian groups, and was headed by Fabian Kier Hardie (who had earlier co-founded the Second International with Karl Marx's writing buddy and sponsor

---

[19] "Tony Blair - New World Order", 9 November 2010.
https://www.YouTube.com/watch?v=Jv17gVF9kMA

[20] CNN, "New world order is emerging", 2 April 2009.
https://www.YouTube.com/watch?v=ZD5Yy9Iq7lg

Friedrich Engels); founded the London School of Economics and Political Science in 1895; helped create the *Labour Representative Committee* in 1900; promoted the introduction of a minimum wage in 1906; founded the *Pan-Fabian Organization* in 1907; promoted the idea of a National Health Service in 1911; founded *Fabian Research* in 1912 (later known as the *Labour Research Bureau);* founded the *University Socialist Federation* in 1912 (later known as University Labour Clubs); founded the *New Statesman* socialist magazine in 1913 (which is still active today); assisted Lenin's Bolshevik revolution in Russia; were involved with the creation of the *Royal Institute of International Affairs* in 1919 (one of the "Big 6" orgs that apparently 'run' the world); were involved in the creation of *The League of Nations* in 1920 (a forerunner of the UN); created the *New Fabian Research Bureau* in 1931; were involved with the creation of the *United Nations* and founded *The International Court of Justice* at the Hague in 1945; and was involved in the creation of the *Socialist International* in 1951.[21] [22]

A piece called "International Government" (1916) was authored by the Fabian, Labour Party member, and journalist Leonard Woolf (1880–1969). This book was the inspiration for the creation of the *League of Nations* a few years later, which was achieved through the society's collaboration with the *Milner Group*. The *Fabian International Bureau* was involved in research and propaganda in international matters and promoted various internationalist schemes like the union of the British Empire with America and Russia.

The Socialist International (SI) was created to control a network of socialist organisations. Its aim was to co-ordinate international socialism and push the One World Government agenda through these groups. In addition, and to this end, these groups would help to strengthen the control of the United Nations. In June 1962, at the *Socialist International Council Conference* in Oslo, the SI famously declared that "Membership of the United Nations must be made universal".[23]

Why "Fabian" Society?

The name "Fabian" was suggested by a FS founding member (likely Frank Podmore). Quintus Fabius Maximus Verrucosus (280-203 BC) was a

[21] McGrath, A, *Wolves in Sheep's clothing* (2012), P. 20.

[22] https://fabians.org.uk/about-us/our-history/

[23] *"Declaration of the Socialist International, Oslo Conference, 2–4 June 1962".*

https://www.socialistinternational.org/councils/oslo-1962/

Roman General tasked with defending Rome from the Carthaginian General Hannibal (247-181 BC) during the *Second Punic War* (218bc-201bc). Hannibal became legendary for such innovative tactics as using elephants to attack the Romans over the Alps! The Carthaginians vastly outnumbered the Romans, yet Fabius defeated Hannibal by employing a guerilla warfare approach—hit-and-run tactics, no direct battles, destroying supply lines etc. Since he held back the Carthaginian advance, he became known as Fabius "Cuncatator" (latin for "delayer"). His efforts allowed Rome to re-organise.[24] A key point here, for our purposes—the Fabians were/are outnumbered by the masses. When you are confronted by superior numbers, it's better to attack using subversive, indirect means to achieve victory.

Fabian symbology

"Beware of false prophets, which come to you in sheep's clothing, but inwardly they are ravening wolves" Matthew 7:15[25]

"I have feasted myself on the blood of the saints, but I am not suspected of men to be their enemy, for my fleece is white and warm my teeth are not the teeth of one that tears flesh my eyes are mild, and they know me not as the chief of the lying spirits"[26]

British occultist Aleister Crowley, *The Vision and the Voice*, 1911

Coat of Arms

The much-used traditional and Machiavellian Marxian tactic of malevolence, disguised as benevolence is perfectly symbolised by the Fabian coat of arms—a wolf in sheep's clothing. The wolf is black, wearing its white sheep disguise, holding a (commie) red flag. Can you think of a more appropriate image to symbolise this concept? It comes disguised as one of you—one of your own, as a friend; but aims to kill you and all your kind. A vicious predator disguised as the harmless prey. In short, this is a hostile attack on unsuspecting victims, using stealth. Apparently G.B. Shaw designed this coat of arms. It was later retracted as it was deemed a bit too blatant (no shit?).

The Fabian Logo

The Fabians also used the tortoise on a (commie) red background, representing a slow, creeping process. The bottom of this logo features

---

[24] https://fabians.org.uk/about-us/our-history/

[25] Matthew 7:15; King James Bible. https://biblehub.com/matthew/7-15.htm

[26] Crowley, A, *The Vision and the Voice* (1911).

some text of their motto "I wait long, but when I strike, I strike hard". This symbolises the patient, subversive style of the Fabians—a slow moving process of installing socialism, rather than an immediate, violent overthrow.

From their first pamphlet: "For the right moment you must wait, as Fabius did most patiently, when warring against Hannibal, though many censured his delays; but when the time comes you must strike hard, as Fabius did, or your waiting will be in vain and fruitless". A great quote from American author Jon Perdue: "The logo of the Fabian Society, a tortoise, represented the group's predilection for a slow, imperceptible transition to socialism, while its coat of arms, a "wolf in sheep's clothing", represented its preferred methodology to achieve its goal".[27]

A 'Religious' Fabian Window

The Fabian Window is a stained-glass window located at the London School of Economics. Designed by G. B. Shaw, it was commissioned in 1910. The window has changed hands and locations several times since then, reaching its final home in the Shaw Library at the LSE. Tony Blair unveiled it at a ceremony there on 20 April 2006.[28] In the window, three Fabians—Shaw, Webb and ER Pease—are pictured 're-forging' the Earth on an anvil, using (masonic) hammers. They are 'shattering it to bits', to remould the world as they see fit...to build 'the new world'. Above the world, we can see the Fabian coat of arms.

This 'reforging' of the world represents the traditional Marxian concept of deliberate destruction of the social order first before it then can be re-built as a 'utopia'. At the bottom there are other FS members 'praying' to their 'scriptures'. The scene depicted evokes the concept of religiosity and worship. The Fabians wanted their internationalist, collectivist totalitarian ideology to be the new 'religion'.

Do we not see this worship of Marxist 'knowledge'/scriptures, in a cult-like fashion today, particularly in academic/intellectual circles? This imagery, and indeed the intention of the Fabians in general, reflects one of the core messages of this book—it's a subversive cult. The window is probably the best physical artefact to symbolise this. The text across the top of the window says "Re-mould it near to the heart's desire". This is from a quatrain by the medieval Persian philosopher and poet Omar Khayyam (1048–1131): "Ah Love! Could thou and I with Fate conspire,

---

[27] Perdue, J, *The War of All the People: The Nexus of Latin American Radicalism and Middle Eastern Terrorism* (2012).

[28] Donnelly, S.,"Hammering out a new world–the Fabian Window at LSE", 13 September 2017.

To grasp this sorry scheme of things entire, Would not shatter it to bits—and then, Re-mould it nearer to the Heart's Desire!".[29]

The Fabian Strategy

The Fabians did not subscribe to the Bolshevik's modus operandi for revolutionary takeover. They weren't so anti-'bourgeoisie', being bourgeoisie themselves. They rejected the idea of a violent 'class struggle' to bring in a socialist society. They felt that reformation was better than revolution. Therefore, the Fabians aimed to bring in socialism by evolution not revolution. This was to be achieved not by direct and instant political action, to obtain immediate results, but by consistent, subtle influence spread out over a longer period. This was a different, indirect method of implementing collectivism compared to other methods that employed violent revolution (e.g. military overthrow/coup by 'Marxist-Leninists').

Quite unlike other interpretations of Marxism—where primarily the working classes were to be manipulated and controlled—the Fabians sought to control the other classes too. In particular, they wanted to use the middle classes to push their agendas, not the 'proletariat', and it was typical of the modus operandi of the Fabians to target the 'bourgeoisie' types. In Beatrice Webb's writings she spoke of conning people; of "catching millionaires". Overall, they wanted to indoctrinate society as a whole, to create "a common opinion in favour of social control... etc.". In other words, to psychologically prime our countries for a takeover by the Marxist cult. During the early years of the society, the Fabians were giving 700 lectures a year, pushing their 'philosophy' of "Gradualism" or "Permeation".[30]

The Fabians specialize in using the democratic system to bring in a totalitarian state. This gradual method is generally well-suited to western 'first-world' countries. They pioneered the concept of democratic socialism—using the democratic system to ensure a pro-socialism mindset in their target countries. Infiltration of the 'power centres' is key, including labour unions, political parties, religious institutions, and groups (including the *New Age* movement), the legal system, media organisations, education systems, civic and financial institutions, industrial corporations etc. On education in particular, Shaw said that they must gain "control over the whole education system from the elementary school to the University...and

---

[29] Khayyam, O., quatrain XCIX https://en.wikiquote.org/wiki/OmarKhayyam

[30] McGrath, A, *Wolves in Sheep's clothing* (2012).

overall educational endowments".[31]

Doesn't all this sound familiar when we look at how western countries have been transformed in recent decades? Have you noticed the rate and pace at which things have changed in your country in recent times; not overnight, but through a gradual process of almost constant change? That's the Fabian way. Gradual, constant progress—like a walking tortoise.

Permeation

Here is G.B. Shaw talking about how the British Liberal Party were targeted using Permeation:

"We permeated the party organizations and pulled all the wires we could lay our hands on with our utmost adroitness and energy; and we succeeded so far that in 1888 we gained the solid advantage of a progressive majority, full of ideas that would never have come into their heads had not the Fabian put them there".[32] Note how this was a mere four years after the society formed.

From *The History of the Fabian Society* (1918) by Edward R. Pease (1857–1955), who served as secretary for several decades: "... a Universities Committee, with Frank Podmore as Secretary for Oxford and G. W. Johnson for Cambridge, had begun the 'permeation ' of the Universities, which has always been an important part of the propaganda of the Society". [33] (Readers may understand the significance of Oxford and Cambridge being mentioned here. They are regarded by some 'new world order' researchers as being an important part of the academic control apparatus).

The Fabians spawned many organisations to extend their reach. From *Occult Theocracy* (1933) by Lady Queenborough (1887–1933): "The Fabians form numerous detached societies, committees, study clubs, associations, leagues, schools, in order to gain the support of non-socialists for such sections of the Socialist programme which might fail to receive public approbation if the connection with the World Socialist-Communist scheme was revealed. Thus the "sucker lists" of capitalistic supporters of socialism are made available for England. The system is the same in

---

[31] Shaw, G.B, "Educational reform", 1889.

[32] Shaw, G.B., Fabian Tract 41 ("The Fabian Society: What it has done and how it has done it"), 1892.

[33] Pease, Edward R., *The History of the Fabian Society* (1918). https://www.voltairenet.org/IMG/pdf/Pease_Edward_R_-_History_Of_The_Fabian_Society.pdf

America ".[34] (Beatrice Webb's statements about conning the bourgeois business types spring to mind).

The Labour Party

> "Labour remained faithful to its long-term belief in the establishment of east-west co-operation as the basis for a strengthened United Nations developing towards world government.. For us world government is the final objective and the United Nations the chosen instrument"[35]
>
> British Labour Party election manifesto ("The New Britain"), 1964
>
> "The Labour Party hate the concept of Englishness... have done for a very long time, can't even stand the concept of patriotism. They think the flag somehow is unpleasant, backward-looking and nasty. People like Emily Thornberry would rather we had that blue flag with 12 stars on it that comes to us from Brussels"—British politician Nigel Farage, BBC News article, November 2014[36]

The British Labour Party evolved from the *Labour Representation Committee* (which the Fabians helped create). Before its founding in 1900, there were two main parties in British politics—the Conservatives and the Liberals. The Labour party was formed from those who belonged to a third category of 'rebels' and outliers who did not belong to the main two (and at that point in history, you can be sure there were plenty of determined cult members wandering around the place!). Sidney Webb wrote much of the party's 1918 constitution, in addition to the *Labour and the New Social Order* programme in the same year.[37]

From the "Our History" page of the *fabians.org.uk* website: "As the electoral significance of the Labour Party grew in the inter-war period, the contribution of the society kept pace. In 1923, over twenty Fabians were elected to parliament, with five Fabians in Ramsay McDonald's first Labour cabinet. Future prime minister and Fabian Clement Attlee received his first ministerial post at this time.". The war period itself saw "the blossoming of local Fabian societies. In 1939 there were just six local societies, by 1945 there were 120 local societies across the country". In 1945, the first UK Fabian PM, prominent cult member Clement Attlee,

---

[34] Miller, E.S. (Lady Queensborough), *Occult Theocracy* (1933).

[35] 1964 Labour Party Election Manifesto "The New Britain".http://www.labour-party.org.uk/manifestos/1964/1964-labour-manifesto.shtml

[36] "Miliband: Thornberry's 'white van, flag' tweet lacked respect", 21 November 2014. https://www.bbc.com/news/uk-politics-30148768

[37] https://fabians.org.uk/about-us/our-history/

took office replacing Winston Churchill. It has been estimated by FS researchers that there was 200 Fabians in the UK Parliament during Attlee's tenure. Under his leadership, the U.K. entered a period of economic decline due to experimentation in socialist policies. As mentioned, the cult/ideology often pushes to take control of countries when they are in a weakened state, such as in a post-war period.

The London School of Economics

The London School of Economics (or LSE) was founded in 1895 by leading FS members Sidney and Beatrice Webb, G.B. Shaw and Graham Wallas. Home of the Fabian Window, it was established to promote the ideology through academia. The official name is "The London School of Economics and Political Science", and it doesn't take a genius to imagine what kind of ideological slant it places on these subjects. The name is amusing too since an economic Marxist institution is an oxymoron. The LSE is known for 'far-left' radicalism, and was once referred to as the "London School of Extremists".[38] Notable Alumni include George Soros and David Rockefeller (1915–2017). The Irish politician and businessman Peter Sutherland (1946–2018) was also attached to the LSE. Sutherland was a central figure in the mass migration agenda of the UN, as Special Representative of the Secretary-General for International Migration (2006–2017).[39] In the late 1920s and 1930s, the LSE received millions of dollars from the Rockefeller and Laura Spellman foundations becoming known as "Rockefellers baby".[40]

Graham Moore

An analyst of note on the Fabians is a London-based researcher and English patriot by the name of Graham Moore. In January 2018, Moore was involved with an attempted citizen's arrest of Fabian Mayor of London Sadiq Khan. The action was attempted by a 'far-right' group called the *White Pendragons* (of which Moore is listed as the leader), while Khan was making a speech at a Fabian Society conference on gender equality (rolls eyes).

Moore's work has covered several areas, including some excellent work on

---

[38] Syal and Hasting, "Al-Qa'eda terror trio linked to London School of 'Extremists'", 27 January 2022. https://www.telegraph.co.uk/news/uknews/1382818/Al-Qaeda-terror-trio-linked-to-London-School-of-Extremists.html

[39] https://en.wikipedia.org/wiki/Peter_Sutherland

[40] Cox, M. "LSE – Rockefeller's baby?", 24 June 2015.

https://blogs.lse.ac.uk/lsehistory/2015/06/24/lse-rockefellers-baby/

the Fabians. At time of writing (Feb 2021), his YouTube channel is nowhere to be seen, but his website *daddydragon.co.uk* is still up.[41] In his several lengthy, detailed videos he made some very interesting observations about the Fabians. Here are some of the key points gathered (via notes) from them when the channel was still active.

Fabians in Government

In 1945, 393 Labour candidates were elected to parliament, of whom 229 were FS members. In 1997, 418 Labour candidates were elected, out of whom 200 were FS members. The Fabians have maintained a consistent presence in the UK parliament and are not only present in the Labour Party. According to the 2012 figures, there were approximately 7000 FS members in the U.K.

Of the 7000, eighty percent (5600) were members of the Labour Party (which is only about three percent of the general Labour party members). The other 20 percent of the FS total membership (1,400) are in other parties such as the Liberal Democrats and the Conservative Party.

In the higher echelons of Labour leadership, the percentage of Fabians dramatically increases, and about fifty percent of labour candidates since the 1940s have been FS members. When we come to the Labour party leadership itself, the proportion of Fabians comes close to one hundred percent. In 1966 the Labour cabinet had 21 members, out of which 17 were FS members.

This proportion has remained constant until today. Nearly the entire Labour cabinet in 1997 (including PM Tony Blair) was composed of Fabians. All Labour governments since 1924 to 1997–2010, have consisted almost exclusively of FS members. Almost all Labour party leaders have been Fabians. All Deputy Leaders of the Labour Party have been Fabians.[42]

From the "About Us" page of the UK Fabian Society website: "Every Labour prime minister has been a Fabian and today hundreds of Labour politicians are members of the society, including Labour leader Keir Starmer MP and more than half his shadow cabinet, as well as senior figures in devolved and local government. Our elected executive

---

[41] "Who are the White Pendragons?", 22 January 2018.
https://medium.com/@RidgewayInfo/who-are-the-white-pendragons-ba75af92d5eb

[42] Crace, J., "The Fabian Society: a Brief History", 13 August 2001.

https://www.theguardian.com/politics/2001/aug/13/thinktanks.uk

committee currently includes five Labour frontbenchers".[43]

Fabian activities globally

Moore also commented that: the Fabians played a role in dismantling the British Empire, using a front organization called *The Fabian Colonial Bureau*, as the empire was an obstacle to worldwide communism; Shaw and Webb pioneered the use of the Hegalian Dialectic in practical terms, in order to manipulate public opinion; the famous book *1984* authored by George Orwell (1903–1950) in 1949, was entitled so as a centenary tribute to the foundation of the Fabian Society in 1884; the Fabians were involved with writing the constitutions of several countries, including Ireland (Republic of) and India.

Moore stated that the famous quasi-messianic figure of Mahatma Gandhi (1869–1948) was involved with the Fabian Society and may have been a member; and that the founders of Pakistan—which was established after the partition of India and its independence from the British Empire—were Fabians.

The world-famous George Orwell (real name Eric Blair) went to Eton College—an elitist private school for teen boys in Berkshire, UK. While there, Blair was a pupil of Fabian Aldous Huxley (1894–1963)—author of the 1932 dystopian novel *Brave New World*.[44] Mahatma Gandhi, who was held-up to the world as another Messianic social justice figure, may remind the reader of Nelson Mandela, who was revered in a similar fashion. Gandhi of course was central to the Indian 'liberation' movement. G.B. Shaw met Gandhi in London in 1931, and they were both admirers of each other's work.[45]

The Frankfurt School

"Obscenity is a moral concept in the verbal arsenal of the establishment, which abuses the term by applying it, not to expressions of its own morality, but to those of another"[46]

---

[43] https://fabians.org.uk/about-us/

[44] Heitman, D., "The Talented Mr. Huxley", November/December 2015.

https://www.neh.gov/humanities/2015/novemberdecember/feature/the-talented-mr-huxley

[45] "George Bernard Shaw". https://www5.open.ac.uk/research-projects/making-britain/content/george-bernard-shaw

[46] Marcuse, H. "An Essay on Liberation", 1969. P. 12.

Herbert Marcuse, "An Essay on Liberation", 1969

"What can oppose the decline of the west is not a resurrected culture but the utopia that is silently contained in the image of its decline"[47]

Theodor Adorno, *Prisms*, 1967

"Socialism has never and nowhere been at first a working class movement... It is a construction of theorists, deriving from certain tendencies of abstract thought with which for a long time only the intellectuals were familiar; and it required long efforts by the intellectuals before the working classes could be persuaded to adopt it as their program"[48]

Friedrich Von Hayek, *The Intellectuals and Socialism* (1949)

Another very important manifestation of subversive Marxism is the now infamous 'think tank' called The Frankfurt School. If you ever wondered why the Western world is riddled with political correctness, "multiculturalism", identity politics, and 'radical' activism; or why concepts like Critical Theory, Critical Race Theory are now popular, or where 'Cultural Marxism', came from; why Marxist 'protest' groups are not immediately crushed and imprisoned by the state; and why the 'education' systems seem to be heavily involved in all of this; this group is of central importance. It embodied the essence of Marxian pseudo-scientific toxic trash that the world (not just the U.S.) is now terminally ill with. It's quite rightly nicknamed the 'School of PC'.

The Frankfurt School (FS) helped to spread the infection primarily via academic, literary means; particularly in sociology, psychology, and 'philosophy'. 'Intellectualising' the ideology has been a very effective way to legitimise it. In this respect, the FS stood apart from other types of Marxist groups. Looking at the spread of the ideology in the U.S. historically, from a panoramic view, it played a certain role. The types of organisations traditionally used by the cult (political parties, labour unions etc.), were already operating and growing in strength even before the FS was established.

Keeping that context in mind, let's take a look at this group. Though it wasn't in existence for that long, it had a huge impact; via one member in particular. Its legacy is a major factor as to why the U.S. (and indeed the

---

https://www.marxists.org/reference/archive/marcuse/works/1969/essay-liberation.pdf

[47] Adorno, T., *Prisms* (1967). P. 72.

[48] Hayek, F.,"The Intellectuals and Socialism", 1949.

https://cdn.mises.org/Intellectualsand20Socialism_4.pdf

west in general) has never been more divided and unstable in this time. (I'm using the same acronym "FS" for the Frankfurt School, as I did for the Fabian Society).

Background

Europe post WW1 proved to be a turning point for Marxism. According to Marxist theory/predictions, the proletariat working classes of Europe would, in the event of war, rise-up and overthrow capitalism; proletarians in one country would unite with their counterparts in other countries etc. However, this did not materialise after the outbreak of war in 1914. Even though the ideology was already spreading around Europe at that point, when it came down to it, generally, the working classes in each country still separated themselves from the working classes in other countries; this resulted in them donning their respective uniforms and fighting each other.

During this period, Marxist 'intellectuals' had to reconcile this reality with the presumptions. Their solution was to adapt the failed theory (as usual), and here the stubborn fanaticism kicked-in, in a particular way. They theorised that the reason why the workers were not being good little revolutionary proletarians—and being passionate about 'class struggle' etc.—was because of the negative influence/mind-control of western culture and Christianity (a concept first expressed by V.I. Lenin in his 1904 work "What is to be done?").

The cult concluded that creating a communist world could not be realised until the structures of Western Civilisation were first destroyed. Prominent proponents of this theory were Antonio Francesco Gramsci and Gyorgy Lukacs.

In 1922, Lukács and Willi Muezenberg (the Soviet's subversion mastermind) attended a meeting of European communists at the Marx-Engels Institute in Moscow to discuss this issue.[49] This meeting shaped the global initiatives that the Comintern would implement to spread the ideology. These post-WW1 interpretations of Marxism marked the beginning of what is called Western Marxism (same ideology; different label). In his "Prison Notebooks", Gramsci championed the idea of the The Long March through the institutions (though he didn't actually coin this phrase himself), or "colonize the superstructure"; to infiltrate and saturate

---

[49] Parrhesia Diaries, "The Marxist "long march" into the age of identity politics", 1 February 2020. https://theparrhesiadiaries.medium.com/the-marxist-long-march-through-the-institutions-and-into-the-age-of-identity-politics-6a7042b235dc

the structures of society with the cult/ideology.[50]

Origins

The Frankfurt School spawned in 1923 in Germany, being associated with the University of Frankfurt. The original intended name for this group was "The Institute for Marxism" but this was a bit obvious now wasn't it? The name chosen was *The Institute for Social Research* (Institut fur Sozialforschung), which sounds a bit nicer. German Argentine cult member Felix Weil funded its establishment. In 1922, Gyorgy Lukács chaired a meeting of intellectuals and sociologists who were sympathetic to the cause.[51]

Since FS members were both obviously on the left of the political spectrum and Jewish intellectuals, the rise of the National Socialists in Germany meant they had to set up shop elsewhere, post-haste. The school moved from Frankfurt to Geneva, eventually fled Europe entirely, and finally settled in New York City in 1934, attaching primarily to Colombia University. They were welcomed by John Dewey (1859–1952) who was on staff there (himself a cult member, connected to the Fabian Society). These 'intellectuals' would then be in a position of influence, making connections with leading colleges and universities around the country.[52]

As they were Marxist intellectuals—what were the chances that once they were in the U.S., they would be able to see the positive things in this new, relatively stable and prosperous capitalistic country they found themselves in? No chance! They couldn't just enjoy being in a nice place that had welcomed them in and show some gratitude; they had to start criticising and deconstructing everything in order to re-make it in their image. They were nothing if not nihilists, and the personification of cynicism. Obviously, the U.S. was nothing like the relatively miserable, unstable shithole they fled from (Weimar Germany).

From Herbert Marcuse's *One Dimentional Man* (1964): "Under the rule of a repressive whole, liberty can be made into a powerful instrument of domination. Free election of masters does not abolish the masters or the slaves. Free choice among a wide variety of goods and services does not

---

[50] Gramsci, A. *Prison Notebooks,* 1950.

https://archive.org/details/AntonioGramsciSelectionsFromThePrisonNotebooks/page/n7/mode/2up

[51] Corradeti, C. "The Frankfurt School and Critical Theory".
https://iep.utm.edu/critical-theory-frankfurt-school/

[52] Ibid.

signify freedom if these goods and services sustain social controls over a life of toil and fear—that is, if they sustain alienation. And the spontaneous reproduction of superimposed needs by the individual does not establish autonomy; it only testifies to the efficacy of the controls". [53] What nonsensical gibberish. Note the obvious digs at capitalism and consumerism, and how such a society is "repressive". (The word "alienation" is in reference to Karlie Marx's ridiculous theory of 'alienation of labour' ("estranged labour"). Essentially, it's the idea that once you produce something (e.g. a product or item in your line of work/employment), that it becomes separate from you; you become 'alienated' from it. Real genius-level stuff (rolls eyes). Have you ever heard of something so stupid?).

Members

The membership of the FS at various times included: Theodor Adorno (1903–1969), Max Horkheimer (1895–1973), Erich Fromm (1900–1980), Henryk Grossman (1881–1950), Otto Kirchheimer (1905–1965), Leo Lowenthal (1900–1993), Herbert Marcuse, Franz Neumann (1900–1954), Friedrich Pollock (1894–1970); in addition to Hannah Arendt (1908–1975), and Paul Lazarsfeld (1901–1975).

In terms of their influences, the ideas of the Frankfurt School has been connected to the works of Karl Marx, Sigmund Freud (1856–1939), G.W.F. Hegel, Antonio Gramsci, and Friedrich Nietzsche (1844–1900). In particular, they fused the ideas of Marx, Freud and Gramsci.[54] To simplify this, this fusion was the application of Marx's principles to society using Freud's psychological techniques, in combination with the tactical ideas of Gramsci. The group's influence spread very quickly throughout the U.S., helped by *The New School for Social Research*, another Marxist trash dispenser established in New York City in 1919 (as part of *The New School*).[55]

Their modus operandi

With the formation of the FS, the ideology would now make the (tranny) transition from being political-sociological-economic theory to spreading in to the 'philosophical'-psychological-cultural via academia. To do this, FS intellectuals had to apply the ideology in a certain way. They departed

---

[53] Marcuse, H., *One Dimensional Man* (1964), P. 7. https://libquotes.com/herbert-marcuse

[54] https://www.britannica.com/topic/Frankfurt-School

[55] https://en.wikipedia.org/wiki/The_New_School

from the traditional concepts of 'class-struggle' and violent revolution of the proletariat; similarly to the Fabians. And like the Fabians, there was no use promoting violent working-class revolution against the bourgeoisie since they themselves were (and associated with) bourgeois types. A 'revolutionary' ingredient, however, would still be required. To find a replacement for those poor godforsaken proletariat workers, they would seek to create 'oppressed' classes throughout society, which provided the activist/revolutionary element that they needed. Herbert Marcuse's work suggested that this could be a coalition of various 'oppressed' groups: "the substratum of the outcasts and outsiders, the exploited and persecuted of other races and other colors, the unemployed and the unemployable".[56]

The Frankfurt School's impact came via criticism of the pillars of Western civilisation—capitalism, Christianity, and culture—which would then have a destructive impact on American society. The 'work' of these cult members subversively inserted self-destructive attitudes into the American psyche. They would suggest the (racist!) idea that majority's relatively have no rights (e.g. white people in the U.S.), but minority's do.

(Of course, even if a person belongs to the white majority, they can still decide to join their minority 'oppressed' group of choice and thereby change their status (e.g. a white male or female being gay, bi-sexual, transgender etc.); or they could change their status by being an activist for the cult, obviously). Another destructive idea they suggested (complimentary to the above idea) is that white people should not be concerned about becoming a minority in their own countries.[57]

Concepts it popularized

Their work paved the way for destructive concepts such as Critical Theory, Critical Race Theory, and what's called "cultural relativism". These terms have been used to popularise the criticism (and inevitable destruction) of various aspects of society that were obstacles for the cult/ideology: the pillars of Western Civilisation, in addition to the family unit and stable, and monogamous, heterosexual relationships etc. "Critical theory" was a weapon created to attack 'problematic' aspects of their target countries culture. Of course, you can destroy the merits of many things with criticism. ("Postmodernism", in the next section, is the assault on anything traditional, basically).

---

[56] Marcuse, H, *One-Dimentional Man* (1964), P. 260.

[57] Corradeti, C. "The Frankfurt School and Critical Theory". https://iep.utm.edu/critical-theory-frankfurt-school/

It's just Marxist mumbo jumbo to hide what it really is—criticism of anything the ideology regards as an enemy. This twisted new form of toxic logic would become part of mainstream discourse, which it has. It would then be open-season on anything in American culture that gave the country strength or stability—the family unit, religion, patriotism, the tradition of military service etc.

This normalisation of self-destructive attitudes is central to understanding the internal chaos of the U.S. today. The brilliant American author Michael Walsh had this to say about this concept: "Critical theory was the notion, promulgated by the cultural Marxists of the Frankfurt School, that simply states there is nothing—no custom, institution, or moral precept—that is beyond criticizing, and destroying. It is license to vandalize, and the fact that it was so swiftly embraced by American academe after WWII remains a national disgrace".[58] Indeed. To put it another way, Critical Theory is anti-patriotism—it destroys a nation/culture/people. If used by the citizens of a country towards their own country, it's a form of treason; if used by those from the outside, it's an attack on the nation.

The old "if you're not Marxist, you must be insane!" trick

Essentially, anything that went ahead with their agenda was 'logical', and anything that went against it was 'illogical'. In political terms, what this meant was: if you believe/support ideas that encourage/manifest the destruction of western civilisation you are being 'logical', and if you try to justify/defend/support any of the institutions or traditions of the west you are being 'illogical'. Critical Theory was, essentially, the politicisation of logic. In other words, making logic itself pro-Marxist. In a sense, the ideology was logic, according to Critical Theory. Partisan to-the-max, but clever, right? Their goal in this regard was that if a person defended any aspect of western civilisation—capitalism, religion, family, culture, nationalism, patriotism etc.—they must be viewed as illogical, non-evolved people. Not 'progressive'. So basically, anyone who believed in what these snakes were saying would end up with a distorted perception of reality (aka crazy), while simultaneously viewing sane, rational people (e.g. you, me) as being insane or 'extreme' etc.! Literally turning reality on its head (inversion)!

Unfortunately, their influence has been diffused worldwide, especially via the education systems. It is no coincidence that the universities are now producing a never-ending conveyor belt of psychotic Marxist activists

---

[58] Walsh, M. *The Devil's Pleasure Palace: the Cult of Critical Theory and the Subversion of the West* (2017).

masquerading as students, completely detached from reality. This level of disproportionate psychosis of college-educated individuals is not natural. It's the result of the indoctrination, and the Marxists snakes are to blame for that.

Herbert Marcuse

> "One can rightfully speak of a cultural revolution, since the protest is directed toward the whole cultural establishment...The traditional idea of revolution and the traditional strategy of revolution has ended. These ideas are old-fashioned...what we must undertake is a type of diffuse and dispersed disintegration of the system"[59]
>
> Herbert Marcuse, *The Affirmative Character of Culture*, 1937

Perhaps the most influential member of the FS was Herbert Marcuse, partly due to the longevity of his presence in the U.S. When most members returned to Germany once WW2 ended (to help 'De-Nazify'/Marxify the German masses), Marcuse stayed. He eventually went on to become the academic icon of the 'new left' in the U.S. in the following decades, ensuring that the 'Cultural-Marxist' virus burrowed deep into the heart of America. At one point, Marcuse worked for the CIAs predecessor—the Office of Strategic Services (OSS)—on anti-Nazi projects. After Columbia, he was involved with Yale, Harvard and Brandeis Universities in Massachusetts, and the University of California, San Diego. So basically he spent much of the 1950s and 1960s spreading his brand of Marxian intellectualism, contaminating countless University staff and students as he went.[60]

The famous phrase "Make love, not war", which emerged during the (Marxist) 'anti-war' movement in the U.S. in the 1960s, was popularised after Marcuse's *Eros and Civilisation* (1955). In addition to exploring the Freudian idea of repressed tendencies (and how they impacted on society), the book was a critique of consumerism and capitalism itself. Naturally, it suggested that capitalism was oppressing society.

This piece of degenerate, Marxian, reality-distorting hocus pocus was summarised brilliantly by American author Daniel J. Flynn in his 2004 book *Intellectual Morons:* "Marx argued against the exploitation of labor; Marcuse, against labor itself. Don't work, have sex. This was the simple

---

[59] Marcuse, H, *The Affirmative Character of Culture (1937)*.

https://monoskop.org/images/1/11/MARCUSE_Herbert_-_Coll._papers_4_-_Art_and_liberation.pdf

[60] https://www.britannica.com/biography/Herbert-Marcuse

message of Eros and Civilization, released in 1955. Its ideas proved to be extraordinarily popular among the fledgling hippie culture of the following decade. It provided a rationale for laziness and transformed degrading personal vices into virtues".[61]

Isn't that a magnificent, powerful message (don't work, have sex)? Hitting two birds with one stone by encouraging the youth (the main target demographic) to be lazy and refuse supporting the evil capitalist system, while being hedonistic, egocentric etc. Exactly what the disciples of the 'radical' drug-taking hippie movement wanted to hear (interestingly, the word "Radical" was a popular term used during the hippie era, meaning "cool", "great" etc. "Radical"?). Cultivating this mentality of laziness, hedonism, and irresponsibility in the youth encourages them towards degeneracy and the welfare state.

(As an aside, referring to the historical section earlier: the Indochina Wars were about to kick-off when *Eros* was released, which would soon become the Vietnam War. It couldn't have been better timing for the global cult/ideology to have the U.S. (its chief military opponent) become engulfed in an internal wave of anti-capitalism, hedonism (interpersonal/sexual degeneracy, drug use etc.), and anti-American anti-war passivity).

Liberating tolerance

> "I still believe that our cause (which is not only ours) is better taken up by the rebellious students than by the police, and, here in California, that is demonstrated to me almost daily"[62]

> From Marcuse's 1969 letter to Adorno on the
> chaos they helped create during the 60s protest era

The intellectual snake Marcuse is famous for advocating a biased, pro-Marxist political environment. In his 1965 essay "Repressive Tolerance", he argued it was necessary to have a system of "liberating tolerance" in society. In practice, this meant that non-Marxists shouldn't have the right to protest (parts emphasised): "I suggested in "Repressive Tolerance" the practice of discriminating tolerance in an inverse direction, as a means of shifting the balance between Right and Left by restraining the liberty of the

---

[61] Flynn, Daniel J., *Intellectual Morons: How Ideology Makes Smart People Fall for Stupid Ideas* (2004).

[62] Marcuse, H., Letter to Adorno, 1969.

https://cominsitu.wordpress.com/2021/08/17/correspondence-on-the-german-student-movement-adorno-marcuse-1969/

Right....Liberating tolerance, then, would mean intolerance against movements from the Right and toleration of movements from the Left. They would include the withdrawal of toleration of speech and assembly from groups and movements which promote aggressive policies, armament, chauvinism, discrimination on the grounds of race and religion, or which oppose the extension of public services, social security, medical care etc".[63]

Essentially, only the 'oppressed' or those who supported the oppressed (cult members) would be allowed to open their mouths! On the other hand, simultaneously, there would be extremely biased promotion of the Marxian causes, speech, groups etc. The overall aim was to not let those evil right-wingers congregate at all, never mind grow in strength and become political opponents.

Marcuse also recommended that students be indoctrinated to perceive the issue of 'free speech' this way. Hence the mentality of "you can only have free speech if you aren't saying hate-filled things!"; in other words, saying anything that contradicts the cult's/ideology's distorted perceptions of ethics. This strategy is the exact opposite of what this book is advocating—completely suppressing the cult/ideology by denying them the rights to do anything, including protest.

Interview with Bryan Magee

In 1977 Marcuse did an interview with British cult member and Labour Party MP Bryan Magee on the "Modern Philosophy" series; this was two years before Marcuse died.[64] At one point, Magee asks him what "defects" he felt the 'new left' had developed. Marcuse's response was two-fold : Firstly, he highlighted the "totally unrealistic strategy" by some, and "the refusal to recognise that we are not in a revolutionary situation in the advanced industrial countries (i.e. western countries)...not even in a pre-revolutionary situation...and that the strategy has to be adapted to this situation".

Secondly, he said there was a "refusal to re-examine and develop Marxian categories", and "to make a fetish out of Marxist theory". Also that Marxian concepts "cannot simply be transmitted...(they) have to be re-examined in accordance with the changes in society itself". His answer encapsulates the

---

[63] Marcuse, M, *Liberating Tolerance* (1965). P. 14.

https://www.marcuse.org/herbert/publications/1960s/1965-repressive-tolerance-fulltext.html

[64] Manufacturing Intellect, "Herbert Marcuse interview with Bryan Magee" (1977).

https://www.YouTube.com/watch?v=0KqC1lTAJx4

skin-shedding snake that is Marxism quite well.

Magee also queried Marcuse's criticisms of Marxism and what it had become; that Marcuse regarded it as somewhat "anti-libertarian", and "didn't take sufficient account of the individual". In his reply, Marcuse said that the nature of the 'proletariat', and its relationship with capitalism had changed (since Marx's time); that the "proletariat" are not what they used to be. He outlined that there was now a "large-scale integration of a majority of the population…in to the existing capitalist system". In fact, that the "working class no longer has nothing to lose but its chains…but a lot more".

He explained that this applied "not only on a material, but also on a psychological basis", therefore the masses were now psychologically dependent somewhat. Essentially, the "consciousness of the dependant population had changed". (this harkens back to a point made earlier—this is how the 'Neo'/'Western' Marxists could explain why the proletariat didn't want revolution; too wedded to capitalism!).

He blamed this on the "ruling power structure", and its negative influence over the masses, that it was able to "manipulate, manage and control, not only the consciousness, but also the subconscious and unconscious of the individuals". Therefore, he and his colleagues at the Frankfurt School "considered psychology…one of the main branches of knowledge that had to be integrated with Marxian theory". So, we are back to cult members thinking they know what's best for the masses again: that revolution was required and mandatory, even if the proletarians didn't know it or ask for it! This means Marcuse and his FS colleagues felt they were the 'proletarian vanguard' of the 'new left'.

Marcuse himself, due to his indoctrinated mind, was a toxic, dangerous man. Exactly the kind of academic personality that needs to be weeded-out of the education system today. We can only speculate how many minds he contaminated.

Toxic intellectuals

Groups like the Frankfurt School capitalise on the naivety of some types of individuals; those who automatically respect academics and 'intellectuals'. People who love knowledge in a conventional sense, love to absorb information, then engage in some chin-stroking pompous discussions, basically. It's pseudo-intelligence. Even dumb people can absorb knowledge and go around the place reciting it.

The damage done by this group to U.S. academia—and through filtration, academia worldwide—is almost immeasurable. They certainly weren't the only subversive force active in the country during their period, but a crucial one. If average everyday Americans understood what these Marxist nuts were up to, and what impact their 'work' would eventually have on the American psyche, they surely would have been lynched; or at the very least, had their rights (to influence anyone) removed (the tactic Marcuse suggested). Indeed, if the authorities knew who/what this mob was, they would've denied them the privilege of entering the U.S. in the first place, before they could do their damage. Toxic Marxist immigrants.

What can we learn from this episode in Marxist history? It should make us more conscious of the hypnotic power of 'knowledge', intellectualism, and academic credentials etc. The ideology still likes to use this particular cocktail; it's very effective at brainwashing people, especially the young and impressionable.

Postmodernism

"(Postmodernism) generates a philosophy of resistance of negation.. (it) is not a logically coherent system, it is systematic distrust, organised scepticism, systematic suspicion"[65]

Dr. Michael Sugrue, presentation on
Postmodernism and Jean-Francois-Lyotard

"Postmodernists completely reject the structure of Western civilisation. They don't believe in the individual, in logic, in dialogue. They believe your fundamental identity is group fostered. For the postmodernists the world is a Hobbesian battleground of identity groups"[66]

Canadian psychologist Jordan Peterson,
Manning Centre Conference, 2017

Another related—and potent—element of the ideology connected with academia is Postmodernism. It maintains a significant presence in the usual infected subject areas, including the humanities, social sciences etc. To be more precise, at this point in time, it drives them. As Jordan Peterson stated at that same conference: "The humanities and much of the social sciences has turned into a postmodern neo-Marxist playground for radicals".[67]

---

[65] "Jean-Francois Lyotard: The Post-modern Condition".

https://www.YouTube.com/watch?v=Xdf41gsESTc

[66] Peterson, J., "2017/02/25: Jordan Peterson: Postmodernism: How and why it must be fought", 5 June 2017.https://www.YouTube.com/watch?v=Cf2nqmQIfxc

[67] Ibid. "2017/02/25: Jordan Peterson: Postmodernism: How and why it must be fought". https://www.YouTube.com/watch?v=Cf2nqmQIfxc

Of course, "Postmodernism" is a term with a broad variety of uses, such as in art, architecture etc.; here we are focusing on it in a 'philosophical' context. At first glance, it seems to be something somewhat tangled-up in 'political correctness'; even that there's a symbiosis between them. You could also say that postmodernist thought is what's becoming the norm; in a sense it is political correctness. It also explains why the cult is full of individuals with heads full of crossed wires, who are unable to reason correctly and face up to reality. This is important because (conventional definitions aside) being detached from reality is one of the two main interlinked characteristics of insanity (the other being a lack of conscience—which postmodernism encourages; the inability to distinguish between right and wrong).

Like other elements of the ideology, post-modernism can be slippery to pin-down at first, and can initially seem to be quite nebulous, and even vague in its message/purpose. As usual, this is just an attempt to obfuscate its purpose. Basically, it's another tangle in the larger tangled ball of red string that is Marxism. Cult members will predictably do intellectual gymnastics and try to dazzle us with 'knowledge', spewing reams of absolute garbage (usually with the most flamboyant language possible), to justify or legitimise this 'philosophy'. Nice try zombies. Let's break this down into simple terms.

What is it?

It emerged as a form of 'philosophy' during the second half of the 19th century to challenge previously-held, common philosophical perspectives formulated during previous centuries—in the areas of science, identity and culture, linguistics, history etc. This encompasses the developments of the *Enlightenment* of the 17th and 18th centuries.

Essentially, this 'philosophy' took up a mainly contradictory (revolutionary) position to what came before, its chief characteristics being: subjectivism, relativism, scepticism, general dismissal of logic and reason, and having a cynical view of what was previously considered valuable for human progress.[6869] In other words, it opposes what has existed/currently exists, and it doubts, criticizes, and de-constructs; it dismantles or destroys. Postmodernistic thought is obviously related to the Critical Theory pushed by the Frankfurt School et al.

---

[68] "Postmodernism", 2001.
https://www.sciencedirect.com/topics/psychology/postmodernism

[69] https://www.britannica.com/topic/postmodernism-philosophy/Postmodernism-and-relativism

Key points

Some of the common philosophical perspectives that postmodernism is opposed to in general are:

That there is such a thing as an objective reality and truth that operates independently of anyone's personal opinions; the idea that logic and reason exist (and that there are universally accepted standards of these things); that there is such a thing as inherent, natural behaviours and psychological attributes that human beings just contain at birth (aka human nature; or that there is a difference between males and females on a psychological level, inherent since birth).

Postmodernism claims that human behaviour is programmed primarily through social conditioning, as opposed to 'human nature' (e.g. gender is a social construct). It also claims that things like reason or logic cannot have universally-acceptable standards, because the perception of these things depends upon the context—or intellectual environment—in which they are used. Certain things which were regarded as being positive and uplifting for humanity—such as technological and scientific advancements—are viewed cynically. From Jean-Francois Lyotard's *The Postmodern Condition* (1979): "In the discourse of today's financial backers of research, the only credible goal is power. Scientists, technicians, and instruments are purchased not to find the truth, but to augment power".[70] (This bitchy 'intellectual' cynicism may remind the reader of Herbert Marcuse).

It uses terms like 'meta-narratives' or 'grand narratives' to describe previously espoused concepts, and terms like 'enlightenment rationality' when describing the modern scientific use of reason and logic (insinuating that these things are not 'progressive' somehow and belong in the past). Invented concepts such as 'hyperreality', 'trace', and 'univocity of being' were used to basically criticise and dismiss those previously espoused concepts (so more intellectual mumbo-jumbo and term-invention to distort reality).

It also argues that traditional philosophical perspectives come from the establishment, and should be viewed with suspicion, as they serve to maintain its level of control (those damn, evil bourgeoisie, controlling our lives via our thoughts! I knew it!). This in part explains why they don't believe in having constructive dialogue with those holding opposing views (i.e. non-cult members). They may view the rest of us as brainwashed cult-members, basically! (giggles)

---

[70] Lyotard, J.F., *The Postmodern Condition* (1979), P. 46.

It denies true independence as an individual but promotes the idea of group identity. As in, what defines us is what group we belong to. For example: a white, heterosexual male can be identified as being part of an 'oppressor' class, while a black migrant female is part of an 'oppressed' class. Another: a white person automatically has (white) 'privilege' because they are white, and a non-white person automatically does not etc. How nauseating.

A simplified explanation

Let's look at how it can warp minds and society at large (which is all that matters really): it's the concept that all opinions/ideas/perspectives have merit; it says that subjectivity is good, and all opinions have some value, or are of equal value (unless you have anti-Marxist views, naturally); since there is no such thing as a universal truth, everything—including reality itself—can be interpreted in an infinite number of ways; everything is subjective and not objective.

"Subjective": coming from inside the self, existing in the mind, or coming from a person's individual perspective. It means being 'internal'—as opposed to being 'external'—where an individual's perceptions are concerned. "Objective": existing outside the mind or coming from a source outside the individual's mind/personal perspective; being external to the individual. From the postmodernist perspective, there is no such thing as an objective/external/universal truth; no such thing as truth that is outside of the self, that is not affected by your personal interpretations.

So why should we care? What does all this mean in practice? It means you can make up your own version of reality, basically! The end product of all this is delusion in the minds of those indoctrinated with post-modernistic thought.

The notion of all ideas being 'equal' is just Marxist egalitarianism being applied to logic. If we compare two people—one is a very calm, knowledgeable, indoctrination-free, intellectually-skilled; and the other is manic, ignorant, indoctrinated, intellectually-unremarkable, gullible; both of their opinions have equal value? This is—objectively and intellectually-speaking—a load of shit. Utter nonsense!

In a way we have one stupid, destructive idea (equality), influencing intellectual thought and leading to the creation of another (post-modernism). As the reader knows by now, the notion of this 'equality' of different opinions is not something that the cult/ideology actually wants (what it really wants is only Marxian thought/opinions).

The notion of equality of different perceptions (being peddled in post-modernism) is just an excuse to allow stupid, insane, reality-distorting destructive ideas to have merit, which then allows them to gain a foothold in the human psyche. It allows reality to be turned upside-down and inside-out, to the benefit of the ideology/cult. "Post-modernise, destabilize, destroy"—Vladimir Lenin, probably.

It helps the ideology to spread

The various sub-agendas of Marxism (explored elsewhere) rely upon a distorted perception of reality and/or history to work. Of course, "history" is just reality in the past, so "a distorted perception of history" is really "a distorted perception of what happened in the past"; of what actually happened. The sub-agendas which the cult is promoting/supporting all adhere to this principle.

In addition, the general mentality of the cult shows us they don't believe in the ideas of objective morality—that there's a universal, pre-existing concept of right and wrong. They do, however, seem to subscribe to the idea of subjectivity—that it's all about your personal interpretation of what you think right and wrong is. As an example, this is how the cult/ideology has convinced millions that abortion is not wrong. All that matters, according to them—where the pregnant female is concerned—is what is 'right' for her. (This concept of Moral Relativism is one of the core concepts within Satanism—what you think 'right' means revolves around your ego and happiness, basically).

Another example would be this ludicrous gender non-binary nonsense. If a male feels, for whatever reason, that he's not male, then apparently this has merit (postmodernism), even though he's actually male and his 'feelings' about the matter are irrelevant! In addition, even though he's objectively wrong, we must respect his 'opinion' ('political correctness')'! Otherwise, we may be branded a _____ phobe (control of language to suppress opposition).

We can see how these combined ingredients of postmodernism, political correctness and partisan suppression are dangerous; they lead to manifest madness. The ideology injects lunacy into every stage of the process. Not surprisingly, these patterns of behaviour/reactions in society lead to distorted perceptions of logic and morality, which itself eventually leads to the breakdown of society.

So, if you want to identity as being 'non-binary', which means you are neither one of the two sex's we all previously thought there was (sarcasm), then this is true because you believe it to be true. Sounds like mental bullshit, doesn't it? That's because it is. From the post-modernistic point of view, the biological fact that what sex you are is imprinted in the DNA inside the nucleus of every relevant cell of your body is not the issue here;

the issue is what you believe the truth to be. Remember, postmodernism rejects logic (!), never mind science.

A person who thinks that they are, somehow, in the wrong sex body needs mental help first; but this requires somewhat of an admittance on the part of the individual that they might have some issues; which requires some sanity, guts, and self-love. Post-modernistic thought allows a person to avoid this challenge/hassle/fear, and instead offers a much easier option— just change reality to what you want it to be! Simples and convenient, right? The price, though, for burying one's head so deep in the sand is very high— delusion/insanity. It's short-term comfort for long-term degeneracy.

Heteronormativity

The recently-invented term "Heteronormativity" is another degenerate post-modernistic outgrowth of 'intellectual' Marxism; it's critical theory applied to sex and gender (Queer Theory).[71][72] The aim is to insinuate the very dangerous, pro-eugenics, society-destroying idea that heterosexual relationships are not 'normal'—since there cannot be such a thing as 'normal'—and that other types of (non-heterosexual) relationships are equal to them. Of course, this is just more reality-distorting, postmodernist rubbish.

A definition from the *European Union Agency for Fundamental Rights*: "Heteronormativity is what makes heterosexuality seem coherent, natural, and privileged. It involves the assumption that everyone is 'naturally' heterosexual, and that heterosexuality is an ideal, superior to homosexuality or bisexuality". [73] And another from Wikipedia: "Heteronormativity is the belief that heterosexuality, predicated on the gender binary, is the default, preferred, or normal mode of sexual orientation. It assumes that sexual and marital relations are most fitting between people of opposite sex. A heteronormative view therefore involves alignment of biological sex, sexuality, gender identity and gender roles. Heteronormativity is often linked to heterosexism and homophobia".

The previously believed 'grand narrative' in society was that non-heterosexuality was, indeed, 'abnormal'. That has progressively changed

---

[71] https://en.wikipedia.org/wiki/Heteronormativity

[72] https://en.wikipedia.org/wiki/Queer_theory

[73] "Homophobia and Discrimination on Grounds of Sexual Orientation and Gender Identity in the EU Member States", FRA, (2009). P. 25.
http://fra.europa.eu/sites/default/files/fra_uploads/397-FRA_hdgso_report_part2_en.pdf

since Marxism appeared on the scene, which means the ideology, once again, is turning things upside down. So, this term "heteronormativity" is challenging that 'grand narrative' and is therefore postmodernistic. Note the amusing "heterosexism" term.

Key figures

Though a large movement, here's some of the more prominent figures historically. Mostly academics, typically, their areas of study were philosophy, political philosophy, sociology, psychology etc. Some big names are Jean Francois Lyotard (1924–1998), Jacques Derrrida (1930–2004), and Michel Foucault (1926–1984).[74]

Jean Francois Lyotard was born in 1924. In 1950, he completed a teaching degree in philosophy at the Sorbonne university in Paris. He began his teaching career in Algeria and was later involved with a socialist group called *Socialism or Barbarism* (Socialism ou Barbarie). His writings during this period were highly critical of French colonialism (what a shocker), and being a staunch supporter of Algerian independence, was involved with several Marxist groups, including the *National Liberation Front*. He was later involved in the Marxist *May 1968* revolutionary movement (an attempted takeover of France).

Lyotard continued his career in 1966 in France at the University of Paris (Nanterre and Vincennes-Saint-Denis), going on to teach elsewhere during the 1980s and 1990s, including the University of California and Emory University in Atlanta, Georgia. He later renounced revolutionary activism, but he clearly spent the first half of his life highly-involved, retaining Marxian attitudes for the rest of his life.[75]

His most famous work is *The Postmodern Condition: A Report on Knowledge* (1979). It was produced at the request of the Canadian *Conseil des Universites* (Council of Universities) of the government of Quebec. In it he suggested that the traditional 'metanarratives' (truth, reason, logic) were too dominant (almost totalitarian), and should be challenged and replaced by little narratives ("petits récits") that would compete with each other. In the introduction, he states "Simplifying to the extreme, I define postmodern as incredulity toward metanarratives".[76]

His work contained some of the usual cynical attitudes towards modernity

---

[74] https://www.britannica.com/topic/postmodernism-philosophy

[75] https://www.britannica.com/biography/Jean-Francois-Lyotard

[76] Lyotard, J.F., *The Postmodern Condition* (1979), (introduction, xxiv).

and capitalism. On page five, he stated "economic powers have reached the point of imperilling the stability of the state through new forms of the circulation of capital that go by the generic name of multinational corporations". [77] This is reminiscent of Marx's belief that capitalism contains within it the seeds of its down destruction.

Michel Foucault

> "There exists an international citizenry that has its rights, and has its duties, and that is committed to rise up against every abuse of power, no matter who the author, no matter who the victims. After all, we are all ruled, and as such, we are in solidarity"[78]

> Michel Foucault, June 1981 press conference

Michel Foucault was born in to a wealthy family in the French city of Poitiers in 1926. During his secondary school years at the prestigious *Lycee Henri-IV*, he was influenced by Jean Hyppolite (himself an enthusiastic student of Marx and Hegel). In 1946 he attended the *Ecole Normale Supérieure* (ENS) and the *Sorbonne* University in Paris, studying psychology and philosophy, receiving the equivalents of B.A. and M.A. Foucault was encouraged to join the *French Communist Party* by his tutor (and cult member) Louis Althusser while at ENS, and was a member for a few years.[79] He worked abroad in Sweden, Poland, and West Germany during the late 1950s, and later taught psychology at the University of Tunis, Tunisia. He returned to France in 1968, working at the *Centre Experimental de Vincennes*. After joining the *College de France* in 1970, due to his sparse lecture schedule, he travelled internationally up until the mid-1980s, and gave lectures in several countries including Brazil, Canada, Japan, and the U.S.

His works include *Madness and Civilisation* (1960), and *The History of Sexuality* (1976). Foucault placed special emphasis on sexuality in his work. He promoted the idea that it was about power. He is also regarded as being one of the major influences in what became 'queer theory'. Predictably, he was also avidly non-hostile to paedophilia, and was involved with petitions

---

[77] Ibid. P. 5.

[78] "The rights and duties of international citizenship", November 2015.

https://www.opendemocracy.net/en/can-europe-make-it/rights-and-duties-of-international-citizenship/

[79] https://www.britannica.com/biography/Michel-Foucault

to lower the age of consent in France.[80]

The History of Sexuality is a magnificent piece of Marxian propaganda, trying to distort people's perceptions of normal healthy sexual behaviour. He suggested that sexual behaviours normally classed as negative—the "world of perversion"—were not only unjustly classed as such, but actually positive since they were the pursuit of truth! By this logic, I would like to point out that if you have sex with a farmyard animal, jagged boulder or perhaps a stinking garbage bag in a refuse skip down an alley, then that becomes part of your 'truth', doesn't it? "Fucking this cow is part of my truth!", or "receiving oral sex from this garbage bag is part of who I am!". You could perceive and describe it however you wish; it doesn't change the fact that you are a disgusting degenerate maniac. He also promoted the idea that the system was oppressive and manipulative (yawn), and that 'scientific knowledge' used by the system/authorities was in reality a form of social control (typical postmodernist attitude).

Marxist activism

Foucault was actively involved in the cult's initiatives throughout his life, including: 'liberation' and 'anti-racism' movements; student protests against the state; protests at the killing of non-whites or cult members (both in France and abroad); supporting Islamism; protesting the imprisonment and extradition of cult members; campaigning for foreign cult members to be given asylum in France. Plus the promotion of paedophilia etc. In fact, he was downright fanatical.[81] Again, the argument that he may have officially renounced communism later in life means nothing. In 1967, during his time at the University of Tunis, during the pro-Palestine riots in which the cult played a role, Foucault actively assisted and protected students who were involved, and later expressed admiration for their conduct during the state's crackdown. He was involved in the University reforms implemented by the Minister of Education Christian Fouchet in 1967, being part of a commission.[82]

During the revamping of the French education system in 1968, new 'autonomous' Universities were founded ('autonomous' = having the ideological red bias). Foucault was appointed to a highly influential position at the *Centre Expérimental de Vincennes,* near Paris as head of the

---

[80] https://en.wikipedia.org/wiki/French_petition_against_age_of_consent_laws

[81] https://en.wikipedia.org/wiki/Michel_Foucault

[82]

https://en.wikipedia.org/wiki/Michel_Foucault#University_of_Tunis_and_Vincennes:_1966-1970 philosophy department; Foucault then employed other cult members to teach there such as openly Communist fanatics Judith Miller (1941–2017) and Alain Badiou (1937-). The courses in this 'radical' philosophy department had a distinctly Marxist-Leninist slant. Almost immediately after this red 'university' was founded, it aggressively clashed with the establishment, since it attracted the most fanatical of students and staff.

Foucault was directly involved in several confrontations with the police: he was arrested in 1972 due to his involvement with protests over the police killing of an Algerian worker (sound familiar?); was arrested and deported in 1975 when trying to protest the Spanish governments execution of cult members there; he protested the imprisonment and extradition of the Marxist East German spy and terrorist Klaus Croissant (1931–2002), along with fellow cult member and academic Jean-Paul Sartre (1905–1980). He even got himself physically injured in an altercation with the police. [81]

Death by gayness

Foucault was a disturbed character (not surprising as "Fou" means 'crazy', en Francais). As a gay man, he had many 'interactions' during his lifetime, including a relationship with a transvestite during his stint in Hamburg. He had an 'open relationship' with his lover Daniel Defert (1937–2023) for much of his life (who was himself a cult member and a fan of Mao Zedong). [79]

In his youth, Foucault was involved in the gay scene in Paris, and continued this theme throughout his life, having unprotected sex with strangers. During his time in the U.S., when he lectured at UCLA and Berkeley in California, he was drawn to the bustling gay scene in San Francisco. He died as the result of AIDS in 1984. [79] The man who had been promoting a cavalier "anything goes" attitude towards sex and sexuality his whole life (the "do what thou wilt" Satanic approach), literally fucked himself to death. What a role model. He is a celebrated intellectual in cult academic circles.

Other characters involved in the post-modernism scene were Jacques Derrida and Jean-Paul Sartre. Derrida was an avid cult member, being involved with many 'leftist' issues including anti-nuclear, anti-apartheid in South Africa. Derrida signed the petition (along with Foucault) to decriminalise under-aged sex in France. [83]

The 'contradiction' of post-modernism

How is it that Postmodernism is also Marxist? Since Postmodernism claims

---

[83] https://en.wikipedia.org/wiki/Jacques_Derrida

to not believe in anything concrete, and Marxism traditionally does (equality, class struggle etc.), then how can post-modernism come from Marxism? This is because the purpose of post-modernism is to deconstruct and destroy what is already established in civilisation, to then allow Marxism to enter the picture as the 'replacement'.

The relativism, criticism, cynicism that postmodernism pushes is obviously not going to be applied to the ideology, the cult or the cult members themselves. They can dish out criticism but not take it (very spoilt brat-ish). According to the cult, their ideology is the answer, and they are the saviours, and any perceptions to the contrary will not be tolerated. No 'subjectivity' will apply in this case.

Not logic, but Marxian 'logic"

Postmodernism is the perversion and trashification of logic. Just another way of deconstructing what exists in order to replace it with Marxist thought, that's all. The rest is just the usual chin-stroking intellectual crap. It serves the purpose of creating psychotic individuals who are detached from reality and who have no conscience—who cannot reason or be reasoned with. Creatures like this are a resource that fuels the cult/ideology, therefore it's in its interest to create as many of them as possible.

It also indoctrinates individuals to be egocentric in the extreme. Notice how it ties-in with a major characteristic of the cult/ideology I've highlighted throughout—the immature spoilt-brat factor. The post-modernistic "make up your own reality" thought process is equivalent to being a spoilt brat on a perceptual level. "All that matters is how I feel, and what I think, and what my feelings are, and what my opinions/perceptions are".

Brats just love to get their own way; being told they are great; never having to be told they are wrong; thinking they are extremely intelligent etc. Postmodernistic thought allows them to invent all types of rubbish and believe in it, without ever being told they are dumb or that they need to grow up (and God forbid, to do something constructive with their lives). It also allows them to believe/support/idolise all sorts of rubbish created by others (including other cult members). It allows them to feel that warm, tingly, cultish feeling they get living their delusional cult member existence.

The prominent component of postmodernism which suggests that everything—including reality itself—can be interpreted in an infinite number of ways, is another piece of feel-good nonsense. It retards the psychological development of a mind, as it prevents the development of genuine perceptual skills; of learning how to see things how they actually are. It rewards stupid and insane thinking, treating it the same as excellent thinking. It's the whole "wanting a medal just because you were in the race" thing encapsulated in a school of thought. It's another thing that needs to banned and removed from academia and literature etc.

Yuri Bezmenov

"Understand what's going on around you—you are in a state of war... and you have precious little time to save yourself"[84]

Soviet defector Yuri Bezmenov,
interview with G. Edward Griffin, 1983

Is your country a receptive target when it comes to Marxist subversion, or "ideological subversion"? What is "ideological subversion" anyway?! Does your country essentially have open borders that anyone—including potential enemies—can cross? Does it have a strong sense of independence/sovereignty; that it's different from other countries? The asking of such questions was encouraged by a man named Yuri Besmenov (1939–1993).

Yuri Alexandrovich Bezmenov (aka Tomas Schuman) was a Russian KGB operative and journalist mainly active during the 1960s. He was born in a Moscow suburb in 1939, into a military family. His father was a high-ranking officer of the General Staff of the Soviet Army, and an inspector of land forces wherever the Soviets had troops stationed (Mongolia, Cuba, Eastern Europe etc.).

Speaking of his early life many years later, he said it was relatively affluent compared to others living under the Soviet regime (due to being brought-up in a military family), and that "most of the doors were open" for him. He was educated at *Moscow State University* in the *Institute of Oriental Languages*, where he became an expert in Indian languages (Hindi and Urdu) and culture, in addition to studying journalism, history, literature, and music. He also underwent extensive military and civil defence training, saying that "each student has to graduate as a Junior Leftenant and in my case it was administrative and military intelligence service".[84][85]

He joined the *Novesti Press Agency* which he described as "a propaganda and ideological subversion front for the KGB", before he graduated in 1963 (Yuri later explained that 75% of the members of Novesti were commissioned officers of the KGB, with the other 25% being agents like him who were co-opted and assigned to specific operations). Students who

---

[84] G. Edward Griffin interview, "Yuri Bezmenov - Deception Was My Job (full interview)". https://www.YouTube.com/watch?v=UrS1qDcgdTk

[85] "Yuri Bezmenov 1983 Interview and Lecture (1080p HD)". https://www.YouTube.com/watch?v=Z0j181tR5WM

graduated "were later on employed as diplomats, foreign journalists, or spies". His first assignment was to India, where he was a translator with the Soviet economic aid group *Soviet Refineries Constructions,* who were building refinery complexes in the states of Bihar and Gujarat. At the end of his first assignment there, he was promoted to the position of public relations officer. His final position was at the Soviet embassy in New Delhi as a press officer.

Yuri defected to the United States in 1970, escaping India by blending-in with the hippie movement. He eventually settled in Canada under the assumed identity of Tomas Schuman, taking various jobs to get by. A turning point came after gaining employment with the *Canadian Broadcasting Corporation* (CBC) in Montreal in 1973, on their overseas service in Russian. The Soviets became aware of this and the ensuing pressure—via the Soviet Ambassador Alexander Yakovlev—got him fired. He alleged that the Canadian PM Pierre Trudeau made a call to the CBC president, and this led to his dismissal. Trudeau and Yakovlev were apparently on friendly terms.[86]

He also taught political science at the *University of Toronto,* Slavic studies at *McGill University,* Montreal, and journalism at *Carleton University,* Ottawa. In one of his presentations, Yuri said he was amazed at how many Marxist books and other "left-wing propaganda" items he could find associated with American and Canadian Universities. These included works by Marx and Engels, Lenin, Frankfurt School 'intellectuals' Erich Fromm and Herbert Marcuse, and *The Indochina Story* (1970). [85]

After his defection, he became openly critical of the Soviet Union's brand of Marxism, authoring books and doing interviews and lectures. He was also a political analyst for a weekly paper called *Panorama.* His written works include *Love Letter to America* (1984)*; Black is Beautiful, Communism is not* (1985)*; No "Novosti" is Good News* (1985)*;* and *World Thought Police* (1986). He died a relatively unknown, isolated man while living in Windsor, Ontario in 1993 at the age of 54 (due to alcohol, apparently, and family issues). [86][87] His defection, his life was essentially a sacrifice in our struggle against Marxism.

He's a very significant character because he openly spoke about some critically important concepts within the ideology. A great analyst and

---

[86] Barrera, J., "Chaos agent", 5 Feb 2022.
https://www.cbc.ca/newsinteractives/features/yuri-bezmenov-soviet-defector-canada

[87] "Soviet Defector had passion for homeland", The Windsor Star, January 6, 1993, P. 5. https://www.newspapers.com/clip/53029092/yuri/

communicator on this subject, he was an expert in Soviet propaganda, popularising concepts such as "Ideological Subversion". With 20/20 hindsight, we can see that his predictions were almost prophetic. Yuri even speaks to us from the grave—he was featured in the trailer for the highly-popular game series *Call of Duty*, in their 2020 release entitled *Call of Duty: Black Ops Cold War.* The tagline of the trailer was "Know Your History".[88]

In 1984, Yuri did a long interview with G. Edward Griffin entitled "Soviet Subversion of the Free-World Press".[84] He also did an interview in Los Angeles in 1983 for the Summit University Forum (SUF), which he followed with an excellent one hour long presentation on the subject of ideological subversion. [85] (these two videos are the main sources for this whole section).

Why he defected

> "One of the reasons not to defect was I was living in relative affluence. Who the hell in their normal mind, would defect and do what? To be abused by your media? To be called McCarthyist and fascist and para-noid? or to drive a taxi in New York City. What for? What the hell for should I defect? To be abused by Americans, to be insulted in exchange for my effort to bring the truthful information about impending danger of subversion"[84]

In the 1984 interview, he listed things that made him question communism, including: the dichotomy between how the United States was an ally of the U.S.S.R. during WW2, as compared to how Soviet propaganda painted it as the enemy afterwards; when the genocidal crimes of Stalin came to light, thanks to Khruschev; and the Soviet invasion of Czechoslovakia in 1968 (which suppressed an anti-communism revolt).

When asked what he specifically objected to about the Soviet regime, he spoke of its behaviour, saying it was: "…a million times more oppressive than any colonial or imperialist power in the history of mankind. My country brings to India not freedom, progress, and friendship between the nations, but racism, exploitation, and slavery and of course economical inefficiency".

In the 1983 SUF interview, he spoke of his defection: "The decision, of course, was very painful and difficult…but on the other hand, I didn't have any illusions about the communist or socialist system…as the most rotten

---

[88] "Know Your History | Official Call of Duty®: Black Ops Cold War Trailer", August 2020.

https://www.YouTube.com/watch?v=zsBRGCabaog

and un-working system in the world…It doesn't matter what label you attach to the system. Basically, if you are a religious person, it's a devilish, Satanistic system, which appeals only to the most primitive, negative side of human nature. The basis of that system is denial of private property, human dignity, and personal responsibility and of course any religious affiliation…to God as a supreme being".

In the same interview, when talking about methods of subversion, he outlined the goal of the Marxist Soviet system (underline for emphasis): "The basic methods are not that much different from activities of any public relation(sic) officer from any big company…but the ultimate purpose is different. The ultimate purpose of the Soviet system is not to sell anything (least of all ideology). It's to destroy the civilisation, on which the affluence and freedom (is) based and replace it with a system of total control over life of human beings. The system of total exploitation—that's the ultimate purpose".

Soviet creation of 'Liberation' movements globally

The Soviets had a school in Moscow called *Lumumba Friendship University*. It was under the direct control of the KGB and Central Committee. In his interview in 1984, Yuri explained that was where "future leaders of the so-called "National Liberation" movements are educated and selected carefully". They were then "dispatched back to their countries to be leaders of the so-called "National Liberation" movements, or to be translated into normal human language—leaders of international terrorist groups".

(Note: in the tables section, we saw all these "freedom" movements springing-up across the world during the 20th century, particularly in lands (formally) controlled by European colonial powers. These were merely Marxist groups who were ostensibly against foreign/imperial control, but who were, in reality, driving their country towards an even more extreme form of control—international Marxist imperialism). [84]

On his functions at Lumumba, Yuri said "language instruction was my so-called extra-curricular activity" which was a role usually given to "young Communists as a non-paid job to prove loyalty to the party". He was giving Russian language instruction to students from Asia, Latin America, and Africa. Then the students entered an indoctrination class, which would brainwash them in Marxist-Leninist ideology, for a period of two to three years.

After a period of further vetting, if the students were suitable, they would then receive a further two years training by the KGB. Then, they would be dispatched back to their native countries to become 'sleepers'. They would lie dormant, so to speak, usually focusing on their usual job or career in the meantime. During the "destabilization" phase of their countries (explained further along), the agents would then become active, assisting Marxism in taking over.

Yuri explains: "Therefore, all of a sudden, you discover well-established lawyers in a country like Nicaragua, who for some strange reason are bitterly against "American imperialism" and idealistically for Soviet Marxist-Leninist imperialism".

Marxist 'Spirituality'

Here is a fascinating connection between the world of 'spirituality' and the subversion conducted by the cult/ideology. During his time in India, Yuri said the KGB were very interested in a 'guru' by the name of Maharishi Mahesh Yogi. This guru became famous in the 1960s and 1970s for his associations with celebrities, including The Beatles, The Beach Boys, and members of The Rolling Stones, to name a few; actors too: "Mia Farrow and other useful idiots from Hollywood visited his school and returned back to the United States absolutely zonked out of their minds with marijuana, hashish, and crazy ideas of meditation".

Yuri explained that this type of "spiritual" training and meditation was something that impacted the U.S. in a way desirable to the Soviets: "To meditate—in other words to isolate oneself from the current social and political issues of your country. To get in to your own bubble; to forget about troubles of the world...Obviously KGB was very fascinated with such a beautiful school, such a brainwashing centre... I was dispatched by the KGB to check what kind of VIP Americans attend this school".[84]

Yuri's function was "to discover what kind of people from the United States attend this school, and we discovered that yes there are some influential members of family, public opinion makers of United States, who come back with crazy stories of Indian philosophy. Obviously a VIP—say, the wife of a Congressman or a prominent Hollywood personality—after being trained at that school, is much more instrumental in the hands of manipulators of public opinion and KGB, than a normal person who looks through this type of fake religious training". This was because "a person who is too much involved in introspective meditation..." (i.e. a person who attended the Yogi's school), was more mentally suitable for serving the Soviet cause" (by being indoctrinated and helping the Soviets to subvert the US). This is true today; you can substitute the word "Soviet" for "Marxist".

He points out the Maharishi was teaching people—including his naive American students—that "the burning issues of today can be solved simply by meditating. Don't rock the boat. Don't get involved. Just sit down, look at your navel and meditate. And that things (the issues)—due to some strange logic, due to some "cosmic vibration"—will settle down by themselves". (this is reminiscent of the concept of 'Detachment" in the world of spirituality, including Buddhism).

Yuri continued: "This is exactly what the KGB and Marxist-Leninist propaganda wants from Americans—to distract their opinion, attention and mental energy from real issues of United States into a non-issues, into a non-world, non-existent "harmony"...Obviously, it's more beneficial for the Soviet aggressors to have a bunch of duped Americans than Americans who are self-conscious, healthy, physically-fit, and alert to the reality".

Pointing out that although Maharishi Mahesh Yogi was not on the payroll of the KGB, Yuri said "whether he knows it or not, he contributes greatly to demoralisation of American society, and he is not the only one: there are hundreds of those gurus who come to your country to capitalise on naivete and stupidity. It's a fashion to meditate, it's a fashion not to be involved".

Indeed, the 'new age' movement has complimented the spread of the Marxist infection very well. It is full to the brim with individuals talking about being 'awakened' (or 'woke') yet not having a clue what is actually happening in/to the world (in addition to not understanding themselves and their own beliefs, behaviours etc.). If that's what being 'awakened' is, I endeavour to be the most unawakened person ever. I wish the same level of 'spiritual ignorance' for you!

Being ignorant and morally irresponsible is not synonymous with true, genuine 'awakening/higher-consciousness'—it's the exact opposite! In addition, the type of psychological mindsets that pseudo-spirituality encourages actually accelerates Marxist indoctrination: excessive feminine/emotional perception; thinking that anger is negative; believing that all forms of conflict/physical force/killing is wrong; believing we are all one (collectivism, solidarity) and equal (equality) etc.

Enemies, recruits, and betrayal

Yuri spoke of the *Secret Department of Research and Counterpropaganda*. This group compiled information on anyone who could influence public opinion—journalists, actors, educationalists and professors, members of parliament, reps of business circles. They were divided in to two groups: those who would "tow the Soviet foreign policy they would be promoted to the positions of power through media and public opinion manipulation", and "those who refused the Soviet influence in their own country, who would be character assassinated or executed physically come revolution".[84]

As an example, Yuri spoke of assassinations like this during the Vietnam War, in the city of Hué. Where the Vietnamese communists were able to round-up and execute thousands of non-Marxists in just a few nights. The CIA were perplexed as to how swiftly this massacre was executed. Yuri explained: "The answer is very simple—long before Communists occupied the city, there was extensive network of informers, local Vietnamese citizens" who knew everything about their non-Marxist countrymen. This is a major recurring factor with the cult—it turns people of the same nationality/group against each other, in the most murderous ways. The infected will kill their own countrymen/women every chance they get.

Another group that was listed as targets by the Soviets were "pro-Soviet journalists with whom I was personally friendly". These types were "idealistically minded leftists who made several visits to the U.S.S.R... yet the KGB decided that, come revolution... they will have to go...". When asked why, he replied "because they know too much. You see the useful idiots, the leftists who are idealistically believing in the beauty of soviet socialist or communist or whatever system... when they get disillusioned they become the worst enemies... ", which is why they eventually have to be taken out (otherwise what they have learned in their dealings with the Soviets could pose a problem later). [84]

He continued, on the types of people the KGB wanted their operatives to target: "That's why my KGB instructors specifically made the point "never bother with leftists, forget about these political prostitutes, aim higher", this was my instruction. "Try to get into large circulation, established, conservative media. Reach filthy-rich moviemakers, intellectuals, so-called academic circles; cynical egocentric people who can look into your eyes with angelic expression and tell you a lie". This (sic) are the most recruitable people". People with no conscience essentially, those who are "lacking in moral principles". People who are "either too greedy or...suffer from self-importance...These are the people who the KGB wanted very much to recruit".

Referring to those leftist journalists that the KGB had on their hit-list, Mr. Griffin asks: "but to eliminate the others, to execute the others... don't they serve some purpose... wouldn't they be the ones you'd rely on?". Yuri responded: "No, they serve purpose only at the stage of destabilization of a nation. For example, your leftists in the United States....professors civil rights defenders... They are instrumental in the process of the subversion only to destabilize a nation...When their job is completed, they are not needed anymore, they know too much... Some of them, when they get disillusioned, when they see that Marxist-Leninists come to power, obviously they get offended—they think that they will come to power".

Smiling, Yuri continues "That will never happen of course, they will be lined-up against the wall and shot...but they may turn into the most bitter enemies of Marxist Leninists when they come to power".[84]

As stated throughout, the Marxist infection proliferates in waves, where the level of fanaticism embodied by the cult members is concerned. In other words, Marxists of one wave are always replaced by more fanatical Marxists in the subsequent waves.

Yuri listed examples of this pattern playing out: "In Nicaragua most of this former Marxist-Leninist's were either put to prison or one of them split and now he's working against Sandanistas. The case of Maurice Bishop in Grenada: "he was already a Marxist, he was executed by a new Marxist, who was more Marxist than this Marxist (referring to Bishop). The same pattern again in Afghanistan "first there was Taraki, he was killed by Amin, then Amin was killed by Babrak Karmal with the help of KGB and in Bangladesh "when Mujibur Rahman—very pro-Soviet leftist—was assassinated by his own Marxist-Leninist military comrades... It's the same pattern everywhere". According to Yuri, once they played their role, all these useful idiots would be either "executed entirely (all the idealistically minded Marxists), or exiled, or put in prisons like in Cuba" (adding that there are many former Marxists in prison in Cuba). [84]

The reality of 'equality'

Later in the interview, Griffin re-inquires about the extermination of these types of individuals, to which Yuri replied, with a great point about how the utopia of 'equality' is just a fantasy: "Most of them, yes. Simply because the psychological shock when they will see in future what the beautiful society of equality and social justice means in practice, obviously they will revolt.. And the Marxist-Leninist regime does not tolerate these people... (they) will be simply squashed like cockroaches. Nobody's going to pay them nothing for their beautiful ideas of equality and it will be greatest shock for them of course".

In his 1983 SUF presentation Yuri stated "You cannot legislate equality". Adding "If we put the principle of equality in the basis of our social political structure, it's the same thing as building a house on sand—sooner or later, it will collapse. And that's exactly what happens".

The Soviet regime and its allies (similar to China/its allies today) were happy to see western countries become obsessed with 'equality', making themselves weaker and unstable, making it easier for the cult to roll in and take over (in the words of Napoleon Bonaparte "Never interrupt your enemy when he is making a mistake"). Yuri added: "The absolute equality exists in Soviet Union...everybody is equal in (the) dirt".[85]

Ideological subversion

> "A long process...which sometimes is unnoticeable to an average person...It's unnoticeable as movement of a small hand of a clock—you know it's going around, but even if you watch it intensely you don't see the movement"

Yuri Besmenov's 1983 SUF lecture in Los Angeles

Perhaps the most important piece of information that Yuri gave us—and most pertinent in relation to this book's message—is something called Ideological Subversion. We've already covered what ideology is, but what about 'subversion'?

In his 1983 presentation, Yuri gave us the Soviet definition of the term 'subversion': it's "a destructive, aggressive activity aimed to destroy the country, nation, or geographical area of your enemy", pointing out that most subversive activity is "overt, legitimate, and easily observable", but also legal — "according to the law, it's not a crime!".[85]

Also (take note!), subversion is a two-way street: "You cannot subvert an enemy which doesn't want to be subverted". (i.e. a nation). There needs to be compliance, indifference or acquiescence to a certain degree. The process can only be successful when there is a "responsive target" (this is the crux of the issue in the world today). Interestingly, Yuri stated that the basics of subversion were taught to "every student of KGB school in U.S.S.R. and to officers of military academies", and that the *Art Of War* was on the recommended/mandatory reading list (the Art of War was authored by the Chinese philosopher Sun Tzu in the 5th century B.C.).[89]

Subversion is a far more efficient way of destroying an enemy: "The highest art of warfare is not to fight at all, but to subvert anything of value in the country of your enemy". Eventually this would lead to your enemy's perceptions being so distorted that "he does not perceive you as an enemy".[85] Does this not summarise the global predicament this book is highlighting, when it comes to how cult members are perceived by the general populace? Are we not surrounded by enemies within our own countries? (i.e. indoctrinated traitors and invaders)

In his 1984 interview, Yuri explained Ideological Subversion as "the process which is legitimate, overt and open—you can see it with your own eyes... There is no mystery; there is nothing to do with espionage... the main emphasis of the KGB is not in the area of intelligence at all. According to my opinion and opinion of many defectors of my calibre, only

---

[89] https://en.wikipedia.org/wiki/The_Art_of_War

about 15% of time, money, and manpower is spent on espionage as such. The other 85% is a slow process which we call either "Ideological Subversion" or "Active Measures" (активные мероприятия) in the language of the KGB—or psychological warfare".[84]

And here is perhaps the most profound part with respect to our struggle against the cult: "What it basically means is to change the perception of reality of every American* to such an extent that, despite the abundance of information, no-one is able to come to sensible conclusions in the interests of defending themselves, their families, their community and their country. It's a great brainwashing process which goes very slow and it's divided in four basic stages". (substitute your own nationality for the word "American").

Stage 1: Demoralisation

Yuri explained that at this first stage of the process, the ideology was inserted in to the various "areas of application of subversion" including religion, education, social life, power structure, labour and employer relations, and law and order.

He described the process of this stage: "It takes from 15 to 20 years to demoralize a nation, this is the minimum number of years which requires to educate one generation of students in the country of your enemy, exposed to the ideology of the enemy. In other words, Marxism-Leninism ideology is being pumped into.. at least three generations of Americanstudents, without being challenged or counter-balanced by the basic values of.. American patriotism... Most of the people who graduated in the sixties—drop-outs or half-baked intellectuals—are now occupying the positions of power in the government, civil service, business, mass media, education system".

Here Yuri outlines the severity of the indoctrination in these types of people: "You are stuck with them, you cannot get rid of them, they are contaminated. They're programmed to think and react to certain stimuli in a certain pattern. You cannot change their mind, even if you expose them to authentic information... you still cannot change the basic perception and the logical behaviour. In other words, (in) these people... the process of demoralisation is complete and irreversible. To get rid society of these people, you need another 20 or 15 years to educate a new generation of patriotically-minded...people, who would be acting in the interests of the United States's society".[84]

Yuri continues: "The demoralisation process in the United States is basically completed already, for the last twenty-five years actually it's over-fulfilled", explaining that the demoralisation has reached areas that Soviet intelligence never even dreamed it would: "Most of it is done by Americans to Americans, thanks to lack of moral standards". This sums up the situation in the U.S. at present.

Stage 2: Destabilisation

The next stage in the process, Yuri explained, is 'Destabilization', saying "it takes only from two to five years to destabilize a nation". During this phase, particular structures within the target country are targeted, including economy, foreign relations, and defence systems. Interestingly, even then in 1984 (the year of George Orwell) Yuri said "you can see it quite clearly…in such sensitive areas as defence and economy the influence of Marxist-Leninist ideas in the United States is absolutely fantastic… I could never believe it 14 years ago when I landed in this part of the world that the process will go that fast".

In his 1983 SUF presentation, he said the goal is to "destabilize all the relations, all the accepted institutions and organisations in a country of your enemy". The areas of application for destabilization is much narrower (than in demoralisation), focusing on specific areas including economy, labour relations, law and order (including military), and media (albeit differently to in the demoralisation stage).

Conflict is generated between groups

A "radicalisation of human relations" occurs at this stage. This is done to trigger conflict between different groups and individuals—even between family members, neighbours etc.—who "cannot come to compromise unless they start a fight". There is "no more compromise", only "fight fight fight". Any of this stuff sound familiar reader? You may or may not experience this with close family members, but this certainly should resonate on a social level. Essentially, the ideology creates division, polarising human interactions.

Yuri continued: "The normal, traditionally-accepted relations are destabilized: the relations between teachers and students, in schools and colleges; relations between labourers and employers are further radicalized, no more acceptance of the legitimacy of the demands of workers". Yuri mentioned the *Greyhound Lines* bus network strikes in 1983.[90] Though these strikes might have looked normal and reasonable at the time, Yuri explained: "The violent clashes between passengers, picketers and the strikers are presented as something normal. 10, 15, 20 years ago, we would be angry and say "Why? Why so much hatred? Today we are not, we say

---

[90] https://en.wikipedia.org/wiki/1983_Greyhound_Bus_Lines_strike_in_Seattle

"Well, it's commonplace". Law and order becomes more radicalized: "where previously people settled their differences peacefully and legitimately", now there is more tension and lack of resolution. It's when "society at large becomes more and more antagonistic—between individuals, between groups of individuals, and the society at large". He added that the media in general becomes more alienated from society, and in opposition to it.

The 'sleepers' wake-up

During destabilization, the 'sleepers' become active. These Soviet-trained recruits would become active in their respective countries, to participate in their de-stabilisation. They get involved in the whole Marxist movement, often openly, as activists or leaders of groups, and become active in the political process etc. In Yuri's era, these "sleepers" were often KGB agents (in our era, they may be operatives/infiltrators from other sources; or traitors within their respective countries).

Yuri mentions those in 'oppressed' groups (e.g. homosexuals, feminists). Whereas before, they were quieter and were less active, in this stage of the process they become more active, vocal and demanding (that society must change to suit them etc.). Now, their personal lives/life choices become "a political issue". They demand "respect, recognition, human rights" and generate unrest, which inevitably leads to conflict, including violent clashes with the police, opposing groups etc. Those in groups like that (feminism, LGBTQ+/'trans' movement, Black Lives Matter etc.) create tension and conflict, adding to the overall destabilisation process. All that matters, Yuri said, is that there is conflict and unrest between different groups. The destabilisation process leads directly to "Crisis".

Stage 3: Crisis

The third stage in the process is 'Crisis', and Yuri explained it may take "only up to six weeks to bring a country to the verge of crisis", referring to what was happening in Central America at the time as an example (i.e. the cults manoeuvring in that region). This could involve a "violent change of power structure and economy" (e.g. a military coup or invasion).

In the crisis stage, the cumulative effects of the demoralisation and destabilisation stages now come to a head. Society collapses. The artificial, bureaucratic groups that are created earlier in the process—riddled with cult members—now may start to claim power, using force if necessary: "In (the) case of developing nations...the process starts when the legitimate bodies of power, the social structure collapses... it cannot function anymore. So instead, we have artificial bodies injected in to society, such as non-elected committees (e.g. 'revolutionary' committees, social or government workers groups, NGO's/non-profits, media organisations etc.)".

Due to the chaos, the population in general may be looking for a saviour at this point. There may be calls for a 'stronger' or more authoritarian government; perhaps even a centralised, 'socialist government'. This 'saviour' can come in the form of an internal, local Marxist group taking control, or the invasion of the country by an external Marxist force. Yuri said this results in either two things—civil war, or invasion.

The civil war scenario basically involves the cult struggling for power against opposing groups. Either the non-Marxists will prevent the cult from taking over, or not. If there is no such internal Marxist group capable of doing this, then the force will come from the outside. Yuri used Lebanon as an example of the civil war scenario, that it "was artificially implanted in Lebanon by (the) injection of force of PLO ".

For invasion, he mentioned the Soviet operations in Afghanistan plus the various occasions that they invaded Eastern European countries. (The PLO (*Palestine Liberation Organisation*), which was supported by Moscow, was active in Lebanon from late 1960s to early 1980s).[91] Trying to reverse the whole process of ideological subversion at this stage, is only possible by strong country-wide support, preventing the civil war/invasion, and preventing the rise of the 'strong government'. Whichever route the crisis takes—civil war or invasion—it leads to the next stage: Normalization.

Stage 4: Normalization

The fourth stage is 'Normalization', which according to Yuri, may last indefinitely. The term "Normalization" is another way of saying "under Marxist control". Yuri explained that this was an ironic term, used by the Soviets after their 1968 invasion of Czechoslovakia, when the Soviet Premier Leonid Brezhnev (1906–1982) said that the situation there was "Normalized".

This 'normalisation' stage is essentially the opposite of the second stage ('destabilization') because "the self-appointed rulers of the society don't need any revolution (and) radicalism anymore". Now, they want stability, calm. Anything/anyone that doesn't comply with this is put down and eliminated with extreme prejudice. It's essentially "stabilizing the country, by force".

---

[91] Brand, W.E., "Soviet Russia, The creator of the PLO and The Palestinian people".

https://www.readcube.com/articles/10.2139/ssrn.2387087

In practice this means that "all the "sleepers" activists, social workers, liberals, homosexuals, professors, and Marxists and Leninists…are being eliminated, physically sometimes. They done their job already, they are not needed anymore. The new rulers need stability to exploit the nation, to exploit the country, to take advantage of the victory".[85] Again, the ideology takes over in evermore extreme waves, washing away the previous ones. It's at this point that all the Marxist traitor cult members—who have helped to destabilise or subvert their own homelands—get their well-deserved surprise of a lifetime.

Solutions for the different stages

At this very late, critical stage of the whole process, when a nation is this far gone (Normalisation), only military force from the outside (by a non-Marxist force) can reverse it. The U.S. invasion of Grenada in 1983 was a (then recent) example of this: "To reverse this process takes enormous effort when today United States had to invade Grenada to reverse the process of subversion". Though many in the U.S. would have objected to this, Yuri argued that the U.S. should have intervened earlier in the whole process, during the first stage of 'demoralisation' (as opposed to waiting till it reached 'normalisation').

The 'PC' objections of 'peace-lovers' and cult members in the U.S. would have opposed this: ""Why not to prevent Maurice Bishop to come in power in the first place?…Why not to stop the process before it comes to crisis? Oh no, intellectuals will not let you—it's interference into domestic affairs. They are very careful not to let American administration interfere in domestic affairs of Latin American countries; they don't mind Soviet Union interfering in its affairs". Indeed. Partisan double-standards! We were told for years (in infected parts of the world) that only America does things like that because it's a horrible, imperialist power. With hindsight, we can see that America would have been right to prevent the emergence of yet another Communist-infected country near their borders. Absolutely right! Of course, once the U.S. waited until the latter stages to invade, they discovered that Grenada was a military base for the Soviets.

To re-iterate Yuri's point: at the 'Normalisation' stage "it takes only and always military force. No other force on Earth can reverse this process at this point".[85] This reflects the gravity of the situation—when you have a country that is under the control of the Marxist cult, it's a dangerous threat to any country that is not yet fully-infected.

Yuri explained that at the 'crisis' stage that "it does not take military invasion of the United States army (note: or any other liberating non-Marxist force), it takes strong action like in Chile: a CIA covert involvement to prevent the 'saviour' from outside to come into power and stabilize the country before it erupts in to civil war...Support the right-wing conservative forces by money by crooks or love—doesn't matter. Stabilize the country, don't let the crisis develop in to civil war or invasion". He also pointed out that, predictably, there would be 'politically correct' (Marxist) uproar from some Americans, saying that early interventions are illegal etc.; but the alternative to such early interventions would be waiting till things get much worse, which is wrong, no matter what the law says. (Above is a reference to *Operation Condor* in Chile, and Augusto Pinochet. Condor was a righteous and justifiable anti-communism CIA-backed operation and involved collaboration between several South American right-wing governments).

Here's a point that's very useful for our current situation: how could we stop the process at an even earlier stage? By suppressing the 'revolutionaries'. At the destabilization stage, Yuri said, there is no need for covert operations or military invasions: "You know what it takes here? Restriction of some liberties for small groups which are self-declared enemies of the society. As simple as that".[85] What a great idea! Again, the hysterical irrational uproar would ensue, with the country's constitution and civil rights of these traitors/cult members/criminals being cited. From a rational perspective, if a person is actively destroying their home civilisation (because they are young/stupid/indoctrinated), they waive their rights to freedom in society! At the very least, these people should be monitored and regarded as potential criminals. We have this attitude towards criminals, so it should be applied to Marxist activist cult members too.

Our maxim on this should be—if you are part of a destructive, anti-humanity cult movement, then you wave your human rights. Again, the Marxian spectre of 'equality' comes in to play here in a problematic way. In the eyes of some, these civilisation-destroying Marxist faux-revolutionaries should have the same rights as normal, everyday, non-indoctrinated, law-abiding citizens. What rubbish! A fatal error of judgement.

Yuri continues: "Ok, if you allow the criminals to have civil rights, go on...and bring the country to the crisis. This is a bloodless way to do (it). Curb the rights. I mean not to put them in prison.. I'm not talking about putting all the gays from San Francisco in the concentration camp...Do not allow them to take political force! Do not elect them to the seats of power!.. It has to be bitten in the heads of American voters, that the person like that, in the seats of power, is an enemy".

At the earliest stage of the process, to prevent demoralisation, Yuri recommended not allowing any foreign or toxic propaganda in to the country in the first place: "If at that point the society is strong, brave and conscientious enough, to stop importation of ideas which are foreign then the whole chain of events could be prevented…The process of demoralisation could be stopped right here…both as an export and an import". In other words, as stated at the beginning "No to Marxism. No exceptions". Interestingly, we can see how the likes of China and North Korea strictly control any foreign ideology or media from reaching—and potentially influencing—their populations, while they actively export the ideology (the former in particular).

We are all in a state of war

In the 1984 interview with G. Edward Griffin Yuri made a statement which should be easier to understand now than back then (underlining for emphasis): "Most of the American politicians, media, and educational system trains another generation of people who think they are living at the peacetime. False. The United States is in a state of war, undeclared total war against the basic principles and the foundations of this system (the Marxist ideology/cult)". (Of course, this applies to civilisation in general, or anywhere that is infected with the ideology not just the U.S.). This system is "however ridiculous it may sound the "World Communist System" or the "World Communist Conspiracy". Whether I scare some people or not, I don't give a hoot, if you are not scared by now, nothing can scare you".[84]

Speaking of the impending doom that the U.S. (and indeed, the rest of the world) was edging towards, he said: "You have literally several years to live on.. unless United States wake up.. the time-bomb is ticking, with every second, the disaster is coming closer and closer.. unlike myself, you will have nowhere to defect to…This is it—this is the last country of freedom and possibility".

When Mr. Griffin asked him what the American people should do about all this, he replied that there were a few solutions: firstly, to educate, on a national scale, in "the spirit of real patriotism", and secondly, to inform of the dangers of Marxist government; adding "If people will fail to grasp the impending danger…nothing ever can help United States". He added: "So.. educate yourself…understand what's going on around you, you are not living at the time of peace…you are in a state of war and you have precious little time to save yourselves….As I said, I am now in your boat if we sink together, we'll sink beautifully together. There is no other place on this planet to defect to". Tick tock, tick tock..

Saul Alinsky

"Hell would be heaven for me. All my life I've been with the have-nots. Over here, if you're a have-not, you're short of dough. If you're a have-not in hell, you're short of virtue. Once I get into hell, I'll start organizing the have-nots over there"[92]

Saul Alinsky, interview with Playboy magazine, 1972

Another notable character is Saul Alinsky—a prominent Marxist active in the United States. Though we are going backwards chronologically (since Alinsky died in 1972, just after Yuri arrived in the U.S.), it's appropriate that we place him after the Besmenov section. This is because Alinsky was the subversive cult member who operated on the ground level, implementing the changes that Yuri spoke about during the Ideological Subversion process. In fact, I can think of no better (or infamous) a person to feature when examining the application of Marxist tactics, particularly among the 'oppressed' minority or 'proletariat' groups.

He was primarily known for being a 'community organiser', or a (Marxist) 'agitator' if you prefer. The kinds of tactics he developed inspired generations of cult members, including the *Occupy Movement* of 2011/12 and *Extinction Rebellion* which spawned in 2018, *Black Lives Matter, Insulate Britain, Just Stop Oil* and many others.

Who was Saul Alinsky?

Saul David Alinsky was born on 30 January 1909, in Chicago, Illinois, and was active from the 1930s to the 1960s. He attended the University of Chicago where he studied sociology and criminology, under the tuition of Robert Park and Ernest Burgess. He also spent some time in the company of Al Capone's mob, in particular with one of Capone's 'enforcers' — Frank Nitti. At one point Alinsky was a fundraiser for the Comintern-controlled *International Brigades*—the Marxist force of international volunteers who fought against the nationalist forces of Francisco Franco in the Spanish Civil War (1936–1939).[93]

Alinsky has been described as an 'activist' and was primarily known for being a 'community organiser', working with various ethnic minority groups including black and Mexican communities, in Rochester, New York and California respectively. He felt it was his role to "organize the poor" (what a nice guy). He was involved in the creation of groups such as the *Back of the Yards Council* in 1939; a national network for community

---

[92] Norden, E., "Saul Alinsky: Playboy Interview (1972)", 1 May 2018.

https://scrapsfromtheloft.com/comedy/saul-alinsky-playboy-interview-1972/

[93] https://www.britannica.com/biography/Saul-Alinsky

groups called the *Industrial Areas Foundation* (IAF) in 1940; and a collection of groups called *The Woodlawn Organisation* (TWO) which came to prominence in the 1960s.

These groups in general had the purpose of attracting, 'radicalising'/manipulating, and mobilising lower-income and inner-city residents (the TWO, for example, targeted black inner-city communities). Was also involved with an organisation called F.I.G.H.T. in Rochester, New York. Alinsky charged a fee for his 'services', to come in and 'help' the communities, and would act like he was invited-in by 'the people'.[93]

Alinsky's particular method of pushing the ideology—by exploiting these 'oppressed' groups—resulted in indoctrination of those who would not normally become so, ensuring that as many people as possible got caught in the big red brainwashing net. This community-targeting method was of great strategic benefit to the cult/ideology: it extended its influence to certain areas that were previously unreachable with the education system, particularly at university level. It's clear to see from Alinksy's own words in *Rules for Radicals* (1971) that the non-white protestors he "encouraged" were getting indoctrinated through the activism he advocated. Ergo, "Complain, and ye shall receive". His other notable (similar) work was *Reveille for Radicals* (1946).

Alinsky died in California in 1972, but his legacy lived on, inspiring the likes of Barrack Obama and Hillary Clinton. Obama, a known socialist, was a protégé of the Alinsky movement in Chicago, doing similar 'community work' there before eventually moving up in the world. An admirer of Alinksy, Clinton did a thesis on Rules for Radicals when she was in college (apparently, she didn't want the thesis becoming widely known during Bill Clinton's presidential campaign). She was a big fan and had several correspondences with him.[94]

What he was

This guy was an easily identifiable Marxist snake, and a master at manipulation. It should have been obvious that he didn't have a genuine empathetic/sympathetic bone in his body, particularly when it came to the well-being of those who had nothing at all in common with him (i.e. black people, Mexicans, Irish Catholics etc.). Was it more likely that he genuinely cared about these 'oppressed' types (who were total strangers to him)? Or that he had an agenda and was feigning concern, then virtue-signalling etc.? His interviews are revealing, but his actions and writings really expose him

---

[94] https://www.lincolninstitute.org/hillary-clinton-saul-alinsky-and-lucifer/

for what he was.

He wrote Rules for Radicals in 1971, not too long after the McCarthyism era, which he refers to early in the book. For this reason, amongst others, he doesn't openly refer to himself as a 'Marxist' or 'Communist'; he was part of the "don't call yourself a Communist" wave. In the book he wrote: "They are now the vanguard, and they had to start almost from scratch. Few of us survived the Joe McCarthy holocaust of the early 1950s and of those there were even fewer whose understanding and insights had developed beyond the dialectical materialism of orthodox Marxism. My fellow radicals (note: doesn't call himself a Marxist!) who were supposed to pass on the torch of experience and insights to a new generation just were not there".[95] Clearly, despite the anti-cult push by McCarthy et al, cult members like Alinsky remained defiant.

In a speech at the Kirby Centre at *Hillsdale College*, Washington D.C. in July 2010, David Horowitz spoke about Alinksy's attitude towards the New Left of the 1960s: "(Alinsky) was critical of the New Left. I was part of the New Left...We had one redeeming grace—we said what we were about. "We want revolution and we want it now! We want America to lose in Vietnam", we said these things. Alinsky thought we were nuts for saying that...(he) said "what you're doing when you say those things is you're telegraphing to people what you're gonna do... and they're gonna understand that you're a threat and that's bad".[96]

Ipso facto, Alinsky regarded himself as a threat, and a subversive one at that. He was simply an operative hidden in plain sight. To those wearing their anti-Marxist glasses, it would've been easy to spot him; to others, he was a benign helper of the poor etc.

Rules for Radicals

In 1971, Alinsky unleashed unto the world his evil book Rules for Radicals: A Pragmatic Primer for Realistic Radicals. It gives us great insight into what he was—psychotic, manipulative, and morally degenerate. It's easy to see how this book has contributed to the fanatical psychosis displayed by cult members today. It was basically an instruction manual for them, which could've been entitled "How to be a Marxist activist and subverter". "Radical" was obviously a good choice, rather than using Marxist (plus it would be appealing to anyone with hippie-ish tendencies). This book was required reading at the University of Texas in 1972, on the "Introduction to

---

[95] Alinsky, S., *Rules for Radicals* (1971) (xiii, prologue).

[96] "David Horowitz: What Conservatives Should Know About Saul Alinsky", Kirby Centre, Hillsdale College, 2010. https://www.YouTube.com/watch?v=GxHrbGPIQ-o

Political Behaviour" course, according to Texan author Richard Pennington.[97] David Horowitz mentioned in the same (above) lecture that the book had a noticeable presence in the many Universities he frequented.

Here is the list of contents by chapter: "The Purpose; Of Means and Ends; A Word About Words; The Education of an Organizer; Communication; In the Beginning; Tactics; The Genesis of Tactic Proxy; and The Way Ahead". I'm sure those will resonate and trigger some curiosities in the reader (and note the obvious references to the Bible).

In the "Of Means and Ends" chapter, Alinksy dedicates a section to convincing the reader that they should not worry about the consequences of their actions, if they believe their goals are noble (i.e. Marxist goals). Obviously, if they are reading his book, they likely already believe their goals are noble. Therefore, reading between the lines here, Alinsky is telling them "don't worry, do whatever you want, because you are right. Ignore those silly critics saying you are being immoral/unethical". Is this attitude not evident in cult members today? On page 126, Alinsky listed his rules:

1 "Power is not only what you have but what the enemy thinks you have".

2 "Never go outside the experience of your people".

3 "Wherever possible go outside of the experience of the enemy".

4 "Make the enemy live up to their own book of rules".

5 "Ridicule is man's most potent weapon. It is almost impossible to counterattack ridicule. Also it infuriates the opposition, who then react to your advantage".

6 "A good tactic is one that your people enjoy".

7 "A tactic that drags on too long becomes a drag".

8 "Keep the pressure on".

9 "The threat is usually more terrifying than the thing itself".

10 "The major premise for tactics is the development of operations that will maintain a constant pressure upon the opposition".

11 "If you push a negative hard and deep enough it will break through into

---

[97] Pennington, R., "Saul Alinsky's "Rules for Radicals"—Required Reading at UT in 1972", 5 April 2019.

https://richardpennington.com/2019/04/saul-alinskys-rules-for-radicals-required-reading-at-ut-in-1972/

its counterside; this is based on the principle that every positive has its negative".

12 "The twelfth rule: The price of a successful attack is a constructive alternative.

13 "Pick the target, freeze it, personalize it, and polarize it".[98]

Rule one sums up the cult quite well—"fake it till you make it". Basically, they make lots of noise and act big, to intimidate the potential opposition, while generating confidence in the organisation etc. This is reminiscent of how young cats play-fight: sometimes they run at you sideways, to appear bigger than they actually are. This is crucial for the non-indoctrinated portion of civilisation to understand—we easily outnumber them, and the cult isn't as big as it acts, so there is nothing to be afraid of!

Rule five sums up their behaviour in public discourse when dealing with their enemies, particularly online. Cult members in the media engaging in character assassination is another manifestation. Rules eight is their attempt to mentally break their targets. Rule nine is more psychological warfare tactics, exemplified in how cult members dish out threats constantly to opponents, but don't do anything physically in most cases. Rule thirteen is more of the same, trying to isolate and slander opponents.

Sneaky snaky wording

One of the easiest ways to see that Alinsky was just a Marxist under the mask was the terms he used. He described the poor, middle-class and rich as the "have nots", "have-a-little, want mores" and the "haves" (respectively). When he said "haves" he meant the wealthy/bourgeoisie (oppressors); when he said "have nots" he meant the 'oppressed' or proletariat class. A blatant—and clearly effective—attempt to re-vamp the oppressor v oppressed principle. Pathetic.

There is a small section called "Class Distinctions: The Trinity": "The setting for the drama of change has never varied. Mankind has been and is divided into three parts: the Haves, the Have-Nots, and the Have-a-Little, Want Mores".[99] The use of the word "Trinity" is just one of the many partisan digs at Christianity contained in the book, typical of a Marxist Jew like Alinsky.

Naturally, evoking the power of suggestion, the 'have nots' are depicted as the oppressed potential revolutionaries, frothing at the mouth for (Marxist)

---

[98] Alinsky, S. *Rules for Radicals* (1971), P. 126.

[99] Ibid. P. 32.

revolution: "On the bottom are the world's Have-Nots. On the world scene they are by far the greatest in numbers. They are chained together by the common misery of poverty, rotten housing, disease, ignorance, political impotence, and despair; when they are employed their jobs pay the least and they are deprived in all areas basic to human growth. Caged by color, physical or political, they are barred from an opportunity to represent themselves in the politics of life. The Haves want to keep; the Have-Nots want to get. Once the fever begins the flame will follow. They have nowhere to go but up.". Note the use of "chained". And that last one is amusing—it's a semi-cryptic nod to what was written in the Communist Manifesto "Proletarians of all countries unite! You have nothing to lose but your chains!".[100]

Targeting the youth

He wrote in a way that pandered to the naive youth and fuelled their egos, by feigning respect and using virtue-signalling language and sentiments: "I salute the present generation. Hang on to one of your most precious parts of youth, laughter—don't lose it as many of you seem to have done, you need it. Together we may find some of what we're looking for—laughter, beauty, love, and the chance to create".[101] He wrote for the 'radicals of today' (in 1971), saying "I hope that these pages will contribute to the education of the radicals of today, and to the conversion of hot, emotional, impulsive passions that are impotent and frustrating to actions that will be calculated, purposeful, and effective".[102]

He encouraged the disrespectful behaviour we see in many youths of today towards older generations. On the generation gap and how older generations could deal with the revolutionary tendencies of the youth: "Unable to come to grips with the world as it is, they retreat in any confrontation with the younger generation with that infuriating cliché, "when you get older you'll understand." One wonders at their reaction if some youngster were to reply, "When you get younger which will never be then you'll understand, so of course you'll never understand".[103] How manipulative: it's highly-destructive for a young person to read that the phrase "when you get older you'll understand" is in any way negative, as often, this phrase is exactly what they need to hear; it can instil some humility, stopping their egos from inflating (and thinking they know what's

---

[100] Ibid. P. 33.

[101] Ibid. P. 18.

[102] Ibid. P. 21.

[103] Ibid. P. 9.

best for humanity, then become activists etc.).

A permanent revolution

Alinsky skilfully pedalled his interpretation of 'permanent revolution' to the reader: "If we think of the struggle as a climb up a mountain, then we must visualize a mountain with no top....And so it goes on, interminably... Simply, this is the very nature of life—that it is a climb—and that the resolution of each issue in turn creates other issues, born of plights which are unimaginable today. The pursuit of happiness is never-ending; happiness lies in the pursuit.". And: "History is a relay of revolutions; the torch of idealism is carried by the revolutionary group until this group becomes an establishment, and then quietly the torch is put down to wait until a new revolutionary group picks it up for the next leg of the run. Thus the revolutionary cycle goes on".[104] He was brainwashing the young and naive reading this in to creating permanent 'revolution' their whole lives; therefore becoming obnoxious problems that the rest of us must solve.

Training Marxist agitators

He referred to the training of Marxist activists: "The building of many mass power organizations to merge into a national popular power force (note: Communist movement) cannot come without many organizers. Since organizations are created, in large part, by the organizer, we must find out what creates the organizer. This has been the major problem of my years of organizational experience: the finding of potential organizers and their training. For the past two years I have had a special training school for organizers with a full-time, fifteen-month program".[105]

On how the Marxist agitator should communicate and mingle-in to their target communities: "He learns the local legends, anecdotes, values, idioms. He listens to small talk. He refrains from rhetoric foreign to the local culture: he knows that worn-out words like "white racist," "fascist pig," and "motherfucker" have been so spewed about that using them is now within the negative experience of the local people, serving only to identify the speaker as "one of those nuts" and to turn off any further communication".[106] This is some sneaky subversive Marxist stuff—hiding their commie nature from those in the communities as they manipulate them.

---

[104] Ibid. P. 35.

[105] Ibid. P. 73.

[106] Ibid. P. 80.

Why the cult needs to have lots of issues/sub-agendas

He highlighted how it's crucial for the cult to engage in multiple issues simultaneously, so there's always something going on: "Not only does a single- or even a dual-issue organization condemn you to a small organization, it is axiomatic that a single-issue organization won't last. An organization needs action as an individual needs oxygen. With only one or two issues there will certainly be a lapse of action, and then comes death. Multiple issues mean constant action and life".[107] Then the cult is like a shark in that it needs to keep swimming in order to get its oxygen. Picture a red commie shark having a permanent revolutionary swim.

This logic can be applied to the Marxist movement as a whole, globally. Is this another reason why they have so many different issues ("sub-agendas") and support them, so they can keep active? Certainly, having so many sub-agendas means the big red net can be cast nice and wide, pulling in many adherents.

The fact that there are lots of different types of issues/sub-agendas to cater to all tastes (as listed elsewhere) ensures this: "There is a way to keep the action going and to prevent it from being a drag, but this means constantly cutting new issues as the action continues, so that by the time the enthusiasm and the emotions for one issue have started to de-escalate, a new issue has come into the scene with a consequent revival. With a constant introduction of new issues, it will go on and on. Keeping that revolutionary energy going". [108] Never-ending revolution eh? how delightful!

Displaying the Marxist control freak mindset

Another example of Marxian obsession with 'revolution': "One of the great problems in the beginning of an organization is, often, that the people do not know what they want. Discovering this stirs up, in the organizer, that inner doubt shared by so many, whether the masses of people are competent to make decisions for a democratic society. It is the schizophrenia of a free society that we outwardly espouse faith in the people but inwardly have strong doubts whether the people can be trusted. These reservations can destroy the effectiveness of the most creative and talented organizer".[109] Well, if they actually needed anything, they would know already! This is Marxist logic: "they don't know what they want, but they do want a Marxist

---

[107] Ibid. P. 86.

[108] Ibid. P. 163.

[109] Ibid. P. 111.

revolution of some kind…because they are the proletariat, so they simply must!". The usual "the proletariat don't know what's good for them, so they should be pushed towards revolution" line of thought.

Being aggressive so people will listen

He pushed the idea of being aggressive and threatening people otherwise they won't listen to you: "You don't communicate with anyone purely on the rational facts or ethics of an issue.. It is only when the other party is concerned or feels threatened that he will listen—in the arena of action, a threat or a crisis becomes almost a precondition to communication.". In short—pay attention to me or I will cause harm. Combining elements like these with the spoilt-brat factor explains the potency of the cult's fanaticism. Rule nine is "The threat is usually more terrifying than the thing itself".[110]

Generating discontent in the proletariat

The Marxist agitator must find things for the community to complain about: "The organizer dedicated to changing the life of a particular community must first rub raw the resentments of the people of the community; fan the latent hostilities of many of the people to the point of overt expression. He must search out controversy and issues, rather than avoid them, for unless there is controversy people are not concerned enough to act". Tellingly, it fits the cult's MO of generating problems, creating tensions, and fomenting hostility. They will literally seek out and exaggerate things to proliferate the ideology. Obviously, encouraging the 'oppressed' mentality is central to all this.[111]

He adds: "An organizer must stir up dissatisfaction and discontent; provide a channel into which the people can angrily pour their frustrations. He must create a mechanism that can drain off the underlying guilt for having accepted the previous situation for so long a time. Out of this mechanism, a new community organization arises. The job then is getting the people to move, to act, to participate; in short, to develop and harness the necessary power to effectively conflict with the prevailing patterns and change them (note: aka 'revolution'). When those prominent in the status quo turn and label you an "agitator" they are completely correct, for that is, in one word, your function—to agitate to the point of conflict".[112]

The cult acting big

---

[110] Ibid. P. 97.

[111] Ibid. P. 121.

[112] Ibid. P. 122.

On the tactic of Marxist groups presenting themselves as big and intimidating: "For an elementary illustration of tactics, take parts of your face as the point of reference; your eyes, your ears, and your nose. First the eyes; if you have organized a vast, mass-based people's organization, you can parade it visibly before the enemy and openly show your power. Second the ears; if your organization is small in numbers, then do what Gideon did: conceal the members in the dark but raise a din and clamor that will make the listener believe that your organization numbers many more than it does. Third, the nose; if your organization is too tiny even for noise, stink up the place".[113]

As covered elsewhere, the cult's tradition of regular public protests gives the visual impression that they are more powerful and numerous than they actually are. Unfortunately, in many instances, even this is enough to intimidate non-indoctrinated average, everyday people in to not challenging and overpowering the cult publicly.

A large anti-immigration protest in Dublin on Monday 5 February 2024 was an example of this. As usual, cult members in Ireland staged a 'counter-protest' ('anti-racism' etc.) outside the General Post Office on O'Connell street. Thousands of protestors showed-up for the patriotic side. The group of patriotic protestors dwarfed the cult group considerably. The Irish YouTuber Keith Woods live streamed the event, which clearly showed this.[114]

Biblical or Occult references

Interestingly, there are many biblical or occult references in the book. In fact, within the first few pages, there is a dedication to Lucifer: "Lest we forget at least an over-the-shoulder acknowledgment to the very first radical: from all our legends, mythology, and history (and who is to know where mythology leaves off and history begins—or which is which), the first radical known to man who rebelled against the establishment and did it so effectively that he at least won his own kingdom—Lucifer".[115]

Not only is the cult/ideology itself inspired by this famous/infamous entity, but it represents it. And what does Lucifer/Satan represent? It represents the defiance/opposition to "God's plan" (i.e. nature/the natural order of things), which the cult/ideology most certainly is. The 'kingdom' of Satan

---

[113] Ibid. P. 131.

[114] Keith Woods, "National Day of Protest – Ireland Belongs to the Irish", 5 Feb 2024. https://www.YouTube.com/watch?v=G-LLcv8xW7s

[115] Ibid. pre-intro (dedications/quotes).

is not some immaterial hell in the afterlife, but the Earth itself if evil (e.g. Marxism) becomes victorious. A kingdom in defiance of God/the Creator. (Note: there are some who believe that "Lucifer" does not represent 'evil', that this is a separate entity to "Satan". This is an ancient, esoteric, colossal subject outside the scope of this book).

There are biblical references in the section titles, such as "In the beginning" and "The Genesis of Tactic Proxy", in addition to several references to apocalypse throughout. "Remember we are talking about revolution, not revelation; you can miss the target by shooting too high as well as too low" ("as above, so below"). [116] The word "apocalypse" (from the Latin "apocalypsis") essentially means 'revelation'. Did he refer to the Bible constantly to allude to some sort of apocalypse; one that the Marxian 'revolution' will assist in bringing about? What did Alinsky know that 'we' don't know? This certainly feels like an apocalypse, doesn't it?

Obviously, these connections would go over most people's heads (certainly the youth, and/or those who have no religious, esoteric, or occult knowledge), leading me to believe that Alinsky was a Satanist. As mentioned at the beginning, Marxism is not the whole picture, or, indeed, the top of the totem pole—the ideology has spawned from something bigger and more sinister..

Final thoughts

Alinsky was a real piece of work—quite obviously manipulative, plus open and proud about it. As Yuri Besmenov recommended, the solution to stopping Ideological Subversion in its tracks is to restrict freedoms for certain types of individuals. Activists cut from the Alinsky cloth often do things that aren't illegal, but yet are disruptive and pressuring etc. The solution for society, then, is to make it illegal to do things of that nature; to make it illegal to be a Marxist activist, essentially. (as Yuri said — "curb the rights").

Why should the rest of us suffer just because there are organised, misguided fools in the world? Obviously, before this could be achieved, the general public—in sufficient numbers—would have to understand the wisdom of this course of action. It would be putting the cart before the horse to expect that level of collective understanding right now, before the message of this book reaches everyone it needs to reach. Let's move on.

Communitarianism

Since we just covered communist 'community organisers', let's continue

---

[116] Ibid. P. 10.

that community theme and look at another deceptive concept (through our brand-spanking-new, magical anti-Marxist glasses!). Another form of Marxism in disguise is communitarianism. Just like with "community organiser" (cheers Saul), it's almost "communist" or "communism", with a few extra letters thrown in.

Definitions

As Wikipedia is the always-being-shoved-in-your-search-engine's-face common source (and therefore in a massive position of influence over people) here's what it says. I've underlined certain words for emphasis: "Communitarianism is a philosophy that emphasizes the connection between the individual and the community. Its over-riding philosophy is based upon the belief that a person's social identity and personality are largely moulded by community relationships, with a smaller degree of development being placed on individualism", and "Communitarianism usually opposes extreme individualism and disagrees with extreme policies that neglect the stability of the overall community".[117]

Sounds lovely, doesn't it? Remember, we are dealing with a skin-shedding snake here. Note the word "philosophy", being used: a typical Marxist tactic to give the concept some intellectual merit; this tends to sucker-in people who are impressed by 'intellectual' things. (As we've seen, whenever you see the word "philosophy" being used in connection with anything 'revolutionary' (Marxist), this often means that someone is conjuring-up ideas with a distinctly Marxian, often post-modernistic slant). You can see the virtue-signalling tone towards the end too. The word "extreme" suggests that anything opposed to this 'philosophy' is negative/unethical (e.g. anything 'right-wing'). This latter part carefully insinuates that communitarianism is benign, collectivist, and that it wants what's best for the group. "Stability" means "the community is ideologically Marxist, and this dominance must not be threatened" ("stability" means "normalised").

Another description from *Brittanica.com:* "Communitarianism, social and political philosophy that emphasizes the importance of community in the functioning of political life, in the analysis and evaluation of political institutions, and in understanding human identity and well-being. It arose in the 1980s as a critique of two prominent philosophical schools: contemporary liberalism, which seeks to protect and enhance personal autonomy and individual rights in part through the activity of government, and libertarianism, a form of liberalism (sometimes called "classical

---

[117] https://en.wikipedia.org/wiki/Communitarianism

liberalism") that aims to protect individual rights—especially the rights to liberty and property—through strict limits on governmental power".[118] So it's anti-individualism and pro-collectivism, basically.

Origins of the word

Apparently, the term Communitarianism was first coined, in 1841, by John Goodwyn Barmby (1820–1881). He was another part of the utopian socialist mob during that period, and apparently (according to Wiki!) he "claimed to have introduced the word communist into the English language as a translation of the French word 'communiste'". He also introduced Friedrich Engels to the French "communiste" movement, and they founded two organisations in 1841—the *Universal Communitarian Association,* and the *London Communist Propaganda Society* (seven years later, the Communist Manifesto appears).[119]

There are connections between this concept of communitarianism and other areas we know are saturated with Marxism, such as sociology, social democracy, philosophy etc. Amusingly, many of the online definitions for it explain that these types of communitarian ideas have been around for centuries, featuring in the Old and New Testaments, Confucianism, Islam ("Shura", meaning "consultation"), and Fabian Socialism, naturally (again, the 'ol "See? We were already Marxist and we didn't know it" trick).

Elements of Communitarianism

One of the modern-day proponents of Communitarianism was a German-born Israeli sociologist called Amitai Etzioni (1929–2023; born Werner Falkin). He was the director of the *Institute for Communitarian Policy* at George Washington University, Washington D.C (it has a whole institute at an American University? Impressive). He authored many academic works and books on the subject including: *The Spirit of Community: The Reinvention of American Society* (1993), *The New Golden Rule: Communisty and Morality in a Democratic Society* (1998), and *From Empire to Community: A New Approach to International Relations* (2004).[120] Looking at those titles, how much revolutionary and virtue-signalling sentiment can you spot? (rolls eyes). The last title is a nod to the fact (noted earlier) that Marxism is a new form or imperialism that simply replaced the traditional colonial variety — "Empire to Community" could

---

[118] https://www.britannica.com/topic/communitarianism

[119] https://en.wikipedia.org/wiki/John_Goodwyn_Barmby

[120] https://www.amitaietzioni.org/

also be entitled "Empire to Communism".

In 1993, he founded an organisation called the *Communitarian Network*. Etzioni had a YouTube channel, and in his video *The Five Minute Communitarian* he had this to say: "It's a rather unusual kind of social philosophy because the term communitarian is not widely known at all.. actually, very few people use it. On the other hand, there is a very large number of people (who) hold communitarian ideas…". After pointing out that these ideas have existed throughout history, he continues by explaining three major elements to it: "One, is the notion that we are members of each other. (!!).. and the second (is) that we need a moral infrastructure.. and thirdly, that the rights and responsibilities go hand-in-hand".[121]

He explains that first one with the catchphrase "The "Me" needs a "We" to be". Expanding, he said that there was plenty of social science data, collected via psychological experiments on various social situations (including prisons, high-rise buildings etc.), to show that when people are isolated, they "suffer a large variety of inflictions—many of them psychological, some of them even physiological". Nothing ground-breaking so far.

He continued: "So it seems that the essence of human nature is not that free-standing, isolated individual—which is often cherished in American history and ideology (note: uh oh.. criticism of America/Americanism again..) — but it's somebody who thrives in the lasting meaningful relationship with others". The solution is that "we need to opportune communities". This would be done by encouraging more social, communal interaction by changing how we build structures, which would force people to interact more (wider sidewalks, more front porches and less back porches, more promenades, having local schools open for community meetings etc.). He also said "If communities are not nurtured, they tend to die, and that leaves us with isolated individuals. That's the first element of communitarian thinking—we need lasting relationships, we need each other".

The second element, Amitai explains, is the moral dimension—the "moral infrastructure". This essentially means that the community encourages certain behaviours in the individuals within that community. As he put it "Communities have norms, not laws, informal understanding which are enforced, but nothing harsher than people shaking the finger sometime(s) at each other, or appreciating when people live up to these norms. And they

---

[121] Etzioni, A., "The Five Minute Communitarian HD", 16 April 2015.

https://www.YouTube.com/watch?v=gKA4JjkiU4A

suffice—in a well-grounded community—to take care of an enormous amount of social business". Therefore, Amitai said, we're much, much better off when the community decides "how much environmental protection is correct?; what should we do if people don't get vaccinated?; how high should we send (sic) the speed limits?; once we have these things in place, the more we can rely on our mutual understanding and informal enforcement, the better we are all off (sic)". [121]

The third and final element is "Rights and responsibilities". Amitai explained that this is the notion that we have individual rights, but that "rights go with social responsibilities and we cannot have one without the other", once again alluding to the fact that America has always had strong emphasis on individual rights. He uses polarising debates as an example here, such as the rights of privacy for individuals vs the states' right to protect the nation from terrorism; also freedom of the press, or issues of public health etc. He says that from the communitarian point of view, it's important that the conversation starts by "not assuming that one side automatically trumps the other and prevails, but to start the conversation by arguing that we do need to be concerned both with cherishing our rights, but also with serving the common good security and serving the common good for example". All of that is just pushing solidarity, basically, and that there should be the resultant consensus on social issues etc. It's suggesting that the traditional American idea of individual sovereignty is not as much a part of 'human nature' as being part of the community.

Should we trust this?

Sure, this is just one person speaking, but his opinion is noteworthy—he has been regarded as somewhat of a 'guru' for communitarianism and was certainly a respected voice. Having said that, doesn't this all sound a bit fishy? What are these communitarian advocates saying? That we need a movement to encourage people to be more social? What a load of horseshit.

Does all of this benefit Marxism? Are they trying to create tight-knit communities of brainwashed Marxist rats, who know each others' business? It this so the sheep can monitor each other, ensuring no one strays from the pack, and everyone in society all thinks, speaks, and acts the same way? This is not about helping the isolated/depressed/mentally ill, this is about ensuring that everyone stays under control, with no privacy from the collectivist social psycho culture that the Marxist cult creates.

Section VI — The Marxist Matrix

"Politics is downstream of culture"[1]

Andrew Breitbart, founder of *Breitbart News,*
"Courrielche: Conservatives' Next Frontier"

Introduction

In *The Matrix* (1999), Morpheus (Laurence Fishburne) and Neo (Keanu Reeves) are about to cross a busy city street. First, we see the pedestrian crossing light showing the (commie) red man. When it changes to green and they start walking through the crowds, Morpheus speaks about indoctrination: "The Matrix is a system Neo, that system is our enemy, but when you're inside, you look around, what do you see? Businessmen, teachers, lawyers, carpenters; the very minds of the people we are trying to save. But until we do, these people are still a part of that system, and that makes them our enemy. You have to understand, most of these people are not ready to be unplugged; and many of them are so inured, so hopelessly dependent on the system, that they will fight to protect it. Were you listening to me Neo? or were you looking at the woman in the red dress?".[2]

The real Matrix is not green as in the film, however, it's red. Marxist subversion has historically been a highly-organised, professional system, that uses tried-and-trusted methods. Here we take a look at the 'transmission belts of culture' that the ideology/cult uses to infect a country/society.

Clizbe and Willing Accomplices

An excellent book about Marxist subversion in the U.S. is *Willing Accomplices: How KGB Covert Influence Agents Created Political Correctness and Destroyed America* (2011); by Kent Clizbe, a former CIA case officer.

Clizbe's work covered some relevant concepts, including the 'transmission

---

[1] Breitbart, A., "Courrielche: Conservatives' Next Frontier", *Daily Wire.*
https://en.wikiquote.org/wiki/Andrew_Breitbart

[2] "Walking through the Matrix". https://www.YouTube.com/watch?v=zDO1Q_ox4vk

belts of culture'; those disseminators of propaganda and influencers of the masses: education, media, and entertainment. Though the cult/ideology has permeated into many areas of society, these 'transmission belts' are perhaps most crucial in facilitating the ideology's spread. (The term 'transmission belts' was used earlier by W. Cleon Skousen in his 1958 book *The Naked Communist;* in his "Current Communist Goals", no. 17).[3]

Clizbe's book brilliantly highlights the early phase of the red rot in the U.S., and the subsequent rise of 'political correctness'. He explained how this was not an organic process, but a deliberate attempt at subversion by the Soviets, starting not in the last few decades or in the 1960s (as some think), but much earlier, with the 1920s being a key period.

This corroborates with the chronological pattern of the spread of Marxism, which accelerated massively after the 1917 revolutions in Russia (as the historical tables earlier showed). Obviously, the period of McCarthyism was to follow later, as a response to this ideological assault on America.

The creation of the Third Communist International/"Comintern" in 1919 was central to this, and they were engaging in subversion professionally during the 1920s.[4] They were essentially experts at this long before the *Office of Strategic Services* (OSS) or the *Central Intelligence Agency* (CIA) were even formed (in 1942 and 1947 respectively).[5] Clizbe put forth the argument that the 'pc progressive' culture in today's America exists due to this deliberate subversion, and that the "hate America first" mentality—propelled by Socialist ex-President Barrack Obama—was part of its legacy. This is the ideological subversion that Yuri Besmenov pointed out. Yuri's and Clizbe's work showed us that eventually this became a weaponised science to the Marxists.

Covert influence 'payloads'

Clizbe's work shows that Soviet operations—to infect American minds—involved inserting covert influence psychological "payloads" into American culture. These were essentially concepts, which encouraged certain attitudes which were destructive to the integrity of American society (self-destructive if adopted by Americans). Attitudes such as: capitalism is oppressive; the U.S. military is a globe-trotting imperial force and Americans shouldn't support it; America was founded on violence, the

---

[3] Clizbe, K., *Willing Accomplices: How KGB Covert Influence Agents Created Political Correctness and Destroyed America* (2011).

[4] https://www.britannica.com/topic/Third-International

[5] https://www.cia.gov/legacy/cia-history/

theft of land and the oppression and murder of native Americans (which instils guilt); there is unjustifiable institutional racism and it's at the heart of American society, and that non-white Americans have historically suffered more than whites; the idea that the U.S.A. is the greatest country in the world is bad and leads to dominance and suffering outside its borders etc. In short, any attitudes which would—if absorbed by Americans and spread throughout society—destroy any healthy patriotism and unity in the nation.

Clizbe wrote: "Using experienced operatives and highly compartmentalized operations, the KGB sought to insert covert influence "payloads" designed to call into question the fundamental bases on which American society and culture had been built. Many progressives eagerly carried out these covert operations for the Communists. Others not involved in the operations received the covert messages and accepted them as gospel".[6] Do we not see these 'payloads' everywhere we look nowadays in education, main-stream media, and 'entertainment'?

Agents of Influence and "Adversary Culture"

Clizbe wrote that certain individuals were targeted by the Soviets based on their "potential as an agent of influence" and chosen "for access to a desired channel of communications (the Comintern intel operators targeted American media, academia, and Hollywood).". These "agents of influence" would then be approached and manipulated by Soviet espionage operatives, leading to them being primed for use (the persons being manipulated may or may not have known who (and indeed what) they were dealing with). It's at this point that the subversive 'payload' can be delivered (underlining for emphasis): "In the actual operation, the espionage officer provides the recruited agent of influence with the payload. The agent of influence inserts the payload into his communications channel. Once the payload is inserted, in the form of a news story, an editorial, a speech, a book, a lecture, a movie, a radio program, a song, a play, or any other form of communication, the payload takes on a life of its own".[7]

This is crucial. These payloads—which are really just bits of propagandised information—may gather momentum and 'snowball' as they spread. They take on a life of their own (as the ideology itself has done). These covert influence "payloads" were linked-in with another term Clizbe used called "adversary culture" (which came from a work by

---

[6] Ibid. vi (preface).

[7] Ibid. P. 113.

Stephen Koch entitled *Double Lives: Stalin, Willi Muenzenberg,* 2004).[8] It was a term used to describe the anti-patriotic mentality of intellectuals who loathed their own country/culture (sound familiar?). This meant that within a target country (i.e. the U.S.) the Soviet subverters could identify these types, who would then be utilised to influence the the masses. Indeed, there will always be individuals like this in every country, which the cult/ideology can take advantage of. Who better to diffuse these payloads than them?

Muenzenberg

Clizbe singled-out a character by the name of Wilhelm "Willi" Muenzenberg (1889–1940) as being central to these subversion operations, calling him "the father of PC". Being a key-player for the Comintern, he used cover organisations, fronts, and "innocent clubs" to spread the Marxist rot: "The communist master of feel-good America hating, Willi Muenzenberg perfected the "Popular Front" operational concept. He and his agents set up multiple organizations with high-minded names and reasons for existence—for example the International Congress Against Fascism and War, and the Hollywood Anti-Nazi League. These fronts gave intellectuals, journalists, artists, and educators a higher calling—while serving as cover to insert covert influence payloads into the targeted cultures. The perceived moral superiority of the Soviet's covert influence messages provided Popular Front members a chance to show "you were a decent human being," in fact, a better human being. Muenzenberg despised these Popular Front members, and called them "innocents".[9]

Clizbe crucially highlighted that even back then any critics of the cult's activities—or anyone they did not like—were publicly labelled fascists, racists, bigots etc. So, their behaviour in recent years is nothing new (of course, Mussolini came to prominence earlier than Hitler and the National Socialists, so "fascist" was popular before "Nazi"). If the cult used a modus operandi like this a century ago, we must accept that it's part of its armoury today, generally speaking. The ideology doesn't devolve; it evolves. This is why the underlined parts are familiar to the reader; same goes for the virtue-signalling tone. The point on racism is crucial, and highly relevant. Today anyone can see there's a nauseating obsession with race/racism in public discourse in the U.S. This is not by accident nor is it naturally-occurring—it's a result of the Soviet operations and the Marxist rot in general. The cult are masters at finding 'weaknesses' to exploit, and since

---

[8] Koch, S., *Double Lives: Stalin, Willi Munzenberg and the Seduction of the Intellectuals* (2004).

[9] Ibid. vii (preface).

the U.S. is multi-ethnic, 'racism' was the obvious choice.

On the overall impact of Willi's efforts, Clizbe wrote (underlined for emphasis): "The result of the Muenzenberg payload's dissemination throughout American society is now clear. A healthy, happy, productive nation of citizens, blended in the great Melting Pot, had set aside their differences when they became Americans. After Muenzenberg's influence op, the same people were converted into a confused mass of self-interest groups, torn apart by PC divisions of race, gender, ethnicity, income, class, language, sexuality ".[10]

Doesn't all of this resonate? That's how you destroy a place like America, that has traditionally had a strong sense of patriotism woven into its culture—you create division among sub-groups, by playing them off against each other, using the Marxian principle of oppressor v oppressed. Of course, this strategy is employed globally. This is what the ideology does: it finds chinks in the armour to exploit.

MSM = MarxiStMedia

"A newspaper is not only a collective propagandist and a collective agitator, it is also a collective organiser"[11]

V.I. Lenin, *What Is To Be Done?*,
"The Plan For an All-Russia Political Newspaper", 1901

"The art of any propagandist and agitator consists in his ability to find the best means of influencing any given audience, by presenting a definite truth, in such a way as to make it most convincing, most easy to digest, most graphic, and most strongly impressive"[12]

V.I. Lenin, *The Slogans and Organisation of Social-Democratic Work*, 1919

"The press must grow day in and day out—it is our Party's sharpest and most powerful weapon"

Joseph Stalin, speech at The Twelfth Congress

---

[10] Ibid. P. 116.

[11] Lenin, V.I., *What Is To Be Done?*, "The Plan For an All-Russia Political Newspaper", 1901. https://www.marxists.org/archive/lenin/quotes.htm

[12] Lenin, V.I., *The Slogans and Organisation of Social-Democratic Work,* 1919. https://www.marxists.org/archive/lenin/quotes.htm

of the R.C.P.(B.), 1923 [13]

We have all noticed how the Mainstream Media has been behaving in recent times—sometimes promoting 'political-correctness', sometimes virtue-signalling, or both. Why do we have countless, brainless, talentless mouthpieces all across the world—from Ireland to Australia, Canada to Sweden, the UK to the U.S.—constantly pumping-out this swill? Have they always been like this, or has this insane behaviour actually intensified? Why are they trying to squeeze-in as many Marxist sub-agendas (causes) as possible into every conversation? If they are not trying to reinforce the climate change scam, they are encouraging people to support Mass Migration or Black Lives Matter. If they're not talking about the gender 'pay gap', they're talking about the dangers of right-wing politics, and that dreaded, ever-present threat to society—the "far-right" (rolls eyes).

Whenever the media are doing their virtue-signalling on their issues of choice, it's (often subtly) suggested it's being done for humanitarian, 'compassionate' reasons etc. In reality, it's being done for the promotion of the various sub-agendas of the ideology. The media is the 'transmission belt of culture' that is responsible for taking real world events and placing them in our consciousness, via our chosen media—TV, radio, print, or online—with a distinctly partisan slant of course.

Propaganda top-ups

In addition to promoting the various sub-agendas independently, or the main agendas at certain times (i.e. mass immigration/'multiculturalism' in the years before Covid, then switching to Covid), the media may 'top-up' propaganda on other issues to re-enforce the levels of indoctrination. This was evident in the Irish media during the Covid lockdowns, when they topped-up the feminist propaganda. It was reported that 'domestic violence' cases (aka men beating up women) were on the increase, as a result of people being locked-up in their houses. This was accompanied by these cringe-worthy domestic violence TV ads—produced in a 're-enactment' style as part of the "Always here" domestic abuse campaign, supported by Ireland's feminist cult member groups naturally.[14] One showed a female talking to a friend online (on Skype or Zoom or something) and her abusive male 'partner' comes out of nowhere, asking who she was talking to etc.; hysterical tears followed. The funniest part was that the male sounded

---

[13] Stalin, J., speech at The Twelfth Congress of the R.C.P.(B.), 1923.
http://marx2mao.com/Stalin/TC23.html#s2

[14] https://www.alwayshere.ie/awareness-campaign/

incredibly camp (he was probably a gay actor).[15]

These propaganda top-ups were used during Covid for the climate change sub-agenda: it was insinuated on the Irish radio that the lockdowns were good for the environment, due to the lack of travel/commuting, and the resultant reduced vehicle emissions etc.! I'm polishing my guillotine…

'Experts' and catch-phrases

> "We must give a scientific explanation of society, and clearly explain it to the masses. That is the difference between Marxism and reformism"[16]

Leon Trotsky, "Discussions on the Transitional Program", 1938

There are cult member 'experts' everywhere you look/listen/read! We see them constantly in the MSM (or entertainment media etc.) as part of the public brainwashing initiative. They will either outright lie to the audience or spout a load of 'politically correct' bullshit or pseudo-scientific crap they absorbed elsewhere; more propaganda to push the various Marxist sub-agendas. Remember, whatever these 'experts' are called, wherever they are from, whatever their 'qualifications' or titles, they are just mouthpieces for the ideology and should be viewed as such. There has always been a steady stream of these types. Obviously, some will listen to them due to their status. Of course, this is mostly effective on those who need to be told how to perceive things.

Cult members created terms like 'vaccine hesitancy'. I first heard this on RTE Radio 1 on 15 January 2021 on *The Clare Byrne Show*.[17] They were discussing how to deal with the 'misinformation' spreading on social media platforms etc., that discouraged vaccine uptake. This is an amusing double-barrelled term. It's similar to "holocaust-denier" or "climate change denier". The cult making up catchphrases again! The media also dutifully discussed/promoted the different 'variants' of Covid: the English variant, South African variant, Brazilian, Multicultural, Roman, Gender-non-Binary Diana Ross Impersonator, Glorious People's Revolution, Wuhan

---

[15] Dept. of Justice Ireland, "StillHere Domestic Abuse Awareness Campaign TV Advert".

https://www.YouTube.com/watch?v=VTcVbHpCTVQ

[16] Trotsky, L., "Discussions on the Transitional Program", 1938.

https://www.marxists.org/archive/trotsky/1938/tp/tpdiscuss.htm

[17] https://www.rte.ie/radio/radio1/today-with-claire-byrne/2021/0115/1189998-today-with-claire-byrne-friday-15-january-2021/

Wutang Clan, and Xi Jinping variants etc.

Anti-RTE protest and "Truth Matters" video

The state broadcaster in Ireland is RTE (*Radio Telifís Eireann* meaning "Radio Television Ireland"). It has long lost any sort of respect from the non-indoctrinated people in Ireland and is now a conveyor belt of treasonous garbage spouted by treasonous whores (much like the rest of the media in the country). The RTE HQ buildings deserve a nice refurb job with a kamikaze truckload of Semtex and red paint.

After a few months of the Covid fiasco, due to RTE's central role in it, a protest was organised to march on this organisation on Sat 29 August 2020. As the procession moved through the streets, the marchers shouted "RTE fake news!" and carried a banner which read "RTE Is The Virus". They then reached their destination outside RTE studios in Donnybrook, Dublin. It was obvious that a significant number of Irish people weren't buying the Covid con.[18]

Soon after this incident, RTE pulled a sneaky Marxist con job, hidden in plain sight. It was a short forty second 'advertisement' that appeared on television, extolling the moral purity of this organisation, called "The Truth Matters".[19] The patronising, virtue-signalling message was essentially this: that the public should not get its information elsewhere (particularly online), and that RTE are the only trustworthy source of information! So, the Marxism-riddled state broadcaster, full to the brim with cult member fuckups, is the only one 'the people' should listen to, hmmm. Queue the Soviet National Anthem. The Irish proletariat comrades should be proud of their great Chief Commissarial Department for Glorious Revolutionary Propaganda in Ireland (R.T.E.)!

Most brazenly, it insinuated that perhaps the general public was getting its information from hate-filled, deceptive, and fearful (info-phobic?) sources. Simultaneously, it told people how to feel; not to feel rage or be afraid. Hmmm, a bunch of Marxist trash-bags trying to control people's perception and emotional reactions, how original! The real underlying message was "Obey the state! We are good people! We are not liars! Don't listen to those hate-filled, lying, and _____phobic others!". (Yes, this actually happened;

---

[18] "Crowds attend anti-RTÉ protest in Donnybrook", 29 Aug 2020.

https://www.rte.ie/news/ireland/2020/0829/1162051-rte-protest/

[19] RTE, "RTÉ News | The Truth Matters", 16 September 2020.

https://www.YouTube.com/watch?v=gZhghn9HaCc

not making this up!).

What was most psychotically Marxist and hypocritical about it, was the insinuation that those other sources of information are negative and almost apocalyptic, which means they regard themselves as being the bringers of uplifting, wonderful, happy news! And this is after months of them jabbering on to the Irish public about this plague-like CovAIDS illness, an ever-rising death toll (without a shred of evidence), and incessantly trying to instil fear. There's an incredible level of psychosis on display here.

The production of the video item was very good (for RTE standards). It shows a girl in a cafe looking at her phone, scrolling through Facebook. She sees a post that says "5G is attacking our immune systems", as the nauseating voice over begins and she is 'transported' to a dark, storm-filled world before our eyes. Poor Alice tumbles down the conspiracy theory-laden fascist Hitler-moustached rabbit hole. Predictably, some ominous music was used, and the imagery contained a variety of suspicious, aggressive, and unhinged characters who are carrying a variety of weapons running towards her (some skinheads, naturally. No sign of Mussolini's black shirts, Nazi uniforms, or copies of Mein Kampf in sight, probably because that's a bit too direct, and funny).

Here is the voice over text: "Before you arrive at your opinion…do you know where your information is coming from? Not everything on your feed can be trusted… You need to move past the rage, deception, and fear; and find the truth about the story". Just as the crowd of characters are about to reach her, she clicks on the RTE app on her phone and is instantly transported back to the peaceful cafe. So RTE is her saviour here, clearly, saving her from all those unruly deceivers and thugs on social media (including her fellow countrymen/women)! Then some text on screen appears, showing these three 2-word messages in sequence: "Integrity/truth/journalism—matters". The outro VO line was "RTE News — the truth matters". Patronising degenerate traitor lowlifes.

It was a work of brilliance in that it showed how much propaganda and mind-control you can fit in to a forty second video clip; a classic countermeasure usually employed by the cult, complete with the usual inversion of the truth, virtue-signalling, and a load of PC nauseousness. It was a direct, tactical response to the aforementioned protest calling RTE out as liars, which highlighted their general traitorous, guillotinable behaviour during the Covaids 1984 shenanigans.

What is "Irish"?

The cult is also masterful at conducting psy-ops using propaganda to distort the masses perception of normally beneficial concepts, even ones that are long-held and (relatively) simple in logical terms, such as nationality and race.

Using the sub-agenda of multiculturalism in Ireland as an example, the postmodernist influence can be clearly heard in the endless flow of traitorous, Marxian, anti-Irish crap coming from the establishment. You will hear the various propaganda pieces contain ideological subversion 'payloads' such as: "...but what is Irish anyway?" or "Is there such a thing as Irish people?" or "All races came from Africa anyway, so Irish people and African people are pretty much the same thing aren't they?". These are some of the psychotic, relativist pieces of nonsense that are pushed.

These subversive soundbites are designed to distort the perception of reality of the target population (in this case Ireland). The aim is to convince people that all races and cultures are the same (equality), and that it doesn't matter if we are all mixed-up ethnically. This distorted perception assists the advancement of this particular sub-agenda (multiculturalism). Marxian concepts of 'critical theory' and 'critical race theory' are related here—they allow the cult to create the required distortion of reality. Of course, if anyone attempts to highlight the fact that being Irish is not just a question of official nationality, citizenship, and passports (but a question of history, ethnicity and culture) the appropriate suppressive label of "racist" is used.

The traitorous Marxist Media in Ireland have constantly bombarded the consciousness of the general public with this crap. Africans and Middle Easterners have been featured proclaiming to be Irish, or participating in Irish things (sports, arts etc.). I once briefly saw an interview segment on Irish state broadcaster *RTE* that showed a female of clearly African origin explaining how proud she was to be Irish. Another segment featured on the RTE YouTube channel in June 2020 entitled "Growing up black and Irish".[20] It showed several mixed-race and black females talking about their racism experiences. In 2017, the YouTube channel of news website The Journal featured a series called "Yes, I'm Irish", featuring various mixed-race or black people doing the same thing.[21]

In October 2021, an RTE news article gleefully reported that Pamela Uba was the first black woman to win Miss Ireland. The article stated she was a former asylum seeker from South Africa, quoting her as saying "It's such a milestone. I'm so proud to say that as a black woman I've paved the way

---

[20] RTE News, "Growing up black and Irish", 16 June 2020.
https://www.YouTube.com/watch?v=R_uT58C-wHw

[21] The Journal, "Yes, I'm Irish: Meet Áine Mulloy", 6 Aug 2017.
https://www.YouTube.com/watch?v=PzKKCZUV6xM

for others who will come after me".[22]

Clearly, to anyone with a brain, Irish people are not the same as sub-Saharan Africans, or Middle Easterners. We are not the same historically, racially or culturally. All we have in common, using simple logic, is that we are humans; but that's the thing—Marxism doesn't do logic! There are no cultures or races in Marxism. It's "One Race, Human Race!" all the way baby. That's the reality, and that's why the indoctrination is needed.

The fact that being Irish has an ethnic and cultural component is something that obviously needs to be suppressed by the cult. These soundbites then force uncontaminated people to say things like "Being Irish doesn't mean just living here!" or "Just because you were born here doesn't make you Irish!". The kinds of things that are blatantly obvious, but need to be said as logic becomes more and more scare, thanks to the cult's/ideology's impact. These reactions are then pounced upon by the cult as evidence of 'racism'.

Instances of this are legion in Ireland. We have seen these bizarre, fake, cringe-worthy bits of propaganda that appear on television; designed to shove the 'multiculturalism' agenda down the public's throats. RTE once did a segment showing a migrant playing the Gaelic sport of Hurling; then he did an interview that displayed how much he loved Irish culture etc.

These little mini cons are designed to make the viewer go "Fair play to him for integrating into Irish society!" and "he's practically one of us now!". I'm sure they have featured (or will feature): Irish-dancing Somalians, violin-playing Afghani's, small Indian men dressed as Leprechauns, ordinarily puritanical Tibetan monks drinking Guinness and doing drugs etc.

A Dec 2016 Irish Independent article extolled the great contributions migrants were making to Gaelic sports. It stated that the Gaelic Athletic Association (GAA) was "keen to accommodate" the changes in Ireland's population.[23]

Another amusing cringe-worthy piece on RTE fake news (unable to locate)

---

[22] Okoh, J. "History-making Miss Ireland proud to 'pave the way", 14 October 2021.

https://www.rte.ie/news/2021/1014/1253565-history-making-miss-ireland/

[23] Crowe, D. "From Laois hurler Paddy Ruschitzko to Mayo's Shairoze Akram: How immigrants are playing increasing role in GAA", 18 Dec 2016.

https://www.independent.ie/sport/gaelic-games/gaelic-football/from-laois-hurler-paddy-ruschitzko-to-mayos-shairoze-akram-how-immigrants-are-playing-increasing-role-in-gaa/35302328.html featured a Polish migrant who was learning the Irish language. Are cult members in the Irish media actually trying to convince us that migrants are going to Ireland to learn local Arts and Crafts? Or to study Irish history, poetry, or the Irish language? Or to play Irish sports? Does anyone in the public believe this? If so, hilarious. I would like to interview them myself!

'Education'/indoctrination

"Education is a weapon whose effects depend on who holds it in his hands and at whom it is aimed"

Joseph Stalin explains to his Fabian interviewer H. G. Wells (1934)[24]

"And your education! Is not that also social, and determined by the social conditions under which you educate, by the intervention, direct or indirect, of society, by means of schools, etc.? The Communists have not invented the intervention of society in education; they do but seek to alter the character of that intervention, and to rescue education from the influence of the ruling class"[25]

Marx and Engels, *The Communist Manifesto* (1848)

"Throughout the West there are large numbers of dons in most disciplines who teach Marxism of one kind or another. A vast number of textbooks, including many used in schools, reflect Marxist concepts. Clearing out this poison, human and printed, will take a long time"[26]

British historian and author Paul Johnson

Many of the cult's prophets and leaders—Markey Marx, Vladimir Lenin, Mao Zedong, Fidel Castro, Ho "Hoe" Chi Minh, Pol Pot and other Khmer Rouge members—were infected ('radicalised') in the education systems. This 'revolutionary' indoctrination-thru-education has been an issue from the early 1800s. So it's no surprise that we are seeing the same thing today—countless, red-minded minions rolling off the production line. The same minds, with the same personalities, all following the same formula. All 'educated' unoriginal losers with no thoughts of their own that are separate from Marxist dogma. What a sad way to exist—having a mind full of crossed-wires, devoid of the wonder and magnificence of creation.

---

[24] Stalin, J. "Marxism Versus Liberalism An Interview With H.G. Wells", *23 July 1934*.

https://www.marxists.org/reference/archive/stalin/works/1934/07/23.htm

[25] Marx and Engels, *The Communist Manifesto* (1848), P. 24.

[26] https://www.quotetab.com/quotes/by-paul-johnson

Traditionally, the universities were the major point of indoctrination for students. As the infection spreads throughout society, it further emboldens the cult, enabling them to promote the ideology (via its sub-agendas) in secondary/high schools and primary schools (I'm not including 'socialist'/'communist' countries here, where the indoctrination of students at all levels was common practice). The German news website *jungefreiheit.de* reported in January 2023 what was being peddled in a German school. It stated that sixth graders in the North Rhine-Westphalia state were "forced to deal with transsexuality and "pansexuality" in class", and that "gender reassignment surgery is aggressively promoted".[27]

The Irish education system seriously stinks of the red rot too, pushing the various sub-agendas on kids: trans and 'gender non-binary' nonsense, feminism, climate change etc. Of course, it's an unforgivable, criminal behaviour to indoctrinate children since they may never recover from it; not to mention it's an infringement upon the principle of free will.

Marxism for kids

On Friday 20 September 2019 a mob of (apparently) about 10,000 children held a 'protest' in Dublin City on the issue of climate change. This was part of the *Global Climate Strike* organised by two student-led mini-Marxist groups—*Fridays for Future Ireland* and *Schools Climate Action Network.*[28]

Thousands of students were permitted to participate in "walk-outs", missing out on school lessons (if this is not symbolic of how the ideology destroys education and turns kids in to brainless Marxist activist minions, I don't know what is!). The protests were called "strikes", reminiscent of the traditional Marxian activism of the labour union movements. The media reported that they were inspired by Greta Thunberg (who I predicted years ago would be used to promote the climate change sub-agenda, as a sort of activist role-model for kids).[29]

Think of all the students being indoctrinated with this, unaware that it's simply a Marxist sub-agenda? What impact does believing in this pseudo-

---

[27] Kinder in NRW werden zu Geschlechtsumwandlungen gedrängt", 23 January 2023. https://jungefreiheit.de/politik/deutschland/2023/cdu-geschlechtsumwandlung/

[28] Halpin, H. "PHOTOS: Thousands of students turn out around the country for climate strikes", 20 September 2019. https://www.thejournal.ie/climate-strike-ireland-4817846-Sep2019/

[29] "Climate change strike: Irish students join millions protesting globally", 20 September 2019. https://www.irishtimes.com/news/world/asia-pacific/climate-change-strike-irish-students-join-millions-protesting-globally-1.4024673

scientific garbage have on the minds/perceptions of youths throughout the world? How inflated will their egos be, and how much of a problem will this be for society when they become 'adults'? From the cult's/ideology's perspective, environmentalism/climate change is a nice, 'soft' issue that is ideal to put young minds on the revolutionary path. Any 'educators' participating in this nonsense should be banned from teaching for life.

The Portuguese six

Here's another incidence of child abuse/neglect. In September 2023, the media reported that a group of six Portuguese youths wanted to sue an entire continent because of climate change via the *European Court of Human Rights* (ECHR). Yes, really! As reported by Euronews on 27 September "The historic trial is the first time so many countries will have to defend themselves in front of any court in the world. All 27 European Union member states, the UK, Turkey, Russia and Norway are among the defendants. The Portuguese youths, aged between 11 and 24, say governments' inaction on climate change breaches their human rights and discriminates against young people".[30] What an absolute disgrace. In a sane society, any culprit parents or teachers would be arrested, and hopefully the kids could be de-brainwashed at such young ages. It would set an example for any further lunacy.

When Henry loves Thomas

Back to school stuff. Another standout incident of kid-focused indoctrination was much reported in late 2018 in the U.K. It was discovered that young children at the Bewsey Lodge Primary School, Warrington were being indoctrinated with the LGBT agenda. A video published by BBC Radio Manchester in September showed the children being instructed to write gay love letters by their 'teacher'.

The commissar of education in this instance ('teacher') Sarah Hopson was quoted as saying "This class of six-year-olds is learning about gay marriage. In this fairytale, the prince wants to marry his servant. And the children are writing a love letter". The Prince "Henry" wants to marry his manservant "Thomas".[31] There was somewhat of a backlash from the non-

---

[30] Jones, and Da Silva, "Six young people sue 32 nations for climate inaction at European Court of Human Right", 27 September 2023.https://www.euronews.com/my-europe/2023/09/27/court-case-over-climate-inaction-against-32-countries-opens-at-the-european-court-of-human

[31] 'Voltaire', "Teacher instructs 6-year-old British primary school students to write 'gay love letters' to get them to accept diversity", 1 October 2018.

indoctrinated portion of the population, but obviously, since the school still functions, it was limited. The school has an LGBT+ page and received an award for its LGBT indoctrination efforts. It has two gnomes outside the main entrance holding the ubiquitous rainbow-coloured flag (they are probably wearing crotchless pants and gimp masks now).

Obviously, this can't be regarded as an isolated incident; if it wasn't for the BBC video the general public might not have been made aware. If it's happening in one/a few, it could be happening in many/most. How can we discover all the incidents like this unless the children are informing the parents? Let's keep in mind, that these fanatic cult members (masquerading as teachers) are university-educated and are approved by the state, education boards etc. In reality though, they are contaminated thanks to the indoctrination, and should be kept well away from children.

Birmingham school

In early 2019, another high-profile (though contrasting) incident happened in Birmingham. As reported on the Guardian newspaper, there were months of protests due to the LGBT indoctrination programme at the Anderton Park Primary School. The vast majority of protestors, according to media reports, were Muslim (not surprising because Marxian degeneracy is not tolerated in Islam). Protestors held signs with messages including the very clever "My Child, My Choice".[32] I say "contrasting" because there were genuine protests this time, and potent ones at that.

The Guardian article featured an exchange that took place outside the school between the author and one of the protesting parents. A mother revealed her daughter had come home from school on one occasion showing clear signs of brainwashing: ""Do you know how hard it is to explain to a four-year-old why she doesn't have two daddies?... She kept pushing it — 'I want two daddies'—questioning me: 'Why can't I?' It was upsetting for me and my child.". To be fair, the reply should have been "because two men can't make a baby, and whoever told you that is stupid, sweetheart".

The article mentioned that the whole controversy centred around the 'age

---

https://theindependent.sg/teacher-instructs-6-year-old-british-primary-school-students-to-write-gay-love-letters-to-get-them-to-accept-diversity/

[32] Ferguson, D. "'We can't give in': the Birmingham school on the frontline of anti-LGBT protests", 26 May 2019.

https://www.theguardian.com/uk-news/2019/may/26/birmingham-anderton-park-primary-muslim-protests-lgbt-teaching-rights appropriateness' of LGBT teaching. I'm sure many would fall for that one. Some might say "well…six year olds are a bit young…but maybe early teens?". This is how the cult/ideology manipulates consent/compliance; the truth is that children shouldn't be 'taught' that rubbish at any age! Predictably, in late 2019, the authorities stepped-in to ban protests outside the school, and an exclusion zone was enforced (ergo, the state is pro-Marxism).[33] As usual, the cult can protest eternally, but they do not tolerate protest of Marxist sub-agendas. The tag-line of the school is "Relationships, Determination, Sparkle" (hopefully that's not a Drag Queen-esque Diana Ross sparkle).[34]

"Good afternoon, girls"

In April 2023, several British newspapers reported on another incidence of infection in an education institution. A female teacher at an expensive private girl's school was found guilty of committing a despicable crime against the oppressed—she said "Good afternoon, girls"! The teacher was then apparently corrected by a bunch of 11-year-olds, some of whom didn't 'identify' as female. Protests were held by some students, with some staff siding with the 'protestors'. The 'oppressing' teacher was forced to apologise to the little brain-washed brats.[35]

As reported in a Daily Mail article on 15 April, she was treated in a humiliating fashion by the school and was eventually 'managed out' she claimed. Interestingly, it was a religion and philosophy teacher. If the school is that fanatical, we can only speculate what kind of degenerate fuckups these young females will grow up to be. Many will swell the ranks of the cult, no doubt. They should've had their arses smacked till they were purple, made to write "there is only male and female" one hundred times, and grounded until they renounced Marxist activism, and that goes for the staff too. I would also say "Good afternoon, cunts" to them every day until they themselves apologised.

Incidents like these—broadcasted by the media in their aftermath—are little coercive 'victories' for the cult. They serve as deterrents for other teachers, who will have to choose between complying with the cult's

---

[33] "LGBT teaching row: Birmingham primary school protests permanently banned", 26 November 2019. https://www.bbc.com/news/uk-england-birmingham-50557227

[34] https://www.andertonparkschool.org/

[35] Manning, S. "Female teacher at £20,000-a-year girls' school is forced to apologise to pupils for saying 'Good afternoon, girls'", 15 April 2023.

https://www.dailymail.co.uk/news/article-11976891/Female-teacher-forced-apologise-saying-Good-afternoon-girls.html activism, or face being made an example of as that teacher was.

Suing the cult

In August 2023, GB News interviewed Dr. Anna Loutfi—an equality and human rights lawyer involved with a group called the Bad Law Project. Loutfi spoke on behalf of concerned parents who desired to file a class action lawsuit against the UK government and the department of education.[36] The discussion focused on the legality (or lack thereof) in teaching school pupils questionable subject matter (aka Marxist degeneracy). She spoke of "rogue actors…posing as charities" (note: Marxist activist groups, NGO's/non-profits etc.) being involved, and that they produced the school educational materials, with no oversight. Also mentioned were self-appointed "experts", who were making the decisions as to the age-appropriateness of certain topics, without parental consent, of course. (Those 'experts' again…)

When presented with the common activist argument that some children 'struggling' with gender or sexual identity issues need to feel protection and inclusivity within schools, Loutfi replied: "we struggle with a lot of things but we cannot as a society adopt a position where we say society will embrace your desire to be something other than you are". She brilliantly pointed-out that society shouldn't affirm negative, self-destructive behaviours in a person who's struggling, adding that these people "are expressing an inner struggle and an idealistic notion of escape from their reality. It is not the business of schools to facilitate that self-harm. The fact that a child is struggling is not a justification for the entire society to facilitate a pathway to self-destruction". The interview highlighted how well-entrenched the cult is in the British establishment, and the collusion between the government, NGO/non-profit sector, and the department of education.

The School of Palestine protests

Sometimes the cultish behaviour doesn't come from within school, it goes to (the) school. In the final months of 2023, there was significant cult activity at the Barkley Primary School, in Leyton, London, UK. GB News reported that children were attending school with Palestinian flags on their clothing. As this school is non-partisan, multi-cultural, multi-ethnic, and "apolitical", it wasn't happy about all this, and the message reached the parents via a letter it issued on Friday 17 November. Some parties involved

---

[36] GB News, "UK Govt to be sued over trans ideology being taught in primary schools | Dr Anna Loutfi", 6 August 2023.
https://www.YouTube.com/watch?v=TxDVAkfGAGo

apparently claimed "Islamophobic" discrimination, and there were reports that staff were threatened. Protests were arranged outside the school, with placards etc. One particular idiot agitator, wearing a Palestinian-coloured mask, was on a megaphone prompting the chant "education is a human right" from the crowd.[37] On 21 December Sky News reported, quoting a school statement, that the school had closed early for Christmas: "In the light of escalating threats against staff and the school, based on factually inaccurate misunderstandings, falsehoods and malicious fabrications", and that there was no evidence of bullying or misconduct.[38]

Cult members framed the whole situation as being the bullying of an 8-year-old boy by the school. According to Sky News, it all started in mid-November when the boy had shown up to school with a very prominent Palestinian flag on his jacket, to be "in solidarity with his mother's family in Gaza". According to his father he was segregated from other pupils and wasn't welcome at the school. The parents refused to remove the patch (or just give him another jacket!), so the drama ensued.

Even if this whole fiasco wasn't a deliberate action planned by cult members from the beginning, the school was right! No Marxist activism of any kind should be permitted in schools, including Palestinians rights, whether internal or external! Zero! The fiasco was just another instance of the cult/ideology wanting to get its own way. A parent allowing their child to adorn their clothing with a Palestinian flag to be "in solidarity", to make a political statement, is a form of indoctrination. The tragedy here is, because Marxist protests are allowed by the state, many children exposed to this situation and the protests etc. may now be indoctrinated. It's another stunning example of how the ideology can cause great division, this time via a piece of clothing material a few inches in size, and then capitalise on it.

On 22 December, GB News featured an interview with a local resident and showed video of masked 'protestors' putting Palestinian flags up on lamp posts near the school, the night before the protests. Tellingly, the police

---

[37] GB News, "Masked Palestine protesters force primary school to SHUT after kids wore Palestine flags to lessons", 21 December 2023.
https://www.YouTube.com/watch?v=CLj9anqykrE

[38] "London primary school forced to close after claims boy was punished over Palestinian flag on coat", SKY NEWS, 21 December 2023
https://www.YouTube.com/watch?v=VsaSEui-C9Y

actually showed-up, and did nothing.[39] Again, in a sane society, 'protestors' wouldn't have the nerve to do things like that, but if they did—they would find themselves introduced to the inside of the back of a police van, headfirst, post haste.

I'm sure the hypocrisy and double standards of all this is not lost on the reader, given the previous items involving schools. The cult obviously doesn't protest the various forms of Marxian indoctrination/child abuse masquerading as 'education' in schools at present across the west; but it will 'protest' over a coloured patch on an 'oppressed' child's jacket.

ShoutOut

One of the increasing number of LGBTQ organisations in Ireland is Shoutout. The landing page of their website alludes to the disturbing situation involving Irish schools (underline for emphasis): "ShoutOut is a registered charity committed to improving life for LGBTQ+ people by sharing personal stories and educating school students, parents & guardians, teachers, youth workers and workplaces on LGBTQ+ issues. Since 2012 we've been delivering workshops in secondary schools across the Island of Ireland which tackle LGBTQ+ bullying, and we've completed over 1,800 student workshops over the past 8 school years. That means we've spoken directly to over 54,000 students!".[40] So the schools are essentially providing the audiences for these types of activist groups to indoctrinate/contaminate children. Even if these numbers are exaggerated, this is a critical situation. It also clearly shows the same collusion between different tentacles of the red monster—schools and non-profit/NGO/'charity' organisations.

Enoch Burke

Irish teacher Enoch Burke made headlines in 2022/2023 for failing to comply with the cult's gender-bending at Wilson's Hospital School, County Westmeath. Burke's family is Evangelical Christian and they have a record of protesting against the cult.

The Irish Times stated on 19 May 2023 that the secondary school "had initiated proceedings last autumn against Mr Burke, because he continued to attend there after he was made subject to a disciplinary process and placed on paid administrative leave. The disciplinary process, based on a

---

[39] GB News YouTube channel, "School closed over Palestine protest - 'It frightens my daughter!' | East London mum reacts", 22 Dec 2023.https://www.YouTube.com/watch?v=z7OViaPGexc

[40] https://www.shoutout.ie

report compiled by the principal Niamh McShane and provided to the board of management, was initiated arising from his response to her request to staff asking that they address a student by their new preferred name and using the pronouns they/them".[41] (This reminds me of a Mr. Jordan Peterson, and the 2016 C16 gender-bending pronoun bill in Canada).

Due to his defiance and refusal to abide by a court injunction requiring him to not attend the school, he got himself in more gender-neutral hot water. The Irish Times article reported he was ordered to pay the school €15,000 in damages. Ironically, at time of writing, he is now being held in the Progressive unit of Mountjoy Prison, Dublin.

Scott Smith

With all the gender-bending being pushed in schools, it was just a matter of time until parents snapped out of frustration. One such instance occurred in Virginia, U.S., to father Scott Smith. His daughter was sexually assaulted by a boy in a female toilet at Stone Bridge High School in May 2021. According to the Daily Mail: "The male student, who was wearing a skirt on the day of the attack, was allowed into the bathroom because he told staff he identified as female. The school's lax policy allowed him to use (it)".[42]

In June 2021, Smith attended a Loudoun County school board meeting. In an interview with Fox News on 11 Sept 2023, he explained that he and his wife were approached and provoked by a female "radical protestor" parent. When Smith mentioned the assault, she accused him of lying, then, in typical cult member fashion, threatened his livelihood, and said "I'm going to ruin you on social media". The instant he retaliated with 'abusive' language; the cops grabbed him. In a sane world, this provocative deranged cult member should have been carted off to the Gulag in Siberia and forced to break rocks wearing the same skirt for 20 years; same goes for the perpetrator student. Smith was charged, was eventually given a tend day suspended sentence, and after a legal struggle, was later pardoned by

---

[41] Carolan, M. "Enoch Burke was validly suspended by Wilson's Hospital school, judge rules", 19 May 2023.https://www.irishtimes.com/crime-law/courts/2023/05/19/enoch-burke-was-validly-suspended-by-wilsons-hospital-school-judge-rules/

[42] Yeatman, D. "Virginia Governor Glenn Youngkin pardons Scott Smith, father of a girl raped in unisex bathroom by a 'boy in a skirt' at Stone Bright High School after he was convicted for erupting in fury over cover-up at board meeting", 11 September 2023.

Virginia Governor Glenn Youngkin in Sept 2023.[43]

This is another type of incident where someone is being made an example of for defying the lunacy of the cult. This dissuades other parents from challenging the schools on their insane bullshit and their denials of any issues surrounding their Marxian activist policies.

Universities—AKA "socialist indoctrination academies"

> "Without revolutionary theory there can be no revolutionary movement"[44]

V.I. Lenin, *What Is To Be Done?*, 1902

The Universities are a serious problem for society, being a key component of the indoctrination machine. This is a critical global issue. In fact, as compared to other institutions within society, they are mainly responsible for this indoctrination, and have no equal in this regard. They need to be cleansed of Marxist elements as soon as possible, once and for all. Perhaps the detoxification process has already begun. In August 2023, NBC News reported that the U.S. state of Florida was banning psychology courses that contained course content on sexual orientation and gender identity.[45] This is good news, but there is still a gargantuan task ahead of us.

The colleges and Universities allow for the indoctrination of young adults and beyond. They also facilitate the recruitment of students to activist groups, including more overtly 'radical' groups such as Antifa and associated groups (or, indeed, the formation of new groups). This is how/where many cult members are spawned, getting their taste of the cult environment for the first time.

There is also the issue of students being academically assessed by their willingness to comply with the ideological bias within the institutions. In other words—if you are not willing to agree with the cult's/ideology's point of view, you will not be allowed to excel. Conversations with non-infected University students confirms this. In other words, there is a cult culture in these Universities.

Useless education = useless graduates

---

[43] Fox News, "Father pardoned by Youngkin: This is about protecting the children", September 11th 2023. https://www.YouTube.com/watch?v=uiM8KEDPj1A

[44] Lenin, V.I., "What Is To Be Done?", 1902, P. 12.https://www.marxists.org/archive/lenin/works/download/what-itd.pdf

[45] NBC News, "Florida bans AP Psychology course due to its LGBTQ content", 5 August 2023. https://www.YouTube.com/watch?v=Vzg31_jhzV4

"Men are born ignorant, not stupid; they are made stupid by education"

Bertrand Russell, "History of Western Philosophy:
Collector's Edition"[46]

University-level (and other post-secondary/high-school institutions) are filling-up with overtly Marxist courses, or other subjects with a Marxian slant. Of course, this renders the 'education' system useless, in addition to gradually 'radicalising' the general population (and all that entails as outlined elsewhere). We are seeing this with the ever-more prevalent Marxist courses like 'Equality' or 'Diversity' studies and various combinations of these terms. How about a "PHD in Equal Diversity and Transgenderised Multicultural Socialist studies"? Or would you prefer to get an MA in "How to stop Nazis from intimidating and controlling other people's lives (by trying to intimidate people and control their lives)"? Of course, they might not be so brazenly named (yet!), but they're still riddled with the ideology.

This has been going on for decades but has become more obvious and outrageous in recent times. At the minimum, anything of a psychological, sociological, or historical nature is more than likely infected. Perhaps even the STEM subjects aren't safe nowadays. How about a "Phd in Gender-neutral Rainbow-coloured Unisex Dildo Engineering"? Or a "Masters in Technological Bionic Maoish Trotskyite studies to prevent Racist Homophobic attitudes towards Gay Paedos"? Or a higher-education Certificate in "Teaching other people how to Prevent the 'Gag Reflex' so they can give better Blowjobs to Others"? We need to cover all the degenerate gaps here (or should I say, "plug the orifices").

In addition to the more blatantly infected courses, students receive useless 'educations' in other areas including those related to the three transmission belts of culture (many forms of teaching, technical/production media course, journalism etc.). How will they make a positive contribution to society since they will only be able to get employment serving the Marxist establishment? That also goes for the social sciences, and political/political science areas etc. Of course, all Universities/higher education institutions will have sociology courses too. Courses that combine different elements allow for indoctrination on several levels. Trinity College Dublin, for example, offers a four-year B.A. course called "Philosophy Political Science Economics and Sociology".[47]

---

[46] Bertrand Russell (2013). "History of Western Philosophy: Collectors Edition", p.578, Routledge. https://www.azquotes.com/quote/254907

[47] https://www.tcd.ie/courses/undergraduate/az/course.php?id=DUBSP-PPES-2F09

In addition, in terms of choices of education courses—and therefore what roles a person can fill in society—western countries will increasingly become like the 'Communist' regimes of the 20th century; as in, the end purpose of education and employment is to serve the regime, to serve the ideology. This is where things are going if the cult's dominance in educational matters is not dealt with immediately.

It would take forever to list all the contaminated courses/societies/groups in the universities, so here's a selection of courses in Ireland that wave the red flag (didn't need to dig deep at all—just visited uni websites, searched for courses using the key Marxist words (equality, diversity, gender, feminism, climate) et voila).

Contaminated courses

Trinity College Dublin (TCD), Dublin City University (DCU), and University College Dublin (UCD) are the major institutions in Ireland's capital. In the heart of the city the famous Trinity College offers: a postgraduate certificate in Diversity and Inclusion in Further Education and Training; a postgraduate two year full-time course called Gender and Women's studies; an undergraduate course in Gender and Sexuality in Early Modern Europe; and an undergraduate course in Stalinism and Society in Eastern Europe.[48] TCD also has an Equality Office, and a branch of the Workers' Party, in addition to groups promoting various Marxist causes.[49]

South of the city, UCD offers: a course module in Feminism and Gender Justice (hilarious); an MA in Gender Studies; an MSc masters in Equality Studies; an MSc in climate change; and a BSc four-year Social Justice course.[50] Imagine doing all of those! Imagine the amount of progressive revolutionary social justice power at your fingertips! Interestingly, the course description for that MA in Gender Studies says this under the "Careers and Employability" heading: "Graduates have become central members of local communities, key members of NGOs, employees in public-sector agencies, education and media organisations in roles such as: social researchers, project development managers, lecturers, journalists, and policy and advocacy officers. Graduates work in Amnesty

---

[48] https://www.tcd.ie/courses/

[49] Grace, A. "Trinity branch of Workers' Party officially recognised", 17 February 2018.

https://trinitynews.ie/2018/02/trinity-branch-of-workers-party-officially-recognised/

[50] https://www.myucd.ie/courses/

International, Immigrant Council of Ireland, Crisis Pregnancy Programme, Médecins Sans Frontières, National Broadcasting Authority, RTE, and the National Women's Council of Ireland".[51] Most of which are riddled with the ideology.

On the North side, DCU offers the following: an MA in Sexuality Studies; a postgraduate certificate in Sexuality Education and Sexual Well-being; an MA in Refugee Integration; an undergraduate in Climate and Environmental Sustainability; an online Equality, Diversity and Inclusion Course. DCU also has a Centre of Excellence for Diversity and Inclusion.[52] So that's Dublin well and truly covered....

Outside Dublin

NUI Maynooth, County Kildare offers an MA in Gender, Diversity, and Inclusion; a certificate in Equality Studies.[53] The University of Limerick offers the Equality, Diversity And Inclusion—Graduate Certificate.[54] NUI Galway offers a BA in Global Women's Studies and an MA in Culture and Colonialism. From the course description of the latter: "The MA in Culture and Colonialism explores literature, politics and culture from Ireland to India, and from Africa to the Middle East. It is a multi-disciplinary taught Master of Arts programme, aimed at graduates from the Arts, Humanities, and Social Sciences. Students analyse imperial ascendancies, race and racial theories, nationalist movements, postcolonial experiences, the rise of neo-colonial thought, multiculturalism and interculturalism, and the implications of globalisation and development for the modern world".[55]

It's obvious that this course will be peddling the usual Marxian perspectives, promoting: anti 'right wing' thought; anti-colonialism; the 'anti-racism' narrative etc., in addition to promoting Marxian concepts like white 'supremacy' and 'privilege' etc.

St. Angela's College in Sligo is connected to NUI Galway. It offers an MA

---

[51] "MA Gender Studies".
https://hub.ucd.ie/usis/!W_HU_MENU.P_PUBLISH?p_tag=PROG&MAJR=W383

[52] https://www.dcu.ie/courses

[53] https://www.maynoothuniversity.ie/study-maynooth/find-course

[54] https://www.ul.ie/gps/equality-diversity-and-inclusion-graduate-certificate

[55] http://www.nuigalway.ie/courses/taught-postgraduate-courses/culture-colonialism.html

in Religious Education and Social Justice.[56] In early 2020, University College Cork ran a short course on the subject of LGBT+ history entitled "From Shame to Pride? A Short Introduction to LGBT+ Irish History (1970s–2020)".[57]

The effects of all the shitty 'education'

What effect does all indoctrination have on a society? If generations of students are now being programmed to be little Marxist revolutionaries, what value are they going to have for society, when they graduate? What skills will they have? They will contribute nothing except to serve the cult/ideology in their respective countries. Aside from this, what else can they do? What other roles could they fill?

In addition to strengthening the ideology/cult by helping the infection to spread, it also weakens and destroys civilisation. Obviously, the more devoid of useful skills the younger generations are the easier civilisation will collapse. Civilisation only functions because (some) people know how to get things done in the real world. Yuri Besmenov (the Soviet propaganda expert) made a relevant point in his 1983 lecture, when explaining "Ideological Subversion": that genuinely useful education courses would be replaced with useless "fake alternatives", that are of no benefit to a nation, during the (second) "Destabilisation" phase.

There is also the economic impact. Aside from the fact that these generations of students will be indoctrinated to hate wealth, profits, and capitalism, they will have no useful, practical skills. This negatively impacts the economy and contributes to collapse; prosperity is affected, and generation of wealth is limited. This point connects with the 'welfare state' issue plus the fact that the Marxist sub-agendas and NGO/non-profit complex drains money from the economy. It all contributes towards the attack on the economic prosperity and independence of a nation (and capitalism in general). The more time, energy, and resources that Universities are permitted to spend peddling Marxian thrash, and the more indoctrinated students are emerging from those institutions, the more these societal effects are amplified.

'Knowledge', ego inflation and hypocrisy

As with the cult/ideology in general, ego is a central issue. University

---

[56]

http://www.stangelas.nuigalway.ie/Downloads/ProspectiveStudents/Brochures/IET47.pdf

[57] https://libguides.ucc.ie/lgbt/gettingstarted

indoctrinated students will receive their 'education' and will then consciously or unconsciously spread the ideology throughout society, thinking that they are educated (or perhaps even 'experts') in their chosen field of study; blissfully unaware that they know virtually nothing of any value. Not only is their knowledge worthless, but it's in fact toxic and often helps to create the opposite effects to what the person believes they do! These types of individuals believe that promoting Marxian equality, diversity, solidarity, multiculturalism, environmentalism, socialism etc. is a benevolent act but is in fact extremely destructive and divisive. The results are destructive and create suffering in the long run. Their 'educations' make them ultra-hypocrites in the extreme.

Cult activity on campuses

The Universities in Ireland are highly contaminated. There's too much cult activity to include, but this example caught my eye. On 13 Sept 2020, the Irish Times newspaper reported on recent events at the National University of Ireland Galway (NUIG). The University had attempted to implement a mandatory requirement for students to sign a "community promise" pledge. This involved students adhering to certain (pro-Marxist) behavioural guidelines. NUIG eventually changed their position and it was no longer a mandatory requirement.[58]

A law student by the name of Simeon Burke (brother of defiant teacher Enoch, mentioned earlier) was a prominent voice highlighting the madness occurring at the university. On the mandatory pledge, Burke was quoted in the article as saying: "I felt it undermined my rights as an NUI Galway student and threatened my freedom to think for myself". Burke decided to run for presidency of the student's union in the elections which took place in April 2021 (albeit unsuccessfully), and inevitably incurred the wrath of cult members there.

In a video on the "Simeon Burke for President" Twitter profile, he spoke about how their campaigning materials were dumped in the thrash. On the atmosphere on campus, he said "Students who don't completely agree with the left, and who speak-up and make their voices heard, get subjected to a torrent of intimidation and serious bullying almost as a matter of course here at NUI Galway. These issues have been raised with the University management time and time again down through the years…yet nothing has

---

[58] O' Brien, C., "NUI Galway drops 'behave responsibly' pledge requirement", September 2020. https://www.irishtimes.com/news/education/nui-galway-drops-behave-responsibly-pledge-requirement-1.4353962

changed. The situation persists, and students continue to be silenced".[59] Predictably, Burke was subjected to the usual ridicule by cult members associated with the University (and beyond); even two cult members masquerading as politicians—Luke Flanagan and Paul Murphy—got involved in the online ritual.[60]

I'm sure readers will have countless examples of such cult activity in their respective countries. What is of note here is the fact that institutions of education are supposed to be places that allow for diverse opinions, debate, the exploration of different schools of thought etc. The conduct and ideological bias of the Universities nowadays makes this laughable. The cult/ideology doesn't tolerate dissent when itself is in the driving seat. Spoilt fucking brats.

'Entertainment'

"Theatricality and deception—powerful agents to the uninitiated"[61]

Bane (Tom Hardy), *The Dark Knight Rises,* 2012.

Any form of entertainment is populated with cult members and used to further contaminate the population. The media used for indoctrination may be TV, movies, 'documentaries', music, plays, live performance, the arts in general etc. The ideology contaminates all. This contaminated entertainment industry produces Marxist propaganda mixed with hedonism.

One is very susceptible to absorbing ideas when one is experiencing pleasure, when being 'entertained'. This is brainwashing 101—get the suckers while they are relaxed and being frivolous, while their guard (whatever guard they have) is down. A contemporary, highly popular example would be Netflix, which churns out a mind-boggling amount of high-level propaganda.

It's par for the course too—with a global Marxist infection—that entertainment and the arts go to shit, as we are seeing. You will see them degenerate further as the cultural environment becomes increasingly infected. Things become more political, but in a Marxian partisan way, of

---

[59] https://twitter.com/voteforsimeon?lang=en

[60] Carolan, M. "Student criticises 'shameful' decision not to investigate TD over tweet", 30 May 2022.

https://www.irishtimes.com/crime-law/2022/05/29/student-criticises-shameful-decision-not-to-investigate-td-over-tweet/

[61] "Batman VS Bane - The Dark Knight Rises Full Fight 1080p HD".https://www.YouTube.com/watch?v=rDuetklFtDQ

course. They can also become blatantly trashier, depending on the medium in question. This can be obvious when we see celebrities engaging in PC talking points, becoming mouthpieces for various Marxist causes.

Cuntry Blues

Ireland's Eurovision Song Contest entry for 2024 is "Doomsday Blue", by a 29-year-old Irish 'non-binary' female 'artist' called Bambie Thug (aka "Bambie Ray Robinson", or "Cuntry Ray Robinson").[62] The song sounds like a few playing simultaneously; three for the price of one (so great value really). It was reminiscent of bad musical theatre, or a pantomime even, that's influenced by Marilyn Manson and Lady Gaga. There was slow heavy metal elements and screeching. The bizarre stage production of the Late Late Show performance was gothic and satanic-themed, featuring two 'demons' and a constant visual stream of pagan and occult symbology. In a Late Late Show video interview segment, Robinson said "Eurovision is such a giant platform…as a non-binary person I do represent a massive proportion of our country that is under represented".[63] In an interview with the *Gay Times*, 'they' said "I like being part of a cool queer rising scene, more queer voices is what the world fucking needs".[64] Another degenerate personality. Another life ruined.

So, a country that punches well above its weight in terms of artistic excellence—with a strong tradition of talented singers and musicians going back centuries—has a relatively talentless 'non-binary' person as its representative? Obviously, the non-degenerate, non-indoctrinated portion of the Irish population can see what's going on here. This fiasco obviously incorporates the 'trans' and destruction of culture sub-agendas.

The loss of meaning

The true meaning of art is lost in a Marxism-riddled society. The infection's impact is twofold—what was once a source of existential stimulation and an expression of awesome creativity becomes neither, in addition to becoming one big propaganda vessel for the ideology. True brilliance is removed, as this defies the Marxian axiom of equality. Art is no longer a

---

[62] https://en.wikipedia.org/wiki/Bambie_Thug

[63] "Bambie Thug - Doomsday Blue | Eurosong | The Late Late Show", January 2024.

https://www.YouTube.com/watch?v=eA2fKlT8Khw

[64] Raza-Sheikh, Zoya, "Welcome to Bambie Thug's witchy soundscape", 21 June 2023.

https://www.gaytimes.co.uk/music/queer-and-now/queer-now-welcome-to-bambie-thugs-witchy-soundscape/

thing of creative, contemplative beauty, but a thing of 'politically correct'(Marxist), predictable ugliness. The relativist influence of postmodernism (covered earlier) ensures that there's no such thing as objective actual beauty anymore—everything becomes subjective. That's why, nowadays, you can see these meaningless expressions of 'art' that are held aloft as being 'progressive' etc. As an extension of that, the relativistic attitude allows the arts and entertainment to be used for propaganda purposes.

Music, poems, documentaries, and art (sculpture, painting etc) become trashy and meaningless. Crappiness becomes the new 'deep' and 'edgy'. Art suddenly requires no creative or technical skill or substance; 'avant-garde' now means 'innovative in a crappy way'. Speaking of crappy, in 2018 giant sculptures of shit were displayed/dumped in the Museum Boijmans van Beuningen, in Rotterdam, Netherlands.[65]

The purpose is to lower standards of excellence, encourage degeneracy and force equality. It's the erroneous, relativist, post-modernist Marxist distortion of reality that everything has value, and nothing is superior to anything else. To imply that one thing is superior to another is to suggest that there is a hierarchy of sorts, and this is something that the ideology/cult cannot allow. Obviously, hierarchies often potentially result in someone getting upset (since not all artists can be great!), and we can't have that can we?

Art should be about presenting something, for another's consideration, who is free to like or loathe it. In a contaminated society, all avenues of the arts start to become saturated in the red stench. Now, instead of merely being presented with things for your consideration, you're also told how to feel about them too. No room for free will—you can't even react how you choose any more! A thing such as the arts now becomes just another tentacle of the ideology/cult. How depressing!

Of course, the indoctrinated types absolutely love all of this. They would surely be brought to tears reading a poem riddled with Marxist dogma about the 'oppression' of the 'oppressed'; or impressed by an 'intelligent' documentary examining the genius of socialism.

They would be inspired by a song extolling the virtues of 'diversity' with a video that contains as many non-white non-heterosexual people as possible; or in convulsions of laughter watching a female stand-up

---

[65] Tidey, A., "These giant poo sculptures prove 'contemporary art is not s***'", June 2018. https://www.euronews.com/2018/06/08/these-giant-poo-sculptures-prove-contemporary-art-is-not-s-

comedian doing a 'cutting-edge' set about her vagina, sleeping around and other trashy subjects; or perhaps being turned-on by a large 10 foot sculpture celebrating the eroticism of anal fisting…"I think it's beautiful!"…"It's so diverse!"; smiling, crying their soy-infused tears and wiping their oestrogenic (red) snots from their noses at the wonderful progressiveness of it all.

Of course, 'art' like this would make a sane person want to puke, put their fingers in their ears, change the channel, or put that garbage in the trash. It reminds me of how exciting it must be for a gang of Satanic paedophiles when the children arrive at their meeting. They are having a good time amongst themselves, but if any sane person was to witness it, they would puke with a combination of disgust and horror (Me? I would let my machetes fly).

So, when people suggest "What do you mean "trash"?!? How can you criticize it when so many other people are enjoying it??", we can respond that hedonism is not the right barometer against which to judge things. We can bring up grooming and paedo gangs, or the drugs culture (including crack houses), or the sex industry—all situations where someone is enjoying themselves in one way or another, and all manifestations of societal degeneracy that cause so much harm. One could also answer with "Trashy people equals trashy art. Trashy art equals trashy people", since the arts are highly influential in societal development while simultaneously reflecting society itself.

Celebrity champagne socialists

Nowadays it seems that everywhere we turn in the arts and entertainment the ideology is present. Though it has definitely increased in recent times, it isn't anything new. The song *Imagine* by John Lennon (1971) is a classic example of the ideology being promoted through song. It promotes atheism, world government/world without borders, hedonism, anti-war/'peace', solidarity, revolution, anti-private property/anti-capitalism and collective ownership, utopianism. All in a three-minute song! Perhaps we can regard it as the benchmark?[66] *One Vision* (1985) by British rock band Queen also promoted some of those themes: "One race, one hope, one real direction… One world, one nation. One vision".[67]

In the 1980s, Irish singers-turned-cult members Bono (aka Paul Hewson) and Bob Geldof began supporting various Marxian causes including the

---

[66] https://genius.com/John-lennon-imagine-lyrics

[67] https://genius.com/Queen-one-vision-lyrics

'Save Africa' initiative and world government. Geldof co-created *Bandaid* in 1984—a collaboration of celebrity artist singers and musicians to highlight the famine in Ethiopia.[68] (obviously, there was no mention of socialism's role in it; or of Marxist factional warfare). Bono, a transparent entertainment figure at the fore of world revolution, considered the late convicted Marxist terrorist Nelson Mandela an inspiration for his own activism, once stating "I've been working for Nelson Mandela pretty much my whole life".[69] An Irish activist celebrity, 'working' for a black African Marxist?

In 1992, the late Irish singer—and lifelong cult member—Sinead O' Connor (1966–2023) famously ripped-up a picture of Pope John Paul II on American TV (anti-Christianity); she later converted to Islam ('diversity'/Islamification of western countries). Her death in July 2023 was treated as the passing of a progressive saint, with thousands of mourners.[70]

There are now countless examples of celebrities endorsing/promoting the ideology, wittingly or unwittingly, whoring themselves out at every opportunity it seems. The higher their profile, the higher their influence. The Marxian sub-agendas that are extremely popular with celebrity types are: feminism, any issues involving sexuality/gender, climate change, veganism, in addition to promoting multiculturalism/diversity/anti-racism and Marxian concepts like equality and solidarity etc.

Other instances spotted include: Leonardo DiCaprio talking about climate change during his Oscar acceptance speech (other 'green' celebs are Cate Blanchett who once appeared on Australian television supporting the carbon tax); William "Caitlyn" Bruce Jenner coming-out as a 'trans woman' (amplified by the high profile of the *Keeping Up with the Kardashians* TV show); actresses Emma Watson, Nicole Kidman, and Anne Hathaway becoming UN Women Goodwill ambassadors;[71] actresses Uma Thurman, Alyssa Milano, Ashley Judd, Linsey Godfrey and ex-Fleetwood Mac singer

---

[68] https://en.wikipedia.org/wiki/Band_Aid_(band)

[69] CBS Mornings, "Bono discusses Nelson Mandela's wisdom and courage", 6 December 2013. https://www.YouTube.com/watch?v=c-lhKwIZYIg

[70] Carroll, R, 'She blazed a trail': thousands gather for funeral of Sinéad O'Connor in Ireland", 8 August 2023.

https://www.theguardian.com/music/2023/aug/08/thousands-gather-funeral-sinead-oconnor-ireland

[71] https://en.wikipedia.org/wiki/UN_Women_Goodwill_Ambassador

Stevie Knicks publicly supporting abortion.

There was also: British TV show host Philip Schofield 'coming out' as gay on the *This Morning* show; actress Ellen "Elliot" Page coming out as gay then deciding she was 'trans'; the cross-dressing comedian Eddie Izzard coming as 'transgender' (who is, shockingly, involved with the British Labour Party); actress Natalie Portman rewriting fairytales for kids to be more 'gender' neutral, and the list goes on and on.[72][73]

The Joker's speech

The sane part of Earth is fully aware that Hollywood is an endless conveyor belt for degeneracy, so nothing it produces should surprise us. Here's another clear, high-profile example of the ideology being peddled on perhaps the grandest stage Tinseltown has to offer—the Academy Awards. At the 2020 ceremony—having won the Oscar for best actor for the movie *Joker*—Joaquin Phoenix gave a rehearsed speech Marx himself would be proud of, ticking a whole myriad of red boxes as he went. He spoke of how being a famous actor gives him (and his colleagues) the "opportunity to use our voice for the voiceless" (the oppressed). What this really means is that they are in a position to peddle Marxian trash, which is exactly what he dutifully did in this speech.[74]

Going in to full Marxian SJW mode, Phoenix said (notes in brackets): "I've been thinking a lot about some of the distressing issues that we are facing collectively (solidarity/collectivism)…and I think at times we feel…that we champion different causes, but for me I see commonality (one revolution). I think whether we're talking about gender inequality (feminism), or racism, or queer rights (LGBTQ) or indigenous rights (native American agenda) or animal rights (veganism) we're talking about the fight against injustice ('oppression'/Marxian virtue-signalling). We're talking about the fight against the belief that one nation (anti-America), one people (several sub-agendas), one race (anti-white people), one gender

---

[72] Cho and Sengwe, "Celebrities Who Have Shared Their Abortion Stories to Help Women Feel Less Alone", 17 October 2023. https://people.com/health/celebrity-abortion-stories-busy-philipps-jameela-jamil/?slide=6764577#6764577

[73] Huston, W. "Natalie Portman Rewrites Classic Fairytales to Make Them 'Gender Neutral' So Children Can 'Defy Gender Stereotypes'", 15 March 2021.

https://www.breitbart.com/entertainment/2021/03/15/natalie-portman-rewrites-classic-fairytales-to-make-them-gender-neutral-so-children-can-defy-gender-stereotypes/

[74] Oscars, "Joaquin Phoenix wins Best Actor | 92nd Oscars (2020)", 11 March 2020.

https://www.YouTube.com/watch?v=qiiWdTz_MNc

(feminism), or one species (anti-human/veganism) has the right to dominate control and use and exploit another with impunity" (oppressor v oppressed).

He said that we've become disconnected from nature, and due to our egocentric world view we then "go into the natural world and we plunder it for its resources" (agriculture and industry, climate change, anti-capitalism etc.); also pointing out that we oppress cows, by artificially inseminating them, stealing their babies and stealing the milk intended for them by putting it "in our coffee and our cereal". By Joaquin's logic, if cows could speak, since they are voiceless, they would speak of this oppression. He said we can develop systems of change that "are beneficial to all sentient beings and to the environment" ('sustainability'), using "love and compassion as our guiding principles" (Marxian moral 'superiority'); he also squeezed in the words "love" (again) and "peace" at the end (all effective Marxian emotional manipulation keywords).

In a speech that was almost four minutes long, Phoenix spoke not one word about the film itself, nor thanked anyone involved in the project which allowed him to win his first Oscar—he was too busy jabbering-on about saving the world for that.

There are hundreds of people involved in producing a Hollywood movie! Stupid brat. It's worth noting the speech was laden with over-emotional, feminine thought, which is of course typical of the ideology/cult in general but it's also typical of vegan males (which he is), due to low testosterone levels.

Interestingly, the Joker movie itself featured many Marxian themes, including mental health/being a victim, anti-capitalism/revenge against the bourgeoisie, and revolution. Anyone familiar with the character knows the Joker represents chaos (aka anarchy, and, by extension, revolution). The end scene showed him dancing atop a car in front of a cheering crowd, with a bloodied demonic smile, as the city burned with the revolution he created. Satan smiles when the world is in flames...[75]

Though the Oscar's viewership has declined massively over the years (perhaps due to the 'wokeness'/Marxist rot, plus Covaids 1984) the figures

---

[75] Flashback FM, "Anarchy in Gotham (Ending) | Joker [UltraHD, HDR]", 8 January 2020.

https://www.YouTube.com/watch?v=NHi_8FGMObQ

were still around the 23.6 million mark.[76] That is a massive advertising platform for the ideology, with all eyes on the best male, best female, and best film awards in particular. Same applies for DiCaprio's climate change Oscar speech in 2016.

Movies

Some examples of films that promote Marxian propaganda, behavioural degeneracy, or 'wokeness' in one form or another:

In the movie *Pimp* (2018), the central character is a black lesbian pimp in the Bronx whose degeneracy level is matched only by that of the movie. She pimps-out mostly white females, one of them being her (kindof) love interest; this relationship with her (almost) girlfriend is obviously inter-racial, yet she's in the dominant position (insinuating that whites should be the slaves of blacks now). As the movie progresses, we see the pimp's two would-be lovers—both very attractive females—fight over this manipulative degenerate person. Obviously those two females would be better off spending their time and sexuality elsewhere. The movie essentially promotes this disgusting, wasteful behaviour to females, attempting to normalise it.[77]

Gay 'icons' and behaviour

We have recently seen the idolisation of gay 'icons'. *Bohemian Rhapsody* (2018) tells the story of Queen frontman Freddie Mercury, albeit in a more sanitised way. Mercury's personal life was one big act of degeneracy—infidelity, promiscuity and drug use—but this was not emphasised in the movie. Despite this and other inaccuracies the movie was a massive box office success (indicative of society's infection level).[78] The following year, the biopic of Elton John called *Rocketman* (2019) hit the big screen. Again, it was highly sanitised, refusing to elaborate on the details. It did however contain some mild gay sex scenes.[79]

The Irish/British movie *Rialto* (2019) is the story of Colm—an average 46-year-old Dublin man with a family, who has a mid-life crisis triggered by

---

[76] Whitten, S. "Audiences for award shows are in steep decline. This chart shows how far viewership has fallen", 2 May 2021.

https://www.cnbc.com/2021/05/02/oscars-2021-nielsen-data-shows-viewers-have-lost-interest-in-award-shows.html

[77] https://en.wikipedia.org/wiki/Pimp_(2018_film)

[78] https://en.wikipedia.org/wiki/Bohemian_Rhapsody_(film)

[79] https://en.wikipedia.org/wiki/Rocketman_(film)

traumatic events (father's death; job loss). He then becomes emotionally and sexually involved with a 19-year-old male called Jay after he is mugged by him(!). This leads to Colm developing a strange sort of victimised, Stockholm-syndrome infatuation with him afterwards; his feelings are not reciprocated.[80]

The movie essentially platforms the notion that heterosexual men can destroy their own lives/family's lives to become emotionally and sexually involved with other men. It also does a good job of evoking sympathy for Colm (victim/oppressed) despite his despicable, irresponsible behaviour. It even manages to squeeze-in a dig at capitalism, as one of the triggers for Colm's downward spiral was the unfair loss of his job (despite being a loyal employee for many years). In addition, it unintentionally shows that mental breakdown can lead a person to engaging in degeneracy, which sums up the ideology/cult very well. A disgusting film that didn't need to be made.

Robot feminism, blue Indians and climate change

The movie *Terminator: Dark Fate* (2019) was yet another instalment of the iconic sci-fi series that did not need to be made. It featured a female-centric cast and plot. Director and writer James Cameron has peddled feminist propaganda previously, with *Aliens* and *Terminator 2* featuring female 'warriors'.[81] Another relatively recent project of his was *Avatar* in 2009—which contained the themes of anti-Americanism/militarism and anti-capitalism themes, plus the resultant oppression/suppression of a tribal, indigenous population by these invaders. Like a sort of *Dances with Wolves* and *Fern Gully* set in space, with blue 'Indians' instead of native Americans.[82]

(*Fern Gully* (1992) was an animated movie about corporate rainforest destruction. Anti-capitalism and climate change agenda aimed at kids.[83] *Dances With Wolves* (1990) is also on the list of virtue-signalling Marxist Hollywood films. Promoting the 'oppression' of the native Americans, it featured an obvious anti-white/anti-American theme, an anti-military theme, and promoted the white guilt agenda. Though an enjoyable movie, it made a contribution to the ideology's attack on America, by emphasising

---

[80] https://en.wikipedia.org/wiki/Rialto_(film)

[81] https://en.wikipedia.org/wiki/Terminator:_Dark_Fate

[82] https://en.wikipedia.org/wiki/Avatar_(2009_film)

[83] https://en.wikipedia.org/wiki/FernGully:_The_Last_Rainforest

the native American issue through a Marxian lens[84]).

Ghostbusters (2016) was a re-make of the 1984 classic, made simply to promote gender equality. This time, opposite to the original, all Ghostbusters are female, but with a male receptionist who is a little bit on the dumb/incompetent side of things, while the women are relative geniuses (feminism/anti-male/male subservience agenda). Targeted primarily at a young female audience plus cult members, the film also features themes including occultism and the apocalypse.

The movie's tagline (as on the movie poster) is "Answer the call" (a subtle indoctrination term to evoke feelings of revolutionary fervour in the minds of the mostly young female audience).[85] It served as another example of the ideology destroying the arts, being a box office bomb and deservedly so.

Political 'comedy' and cult member idols

A Marxist political 'comedy' film called *Irresistible* was released in 2020. Essentially it was a mockery of anyone right-wing, including Republicans and Donald Trump supporters elsewhere.[86] It's an example of 'art' created by cult members that only other cult members would love, and be in convulsions of laughter over. It was directed and written by the former *Daily Show* host Jon Stewart (Leibowitz).

Another 'woke' movie entitled *Seberg* was released in 2019. It was about the actress Jean Seberg who got involved with a Marxian sub-cult—the Black Panthers. She also made donations to the *NAACP* (*National Association for the Advancement of Coloured People*)—a central Marxian group that helped to kick-off the black rights movement in the U.S. She was married to the ex-Marxist terrorist Romain Gary who fought the Nazis in WW2 France, though she had numerous affairs. The marketing tagline for the film was "Actress. Activist. Adversary", making it loaded with propaganda. Due to her anti-American activities, Seberg was the target of FBI surveillance and demoralisation operations in its fight against the cult. So Seberg is just another misguided SJW lefty entertainer being held up to audiences (particularly young females) as a role-model, rebel, hero etc.[87] (As an aside, the tag-line for *Seberg* contains another reference to the devil. The word "Satan" (pronounced "sha-tan") is the Hebrew word for

---

[84] https://en.wikipedia.org/wiki/Dances_with_Wolves

[85] https://en.wikipedia.org/wiki/Ghostbusters_(2016_film)

[86] https://en.wikipedia.org/wiki/Irresistible_(2020_film)

[87] https://en.wikipedia.org/wiki/The_Glorias

"adversary").

In 2020, *The Glorias* was released: a film about cult member Gloria Steinem—a central figure of 'second-wave feminism' in America's hippie era.[88] In the same year, the movie *Miss Marx* was released about Eleanor Marx, the youngest daughter of Karlie Karl. Reading the synopsis, it sounds like she's depicted as an oppressed heroine, held back by all the males in her life (rolls eyes).[89] No mention of how she was the child of Satan personified, and that's what ruined her life. Also in 2020, a feminist revenge thriller called *Promising Young Woman* was released.[90] And on and on it goes…

Superheroes for equality

The presence of the indoctrination in society means artists/performers aren't respected for producing excellence anymore; they are applauded (by the indoctrinated) because of the 'oppressed' group they belong to. And the rest of us, not wanting to go along with the 'PC' crowd, tend to resist giving respect to those who might actually deserve it. The ideology just imbalances the whole situation. Not only does it turn the arts to shit, it can warp the perception of anything good that is contained therein.

In movies, the indoctrinated types will go hysterical over watching someone like Israeli actress Gal Gadot in the *Wonder Woman* movies. Any actual greatness in the actor's performance is tainted by the virtue-signalling undertones present due to the indoctrination. By simply even being in that position, according to the cult/ideology, she deserves to be lauded. That's ludicrous! This doesn't empower females, it disempowers them. Greatness should be judged on greatness. When we hear things like "she's such a great role model for girls/women", it becomes obvious what's afoot here. Do we hear the same things when Henry Cavill plays Superman? No.

The 2020 movie *Wonder Woman 1984* (take a bow Orwell) included a sequence near the film's end where she delivers an evocative monologue straight into the camera lens, encouraging the viewers—including millions of young impressionable females—to be revolutionary saviours, warriors etc. It starts as a dialogue with the movie's antagonist, then she speaks straight to the audience, breaking the 'fourth wall'. It includes lines like "you're not the only one who has suffered", and "you must be the

---

[88] https://en.wikipedia.org/wiki/The_Glorias

[89] https://en.wikipedia.org/wiki/Miss_Marx

[90] https://en.wikipedia.org/wiki/Promising_Young_Woman

hero...only you can save the day"; it talks about fear, isolation (all things the 'oppressed' must feel, right?), and utopia, naturally.[91]

Perhaps in the next sequel we'll see Wonder Woman quoting feminist authors like Emmeline Pankhurst and going after the NWO banking elites, with a Lenin-esque shaved bald slap-head and goatee beard? (that would totally end my interest, since Gadot's physical beauty was the best thing about those films). Also of note is the Captain Marvel character in the Marvel Cinematic Universe, played by avid feminist, cult member, and YouTuber Brie Larson.

Princesses and dolls

Gal Gadot also stars in a live-action remake of Walt Disney's animated classic *Snow White and the Seven Dwarfs* (1937), entitled *Snow White* (2024).[92] This film will feature an 'empowered' main character. According to the actress playing her, Rachel Zegler, in an interview with *Variety*, she's "not gonna be saved by the prince and she's not gonna be dreaming of true love. ...she's dreaming about becoming the leader she knows she can be".[93] Popcorn or puke bucket, anyone?

One of the screenwriters for *Snow White* is Greta Gerwig, who directed *Barbie* (2023)—a piece of disgusting, spiteful feminist trash directed primarily at young females. Perhaps the most disturbing and insidious thing about this was that it was cleverly marketed as a 'family comedy'.[94]

The movie is based on the famous Barbie doll, released by toy company Mattel in 1959.[95] This 'fashion' doll helped to replace the traditional baby doll as a toy for girls, being symbolic of the psychological warping/conditioning of the modern female with superficiality/ego, hyper-sexuality etc. In addition, a 'fashion' doll, with a clearly sexual element, obviously objectifies the female, literally. Mattel was founded by Jewish couple Ruth and Elliot Handler.

An opening scene (also used as a trailer) in *Barbie* features a strange

---

[91] Movieclips, "Wonder Woman 1984 (2020) - Wonder Woman's Speech Scene (10/10) | Movieclips", 9 March 2022. https://www.YouTube.com/watch?v=7ofZ_Ij4HaE

[92] https://en.wikipedia.org/wiki/Snow_White

[93] Variety, "Rachel Zegler and Gal Gadot on Bringing a New Modern Edge to 'Snow White'", 10 Septermber 2022. https://www.YouTube.com/watch?v=2RVg3yetTE4

[94] https://en.wikipedia.org/wiki/Barbie_(film)

[95] https://en.wikipedia.org/wiki/Barbie

homage to an iconic scene in Stanley Kubrick's *2001: A Space Odyssey* (1968). The original scene featured a bunch of proto-human apes (hominins), going bananas around a mysterious alien monolith, which inspires them to learn how to use a bone as a tool or weapon; suggesting a great leap in evolution.[96] In Barbie, a bunch of young girls—holding baby dolls—discover a giant Barbie doll. They then smash the baby dolls, screaming "fuck the patriarchy!" (no not really), but they do smash the dolls. The blood boils..[97] This is mainstream anti-humanity Satanism, aimed at girls.

In the movie, Barbie's world is depicted as a sort of feminist utopia, where males ("Ken"'s) are relegated to second-class citizens essentially. The Ken's turn the tables and manage to temporarily create a 'patriarchy' for themselves, until a feminist 'counter-revolution' by the females (giggles). Gerwig performed the writing duties, along with Noah Baumbach. Barbie, once regarded by some feminists as a negative role model for girls (as it set beauty standards unrealistically high), is now a bitch of the ideology. Another example of how the ideology/cult can co-opt things and mould them to its whims.

According to Wiki, the movie took just under $1.5 billion at the box office.[98] Imagine those millions of little girls' eyes… those shiny bright colours flowing down all those optic nerves…and all that degenerate feminist propaganda being faithfully reproduced by their ear drums, to be decoded in their vulnerable minds, potentially warping their minds and ruining their lives. This was child abuse, and parents were complicit in this.

Greedy Steve Coogan

Another example of the cult's evermore brazen propaganda was in the British movie *Greed* (2019) with comedic actor Steve Coogan.[99] No prizes for guessing which Marxian sub-agenda is being pushed here. If you could use just one word to cynically describe materialism and wealth while criticising it from a position of apparent moral superiority, wouldn't that be it?

---

[96] FilmScout, "2001: Space Odyssey Best Scenes - The Bone As A Weapon", 30 November 2014. https://www.YouTube.com/watch?v=T0vkiBPWigg

[97] Warner Bros. Pictures, "Barbie | Teaser Trailer". 16 December 2022.

https://www.YouTube.com/watch?v=8zIf0XvoL9Y

[98] https://en.wikipedia.org/wiki/Barbie_(film)

[99] https://en.wikipedia.org/wiki/Greed_(2019_film)

The plot centres around a rich, white, middle-aged male (of course) played by Coogan named McCreadie (mcGreedy), who amassed his wealth by oppressing others (yawn). He is predictably portrayed as a dominating scumbag who treats others like garbage (toxic masculinity) and who wants to have sex with his ex-wife despite being married (feminist "men are bastards" mindset). Disguised as 'satire', it promotes: anti-bourgeoisie/anti-capitalism; anti-oppression of the oppressed (migrants); the exploitation of workers (sounds familiar, right?). Interestingly, one of the characters in it is called Fabian.

McCreadie is mauled to death by a coked-up Lion while he's drunk at a party (yes, really). The Lion was let out of his cage, during this opportunistic moment of revenge committed by the character Amanda. Amanda's mother was a worker who was essentially exploited/worked to death by McCreadie's business (cringeworthy I know), so this was her moment of retribution. The unoriginal, traditional commie message here is—kill the bourgeoisie because they deserve to die for oppressing the poor oppressed proletariat. It's also saying men should die for oppressing females. So, the Lion essentially delivered a double-whammy for the great proletarian utopian revolution when he tore Mr. McGreedy's face off! Lenin the Lion! A big cat that goes meow meeoow Meeaao Mao.

Rather cringely, at the end of the film when the credits roll, some Marxian 'facts' appear on the screen—blatant propaganda highlighting 'oppression' in the fashion industry. Obviously, no mention of the fact that the bulk of the trashy fashion industry itself only exists because of females, female superficiality/ego, feminism/women's 'lib', and gay men. Same goes for the cosmetic industry. No industry = no oppression contained therein. In addition, no mention of the fact that those industries would struggle to function without using animal fur for clothes, animal testing for make-up etc. (a cause championed by the animal rights/veganism sub-agenda).

"Kneel before Marx!"

Sports go in to the 'entertainment' category. Have we seen the sports world being used as a platform by the cult/ideology to generate the social justice warrior mentality? Absolutely. In particular the "no to racism" agenda.

The Marxist cult ritual of 'taking a knee' was seen across the world, in 'solidarity' with the anti-racism or Black Lives Matter agenda. The Marxist clenched fist that was used in Marxist BLM street 'protests' was (mostly) absent in this sporting 'protest'. Still, when you see sporting figures across the world taking part in a Marxist cult ritual this is another sign that the infection is permeating deeply throughout society.

In the U.S. in 2016, dumb NFL players engaged in the ritual to 'protest' racism/race inequality and 'police brutality', taking their knees during the playing of the national anthem before football games (which has an obvious anti-nationalistic/anti-American treasonous tone).[100]

The Irish international soccer team faced Hungary in a friendly match in Budapest in June 2021. At kick-off, like idiots, the Irish team took a knee to protest racism only to be amusingly booed by the crowd. It was a brilliant display of hostility towards Marxist activism by the crowd. The Irish team manager Stephen Kenny was quoted in the Irish Times as saying "The fact that it was booed is incomprehensible really".[101] Correct—if you are brainwashed it most certainly would be.

One of the players, Chiedozie Ogbene, the first Republic of Ireland player to be born in Nigeria, spoke of the booing: "This is something black people have been fighting for many years. Discrimination and racism, there is no place for it in any sport or in any place... we stayed strong. I am so happy that we, as a team took the knee, to show solidarity between us all". Ireland always has thousands of talented young Irish men who are constantly denied the opportunity to pull on the green jersey. 'Diversity' and mass immigration will be a further insult to them. The behaviour was also seen at club level—English Premier League teams were obliged to kneel before Marx before matches during the 20/21 season.[102]

Online and social(ist) Media

In addition to the media, education, and the entertainment industry, the 'transmission belts' now include the newer element of online and social media etc. This is an important virtual battleground. Thanks to smartphones, we can step on to it at almost any moment during our waking day. Socialist media serves many roles that benefits the cult/ideology including indoctrination; controlling public discourse; surveillance and threat assessment; and the dissemination of degeneracy, creating such personalities on a massive scale.

---

[100] Haislop, T. "Colin Kaepernick kneeling timeline: How protests during the national anthem started a movement in the NFL", 13 September 2020. https://www.sportingnews.com/us/nfl/news/colin-kaepernick-kneeling-protest-timeline/xktu6ka4diva1s5jxaylrcsse

[101] Cummiskey, G., "Stephen Kenny: 'The fact that it was booed is incomprehensible really'", 9 June 2021. https://www.irishtimes.com/sport/soccer/international/stephen-kenny-the-fact-that-it-was-booed-is-incomprehensible-really-1.4587995

[102] "Premier League players to continue taking a knee in 2021/22 season", 4 August 2021. https://www.skysports.com/football/news/11661/12371928/premier-league-players-to-continue-taking-a-knee-in-2021-22-season

Population control & censorship

Most obviously, socialist media allows for a tremendous level of control over public discourse. Anyone who doesn't conform to the Marxist status quo can be profiled, monitored, and censored. These dissenters can then become targets for cult members in the real world (harassment, threats, violence, losing their jobs etc.). In recent times, we are seeing the purging of any 'right-wing', 'far-right' or 'conspiracy theorist' (non-Marxian) voices/profiles/channels from online/social media platforms. This is all simply one big act of neutralising the political/ideological opposition, enabling the cult/ideology to dominate the landscape. Social media also allows cult members and organisations to study the behaviour of their enemies, helping them to maintain a tactical advantage.

It's a tradition of commie totalitarianism to use surveillance to maintain ideological control of public discourse, as part of a pre-emptive strike on its enemies. Since the cult must know who the dissenters are, they must know what you're saying to others, and social media is a constant act of expressing your opinions through text, video, audio etc. Furthermore, when we express ourselves in this way, they can find out what we are thinking. This is a form of threat-assessment, allowing them to zero-in on dissenters before they even open their mouths on the public stage. If we are allowed to do this, we may influence others, so the cult must stop us before it gets to that. Social media helps to 'flush-out' or expose these dissenters. This flushing-out process has already begun in western countries. We have seen many examples of this in Australia, UK, U.S. etc. where police are showing-up at people's houses over 'non-pc' social media posts. There are now too many examples to list.

A 2016 article in the *Independent* UK newspaper spoke of "online crimes of speech". It said: "According to the Register, a total of 2,500 Londoners have been arrested over the past five years for allegedly sending "offensive" messages via social media. In 2015, 857 people were detained, up 37 per cent increase since 2010.". These messages were deemed illegal due to the (commie) Communications Act 2003. It added: "The legislation has been used to arrest Twitter users responsible for racist hate speech. According to Vocativ, among many recently arrested was a Scottish citizen who had posted hate speech about Syrian refugees on his Facebook page. A recent study found the words 'slut' and 'whore' were used by UK Twitter users 10,000 times in three weeks.".[103] Those three issues referred-to here—anti-

---

[103] Gale, S. "Arrests for offensive Facebook and Twitter posts soar in London", 4 June 2016. https://www.independent.co.uk/news/uk/arrests-for-offensive-facebook-and-twitter-posts-soar-in-london-a7064246.html

racism, mass migration, and feminism—are all coming from the ideology of course.

If you say anything online that displeases the cult, they can report you to the likewise-infected authorities. It's collusion between casual cult members in the public and those working within the system (in government, policing, civil service, non-profits/NGO's etc.). It's all about overall control over the narrative. A more advanced stage of the same system/process exists in the glorious People's Republic of China (ruled by the Chinese Communist Party), where social media (as it exists in the west) is not allowed. This is because there is no need to flush-out dissenters or control the ideological environment there—the ideology is already sufficiently dominant. The (virtual) ban on foreign social media also helps to keep any non-Marxian influences out of their society. Twitter, Facebook, YouTube are blocked via China's "Great Firewall"; but they are many Chinese platforms for the one billion plus users to get hooked on.[104]

The conduct of social media platforms during the Covid Pan(lucifer)demic has been nothing short of criminal, banning those questioning the narrative because they were spreading "vaccine misinformation". This is classic Marxian snake-like manoeuvring—lying while they censor others and label them as liars, in order to 'protect' us all, ostensibly for our own benefit.

Also, the official reason/justification for them doing this is that some in society are impressionable and are easily led down the wrong path (the exact mechanism that the ideology relies on to spread from mind-to-mind!). Psycho hypocrisy to the max. That commie-red-coloured virtual bitch of the ideology—YouTube—showed us very clearly what its role was during this 'pandemic', by not only banning any content opposing the official narrative but actively promoting it.

Pleasure/hedonism

All social media platforms are primarily based on pleasure—the user gets a little dopamine fix via the reward system of the brain. This benefits the ideology/cult greatly; hedonism provides a clear avenue for it to gain influence over a mind.

The creators of Facebook said they were aware of what they were doing when making people pleasure/approval junkies. The Sri-Lankan venture capitalist Chamath Palihapitiya commented on this during an interview at Stanford University's Graduate School of Business, in November 2017; he

---

[104] Thomala, L. "Social media in China – statistics & facts", 20 December 2023. https://www.statista.com/topics/1170/social-networks-in-china/

essentially stated social media was destructive for society. Palihapitiya was an early executive and Vice President of User Growth at Facebook. He said: "The short-term, dopamine-driven feedback loops that we have created are destroying how society works. No civil discourse. No cooperation. Misinformation. Mistruth. And it's not an American problem…This is a global problem". He added: "I feel tremendous guilt…In the back, deep, deep recesses of our mind, we kind of knew something bad could happen".[105]

As mentioned, when people are feeling pleasure, their defences are down, and are therefore easier to indoctrinate (the youth in particular). It can also disseminate ideas around society very quickly, offering users instant interaction with society, constantly attaching them to the collective, and encouraging them to conform as it's more pleasurable to do so. It offers them a level of control, customisation, and interaction that traditional media has not. For these reasons social media is unique, and arguably more useful for the cult/ideology than traditional forms of media.

Ego degeneracy

Social media platforms are built around the ego (which itself can be the central source of pleasure for the individual). Facebook, Twitter, Instagram, Snapchat, YouTube—anything where you have a profile and you can get 'likes'—all help to encourage certain interlinked behaviours in the masses, including:

Being liked/accepted by others (aka popularity)

This conditions us to feel pleasure by being part of a collective, via getting approval from others. This can create weak, dependent, superficial people. There's nothing wrong with being admired by others in our lives, but unwise to make it the focal point of our existence (or our daily routine)! Obviously, if the collective is composed of a significant amount of indoctrinated cult members, then there is a strong incentive to 'join the cult' somewhat, or at least comply with it, and, most importantly, not oppose it. This connects with the fact that those prone to indoctrination are full of fear since they don't have the courage to refuse to conform. They fear being isolated, or lack the self-esteem to be a genuine individual, reasonably independent from the collective.

Social media can encourage a person to become addicted to conformity,

[105] Kovach, S. "Former Facebook exec feels 'tremendous guilt' for what he helped make", 11 Dec 2017. https://www.businessinsider.com/former-facebook-exec-chamath-palihapitiya-social-media-damaging-society-2017-12?r=US&IR=T

leaving that person with (almost) no choice but to do so. That is, unless they want to deny themselves access to the mind drug of acceptance by the collective and endure the horrors of cold turkey (the horror!). Obviously, it doesn't have this effect on everyone (e.g. you, me, or anyone who didn't start using social media as an adolescent), but it surely does on many in society. We can only speculate how many, and to what degree.

Being idolised

Same thing as the previous only amplified considerably (if enough people pay attention to you). Being idolised then puts you in an influential position, where you may influence others to become like you, as they will influence others to be the same, ad infinitum. Idolisation allows a person to have their own little cult, in a sense. This cult worship factor helps to accelerate the diffusion of the ideology throughout society, as the impressionable idolisers will be keen to follow the example of their idols (even if their idols are absolute morons or whores for Marxian sub-agendas. Example: indoctrinated celebrities). Social media also encourages the manic hysteria that fuels cult worship and the ideology/cult in general. This is evident when we see those pushing Marxian sub-agendas being held aloft on the public stage as 'heroes', or 'brave' or 'strong' etc., which triggers the outpouring of adoration and emotion from the gullible. This idolisation process includes the idol/idoliser relationship, similar to the master/slave relationship (oppressor/oppressed).

Being self-absorbed and spoilt

Self-absorbed: this can be the opposite of/antagonistic to having a sense of duty (e.g. the duty towards your own family, people, race, nation etc). Essentially, it's putting yourself, your desires, and opinions above all else. Spoilt: this is the result of excessive attention, pampering, 'nice'/not critical social interaction that's pleasurable to the recipient. As mentioned elsewhere, the ideology/cult heavily relies on the spoilt brat factor to swell its ranks.

Obviously these above are all inter-connected and fuel each other, centring around the ego, pleasure, self-esteem, fear, a lack of conscience, stupidity, immaturity, and being miserable on the inside etc.

Retards normal psychological development

Social media can retard a person's development in other areas too. It conditions people to be scatty, with poor concentration spans. This can lead to the inability to learn anything of value and a tendency to become stressed-out or overwhelmed when having to do any serious thinking!

This includes, crucially, the inability to examine your own

personality/behaviour, to assess yourself, and engage in some constructive criticism (example: "am I in a cult?" or "am I brainwashed, fanatical" etc?). This benefits the cult/ideology tremendously because the enemy of indoctrination is a person who has the brains, guts, persistence, and patience to question themselves and their beliefs.

Of course, if a person is addicted to pleasure and 'nice' comfortable feelings (including thinking they are amazing, flawless etc.) it becomes too uncomfortable—or even painful—for them to criticise themselves in any meaningful or constructive way. The idea that they may be flawed in some way is too much for their deficient, internally weak minds to handle. This type of psychological cowardice and immaturity is at the crux of the matter! Social media encourages it; it can make a person weak. It can also keep us constantly distracted with its virtual collectivism, which makes any sort of reflective behaviour much less likely (particularly the solitary kind).

YouTube

It's fair to assume that the consolidation of power we are seeing now was always part of the plan. YouTube has become the biggest video platform in the world, sucking-in billions of eyeballs every day. Clearly, it's ideologically biased against non-Marxian perspectives, and the channel culls in recent times have clearly shown this. Previously it was an indispensable platform for alternative media. It seems like this was the timeline of YouTube: present the platform, promote it and grow the user base; consolidate its position as number one; encourage users to earn an income from it, and even become financially dependent upon it; then start pulling the rug out from under certain users, removing those who don't conform to 'hate-speech' and 'community guidelines' (aka Marxism). Et voila — it runs the show, literally. Now, there's all sorts of degenerate trash on the platform, including purveyors of Marxist propaganda, but they won't be removed—their subscriber counts and views will continue to soar (explored later).

YouTube's new initiative to clamp-down on content officially began in 2016, with 2017 seeing the use of improved machine learning/algorithms to flag 'extremist' or 'inappropriate' content. Who is deciding what is extreme and inappropriate, and what's their ideology? From YouTube's May 2019 video "Hate Speech Policy: YouTube Community Guidelines" (underline for emphasis): "Hate speech is not allowed on YouTube. We remove content promoting violence or hatred against members of protected (note: 'oppressed') groups, including but not limited to—race, gender, sexual orientation, or religious affiliation". [106] Commie community guidelines. The word "protected" is key, and it makes all the difference in how the whole sentence is perceived. "Protected" = 'oppressed', but using the word oppressed is a bit too obvious. And which groups are "protected"? Who's to say who's in a "protected" group and who isn't? Cult members, that's who. YouTube is virtue-signalling here, trying to come across as being universal and unbiased, but we know the ideology doesn't work that way—it only gives certain groups 'oppressed'/'protected' status. The word "hatred" is key too. It's very flexible in that even criticism of one of these "protected" groups can be construed as "hatred".

A 12 December 2023 post on the *statista.com* states: "During the second quarter of 2023, a total of approximately 7.4 million videos were removed (from YouTube) This includes videos that had been automatically flagged for violating the platform's community guidelines. In comparison, only 507.7 thousand videos were removed via flags from non-automated flagging systems". The graphs shows figures from 2017–2023, with the highest peak in 2020 showing that over eleven million videos were removed via automation (prob due to videos defying the Covid narrative).[107]

As for channels being removed, there's too many to mention here, but a notable, relatively high-profile casualty was the popular and outstanding U.S.-based alternative media platform *Red Ice TV*; hosted by Henrik Palmgren and Lana Lokteff. In Ireland, in an obvious cull, prominent voices Dave Cullen ("Computing Forever"), Grand Torino (aka Rowan Croft), and former journalist Gemma O' Doherty all lost their channels. Obviously, YT did not remove videos promoting a myriad of destructive, evil things such as feminism, socialism, climate alarmism, veganism, or Covid-related scaremongering etc.

Despite these culls of the major 'right wing' channels, obviously it still wasn't enough for some Irish Marx-worshippers. On 21 February 2023, fanatical Irish cunt member Mark Malone made an appearance before an Oireachtas Joint Committee on Children, Equality, Disability, Integration and Youth. Highly-involved with several groups in Ireland, including Antifa, on this occasion Malone spoke as a 'researcher' with the benign-

---

[106] YouTube Creators, "Hate Speech Policy: YouTube Community Guidelines", 24 May 2019.

[107] Ceci, L. "Number of videos removed from YouTube worldwide from 4th quarter 2017 to 2nd quarter 2023", December 2023.
https://www.statista.com/statistics/1132890/number-removed-YouTube-videos-worldwide/

sounding group "Hope and Courage Collective" (formerly FRO/"Far Right Observatory"). The topic was essentially how they could remove even more 'right-wing' content from online platforms, under the pretence of combating 'misinformation' (about migrants and refugees etc.). He suggested they should pre-emptively stop this misinformation before it had an effect.[108]

Amusingly, Malone forgot the group's new 'nicer' name, when he said "we're as FRO... part of trusted flagger status on every one of the main platforms", and that these platforms have "failed regularly to remove content as reported". According to the *inhope.org* website, Trusted Flaggers are "Organisations that are formally recognised as trusted for identifying and reporting illegal content", under the Digital Services Act (DSA).[109] A bunch of Marxist activists regarded as 'trusted flaggers' by ostensibly capitalistic big tech platforms? That's collusion. Malone added there was "a possibility of organisations working to take some responsibility some action to mitigate what's happening and we're not seeing that". The cult will never be satisfied until all non-Marxist content is purged from the internet.

The former CEO of YouTube Susan Wojcicki is regarded as being the driving force of the decline (Marxification) of the platform. She was involved in Google's buy-up of it in 2006, becoming CEO in 2014. Wojcicki is an avid cult member, supporting the mass immigration and feminism sub-agendas.[110] Her sister Anne Wojcicki is the co-founder and CEO of the direct-to-customer genetic testing service *23andMe* (one of many groups promoting the racial 'equality'/'multiculturalism' sub-agenda).[111] I'm sure if I used that 'service' my results would come back 50% sub-Saharan African, 20% Arabic, 20% Apache, 5% Latino, 5% Aboriginal, and yet 100% Irish.

Capitol hill and censorship of Trump

There's plenty of examples of partisan behaviour on other platforms too. The aftermath of the 2020 U.S. presidential election included the violent events at the Capitol in Washington on 6 January 2021, during the formal

---

[108] Hope and Courage Collective, "Mark Malone | Researcher | Hope and Courage Collective Ireland", 7 March 2023.
https://www.YouTube.com/watch?v=uQAXrck9ouk

[109] "What is a Trusted Flagger?", 11 November 2023.https://www.inhope.org/EN/articles/what-is-a-trusted-flagger

[110] https://en.wikipedia.org/wiki/Susan_Wojcicki

[111] https://en.wikipedia.org/wiki/23andMe

counting of votes to confirm Joe Biden's 'victory'. The patriots knew something stank and went on the offensive, and this was no doubt fuelled by the claims of election fraud by President Donald Trump.

Predictably, the directors of social media/online platforms then seized this opportunity to ban him from several including *Facebook*, its property *Instagram*, and *Twitter* amongst others. The CEO of Facebook Mark Zuckerberg announced that they would block Trump, as his posts might incite further violence, calling the events at the Capitol "shocking".[112]

On 8 January, Twitter announced in a well-crafted piece of Marxian propaganda that Trump's account was now "immediately and permanently suspended" from the platform, officially "due to the risk of further incitement of violence". This one short, petty post is enough to show you they are riddled with the ideology. It described the events at the Capitol Building as "horrific" and "criminal acts", citing the usual violation of rules by the @realDonaldTrump account. Their statement of judgement was based on what Trump tweeted on the same day: "The 75,000,000 great American Patriots who voted for me, AMERICA FIRST, and MAKE AMERICA GREAT AGAIN, will have a GIANT VOICE long into the future. They will not be disrespected or treated unfairly in any way, shape or form!!!". He also tweeted: "To all of those who have asked, I will not be going to the Inauguration on January 20th".[113]

They cited their spurious "Glorification of Violence Policy" (anti-Marxist violence). They stated that the second tweet encourages the idea "that the election was not legitimate", and that it "may also serve as encouragement to those potentially considering violent acts that the Inauguration would be a "safe" target, as he will not be attending". According to Twitter, the first tweet, by using the term "American patriots" was highlighted as being supportive of "those committing violent acts at the US Capitol" (which it was, and rightly so). Finally, it stated that plans for more violent protests were appearing on the platform. Obviously, the main issue the cult members at Twitter, Facebook etc. had with Trump's tweets is that they didn't condemn what happened at the Capitol, and this was used as the excuse. I'm sure Trump leaving the picture emboldened them to censor him. Another factor is the spoilt brat mentality—and what happens if they don't

---

[112] Palmer, A. "Facebook will block Trump from posting at least for the remainder of his term", 7 Jan 2021. https://www.cnbc.com/2021/01/07/facebook-will-block-trump-from-posting-for-the-remainder-of-his-term.html

[113] X, "Permanent suspension of @realDonaldTrump", 8 Jan 2021.

https://blog.twitter.com/en_us/topics/company/2020/suspension

get their own way. Trump didn't condemn the protestors and respond how they wanted, so they have a tantrum and ban him. Pathetic. Keeping in mind here, that the Biden administration coming to power was nothing more than a Marxist coup (which is genuinely "horrific", "shocking" and "criminal"), and these online platforms have clearly shown their true (red) colours by being complicit with the treason.

How dare Zuckerberg et al behave in that way! In a sane, healthy (Marxism-free) nation, people like him would be immediately arrested for treason (if they managed to get in to positions of power in the first place). It's "horrific" that they get away with this. These online platforms are a crucial part of the cult's operations—playing a central role in creating the chaos, division and violence engulfing the country—yet when the consequences manifest in actions against them, they take up a position of virtue-signalling moral superiority! This is totally unacceptable. And then there's the partisan double-standards of who is allowed to use their platforms, and in what capacity. Obviously, innumerable Marxist voices have been allowed to operate on them since the beginning. Can you imagine the likes of cult members Bernie Sanders, Alexandria Ocasio-Cortez etc. being banned, despite the amount of anti-American drivel they spew? Not likely! (At time of writing June 2022, Sanders is tweeting promoting degeneracy about legalizing marijuana; talking about the bourgeoisie; the rights of the proletarian workers; big business etc.)

Or what about the multitude of fanatical Marxist groups using social media platforms (Antifa, Black Lives Matter, Extinction Rebellion etc.)? Don't they use them to generate violence/social unrest/disruption, in addition to monitoring non-Marxist voices to harass or commit crimes against them in the real world? The ideological double-standards are evident—violence and unrest are fine when they're Marxist in origin, but when they're anti-Marxist they're "horrific" and "shocking". Another thing that's "shocking" is that the likes of Zuckerberg et al have control over three massive social media platforms—Facebook, Instagram, and Whatsapp. Hmmm, what's that called, when things become increasingly centralised, accompanied by the suppression of free speech? Is that capitalism or communism?

Telegram and Parler

The *Telegram* platform had a massive surge of users after the banning of Trump in early 2021, attracting many trying to escape the contaminated platforms mentioned earlier. It had a reputation of being a genuine free-speech and privacy-centric platform, so it inevitably attracted many on the right. In fact, it became the primary platform even compared to other right-friendly alternatives such as *Parler*. Of course, this was not tolerated by the cult, and further steps were taken to suppress the enemy. A lobby group called *The Coalition for a Safer Web* (CSW) became involved ("safer" = funny). The emergent strategy was to target the likes of *Apple*—those who control the operating systems software on smartphones—rather than solely trying to go after social media platforms themselves. This centres around the fact that on both Apple's iOS and Google's Android systems, users required the app installer programme (*App Store* and *Play Store* respectively) to download the actual apps (e.g. Telegram). The CSW then filed a lawsuit against Apple, in order to gain leverage over Telegram, to essentially make it conform.[114]

The CSW founder Marc Ginsberg is a Jewish lawyer, with decades of experience in the political and corporate sectors. The 'anti-semitism' card was played by him in his attack on Apple, citing the 'religious threats' (towards Jewish people) being expressed by some Telegram users. The *coalitionsw.org* website is a nauseating, virtue-signalling Marxian read, including the usual jabber of 'far right', 'extremism', white nationalists, 'racists', the promotion of 'hate' etc.[115]

Economic blackmail

The *Stop Hate for Profit* campaign was formed by the cult in the wake of their highly-advantageous moment—the death of George Floyd. That name—Stop Hate for Profit—is obviously Marxist; anti-capitalism and virtue-signalling combined. This one allowed the cult to combine their control of social media with their anti-capitalism sub-agenda. It involved such companies as Unilever, Starbucks and Verizon and used advertising boycotts to force Facebook to essentially go more Marxist. Interestingly, regardless of how sympathetic Zuckerberg's Facebook had previously been to the ideology, it still wasn't good enough! As a result, the CEO promptly announced that the company would change its policies to probit 'hate speech'.[116] The cult's fanaticism comes in waves...

The Rogan-gate affair

Another example of the cult's fanaticism, this time involving the famous

---

[114] Duden, T.,"Lobby Group Sues Apple To Remove Telegram From App Store For Allowing "Hate Speech"", 19 Jan 2021.
https://www.zerohedge.com/technology/lobby-group-sues-apple-remove-telegram-app-store-allowing-hate-speech

[115] https://coalitionsw.org/

[116] Hern, A., "How hate speech campaigners found Facebook's weak spot", 29 June 2020. https://www.theguardian.com/technology/2020/jun/29/how-hate-speech-campaigners-found-facebooks-weak-spot

podcast host, comedian, and UFC commentator Joe Rogan. It happened after he signed a massive exclusivity deal with the audio streaming giant *Spotify* in May 2020 to feature his show—the *Joe Rogan Experience.*

The horrific crime he committed was doing an interview with Abigail Shrier, the author of an important book on the trans agenda called *Irreversible Damage: The Transgender Craze Seducing Our Daughters* (2020).[117] Shrier's noble work highlights several important aspects of that sub-agenda including that the pop culture contributes greatly to young females identifying as 'trans', and that vulnerable females are prone to getting swept-up in the craze (e.g. those with anxious or depressive tendencies). In other words, she explores areas that contradict the cult's narrative (i.e. that the issue is all about 'compassion' for the 'oppressed').

This unforgivable injustice sparked the glorious inner revolutionary in the Spotify staff since many of them were LGBTQ etc. An 8 October 2020 article on *the musicnetwork.com* stated: "In a statement, Spotify CEO Daniel Ek expressed that the company had reviewed the episode, ultimately deciding against removing it from the platform. "In the case of Joe Rogan, a total of 10 meetings have been held with various groups and individuals to hear their respective concerns," Spotify CEO Daniel Ek said. "And some of them want Rogan removed because of things he's said in the past"".[118] I'm surprised they didn't strike to try get their own way! I would've welcomed them to work in the morning with a full-blast ice-cold genitalia-slicing firehose in the transgenderised crotch, making them drop their skinny ethically sourced oppression-free vegancino latte coffees. Morons.

In one subsequent episode featuring Tim Dillon, Rogan commented: "They have literally said nothing to me about it. Now, is there someone at Spotify that's complaining about the episode? I'm sure. Is it a transphobic episode? It's not. They're wrong. It's nothing to do with that. It has to do with the fact that human beings are actually malleable. We all know that. That's why cults exist".[119] Indeed. Interestingly, when Rogan's show arrived on Spotify in September 2020, some episodes didn't survive the migration from YouTube. These featured interviewee's such as the 'right-wing'

---

[117] JRE Clips, "Why Abigail Shrier Took on the Transgender Craze Amongst Teenage Girls", 16 July 2020. https://www.YouTube.com/watch?v=6MYb0rBDYvs

[118] Gray, G. "Joe Rogan has weighed in on Spotify employees looking to censor JRE", 8 October 2020. https://themusicnetwork.com/joe-rogan-spotify-controversy/

[119] Powerful JRE, "Joe Rogan Experience #1525 - Tim Dillon", 14 August 2020.

https://www.YouTube.com/watch?v=h9XzuUXj6Gc

commentator Gavin McInnes and Alex Jones.

Overtly Marxist platforms

An example of an absolutely disgusting garbage website is *Rational Wiki*. Most of its 'articles' are pages of propaganda, specifically written to counter, mock, or dismiss any non-Marxist voices in society. The writing style is predictably highly intellectualised, featuring overly flamboyant language to maintain the veneer of intelligence (classic cult member behaviour). No doubt it's effective at entertaining cult members due to their bitchy tendencies, and at keeping the average Joe/Jane (already indoctrinated or not) from waking up to what the 'Left' is. The cult members involved should be incarcerated, and sites of this kind should be purged from the internet with extreme prejudice.

From "About RationalWiki" on the site's homepage (formatted, notes in brackets): "Our purpose here at RationalWiki includes: 1. Analyzing and refuting pseudoscience and the anti-science movement (they support the Climate con, evolution etc.); 2. Documenting the full range of crank ideas (countering 'conspiracy theories' involving population replacement migration, Covid etc.); 3. Explorations of authoritarianism and fundamentalism (anti-'right wing'); 4. Analysis and criticism of how these subjects are handled in the media".[120]

The Irish website *The Beacon* is another example. On the homepage, we see a red and black lighthouse, on a black background; the tagline under it is "Reporting on the Far Right". From the "About" page: "The Beacon was founded in August 2019 and is dedicated to anti-racist and anti-fascist principles. It reports on and investigates the far right in Ireland and further afield".[121] It's a simple but well-constructed website, with many articles pumping out Marxian swill. The writing is technically competent, but you can clearly see that it's ultra-partisan. Much use of the terms "far-right" and "conspiracy theorists" etc. The ignorant/impressionable would definitely be influenced by this propaganda.

There are countless sites like these. The most fascinating thing about them (similar to other cult groups) is how they can type endless pages of this rubbish and not realise they're lowlife brainwashed fanatics; literally going out of their way to use whatever intelligence they have to betray humanity. There's enough intelligence there to construct points and present them etc., but not enough to realise what they are and what they are doing (to

---

[120] https://rationalwiki.org/wiki/Main_Page

[121] https://the-beacon.ie/about/

themselves/us). Sad zombies. It really is fascinating.

Non-Governmental Organisations/non-profits

While so called 'Non-Governmental Organisations' (NGOs, or "non-profits") are not necessarily one of the traditional 'transmission belts of culture', they are an equally important component of the big red machinery (non-contaminated groups excluded, of course).

They play a critical role in furthering the spread of the ideological infection in a country, allowing the 'ordinary' Joe/Jane citizen to become 'heroes' in the fight to create a Marxist utopia. By their nature as 'non-profits' they are not businesses, and no doubt this is somehow noble in the mind of capitalism-hating cult members, making them attractive, worthwhile endeavours. So basically they are sucking wealth—via donations and funding—to help destroy the countries in which they operate (by promoting/supporting various Marxian sub-agendas)!

They may be involved in the multitude of sub-agendas: fighting 'racism' and 'hate speech' or 'hate crimes'; promoting abortion as healthcare; playing a role in the importation of immigrants—legally or illegally—and fast-tracking their addition to the general population; promoting LGBTQ issues in schools and communities; supporting the construction of Mosques in various western countries (despite any local objections); promoting the climate change sub-agenda; promoting and re-enforcing feminist propaganda etc. In many cases, they combine them, and promote several at the same time. Regardless of the bells and whistles and different names, logos, colours etc. of these groups, they're all part of the one big cult movement.

Some will play roles in different capacities at different stages of the same sub-agenda. For example, the Israeli NGO *IsraAid* has been involved in the mass migration sub-agenda, helping to bring migrants from Africa in to Europe, via the Mediterranean; same for the German NGO *Sea-Watch*.[122]

Then we have the *European Network Against Racism* pushing the sub-agenda on a European Union level, via its multitude of sub-organisations on the national level. From their "Our members" page of the website: "ENAR is about connecting local and national anti-racist NGOs throughout Europe and bringing their voice forward to bring lasting change at European and national levels. We are a strong and dynamic network of over 150 NGOs working to combat racism everywhere in Europe. Our member organisations are our strength: the bedrock of our expertise and the voice

---

[122] https://www.israaid.org/; https://sea-watch.org/en/

of victims of racism and discrimination throughout Europe".[123] "Anti-racist", eh? These types of NGO's between them—as part of an internationalist Marxist network—help to ferry migrants into Europe, then ensure they are housed/accommodated and receive financial benefits in their destination country, in addition to suppressing any opposition to the process (via 'anti-racism').

The terms such groups use identify them as Marxist. The *Migrant Rights Centre Ireland*, which combines several sub-agendas, states this on the home page: "MRCI is a national organisation working to advance the rights of migrant workers and their families at risk of exploitation, social exclusion and discrimination". Socialism/anti-capitalism, mass immigration and 'anti-racism' combined. Is that "exploitation" the "naked, shameless, direct, brutal" kind described in the Communist Manifesto? (rolls eyes). It also works "with migrants and their families in Ireland to promote justice, empowerment and equality".[124] Yawn.

Note that the organisations mentioned in the following pages do not call themselves "Marxist" or "Communist" (or even the 'nicer' name of "Socialist", in most cases)! A skin-shedding snake…

Irish NGO's

There's a large network of N.G.O.'s in tiny Ireland; an inter-connected web in fact. We won't be delving deep into this, but here are some titbits:

The *Irish Network Against Racism* is a branch of ENAR. According to the "Our members" page on their website, they have approximately 132 member groups in Ireland.[125] They also campaign for legislation against 'hate crime', via their #Lovenothate campaign. Tellingly, this group encourages members of the public to report incidents of racism, using the *iReport.ie* system.

From the iReport.ie page (formatted differently to save space, and underlined for emphasis):

"iReport.ie Racist Incident Reporting System: Enables people who experience or witness racism and/or those supporting them to do something about it and break the silence; national, confidential and user-friendly way to report racism from any online device; used for monitoring racism in Ireland; Provides evidence and data on racism in Ireland; Counters an

---

[123] https://www.enar-eu.org/Members

[124] https://www.mrci.ie/; https://www.mrci.ie/about-us/

[125] https://inar.ie/membership/inar-members/

increase in racism and hardening of racist attitudes; Responds to the need to focus the discussion on finding solutions to racism".[126]

The *Racist Incident Reporting System* bit sounds even funnier if you read it in a robot voice (as I did). As it's a confidential system, this potentially means that an unlimited amount of 'reports' could be received (plenty of brainwashed cult members in Ireland, so I don't think "unlimited" is an exaggeration). Droning robot voice:"re-port on your fel-low ci-ti-zens like a good li-ttle Marxist ro-bot com-rade". Being a rat is noble, of course, if you're a Marxist SJW rat.

Another is the *Immigrant Council of Ireland*. From "Our Values" (formatted to save space): "The values which inform and drive the work of the Immigrant Council are: We are rights based, supporting justice and equality for all; We respect and support the empowerment of migrants and work in solidarity; We embrace and promote diversity and inclusion; Gender equality is central to our work; We work in partnership and collaboration to achieve our goals". [127] So included are the Marxist concepts/interpretations of equality, justice, 'empowerment' of migrants (including political power), solidarity, diversity and inclusion, and feminism.

Comhlamh

Cómhlámh is primarily a volunteering organisation but is involved in other activities too. The word "Comhlamh" is an Irish language (Gaelic) word meaning "together" (aka solidarity). Typical red snake deception— Marxism masquerading as patriotism, all contained in one word! (Irish readers know that using the Irish language is a good way of feigning Irishness in Ireland. This is somewhat unique in western countries, as Ireland is a primarily English-speaking country with its own (essentially) indigenous language spoken by white people. Perhaps the same tactic is used in Scotland (which has its own Gaelic language) and Wales. Non-Irish/Scottish/Welsh readers may not have an equivalent of this type of deception in their own countries).

On their red-soaked website we see the taglines "Action for Global Justice" and "In Global Solidarity". From the "About Us" page: "Comhlámh is a member organisation that works to mobilise for an equitable and sustainable world. As the Irish association of development workers and volunteers, Comhlámh promotes responsible, responsive international

---

[126] https://www.ireport.ie/

[127] https://www.immigrantcouncil.ie/vision-mission

volunteering. We support people in working for social justice. We work with returned volunteers, partner organisations and member groups to foster just, inclusive societies, through progressive grassroots activism in Ireland and internationally".[128] Now look at all those blatantly Marxian keywords, yet the words "Marxism", "socialism" or "communism" are nowhere in sight! This is exactly the kind of shit I'm talking about! Sneaky cult bastards. The uninformed would have no idea that this organisation is part of the international red cult.

The introductory video (on the same page) is called "40 years of Solidarity". After highlighting that most of its work takes places in the southern hemisphere, the voice-over states "but many of the root causes of global inequity, poverty, and oppression, have their origin right here—in the industrialised north... So our real work begins when we come back home". Uh oh... "real work" is code for 'revolution'. Note the usual virtue-signalling dig at capitalism and 'oppressor' Western countries. Obviously, the fact that socialism was a major factor in creating the mess that much of the third world is in is incomprehensible to these people. These volunteer idiots will be coming back to Ireland (or wherever) determined to revolt against the evil bourgeois capitalist system, inspired by the suffering/oppression they saw on their travels.

Other orgs by group

Some other Marxist groups in tiny little Ireland:

Feminist groups: *Irish Feminist Network*; *National Women's Council of Ireland*; *Women's Aid*; *Actionaid*. Many of these organisations spawned from earlier groups like the *Irish Women's Liberation Movement,* which was founded in 1970.[129] (An amusing title—sounds like the many Marxist terrorist groups mentioned elsewhere, does it not? It dramatically insinuates women have been imprisoned (in Marx's words, kinda, "women have nothing to lose but their chains!"). The IWLM published a manifesto called "Chains or Change" and its members went on to form other groups. It's classic Marxian use of the oppressor v oppressed principle).

Climate change groups: *Stop Climate Chaos*; *Climate Ambassador*; *Friends of the Earth*; *Irish Environmental Network*; *Environmental Protection Agency*; *Environmental Pillar*; *Friends of the Irish Environment* (cringe!).

Pro-abortion groups: *Together For Yes*; *Rosa (Reproduction rights, against*

---

[128] https://comhlamh.org/about-us/

[129] https://en.wikipedia.org/wiki/Irish_Women's_Liberation_Movement

Oppression, Sexism & Austerity).

From the "About Rosa" page on the red-bannered *rosa.ie* website: "ROSA is a socialist feminist and pro-choice activist group. ROSA is named after Rosa Parks, the inspirational black campaigner who famously refused to give up her seat for a white passenger, sparking the Montgomery bus boycott of the Civil Rights Movement. And also after Rosa Luxemburg, exceptional and leading socialist theoretician and activist of the early 20th century, killed for her revolutionary politics in 1919".[130]

That says it all really—socialism, feminism, abortion, plus it even manages to squeeze-in some minority rights in the U.S., plus the Jewish Communist and 'martyr' Luxemburg (the patron saint of "Luxemburgism"). This group's website shows us how the ideology makes people do weird things. Essentially, it's a bunch of 'Irish' people being weirdo Marxist cult members, by worshipping many things outside of their own country/culture! That's what the ideology does to people's brains. What on earth has black rights in 1950s America or the attempted Communist takeover of post-WW1 Germany got to do with present day Ireland and young Irish females, Marxist indoctrination aside? Absolutely nothing! Weirdos!

LGBT organisations: *LGBT Ireland*; *Belongto*; *NXF—National LGBT Federation*; *Outhouse LGBT Community Resource Centre*; *Transgender Equality Network Ireland.*

Many of these groups have team photographs or member shots, full of happy, smiling faces. We can see the cult principle in action here. Being a member of a Marxist organisation gives a person a sense of belonging; a sense of warmth and 'love'. Just like being in a cult surrounded by fellow cult members.

---

[130] http://rosa.ie/about/

Section VII—Excuses (Marxist) People Make...

"Antifa is an idea, not an organisation"[1]

> Joe "Patriot" Biden patronising the American people during a presidential debate by suggesting the notorious treasonous cult group doesn't exist, 29 September 2020

Introduction

Now for some common excuses or justifications we will hear from cult members. Since there are many aspects to the ideology, and so many cult members, with so many interpretations, it would take a whole book to list all possible excuses. Therefore, we will focus specifically on 'socialism'/'communism'.

As should be clear by now, there's no point engaging in debate with brainwashed fanatics, but I'll leave that up to the reader's discernment. Not every mind is contaminated/indoctrinated to exactly the same degree. Whether or not a person is to be regarded as a lost-cause, I'll leave up to you. Doing it in order to suppress, or for entertainment or practice purposes, or to ridicule is one thing, but to actually expect them to change is another (most often it's futile). The purpose of this section (and indeed the book itself really) is to highlight the behaviour, which can help us to identify who is indoctrinated—and to what degree—and who isn't. To draw that line in the sand and point the finger at the enemy.

As we move through the list, we should consider the "Theory v Reality" problem—how Marxist/socialist/communist theories don't produce the results that cult members expect in the real world, in reality (whether they can accept this or not, or whether they are aware of it or not).

"The real Communism/Socialism hasn't really been tried yet!"

---

[1] National Review, "Biden Says Antifa Is 'An Idea, Not An Organization' during Presidential Debate", 30 September 2020.
https://www.YouTube.com/watch?v=UaWsYjBOXdg

A variant of this is "Communist countries have never existed! So no, communism or socialism are not failures!". This argument centres around what Karl Marx, Friedrich Engels, and other early 'communists' had envisaged what 'communism' is, in general. In general, they envisaged an egalitarian, classless, moneyless, stateless, atheistic, materialistic, society where the resources, industry and means of production are owned and controlled by the proletariat (workers); the 'community'. A reminder here—socialism is (generally regarded as being) the transitional period in the process towards this Communist utopia. In the short term, in a socialist society, those things listed would not be necessarily achieved (!).

Marx and Engels also believed that the state itself was a form of oppression, so if we are to hold them to their position (and take them at their word!), they would (apparently) disapprove of the various 'socialist' and 'communist' regimes that manifested since their time. This particular point is raised by Marxist apologists often when attempting to counter criticisms of Marxism, but it's irrelevant in the grander scheme of things, as I will explain in the following paragraphs. All of the so-called 'Communist' regimes that ever existed (starting with V.I. Lenin's Bolshevik Soviet Union), did not conform to the above definition/parameters obviously, since they all had a working leadership/state.

They may have claimed to be representative of the people, but they were simply a bunch of 'men' (thugs) at the helm of the country, directing its affairs, which eventually constituted a 'state' (of course, it's now common knowledge the Bolsheviks took control of Russia thanks to help from the outside, financial and otherwise. There was nothing Russian about the 'Russian' revolution. Most of them were Jewish cult member 'revolutionaries' from abroad).

Also, the fact that Lenin's 'Vanguard' were in a position of control, means there was a class system of sorts; a power differential between him and his cronies, and the general public. And there were many other discrepancies. We can view all the other 'communist' and 'socialist' states that existed since Lenin's Soviet Union through the same lens.

So, do these apparent discrepancies between what Marx and Engels et al said, and what actually transpired in those instances, mean that this first Marxist excuse has some validity? No! This excuse ("the real communism/socialism has never been tried") primarily comes from not realising that Marx's and Engels' ideas were just theoretical fantasy. Trying to have an egalitarian, classless, moneyless, stateless, atheistic, materialistic society where the resources, industry and means of production are owned and controlled by the proletariat (workers), the 'community', is not going to work because it is detached from reality and human nature.

Human beings are not equal; there will always be someone in charge as nature itself is built around hierarchies; currency and trade have existed (in one form or another) for millennia; humans need some sort of spirituality or religion; there is more to life than materialism, and human beings are not robotic commodities or worker bees; the community cannot have collective ownership of things, because that's not how ownership works (see the earlier section on socialism). Obviously, people who give this first excuse can't see all that.

Slippery slope and power vacuum

The idea of a classless, stateless society is just a fantasy because there will always be someone/some group at the helm. Hierarchies have been a feature of human existence since the beginning. Whatever the original intentions of all those Marxists who participated in all those successful 'Communist' revolutions (and subsequent regimes) throughout the 20th century, inevitably, the reality sets in later. Revolution can be a slippery slope; one thing leads to another. A power vacuum is created by overthrowing the establishment, and it matters not your original intentions: when you tear-down the existing system, something/someone is going to take its place. You end up with a power structure again (the beginnings of a new state), even if it's a Marxist 'revolutionary vanguard'.

There are many other reasons why the genuine, original idea of communism is flawed. Whatever Marx or Engels envisaged, or what Lenin thought of what Marx said etc., does not matter at this point (in the present day). It must be re-iterated, that in all cases where the theories of Marx, Engels, and early Communists were put in to practice, it resulted in disaster and the breakdown of society, sooner or later. The central tenets of 'class struggle', collectivisation and 'communal ownership', egalitarianism (via coercion!), the elimination of religious beliefs etc., all produce destruction to one degree or another. Again, the theories themselves are failures.

Bottom line

We're not going too in-depth to the counter to this excuse here, as it's repeating what's highlighted elsewhere (e.g. the implementation of socialism; how equality is destructive; about power and hierarchies etc.). However, this is essentially the main point—the apologists will compare Marx's and Engel's vision for communism to all of those so-called socialist or communist regimes and will say "that wasn't real communism". Compared to what Marx and Engels envisaged, in a sense, they are correct; but you know what? It. Does. Not. Matter! Who cares what they envisaged?!

The theoretical fantasies of Marx, Engels, Lenin etc. have no place in the real word. So overall point is—even their concepts of communism or socialism are still useless to society in any practical way. The Marxists/apologists will insist we hang on to them, as they have some value. Wrong! Besides, the hypothetical value of these concepts (according to Marxists) is outweighed by their actual destructive impact in the real world today (as this book shows).

A key point: of course, no regime or form of state organisation (called by the label 'socialist' or 'communist' or anything else) could ever match what Marx and Engels envisaged! Therefore, what they called communism can never materialise in the real world, and cult members will keep insisting that it needs to be tried. It's a destructive, perpetual cycle of hypothetical theory leading to non-materialisation. This is why we are constantly stuck in a never-ending debate with this cult (while they actively destroy civilisation). This cycle must be broken, or we may all just forget about any sort of respite from the madness; never mind lasting freedom!

This first excuse is an important, often used one. It's the universal, "get-out-of-jail-free" card, eternal excuse we hear from them, time and time again; it's constantly used to justify keeping this toxic ideology in our societies. They will be happy for it to be tried a million different ways, regardless of the destruction it causes, as the utopia is always just around the corner! And you know what? No matter how many times it fails, these intellectualising idiots will still use the same excuse (see "Theory v Reality" problem). Never-ending.

"They were just dictators. They weren't real Marxists/Socialist/Communists!"

This is used by cult members (wittingly or unwittingly) to attempt to distance themselves from the many Marxism-inspired, horrific, dictatorial regimes throughout the 20th century. It's PR damage control. Even if this excuse was 100% true and not up for debate in all the "socialist" or "communist" regimes; once again, it's irrelevant!

The main point here is that the ideology itself helped these people get in to power, because others mistakenly thought it was benevolent and that they were helping a fellow 'comrade' to do a myriad of wonderful things for the benefit of 'the people'. Then these dominant characters assume power, with a leader, atop a hierarchy. It doesn't matter if they precisely implemented Marxian theories or not (according to Marx's, Engel's, Lenin's etc. wishes); the ideology itself is what started and/or perpetuated the 'revolution', regime, and subsequent destructive process.

Of course, where cult members are concerned, there's a lack of understanding of what Marxism-inspired revolutions really are, and what they lead to. When the power vacuum I described is created by the 'revolution', it will inevitably attract power-hungry control freaks/psychopaths. These personality types may have been part of the instigating forces of the revolution, or they emerge at a later point to take the reins.

When a contaminated society starts to collapse, there will be chaos and violent upheaval. The psychopaths revel in this process: their lack of empathy to the commonplace suffering allows them to remain comfortable, calm. At an opportune time, they will take the reins, and no-one will be able to stop them. Since the 'revolution' is inspired by Marxism, and instigated by cult members, inevitably, once they gain the upper hand, they will start to implement Marxian principles including: forced egalitarianism through coercion (especially violence), collectivism, centralisation of power on behalf of 'the people', elimination of political opposition, incarceration or liquidation of dissenters etc. Of course, the cult members surrounding them will not object (!).

Once this centralisation of power happens, the more brutish and ruthless personality types come to the fore (e.g. Stalin, Pol Pot etc.), and the more extreme Marxists will be put in key positions to compliment the central leadership. In short, having a centralised system like this is extremely risky while we have a little-discussed and critically important issue in our world—the presence of psycho control freaks!

The apologists try to distance themselves from all those dictatorial regimes by compartmentalising the whole cult movement: 'Stalinism', 'Maoism', 'Castroism' etc. They either can't see (or are in denial of) the fact that the original causal factor was the ideology itself. Without an acceptance of the ideology, these dictatorships would not have emerged. One man is nothing if his ideas are not accepted as good, or if the ideas are viewed as toxic.

Sure, many of these 'people's' revolutions were often encouraged by external parties, but the point still stands: without any sort of support for the ideology (and ideally a hostility towards it!), these 'revolutions' would not have been able to do the damage they did (with "external parties" I'm not just referring to the numerous revolutions in Africa and South America, for example, that were supported by Russia, China, Cuba etc. I'm referring to how Lenin and Trotsky's Bolshevik revolution may have been funded by non-Russia parties, including the international bankers. Same goes for Mao.).

I think if Marx himself had the power to implement his theories during his lifetime, that would have settled a lot of these debates before they could even arise. And that goes for the other Marxist theorists too. Judging from his rotten, conceited personality, I think Marx would have been as evil as any of the other nuts in the commie hall of fame; perhaps worse.

"Many people have socialist values"

Another way of saying this is "Don't you want a more equal, humanitarian society and a better standard of living?!?". Which boils down to "don't you want a better world/life?!?". (Note: "you want"—back to the ego again! Just because we want something, doesn't mean we can have it—the world/life/reality does not revolve around our egos! It's also virtue-signalling coercion: "Are you not a good person? Don't you care about other people?!?").

These types of statements, again, come from a distorted perception of what Marxism is. It's not a humanitarian movement—it's a pseudo-humanitarian movement. Just because a person (of any stripe, politically or otherwise) happens to believe in certain principles or has certain wishes for society, doesn't equate to meaning that Marxism/socialism are good! Reality doesn't work that way.

Obviously, anyone who makes that statement is making major assumptions. Are they correct though? Of course, any rational person wants a better quality of life for themselves and their folk and would be happy to see things run more efficiently in their countries! Of course, people love to be told that they can get things for free (wealth, services, property etc.); even many wealthy people—who may not be wanting of anything materially— just love to hear this!

Some of the assumptions might just be coming from the indoctrination itself though. They assume that everyone does (or should) think the way they do, since they're obviously right (aside from any evil 'right-wingers', 'racists' and 'fascists', of course). For example, we know that the cult is, in general, in favour of a world-without-borders. Trying to say that everyone wants to go along with that is a massive assumption to make. Another assumption they might make is that all of us believe we should take money off the rich and distribute the wealth more equally. Another is that we all believe in the ideas of 'social justice'—that there's a serious problem with 'oppression' in the world.

Marxism seems to sound lovely and humanitarian, for the 'greater good' and for the benefit of the downtrodden, but it isn't, and non-cult members can see that. The indoctrinated ones, however, believe that it is benevolent. In their mind—due to arrogance and ignorance—they believe they have the solution, and everyone else needs to catch on, and be 'with it' and 'woke', just like them. That's how they can imply that "everybody agrees with socialism really, on some level" etc. Their thought process goes like this: Marxism and socialism = good. Marxian concepts and perspectives =

humanitarian, nice, progressive, positive etc. Ergo, others naturally should agree.

Again, the 'ol "See? You're already a Marxist and you didn't even realise it!" trick. I think if the average person in the street fully understood what Marxist socialist 'values' mean in practice, they would acknowledge that they're mistaken (at whatever depth of their being they held those values).

Bottom line—so what if people are holding values that can be interpreted as being socialist? So what? Doesn't mean they are correct to do so; doesn't mean we should now embrace socialism! Another point is that the ideology is very good at hijacking genuine, honest grievances the masses have and co-opting them into the agenda for its own ends. What cult members are suggesting (by saying "everyone has socialist values deep down") is that the fact that these grievances merely exist justifies the existence of the ideology, since the ideology (naturally) provides the solutions to them. This is nonsense! We don't need Marxism as a solution to anything!

In addition, of course there will be lots of people walking around in society with Marxian ideas in their heads (such as socialism), as the Marxist rot has permeated throughout our societies. In today's world, saying that many people have socialist ideas in their heads is like saying many cows think about eating grass.

"It hasn't succeeded because there's been too much right-wing thinking!

Variant 1: "communism/socialism/Marxism has failed because we've had too much right-wing thinking!". Variant 2: "Socialism has failed because we've had too much right-wing thinking, and therefore we have never been able to reach communism! And if we continue to have too much of it, we probably never will!". Let me say that again—Marxism/socialism has never succeeded because there has been…wait for it: too much right-wing thinking! Another classic! Well, how-fucking-convenient! This is like blaming the other teams because you've lost the matches (many times in a row). Over the years I've personally interacted, face-to-face, with say 15–20 brainwashed university students who've handed me this one.

Again, this excuse comes from a distorted perception of the truth—believing that Marxism/socialism is good (and it isn't); the point of view that Marxism is a fantastic, benign thing, and that it's failures must be due to all sorts of reasons, other than the only one that matters (i.e. the ideology itself is toxic and a failure by its very nature). This excuse is deeply embedded in the indoctrination.

Those who utter this justification are convinced that Marxian principles (including socialism, equality, 'social justice', 'anti-racism' etc.) are the way forward for society. Therefore, it's totally inconceivable that the ideology is not more popular because: these principles are flawed, and/or that the masses start to reject the ideology when they can see how toxic it is in practice. Hence, there must be some other reason why Marxism is not 100% universally accepted, and the world is not full of Marxist cult members (just like them). The result is that the 'right-wing' scapegoat is wheeled out.

Interestingly, this argument is the opposite of the actual truth of the matter. It's based on the presumption that Marxism/socialism/communism is capable of improving/liberating/freeing society etc., while also insinuating that 'right-wing' thinking is stopping this process. This is backwards. It's clear that Marxism is what's preventing those things from materialising, and that 'right-wing' thinking can make them materialise (at an individual, social, national, and global level). We reach this conclusion when we look at world affairs and see that Marxism is the dominant ideology in the world today (a fact invisible to most due to the reality-distorting effects of the indoctrination).

I suppose if you think something is good, and you are absolutely convinced about it, then you will do all sorts of mental gymnastics rather than consider the possibility that it's simply a failure unto itself. This justification is also typical of how the ideology operates: it will take every opportunity (via the cult member's 'minds') to spear its ideological rival—right-wing thought—while simultaneously deflecting from the fact that it's a toxic failure of an ideology. It's also petty, which is another typical attribute of the cult.

Finally, in a sense, the excuse is accurate—it's true that Marxism has not succeeded—as in, does not have complete control over the world yet—since there are too many people with 'right-wing' (non-Marxist) stances. For humanity's sake, this is good. Let's keep it that way, shall we?

"Anti-Marxist/socialist attitudes stem from having a fascist mentality"

We don't need to do a deep analysis of Marxism v fascism for this phrase, and it's linked to the previous item. It can be translated as: "If you don't agree with me/us, you're obviously wrong, there must be something wrong with you, and you're probably insane and evil"!".

This type of response is familiar, isn't it? It appears throughout the history of the cult. It's a very lazy, immature response to criticism. Again, it comes from the erroneous fanatical belief that Marxism is benevolent, ergo, any opponent of it must be evil.

When they say 'fascist' they mean authoritarian, aggressive and not representing 'the people' (which Marxism ostensibly is, right?), in addition to being unethical (xenophobic, not 'progressive', not 'compassionate' etc.), with backward 'racist' nationalistic ideas of ethnic homogeneity etc. Essentially, 'fascist' = bad, and the Marxist ideology/cult = good.

There is a much deeper, more interesting reason why we hear this phrase being dished out. Essentially, the justification shows us that fascism and Marxism are ideological opponents (expanded upon in a later section about 'right' v 'left'). Those who utter this one are really saying "If you don't agree with Marxism you must be a horrible, imperialistic, war-mongering, xenophobic, white-supremacist, coz that's what fascists are!".

"Some of our greatest patriots were socialists, or had socialist ideas"

Even if that's completely true, so? So what? Human beings are fallible. And besides, what has that got to do with now? Just because someone has been attracted to, or espoused, Marxian socialist ideas doesn't mean that we should too. People can be mistaken! This applies even more so to those in the past. Why? Because the ideology is not what it was when Marx was still alive, or at the dawn of the 20th century. It's not what it was 100 years ago. It has evolved in its variations. It has saturated the societies of the world to the core, as it has penetrated deep into the minds of the unsuspecting.

This particular phrase/mindset is often wheeled-out in Ireland in debates over the cause for Irish freedom and the role of socialism; James Connolly (1868–1916) promoted it in the late 18th/early 19th century. He wasn't the only pro-socialism voice in this period, but certainly a prominent one. He was highly active in the labour union movement and established several socialist groups/pre-cursor groups (including the Irish Labour Party, which still exists today). Most significantly, in terms of his notoriety, he also participated in the Easter Rising of 1916 as Commandant of the Dublin Brigade and was executed afterwards. Connolly was born and raised in Scotland by Irish parents but came to Ireland to push socialism and help the anti-Imperial anti-British revolution.[2]

Considering the state of affairs in Ireland during Connolly's lifetime (being under British rule), it was understandable that the ideology would enter the picture as an alternative. We can therefore understand and forgive anyone, to a degree, who pushed in that direction—if they had genuinely good intentions and were not simply a subversive cult member masquerading as an Irish 'patriot' (note: Ireland was like the multitude of other countries in

---

[2] https://www.britannica.com/biography/James-Connolly

the world during this period, being under the control of a foreign imperial power. Considering the tables in the historical section, the Easter Rising of 1916 is consistent with the worldwide spread of the ideology).

Idolisation can be bad; particularly of someone who existed in a different time (or age!). A person may be right somewhat and have good intentions, but we must also consider that their opinions may be more appropriate for their time, not ours. James Connolly was shot on the 12 May 1916, the year before the Russian revolution—a major milestone in the spread of the ideology. He was in no position to understand what socialism really was, or what it would lead to!

With hindsight, we have the benefit of learning from over a century of Marxist failures, in addition to the access to information that our technology provides, to give us a superior understanding. It must be added that participating in a revolution/military uprising and getting yourself shot doesn't make you omniscient! We shouldn't idolise anyone who doesn't understand the ideology fully. Again, we must place the opinions of historical figures in their correct context of time and place.

In our current predicament (a high level of global infection), it's counter-productive to idolise anyone who assisted the spread of Marxism, even if they were right about some things and had good intentions, good intelligence etc., as it only serves the ideology/cult.

On a global scale, the cult will, predictably, emphasise characters like this and use them to attach themselves to legitimate patriotic causes today (by wheeling out "some of our greatest patriots were socialists" etc.). Or, in the case of Ireland, they don't need to—others (non-cult members) are already doing this for them. It's downright foolish and suicidal to help them! Many countries have their equivalents to Connolly, so I would recommend you take a similar approach towards them/their legacy. They won't be offended, don't worry—they're dead! Bottom line—who cares if past figures thought the ideology was benevolent. In this world we have today, it is anything but. So, any historical approvals of it are irrelevant, regardless of their origins. This excuse is another fail.

"If you're against socialism you're supporting the capitalist bourgeoisie!"

What does this even mean? Who are these bourgeoisie anyway? Rich people in general? The political elites? The wealthy corporate, business types and landowners that cult members love to jabber on about? This one can be quite nebulous, so I will take the definition of capitalist bourgeoisie to mean those who are extremely wealthy and who (apparently) wield tremendous power in society, and who abuse their position of power and influence.

This is a classic Marxist comeback. They're programmed to react in this way. They think this because, remember, they believe that they are the good guys, the rebels, the 'radicals' etc. If you oppose them, you are naturally on the wrong side, right? Obviously, if you are criticising Marxism, you must be a little subservient lackey for the capitalist bourgeoisie oligarchs, right? No, not necessarily. Perhaps we are criticizing Marxism because we know it's a step in the wrong direction (they erroneously believe the opposite), while simultaneously being opposed to the globalist 'elites'. There is nuance here. We—those who are opposed to the ideology/cult—know that the issues (real or perceived) present in a capitalist system can be resolved other ways, without needing to turn to Marxist ideas. Maybe we would like to throw Marxism (and its derivatives) in the trash because it's more trouble than it's worth? (sarcastic, rhetorical question).

This is the upside-down (inverted) logic of your garden variety Marxist: if you oppose them, you must obviously be serving the bourgeoisie globalist elites, when cult members are, in fact, serving them/internationalist totalitarianism. To use the author as an example—there ain't nobody on Earth more opposed to these 'elites' and internationalist totalitarianism, yet I understand that the Marxist cult/ideology is the enemy too, as they serve that agenda, wittingly or unwittingly. There are many who think the same way, so this comeback is a fail with a capital F.

"We need Marxism/Socialism to stop the oppressive evils of Capitalism!"

No, we don't! I have expanded on the economic/anti-capitalist justifications for Marxism/socialism in a different section. For now, the short answer to this one is: Marxism has never had any merits or benefits economically; it's a failure in many ways, but especially economically; the minute a country allows Marxist theories to be implemented economically, disaster looms. So, the idea that we somehow need the ideology (via socialism) to maintain alternative views on economic matters nationally or internationally is just more propaganda.

Again, the solution to many of the problems (perceived or otherwise) in our countries involving capitalism—economics, employment, trade etc.— is to have a Marxism-free, sovereign, genuinely patriotic state. Marxism is anti-patriotism, being antagonistic to prosperity (the cult will advertise the opposite naturally). How can anything that destroys a country's prosperity be considered patriotic? No, the ideology (via socialism) is not the answer since it would only make matters worse.

Final words

This section covering some excuses is not comprehensive, nor is it intended to be. Your garden-variety Marxist 'intellectual' could keep you debating almost endlessly on just one of those sub-topics. This cult thrives on never-ending debate! Let's not waste time engaging with them! The purpose of this section is to help to identify the indoctrination in others, via their behaviour/speech.

Remember, we could literally have books full of all the excuses and justifications that cult members come up with, and they would still come up with more. As long as they have breath in their lungs or fingers to type, they would keep churning them out, like their lives depended on it. That's the existence of a cult member—constant justification of their existence and persistent promotion and defence of their cult and ideology.

Section VIII — The Scarlet Formula

"If you know the enemy and know yourself, you need not fear the result of a hundred battles. If you know yourself but not the enemy, for every victory gained you will also suffer a defeat. If you know neither the enemy nor yourself, you will succumb in every battle"[1]

Sun Tzu, *The Art of War*, 5th century BC

Introduction

The cult uses a variety of tactics while initiating its civilisation-destroying 'revolution'. Some have been part of the ideology since its earlier manifestations, while others are the handiwork of the Frankfurt School, the postmodernist brigade or agitators/manipulators like Saul Alinsky. These include: the control of language; controlling/distorting our perception of history, reality and morality; using emotional manipulation tactics; introducing insane double-standards; using the very effective oppressor vs oppressed formula, as a divide-and-conquer tactic; promoting Marxist fanaticism; and encouraging pro-Marxist cult-like insane behaviours within societies including 'political-correctness' (an old favourite), virtue-signalling and the extremely dangerous pathological altruism.

How to speak Marxist

The cult's/ideology's control of speech is an extremely serious matter being absolutely crucial for its dominance; therefore, this section will be somewhat comprehensive. The following key terms are organised into tables. Some we hear daily and are often repeated by cult members, ad nauseam, to promote the ideology (e.g. solidarity, progressive etc.). Others are (tactically) offensive terms used to engage the cult's enemies (e.g. far-right, 'fascists', 'Nazis' etc.), in order to demoralise, ostracize, and convince the 'neutrals' in society to shun them.

The reader should pay attention to the patterns, so we don't miss the forest for the trees. There's a multitude of terms, which can almost be distractionary, but what's important is the strategic goal behind their use.

---

[1] Sun Tzu, *The Art of War*, circa 5th century BC.
https://www.utoledo.edu/rotc/pdfs/the_art_of_war.pdf

As in, what are they really insinuating when these terms are used, and what are they really trying to achieve. As a simple example, the terms "homophobe", "transphobe" etc., are designed to attack/suppress anyone who is opposed to the relevant Marxian sub-agenda in this area: the promotion/normalisation of LGBTQ and 'gender non-binary' issues and behaviour, etc. These terms insinuate that the person is a hate-filled person or is afraid of something. From the Cambridge online dictionary: "Phobe—Someone who hates or has a fear or something, especially in a way that is extreme or not reasonable".[2]

The use of the word "phobe" from the Greek "Phobos", evokes the notion of fear (in Greek mythology, Phobos was the God of this emotion). It implies that the target/person being labelled is essentially a coward. This is typical Marxist ridicule-and-con language. They insinuate that you are the one with the problem if you don't agree with them. In this case, the implication is that you are either consciously or subconsciously afraid of those in a particular group (LGBTQ people etc.) and your fear is manifesting in unjustifiable hatred, judgement etc.

Using "phobe" also implies a phobia—an irrational fear of something. Or that you are afraid of change in society (aka anything 'progressive'). The cult implies all that just by using those five letters and sticking them to the end of various words! The new words are then used as a weapon to ridicule any dissenters while simultaneously promoting the sub-agenda in question (in this example—the LGBTQ movement and non-binary nonsense).

As we go through the tables, note how they have a term for virtually every single possible form of threat (i.e. anyone who objects to a Marxian sub-agenda or the cult/ideology itself). In the spirit and tradition of the ideology, the terms cover a diverse range of subject areas, including politics, sexuality, religion, science, racism, sexism, antisemitism, vaccines, conspiracies etc.

We must remember Saul Alinsky's fifth rule here: "Ridicule is man's most potent weapon. There is no defence. It is almost impossible to counterattack ridicule. Also it infuriates the opposition, who then react to your advantage". Naturally, all the pejorative terms the cult uses involve ridicule. You could also say that some of Alinsky's other rules come in to play here too, such as rule six — "A good tactic is one your people enjoy". The fact that cult members will enjoy being in a pack and use these types of terms to ridicule their opponents is symbolic of how Marxism brings out the worst in humanity: a bunch of mentally ill anti-humanity sub-human

---

[2] https://dictionary.cambridge.org/dictionary/english/phobe

fanatics mocking their fellow humans as they betray them (!).

This all explains the constant labelling and bitching from cult members about those who oppose them/the ideology. They're trying to silence their opponents with ridicule to achieve ideological dominance. The effect on society is that the Marxian perspective on things becomes the norm, due to the emotional manipulation that ridicule allows. This then leads to what is called 'political correctness', which is really just code for 'the Marxian perspective'. It forces the masses to conform to the ideology's/cult's whims and sub-agendas, through socio-psychological pressure. The result is that the ideology/cult becomes ever-more dominant. It's intimidation; it's terrorism.

Let's use a non-personal issue as an example—the subject of 'climate change'—in a particular society: if everyone who publicly expresses a lack of belief in 'climate change' (that human behaviour is affecting the weather; that the planet is 'in danger!' due to pollution etc.) are constantly ridiculed by the majority until there are no such opinions being expressed, then a new Marxist norm is created, where the only opinions being expressed are supportive of the climate change con.

It's the enforcement of equality and uniformity (of opinions), using emotional manipulation, via ridicule. The term used to ridicule the 'deniers' is the amusingly unimaginative "climate change denier". On the Covid issue, they have invented the terms "Covidiots" and "vaccine hesitancy" for those refusing to go along with this sub-agenda.

Despite the fact, of course, that trying to achieve this level of control over a population is impossible and absolutely stupid, it's never stopped the cult from trying! Indeed, they've always found a way of creating the illusion of these things, by neutralising/liquidating those who didn't conform. This then makes it seem that everyone agrees with the cult, since everyone else has been silenced through imprisonment, death, exile etc. The few who are spared are intimidated into silence. Thus, the new 'norm' is that everyone agrees with the wondrous 'people's' revolution! We see this being played out in North Korea and China today.

Other terms are used to feign benevolence, which is part of the Red Trojan Horse principle, essential for the cult in maintaining that seemingly positive veneer of 'progressiveness'. An example of that is when they say that abortion is 'compassion' for women, or when they call abortion services 'care' or 'healthcare'.

Commie sticks and stones: Marxist "insults" and other terms

The insult	Marxist meaning	Actual meaning	Intended effect
Far-Right/ Nazi/Fascist	Person who is Xenophobic/racist, hate-filled, authoritarian, uncompassionate, evil etc.	One who isn't Marxist, or objects to Marxian sub-agendas, especially nationalists/right-wingers/genuine patriots.	They're viewed as troublemakers who should be shunned, abused, and stripped of their rights, including free speech.
Reactionary	Person who is not progressive, or who opposes progressivism. Their beliefs are outdated and have no place in the modern world.	One who opposes the cult/ideology, with beliefs that are usually traditionalist, conservative, right-wing etc.	They/their views are ignored, treated as being backward, outdated, associated with oppressive, 'primitive' concepts like religion etc.
Racist	Person who fears/hates other races; who doesn't believe all races are equal; may believe their race is superior to other races.	One who doesn't agree with the 'diversity'/ 'multiculturalism'/ mass migration sub-agendas.	They are viewed as narrow-minded, backward, uncompassionate, immoral bigots.
White Supremacist	A racist who thinks that white people/groups are racially superior to other races (e.g. black, native American, aboriginal etc.). They don't believe in the idea of 'racial equality'.	One who believes that white people/cultures should be celebrated and preserved (as much as other races are); who may believe that whites have contributed more to the development of civilisation.	They are viewed as evil, racist, oppressive, possibly imperialistic types who believe the white race should oppress other races (like the Nazis, European empires etc.).
Misogynist	A male who hates/oppresses	Male who does not agree with	These males will be ostracized by

	women and doesn't believe in gender equality; someone who is wittingly/unwittingly part of the 'patriarchy'.	feminism, or who criticises females (particularly indoctrinated females).	society in general, especially females. Criticism of feminism will be ignored.
Islamophobe	Person who fears/hates Islam/Muslims, due to racism or religious bigotry (usually Christians with bigoted religious supremacist views). Their attitude is related to racism.	One who criticises Islam/Muslims; who doesn't agree with the 'Islamification' of western, non-Islamic countries; or its promotion at the expense of their own religion.	Criticism of Islam/Muslims is ignored. The anti-Christian/Pro-Islam agenda in Western countries is ignored. The mass immigration sub-agenda is benefitted.
Homophobe	A backward person who fears/hates gays/lesbians, perhaps due to oppressed gay feelings, religious indoctrination, or ignorance etc.	One who criticises homosexuals/homosexuality or objects to the promotion/normalisation of homosexuality (particularly where the young are concerned).	Any criticism of gays/homosexuality, or the promotion of sub-agendas involving this in society is ignored. Gender non-binary nonsense also goes unopposed.
Transphobe	Person who fears/hates trans people, and/or thinks there are only two genders. Usually a person with dogmatic religious views.	One who criticises 'trans' people/the trans movement, or objects to the promotion/normalisation of transgenderism (especially to the young).	Any criticism of the 'trans' movement/'trans' people is ignored. The gender-nonbinary nonsense benefits and continues unopposed.
Xenophobe	Person who fears/hates anyone different to them.	One who has objections to any sub-agenda involving ethnicity,	This term covers the rest of the bases. Used when other terms won't

		nationality, creed, culture etc.	do the job.
Conspiracy Theorist	A gullible, paranoid, tin-foil hat-wearing idiot who believes in stupid things they read or saw on the internet (e.g. 'climate change deniers', holocaust deniers, 'Covidiots' etc.).	One who doubts the official explanation for things; who is sceptical of official narratives peddled by authorities/govern ment.; who doesn't believe the 'pc' Marxist narrative.	They're ignored and regarded as gullible fools. Discourages others from doubting official state- approved narratives. Encourages people to simply believe what they're told (by the cult).
Climate Change Denier (climate denier)	An idiot conspiracy theorist who doesn't believe human behaviour creates climate change; who thinks they know better than climate experts; someone who doesn't care about the planet, and is against 'green' energy etc.	One who doubts the official narrative on this subject (including the 'opinions' of 'experts'); who doesn't believe human behaviour makes the climate change.	Any doubters/disbelieve rs of the 'climate change' narrative are ignored and ridiculed as ignorant, unscientific idiots. This helps create a society where the norm is to believe the con.
Anti-Vaxxer	Another type of irresponsible, paranoid conspiracy theorist, who thinks Bill Gates wants to inject them with a tracking device; someone who dismisses centuries of scientific knowledge etc.	One who doesn't support the 'vaccine' sub- agenda; who doesn't want to submit to authorities while poisoning themselves via these unnecessary 'vaccines'.	These views are regarded as 'dangerous', and must be suppressed, ignored, ridiculed etc.; they are also ostracised (potentially) on health grounds.

Emotional blackmail

On a deeper level, these terms of ridicule are a form of emotional blackmail, in the most insidious way. In fact, it's a threat. We all, as human beings (unless we are damaged somehow psychologically) enjoy or crave respect, admiration, acceptance, affection, love etc., for at least some of our lives. The opposite to those is hate, disrespect, being abhorred, ostracization or isolation etc.; things which no-one in their right mind craves from others or for themselves.

It's for this reason that pejorative terms (racist, fascist, conspiracy theorist etc.) are very effective weapons used by the cult within the Marxism-riddled system. The message for persons labelled as such is "if you understand the system and are trying to share your understanding, you will not get any admiration/respect/love from other human beings, and you will suffer". Or "if you continue to criticize the cult/ideology/system, you will suffer". "Conspiracy theorist", for example, is a very evil manipulation of the above universal tendency we have as human beings, and of the reality of human existence. In short, the threat is—you will not be accepted by the collective if you express certain non-Marxian opinions or engage in certain behaviours.

Climate change denier (or climate denier)

This one is probably the most childish on the list. It's based on the old classic — "Holocaust-denier". If you doubt the official, government-approved explanation for something—as in, you believe that lies are being told about a particular subject—this term is used to counter your argument. It's used to silence any doubt; to stop any further investigation; to cover-up things.

So, if you don't believe in 'climate change' (i.e. that human behaviour, pollution, CO2 levels etc. are affecting the weather patterns or increasing global temperatures significantly), then this term insinuates that you are in denial about this unquestionable, (apparently) universally accepted truth. Not only that, but you are insane for doing so (the ol' "if you don't agree with us, you are crazy!" trick), which we can see in the use of 'denier'/'denial'. It insinuates that you are detached from reality and are therefore crazy.

It's also an inversive term, since it insinuates this person doesn't care about the planet, which is the opposite of the truth—anyone who opposes Marxism/Marxist sub-agendas clearly does (while cult members are wittingly/unwittingly actively destroying the planet and humanity). In addition, by them insinuating that you—the target (of the term)—are crazy when actually you're the sane one is also inversive.

Intended effect: a new 'revolutionary' class system

The "Intended effect" column in the table shows how the cult is creating, ironically, a new type of class system. Individuals who are categorized as being in this column are to be shunned, ostracized, destroyed, incarcerated, exterminated etc. Of course, this class of people deserve this kind of treatment because they're evil anyway, right? They are to be treated as second-class citizens (if they are lucky). Ironically, they will become the new (genuinely) oppressed class, which is, again, a type of inversion (and hypocrisy!).

It's about putting the superior minds/personality types in society in an inferior position with no basic rights, never mind power/influence of any sort (which leads to the dominance of the ideology and the breakdown of civilisation). The cult has always eliminated the 'intelligentsia' throughout its history.

The ideology convinces its adherents that it's a noble endeavour to create a revolution, where, amongst other things, the traditional class systems are abolished. Not only is this irrational and destructive, it's also hypocritical (in that unique, Marxist sort of way). The cult/ideology has always sought to create a new class system, with itself in the dominant position, using all the weapons at its disposal. For decades now, they have been striving to have anyone who does not conform to the Globalist's plans as second-class citizens. Which is not equality! Remember their travel bans on those who didn't get the 'vaccines', and those whose livelihoods were destroyed through job loss etc.

Nazis, Fascists, and 'Far-Right'

The use of terms like Nazi/fascist/far-right are absolutely crucial to stamp out any opposition to Marxism the moment that it appears in society. They dish these labels out like their lives depends on it. The cult has been using this tactic since the birth of fascism in the post WW1 period (note: this might confuse some, who may believe that fascism and Nazism ('National Socialism') are forms of Marxism, but this is a common erroneous, distorted perception that benefits the cult/ideology. They are not the same (again, covered later).

"Nazi"

The word "Nazi" of course, comes from the National Socialist movement in Germany during the 1920s until the end of WW2. The party led by Adolf Hitler was the *Nationalsozialistiche Deutsche Arbeiterpartei* (NSDAP) or *National Socialist German Workers' Party*.[3] The term "Nazi" emerged as a

---

[3] https://www.britannica.com/topic/Nazi-Party

derogatory term to describe this movement. A while back, Nazi used to mean "control freak", comparing a controlling person to the Nazis of Germany during the Hitler era. Now, "Nazi" means anyone who is a conservative, nationalist, patriotic etc.; basically, anyone who doesn't comply with or opposes the cult/ideology/its sub-agendas. It's like someone flicked a (red) switch, and the meaning for that word changed. Now, the Marxists are clearly the control-freaks, and yet they are calling everyone else Nazis; it's funny. So, the word Nazi—which used to mean "control freak"—is now coming from the control freaks and is used as a way of controlling any resistance to the real control freaks—the Marxists. What is this insane shit? It's more hypocrisy/double-standards.

So essentially "Nazi" used to mean "control freak", but now it means (if we look at those who the Marxists give this label to) "someone who doesn't want to be controlled by Marxists". In this context, actually, it's a great compliment, but the cult members are too dumb/brainwashed to grasp this of course. We'll give everyone else a pass, as this truth is not widely understood yet.

"Fascist"

A very important, revealing term, extremely valuable to the cult, so we will devote some time to it. The vast majority of people (could be eighty or even ninety percent) who use this word all over the world every day have no idea what it really means, or where it comes from. Nor do they understand the true significance of it in terms of combating the cult/ideology. The increasing dominance of the cult/ideology in western civilisation since the 19th century has conditioned the masses to perceive this word in a certain way. It generally evokes thoughts of dangerous ultra-nationalism, warmongering, pro-bourgeoisie authoritarianism, racism/xenophobia, brutal oppression of certain groups etc.

The last few decades in particular (as the cult is now numerous/strong enough to be more open and vocal), have seen an increase in the use of this word as part of the ridicule tactic. It's used to suppress ideological opposition before it has a chance to form. It's also linked to the virtue-signalling, hypocritical aspect of the cult: they label their enemies as "fascists" because it has evil connotations, and they want to appear to be the benign, virtuous saviours. When they are calling people "fascists", they are really saying "don't listen to them, they are evil; listen to us, we are good". Juvenile.

The evilness of "Nazi" and "Fascist"

The evil connotations these terms have come from association with the beliefs/ideology   and   actions   taken   by   certain   types   of individuals/regimes/groups in the past: most notably starting with the rise of fascism in Italy under Benito Mussolini and the rise of National Socialism in Germany under Adolf Hitler (both during the inter-war period). Other notable historical figures described as 'fascists' by the cult, to name a few, were Generalissimo Francisco Franco in Spain after the Spanish Civil War; Augusto Pinochet in Chile during the 1970s and 1980s; and Antonio Salazar in Portugal from the 1930s to the late 1960s. We are constantly reminded that these men were evil dictators, perhaps the evillest kind. Hence association with those leaders and their movements is an association with evil itself, which has made the term 'fascist' so effective. Interestingly, despite the amount and impact of Marxist dictators in the 20th century, they are not placed in the same category of the so-called Fascist leaders overall.

Etymology of "Fascist"

The English term "fascist" comes from the Italian "fascismo", itself coming from "fascio" ("league") or "fasces" meaning "bundle of rods or sticks". This had earlier origins in the "Fascio Littorio" of the Roman empire era (latin: "Fascis", and "Fascia"), as a weapon and symbol of authority. [4] Benito Mussolini's pioneer 'fascist' movement chose these Fasces as a symbol of strength and authority. In 1919, this symbol led him to create an organisation called *Fasci Italiani di Combattimento* or *Italian Fasces of Combat*. This was succeeded by the *Partito Nazionale Fascista* or *National Fascist Party* (which ruled until the fascist government collapsed in 1943). [5] So, nothing evil in the word "fascist" itself or its origins, but in the connotations evoked, and associations with those figures in the past. Of course, the perspective that this word is evil is coming largely from a Marxism-influenced partisan perspective.

Non-cult members using it

The ideology's influence can even affect how non-cult members talk. Even when a person is generally being a genuine patriot or nationalist (choose your label), they can still talk like cult members, and use some of their terms. This is just one of the countless signs of how well-entrenched Marxist indoctrination is. For example, the word "fascist" is often used to describe totalitarian behaviour, including 'police-state' behaviour (encapsulated in "fascist police state"). The despicable, traitorous, Covid lockdown-enforcing protest-suppressing behaviour of various police forces has been described in this way. In recent years, it is also used to describe

---

[4] Cartwright, M., "Fasces", 8 May 2016. https://www.worldhistory.org/Fasces/

[5] https://www.britannica.com/biography/Benito-Mussolini

the behaviour of Antifa and other Marxist spawn organisations ("they're the real fascists/Nazis!" etc.).

So, it's used universally in more or less the same way, and all those who use it don't understand what it really means (not just etymologically but symbolically, as we'll see later).

Why don't we hear the terms "Marxist police state" or "Socialist Police State" or "Communist Police State"? When we look at the amount (and fanaticism!) of authoritarian behaviour by Marxism-inspired regimes in the 20th century alone ("Socialist"/"Communist") as compared to the so-called 'fascist' regimes, there is simply no competition between them in terms of authoritarian 'police-state' behaviour (Marxist propaganda aside), in terms of the amount of people and countries affected by it. Yet, authoritarianism, dictatorships, and militaristic state control are associated with the word "fascist" by those all across the political spectrum.

Why this one-sided/imbalanced labelling? This is due to the influence of Marxism over how we speak, and therefore how we perceive the world around us (aka reality). It also shows than even rational, ethical, good-natured people may be infected with Marxism slightly, though they may not be aware. Again, this is no personal offence to anyone; it's just representative of how well-entrenched the ideology is in our culture. (see "Right v Left" section later).

Anti-Fascist

The term "Anti-Fascist" is another deceptive, traditionally used Marxist term. When they label themselves "Anti-Fascist" this is another sleight-of-hand, to distract the attention away from what they are. It immediately makes the ignorant focus on their enemies, as it implies "We are against those evil people, but we are good". As the non-indoctrinated portion of the world is finding out, these 'anti-fascists' are the real troublemakers in our societies (a fact which supports the premise of this book). This term really means "group who is against those who resist Marxism", or "anti-anti-Marxists". That's all it means. Thanks to those incinerateable Marxist zombies *Antifa*, the term is never too far from public discourse.

White Supremacist

The "White Supremacist" label is another anti-white slur towards whites who know 'diversity' and 'multiculturalism' is anti-white. The constant "racism!" talk coming from cult members (the real racists) cleverly disguises the anti-white racism of Marxism! This is typical Marxist distraction/deflection—they go on the attack first, to put you on the back foot. When they are the real racists.

Conspiracy Theorist

This is certainly one of the most powerful and important terms being used today (to keep the masses in check). A very powerful ridicule term. Reminiscent of "Abrahadabra!"—a sort of spell to make a person's mind switch off and go back to their zombie-like slumber. It says "Nothing to see here folks!", and "Shut up! Do what the state/system is telling you to do!", or "Believe what the government and media is telling you!".

Not only can this term dissuade people from understanding how the control system works in a bigger picture sense, but it also stops a person from understanding the conspiratorial nature of Marxism, which is essential for any society that wants to stop the ideology. They have always engaged in conspiracy to destroy nations/the establishment and enforce their will. So, in short, it's in the interests of the cult to call people "conspiracy theorists" and have them ostracized. It helps to stop the rest of us from exposing their actions and taking countermeasures against them.

Funny how, in a Marxism-riddled society, you will be giggled or laughed at for talking about things that are considered 'conspiracy theory', since you're obviously a nut who's detached from reality, right? Yet if you come out with one of the countless insane things approved by the cult, you can be commended, respected, and even idolised.

For example, if you suggest that the Covid scamdemic was a Communist attack on western capitalism plus a ploy to get some 'vaccines' in to people, or that mass immigration is anti-white population replacement, the cult will try to ridicule you in to silence; but if you're a man who 'comes out' as being actually female (after years of denial, apparently), they won't be able to get the microphones and cameras in front of your freshly-manicured face and freshly-created tits quickly enough! Likewise, if you are jabbering-on about climate change, the patriarchy, rape culture or any other Marxist fantasy/conspiracy theory/distortion of reality.

Being conspiratorial is as much a part of the Marxist heritage as is class struggle, or believing in an egalitarian utopia, or hating Christianity and capitalism. So of course, they don't want anyone thinking they are conspiring or engaging in Ideological Subversion. It's no wonder that they love to call people 'conspiracy theorists' and have us ridiculed when we try to expose these traitorous troublemakers in our countries, by highlighting their subversive activities!

The fact that Marxism has infected the structures of society—politics, media, education, NGO's/non-profits, policing, religion, international organisations etc.—and that there is deceptive, covert collusion between them, is a prime example that conspiracies exist. It's the definition of a conspiracy. Therefore, "conspiracy theorist" is an essential tool for the cult.

Classic Marxist terms

Here's some of the cult's classic dog-whistling terms. They are the ubiquitous calling-cards of cult members all around the globe (a reveille for 'radicals'), a kind of ideological branding. They also contain an element of virtue-signalling, suggesting those who use them are convinced they know what's best for society, being the wonderful revolutionary saviours that they are.

When they are spoken, you can literally see the ego and assumptions in their (wide-eyed, often smiley) faces, and hear it in their voices, almost as if they are proclamations of virtue itself! It's manic, cultish behaviour on full-display—thoughts, words, actions, all in beautiful synchronicity. Also, the Trojan Horse element is woven-in to each word, which is quite fascinating. It goes without saying that if you are hearing these terms being used constantly in your country, you have a serious Marxist infection.

Term	Meaning	Meaning/effects
Progressive	Good, making things even better (much better than in the shitty, traditionalist past). Anything progressive is for the improvement of society, particularly the 'oppressed'. It means working towards a better, more ethical world (according to the cult/ideology).	Gives the false impression that society is being transformed in a positive way. Also, it conditions people to accept constant change, constant revolution (via 'progression'), and in to accepting the removal/replacement of traditional (non-Marxist) things.
Diversity	Western societies should have as many different varieties of people as possible with respect to sex, sexual orientation, religion, ethnicity etc. All groups are equal. A 'diverse' society is a more ethical, oppression-free society.	Used in western populations to suggest there are too many white people (particularly heterosexual males), in any given social environment; conditions these

		populations in to accepting mass immigration; facilitates 'anti-racism'/'multiculturalism'. Leads to mono-cultural Marxian societies.
Equality	Equality equals morality and justice. We are all the same. There shouldn't be hierarchies because that leads to oppression.	Everybody becomes equally unremarkable, drone-like, subservient to the state/authorities etc. (aka uniformity).
Solidarity	Let's be united in a big collective, the bigger the better, and agree with each other.	We must all think, speak and act the same; as one unit. Anyone who does not align with us is an opponent/enemy.
Social Justice	Some people should be treated better in society. There should be more equality, compassion, solidarity, diversity, progressiveness for everyone!	Society conforms to Marxist ideas of right and wrong. In other words, it becomes an insane shithole. It leads to the enforcement of 'equality'/uniformity, via coercion.

Feminist and Marxian Racist terms

We could also call these Marxist conspiracy theory terms since they almost fit that bill. A conspiracy theory, in this context, being something that is a made-up idea involving some sort of evil or injustice being committed, often clandestinely, by one group against another group, without concrete proof that it exists (unless Marxist propaganda in the form of 'research' or 'studies', or Marxism-biased 'science' counts as evidence). The first two — "rape culture" and "patriarchy"—come from the feminist movement, and the term "white privilege" is Marxian racism against white people.

Term	Marxist meaning	Intended effect	Target group

Rape Culture	Males are culturally indoctrinated to rape women. All men are potential rapists!	Males must be 'educated' not to be rapists via the 'education' system. It demonises males; destroys masculinity; weakens society.	Males of all ages (indigenous/white males in particular. Not migrant/non-white males, as this is 'racist').
Patriarchy	Men have dominated women in the past via this society-wide oppressive structure.	Women must now be given priority over men in as many areas of society as possible, in the name of 'equality'. #	Males of all ages (indigenous/white males in particular. Not migrant/non-white males, as this is "racist"). **
White Privilege	Generally, white people have been/are privileged, and non-whites have not been/are not.	Generates racist animosity/bitterness in non-whites towards white people.	White people, regardless of age, sex, sexual-orientation, nationality, wealth etc. (unless they are cult members).

Males are made second-class citizens, by first putting females in the 'oppressed' category and males in the 'oppressor' category; to effeminize society etc.

** These evil 'patriarchies' are the creation of white heterosexual males, according to the cult

Again, the only type of person who fits in to the target group of all three terms are heterosexual, white males. In the case of 'white privilege', this can apply to white females too (but not those who are part of the cult of course, since they can avoid this attack by stating they are in 'solidarity' etc.). Essentially these are all propaganda terms directed at white people, and white heterosexual males in particular, but they don't apply to cult members of either gender (or the multitude of other 'genders' like commie tranny non-binary unicorn fairies etc etc.).

Using the oppressor v oppressed formula, we can conclude that the 'oppressor' class in the first two initiatives are white, heterosexual males, with white females being added in the third. Of course, the 'oppressed' class in the first two are women; non-whites in the third.

White privilege

Another Marxist term that's based on a distorted perception of history and reality. This term is complimentary to the slogan of "Black Lives Matter", as they both exist to generate conflict between these races. The concept of 'White privilege' is racist propaganda towards white people. Millions of idiots have been conned by this and have repeated it; particularly in the U.S. where it was unleashed to create chaos. Using the term in the pejorative is simply a criminal act. It's an incendiary incitement to racial hatred.

'White privilege' is an add-on to the oppressor v oppressed formula expressed in Black Lives Matter, because it generates extra hatred towards white people/the 'oppressor' from non-white people/the 'oppressed'. I say "extra" because the oppressor v oppressed formula already contains hatred towards the oppressor anyway!

'White privilege' is a very dangerous, racist term as it allows non-whites to place themselves in the 'oppressed' category, while generating 'justifiable' hatred towards whites. It also encourages violence, rape, murder, and genocide of white people. We can see this in the BLM movement, and also in South Africa.

It's dangerous because it tells non-whites that they're victims by default, and that they have a common, racial enemy. It triggers off any 'us-against-them' tribal tendencies in the 'oppressed' group and will also trigger-off the sociopathic element within that community (all groups have them to one degree or another).

Of course, the term is based on a distorted perception of history and reality (covered later in the BLM section). There are plenty of bitter, resentful, damaged individuals of African persuasion in the U.S. (and elsewhere), and Marxist soundbites like "White privilege" are the perfect tool for those types, allowing them to blame something outside themselves for their own shortcomings.

Again, the ideology brings out the worst in humanity. There are, of course, countless bitter, resentful, damaged individuals all around the world who are white, but they are not provided with this type of racial excuse. There is no such outlet for their issues.

Other terms

Term	Marxist meaning	Meaning/purpose
Gender non-binary (or 'non-cis' gender). *	Person who believes they are neither male nor female, and who can now identify as being some other 'gender' of their choosing.	A person who is different to a typical male or female (due to genetic, epigenetic, or environmental factors), and/or who has psychological issues that have distorted their perception of their sexual identity.
Gender fluid	The concept of gender doesn't apply to this person. They can change their gender at will. #	As above, when it's uttered by someone who fits that bill.
Hate-filled	This opinion/person is bad, potentially evil. They are also irrational and unable to control their negative emotions. They have no love in them! They are creating division, not unity (aka solidarity)!	This opinion/person is not conforming to Marxist ideas of ethics. They don't feel the cult-like Marxist 'love'. They are not pro-equality/unity, so they/their opinion must be suppressed, as they are critical of certain Marxist sub-agendas.
Victim-blaming	Any examination, analysis, or criticism of the behaviour of females who have been sexually assaulted/raped is always wrong.	You must not insinuate that anyone in an 'oppressed' group needs to change their behaviour, or to stop putting themselves at risk (in situations where this applies).
Slut-shaming	Any criticism of the	Marxism (via

	behaviour of women sexually—especially promiscuous, exhibitionist, or 'trashy' behaviour—is wrong.	feminism) encourages degenerate behaviour in women, so this term is designed to prevent criticism of women who engage in such behaviour.
Mansplaining	A male explaining something to a female in a condescending manner. This behaviour is linked to the patriarchy. It oppresses women (rather than empowers them), and it does not conform to equality.	A man must not be allowed to act superior to a female. Since females are in an 'oppressed' class, they may not be treated as inferior, criticised, or even have things explained to them by males. This is linked to the pampering of those in 'oppressed' groups, ego inflation etc.
Discrimination (linked to Exclusion)	A person is being treated unfairly due to the group that they belong to (sex/gender, sexual orientation, race, religion etc.)	A person is being mistreated due to being in a Marxism-approved 'oppressed' group.

* There are many terms for this Marxian gender-bending sub-agenda. Note how we are seeing the increasing use of terms like 'non-cis gender', 'gender-queer' etc. in recent years, in addition to the insistence that we need to call people by their chosen pronouns.

Is this a type of superpower?

"Hate-filled" and schizo hypocrisy

One of the most ludicrous things they come out with, it's wheeled-out often. Any non-Marxist person/group criticising anything is labelled "hate-filled" (especially if that criticism is directed at the cult's activities). So, if you oppose mass immigration, feminism, the great revolution in general or the cult/ideology itself, they you must be "hate-filled". The implication is that the cult is not "hate-filled", but a benign, positive, progressive humanitarian movement of 'love' (ostensibly the polar opposite emotion of hate). So, if you oppose them—and they represent what is good—you must be the opposite (evil). Marxism is love, right?

"Hate-filled" is also linked to the oppressor v oppressed principle, since if you disagree with giving certain groups their oppressed status, then you surely must have hate for them, right? (you are devoid of 'compassion' and 'love' etc.). This applies to any sub-agenda directly involving people/groups (feminism, LGBTQ, mass migration etc.), or animals (vegetarianism and veganism).

There is also, not surprisingly, a schizophrenic, hypocritical element to the term "hate-filled"; it's typical of the cult's persona, and yet another inversion of reality. The indoctrinated ones will think that what drives them is (their interpretation of) love, unity, virtue, ethics, compassion, harmony, nobility, duty, altruism etc. None of those things are the primary driver of this ideology. This is the usual egotism and naivety we can expect from them—everything about them (including their beliefs) boils down to them being wonderful and things being 'positive' and 'nice'. They are completely mistaken! Hate is at the core of Marxism. It's the precursor to its destructiveness. It's not merely hatred for things not Marxist, but hatred of humanity and life itself.

Is the cult/ideology not 'hate-filled'? Are cult members (consciously or unconsciously) not hate-filled for their own identities, nations, cultures, heritage, and peoples (since they are destroying them)? Are they not hate-filled for those who disagree with them (especially anti-Marxists/genuine patriots!)? Being indoctrinated, they will spew hate for those of us who are anti-'globalist', while simultaneously serving the same elitist globalists (who hate us all). Is this not hate-filled? Imagine hating other slaves more than you hate your slave master? This is worse than hate!

We wouldn't be living in this shitty, Marxism-infected world if it wasn't for their hate and their hate-filled ideology, so using the term "hate-filled" is the ultimate deflection/distraction. Those of us not fuelling the hate-filled Marxist cult/ideology would have no reason to express hatred towards it (and its hateful effects) if it didn't exist! Without the cult/ideology and its constant, manipulative, controlling, shit-stirring, divisive tendencies there would be very little cause for hate on the planet at this time, especially in the west!

Conversely, patriotism/patriots (whether they identify as nationalistic or not) are genuine expressions of love for their own peoples, cultures, countries etc., since they are seeking to preserve those things, by protecting them from the ideology's unloving, non-compassionate, hate-filled assault on them.

Using "hate-filled" is also the typical arrogant virtue-signalling we can expect from them; it says "we are the arbiters of right and wrong attitudes or behaviours, and this hate-filled opinion/person is inferior to us. They don't make the cut as humans, and they deserve to be condemned". It's yet another stupid, childish, virtue-signalling term, used by indoctrinated people to silence any opposition to the genuinely hate-filled agendas of the cult/ideology.

"Hate-filled" as mind control

Expressing anger towards the consequences of a Marxist infection in society can attract this label, even if the person is not actively criticising the cult/ideology or its sub-agendas. For example, a sane person could express anger towards the seemingly never-ending parade of psychotic things that cult members will say or do. And it's absolutely their right to do that! They are correct to do so! But this sort of reaction cannot be allowed to stand (from the cult/ideology's point of view). The term "hate-filled" is designed to make the person being targeted seem like they are the problem, especially in the eyes of others. It's a form of subtle, psychological intimidation; to ensure others don't imitate the behaviour.

The cult/ideology wants us to be smiling, docile morons and be 'positive' and 'compassionate' etc.; to just accept the destruction it imposes on us, on society. Any type of hatred for this lunacy is to be viewed as the negative psychological issues of the person expressing this very natural, rational, and constructive emotional response! Being angry in the right context is about ethics, justice, and intellectual consciousness. If you are angry at an individual/group for destroying what's good, and if you express that anger in front of others—thereby setting an example for them to follow—you are righteous. If others are too dumb, too cowardly, or too far gone to appreciate that, then fuck them!

The term "Mansplaining"

Though feminism has its own separate section, this stupid divisive term deserves to be included here. From *merrian-webster.com*: "Mansplaining is.. what occurs when a man talks condescendingly to someone (especially a woman) about something he has incomplete knowledge of, with the mistaken assumption that he knows more about it than the person he's talking to does".[6] This is just another invented term—a piece of childish anti-male propaganda coming from the feminist movement. A single 'word' to generate conflict between the sexes by designating males as the oppressive target group; particularly knowledgeable, confident, take-charge masculine males. The term is very destructive, and an add-on to Marxian feminist programming. It's a top-up to the indoctrination, basically, and another layer of bullshit that we have to deal with. It generates animosity towards/suspicion of males in the minds of females.

The term also attempts to conceal a truth that cult members in general, feminists, and others are unwilling/unable to accept—men have an advantage over women generally when it comes to perceiving bigger picture issues clearly, and technical and mechanical things (indeed, reality itself is technical and mechanical. Even 'bigger picture' issues, history, science, geo-politics have technical and mechanical elements to them). Concurrently, men in general tend to be more interested in those things during the course of their lives, and they accumulate more knowledge because of this, giving them a massive advantage over females.

More knowledge equals more ability to teach/explain things, particularly to someone who knows less! Hence why men are often explaining these types of things to women (and not the other way around). This should be obvious! It's one of the fundamental differences between the sexes that the cult/ideology tries to mask. Obviously, this dynamic can exist between males too, but males are not allowed to cry 'oppression' when another more knowledgeable, skilled male is explaining things to them! Again, there's no need for anyone to choose the weakling's path (denial), and be 'offended' by this, as it's simply the truth. Men and women are not the same. The term "Mansplaining" is just another way of obscuring the truth, and pushing the erroneous and damaging concept of equality, through propagandised language. It also attempts to deny the existence of hierarchies (of knowledge/skill), upon which civilisation has been built. It is therefore an attack on civilisation itself.

Mansplaining and criticism

"Mansplaining" encourages women not to listen to men, insinuating that they will be somehow more 'empowered' if they don't (the opposite of the truth). In particular, they should not accept any criticism from males, even if they deserve to be criticized! Can you see how this mentality is going to be a real problem when a non-indoctrinated male is interacting with an indoctrinated female?

---

[6] https://www.merriam-webster.com/wordplay/mansplaining-definition-history

The term helps to prevent any criticism of females who may be engaging in degenerate behaviour, due to Marxian feminist indoctrination, particularly if that criticism is coming from males (who are more likely to try to 'snap them out of it' anyway). In addition, the term helps to ensure these women stay that way (as they opt to choose the weakling's path and ignore the males), by being stubborn and digging their heels in.

In a sane, balanced, non-contaminated society, males and females can balance each other out in a complimentary fashion, which includes constructive criticism sometimes. The masculine and the feminine provide balance to each other, in a symbiotic relationship (ergo, men and women are supposed to be complimentary, not equal). Whether the male or female is delivering this type of criticism, it's a primarily 'masculine' act. This is natural; Marxism is anti-nature.

It also connects with a point made elsewhere—that criticism of anyone/any group with 'oppressed' status (in this case females) is not permitted. In this case, it is taken to a psychotic extreme where even any hint of a suggestion that the oppressed are inferior in some way to the oppressor (males) is an act of war! An act of oppression against the oppressed, coming from the patriarchy itself! It proves my point that the goal of giving a group 'oppressed' status is not to help, but to actually inflate their egos to the point they become spoilt and insufferable, and any hint that they are imperfect is intolerable.

"Mansplaining" is a nauseating, pampering term, and a good example of the nonsense that appears as 'language' when Marxism takes hold. It's a term that says "How dare you not treat females as all-knowing perfect goddesses!". (As mentioned, this spoiling factor also applies to those in other oppressed groups, not just females; it's highly problematic).

Victim-blaming

A very dangerous, anti-women Marxian term, used by cult members within and without feminism. It's also linked to the above points, and how any criticism—or attempts at controlling—the behaviour of females can be countered by the ever-virtuous cult with another catchy catchphrase. This term actually puts girls/women at more risk of being sexually assaulted/raped, because it sends out the wrong message—that females don't have to pay attention to their behaviour at all, including ones that may put them at risk of such things (for example, young females dressing up sexually, going out in public, and getting themselves severely inebriated with alcohol, making themselves an easy target for any sexual predators in society). It's also linked to the 'liberalisation' of women/women's sexuality; an apparent 'achievement' of feminism.

Marxist "Pride" Terms

> "Until my dying day I will look back with pride that I found the courage to come face to face in battle against the spectre which for time immemorial has been injecting poison into me and into men of my nature.. Indeed, I am proud that I found the courage to deal the initial blow to the hydra of public contempt"[7]

> Karl Heinrich Ulrichs, 19th century Germany proto gay rights activist

You can't have a cult without the members complimenting each other on their brilliance as human beings or patting each other on the backs for doing nothing (or in this cult's case, destroying the earth)! Let's try to analyse these terms without giggling at the OTT dramatic ridiculousness. You will hear them being dished-out to those who participate in/promote Marxist initiatives. You might hear them when someone 'comes-out' as being gay or 'trans' or 'non-binary', or who has 'transitioned', usually on a public platform, naturally. An example of this would be William Bruce "Caitlyn" Jenner—a voluptuous, sensuous beauty with a strong jaw, rough voice, powerful pole-vaulting hands, Adam's apple, and shoulders.

Even though it's never been easier to do all these things (due to the decline of civilisation towards complete degeneracy, thanks to Marxism), these persons must be congratulated for their super-human endeavours! Of course, the myth of these groups (gays, trans) being 'oppressed' makes it seem (to some) that these acts deserve such adulation.

Term	Marxist meaning	Actual meaning	Intended effect
Brave	You have shown courage because what you have done is scary to do. You were brave to go on, enduring the oppression for so long on your own without support!	You have said/done something that promotes/supports a Marxist sub-agenda. It was very easy to do and required zero courage or effort as it's in line with the Marxist	It shows others that if they engage in this behaviour, they will be showered with respect/admiration/'love' etc. (by

---

[7] Quoted in: Keith Stern, K., *Queers in History: The Comprehensive Encyclopedia of Historical Gays, Lesbians and Bisexuals* (2013). P. 460.
https://en.wikiquote.org/wiki/Karl_Heinrich_Ulrichs

	culture.		indoctrinated people/the cult). It promotes more of the same cultish behaviour by encouraging it in others.
Strong	As above, and you have shown mental strength!	As above but add 'mental strength' to the compliment.	As above.

If a population becomes convinced that doing things like 'coming out' or 'transitioning' makes a person brave and strong, this then becomes part of the populations' perception of what bravery and strength is. A new norm is created where you are 'brave' and 'strong' if you engage in behaviours that are accepted by the collective. You are rewarded for making a 'sacrifice' in honour of the cult. 'Coming-out' is a cult ritual.

Core elements

Some core elements of the ideology:

Oppressor v Oppressed—a main ingredient

Since this is so central to the ideology/indoctrination, it must be dissected further. The oppressor v oppressed principle is a chief ingredient used time and again, and we can see it in all the cult's sub-agendas. Its impact is primarily twofold—it generates strong emotional reactions in the affected and creates divisions. Combined these two elements lead to absolute chaos. The mayhem we are seeing in the world today would not exist without this dynamic.

This principle has been a cornerstone of the ideology since the very beginning, though over time, its application has changed (via Marxism-Leninism, Frankfurt School and post-modernism etc.). We should be in awe of how the cult have continuously managed to recycle/re-use this principle for its diabolical ends. "If it ain't broke, don't fix it!", right? What's not changed, however, is how it operates: it uses emotional manipulation to produce strong, psychological reactions, with catastrophic results for society. In addition, it supports sociopathic cult-like behaviour.

First, it creates a clear division between two different parties, placing them on opposite ends of a spectrum. It labels one as the 'oppressor/dominator/controller/perpetrator' and the other as the 'oppressed/dominated/controlled/victim'. Then it encourages excessive combative 'masculine' emotions towards the party labelled as the 'oppressor' (negativity, hatred, judgement, suspicion etc.); while encouraging excessive 'feminine' emotions towards the party labelled as the 'oppressed' (positivity, warmth, empathy, sympathy and compassion, trust etc). In other words, it triggers certain perceptions, by default, that creates double-standards. This can lead to the breakdown of true justice/ethics/morality in society. Divide and conquer all the way baby.

This is arguably the single most important aspect of the ideology since it explains its toxicity. It would have no potency at all if it were not for this emotional dichotomy. It's part of its 'DNA', so to speak.

Virtue-signalling while judging?

Amusingly, and somewhat typically (due to the ideology's tendency to invert), there is further double-standards built-in to the oppressor v oppressed principle.

It's amusing because virtue-signalling is a big part of the ideology's shtick; it claims it's all about justice, ethics etc. It says that any form of criticism or abuse of anyone in an 'oppressed' group is wrong, evil, discriminatory, misogynistic, racist or xenophobic etc. If you are not being directly shouted down by them for engaging in this criticism/abuse, your behaviour will be at least frowned upon. You may be confronted with the sentiment that judgement is wrong: "you should not judge!" or "you should have more compassion" etc.

We usually get this response from those who are indoctrinated without them (or perhaps even you) realising it. Yet the oppressor v oppressed principle itself relies on you judging the person/group in the 'oppressor' class! It wouldn't function without judgement! Therefore, if the oppr. v oppr. principle is crucial for the operation of the ideology, then judgement is a crucial part of the ideology; it allows the cult to operate and proliferate. In a sense, Marxism is judgement.

Now, considering all the virtue-signalling nonsense, isn't that funny? Of course, their response would be that some deserve to be judged, and others don't. And here we come to see what the cult/ideology is really up to: attacking certain groups, whom it designates as problematic. More hypocrisy. It's trying to be the arbiter of right and wrong behaviour/attitudes. And of course—it seeks to create a new norm where Marxian ethics are the only kind: you must judge those in the group the cult has designated as the 'oppressor', and you must not judge those in the group they designate as the 'oppressed'.

It is correct that some in society deserve to be judged by that society, but a destructive cult/ideology is in no position to assume this role! This all serves as another reminder that the cult/ideology is good at addressing tendencies society has (passing judgement) and satisfying them. It provides fake/inferior alternatives to something which is good—the judgement of certain individuals or groups within society for the benefit of that society/nation (example: traitors or subversives, purveyors of degeneracy, brainwashed destructive types).

Emotional manipulation

Here is a crucial item to explain how Marxian indoctrination works. The emotional manipulation effect at the core of the oppressor v oppressed principle ('oppressor'=negativity/hatred/judgement; 'oppressed'=positivity/sympathy/empathy), generates conflict in society by emotionally charging those affected. More precisely, the conflict comes from the misguided emotional reactions of the cult members.

The overall effect, not surprisingly, is that the affected (or infected) person feels that an injustice is being committed from one group/individual towards another group/individual, and therefore, they desire revenge/vengeance on the 'oppressor' (on behalf of the 'oppressed'); essentially, they feel a duty of care towards the 'oppressed'. Then it's "me/us to the rescue!", the ego takes over, and the activism begins..

In the mind of a person who perceives issues/society through the oppr. v oppr. lens, they are feeling these two polar opposite types of emotions towards those two different groups, at the same time: negativity/hatred/judgment towards the 'oppressor' group, and positivity, sympathy/empathy, 'love'/'compassion' etc. towards the 'oppressed' group. A type of scizophrenic schism of the mind is created. In other words, the oppr. v oppr. principle triggers a "grrrrr" mentality towards the 'oppressor' and a "nawwwwwww" mentality towards the 'oppressed'. "Naawwwww" or "aawwwwww" being the sound someone might make when looking at a cute baby or a gorgeous puppy. It's the mothering instinct on crack but warped. It's extremely dangerous for society and is of course connected with the destruction of masculinity/feminisation efforts of the cult.

A clear example of this warped mothering instinct is found in the mass-immigration (or 'multiculturalism'/'diversity') sub-agenda, when indoctrinated people in Europe expressed emotions of warmth and a duty of care towards migrants whom they've never met! This is linked to the problem of Pathological Altruism in contaminated societies; trying to 'save the world' at your own expense, and that of your own country, ethnic group etc. (this is just one example—the warped mothering instinct/'compassion' mentality is the culprit in other sub-agendas too). Of course, Pathological Altruism only exists because of the oppr. v oppr. principle.

Back to the oppr. v oppr. dual emotional reactions: those are two highly charged and highly contrasting emotions to be feeling at the same time, when contemplating a particular issue/Marxist sub-agenda (i.e. feminism, mass migration, racism etc.). To reason correctly, a person needs to be calm and not let emotions be the foundation of their reasoning, but when a person is 'triggered' in to those two base types of emotions, it reduces their ability to reason and to see reality as it actually is (aka the truth of the matter). Their mind has been forced on to a lower level of function/consciousness, thanks to these very strong and contrasting emotions.

Since their minds are now functioning on this lower level, they are now easier to control, and their behaviour is predictable. The indoctrination has them! They are now locked to certain behavioural patterns, primed to react to certain stimuli in a certain way (as Yuri Besmenov explained). These points are crucial to understand the nature of the indoctrination, why this cult is so intense and fanatical, and why there is no turning back for many…

Of course, these above factors don't apply to intelligent, mature, confident individuals who know how to stay calm and form their own clear, accurate perceptions of any given issue. Well, those are the types who don't get suckered-in to Marxist indoctrination! For those who do, their inability to control their emotions and a lack of intelligence is a major contributory factor in what makes them fall for the indoctrination.

Distorts perception with inversion

The oppr. v oppr. formula also distorts perception of reality in even more significant ways. This can be done to such a degree, that things are turned completely upside down. Hence "inversion".

This can be applied to any sub-agenda where there's an 'oppressed' class. Feminism, for example, advertises itself as being pro-female. It is, however, anti-female. Same goes for abortion, as an extension of feminism. It's marketed as pro-female 'compassion' or 'healthcare', but it's actually anti-female (an assault on her body/life/mind). The number of females who end up with lonely, broken, empty lives due to feminism and abortion may never be honestly evaluated and collated; especially not while we still have a strong Marxist infection in our societies. By the time a female realises that the abortion she had was not 'healthcare' or 'compassion', it may be too late (this is why delusion/denial is a much easier option).

Same goes for Black Lives Matter. It does not empower black people; it only disempowers them. The victim mentality and sense of entitlement that this sub-agenda brings never leads to 'empowerment' of any kind; only to further irresponsibility, victimhood, spoiling, and immaturity/degeneracy. Furthermore, it markets itself as being anti-racism, but as we've clearly seen, it generates racial tensions and breeds racism towards the 'oppressor' whites. It also breeds racism towards blacks—if a large portion of them start advocating or supporting the civilisation-destroying Marxian B.L.M. sub-agenda, or start being 'anti-establishment', anti-police etc.

In the mass immigration/multiculturalism sub-agenda: it's not going to be beneficial for Africa or the Middle East, it is going to be detrimental (speaking of the European migrant influx here obviously, but same principle applies to the mass immigration sub-agenda in other parts of the world). It's often said by honest, intelligent analysts, and quite correctly so, that the best thing to improve these peoples/countries is for them to help themselves (or be helped) in their own countries; not for their youngest and fittest males to simply be transplanted elsewhere, which is of no benefit to either their home countries or their chosen destination.

These are the results when you disturb the natural balance of things by trying to enforce artificial 'equality' (racial or otherwise). Of course, this argument is for those who think that this encouraged mass immigration is actually about humanitarianism (which it isn't). What we're focusing on here though is the inversion of truth; how victimisation (having an 'oppressed' status) only leads to disempowerment, not empowerment.

This extreme inverting effect of the ideology is yet another aspect that makes the indoctrination so potent: if someone becomes indoctrinated and their perception of something is so completely backwards/upside down (and remains that way for an extended period), it may be literally impossible for them to grasp the truth. They are beyond help; it's too late for them.

The 'Oppressed' becomes the 'Oppressor'

The oppressor v oppressed principle also inverts things by turning the 'oppressed' class into the oppressor and makes the 'oppressor' class the oppressed.

We can see this with the Europe-wide migrant influx. Many of the migrants have bought-in to the Marxian narrative that they have suffered historically, so if they make their 'oppressors' (European whites) suffer, this will somehow be fair and equal. The results are clear to see—assaults, rapes, and murders of Europeans by migrants. The (Marxist) narrative insists that indigenous Europeans somehow deserve this treatment at the hands of these 'oppressed' migrants! We have seen many in this group literally getting away with murder since the migrant waves have started, thanks to this oppressed-becomes-the-oppressor characteristic. Another example is in the feminism sub-agenda, and the open hostility (misandry) emanating from these 'oppressed' females towards their 'oppressors' (white heterosexual males), and the 'patriarchy'.

This characteristic (oppressed-becomes-the-oppressor) is linked to the sense of entitlement (aka being spoilt) that those in the 'oppressed' class often feel. Feeling entitled/being spoilt and being aggressive go hand in glove, partially because spoilt people usually become miserable which can often lead to anger. This is because they're trapped in the cycle of continuous short-term-pleasure-fix spoiling (erroneously believing that further spoiling will make them happy), which only increases their long-term misery, and they may stupidly lash-out due to the frustration. This happens because they are either too dumb or cowardly to see that they are the problem, not those around them. Perhaps they are somewhat aware of how weak and rotten they are on the inside, which fuels the frustration, but their minds are wired to being addicted to the spoilt mentality and they can't help themselves. Habits are a bitch.

Essentially, spoiling tends to make a person unhinged, due to being stuck in this downward spiral. This is why they may eventually become insufferable and crazy (no empathy plus detached from reality).

Obviously having an inflated ego is another by-product of spoiling, and lack of humility usually leads to degenerate social behaviour of one form or another (e.g. lacking respect for others). In addition, they have no incentive to treat others with respect because there are virtually no consequences for them if they don't (due to their 'oppressed' status). This is another toxic, civilisation-wrecking effect of the opp. v opp. principle. Spoilt brats should be made to suffer, whether it reforms them or not! That is social justice.

Distorts perceptions of history and reality

Of course, many of the sub-agendas—feminism, 'anti-racism' and BLM, multiculturalism/diversity, LGBTQ rights—are based on the idea that those in the 'oppressed' group deserve this status because of the apparent mistreatment of those groups in the past. In other words (according to the cult/ideology), women, non-whites, and LGBTQ types, have all suffered more, historically, than those not in those groups (e.g. males, white people, heterosexual people, heterosexual white males); and by extension, they still suffer more than those in other groups in the present (so the cult says). A crucial point, again, is that this suffering is apparently caused by the 'oppressor' groups involved. So because of this apparent intolerable, unequal proportion of suffering (!), society must be transformed via 'revolution' or reformation etc., to make things 'fair'.

Now, anyone with a non-indoctrinated, rational perspective can see that people in all groups have suffered in the past, and still suffer! (Indeed, life is suffering, and always has been! Everybody suffers!). So, in order for this process to work, Marxism needs to create a distorted perception of history and the present to conform to its false narrative. In fact, creating a distorted perception of the former is crucial to creating one of the latter. This distortion is needed to show the apparent unequal distribution of suffering in the past/present, which emphasises more suffering in only certain designated groups in a way that benefits the cult/ideology. Propaganda.

Feminism, for example, relies on a distorted perception of history to convince people that women have traditionally suffered more than men, due to being 'oppressed' by them etc. There are some people in Ireland, for example, who actually believe that. But anyone who spends even a five-minute honest study of Irish history will find a lot of suffering, but it's not along the gender divide! The notion that women have suffered more in that country is absolutely ludicrous! If an indoctrinated person in that country actually believes the Marxian lie that claims otherwise, they will be inclined to see the merit of feminism; they will feel that, now, women deserve preferential treatment.

And that is one of the battle fronts through which the ideology does its damage, since now the males should be neglected to prioritise females, as this is somehow 'fair' and 'equal' etc. This is destabilizing and is detrimental for society. Where the impact of feminism is concerned, the result is a destructive divide, creating tensions, attempting to split society right down the middle on gender lines (the most universal divide in the world), and it's all based on a distorted, pro-Marxian perspective of history.

Preferential treatment

There are certain consequences whichever group is given the 'oppressed' status, but perhaps the following effects seem to be most potent when it's women, non-whites, or migrants (as in feminism, racism/BLM, or multiculturalism/mass migration):

In addition to the 'oppressed' group becoming imbalanced/damaged/spoilt, and therefore becoming a problem for society (since now they are receiving preferential treatment), the 'oppressor' group will be imbalanced/damaged/neglected, and therefore will not be able to contribute to society as much as they could. The neglect can also result in further destructive effects on that group (physical and mental health problems, suicide etc.). Example: boys being neglected due to feminist initiatives in schools.

In addition, a sense of disenfranchisement is created in the 'oppressed' group, and generally the sentiment develops that they are owed something, which perpetuates the preferential treatment. They also become dependent on it and have no incentive to develop self-sufficiency (which would be true 'empowerment', ironically). More examples of preferential treatment: women being promoted in to influential positions in society due to gender quotas, rather than their merits; migrants being treated better than the indigenous people in similar dire straits (as in Ireland); non-white students being given extra marks/credits to enable them to enter U.S. colleges, simply because of their race etc. (a reference to *Affirmative Action* in the U.S.—an attempt by the cult to enforce artificial racial equality in University admissions). Notice that those not in the privileged 'oppressed' groups, in each instance, are demoralised, neglected, or otherwise affected. The principles of 'equality' and oppr. v oppr. combined are at play in these scenarios.

Anger venting

On top of all of that, now the 'oppressed' group has someone/some group to direct any pent-up animosity towards. The oppr. v oppr. principle offers them a built-in excuse, due to the class they belong to, and any sort of attacks on the 'oppressor' class are seen as justified. We saw this during the Black Lives Matter 'protests' in the U.S. This one is important, because it allows unethical, destructive, and even criminal behaviour that's not going to be adequately condemned for what it is by society. This is one of the ways that the cult/ideology directly attacks civilisation. It's the breakdown of law and order, and normal, civilised behaviour. This uncivilised behaviour would normally prompt a reaction of universal condemnation, but the cult/ideology doesn't allow for that.

Obviously, the non-indoctrinated portion of the population will call a spade a spade and condemn this thuggish behaviour as criminal; cult members will refuse to. Obviously, the more dominant the cult is in any region, the less condemnation there will be of such unrest. This is, overall, how it works, and that's exactly what's been happening.

The anti-racism and BLM example

"Blacks were not enslaved because they were black but because they were available. Slavery has existed in the world for thousands of years. Whites enslaved other whites in Europe for centuries before the first black was brought to the Western hemisphere. Asians enslaved Europeans. Asians enslaved other Asians. Africans enslaved other Africans, and indeed even today in North Africa, blacks continue to enslave blacks"[8]

Black American author, economist, and academic Thomas Sowell

The anti-racism sub-agenda and Black Lives Matter movement rely on a distorted perception of history, convincing people that non-whites (particularly those with African genetics) have historically suffered more than white people. This is totally false, and an honest, unbiased assessment of history confirms this. It's a divisive, racist lie!

Cult members will cite things like historical racism and slavery of black people by whites, while totally disregarding that all other races have engaged in racism and slavery too (and even slavery of their own race!). Racism and slavery have always occurred between the races to some degree, and still does. The Marxist argument is that the whites have engaged in it more than others, which is just biased, racist nonsense.

The Sumerians (5th—2nd century BC), Babylonian (2nd century BC—1st century AD), and Assyrians (3rd century BC—1st century AD) all had slaves at various points. Ancient Egypt (4th century to 1st century BC) had slaves. Examples of slavery in China (of Chinese) go back as far as the 5th century BC. The ancient Greeks (12th century BC—1st century AD) and the Romans (1st century BC—1st century AD) had slaves.[9]

Islamic slavery goes back to the time of Muhammed (6th century AD), up until the Barbery slave trade (16th—19th centuries): "European slaves were acquired by Muslim Barbary pirates in slave raids on ships and by raids on coastal towns from Italy to the Netherlands, Ireland and the southwest of Britain, as far north as Iceland and into the Eastern Mediterranean".[10]

In South America, the Mayans (1500 BC approx to end of 1st century) and the Aztecs (14th—16th century) had slaves. In Europe, the marauding Vikings took white slaves during their expeditions to north-western Europe, between the 8th—11th centuries. The Native tribes of North America enslaved each other throughout history, including the Pawnee, Comanche, Klamath, Haida, Yurok, and Tinglit (and i'm sure others). African tribes engaged in the trade of Africans as slaves, before and during the

---

[8] . Sowell, *Barbarians Inside the Gates - and Other Controversial Essays* (1999), P. 164.

https://libquotes.com/thomas-sowell/quote/lbg2t4v

[9] "Slavery in history". https://www.thehistorypress.co.uk/articles/slavery-in-history/

[10] https://www.britannica.com/topic/Barbary-pirate

transatlantic slave trade.[11] These examples are not difficult to find, despite the amount of Marxian counterpropaganda one has to wade through on this subject (which obviously tries to comparatively minimise or trivialise those instances).

Singling out the white Europeans race as being the main culprit, again, is simply biased historical cherry-picking and a distortion of the past/present. In addition, the cult focusing on only white-on-black slavery for profit allows it to criticise two of its old foes—European colonial imperialism and capitalism. Predictably, a Marxist 'politically correct' partisan 'education' of history is only going to provide a biased perspective. Indeed, there is a whole lot of history to confirm all this, but you won't be taught it in a Marxism-riddled University! We noted the worthlessness of Marxian 'education' earlier.

Having this distorted perception of history (via the oppr. v oppr. formula) results in a destructive divide, creating tensions, splitting society along racial lines. This sub-agenda ('anti-racism' and BLM) is obviously going to have a massive impact in countries that are multi-ethnic enough for it to work, and where there is a sufficient number of non-whites (e.g. the U.S.). Conversely, this kind of sub-agenda would not be as effective in a country that is more ethnically homogenous, like Ireland for example, as historically there have simply not been enough non-whites in Ireland (admittedly this is rapidly changing).

Uses the group defence/retaliation mechanism

In a contaminated society, criticism of a single person in an 'oppressed' group is seen as an attack on the whole group, the collectivist mindset. It's in the ideology's interests that any criticism of anyone in an 'oppressed' group is countered, to allow the ideology to do its damage unopposed. Feminism is a classic example of this. Since a high proportion of women have fallen for this one, it needs to be said. As mentioned, if you criticise feminism, you are actually arguing for the benefit of women (and society as a whole etc.), yet obviously you will be criticised for doing this by the brainwashed. Since the inversion exists that feminism is not to the benefit of women, but to their detriment (the opposite of what an indoctrinated mind thinks), you will be criticised for pointing that out. Nothing amazing about that; it's just the brainwashing doing its thing. If you attack/criticise feminism/feminists in a society, and the Marxist brainwashing is strong

---

[11] "Slavery before the Trans-Atlantic Trade".

https://ldhi.library.cofc.edu/exhibits/show/africanpassageslowcountryadapt/introductio natlanticworld/slaverybeforetrade enough, it's taken as an attack on all women. The indoctrination and group defence aspect combine to suppress your criticism.

Obviously, you are not attacking all women by criticising/attacking feminism/feminists, since there are plenty of women out there who are smart enough to reject feminism! The indoctrinated types, of course, presume that all women (that matter) are feminists. I'm sure you have noticed this one.

The ideology/cult needs women to be indoctrinated to the point that feminism is regarded as being not only pro-female but being female itself! Synonymous is not the word. The ideology's goal here is that any criticism of females/feminism is perceived as an insult/threat to every female, and that they will respond with being offended, shocked, upset etc. (which leads to a reaction from the whole group).

This group counterattack is a clever trick and is no accident—it's built-in to the oppr. v oppr. formula as a defence mechanism. Clever, right? Any criticism of any members in the oppressed groups must be met with a counterattack by the whole group. The purpose is, again, to prevent any criticism of that group. This lack of criticism (when it's deserved/justified) leads to the inevitable downward spiral of that group mentioned earlier: the preferential treatment, being spoilt, degeneracy, insanity etc.

This group defence tactic is used in various other sub-agendas, including anything involving race, socialism, the political 'left' etc. Any public criticism of black-on-black and/or gang-related violence in the U.S. (uttered by non-black people), is met with the "racist" label by the cult members in the general public and MarxiStMedia. Again, the purpose is to get all black people to take offence, as a collective, and to take the Marxist road (and bait!)—to suppress and counter the criticism, thereby helping the ideology dominate the narrative. Same happens throughout Europe when migrant crime is highlighted, or there are criticisms made of Islam or Muslims in Europe. It's a manipulation of the tribal tendencies we may have as human beings.

The ideology/cult needs people to get 'offended' en masse in order to proliferate. On a group level: same emotions, same thought, same words, same actions, and same re-actions. On an individual level: if a person is offended, they become emotionally charged, and are more inclined to want to retaliate. This makes them potential 'revolutionaries'. If you belong to an 'oppressed' category of person, explain the above to others; tell them not to fall for the deception by taking the bait!

How the principle works with propaganda/indoctrination

So, the oppressor v oppressed principle is a divide-and-conquer tactic and can be used to imbalance/destroy both groups, particularly those that are somewhat complimentary/symbiotic (i.e. heterosexual males and females); but of course, it's used in particular to destroy those in the 'oppressor' class. To zoom out for a moment, from the ideology's point of view, both the 'oppressor' and 'oppressed' are being destroyed: the 'oppressed' destroy the 'oppressors' through psychological/physical abuse/attack, while simultaneously destroying themselves through degeneracy.

Propaganda and indoctrination can be employed to create a differential in public perception of how the 'oppressor' group and the 'oppressed' group are perceived. Naturally, the goal is to create/reinforce a negative perception of the 'oppressor' group (hatred, judgement, suspicion etc.), and to create/reinforce a positive perception of the 'oppressed' group (empathy, sympathy, 'compassion', 'love' etc.), as mentioned earlier.

Targeting the worst aspect of the 'oppressor'

The feminism sub-agenda focuses in on the worst attributes/behaviours of the 'oppressor' class and exaggerates them. Any type of attributes/behaviour will work, but one that affects the oppressed class in particular, in a negative way, are ideal (i.e. rape). This is classic Marxist propaganda stuff—you must exploit any potential weaknesses in the enemy! Constant repetition of this narrative, and the creation of catchy catchphrases (e.g. "rape culture") are used to reinforce the message and keep drawing attention to that negative behaviour (which is rape). Eventually, it gets to a point (if the ideology is sufficiently dominant in society) where this negative behaviour becomes synonymous with the target group. The result is that men as a collective are viewed as rapists/potential rapists! Have you not witnessed this happening in western countries?

Rape is ideal for this purpose, because it generates suspicion of the 'oppressor' class, by playing on the fears of females, amongst other things. It's also something (anatomically speaking) that only males can engage in, that females can't, so immediately, it's going to be one-sided and only one-way, which is ideal for propaganda purposes. (Yes, lesbians and gay men can engage in sexual assault, but those are not the issue here—we are talking about the dynamics between heterosexual males and females, and feminism. Attacking those groups is not part of the Marxist agenda, but attacking heterosexual males is, so those issues will not be emphasised by the cult/ideology and are irrelevant here. Obviously, they cannot be emphasised by the cult/ideology because it needs to associate the concept of rape with heterosexual males only).

Rape is also ideal for propaganda purposes because it can be hard to tell in some cases, from a legal point of view, if a genuine rape has been committed or not. Obviously, some naked, psycho guy in the bushes waiting to pounce on an unsuspecting female in broad daylight is a cut-and-dried case, but there are other variations of scenarios that are not so clear.

There are clearly genuine rape/sexual assault cases, but there are also false rape allegations, which are both equally serious crimes, but you won't hear the cult emphasising this fact. Rape can potentially ruin a woman's life (and it has), just as false rape allegations can potentially ruin a man's life (and they have). Perpetrators of both should get the rope in my view, but in our current Marxism-infected societies, enforcing this is not viable or wise. Not surprisingly, the rising number of false rape allegations in recent decades is due to the effects/dominance of the ideology, via feminism—the sense of entitlement/female privilege, being spoilt to the point of psychosis (and the resultant lack of consequences for negative behaviour), in addition to the misandrist, sexist hatred towards men.

The ideology benefits greatly from using this often-complex issue (of rape), as it's difficult to establish what the actual truth is and what the actual figures are, where these figures are coming from and if they can be trusted. It's in this environment that the ideology can excel, encouraging people to believe what they choose to believe about the issue (post-modernist influence). Using rape or sexual assault allegations is also a useful weapon for the cult to employ, particularly against males who the cult considers an enemy (i.e. 'right-wing' males).

It also allows the cult to try to equate rape with masculinity. Rape is nothing to do with masculinity! In fact, it's the opposite of masculinity. True masculinity is about genuine strength and power, while rape is representative of weakness, more akin to an unethical form of dominance. A man who rapes a woman is not a 'real man'. It's a violent, sociopathic act, and should be treated as such.

The only thing a rapist has in common with a 'real', ordinary, regular man is that they are both male! Treating all males as potential rapists because of the actions of a few desperate, trash males is as stupid as it is destructive. It shows a fundamental misunderstanding about what rape is (by those who claim to be feminists/guardians of women's rights!), and how to fix problems in society. It's also extremely sexist. In fact, it's the definition of sexism—mistreating a person due to the group they belong to (by insinuating their default nature might be harmful and needs to be altered).

Of course, the three transmission belts of culture—media, academia, and entertainment industry—are instrumental in all this, as are the various Marxist feminist NGO's/non-profits. They all constantly draw attention to this negative view of the 'oppressor' class (in this case males). The propaganda generates as much hatred and suspicion of the oppressor class as possible, while repeating the victim status of the oppressed class (generating only empathy/sympathy for this group). Simultaneously, all positive aspects of the oppressor class in the equation (men) must be downplayed, ignored, or hidden, to create the illusion that the oppressor group is bad overall. And, hey presto, we have men as a collective being viewed as problems for society—potential authoritarian personalities with 'toxic masculinity', aggressive troublemakers, potential rapists etc. Of course, even if we could prove to cult members that this is what they are doing, many would feel that this mistreatment of males is 'fair', considering the apparent sexist mistreatment of females in the past.

It's this sleight-of-hand that results in the idiotic initiatives of the so-called 'education' system throughout the west ("consent" education), which is now treating young boys as potential rapists. This creates the situation where males are mistreated (aka oppressed!) simply because of their sex (unless they are homosexual, or 'non-binary' of course), which is (drumroll) sexism! Interestingly, if boys decide to conform to the cult/ideology and decide that they are gay or 'gender non-binary', or trans suddenly, this mistreatment/oppression will stop… Well how-fucking-convenient, right? This primarily psychological attack on the 'oppressor' class is now setup, and will start draining the confidence, health, and well-being of those in that class, unless they are willing to comply with the cult/ideology and alter their behaviour/persona accordingly. That's ideological coercion.

In summary, from a tactical point of view: the ideology identifies a weakness in the target 'oppressor' group (males), in the form of a serious, negative, criminal behaviour towards the 'oppressed' group (e.g. rape); the indoctrination (via the feminism sub-agenda) convinces a sufficient amount of people via the Marxism-infected system, that there's a rape epidemic in western countries; cult members then insist that the solution is to suppress males and masculinity, treat them as potential rapists, prioritise females instead etc. Though this is done in the name of humanitarian, equality, 'compassion' etc., this is a psychological attack on the 'oppressor' class (in this case males).

So essentially what's happened here is that the cult has managed to mount an attack on the 'oppressor' group using propaganda, based on the idea that there is a problem, which produces a reaction, which is then capitalised upon when the cult presents their 'solution'. "Problem. Reaction. Solution" (Hegelian Dialectical mechanics). Fabrication of a 'problem', then evocation of emotions (which forms the reaction), followed by capitalisation upon this reaction.

The fallacy of 'equality'

"Building a society on equality is like building a house on sand—sooner or later it will collapse"

Yuri Besmenov, Summit University
Forum lecture in Los Angeles, 1983[12]

"Let it be very justice for the world to become full of the storms of our vengeance"—thus do they talk to one another... "Vengeance will we use, and insult, against all who are not like us"—thus do the tarantula-hearts pledge themselves..."And 'Will to Equality'—that itself shall henceforth be the name of virtue; and against all that hath power will we raise an outcry!". Ye preachers of equality, the tyrant-frenzy of impotence crieth thus in you for "equality": your most secret tyrant-longings disguise themselves thus in virtue-words!"[13]

Friedrich Nietzsche, "The Tarantulas",
Thus Spoke Zarathustra (1880s)

Equality does not create 'diversity' (ironically), but uniformity. It helps to create a society of unremarkable comrade minions who believe the same things and have the same views. No coincidence that this matches the stereotype of the various Marxist regimes throughout history. No freedom to think, speak, or act however you want—you are obliged to conform to the collective. This reality of a dull, unnatural existence is not just part of life in some historical, far-away Communist regime—we can see this process in society today. Are you free to comfortably think/speak/act however you like, or have views different from everyone else? Or are you conscious of a social pressure to conform? This proves the overall premise of this book. It doesn't matter what label you put on your society—if you don't have this freedom, the society is infected with Marxism. 'Equality' equals conformity, and eventually leads to 100% totalitarian control of you and your society. Whatever anyone thinks or 'feels' equality is, is irrelevant.

Equality is constantly pushed as a benign, virtuous thing, using the Red Trojan Horse principle—evil disguised as good. In addition to uniformity, it inevitably results in mass consensus, lack of individuality/individual

---

[12] Absolutely Subversive, "Yuri Bezmenov 1983 Interview and Lecture (1080p HD)", 8 August 2022. https://www.YouTube.com/watch?v=Z0j181tR5WM

[13] Nietzsche, F., "The Tarantulas", *Thus Spoke Zarathustra* (1880s).

http://4umi.com/nietzsche/zarathustra/29

freedoms, the suppression of genuine individual excellence, and the suppression of true leaders in society. Equality leads to the breakdown of society, and that's the primary reason why the ideology places so much emphasis on it. It's relationship to the oppr. vs oppr. principle is that the principle serves it; once the principle is utilised throughout society for an extended period (via the various sub-agendas), this wonderful 'equality' is then being realised, leading to societal breakdown.

Equality is not natural

Equality is not naturally occurring. It's anti-human and anti-nature. It's not humanitarian, it's pseudo-humanitarianism. Therefore, to have any hope to achieve it, it must be enforced via coercion of one form or another (something which the horrific history of the cult confirms). Trying to enforce equality, since it's not natural, only leads to the destruction of life (in a biological, existential sense), because it doesn't conform to the naturally occurring principles of life. 'Equality' in this case is the square peg being shoved into the round hole of reality, by the cult.

Nature, of which human beings are a part, doesn't care about man-made theoretical ideas like 'equality'. In a sense, it doesn't care about what humans do at all, whether they are brainwashed Marxists or not. Nature simply 'is', just like gravity. As the famous Italian astronomer Galileo Galilei once said "Nature is inexorable and immutable; she never transgresses the laws imposed upon her, or cares a whit whether her abstruse reasons and methods of operation are understandable to men".[14] The enforcement of equality brings the destruction of civilisation, and life in general. While you could say that man-made civilisation is not a part of nature in a biological sense, it is natural in that mankind—via men, who are a part of nature—create civilisation; so civilisation is an extension of nature.

It's a very natural part of life for men to design and construct the structures that form society (this has been the case for millennia). Men also have the responsibility of fighting to protect these civilisations, and their folk within. Without men—masculine men—to perform these roles, civilisation collapses. Interesting, then, that Marxism has shown a keen interest in destroying men using its weapons of feminist 'equality' and the attack on masculinity. Coincidence? In addition, men usually perform these roles using/participating in unequal hierarchies, involving a chain-of-command of some kind (another thing the cult/ideology ostensibly opposes).

---

[14] Galilei, G. "Letter to the Grand Duchess Christina of Tuscany", 1615. https://sourcebooks.fordham.edu/mod/galileo-tuscany.asp

Marxism also targets women, in order to destroy civilisation and life. It drives down the birthrates by indoctrinating them (via hedonism, feminism, abortion, lesbianism, the gender-bending movement, pop culture, pornography etc.) to not start families (or delay until it's too late) in the name of 'equality' and 'empowerment'.

Women not having children—or having a diminished mothering instinct or being devoid of a willingness to have children—is pretty abnormal/unnatural too (obviously no offence to women who physically cannot have children; this is outside their control). In other words, the ideology encourages the indoctrination/creation of women who behave in unnatural ways (of course, many of these above listed things have existed longer than the ideology, but its presence exacerbates this problem). Females competing with males—trying to be 'equal' to them—is also an unnatural behaviour that exists because of Marxism (via feminism).

A popular concept on this topic is "equality of opportunity vs equality of outcome". We who are not indoctrinated generally subscribe to the former, and the cult/ideology generally pushes for the latter. The "equality of outcome" part is, in a word, uniformity. It implies that regardless of a person's actions or how they contribute to society (or not) they will receive the same treatment as everyone else.

We can see how this would be detrimental to a society, because individuals/groups would not be judged on their merits/effects. It would lead to the breakdown of civilisation, including normal social behaviour, justice, relationships etc. Obviously, we can see how "equality of outcome" is problematic in the context of socialism—it leads to the destruction/retardation of economic prosperity.

'Equality' is bad for the mind

> "The doctrine of equality! But there is no more poisonous poison: for it seems to be preached by justice itself, while in fact it is the end of justice.. "Equal for equals, unequal for unequals"—that would be the true voice of justice. And its consequence: "Never make unequals equal". The fact that this doctrine of equality was surrounded by such horrors and blood has given this "modern idea" par excellence a sort of glory and radiance, so that the Revolution as a spectacle has seduced even the noblest of spirits"[15]

---

[15] Nietzsche, F. Twilight of the Idols (1889), P. 49.

Friedrich Nietzsche, *Twilight of the Idols*, 1889

This idea of equality is very toxic for the mind. It makes people equal alright—equally predictable and banal. Sure, if you are talking about equality in terms of rights in society (which we already have to a sufficient degree!), and 'equality of opportunity', that sounds somewhat reasonable right? However, when it comes to what human beings actually are, then it starts to become ridiculous real fast. Let's put sociological and economic concepts aside. There are many adjectives that we can apply to people, but this one is the most ridiculous and inaccurate once we examine it.

When a person becomes indoctrinated into this equality mindset, and they keep repeating this concept repeatedly in their minds, this is very damaging for the psyche. Reality is not 'equal' and uniform, neither are people, regardless of how they can seem to be sometimes (many cult members aside). Behaviours and their level (ethics-wise) are not equal either. Reality is nuanced and varied, so people's mindsets and perceptions should be this way too.

When it comes to personal development, making this concept of 'equality' the cornerstone of a person's ethical framework is ludicrous. It's an ideological propaganda term designed to push an agenda and should be treated as such. 'Equality' equalizes things, makes them somewhat identical, and doesn't acknowledge whether things are (objectively) positive or negative. This is of no use to the individual. Viewing reality through the 'equality' lens blinds a person to the nuance in reality, particularly when it comes to what is objectively true and what isn't and what is objectively right/ethical and what isn't.

All of this diminishes a person's ability to distinguish between one opinion and another; one perception and another; one group and another etc. The result is that this person cannot think independently, never mind actually judge correctly. So how can they then accurately process whatever is in their surrounding reality? They can't, and now they have a void in their personality. The ideology—with its pre-packaged set of 'values and 'ethics'—can fill that void. No need for the burden of thinking since it's done for them!

The person can then form an opinion of any given thing based on: if it's coming from a cult member in a position of authority, or how good the thing makes them feel (if the opinion is acceptable to their programming).

https://www.faculty.umb.edu/gary_zabel/Phil_100/Nietzsche_files/Friedrich-Nietzsche-Twilight-of-the-Idols-or-How-to-Philosophize-With-the-Hammer-Translated-by-Richard-Polt.pdf

In short, thinking with 'equality' on the brain makes people dumb, gullible and easy to manipulate.

'Equality' or Fairness?

We should not be pro 'equality', but pro-fairness (aka equity). There is a difference. Fairness is, in reality, what some (indoctrinated people) think equality is, which is why they want this 'equality'. They want this because they have some sense of concern for others and want them to be treated fairly. So great—let's have more fairness! Let's not, however, support the idea of 'equality' because of the destruction it leads. Obviously, those who are indoctrinated cannot understand this—the indoctrination tells them that equality is fairness. In a sense, according to the indoctrination, equality is the epitome of ethics itself. For those people, their misconception is the real issue here, but we'll cover the psychological factors elsewhere. Being able to decide what is fair/justice and what isn't is dependent upon how developed our sense of conscience is—something that is essentially retarded or amputated in indoctrinated people.

'Equality' does not help to create fairness; it actually creates unfairness. This misperception is a major causal factor of the mess society is in right now. It's the inversion of what is right/ethical and what is wrong/unethical.

Equality of criticism: a bad-habit

The equality mindset fuels bad habits. Feminism can indoctrinate females in to becoming a problem for society, and they start being destructive towards it (wittingly or unwittingly). Whenever they are criticised for behaving this way (and justifiably so), other indoctrinated types will come to their defence. This stops the justifiable criticism from having an impact and potentially preventing more destructive behaviour. This criticism is especially important where young females are concerned, because it can keep their behaviour in check if it's sufficiently potent and universal.

An example would be promiscuity. Whenever this is highlighted as being essentially degenerate, trashy behaviour, justifiers will try to 'equalise' things and retort that males have been doing this for ages, so why can't females do it now? It's to make them both seem 'equal' basically. I'm sure the reader has encountered this frustrating and unconstructive mindset!

Here the ideology perpetuates itself—it creates the issue in the first place (negative, crazy, destructive behaviour in females), then doesn't allow us as a society, to prevent those damaging effects. It's a self-perpetuating system. Whenever we try to fix a problem that originates from the ideology, we are met with this bizarre attitude which prevents us from resolving the issue(s). Same goes for any other indoctrinated 'oppressed' group whose behaviour gets out of control. The cult cannot allow any criticism of those within that group. It doesn't matter what the person has done, the group they belong to absolves them, and any criticism of this group must be met with countercriticism of the opposing group as this is somehow 'fair' (since 'equality' is regarded as 'fairness'). The mass immigration problem in Ireland shows this: whenever a migrant commits a violent crime, the cult will remind us that Irish people have committed/do commit these crimes against other Irish people.

This is a rotten psychological habit that prevents any true justice and order from prevailing. Even individuals who are only mildly indoctrinated are guilty of this one. Often the person engaging in it presumes they are being intelligent and virtuous, which is completely backwards. It's incredibly dumb! The ideology/indoctrination prevents people from being judged and punished, which is anti-justice.

Equality and Consciousness

Equality is a nonsensical, irrational idea, when it comes to the most important barometer by which to measure/judge a person—consciousness. We are not all equal in terms of consciousness. Let's first define what this means, and it would help if the reader would put aside any preconceived ideas (particularly those who may have distorted perceptions of 'spirituality', usually originating from the 'new age' movement). Consciousness is, quite simply, how genuinely aware, awake, lucid, perceptive a person is—how truly intelligent they are. Firstly, it's how well a person can process reality (reality being the actual truth about ourselves, others, our environment, how the world works etc). The second component of consciousness—which is inextricably linked—is conscience/morality, which we could also say is a high sense of ethics. A sense of right and wrong. Not according to what we perceive right and wrong to be, but what is actually right and wrong, in an objective sense.

Consciousness is true, genuine intelligence, but let's not use the word "intelligence" because it can be interpreted incorrectly. Indeed, when you say the word "intelligence" it can often trigger off erroneous, even distractionary perceptions (many coming from the Marxism-infected system itself!) of what intelligence is—such as a person's level of education, their IQ score, whether or not they are in *Mensa* etc. Of course, there are countless people in the world who are 'educated', 'rich', 'powerful' etc. who are absolute morons. In the grander scheme of things, these labels mean nothing—they may be neither educated, rich or powerful in any real sense. Conversely, there are people devoid of those attributes who can have a high level of consciousness.

Unequal signs of life in the 'living'

'Consciousness' is also how truly alive someone is; or how truly 'with it' someone is. Shocking a concept as this might be to some at first glance, it's extremely useful to those trying to make sense of the madness around them; it should resonate deeply. A certain amount of emotional control is required to do this, and it's recommended to momentarily switching off any feelings of 'sympathy'.

It's true that we are all alive in a certain sense, we all have a heartbeat, we can eat, speak, talk, walk, reproduce etc. (most of us can). Yet it's also clear we have a serious problem in the world with zombie-like individuals who are not really here; they are not really present in this world and are therefore not fully alive. They are not a fully functioning human being. This is an understanding of paramount importance but is not often discussed in these terms. Toxic ideologies have a role to play here, since they can transform the human being into these un-present/undead zombies.

The concept of 'equality' is an insult to those of us who don't fit in to this zombie category. The Marxism-riddled system has obscured this truth from us via this concept. When we look at the true nature of human beings, 'equality' is one of the most ridiculously erroneous terms we can use. The Marxist cult shows us quite clearly that we are not all equal! They are the evidence that equality doesn't and cannot exist, in terms of the most important yardstick against which to measure a human being— consciousness.

At the same time (and most interestingly, and unintentionally) the ideology/cult creates a new type of class system, with those of us who are not indoctrinated in the superior class; a fact that the cult members are totally oblivious to. Marxism-infected people are not truly present, alive, sane individuals; the ideology makes a person insane, to one degree or another.

Conversely, those who are fully lucid and are against the Globalist totalitarianism we see sweeping across the world—these people are on a different level. These people are truly alive! They generally display intelligence, consciousness (higher perception and conscience), and love. It's not fair to compare these groups. One of these groups are genuine, relatively fully-functioning, sane human beings; the other is not. On the flip side, it's interesting to note that cult members have been trying, for decades, to get their enemies certified as being insane! They peddle notions that expressing 'racism', having nationalistic or conservative or 'right-wing' perspectives is synonymous with mental illness etc. ("If you don't agree with me/us, you must be insane!"). The ideology's/cult's control of the education and healthcare systems has allowed it to decide what sanity is. Trying to get anyone who doesn't agree with Marxism to be labelled as 'mentally ill', will be par for the course in the future. And, even more extreme, they will endeavour to get these enemies treated as sub-human (which they themselves are). Inversion again.

Other elements

Some other general observations about how the cult/ideology/indoctrination operates:

Turning up the red heat...

"Boil a Frog" is an old metaphor used to describe a process of a slowly building threat. The story goes that a frog, if chucked into some boiling water, will obviously jump out asap. Most living things have this built-in safety reaction ("Reflex Action"), in some form, right? Apparently however (as the metaphor/story goes) if you put the frog in cooler water, then slowly turn up the heat until the water is boiling, it will not notice and will be cooked. In other words—the frog did not perceive the threat because things changed slowly, or more precisely, the environment changed slowly. This is a Fabian-style tactic, symbolised in the logo of the tortoise, symbolising a 'slow, (almost) imperceptible transition to socialism'.

It's also a factor in the various other manifestations of Marxism we looked at earlier: the 'Cultural Marxism', postmodernism, and 'ideological subversion'. All of these manifestations affect the target society, incrementally, over a certain period of time. 'Boil a frog' means a country/population is not suddenly attacked. The process is gradual, incremental, so it's not perceived as a threat. This strategic pace also allows for newer generations of a nation to be indoctrinated from an early age to be cult members, replacing the older, possibly resistant ones.

This perfectly sums-up the strategy used in the mass immigration sub-agenda in Europe. It has not been a (relatively) massive importation over a very short period; rather, the numbers have been spread out. I say "relatively" considering the populations of African and the Middle Eastern countries! At time of writing, the population of (the island of) Ireland is over 6.5 million, while the total population of sub-Saharan countries is in the hundreds of millions: Nigeria is 206 million, Ethiopia is 114 million etc. A Middle Eastern example is Afghanistan with 38 million. Obviously Ukranian refugees are in addition; that country's population is almost 37.5

million.[16] Turning up the heat slowly on indigenous populations in Europe using this sub-agenda, also creates a situation where migrants can become involved in politics, which only accelerates the process (of course, they may be/become cult members themselves).

In the still relatively ethnically homogenous country of Ireland, migrants have been shipped-in and implanted into various towns and locations all around the country. For the sleepy portion of the Irish public who still do not see mass immigration as an existential threat, this dispersal of the placement of the migrants keeps many in their slumber. They are the frog sitting there in the pot...unaware that the heat is being turned-up... If however, massive amounts of migrants were shipped-in to only one location (Dublin or Cork) even those sleepy Irish would notice so much easier. The water is beginning to rise up around the necks of the indigenous folk now, ethnically speaking, and it has been a relatively slow creep for the most part.

Everyday fanatics who defend their cult/ideology

The indoctrination turns average everyday people in to often-aggressive fanatics, who are programmed to react to certain stimuli. In a sense, they become like robots. (robot voice) "I am... o-ffen-ded!!". As mentioned, those infected may perceive any form of aggression or criticism towards a person in a 'victim' group as 'oppression'. Not only do they believe that this aggression/criticism is wrong, but they will actively try to suppress it, regardless of why the aggression or criticism occurs. I'm sure you have experienced this at some point. Example: if you express criticises of anyone in an 'oppressed' group, the indoctrinated person will 'correct' you. You may get this reaction whether you are actually right or wrong in your criticism. This can even happen if the person you are criticising is not even in the room! It could be a total stranger, someone on TV, online etc. In other words, no actual harm is being done by you, yet you are being 'corrected' because you have triggered the indoctrinated person (who obviously thinks you are doing something wrong). This is the cult's ideological control at the ground level. In this instance, the indoctrinated person will be the little commissar of the regime and will dutifully police the other sheep. If you find yourself being 'corrected' like this, then you are probably dealing with a cult member (whether you/they have realised it or not).

The cult's hypocrisy is present here: they think you are doing something wrong, and they will try to 'correct' you/control your behaviour (which is actually wrong). Obviously, this ties-in with the spoilt brat factor too, as

---

[16] https://www.worldometers.info/world-population/population-by-country/

brats love to control their environment (including other people)! It can also be linked to some good old nagging, which is linked to being spoilt/immature too. If you are unfortunate enough to be in the company of someone who is spoilt, likes to nag, and has the Marxist infection, you have my sympathies.

Pathological Altruism

When a society is infected with Marxism for a prolonged period, it can develop something called Pathological Altruism—the insane child of the oppressor v oppressed principle. The constant emphasis in society (thanks to the indoctrination) on 'oppressed' groups leads to this psychotic over-indulgence in feminine emotions. The result is an excessive amount of empathy/sympathy, by default, towards whichever group is given 'victim'/oppressed status by the cult. This in turn leads to the aforementioned distorted perceptions of those groups, including their behaviour. This imbalanced perspective becomes engrained in the minds of many. It's that "naaaaaaaaw" attitude gone nuts, encapsulated in the cult's word of choice — "compassion". It manifests as the inability to control emotions and have a rational approach to issues. Taken to its conclusion, pathological altruism is when a person/group/nation helps (or attempts to help) others even if it means their own destruction.

"Pathological" from the Greek "Pathos" meaning suffering, or experience, or emotion. It's related to pathology or illness. When we apply this mindset to a nation, it means the manifestation of self-destructive tendencies of that nation, particularly with respect to its internationalist 'humanitarian' endeavours (i.e. immigration policies, NGO/non-profit initiatives etc.). This element works with the highly important oppr. v oppr. principle by being the emotional fuel that allows it to function (and therefore cause chaos, destruction, imbalance etc.).

"Altruism" essentially means to perform actions for the benefit of others. From the *Oxford English Dictionary*: "Disinterested or selfless concern for the well-being of others, esp. as a principle of action. Opposed to selfishness, egoism, or (in early use) egotism".[17] From a purely feminine emotional point of view, this might seem very noble; but is this noble if that altruistic act is destroying not only the performer of that act, but their folk, their society, their heritage? No! In other words, sacrificing the well-being of one group (your own!) for another? No, that's not noble; that's hypocritical! You either respect life/people/races/cultures or you don't!

---

[17] Oxford English Dictionary - "Altruism".
https://www.oed.com/search/dictionary/?scope=Entries&q=altruism

Obviously, we are referring to mass immigration here, which is perhaps the most serious manifestation of this masochistic, psychopathic mentality. Of course, no-one is suggesting that there's no such thing as the correct application of altruism, but there's a time and place.

It's also true that we don't have the right to practice this supposed altruism on a big scale like that (as in mass immigration) to the detriment of our own nations, people etc. Nobody has that right, certainly not some piece of trash conscience-less politician, NGO chief or Marxist activist!

Pathological altruism can be applied to the other Marxist sub-agendas: males who support feminism are participating in something anti-male, helping to make males (including themselves) in to second class citizens; in veganism, people are participating in the destruction of their own bodies, minds, race and nation for the supposed benefit of agricultural animals who don't even know that the vegans exist (never mind care about them); in the climate change con, by forcing themselves to reduce their CO_2 emissions to insanely low levels, countries will only damage their industries and cripple themselves financially, in order to help 'save' the planet. It's actual self-destruction due to being 'nice'.

'Compassion'

Related to the last item, here is a common virtue-signalling term you often hear being thrown around by the indoctrinated: compassion. Another Marxian marketing con word, used to emotionally manipulate.

It's related to the oppr. vs oppr. principle, because, again, the cult/ideology needs to get the masses over-emotional about anyone in the 'oppressed' classes (to manipulate them). Naturally it also employs the Red Trojan Horse principle because it seems so benevolent, humanitarian, conforms to 'social justice' etc. It also assists in the prioritisation of those in the 'oppressed' classes over those who are not, which itself helps in the enforcement of artificial, destabilising, destructive equality. Furthermore, the concept of 'compassion', as used by the cult, has the role of justifying their 'revolutionary' actions, in addition to encouraging more of this wonderful 'activism'. It's an extremely effective multi-purpose word, perfect for the cult's constant virtue-signalling, hence it's common usage.

In 2018 in Ireland, there was a constitutional referendum to repeal the (1983) 8th amendment of the constitution (which made abortion illegal unless in certain circumstances), thereby making abortion more widely available and socially acceptable. Obviously, cult members in Ireland in general, not just the feminists, brought in this change.

After the referendum, the unelected 'leader' of Ireland—the living abortion

Leo Varadkar—used the word three times in a short, typically nauseating speech: "We have voted to provide compassion where there was once a cold shoulder, and to offer medical care where once we turned a blind eye." And: "Listening to the arguments on both sides over the past few weeks I was struck by what we had in common, rather than what divided us ('solidarity'). Both sides expressed a desire to care for women in a crisis, both sides wanted compassion, both sides wanted to choose life.". And: "Everyone deserves a second chance. This is Ireland's second chance to treat everyone equally and with compassion and respect".[18] Of course, "everyone deserves a second chance" while the unborn foetus doesn't even get one chance, or an ounce of 'compassion' for that matter. You can just picture the smiling, watery-eyed emotional degenerates reacting to his speech, feeling fuzzy-warm feelings.

Interestingly, Varadkar's speech started with the line "Today is a historic day for Ireland. A quiet revolution has taken place, and a great act of democracy." This sums-up the Fabian strategy of a covert Marxian takeover, highlighting how the cult uses 'democracy' to take control. They make it seem like it's the wishes of 'the people', but it isn't—it's the wishes of the cult. In a Marxism-riddled country like Ireland, at that point, only the cult members were motivated to get out there and vote en masse, so it's not exactly a level playing field; many are understandably disillusioned with the system.

The word compassion insinuates that if you don't go along with the various Marxist sub-agendas, that you don't care about other human beings or their suffering; that you are a sub-standard human being. "If you don't have compassion for (X), you are a bad person!". They are saying: "I am a better person than you. We are better than you because we support this". There is a simple way to counter all of that: Marxist cult members are in no position to lecture anyone about ethics/morality! So don't worry about cult members accusing us in this way. They are hypocrites of the highest order. What they are really saying (with the word "compassion") is: "if you don't agree with this Marxist sub-agenda, you are a bad person", which translates to "Marxism is ethics itself". Cult talk.

If you object to your little boy or girl in school being taught about homosexuality (by their infected Marxist 'teacher'), then you might be

---

[18] "Speech by An Taoiseach, Leo Varadkar following the declaration on the Referendum on the Eighth Amendment", Sun 27 May 2018.
https://merrionstreet.ie/en/news-room/speeches/speech_by_an_taoiseach_leo_varadkar_following_the_declaration_on_the_referendum_on_the_eighth_amendment.html

accused of lacking compassion for gay people. If you object to drag queen story time, you lack compassion for drag queens; if you object to 'saving the planet', you lack compassion for the planet (again, giggles); if you object to veganism, you lack compassion for the cows, chickens etc.; if you object to BLM, you lack compassion for black/non-white people; if you object to socialism, you lack compassion for 'poor' people etc. And on and on it goes…

Again, this 'compassion' is very selective, being only applied towards certain Marxism-approved groups/individuals. Obviously a 'poor' person who is opposed to socialism is a fascist, Nazi, racist etc. (or a 'self-hating proletarian'?).

There is almost a pseudo-spiritual element involved here too. As in, if you don't have this Marxist 'compassion' you are lacking something on a deeper level. Not only are you a bad person, lacking in conscience, but you are not a fully developed, progressive human being. In fact, you don't belong in this new superior class of human being that the Marxist culture is creating.

Finally, this term ties-in to the tactic of overloading society with femininity. It's just more jargon to con people via their emotions and egos, and many have been suckers for it. It's all really quite cringe, pathetic and juvenile.

'Social(ist) Justice'

Another virtue-signalling term is "social justice". Just say it loud for a second go on…even whisper it with your eyes closed can you feel that? Can you feel the revolutionary power in your soul deep within your loins? (rolls eyes, fucks sake). Of course, 'social' justice, really means Marxist 'justice': society being structured according to twisted Marxian 'ethics' and principles (permanent revolution, equality, solidarity, diversity, 'compassion' etc.).

Here's another example of the hypocritical double-standards: if you talk about things like right and wrong and morality, you will get accused of being misguided—that your ideas come from outdated non-progressive ideas, like religion etc. You may hear things like "…but what do you mean by "right" and what do you mean by "wrong"?", and become dragged-in to subjective, relativist debates with them (a lá postmodernism).

Basically, they will criticise your ideas about right and wrong and say you cannot have these beliefs, and then come the categorising insults (far-right, Nazi, fascist etc.). So momentarily you are given the impression that there is no system of ethics in the cult, that even the idea of ethics itself might not hold any meaning for it.

Then the situation becomes flipped, when you hear them go and use virtue-signalling terms like "Social Justice"; a term which implies that they have a system of ethics. And not only that, they're so sure of the righteousness of their system, they believe they have the right to impose their beliefs on the whole of society(!). They will claim that their ethics come from (Marxian) 'science' (including the social sciences and whatever other conduit the ideology can use), and not from relatively 'silly' ideas like traditionalism, conservatism, religion etc. This makes their system of ethics superior, apparently. "Social Justice" is just another verbal manifestation of that spoiled-brat psychosis: "we are right, and you are wrong! We are the best, we are special! It's all about us getting our own way!" etc. Cult member talk.

Virtue-Signalling

Virtue-signalling is when someone does something (i.e. makes a statement) to convince other people that they're wonderful: "Look at me! I'm saying/doing this because I'm a good person, and if you want to be a good person, you should be saying/doing this too!". Is this what virtue-signalling is all about? Immaturity? Narcissism? Petty self-aggrandizement? Or is there a deeper significance in terms of the ideology itself? All those, but the latter too, which is much more insidious. That speech mentioned earlier by Leo Varadkar (after the cult's abortion referendum victory) was a good example of a public figure virtue-signalling. A politician, using words like "care" and "compassion" etc. I'm sure that person has some issues with immaturity, narcissism, and self-aggrandizement, but those are not the only reasons why we hear a 'person' like that speaking in that way.

This behaviour is coming from the Marxism-infused system, to attempt to control the thoughts/words/actions of the masses. It's no accident that pretty much every public figure you see is now doing this, and all more-or-less at the same time, all over the world! From politicians, to actors, to journalists, to authors, to talk show hosts etc. We are seeing so much of it currently because it's promotion and suggestive programming.

It's a way of telling people how to feel about things, and how to behave through demonstration. It relies on the monkey-see, monkey-do sheep-like aspect of human behaviour. It shows those witnessing the act of virtue-signalling "See? When you show (Marxist) care and compassion for those who deserve it (especially publicly!), others (other cult members) will give you admiration, respect etc.". (well, this prob doesn't apply in Varadkar's case; nobody likes him).

Virtue-signalling is very effective at conditioning the impressionable portion of the general public through their emotions and egos, and works on two levels:

Firstly, it programmes the audience with the programming itself—in this case (in Varadkar's 'compassion' speech) the programming is that abortion means healthcare for women, or whatever the programming is, the sub-agenda being promoted is (e.g. multiculturalism and diversity = positive, progressive etc.). It's the promotion of a particular Marxist sub-agenda.

In addition to promoting the Marxist sub-agenda (in this case abortion), it also conditions the audience to believe that supporting the sub-agenda is the morally/ethically correct thing to do. This serves the purpose of discouraging any sort of doubt in the minds of the audience that the right thing has been done (in this example: that the law will be changed to make it much easier for women to have abortions in Ireland). Promotion, then reassurance/reinforcement. This promotion component, of course, also re-enforces the Marxist feminist brainwashing that having an abortion is a normal, rational, socially acceptable thing for a female to do. In short, the speech encourages women to have abortions, by suggestion.

Secondly, it programmes the audience to engage in virtue-signalling themselves, as there are benefits to be had—adoration, respect etc.—from other idiots. The mere fact that a public figure is doing it activates the "monkey-see, monkey-do" mechanism. It's the Marxist ideology using the superficial celebrity culture to its advantage. Now, I know that many people hate a character like a Leo Varadkar, and would give him abuse even after a speech like that (regardless of their ideological leanings), but there are also others who would pander to and fawn all over him afterwards.

Those are the types I'm talking about, whether they are close to him or in the audience. I'm pointing that out because obviously this second level (that virtue-signalling works on) doesn't apply to anyone who doesn't trust or respect the person engaging in it.

There's also a (progressive red) snowball effect with virtue-signalling because the more people get sucked-in to the cult (wittingly or unwittingly), the more of a sympathetic, idolising, fawning audience there will be for those who publicly engage in virtue-signalling. Again, it comes back to the ego and emotions, craving love/admiration/respect etc.: "I want people to see how great and special I am! How compassionate, caring, brave, strong I can be!". It's comparable to how cult members give each other respect/adoration/love: the bigger the cult, the more of those things you can get! Therefore, it's in the self-interest and collective-interest of all cult members to virtue-signal since they benefit from it. It's their nectar. Consider them addicts.

A truly 'progressive' system

The cult may start with one thing and move to more extreme things as part of their revolutionary master plan for society, during the destabilisation process (thanks Yuri). In Ireland, there was a gay marriage referendum in 2015, and a pro-abortion referendum in 2018.[19] Perhaps if every (non-indoctrinated) person in Ireland knew how serious the seemingly frivolous issue of gay marriage was, they would have opposed it.

Since much of the general public was unaware of the significance of this milestone, there was no need for the internationalists to force anything—the people consented in sufficient numbers. The referendum's affirmative result also showed the internationalists that the indoctrination was working, and that Ireland was now 'progressive' enough to accept more drastic changes (i.e. abortion).

Then you eventually have the promotion/normalisation of even more bizarre and degenerate behaviours like the hyper-sexualisation of children and drag-queen story time, which assists in paving the way for the normalisation of paedophilia etc. If you've been around for a few decades, I'm sure you've noticed how there has been an incremental intensification of these 'progressive' changes in recent years in the west, particularly the past decade. A slippery slope of degeneracy..

It's as if the population is being tested somewhat; if it's gullible enough to fall for one con, it shows that it may be ready to fall for another one. In Ireland, the gay marriage referendum came before the abortion referendum. The public's response to the former had a bearing on the manifestation of the latter. Perhaps the Marxism-riddled state wouldn't have bothered to try the abortion move if the public's response to 'progressivism' up until that point was much less welcoming.

Hypocrisy and double-standards if you oppose the cult

Even though the inherent hypocrisy seems like a flaw of the cult, in a sense, it's a strength (from their point of view), because it breeds extreme, insane fanaticism, making the movement more powerful. This in turn accelerates the ideology's destructive impact on civilisation long-term. We can see these contradictions in the behaviour of the cult/ideology in general, and in the instances mentioned earlier.

As another example—if a woman publicly expresses patriotic, conservative, or 'right-wing' views, she will be attacked by cult members for doing so. Why is she attacked if she belongs to an 'oppressed' group?

---

[19] https://en.wikipedia.org/wiki/Thirty-fourth_Amendment_of_the_Constitution_of_Ireland

This can also even apply in an instance where a non-Marxist female was defending herself from a Marxist/pro-Marxist male (who was being abusive psychologically/verbally etc.).

Bizarrely, the attacks would also include those Marxists who describe themselves are feminists. The fact that she's female is irrelevant when she's being a dangerous fascist with right-wing views. The fact that she is not Marxist is the real issue that must be addressed and countered by the cult. That you belong to a group with 'oppressed' status doesn't trump the fact that you are a threat to the ideology. Indeed, indoctrinated females would see you as being a 'traitor' to women! Lana Lokteff of Red Ice TV, for example, was regularly criticised by female cult members when their YouTube channel was at the height of its popularity.

The same would apply to a person belonging to any other designated 'oppressed' group—migrant, gay person etc.—who espouses views that contradict Marxist ones. The minute criticism is levelled at the cult/ideology, the 'oppressed' status that this person would normally be entitled to evaporates. The instance that you attack Marxism/PC culture etc., you are instantly 'moved' from that 'oppressed' group to a new (bad!) group, depending on what you've said/done. So basically, you can now be 'attacked' by Marxist minions without them having to face their own hypocrisy (as you are now, technically, no longer 'oppressed'; you're now the 'oppressor'). If you are not Marxist and/or opposed to Marxism, they will mock you, suppress your opinion, try to harm you etc. (to a degree that matches the level of threat you present). An example of this would be British author Douglas Murray who is also gay—his opinions on many issues, including homosexuality, has drawn fire from cult members in the LGBTQ movement.

You may even be part of an 'oppressed' group, and have assisted the cult/ideology, but you are simply not 'revolutionary' enough. Take the case of the ultra-successful and famous British author J.K. Rowling, who wrote the *Harry Potter* series. Over the years Rowling has avidly supported many causes that benefit the cult/ideology, including creating female-orientated NGO/non-profits, donating to the British Labour Party, and opposing the Brexit campaign.[20] However, she stopped short of going along with the more extreme gender-bending initiatives of the cult, incurring their wrath.[21] Basically, she didn't agree that 'trans women' are in fact women, and

---

[20] https://www.britannica.com/biography/J-K-Rowling

[21] Rowling, J. "J.K. Rowling Writes about Her Reasons for Speaking out on Sex and Gender Issues", June 2020. https://www.jkrowling.com/opinions/j-k-rowling-writes-about-her-reasons-for-speaking-out-on-sex-and-gender-issues/

supported the late Magdalen Berns (1983–2019)—another cult member who fell afoul of the tranny extremists. Amongst other things, Berns took issue with the idea that lesbians who didn't want to have sex with 'trans women' (men with penises) was due to them being transphobic etc. (queue gender-queer circus music).[22] I'm digging the mass grave now, petrol cans at the ready.

Rowling's case is a reminder that there are levels of fanaticism at work here. It shows that if you're not extreme enough and disagree somewhat, regardless of wealth or notoriety, you will be forced to conform, or you will be attacked. And labelled too—she has now been placed in the *TERF* (trans-exclusionary radical feminist) category by more extreme cult members.[23] Crazy. The ideology creeps up the shore in every increasing waves…

[22] https://en.wikipedia.org/wiki/Magdalen_Berns

[23] https://en.wikipedia.org/wiki/TERF

Section IX — The Sub-Agendas It Supports

"History is a relay of revolutions; the torch of idealism is carried by the revolutionary group until this group becomes an establishment, and then quietly the torch is put down to wait until a new revolutionary group picks it up for the next leg of the run. Thus the revolutionary cycle goes on"[1]

Saul Alinsky, *Rules for Radicals*, 1971

Introduction

Listed in this section are the various destructive sub-agendas active in our world today, supported by the cult/ideology; the different components within one integrated machine—the internationalist globalist Marxist system. They all serve the ultimate agenda of the ideology, which is world domination.

It's important to remember that while these (sub-agendas) are all seemingly disparate issues (and may be regarded as such by the vast majority), they are all in fact joined at an ideological level by Marxism; they only seem disparate on the surface. This is a crucial point and must be widely understood by the previously uninformed masses. In addition, the sub-agendas are all, quite obviously, forms of 'revolution', being arguably the most visible part of the Marxist system, even to the layman. The international Marxist movement has either created these sub-agendas or supports them. Indeed, if we suddenly removed the ideology from the world, it would be hard to see how these sub-agendas could gain any sort of real traction or even make any impact at all, never mind maintain the prevalence they do in the public consciousness. In addition, it must be pointed out that these sub-agendas are what actually causes the damage to civilisation in real-world terms, more so than the ideology itself. The damage the sub-agendas do is the end-product manifested by the ideology. This damage is what's 'waking' people up to this crazy revolutionary

---

[1] Alinsky, S., *Rules for Radicals* (1971), P. 35.

activity.

Some things supported by Marxism, such as mass immigration (and the related one-world government concept), are much bigger and older than the ideology, in the grander scope of things. Others, such as the 'Islamification' of western countries, obviously is the crossover between two ideologies: Marxism and Islam. Obviously since Islam predates Marxism considerably, we can't say that Marxism created it (approximately twelve centuries earlier, if we measure from the death of Muhammed to the authoring of the Communist Manifesto). However, the aim of this section is to highlight that the ideology plays the central role of allowing the various sub-agendas to transform the world, especially western civilisation. Whether or not Marxism has actually historically created the sub-agenda in question is not the main issue here—we need to be focused on the destructive, enabling, central role of the ideology in the present.

(As an aside, the above is connected to "Islamo-Socialism"—the co-operation between certain elements of Islam and those of the cult. Since these elements both shares similar ambitions of world domination and contain anti-Western anti-Christian sentiments, it's only natural for them to be in alliance.[2] This also explains why cult members won't criticise and attack Muslims/Islam the way they would Christians/Christianity. And naturally it's another reason to explain why the cult has been pro-Palestine/anti-Israel over the decades).

All sub-agendas, to one degree or another, are based on the original oppressor v oppressed principle as featured in the Communist Manifesto. They are simply variations of the same original 'class struggle' of the rich/bourgeoisie/oppressor group v the poor/proletariat/oppressed group. And just like the original, there are usually two groups involved, being placed in either role.

Within the indoctrination component, the sub-agendas also produce the same emotional responses and results (outlined earlier), more or less. Combined with other factors (e.g. the 'revolutionary' mindset that Marxist activism encourages), these emotional responses lead to calls for (pro-Marxist) action, which then gives the sub-agendas traction in our societies. Of course, without action there can be no impact. Indeed, if the ideology purely remained in intellectual, philosophical, or academic spheres, and never manifested in real word action (leading to the inevitable

---

[2] https://www.encyclopedia.com/social-sciences/applied-and-social-sciences-magazines/socialism-islamic

consequences), this book would not be required. The ideology/indoctrination demands 'revolutionary'/'progressive' action.

Ticking commie red boxes....

Throughout this section, we'll keep in mind the various elements of Marxism we've looked at so far. They're all interconnected and there's some crossover between them. Basically, we are looking at how many commie red boxes each sub-agenda ticks. On a bigger-picture level, having this approach is key to sniffing-out the presence of the cult/ideology in our world.

Here are the elements we are looking out for when we examine each sub-agenda; we have to ask ourselves:

Does it use the oppressor v oppressed/divide and conquer principle?

Does it feature two groups, setting one up as the oppressor/dominator/controller/user/evil perpetrator, and setting the other up as the oppressed/dominated/controlled/used/innocent victim? Does it create tension, conflict, and division by doing so? Does it specifically target certain groups within society by placing them in the 'oppressor' group? Does giving these 'oppressed' groups this special status ensure preferential treatment for them? Does it brainwash people by triggering off the two main emotional responses towards the two groups? (negativity, judgement, hatred, contempt for the 'oppressor'; positivity, sympathy, empathy, 'love', 'compassion' for the 'oppressed').

Does it create a new class system, and contain double-standards/hypocrisy?

Does the sub-agenda attempt to create a new category of person, who'll be essentially treated as second-class citizens? Do standards of behaviour that apply to the 'oppressor' group not apply to those in the 'oppressed' group? Does it apply preferential treatment to one group (the 'oppressed'), which damages the welfare of those in the 'oppressor' group? Does the preferential treatment of those in the 'oppressed' group become so extreme, that those in the 'oppressor' group become completely neglected or mistreated, and may develop a tendency to self-destruct?

Does it use the Trojan Horse principle?

Does the sub-agenda embody negativity, yet it's disguised as positivity; malevolence, disguised as benevolence? Is there anything in how the sub-agenda is labelled, or in the associated words, to give this false impression? Does its destructive nature become apparent later, after considerable damage has already been done?

Is it based on a distorted perception of history and/or reality in the present?

Does it rely on the ignorance of history (reality in the past) to create a new false narrative that serves Marxism to 'create' a new (reality in the) present? Does it distort the nature of things in modern history or in recent times for the same reason?

Is it promoted/supported by the system?

Does either the government, transmission belts of culture (education, media, entertainment industry), NGO's/non-profits, or other institutions/organisations promote or support it? Or, most tellingly, do they all simultaneously promote/support it in a co-ordinated fashion, even on an international scale? (this is a key factor, showing the internationalism and conspiratorial nature of the cult/ideology, in addition to showing its dominance).

Does it attack the pillars of western civilisation: Capitalism, Christianity, Culture?

Does the sub-agenda in question contribute to the destruction of these things in any way, even only in reputation? Obviously, something as nebulous as capitalism can't be destroyed, but the cult will openly criticise it as much as they can and promote socialism as the alternative.

Therefore, if the sub-agenda promotes socialism, it can be construed as an attack on capitalism. Same goes for if the sub-agenda engages in propaganda against Christianity or Christians, or deliberately promotes things which goes against genuine Christian values (e.g. abortion, polyamory, gay marriage etc.)

Does the sub-agenda try to attack culture in a given country? Does it de-emphasise traditionalism, national heritage in any way? Does it criticize, 'deconstruct' or replace aspects of a country's history, usually to replace that with Marxian interpretations? Does it try to create a reality where the actual unique attributes of different groups—whether they be racial, cultural, national, or religious—are either ignored or suppressed, being covered up by a Marxist red politically-correct gloss?

Does it attempt to enforce 'equality'?

Does the sub-agenda try to enforce the artificial and hypothetical Marxist concept of 'equality', particularly between different groups? Does it try to create uniformity between them? Is it attempting to destroy any sort of genuine outstanding unequal brilliance or strength in society by suppressing it (as this works in opposition to the erroneous concept that we are all equal)?

Does it involve virtue-signalling?

Do we see virtue-signalling being employed to push this particular sub-agenda? Is there emotional manipulation present? Is the propaganda telling us that this sub-agenda will be of benefit to certain groups, our societies/nations, and even humanity as a whole?

The sub-agendas and the oppressor v oppressed principle

A table to show some of the sub-agendas laid out according to the oppressor v oppressed principle:

Agenda	Oppressor	Oppressed
Abortion	Unborn child/patriarchy/males *	Women #
Anti-Capitalism	Capitalism/capitalists/rich people (the bourgeoisie) *	Non-wealthy/working class/proletariat and socialists #
Anti-Christianity	Christians, Roman Catholic Church	Non-Christians, Catholics ^ #
Black Lives Matter	Whites *	Blacks/non-whites in general #
Climate Change	Humans *	Earth (again, giggles).
Feminism	Heterosexual males */the patriarchy	Females #
LGBTQ	Anyone not in these categories *	Those in these categories #
Multiculturalism/Mass Immigration/Anti-Racism	Whites/capitalists/Imperialists **	Non-whites from Africa, Middle East, Far East, Latin America #

Paedophilia	Non-paedophiles *	Paedophiles
Palestinian rights	Israelis/Israeli sympathisers/U.S. *	Palestinians #
Veganism	Animal product producers/consumers	Animals

* Cult members exempt obviously, as they show their 'solidarity' with these 'oppressed' groups and will have 'compassion' for them.

** White Europeans in particular, because they're the ones who created all the oppressive evil empires, right?

Unless these people are 'evil right-wing fascist Nazis (i.e. non-cult members), in which case they are given 'oppressor' status instead.

I include "Catholics" here because the cult will highlight the paedophilia issue in the Catholic Church, and that the victims are Catholics/former Catholics. Again, they are not allowed 'oppressed' status if they are anti-Marxist (which many Christians are). The Catholics in this instance are given merely a token 'oppressed' status, as the ideology doesn't care about Catholics/Christians of course (!), but it feigns it to destroy the Church. A more comprehensive breakdown of (some) of the sub-agendas in more general terms is further along in the section.

Ingredients in the mixture

Arguably no individual sub-agenda listed is more serious than the others, therefore they're in no particular order overall. They are, however, grouped together by type in some instances. They all work together, like parts in a commie machine, or ingredients in a commie stew. One could argue that, say, mass immigration is a very serious, existential threat to the integrity of civilisation; indeed, it is.

However, this sub-agenda does not exist on its own; nor was it initiated or been perpetuated on its own; and, despite its obvious disastrous consequences, we certainly cannot hope to stop this while ignoring all the other sub-agendas (!).

Since a major objective of Marxism is to destroy civilisation (and rebuild it as a commie 'utopia'), then logically, all of the following sub-agendas contribute towards this process in various ways or quantities; and/or at different stages of the overall process. Similarly, all these sub-agendas contribute towards the One World Government super-objective—with which the ideology is interlinked.

With Marxism, we are dealing with an organic, psychological, ideological monster that can be rudimentary and predictable, yet simultaneously complex and multi-faceted; and each sub-agenda may connect to others in various ways. Sometimes they are synchronised; sometimes not. Sometimes some (seemingly) lay dormant, while the others are fully active.

The various sub-agendas support and perpetuate each other

The various sub-agendas have an almost symbiotic relationship. They support each other in such a way that their success/dominance individually is greatly assisted by the success/dominance of other individual sub-agendas; and by extension, the success/dominance of all of them combined. A quick blend of examples:

Feminism, LGBTQ, and the attack on Christianity, all contribute towards the destruction of marriage and the traditional nuclear family unit. This helps reducing the population in affected/infected countries which are normally white, western countries (anti-white agenda). Feminism also increases abortion levels in the infected country (due to normalisation/popularisation), in addition to encouraging/influencing females to wait until later in life to have children. These also help to reduce the birthrates in the population. The destruction of the family also gives the Marxism-riddled system more control over the minds of the young (since parents are progressively removed from the equation), which benefits all the sub-agendas since the young will be indoctrinated in to supporting them.

Feminism and veganism combine to help to destroy testosterone levels which leads to a societal masculinity/femininity imbalance. This feminising effect leads to the dominance of feminine attitudes towards issues/people/society involving 'oppressed' groups (migrants, LGBTQ, gender 'non-binary' etc.), which the oppressor v oppressed principle is reliant on.

Veganism helps to (nutritionally) reduce testosterone levels in society since it's a cholesterol-deficient and low-in-saturated-fat diet (which, amongst other things, negatively impacts the human endocrine system, responsible for creating hormones). The brainwashed may think this is great, as it apparently helps to reduce 'toxic-masculinity' in men. The dwindling levels of testosterone exacerbates the problem of male suicides (due to the depression the deficiency creates), which combined with the suppression/neglect of males (thanks to feminism), assists the artificial, unequal societal prioritisation/dominance of females which makes the cult/ideology stronger. A testosterone-deficient physically and mentally weak society is also obviously much easier to invade/destroy and dominate/control.

Veganism massively increases infertility in the target population (due to the damage it does to hormone production), helping the anti-white agenda. It also assists in the destruction of western civilisation from an infrastructural/organisational point of view, because masculinity (and how it manifests in men's actions every single day) is required for civilisation to function.

Masculinity is required for a society to defend itself from attack. The impacts of the ideology (and its various sub-agendas) primarily applies to western, predominantly white and traditionally Christian countries. Since the ideology doesn't have a weakening impact on the migrant population, a differential is created in all the areas that are affected by the various sub-agendas. In other words, the migrant populations will not experience the destructive effects of feminism, abortion, multiculturalism, veganism etc. They will not experience fertility issues and falling birthrates, the dominance of feminine/over-emotional attitudes, the suppression/feminisation of their males etc.! Indeed, western females have much lower birthrates compared to Muslim women specifically, allowing Muslims to outbreed westerners very easily. The 'Islamification of the west' agenda, of course, is assisted greatly by mass immigration, feminism, LGBTQ etc.

The Anti-Christianity agenda is helped by the Islamification agenda. Islam/Muslims will dominate in traditionally Christian countries by simply demographically replacing Christianity/Christians through superior breeding rates (a situation helped by the ideology's other anti-reproduction sub-agendas). On a religious level, Islamification fulfils a major goal of the ideology, and the destruction of a pillar of western civilisation: Christianity. Also, the Islamification sub-agenda helps the anti-white sub-agenda. Non-white migrant males—Muslim or otherwise—won't have problems with reduced testosterone levels (nor will they be vegan!) meaning that the western nations they inhabit are wide-open to domination by migrant males. This differential in masculinity, combined with the multiculturalism/diversity sub-agenda also creates a situation where (some) indoctrinated white females may choose migrant males rather than their white indigenous counterparts, leading to wide-spread race mixing or miscegenation (which the ideology promotes/supports, since it's anti-white people).

Veganism also helps to destroy hormone levels in the young, which helps the gender-bending transgender sub-agenda and creates more children with psychological sexual identity issues (greatly benefiting the cult/ideology). Veganism at any age (eventually) leads to degeneration of brain tissue and the associated conditions: inability to control emotions and anxiety; mental health/brain health issues (including early-onset Parkinson's, Alzheimer's); the aforementioned hormonal dis-function; compromised immune system; and reduced lifespan. These effects contribute to an overall weakened society, psychosis, and population replacement. The more emotionally unstable and insane individuals there are in society, the better for the cult/ideology; veganism helps to achieve this on a dietary level, as the above effects are congruent with an unnatural diet deficient in animal fats and high-quality animal protein with a complete amino acid profile.

Veganism is also used in combination with the climate change con. Going vegan is seen as better for the planet, more 'sustainable' (anti-capitalism) etc. This allows the cult/ideology to use one sub-agenda to promote the other and vice-versa. Vegan activists often refer to 'farming for profits' and the 'oppression and exploitation' of animals (anti-capitalism).

The Palestinian rights sub-agenda traditionally championed by Marxists also helps the mass immigration and Islamification sub-agendas. It allows the cult to place non-white Muslims (as a collective) in the 'oppressed' category.

It can also tie this in with their traditional anti-America agenda, as the apparent displacement of 'refugees' from 'war-torn' areas in the Middle East (apparently due to racist, bourgeois capitalist 'American imperialism') is part of the official narrative of the cause of mass migration. As the U.S. supports Israel, the cult supports the Palestinian 'cause' by proxy, and of course, the world-wide cult/ideology would benefit greatly from the annihilation of a western military ally and 'democracy' in the Middle East. Again, Marxism doesn't care about people (e.g. Palestinians, Muslims, Afghanis etc.), it only cares about perpetuating itself.

The Black Lives Matter movement, quite symbolically, led to blatant attacks on businesses and business owners during the unrest (anti-capitalism), in addition to theft or destruction of private property. It also led to attacks on the police, which is an attack on the state ('revolution' and 'anarchy'). It obviously supports the anti-white people agenda, placing them in the oppressor category.

The LGBTQ 'Pride' movement promotes unusual, unconventional, non-traditional heterosexual behaviour, which paves the way for more unusual and sinister things such as the hyper-sexualisation of children and the normalisation of paedophilia. In other words—it destroys the perception of what is normal or usual (hence the word "queer"). This movement also helps to promote the extremely central, toxic, 'progressive' concept that sex is about hedonism, not reproduction; this severely conditions the general population, especially the young, when it comes to their attitudes about sex/sexuality. The message is that any sort of sexual behaviour is good, provided someone is enjoying it, which then allows (some) to argue that paedophilia is ok. This is why we are seeing these degenerate scum notions appearing in society in recent times that children can enjoy sexual experiences with adults etc. If this is accepted as reasonable, then both parties involved are enjoying the act, thereby legitimising paedophilia. The LGBTQ and 'non-binary' sub-agendas attempt to enforce equality when it comes to sex, sexuality, sexual preferences, and gender.

The 'transgender' agenda preys on young (often pre-pubescent) males and females who have mental problems ('gender dysphoria' etc.), which results in them having hormonal treatment and 'gender reassignment' operations. This results in their reproductive system being destroyed which makes them infertile, which in turn helps to lower the birthrates (population control/reduction). The trans sub-agenda seeks to destroy the biological differences between males and females, which is the enforcement of equality on a biological level. Finally, the cult/ideology created/supports the LGBTQ sub-agenda because the apparent 'oppression' of these groups comes from the 'Cis' male-dominated patriarchal bourgeois capitalist system.

The climate change sub-agenda has genocidal anti-human/humanity undertones, telling us that human beings are too numerous on the Earth. It claims we need to reduce our 'carbon footprint', and that a reduced population would be constructive, encapsulated in the idea that having smaller families is somehow the responsible thing to do (there's that inversion again). Obviously, and tellingly, this does not apply to non-white migrants coming in to western countries from Africa and the Middle East—they'll not be encouraged to have less children (a racist double-standard)! In addition, the Marxist watermelon 'Greens' (commie red on inside, green on outside) will insist that western countries should take in millions of migrants, which requires a colossal scale of transport overall, in addition to the construction of housing etc. which is not environmentally friendly or 'sustainable'! (Note: admittedly not all melons are red on the inside, such as Rock melon (Cantaloupe). Let's not engage in fruitist stereotyping).

This is merely riffing; the connections are endless. You could go cross-eyed analysing them fully (it would require an elaborate graphical display). As stated, it's an organic, multifaceted monster. We will see how the cult has been involved in each sub-agenda as we go along.

Mass immigration

"Migration should not be governed by an international body unaccountable to our own citizens. Ultimately the only long-term solution to the migration crisis is to help people build more hopeful futures in their home countries"[3]

> President Donald Trump's UN General Assembly address,
> September 2018

Journalist: "What is the solution for the problem of migration?"

Orban: "Don't let them in, and those who are in, send home"[4]

> Hungarian Prime Minister Viktor Orbán responds to journalist

"Rather than bring peace and harmony, the EU will cause insurgency and violence"[5]

> British politician Nigel Farage on the
> European Union winning the 2012 Nobel Peace Prize

The cult/ideology obviously supports the extremely destructive, critical sub-agenda of population replacement level migration, while driving the various sub-movements that support it. This sub-agenda attempts to achieve cross-national Marxian equality and uniformity by eliminating ethnic and cultural differences, in addition to creating a borderless socialistic world 'federation' (aka world government). Tellingly, this sub-agenda primarily targets historically/traditionally white Christian western countries.

For the record, I'm not saying that Marxists/Marxism are solely responsible for the mass immigration sub-agenda affecting the western countries at this time (there are ethnic, 'religious' undertones to the issue, to put it mildly). The cult/ideology are the chief enablers, on the ground level in these countries. Without the cult and the indoctrination, the peoples of western countries would totally reject mass immigration, leaving the internationalists behind it powerless. The sub-agenda would make no headway, none, because a healthy nationalistic mindset in each western country would see to this.

Many have woken-up to the reality that this is an orchestrated, global agenda; not some sort of unfortunate, accidental 'humanitarian crisis' (well,

---

[3] C-SPAN, "President Trump addresses U.N. General Assembly - FULL SPEECH (C-SPAN)", 25 September 2018. https://www.YouTube.com/watch?v=KfVdIKaQzW8

[4] "Viktor Orban:Solution For The Problem Of Migration?Don't Let Them In, And Those Who Are In,Send Home", 19 September 2020. https://www.bitchute.com/video/3gSDzk1SYrr8/

[5] BBC, "Nobel Peace Prize awarded to European Union", 12 October 2012.

https://www.bbc.com/news/world-europe-19921072

it is a humanitarian crisis, in a sense, but not for the reasons we're told). Many see that the world's largest organisations are in support of this sub-agenda, including the UN and the European Union (both Marxist). Additionally (and crucially), some also understand that not only has this 'crisis' been deliberately orchestrated, but that its being pushed to produce certain demographic outcomes.

Cult members often like to call these people—being true to form as the eternal traitors that they are—'conspiracy theorists'. Yet big orgs like the United Nations are hardly hiding it, having produced several documents stating their intentions, including the now infamous "Replacement Migration: Is it a Solution to Declining and Ageing Populations?" in 2001.[6]

Commie checklist

This sub-agenda uses the oppr. v oppr. principle, which is crucial to cultivate the pathological altruism necessary (in western countries) that allows the mass influx of migrants. Indeed, support of mass immigration into a given country is the result of a prolonged Marxist infection. The emotional indoctrination at the core of the oppr. v oppr. principle (as outlined earlier) is just as central to this sub-agenda as it is in others; it would not function without it.

Interestingly, mass immigration literally forces peoples together, but simultaneously creates so much division and destabilisation. According to the official (Marxist) narrative, the migrants are 'oppressed' refugees, coming from war-torn areas (which is conveniently blamed on U.S. military exploits/'imperialism') not simply economic migrants coming to western countries to have a higher quality of life.

It also says that not only do we have an obligation to take them in for humanitarian reasons in general, but because western countries historically have been the 'oppressors' responsible for the situation in those countries in the first place. Basically, westerners owe them, so we simply must. A refusal to comply is based on having an uncompassionate, racist, right-wing mentality, of course. The virtue-signalling is pushed to the max as the cult insists that supporting mass migration is the height of virtue.

This sub-agenda helps to create a new class system in several ways: Firstly, the indigenous groups will eventually become ethnic minorities in their

---

[6] UN, "Replacement Migration: Is it a Solution to Declining and Ageing Populations?" (2001), 21 March 2000.

https://www.un.org/development/desa/pd/sites/www.un.org.development.desa.pd/files/unpd-egm_200010_un_2001_replacementmigration.pdf own countries. In addition to being outnumbered, they will have increasingly less political power as the sub-agenda progresses, and the migrant groups will generally only support representatives from their own ethnic groups.

Secondly, it divides supporters of mass immigration from those who don't: the politically correct Marxism-infected 'humanitarians' from the politically incorrect non-infected 'racists'. The more migrants there are in the country, the harder it is for someone to openly state that they are opposed to this sub-agenda. They would be literally placing themselves in the second-class citizen position (racist, fascist etc.). Eventually, people like this would be denied employment, education, services, with the migrants receiving preference etc.

This sub-agenda includes double-standards/hypocrisy because it leads to the destruction of indigenous ethnic groups/cultures in the countries absorbing the migrants. A country (and a people) that allow this to happen to themselves/their country are participating in a crime against humanity. The virtue-signalling and pathological altruism the cult employs is based on the idea that a people should not suffer, die, or be ethnically cleansed etc. Therefore, the double-standards/hypocrisy are off the charts here.

For example: cult members in Ireland probably get teary-eyed at the idea of an African, Middle Eastern or South American ethnic group being annihilated in their own lands, yet cannot see, refuse to acknowledge, or simply don't care that mass immigration will destroy the Irish ethnic group in Ireland (and that goes for indigenous Europeans in other European countries too). Isn't this waycist?

The Red Trojan Horse principle applies in various ways: we are told mass immigration is needed to address the problem of falling birthrates; that it's necessary for economic health and prosperity; that it will result in a better, more 'diverse', happier society etc.

This sub-agenda relies on a distorted perception of reality/history in several ways: that non-whites have historically suffered more than whites, due to whites, and that whites are obliged to sacrifice themselves/their countries to 'save' them (distortion of history); that socialism is the real reason why Africa is in a dire state of affairs today, not the imperialism of the past (distortion of history and reality); that European/Western countries can accommodate mass amounts of migrants from different ethnic and cultural backgrounds, and that everything will work out just fine (distortion of reality) etc.

This sub-agenda is quite clearly supported by all facets of the Marxism-riddled system: on a national level by governments, the transmission belts of culture (education, media, entertainment), NGO's/non-profits etc. In the case of Europe, it's also supported on a continental level by the Marxist European Union, and internationally it's supported by the Marxist United Nations.

Of course, it's a gargantuan understatement to say the EU simply 'supports' mass migration. It's one of the primary reasons why it was established in the first place. The other being that the formation of this pan-European entity is a major step towards world government (the reader may research Count Richard Nicholas Eriju Von Coudenhove Kalergi (1894–1972) and his pan-European movement of the 1920s.[7]

Kalergi is regarded as the 'godfather' of the European Union, but it's also apt to view him as the front man. He was obsessed with the idea of a 'multicultural' Europe, perhaps due to the fact he was mixed-race himself. His 1925 book *Praktischer Idealismus* ("Practical Idealism") confirms he was contaminated with the ideology.[8] It was his suggestion to use Beethoven's "Ode to Joy" as the EU's 'national' anthem; same for the EU flag design[9]).

In 2015, then German chancellor and communist-in-chief Angela Merkel stated "Wir schaffen das" ("We can do this") to proliferate this 'crisis', heralding Germany's open door policy; Germany accepted over 1 million migrants.[10] ("We can do this" is reminiscent of the famous slogan of Saul Alinksy fan and former U.S. President Barack Obama's slogan "Yes we can").[11]

Mass migration attacks the pillars of western civilisation in several ways:

Capitalism

It destroys the relative economic stability, prosperity, and quality of life by bringing in massive amounts of economic migrants who will be unable to

---

[7] "Pan-Europe". https://www.europarl.europa.eu/100books/en/detail/18/pan-europe?edition=fr&info=en

[8] Kalergi, R., *Praktischer Idealismus* (1925).

https://archive.org/details/Coudenhove-Kalergi-Praktischer_Idealismus-1925

[9] https://en.wikipedia.org/wiki/Anthem_of_Europe

[10] "Angela Merkel says "Wir schaffen das" on accepting refugees", 6 June 2023.

https://www.history.com/this-day-in-history/angela-merkel-says-wir-schaffen-das-on-accepting-refugees

[11] https://en.wikipedia.org/wiki/Barack_Obama_2008_presidential_campaign#Slogan

integrate into society, never-mind contribute financially. This results in an over-loading of pressure on the welfare system, which in turn further damages western countries fiscally. On a bigger-picture scale, it encourages tens of millions of people from generally less-wealthy parts of the world to relocate to generally more-wealthy parts, thereby trying to enforce financial equality by reducing prosperity in the western countries. Naturally, any financial burden or loss of quality-of-life incurred by those in the more prosperous west (due to mass immigration) is deemed totally fair and justified in the eyes of the cult.

The migrant influx puts tremendous amount of strain on services in western countries including housing, medical care, crime etc. Considering that the cult will insist not only that western countries take in millions of migrants, they will also insist that housing, medical care, and welfare should be provided to them for free, this is yet another attack on the capitalist system, through overloading If you wanted to collapse the economies of western countries, is mass immigration not a great way to do it?

Christianity

Though decades of Marxist indoctrination, propaganda, and subversion have gone a long way to destroy Christianity in western countries, mass immigration will be the final nail in the coffin, due to demographics. Focusing on Europe in particular, a massive proportion of migrants coming in are Muslim. This process expedites the destruction of Christianity/Christians.

Culture

Mass immigration will also be the final nail in the coffin for indigenous culture, again, due to demographics. The wonderful, unique aspects of each European country's cultural heritage will be continually saturated by Marxism-riddled 'diverse' nonsense, progressively replacing them by the culture of migrant groups.

As a final item in our checklist, this sub-agenda attempts to enforce equality by acting as if there's no difference between different ethnic, religious, and cultural groups. It's based on the erroneous idea that not only can vastly different groups of this nature co-exist 'equally' in the same areas without causing destabilisation and/or serious problems, but that it's actually 'progressive', desirable for them to do so.

Miscegenation

Related to culture and 'equality' is a country's ethnic makeup. This is no offence to anyone personally, but it's an important, sensitive subject that needs to be understood. Miscegenation is race-mixing—two people from different races producing children. I personally don't treat a person any less for being mixed-race, of course not; I judge a person based on their level of consciousness. However, we need to be suspicious of anyone encouraging miscegenation particularly where entire races are concerned, because of how it affects countries! When any weirdo internationalistic control-freaks start encouraging this on a mass, unprecedented scale, it's not for benevolent reasons! This should be obvious!

If we acknowledge the anti-white element to the cult/ideology, combined with the fact that it's the chief enabler of non-white mass migration in to traditionally white Western Christian countries, it's obvious something is afoot here. The 'multiculturalism' concept is frequently used to promote miscegenation. So essentially the cult/ideology is behind mass immigration to western countries, while also indoctrinating the indigenous populations with 'multiculturalism' programming. The fact that both have been happening simultaneously in a co-ordinated fashion shows us that the same ideology is behind both (that goes for the other sub-agendas affecting birthrates in primarily white populations too: feminism, abortion, veganism, LGBTQ/gender non-binary etc).

The real issue here is the structural, demographic integrity of certain ethnic groups around the world. This forced, unnatural, manufactured mass immigration results in the effective genocide of indigenous peoples, particularly those of European heritage. From a global perspective, we can see this distinctly anti-white pattern since it's being inflicted only on western countries. Therefore, organised, political, globalist miscegenation equals racism against indigenous white peoples. Again, breeding to produce certain outcomes is a form of eugenics, and the outcome in this case is fewer white people and no mostly white countries.

A predictable response: "but the Irish emigrated too!"

The excuses that cult members use to justify an insane, destructive sub-agenda like mass immigration gives us insight into the destructive effect of the cult's concept of 'equality'.

In Ireland (and I'm sure elsewhere) 'anti-racist' cult members insist that Irish/indigenous people should accept mass immigration because they have themselves migrated in the past. Things like: "Didn't we migrate to other countries?!? How would you like it if they wouldn't let you in?!". How juvenile. So that's it?!? That's the justification for supporting massive movements of people around the globe and accepting tens of millions of migrants into western countries??

This Marxist deception has been repeated in Ireland ad nauseam, and you are regarded as being hypocritical if you do not agree with this sub-agenda.

In a sense, you are accused of not being genuinely Irish, or lacking an understanding of Irish history! This is exactly the sort of messed-up perception gymnastics that the cult/ideology relies on to destroy unsuspecting peoples! This distorted perception of reality comes from the 'equality' concept. When we combine this with the fact that the ideology does not do (constructive) practicality, we understand why Marxist thinking leads to chaos and destruction. Central to this is the concept of 'equality' as applied to different cultures, races etc.; that they are all the same. This is false. It's 'politically correct' Marxian feel-good mumbo jumbo to say otherwise.

What they're claiming is that a historical situation is the same as this present situation; but clearly, they're not. Irish migrants (or any European migrants) leaving Europe to settle in other countries historically is nothing like African and Middle Eastern migrants entering Europe today (or any other migration facilitated by the cult/ideology). It's totally different for ethnic, religious, cultural, political, and financial reasons. This is one of the blind-spots of Marxist indoctrination: it disregards race, culture and religion (and economics!). It only sees whether someone is an 'oppressor' or 'oppressed'; whether they belong to the bourgeoisie or the proletariat. The indoctrination on this issue explains why Marxists all over Europe cannot accept that mass migration brings with it nation-destroying instability and a crime wave, which is detrimental for Europeans. It leads to an ethnic and cultural clash, but Marxism doesn't do ethnicity or culture.

The indoctrination insists that Irish migration to the U.S. during the 1840s is just like the migrant waves of recent years. Rubbish! One situation has nothing to do with the other! Firstly, unlike migrants coming into Western countries today, Irish people did not emigrate to the U.S. with the help of Marxist cult members and organisations, whilst being told they were victims of oppression, and they were now owed something (with some migrants looking to take revenge on the Native Americans for oppressing Ireland!). Same goes for other historical migrations of that nature (i.e. by other European groups to America).

Secondly, Irish people emigrating to the U.S. were not Muslims! Many of the migrants now entering Europe are coming from primarily Muslim countries. So far, we have two ideologies in the mix here that are bad news for white Europeans. Thirdly, it is now (almost!) common knowledge that most migrants travelling to Europe are not fleeing war-torn areas. They are economic migrants, coming for 'a better standard of living' which means use of the welfare system (a system the cult/ideology created in the first place), plus the services and comforts that life in a western country can provide.

Irish migrants of the mid-19th century had no such attractive incentives—the majority settled in North-Eastern American states and Canada. They were not put-up in Irish hotels, given welfare, or the myriad of other supports today's migrants are. Lastly, they were not given these things at the expense of Americans needing the same things!

Even just these few areas of examination, and the Marxist deception starts to become obvious. And that is just scratching the surface here. As mentioned, this is why the equality brainwashing makes people dumb—they are unable to distinguish between one thing and another. If a person spends their whole life looking at individuals/races/cultures through the lens of 'equality', then they will never be able to fully appreciate the differences between them; all the nuances for good or for bad.

Irish PM Leo Varadkar used the above technique/justification (for mass immigration) in a speech in Dublin, following a meeting with European Parliament President Roberta Metsola. In early 2023, there was some unrest in Ireland. It included several anti-migrant protests against the influx of Ukrainians, notably at East Wall in Dublin. When commenting on these events, Varadkar stated "I'm very concerned about the rise of the far-right…and indeed the rise of racism in Ireland", adding "refugees are welcome here". He continued that being opposed to the migrant influx was "not the Irish way", referring to the Irish diaspora and the migrations of the past.[12] Good globalist doggie. Note "refugees", to prop-up that official narrative; most know the majority are economic migrants.

Feminisation of our nations and female activism

We've noted the over-feminising effect the ideology has on a society, when it comes to how various issues are perceived. It works with the oppressor v oppressed principle, eventually leading to pathological altruism: the self-destruction of a people/nation through misguided attempts to 'help' other groups/countries/continents. Having overly feminine attitudes towards particularly serious issues (such as mass immigration) is lethal for a nation and its indigenous population. In fact, it's suicidal, from a nationalistic point of view.

Look at what's happened to Marxism-ravaged Sweden. The influence of indoctrinated women in Swedish affairs was exemplified during the migrant influx. The migrants were being greeted at the airports by these groups of virtue-signalling, smiling brainwashed idiots holding up

---

[12] EU Debates, "'Not the Irish way' Taoiseach Leo Varadkar concerned about the rise of the far right in Ireland", 4 February 23.
https://www.YouTube.com/watch?v=RpGCob69n4c

"Welcome Refugees!" cards. Giving hugs and kisses to total strangers...how insane and naive! This is the equivalent of rolling over and showing your belly to a predator, as a nation. Short-sighted, nation-killing, over-emotional, nonsense. You are literally begging to be overrun and conquered by outside forces. In 2014, when the (manufactured) migrant 'crisis' was in full swing, then Swedish PM Fredrik Reinfeldt encouraged the Swedes to "open their hearts" to them.[13] Marxism = love.

Such things contributed to the assault and sexual assault epidemics in countries like Norway, Germany and Sweden. Amazing that any females in those countries—particularly feminists—would still support mass immigration, but that's indoctrination for you. Anti-women feminists. The statistics for these incidents in Norway in recent decades show that the vast majority of rapes are committed by "non-European" men (i.e. Africans or Middle Easterners) against indigenous women.[14] Similar situation in Sweden.[15] Predictably, these anti-female crimes are either being actively covered-up by the Marxist traitors in governments and the media, or they will try to turn this into a feminist issue (i.e. that it's nothing to do with immigration).

In addition, most migrants are young men of fighting age. Many of whom come from Muslim cultures, who are looking at those non-Muslim females—those welcoming them in—as pieces of meat, there for the taking. And they have taken. Those virtue-signalling "Refugees Welcome" sign-holders mistakenly assumed they were being viewed as 'good people'. A hell of an assumption to make. Many of these migrants have since shown us they did not appreciate this 'hospitality', as the naive ones thought they would.

Regardless of how many women get assaulted by migrants in these countries, cult members will still call us racists and Islamophobes as they welcome migrants with banners or signs, and open arms. Dumb, aiding and abetting behaviour. Even if these virtue-signallers themselves (or those close to them) become victims of these crimes, they will still be unable to face the truth, due to the indoctrination. Some of these 'feminists' may,

---

[13] Local Sweden, "Reinfeldt calls for tolerance to refugees", 2014.

https://www.thelocal.se/20140816/reinfeldt-calls-for-tolerance-to-refugees

[14] Reijden, J., "Norway: 95% of violent street rapes since early 2000's carried out by Africans and Muslims; covered up by authorities", 4 Sept 2017. https://isgp-studies.com/immigration-the-rape-of-norway

[15] "Sweden rape: Most convicted attackers foreign-born, says TV", 22 August 2018.

https://www.bbc.com/news/world-europe-45269764

soon after getting back from the airport (and the dopamine hit from their 'good deed' wears off), will resume with their discussions about 'rape culture' and the 'patriarchy' being imposed upon them by the evil oppressive indigenous males; males who are generally the same race as them!

In 2018, in another example of indoctrinated 'empowered' female activism, 22-year-old Swedish student Elin Ersson started some drama on a plane because a convicted criminal of Afghani origin was being deported. She (apparently) intended to protest the deportation of a different migrant, but he was on a separate plane.[16] A stunning example of how the brainwashing turns people in to traitors against their own country, preventing the deportation of criminals!

This stupid brat Ersson should've been physically removed from the plane and banned from airports for life (unless she publicly renounced being an 'activist'). Better yet, she should've been sedated and exiled to Afghanistan, with her new migrant criminal friend as her host. Ersson, from a socialist background, was studying to be a social(ist) worker at the time of her glorious revolutionary action.

Deflecting blame away from itself

Though the cult has been pivotal in creating and perpetuating this mass migration 'humanitarian crisis' and attempting to suppress any patriotic/nationalistic pushback against it, they have often peddled the narrative that the migrants are mostly 'refugees' from war-torn areas (often blaming U.S. foreign policy). Essentially, the cult/ideology created the situation we are in, tries to prevent us from doing anything about it, and then assigns blame elsewhere. Sharpening my sword… We now know that the vast majority are economic migrants, not refugees fleeing war. In addition, even if it were true there were millions of people fleeing war zones and headed for Europe, their admittance to these countries is down to the countries themselves. Obviously, EU membership makes it virtually impossible for countries to choose to close their borders or implement a robust entry/visa system.

Of course, not only would joining an entity like the EU not happen without a Marxist infection present, the EU would not exist in the first place! Besides, U.S. foreign policy has nothing at all to do with European countries managing their own borders! It's a scapegoat. Cult member

---

[16] Crouch, D., "Swedish student fined for anti-deportation protest that went viral", Feb 2019. https://www.theguardian.com/world/2019/feb/18/swedish-student-elin-ersson-fined-after-broadcasting-plane-protest-against-asylum-seeker-deportation

Anders Borg was the Swedish Minister for Finance from 2006–2014. He spoke at the *Peterson Institute for International Economics* (PIIE), Washington D.C. in 2013, and said this on the migration influx: "Basically the U.S. is providing these flows for us—you make war and we get the refugees"; adding "and we think that this is basically an asset for the Swedish society".[17] Propaganda tricks like this are very significant. The perceived reason(s) why mass migration is happening is pretty crucial with regards to the general public's perception of it (in any given western country). If the perceived reason is erroneous, then the truth remains hidden; and in this scenario, the cult/ideology evades the brunt of the blame.

Critically, the cult blaming mass migration on the bogeyman of 'U.S. imperialism' helps to convince (some of) the public that they have no control over the situation; that it's some external force or factor, which in this case is simply not true! It's a form of demoralisation. It's just another Marxist deflection, to hide the fact that the cult/ideology is the real culprit here. It's destroying Europe, through the brainwashed cult members serving it across the continent. The key to curbing any incoming destructive migration is controlling a country's borders, obviously. As stated, whether or not this action will be taken is dependent upon the level of ideological infection within the country. And that's something that can be controlled.

Irish anti-immigration protests

In 2022/23, there were several anti-mass immigration protests at migrant centres around Ireland. On 18 February 2023, cult members held a counter-protest in Dublin called "Ireland for All". Marchers were carrying red-coloured signs saying "Smash Racism" and "Everyone is welcome".

An article on the *Common Dreams* website stated: "The rally was organized by the rights coalition Le Cheile, along with groups including United Against Racism, National Women's Council of Ireland, the Irish Congress of Trade Unions, and the Union of Students Ireland".[18]

In Irish Gaelic, the words "Le Cheile" means "together" (aka solidarity); another example of the cult/ideology feigning respect for Irish culture. Also note the different infected group types—an 'anti-racism' group, a feminist group, a union group, and the biggest student union organisation in the

---

[17] "Swedish Minister to the US: "You Make War, We Get the Refugees!" - It's a Win-Win", 12 Nov 2013. https://www.YouTube.com/watch?v=zU0_6yPVCPQ

[18] Conley, J. "'Ireland For All': Tens of Thousands March in Dublin to Support Refugees", 18 Feb 2023. https://www.commondreams.org/news/ireland-refugees-march

country.

Prominent Irish cult member and *People Before Profit-Solidarity* TD Paul Murphy tweeted about the march: "What a powerful response to the attempts to spread division and hate. There are enough resources in this country for everyone to have a decent home, job and services and welcome refugees. We need to unite against those who currently hoard that wealth". That's the solution? Well why didn't you say so pal?! Everyone—it's time to revolt against the bourgeoisie! Grab all the hammers and sickles you can find!

In that same month, an opinion poll was run by the *Irish Times*, (apparently) composed of the views of 1,200 adults interviewed over a two-day period. The summarising article stated that the poll highlighted "strong concerns to help and protect refugees and people seeking asylum, but also a concern about Ireland's ability to cope with the large numbers that have arrived in the last 12 months. As well as more than 70,000 refugees from the war in Ukraine, there has been a surge in people arriving from elsewhere who are seeking asylum here under international law, with in excess of 13,000 arriving last year".[19]

If it wasn't for the cult, and the climate of social fear it creates, more everyday Irish people would be publicly voicing their opinions against mass immigration.

Aiding, abetting, mass immigration and migrant crimes

Of course, migrant violence against (primarily white) westerners serves the cult/ideology well—it demoralises, destabilises, generates perpetual conflict, in addition to fanning the flames of racial tensions, which plays in to the hands of the cult/ideology further. In their noble quest to stop that most horrific, criminal behaviour of racism at all costs (sarcasm), the cult has shown relentless determination to suppress crimes committed by migrants. Though this is a global issue, here's some euro-centric examples:

Ireland

On the night of Saturday 6 June 2020, a vicious assault took place in Carrigaline, County Cork. A 17-year-old Irish male was assaulted by a gang of black youths, and stabbed when he was lying on the ground. The incident was filmed by these animals and made its way on to social media via

---

[19] Leahy, P., "Irish Times poll: Majority of voters support ban on protests at refugee centres", 23 Feb 2023. https://www.irishtimes.com/ireland/social-affairs/2023/02/23/irish-times-poll-majority-of-voters-support-ban-on-protests-at-refugee-centres/

Snapchat. In the disturbing video, you can clearly hear the psychotic mindset of the perpetrators, who sound fascinated by the sight of blood. They enjoyed what they were doing.

Detective Garda Healy who was involved with the case said that the victim was "asked for €2 for a bus by a youth. When he refused he was punched to the ground and kicked on the ground. The defendant then spoke to the first youth involved in the assault. He went over to the injured party lying on the ground and smashed a 70cl vodka bottle over the head of the injured party. He then picked up the neck of the bottle that had been broken and stabbed him six times".[20]

Predictably, cult members in Ireland—including a local Sinn Fein party TD, and their allies in the traitorous Irish media—tried to suppress any subsequent outrage. These types claimed that sharing the video of the assault would cause further upset to the victim and his family. Insane traitor scum. When a GoFundMe was created to raise funds for the teenager, cult members succeeded in pressuring the company to shut it down.

PJ Coogan of Cork's *96FM* stated: "And there was a Gofundme flying yesterday as well purportedly set up for the victim. In fact it had nothing to do with the victim. It was setup as a front by a far-right group and when a little bit of investigation was done, it was taken down". On 21 December of that year, the Irish Examiner reported that one of the youths involved was jailed for 18 months (two years and six months sentence, with one year suspended).[21] Pathetic judgement. The sentence for a sociopath—of any age—trying to kill someone over two euro should be a public hanging, followed by immediate cremation.

Stabbings and riots

In September 2023, it was reported that an Angolan man randomly attacked another man at Dublin Airport. Kasonga Mbuyi, 51, used a penknife to stab a German tourist who was alone smoking a cigarette outside departures. Gript media reported that the migrant may have been angry over his welfare

---

[20] "Video: Irish Teenager Stabbed Over Two Euro Bus Fare by Gang of Teens", 8 June 2020. https://nationalfile.com/video-irish-teenager-stabbed-over-two-euro-bus-fare-by-gang-of-teens/

[21] Heylin, L., "Video 'added another layer of hurt' - Teenager jailed for Carrigaline stabbing", Dec 2020. https://www.irishexaminer.com/news/courtandcrime/arid-40194798.html

benefit situation.[22] A court heard the attack was "a cry for help". The Irish Times reported he had Irish citizenship since 2014.[23]

On 23 November 2023, a violent incident occurred outside a primary school in Dublin city centre in broad daylight. Three children and an adult were stabbed and injured, with one five-year-old left in a critical condition. The attacker was an Algerian-born adult male, who was then subdued and disarmed.

That evening riots erupted in Dublin, with widespread property damage and assaults on police. The media and state then sprang in to action, blaming the riots on the 'far-right'.[24] In a statement outside Garda (police) headquarters, the Garda Commissioner Drew Harris stated that : "We have a complete lunatic hooligan faction driven by far-right ideology...engaged in serious violence".[25]

They also used some damage control. Rather pathetically, the traitorous Irish media hailed a Brazilian migrant—who helped disable the attacker—as a hero. They were suggesting "See? Migrants can be good people too!". If it wasn't for the cult/ideology, such incidents would not happen in the first place.

In a statement on Friday 24 November, Comrade Leo Varadkar alluded to new 'hate speech' legislation: "I think it's now very obvious to anyone...that our incitement to hatred legislation is just not up to date...for the social media age, and we need that legislation through...in a matter of weeks because it's not just the platforms that have a responsibility here it's also the individuals who post messages and images online that stir up hatred and violence. We need to be able to use laws to go after them

---

[22] De Barra, M., "Dublin Airport stabbing: African migrant suspect may have been angry over welfare dispute". 18 Sept 2023. https://gript.ie/dublin-airport-stabbing-african-migrant-suspect-may-have-been-angry-over-welfare-dispute/

[23] Tuite, T., "Random knife attack at Dublin Airport was 'cry for help', court told", 23 September 2023. https://www.irishtimes.com/crime-law/courts/2023/09/23/random-knife-attack-at-dublin-airport-was-cry-for-help-court-told/

[24] Fletcher, L., "Gardaí attacked during violent unrest after stabbing", 24 November 2023.

https://www.rte.ie/news/dublin/2023/1123/1418216-protests/

[25] GB News, "'There is No Failure here': Garda Commissioner, Drew Harris, addresses public on the Dublin riots", 24 November 2023. https://www.YouTube.com/watch?v=rFlNHcweOOs

individually aswell".[26]

Being first introduced in November 2022, the legislation in question is the Criminal Justice (Incitement to Violence or Hatred and Hate Offences) Bill 2022. This legislation makes it a crime to share or store any material regarded by the state as 'hate' or inciting violence in any way. It also allows the police to search homes and confiscate items that may store such materials, while also forcing these 'criminals' to provide passwords for them etc.[27] Traitorous scum. At time of editing (Dec 2023) it is now almost through the Irish parliament.

Some suggested that this whole situation was planned. Whether the riots were encouraged or manufactured somehow by the state (same goes for the actual stabbing), or indeed a genuine reaction to recent migrant crimes is beside the point—neither would take place without the cult/ideology directing the country's affairs. An ideologically contaminated country means a state composed of brainwashed mouthpieces, either oblivious or indifferent to the chaos they are creating.

The Irish discontent at migrant influx

Of course, the truth bubbling under the surface is that the Irish public are starting to resist the Irish government's (and therefore the European Union's) mass migration sub-agenda. In an interview with *GB News* on 3 Dec 2023, Irish journalist David Quinn commented on the events in Dublin, giving a fair analysis.[28]

The host Andrew Doyle asked him if there was discontent on this issue in the Irish public. Quinn highlighted that the population growth in Ireland was almost the highest in Europe (due to immigration), saying "this is an unprecedented level of change of a small country in a short amount of time". He added that this tends to put pressure on the state (lack of services, housing etc.), and that people in more "disadvantaged areas" tend to feel these effects more: "So it's easy for somebody like me in a middle-class area to lecture people in disadvantaged areas about their attitude towards immigration, but I don't live with multiculturalism, I don't live with multi-

---

[26] Sky News, "Dublin stabbings 'horrifying act of violence', says Taoiseach Leo Varadkar", 24 November 2023. https://www.YouTube.com/watch?v=5Be6DoUL0y8

[27] Criminal Justice (Incitement to Violence or Hatred and Hate Offences) Bill 2022.

https://data.oireachtas.ie/ie/oireachtas/bill/2022/105/eng/ver_b/b105b22d.pdf

[28] GB News, "David Quinn talks the Dublin riots and Ireland's political class placing blame on Conor McGregor", 3 December 2023.
https://www.YouTube.com/watch?v=MSjUwfRG4fc

ethnicity, I don't live with high-levels of immigration but the people in these other disadvantaged areas typically do.. and essentially, they're not allowed to have an opinion about it… because if you express any concern at all you're accused of hate…and racism, and that frustrates people".

The death of Ashling Murphy

On 12 January 2022, a 23-year-old Irish woman, Ashling Murphy, was murdered beside the Grand Canal in Tullamore, County Offaly. The killer (who recently received life in prison in November 2023) was then 31-year-old Jozef Puska—a Slovakian of Romani heritage. The murder became an international incident of mourning, and it seemed everybody including the Irish Taoiseach (PM) and Irish President were coming out making statements on it. Vigils were held across the world.[29]

Cult members in Ireland used Murphy's death for their own nefarious ends, and, predictably, attempted to spin the incident into a feminist issue. Essentially, the murder was callously used to deflect blame away from the migrant influx caused by the cult and government policies. The bizarre international vigils were reminiscent of the cult's tactics when George Floyd died; they took place in the UK, Australia, Canada, and the U.S. It became a Floyd-esque event, except used to promote the ever-prolific feminism sub-agenda rather than BLM.

In a statement on 13 January 2022, then Taoiseach and prolific super-traitor Michael Martin said: "There is no place in our society for violence, particularly violence against women. It cannot and will not be tolerated…The safety and security of women is at the core of our society's values".[30] Deceiving snake bastard.

On 14 January, only two days after the incident, he made an appearance on Irish TV on *The Late Late Show*,: "… men want to be part of the solution…men need to listen more to women…I think men want to step-up to the plate here, and make sure we can create a different kind of society…where people do feel safe where we can transform the culture that

---

[29] Moloney and Feehan, "Remembering Ashling Murphy: Details of minute's silence and vigils nationwide as events take place as far away as Australia", 14 Jan 2022. https://www.independent.ie/irish-news/remembering-ashling-murphy-details-of-minutes-silence-and-vigils-nationwide-as-events-take-place-as-far-away-as-australia/41239338.html

[30] "Statement by Taoiseach Micheál Martin on the death of Ashling Murphy", January 2022. https://www.gov.ie/en/press-release/8979d-statement-by-taoiseach-micheal-martin-on-the-death-of-ashling-murphy/

underpins bad behaviour, and violence towards women".[31] What utter nonsense! Her death is nothing at all to do with average, everyday Irish men, or Irish culture! Despicable!

The Irish President Michael "Last of the Leprachauns" D. Higgins is another prominent Irish cult member and fan of the late Cuban commie dictator Fidel Castro. In a statement on Friday 14 January 2022, he said it was of "crucial importance that we take this opportunity to reflect on what needs to be done to eliminate violence against women in all its aspects from our society, and how that work can neither be postponed nor begin too early... Let us respond to this moment of Ashling's death by committing to the creation of a kinder, more compassionate and empathetic society for all, one that will seek to eliminate all threats of violence against any of our citizens, and commit in particular to bringing an end, at home and abroad, to violence against women in any of its forms".[32] More indoctrination and bullshit.

Comrade Michelle O' Neill—Deputy Leader of the ultra-Marxist pseudo-patriotic Sinn Fein party—spoke at a vigil held for Murphy at parliament buildings in Stormont, Belfast.

She stated that "Domestic, sexual and gender-based violence is an epidemic", and "we need to develop an enforceable zero-tolerance approach towards misogyny and sexism".[33] Absolutely disgusting virtue-signalling opportunism, capitalising ideologically on the death of a young woman! An "enforceable zero-tolerance approach towards misogyny and sexism'? You can imagine how bad Ireland would get with these nutcase fanatics in power.

Another Irish cult member is media personality Muireann O' Connell. On the *Ireland AM* TV show, the day after the murder, she said "Violence against women perpetrated by men is a pandemic... ", adding "we have to

[31] The Late Late Show, "An Taoiseach Micháel Martin on the murder of Ashling Murphy | The Late Late Show | RTÉ One", 15 January 2022. https://www.YouTube.com/watch?v=SA3W3wrQKl0

[32] "Statement by President Michael D. Higgins on the death of Ashling Murphy", 14 January 2022.https://president.ie/en/media-library/news-releases/statement-by-president-michael-d-higgins-on-the-death-of-ashling-murphy

[33] "'An attack on all women': North's politicians hold vigil for Ashling Murphy", 17 Jan 2022. https://www.irishtimes.com/news/crime-and-law/an-attack-on-all-women-north-s-politicians-hold-vigil-for-ashling-murphy-1.4778873

do something about teaching the boys and men in our society".[34] Amusing. No comment needed.

They are still doing it now, almost two years later. A 'news' segment by RTE news in November 2023 re-reported the murder, as a feminist propaganda top-up.[35] By spinning the incident into a feminist issue, the cult members generated suspicion (and hatred) towards males as a collective in Ireland (in the minds of people not seeing the incident for what it really was—a migration issue).

Ryan's Victim Impact Statement

Ryan Casey, Ashling Murphy's boyfriend, made a victim impact statement at the Central Criminal Court, Dublin, before the killer was sentenced.[36] He spoke a lot about his wonderful relationship with Aishling, but when he let the punches fly, he spoke of Puska being a "burden to society...lowest of the low". He also spoke of the (red) elephant in the room: "It just sickens me to the core that someone can come to this country, be fully supported in terms of social housing, social welfare, and free medical care for over 10 years...never hold down a legitimate job and never once contribute to society in any way shape or form [and] can commit such a horrendous, evil act of incomprehensible violence".

He added "I feel like this country is no longer the country that Ashling and I grew up in and has officially lost its innocence when a crime of this magnitude can be perpetrated in broad daylight. This country needs to wake up; this time things have got to change this country is simply not safe anymore. This time, if real change does not happen, if the safety of people living in this country is further ignored, I'm afraid our country is heading down a very dangerous path and you can be certain that we will not be the last family to be in this position". He paid tribute to her in the best way— by telling the truth.

His anti-Marxism comments were deemed offensive to Irish cult members and were not exactly emphasised by the MSM. Obviously, it alluded to the migrant influx and the welfare state—two things that often go together and

---

[34] Virgin Media Television, "'Violence against women perpetrated by men is a pandemic' - Muireann O'Connell", 13 January 2022. https://www.YouTube.com/watch?v=nG8n3fe0ynM

[35] RTE News, "Boyfriend, Ryan Casey, remembers 'vibrant, intelligent' Ashling Murphy", 10 Nov 2023. https://www.YouTube.com/watch?v=WSZpPsXsLjQ

[36] "Ashling Murphy murder: Boyfriend Ryan Casey's Victim Impact Statement in Full", Nov 2023. https://www.newstalk.com/news/ashling-murphy-murder-boyfriend-ryan-caseys-victim-impact-statement-in-full-1615521

are central to the cult's plans for transforming European countries. On Thursday 30 November 2023, cult member and Irish Times journalist Kitty Holland appeared on *The View* (BBC TV, UK).

She stated that Casey's statement contained "incitement to hatred", and attempted to justify the MSM's censorship of it, before adding "the race and nationality of the man (Puska).. is irrelevant".[37] This is incorrect. Besides, only a cult member—who thinks all people (or men) are equal, regardless of those factors—would say such a thing.

This whole situation is another example of how the cult/ideology really has no genuine 'compassion' (even for a murdered female, or her boyfriend), since the most important thing in this case is that the ideology (and its sub-agenda of mass immigration) is not criticised publicly. Essentially, the truth must be suppressed if it opposes/exposes Marxism; that's why the traitor cult members listed above tried to present the murder as a feminist issue. An 11 November 2023 article on the *Extra.ie* website entitled "Puska was a convicted sex offender and 'person of interest' in two other assaults on women" drew attention to Puska's past before he entered Ireland.[38]

Solution

The immediate solution for migrants attacking or murdering indigenous people in their host countries, is to offer immediate permanent exile or a mandatory death sentence. When you are dealing with violent, degenerate trash like those listed above, you need to send out a strong message. This would at least curb these attacks until mass immigration is stopped and deportations take place. Best of luck trying to impose such swift justice while the cult still has a hold on the state!

Every victim of the ideology's sub-agendas—mass immigration included—is viewed as a martyr of sorts by the cult. I'm sure, deep down inside, many of them enjoyed the 'mourning' process for Aishling Murphy's death (and George Floyd etc.). Since the end justifies the means, every death is another step towards utopia. As the cult marches on unopposed, attacks and murders like those listed above will increase in frequency and ferocity.

---

[37] Gript Media, "Kitty Holland: Ashling Murphy's boyfriend expressed "incitement to hatred", 30 November 2023 (from BBC's the View on 30/11/2023). https://www.YouTube.com/watch?v=PnucUQTy-SA

[38] MacNamee, G., "Puska was a convicted sex offender and 'person of interest' in two other assaults on women", 11 November 2023. https://extra.ie/2023/11/11/news/puska-record

In 2022, the Irish media reported on a killing spree, this time in the north-western county of Sligo. An Iraqi Muslim migrant named Yousef Palani murdered two Irish men and attacked a third. He "tracked the men down using an LGBT dating app before stabbing them to death in their homes and mutilating their bodies". He cult off the head of one his victims and left it on the bed. Palani pleaded guilty to two counts of murder, and was sentenced to 'life imprisonment'.[39]

Again, the traitorous Irish media tried to spin the incident as merely a 'homophobic' issue essentially, and not a mass immigration and Islamic issue (the court heard that Palani told the police that Islam forbade homosexuality). Where are all the LGBTQ marches and organisations demanding action with regards to immigration, so this can't happen again?

Sweden

Tragic Sweden, due to a high level of infection, has seen a breakdown of law and order. The country has endured a massive increase in violent crime and social unrest in general, with several no-go policing zones.

Much earlier in the process, these glorious revolutionary changes were highlighted by a senior detective there in early 2017. Peter Springare, a 47-year veteran, described a week's police activity in the small city of Orebro in a Facebook post: "Here we go; this is what I've handled from Monday-Friday this week: rape, rape, robbery, aggravated assault, rape-assault and rape, extortion, blackmail, assault, violence against police, threats to police, drug crime, drugs, crime, felony, attempted murder, rape again, extortion again and ill-treatment ". He added that virtually all the suspects were African and Middle Eastern migrants: "Suspected perpetrators; Ali Mohammed, Mahmod, Mohammed, Mohammed Ali, again, again, again, Christopher.. Mohammed, Mahmod Ali, again and again"(Christopher was the only Swede). He listed the countries represented: "Iraq, Iraq, Turkey, Syria, Afghanistan, Somalia, Somalia, Syria again, Somalia, unknown, unknown country, Sweden. Half of the suspects, we can't be sure because they don't have any valid papers. Which in itself usually means that they're lying about their nationality and identity".[40] Orebro was once a relatively

---

[39] Galagher and O' Riordan, "Yousef Palani jailed for life for murder of Aidan Moffitt and Michael Snee in Sligo", 23 October 2023.

https://www.irishtimes.com/crime-law/courts/2023/10/23/double-murderer-yousef-palani-jailed-for-life-for-attacks-on-gay-men-spurred-by-hostility-and-prejudice/

[40] Newman, A., "Swedish Police: Government Covering Up Huge Migrant Crime Spree", 22 Feb 2017. https://thenewamerican.com/swedish-police-government-covering-up-huge-migrant-crime-spree/ ; https://en.wikipedia.org/wiki/Orebro

quiet Swedish town, and has an approximate population of 129,000.

The city of Malmo, just across the water from Copenhagen, Denmark, is now an infamous multicultural shithole. In January 2017, the police chief Stefan Sinteus published an open letter, pleading for help to deal with a crime wave: "I can assure you that the police in Malmö are doing everything we can for suspected perpetrators to be held accountable. But we cannot do it on our own. We depend on you, and your witness statements, to solve these violent crimes. Therefore I appeal now to you: Help us". He added: "Malmö police are currently investigating 11 murders and 80 attempted murders. Add to that other crimes of violence, beatings, rapes, thefts and frauds". There were also apparently 52 grenade attacks reported in 2016. The population of Malmo in 2022 was approximately 357,377.[41]

In August 2018, the Daily Mail reported on figures featured in a documentary by *SVT* (Sweden's public service channel): "More than half of those convicted of rape or attempted rape in Sweden last year were born in a foreign country, new statistics reveal. In cases of rape where the victim was set upon and did not know their attacker or attackers, the figure rises to 85 per cent. Four in ten had been in Sweden less than a year"; and: "Their findings revealed that where the victim did not know the offender 97 out of 129 convicted were born outside Europe". The compiled figures— spanning the period of 2013–2018—were based upon convictions all across Sweden for rape and attempt rape in the district courts.[42]

In October 2016, a notable incident took place in the town of Visby on Gotland—an island SSE of Stockholm in the Baltic Sea. A disabled woman was gang-raped by migrants, which incensed the locals. After the suspects were released, protesters 'attacked' a refugee centre. More protests prompted authorities to deploy extra police to the town. The *Sweden Democrats*—an anti-immigration party—held a demonstration in Visby shortly afterwards. In response, cult members from *Feminist Initiative* held a counter-protest.[43] A feminist group, essentially counter-protesting those

---

[41] "Swedish Police Overwhelmed by Muslim Violence", 28 January 2017.

https://www.eutimes.net/2017/01/swedish-police-overwhelmed-by-muslim-violence/

[42] Thompson, P., "Eight out of 10 'stranger' rapes in Sweden are carried out by migrants, with more than half of all rape convictions to foreigners, study reveals", 24 August 2018.

https://www.dailymail.co.uk/news/article-6095121/Eight-10-stranger-rapes-Sweden-carried-migrants-study-reveals.html

[43] "Police send backup to Gotland after reported rape fuels anger", 7 October 2016.

who are protesting a rape! Feminism isn't about the well-being of women.

An honest Swedish journalist

On 28 September 2023, Swedish journalist Lars Aberg, spoke at a conference called "The Diversity Obsession: Can Europe Survive Multiculturalism?" in Brussels, Belgium.[44] Aberg outlined the extreme changes Sweden had undergone, painting an honest and grim picture, highlighting that billions had been spent to integrate migrants, calling it "multiculturalism with a friendly wallet". He commented "migration has changed the nature of Sweden", and that the situation might have been different if the Swedes had "a less idealistic view of the world and Sweden's place in it". Making some brilliant observations, he added "… we could have defined terms like integration much clearer… we could have told people to learn Swedish and to get a job… we could have avoided regarding people from faraway countries as exotic victims… but a combination of fairly open borders, a generous welfare system, and no serious demands on newcomers to become part of society has been an invitation to trouble for all of us".[45] Indeed.

Emily Jones

Mass immigration also results in the importation of dangerous sociopaths and psychotics. On 22 March 2020 (Mother's Day), in Bolton, UK, a 7-year-old-girl named Emily Jones was killed in broad daylight in front of her parents while playing in a park. Her throat was slit with a craft (carving) knife. The killer was Eltiona Skana (30)—an Albanian migrant with severe mental issues—who arrived in the UK in August 2014. A paranoid schizophrenic, she claimed she was a victim of human trafficking (aka 'oppressed').[46]

Emily's father, Mark, assigned blame to the Greater Manchester Mental Health NHS Trust who were aware of Skana, yet was allowed to roam free,

---

https://www.thelocal.se/20161007/police-send-backup-to-gotland-after-reported-rape-sweden

[44] "The Diversity Obsession: Can Europe survive multiculturalism".
https://brussels.mcc.hu/event/can-multiculturalism-survive-21st-century-europe

[45] MCC Brussels, "What happened to our country? Sweden has been transformed by multiculturalism - Lars Åberg", 26 October 2023.
https://www.YouTube.com/watch?v=MhZ3QdJ1xe0

[46] "7-Year-Old Girl Stabbed to Death by Woman in UK Park on Mother's Day", 5 April 2020. https://nationalfile.com/report-7-year-old-girl-stabbed-to-death-by-somali-migrant-in-uk-park-on-mothers-day/

subsequently committing this horrific crime. Cult members all across the UK—in the state, mental health services, and in the general public—are to blame for such things. In December of that year, Skana was sentenced to life, but may just serve a lengthy sentence. In May 2021, the Daily Mail reported that Skana received almost £70,000 in legal aid (!).[47] I can think of an easy way to save money here, can you? (a witch burning in the middle of Manchester would cost considerably less than 70k).

Obviously, child murderers get taxpayer funded legal aid because of the cult's influence and 'compassion'. Makes me want to slit some throats. Innocent little Emily died two months before George Floyd, but most of you have probably never heard of her. There were no Marxist demonstrations or vigils in her honour around the world.

Victims of migrant crime across the west are too numerous, and it's not possible to honour them all. We must move on. Clearly, there's a lot of murderous anger towards white people in the host countries... wonder where that's coming from..

LGBTQ, trans/'non-binary', sexuality etc.

"I'm coming out... I want the world to know... got to let it show"[48]

Diana Ross, "I'm coming out", 1980

Commie checklist

Obviously, this sub-agenda uses the oppressor v oppressed principle by attempting to convince us all that LGBTQ people have been, and still are, unjustifiably mistreated (aka 'oppressed') in some way; and therefore now deserve preferential treatment. It creates a new class system by placing anyone outside this 'oppressed' group (especially anyone opposed to this sub-agenda) in the 'oppressor' category (unless they are cult members, or at least comply).

The Trojan Horse principle is evident since the promotion of LGBTQ is seen as something beneficial for society, even though the effects are devastating. The sub-agenda is cloaked in 'compassion', so is ostensibly about caring for people with gender/sexuality issues (this is the virtue-

---

[47] "Killer who slit the throat of seven-year-old Emily Jones in Mother's Day murder was awarded nearly £70,000 in taxpayer-funded legal aid", 20 May 2021. https://www.dailymail.co.uk/news/1article-9600547/Emily-Jones-Killer-awarded-nearly-70-000-taxpayer-funded-legal-aid.html

[48] *"Diana Ross-Im Coming Out (Lyrics)"*. https://www.YouTube.com/watch?v=ZuvGXxf7oNI

signalling aspect). Even though there may be an increase in those who identify as being in these groups in modern times, they still represent a small minority within society (almost negligible in the case of 'trans' and 'non-binary').

So essentially, this sub-agenda is helping to contribute to a major existential crisis that will impact on the whole of society (low birthrates, infertility, increase in mental health issues etc.), merely for the perceived 'oppression' of a handful of people! In addition, the lie that people can change their biologically determined gender is destroying countless lives (again, particularly the young/naive). It won't help them; it will ruin them. Essentially, nobody wins. True to its destructive form, here the ideology is destroying people's bodies (albeit through indoctrination, hormones and surgery rather than direct assault or murder). Ergo, it's a Trojan Horse.

It relies on a distorted perception of reality because it promotes the idea that there are more than two sex's/genders, that this can be changed (via the above means), and, most insidiously, that this person will be happier after the process is complete—an absolutely horrific, criminal lie. 'Trans' people have a disproportionately high level of mental health issues, with higher suicide rates. Of course, cult members will retort that this is due to the crisis of identity/gender (e.g. gender dysphoria) that they are experiencing in the first place. This is untrue, and the proof is in the mental health state of those who have undergone the 'transitioning' process before and after: they are never cured, and 'transitioning' was a mistake.

Obviously, if puberty-blockers, hormonal 'treatments', and surgery have been used, there may be no turning back. Sterility is common. Many who've been through this process simply disappear from public view. However, there have been some noble, brave characters who've come forward. Walt Heyer springs to mind. Walt developed a fixation with being female when he was a boy. As a 4-year-old, his wise grandmother "repeatedly, over several years, cross-dressed me in a full-length purple dress she made especially for me and told me how pretty I was as a girl. This planted the seed of gender confusion and led to my transitioning at age 42 to transgender female".[49]

(Now think of all the brainwashed degenerate parents/guardians in the world today encouraging this behaviour in their kids, whom they apparently 'love'). Heyer 'transitioned' to being a woman, lived as one, but

---

[49] Heyer, W., "Hormones, surgery, regret: I was a transgender woman for 8 years — time I can't get back".
https://eu.usatoday.com/story/opinion/voices/2019/02/11/transgender-debate-transitioning-sex-gender-column/1894076002/

eventually transitioned back. He has spent years speaking out on the issue.[50]

Another is Katie Lennon Anderson—an American biological female who attempted to 'transition' to male, having a hysterectomy and double mastectomy (which left her a "mutilated and abused version" of her old self). She now describes herself as a "de-transitioner".[51] A truly 'brave' and honourable person, she also now speaks publicly on the subject. Cases such as these are very common unfortunately, and their frequency is going to increase dramatically due to the dominance of the cult/ideology. This sub-agenda also tries to push the narrative that 'transgender' people have been 'oppressed' historically, so it also ticks the distorted perception of history box. This narrative is often jumbled-up with the other babblings of the cult, including the oppression of homosexuals etc. The idea that 'trans' people have been oppressed historically is just another blatant distortion of the past, which benefits the cult.

Clearly, this sub-agenda is promoted and supported by the system. When you have the gay Justin Trudeau as Prime Minister of Canada during the same time frame as Ireland has the gay Leo Varadkar as Taoiseach (Prime Minister), plus a parade of other gay/lesbian characters in positions of power/influence all over world, this is obvious. Of course, they are in those positions to promote the sub-agenda; they suit the times. In addition, the more LGBTQ characters there are in positions of power, the more they will help push the agenda forward. They will 'empower' other 'oppressed' types like them to get involved in helping the ideology dominate. Within the greater cult, it's a bizarre form of cult-like tribalism—they will help 'their own'. Additionally, the sub-agenda is promoted within the education systems, the NGO/non-profit complex, and within the media and entertainment industry. We can all see it, no need for examples.

Does this sub-agenda attack the pillars of western civilisation? It certainly aids in destroying traditionalism and any sort of religious programming that may be present in a society, particularly in the areas of sexuality, relationships, love, monogamy. marriage etc. It's obviously a big (gay) fuck-you to Christianity, typical of Marxism.

It attempts to enforce equality by peddling the lie that all sexual orientations are of equal value to society, and that it's equally positive for

---

[50] https://waltheyer.com/

[51] "Detrans Katie Lennon speaks in support of NH Parental Rights Bill", 20 April 2023.

https://www.YouTube.com/watch?v=cK_WeOe7OVI

someone to spend their lives in same-sex relationships/marriages as in heterosexual ones. Again, it's an assault on the best type of relationships for a healthy, balanced, strong society—heterosexual child-bearing ones.

Even if this sub-agenda succeeds in reducing the number of traditional relationships, this is a victory for the cult/ideology.

Finally, 'trans' and 'gender non-binary' is a form eugenics, since it increases sterility and reduces birthrates in primarily white populations. It is therefore anti-white.

Marxist history of LGBTQ

This sub-agenda would not exist without the Marxist cult first being established. An examination of the formation of the inter-connected feminist, gay rights, and LGBTQ movements shows the common red thread: people describing themselves as Marxists, socialists or communists creating and/or supporting these movements. Some are merely in the cult's activist movement, in the world of Marxist academia, or both. (Of course, there's considerable crossover between the LGBTQ and feminism sub-agendas, but feminism has its own section). Overall, we can say that the gay rights and feminist movements were separate and already established before the more modern 'trans' phenomenon came to the fore. Therefore, we can say that those movements paved the way for the 'transgender' movement. The 20th century saw the production of ship loads of books by Marxist cult members promoting those movements. It would take ages to list all these figures and the connections between them (the story goes back to the 19th century and beyond), but here are some events, groups and names:

Edward Carpenter was a Fabian Socialist and LGBT activist. He authored *The Intermediate Sex: A Study of Some Transitional Types of Men and Women* (1908);[52] Lily Braun—led a German organisation called *League of Progressive Women's Associations (Verband Fortschrittlicher Frauenvereine)*, which was pro-gay rights (late 1800s/early 1900s);[53] The *Mattachine Society,* founded in the U.S. in 1950, was a gay rights organisation formed by cult member and trade unionist Harry Hay. Structurally, it was organised in a similar fashion to the Communist Party itself;[54] Bayard Rustin was a socialist, civil rights and LGBTQ activist. He

---

[52] Carpenter, E., *The Intermediate Sex: A Study of Some Transitional Types of Men and Women* (1912). https://archive.org/details/intermediatesex00carpgoog

[53] https://de.wikipedia.org/wiki/Verband_Fortschrittlicher_Frauenvereine

[54] https://en.wikipedia.org/wiki/Mattachine_Society

was an associate of black American cult figure Martin Luther King;[55] Herbert Marcuse's *Eros and Civilisation: A Philosophical Inquiry into Freud* (1956) should be mentioned here, since it pushed 'sexual liberalism'.

The "Gay Liberation" movement saw the creation of groups such as the *Gay Liberation Front (*a very Marxist-sounding quasi-terrorist militant name!), and the *Gay Marxist Group*. The *Gay Left* was active from 1975–1980 in London, UK.[56] Another was the French group *Homosexual Front for Revolutionary Action (front homosexuel d'action revolutionnaire.* Again, giggles). It was active from 1971–1974; [57] *Towards a Gay Communism* is a 1977 book by Italian author Mario Mieli. One of the things he insinuated was that capitalism oppresses gay men (rolls eyes);[58] weirdo David Fernbach wrote the amusingly titled *The Spiral Path: A Gay Contribution to Human Survival* (1981). He studied at the London School of Economics and a Maoist.[59][60]

Leslie Feinberg was a Jewish American lesbian and trans activist, active from the 1960s. She was openly committed to the cult as a member of the *Workers World Party*—a Marxist-Leninist group. Her 'writings' include *Transgender Liberation: A Movement Whose Time Has Come* (1992); *Transgender Warriors: Making History from Joan of Arc to Dennis Rodman* (1996); and *Rainbow Solidarity in Defence of Cuba* (2009).[61]

Homosexuality in 'Communist' countries

The Bolsheviks in Russia decriminalised homosexuality in December 1917. Bizarre considering they surely had more important things to do (like learning how to run a country without having to murder everyone perhaps?). It was re-criminalised under Stalin in 1933.[62] This marked a new phase where Communist states were anti-gay, and this has been well-documented (even by some who are ideologically Marxist cult members). Any

---

[55] https://www.britannica.com/biography/Bayard-Rustin

[56] https://en.wikipedia.org/wiki/Gay_Liberation_Front; https://en.wikipedia.org/wiki/Gay_Left

[57] https://en.wikipedia.org/wiki/Front_homosexuel_d'action_revolutionnaire

[58] https://www.plutobooks.com/9780745399515/towards-a-gay-communism/

[59] https://archive.org/details/spiralpathgaycon00fern

[60] https://www.haymarketbooks.org/authors/41-david-fernbach

[61] https://en.wikipedia.org/wiki/Leslie_Feinberg

[62] Englestein, L., "Soviet policy toward male homosexuality: its origins and historical roots", 1995. https://pubmed.ncbi.nlm.nih.gov/8666753/

'undesirables' would be treated as such by the state.

Yuri Besmenov mentioned that gayness etc. was only needed during the Destabilisation phase (of the ideological subversion process). Since Communist states were all about attempting to create national strength, surely they realised that promoting gayness in males was not in those interests (less birthrates, less masculinity etc.). So essentially in a 'socialist'/'communist' state they are hard on gays because the charade—that Marxism cares about minorities—is over.

The work of Cuban author and journalist Reinaldo Arenas referred to this process. He spoke of how homosexuals like himself were incarcerated by Castro's regime. He was imprisoned at one point for not towing the ruling party's ideological line (the *Partido Comunista de Cuba)*. He later managed to escape the regime and continued to be a vocal critic. He is regarded as a pro LGBT hero.[63]

As an aside—as mentioned, we can't get caught-up in labels here of how a state, country, or regime is described; we must focus on the ideology at work under the surface. So, the idea that Castro's Cuba (or any other red state) may have been hard on anyone in LGBTQ categories does not contradict this book's message—that the LGBTQ movement is a sub-movement of Marxism. We can't compare Castro's Cuba to a western country today in this regard: that was a time and place where the ideology took a certain form and produced certain effects. At present, the LGBTQ sub-agenda is used by the ideology as part of the Destabilisation process now in Western countries.

Not tarring everyone with the same brush

On these kinds of topics, we should judge people as individuals based on their level of consciousness, and on if they are indoctrinated or not (and to what degree). Certainly, there are many gay and lesbian people who don't support this current extreme 'LGBTQ'/trans/'non-binary' movement, so it would be unfair to blame what's happening on everyone who isn't heterosexual, as if they are all the same! They may not support the more 'radical' aspects of this sub-agenda including pushing homosexuality on children in schools, and drag-queen story time, or encouraging children to 'transition' etc). Well then, those people are not the issue here; they may have the attitude of "live and let live" and are not interested in pushing their behaviour on anyone. It's the controlling, fanatical ones we need to be concerned about right now.

---

[63] https://www.britannica.com/biography/Reinaldo-Arenas

It has been noted by some analysts that the "T" for "trans" has almost piggy-backed itself on to the Lesbian Gay Bisexual movement; and it can clearly be seen in the rift in opinions mentioned above. However, the fact remains that the 'gay rights' movements in the 20th century laid the foundations for this tranny 'non-binary' sexual hellscape we find ourselves in today, and those involved in those movements are responsible somewhat. Again, 'revolution' makes progress in waves.

So, if it's true that there is such a thing as 'normal' (in terms of healthy, sexual behaviour and sexual identity etc.), and that those in LGBTQ categories are indeed not 'normal', then we should not be re-structuring society to adapt to them or moulding the youth in their image. This will have catastrophic effects, and that's exactly what's transpiring now. Where is the rationality in such an outlandish claim, as some might inquire? Well, if we have too many people in a particular nation/society/ethnic group engaging in same-sex, childless relationships (sexual or otherwise), it would lead to the extinction of that group. If an existential reason is not good enough to put the brakes on this movement, then what is?

Author's take on LGBTQ

Certainly, homosexuality and bisexuality didn't just arrive on the planet when Marxism did; they've been around for eons. Though it's hard to quantify, perhaps there's been an increase in the recent era. And then we have the much newer phenomenon of individuals with confusion about their 'gender', which seems to be something different. Perhaps there's been a massive increase in Gender Dysphoria, 'trans' and other types of sexual abnormalities in recent decades due to a hormone-imbalancing toxic cocktail of factors, particularly in the more developed countries. Amongst other things, they have affected the genetic material of both sexes (chromosomes) and impacted on child-bearing females and their children.

On a physiological level, they include: genetic and epigenetic factors; modern low-fat high-carbohydrate diets with GMO and processed foods, including the phytoestrogenic testosterone-decimating vegan diet, the wide-spread use of herbicides (e.g. glyphosate), and the consumption of non-organic dairy products/meats (laden with hormones, pain-killers, additives etc.); alcohol, smoking, and drugs (legal and illegal); the oestrogenic contraceptive pill (i.e. progesterone); contaminants—including fluoride, hormones, and pharmaceutical drugs—in the water supply; the modern lifestyle—potentially higher stress levels, not being physically active enough, relatively weak immune systems, reduced exposure to sunlight (and the resultant Vitamin D deficiency, which impacts the hormone-producing endocrine system); exposure to various vibrations/radiation produced by modern technology (mobile phones, Wifi,

TV, microwaves etc). Combined these factors are instrumental in diminishing healthy hormone levels and affecting DNA in a society, for generally the whole of society where the factors are present. The affected genetic material within the population then contributes to the sexuality of those being born within it. Note also how these factors emerged pretty-much simultaneously, in the modern age.

On a psychological level, in combination with the above factors, society has been impacted with the imbalancing effects of the ideology. Already stated is the demonisation of masculinity and testosterone, along with the accompanying increase in over-femininity (both encouraged by various Marxist sub-agendas, and the oppressor v oppressed conditioning).

In addition, emerging science is showing us that we can affect our genetics through our thoughts/beliefs/mentality, by turning on or off certain genes, under certain conditions ('gene expression').[64] Perhaps the mindset of indoctrinated females—before and during pregnancy—is contributing to this issue by affecting the sexuality of their offspring. If we have a society that demonises masculinity, then the individuals that make up society will increasingly reflect this cultural climate on a physiological level.

These are all in addition to the overall promotion of degeneracy that an infection of Marxism brings, when it comes to natural, healthy attitudes towards relationships and sexuality. In summary—the cult/ideology brings about and amplifies the imbalanced, unnatural conditions where more non-heterosexual people/behaviour will appear, then says "look at all these oppressed people! It then suggests "We need to transform society—via a progressive sexual revolution—to accommodate them! In fact, let's have more gayness and gay people to show how much we are against homophobia and transphobia! Hetero people should be gay too as much as possible, so we are in solidarity!" etc.

Black Lives Matter and 'anti-racism'

> "The white liberal differs from the white conservative only in one way is more deceitful, more hypocritical than the conservative...is the one who's perfected the art of posing as the negro's friend and benefactor. The white liberal is able to use the negro as a pawn or weapon"[65]

---

[64] Mukherji, S., "Mindset and Gene Expression", 15 February 2020.

https://www.psychologs.com/mindset-and-gene-expression/

[65] "Malcolm X : White Liberals and Conservatives".
https://www.YouTube.com/watch?v=T3PaqxblOx0

Black rights activist Malcolm "X" Little, 1963

"When I was on streets...whenever I spoke to black people... Very few people had hang-ups about Communism"[66]

Angela Davis, avid cult member and feminist activist, 1972

"African Americans have been brainwashed into not being open-minded, not even considering a conservative point of view. I have received some of that same vitriol simply because I am running for the Republican nomination as a conservative. So it's just brainwashing and people not being open-minded, pure and simple"[67]

Black American businessman Herman Cain,
CNN interview, October 2011

This sub-agenda uses the oppressor v oppressed principle by placing whites as the oppressor, non-whites as the oppressed. It obviously creates incendiary racial divisions, whether it exists in countries with historical racial divides (e.g. the U.S., France, U.K. etc), or those with relatively new 'diversity'-created ones (e.g. Ireland). It also specifically designates the state—via the police force—as the fascist, racist, authoritarian 'oppressor'.

This sub-agenda contains virtue-signalling and was a Trojan Horse for black people in the U.S. in particular, as it was ostensibly for their benefit, though ultimately it would only harm them and hold them back.

It also involves a distorted perception of history/reality, being based upon the false notion that the U.S. establishment—policing in particular—is inherently racist against black people. It also attempts to hide the fact that the black racial group commits a disproportionate amount of crime compared to other groups in that country (partly due to the ideology's influence in black communities). In addition, it encourages anti-white racism, plus the racist narrative that whites should now be subservient to blacks, in the name of 'social justice' (a new class system).

It was supported by the system in all the usual ways and was an attack on capitalism and culture—during the 'protests' that this sub-agenda inspired, since businesses and landmarks were attacked.

---

[66] Angela Davis - Why I am a Communist (1972 Interview).

https://www.YouTube.com/watch?v=cGQCzP-dBvg

[67] Martin, R., "Herman Cain denies GOP's horrible history with blacks", 3 October 2011.

https://edition.cnn.com/2011/10/01/opinion/martin-cain-brainwashed/index.html

The Rise of BLM

George Floyd died on 25 May 2020, and became a martyred catalyst for the cult/ideology. The Black Lives Matter (BLM) movement, though originating before-hand obviously, then majorly rose to prominence. Floyd's death prompted a cascade of glorious revolutionary actions across the world in almost 60 countries spanning the summer, the majority being in the U.S. and Europe. Many turned violent; those in London and Paris spring to mind. The London 'protests', which went on for many weeks, turned violent particularly when right-wing groups got involved after cult members started attacking landmarks.[68][69]

In Ireland, a protest was organised by several cult groups, including *Black Pride Ireland*. From their website *blackprideireland.ie*: "We are…an LGBTQIA organisation by Black queer people, for Black queer people in Ireland".[70] People all over the world were expected to 'take a knee' in solidarity. Some non-white cult members even filmed themselves approaching white people, insisting they essentially bow down to them and apologise for 'white privilege' (an act that symbolises turning the 'oppressor' class in to the subservient 'oppressed').[71]

Obviously, due to the aforementioned public ignorance, too few were blaming Marxism for this insanity. It wasn't until later that the penny dropped for many. Cult member and BLM co-founder Patrisse Khan-Cullors did an interview on *Real News Network* in 2015, which then re-surfaced during the unrest stating: "…we actually do have an ideological frame…myself and Alicia in particular are trained organisers, we are trained Marxists, we are super-versed on ideological theories. And I think that what we really tried to do is build a movement that could be utilized by many, many, black folk".[72] (in other words, "we are brainwashed, we've

---

[68] BBC, "French police clash with anti-racism activists in Paris", 13 June 2020.

https://www.bbc.com/news/world-europe-53036388

[69] BBC, "London protests: More than 100 arrests after violent clashes with police", June 2020.https://www.bbc.com/news/uk-53037767

[70] The Irish Times, "Black Lives Matter protest takes place in Dublin", 6 June 2020 (video). https://www.irishtimes.com/news/black-lives-matter-protest-takes-place-in-dublin-1.4272820

[71] "BLM YouTuber forced white girls on their knees to apologise for 'white privilege'". 3 June 2020. https://www.YouTube.com/watch?v=RKF5LsTe6KM

[72] Real News Network, "A Short History of Black Lives Matter", 23 July 2015.

https://www.YouTube.com/watch?v=Zp-RswgpjD8

read a lot of Marxist theory, and we want to brainwash lots of other black people").

The Black Lives Matter Network (officially) was formed by Cullors, Alicia Garza and Opal Tometi in 2013. [73] These brainwashed nuts are personifications of the legacy of Saul Alinksy—black community 'organisers'. The "About" page of the *blacklivesmatter.com* website uses some revealing terminology. The group who's "whole mission is to eradicate white supremacy" describe themselves as a "collective of liberators" (insinuating that black people are being enslaved/oppressed, naturally). They claim "we must move beyond the narrow nationalism that is all too prevalent in Black communities", and affirm their "resilience in the face of deadly oppression" (in other words, "there's too much American patriotism for our liking"). [74] The "Take Action" text says "Join the Movement to fight for Freedom, Liberation and Justice". We don't need to pull-out the Marxist-to-English dictionary here.

Black Lives Matter Inc.

Another aspect of BLM that was typically Marxist was the obvious criminality—rioting, theft, assault, property damage, and fraud. The organisation took in an estimated approximate of $90 million in donations in 2020, depending on the source.[75] 90 million dollars to a bunch of anti-American anti-white cult members! Affluent treason!

Cullors was exposed as a hypocrite and profiteer. It was reported that she purchased a $1.4 million property in Los Angeles. The home is located in Topanga Canyon, a rich, predominantly white area, a short drive from the beaches in Malibu.[76] Now if that's not sticking it to the bourgeoisie, I don't know what is! Crime does pay it seems. The New York Post reported that Khan-Cullors also purchased homes in Inglewood, Los Angeles, and another in the city, bringing the total to $3.2 million dollars. [77] What

---

[73] "Black Lives Matter Movement".
https://library.law.howard.edu/civilrightshistory/BLM

[74] https://blacklivesmatter.com/about/

[75] Morrison, A., "New Black Lives Matter tax documents show foundation is tightening its belt, has $30M in assets", 27 May 2023.
https://apnews.com/article/black-lives-matter-donations-george-floyd-protests-ddcf0d21d130a5d46256aa6c5d145ea7

[76] "Marxist BLM leader buys $1.4 home in predominantly white neighborhood", 10 April 2021. https://www.lawofficer.com/marxist-blm-leader-buys-1-4-home-in-predominantly-white-neighborhood/

[77] "BLM co-founder spent $3.2M accruing homes in past few years", 11 April 2021.

happened to "take from the rich and give to the poor"? Or, to quote the great Marx himself, what happened to "from each according to his/her/their ability, to each according to his/her/their needs"? Aren't profits evil?? I suppose 'donations' are different, right?

A 24 June 2020 article on Breitbart.com delved in to the background of Cullors, saying she "was the protégé of a communist-supporting domestic terrorist for over a decade, spending years training in political organizing and absorbing the radical Marxist-Leninist ideology which shaped her worldview". The cult member in question was Eric Mann who "mentored Cullors for over a decade in community organizing, was a member radical-left militant groups: Students for a Democratic Society and the Weather Underground, which bombed government buildings and police stations in the 1960s and 1970s.[78]

One of the organisations behind BLM is called *Thousand Currents*. Susan Rosenberg is the vice-chair of the board of directors. Rosenberg was a highly-active Jewish cult member and anti-American domestic terrorist who spent most of her life involved in 'revolutionary' activities.

These included bombings and shootings, and the shooting-dead of a security guard and police officers in a Brinks heist in 1981. She was an active member of the *May 19th Communist Organisation*, which conducted a domestic terrorism campaign against the U.S. state. This distinctly feminist group supported Marxist black power groups such as the *Black Liberation Army*. Rosenberg should still be incarcerated but was essentially pardoned by Bill Clinton on his last day in office.[7980]

The death of Floyd and the emphasis on BLM was a massive PR boost for the cult. An article on *uk.pcmag.com* on 20 July 2020: "the #BlackLivesMatter hashtag has been used 47.8 million times on Twitter from May 26 to June 7 2020. That's just under 3.7 million times per day!".[81]

---

https://www.lawofficer.com/blm-co-founder-spent-3-2m-accruing-homes-in-past-few-years/

[78] Klein, J., "Black Lives Matter Founder Mentored by Ex-Domestic Terrorist Who Worked with Bill Ayers", 24 June 2020.
https://www.breitbart.com/politics/2020/06/24/black-lives-matter-founder-mentored-by-ex-domestic-terrorist-who-worked-with-bill-ayers/

[79] https://thousandcurrents.org/

[80] https://en.wikipedia.org/wiki/Susan_Rosenberg

[81] Cohen, J., "#BlackLivesMatter Hashtag Averages 3.7 Million Tweets Per Day During Unrest", 20 July 2020. https://uk.pcmag.com/why-

Also, according to Forbes on 2 June 2020, an estimated 28 million Instagram users posted a plain black square along with the hashtag #blackouttuesday. Another was #TheShowMustBePaused, used by the multitude of idiots in the music industry.[82]

Candace's "Greatest Lie" doc

In October 2022, Candace Owens made an appearance on *Tucker Carlson Tonight*. Owens is a great example of a fantastic black American female who is not only not indoctrinated, but a talented, prolific opponent of the cult/ideology. In the interview, she discussed BLM and a documentary expose she produced entitled "The Greatest Lie Ever Sold". She was sporting an amusing t-shirt featuring the Marxist clenched fist, holding a nice wad of cash. On the issue of the colossal amount of funding BLM received, she said: ".. they robbed Americans, robbed American's emotions, extracted emotions, they used black pain to create confusion and to take tens of millions of dollars from people".[83] She also stated that a large amount of the funding actually went to the LGBTQ movement (more evidence that it's all one big cult).

When Carlson asked if any everyday black people benefited from BLM, she replied that not only did it not benefit anyone, it actually harmed black communities: in the aftermath of the rioting, many businesses left these areas (attack on capitalism), and that there were 'no-go' policing zones. Interestingly, she mentioned that shortly after the trailer for the documentary was released the IRS (Inland Revenue Service) essentially threatened her charity—*Blexit*—with investigation. Commie double-standards, anyone?

The testimony of a black cop

On 10 July 2020, a video interview appeared on the *KGW News* YouTube channel featuring Officer Jakhary Jackson of the Portland Police Bureau, in which he gave his first-hand insight in to the BLM unrest. His

---

axis/127817/blacklivesmatter-hashtag-averages-37-million-tweets-per-day-during-unrest

[82] Monckton, P., "This Is Why Millions Of People Are Posting Black Squares On Instagram", 2 June 2020.
https://www.forbes.com/sites/paulmonckton/2020/06/02/blackout-tuesday-instagram-black-squares-blackouttuesday-theshowmustbepaused/

[83] Fox News, "Owens details shocking documentary exposing Black Lives Matter funding", 13 October 2022. https://www.YouTube.com/watch?v=5JfMiXbVH4U

professional, eye-witness account was revealing.[84]

In his attempts to speak to black protesters, he was always interrupted by white cult members, who informed them not to speak to police officers like him (this is done because black police officers are obviously the ones most likely to talk some sense into the black protesters). Jackson graduated from Portland State University with a history degree and noticed that the protesters he was dealing with had no clue about history (in other words, they were babbling erroneous Marxist rhetoric, aka propaganda).

He gave examples of white 'protesters' shouting racist things at black officers, at supposedly anti-racist 'protests'. He also noted that black people were leaving these protests, aware that something else was driving the unrest other than black rights. Something else indeed... "It says something when you're at a Black Lives Matter protest, you have more minorities on the police side, than you have in a violent crowd", he said. He also spoke about being patronised by white cult members—being told to quit his job, that he was hurting his community etc.; and the hypocrisy of a "privileged white person telling someone of colour what to do with their life" (at a protest ostensibly about black equality, rights, empowerment etc!).

This is an instance of the (virtue-signalling) mask of the ideology slipping. Again, the cult/ideology doesn't care about people, black or otherwise. If you are not part of the great revolution, regardless of race, you are the enemy. Floyd's death was just the excuse for cult members to do what they do—destroy. What happened to Portland is an absolute disgrace! A stunning, infuriating example of what happens when you don't stamp-out Marxist unrest immediately, with extreme force. A hotbed of Marxism in modern day America!

American George and Irish George

George Floyd was hardly a model human being. In fact, he was a degenerate criminal and junkie. An absolute mess of a man, he was drugged-up to the gills on that fateful day and was approached by police for using a counterfeit $20 bill. Though Officer Derek Chauvin was incredibly stupid to kneel on him that way, Floyd died because he couldn't follow basic instructions from police. The bodycam footage of his arrest proves this, and shows some of the most frustrating, pathetic behaviour you will ever see from a person. The footage (available on the *Police Activity* YouTube channel) highlights the incredibly difficult job police have to do

---

[84] KGW News,"KGW: What it's like to be a Black officer policing Portland protests | Raw interview", 10 July 2020. https://www.YouTube.com/watch?v=ha-7SETmJD4

every day in that country.[85] (The YT Channel *Police Activity* documents police incidents and arrests across the U.S. It gives the viewer a clear idea of who and what the police have to deal with constantly. Amusingly, while being arrested, many black arrestees make the "I can't breathe" plea—a trend started since George Floyd).

Should we get upset if someone like that dies? Certainly, it's ludicrous to treat this as the passing of a saint. People die all over the world constantly, but the Marxist programme, of course, demands that the whole world should be sorrowful about this one. If the guy was white, there would be no reaction from the cult of course, as it's not advantageous. Also, if a white person is killed by, say, a black migrant, they would do their utmost to suppress it; they would pull all the strings they could to stop it reaching the public consciousness, or they would spin it in such a way to benefit the cult/ideology by doing some PR damage control. In Floyd's case, the cult pounced on the opportunity.

Cult members in Ireland have used the same tactic—capitalising on the death of a non-white person. George Nkencho was shot dead outside his home near Clonee on the Dublin/Meath border on 30 Dec 2020 by Gardai (police). The 27-year-old had assaulted a manager and threatened staff with a knife at Hartstown Shopping Centre. He threatened members of the public and the police who arrived on the scene. He was then followed home by the regular, unarmed Gardai, who advised him to drop the weapon.[86]

The ASU (armed support unit) were on scene and, after attempts to use non-lethal force had failed, Nkencho was then shot as he lunged at them wielding a large blade (a video of the incident confirms this). It followed the usual pattern in such circumstances (particularly noticeable in the U.S., as the Police Activity YT channel shows): a young black man engaging in crime or assaulting someone, brandishing a deadly weapon, refusing to put the weapon down when ordered by armed police, and going down in a hail of bullets.

Tellingly, on the very next day, the cult members in Ireland staged a protest outside the Blanchardstown Garda (police) Station! Well, what a fucking shocker, right? You can imagine these idiots just dying for such an event to

---

[85] PoliceActivity, "Full Bodycam Footage of George Floyd Arrest", 10 August 2020.

https://www.YouTube.com/watch?v=XkEGGLu_fNU

[86] Hussey, S., "Man dies after being shot by gardaí in west Dublin", 30 December 2020.

https://www.rte.ie/news/crime/2020/1230/1186988-shooting/

happen so they can break-out the anti-establishment placards! An image of the 'protest' featured in the *Sunday World* newspaper on 3 January showed the commie clenched fist being used.[87]

In typical fashion, cult members—especially in the media—stated and re-emphasised how Nkencho had 'mental health' issues, attempting to paint him as the victim (oppressed). If this was true, what difference does that make? There are literally hundreds of millions of people all over the world suffering with 'mental health' issues and the majority are not engaging in violent crime; certainly, they are not getting themselves shot while aggressively wielding a knife and charging armed police! Same for Ireland itself—big problems with depression/mental health, particularly amongst young males—yet they are not acting like that. Must be institutional authoritarian fascist racism towards black people, right? And what about the mental health—and unspoken lifelong, mental scars—of the people terrorised and assaulted by Nkencho that day?

High-ranking Irish political figures and cult members expressed condolences towards the family, as all involved emphasised that Nkencho didn't have a criminal record but had those darn 'mental health' issues. Obviously, these sentiments dominated the official narrative, and the armed police were not officially publicly congratulated for doing their job in any meaningful way. On social media, however, there was great support for the actions of the officers that day.

In a sane society, after such an incident, a public warning (and guarantee) should be issued by the state that such criminal activity would be met with the same response in future. Play stupid games, win stupid prizes.

The out of proportion black anti-social behaviour

In the U.S., the cult/ideology tries to hide the fact that blacks (as compared to whites) tend to commit more crime, get arrested more, and engage in more anti-social behaviour (including murder, drug related crime etc.). In addition, there is more black-on-white crime and murder than the other way around. The cult/ideology tries to distort and invert this reality. This is why it's necessary for them to pounce on every killing of a black person by whites, to paint a picture the opposite of the truth. It must also be unequivocally stated that, the Marxist 'victim' programming is a major

---

[87] O' Connell and Foy, "False Claims: Family of George Nkencho pursuing legal action over 'vindictive assertions' circulating online", 3 Jan 2021.

https://www.sundayworld.com/news/irish-news/family-of-george-nkencho-pursuing-legal-action-over-vindictive-assertions-circulating-online-39925190.html causal factor of all this.

This truth was highlighted by the brilliant work of the late Irish American author and former journalist Colin Flaherty (1955–2022). His works included *White Girl Bleed a Lot: The Return of Racial Violence to America and How the Media Ignore it* (2012), and *Don't Make the Black Kids Angry: The Hoax of lack victimisation and those who enable it* (2015).[88] Obviously his work drew consistent fire from the cult. It has also drawn support from many quarters. Thomas Sowell—the legendary, eminent, brilliant black intellectual—praised Flaherty's work.[89]

According to Flaherty when black-on-white violence occurs, the cult will respond in several ways including: denying it's happening; they will claim that white people equally engage in such violence; or they may suggest that white people deserve it somehow (the vilest of the three). Of course, these all stink of Marxian 'logic' (psychosis), and none contain an ounce of condemnation for the perpetrators/acts (and all this while believing they should be the arbiters of societal ethics!). His work also highlighted how the Marxian narrative has claimed for decades that there's institutional racism and hostility from the white population towards blacks. So you would expect to see a lot of white-on-black violence, but in fact you see the exact opposite. [90] The only thing that is systematic and 'institutional' here is the hatred towards whites. More inversion.

Once again, the oppressor v oppressed principle is central: the indoctrination convinces those in the 'oppressed' group that they are victims, which encourages degenerate behaviour within that group (especially if this indoctrination has existed for decades). When this behaviour occurs, if those in this group are not corrected or at least have their behaviour condemned by society, it will get worse and eventually drag society down with it (same as in other sub-agendas). In addition, they feel that they are owed something by society. The degenerate, troublesome behaviour puts many on a collision-course with authorities, including police (the 'fascistic oppressors'). The consequences of their actions (i.e. punishments, arrest, incarceration etc.), allows them to cry oppression again. And the cycle continues…

The ideology's influence brings out the worst in humanity, in any given group. The Marxist infection in black communities creates this cycle; BLM perpetuates it. BLM is anti-black, as it enslaves many black people to this

---

[88] https://www.thriftbooks.com/a/colin-flaherty/1019415/

[89] https://en.wikipedia.org/wiki/White_Girl_Bleed_a_Lot

[90] Notes gathered from his online videos and interviews.

cycle of victimhood. Things like 'Affirmative Action' and reparations are just there to further the Marxist cause, by demonising the 'oppressor' groups (whites) which adds to the indoctrination of the masses in general; plus, they give preferential treatment to those in the 'oppressed' group (black), which leads to all the problems listed already.

Essentially, this preferential treatment further panders to the 'oppressed' group, by catering to the mental degeneracy brought-on by the Marxist indoctrination in the first place. Obviously, it benefits the ideology/cult to create 'white guilt', as it reinforces the narrative.

(As an aside, another example of guilt-tripping is the *Sorry Day* in Australia. This annual calendar event suggests that those of European/Caucasian stock should apologise for mistreatment of Aboriginals in the past. Another Fabian Marxist manoeuvre by the traitors in that country to inject some white guilt into the population. It serves no other purpose! Giving the indigenous Aboriginals the status of 'oppressed' does nothing for them. Fabian Prime Minister Kevin Rudd apologised on behalf of the Australian government in 2008).[91]

Another major contributory factor in black degeneracy and black crime (including black-on-black crime) is the moronic black gang culture; something that is propelled primarily by black people. And the black drug gangs damage primarily black communities. Some black criminals may even be venerated or held aloft as 'rebels' of some kind for engaging in crime and attracting the attention of law enforcement. Well how-fucking-noble! Being a degenerate thug and criminal is 'cool' is it? Isn't it amusing to see people claim they have no choice, and are essentially forced to choose a life of crime, dealing drugs etc? Criminal gang members and drug dealers (of all races), you do have a choice: do the world a favour and kill yourselves! That would be more noble than destroying your communities and ruining people's lives. If that's a bit too extreme, how about getting a (real) job?

'Racist' policing

As part of their efforts to hide this truth from the masses (the out of proportion black crime rates), the cult needs to control the police forces. This is happening across the west right now: police are being indoctrinated to think that they are inherently biased against non-white people and arresting too many of them etc! The cause is institutional white racism, naturally, right? Of course, black suspects getting arrested has nothing to do with the behaviour of the individuals in question (and insinuating so

---

[91] https://en.wikipedia.org/wiki/National_Sorry_Day

would be 'racist'). In the UK in March 2023, a 'report' by cult member Dame Louise Casey was released. It essentially stated that the Metropolitan Police Service (MPS, or "Met") of London, is institutionally racist, misogynistic and homophobic. Predictably, the report took issue with the fact that the Met's "Stop and Search" initiative was not racially equal, with black people being stopped more by police.[92]

An article by the Guardian newspaper on 21 March included the response of Fabian Socialist Mayor of London Sadiq Khan, who said: "The evidence is damning. Baroness Casey has found institutional racism, misogyny, and homophobia, which I accept. I'll be unflinching in my resolve to support and hold the new commissioner to account as he works to overhaul the force ".[93] Uh oh... a new commie police force? Anyway, all that happened here was one cult member created some propaganda, and another one agreed, insinuating that the first cult member is an 'expert' of some sort.

Any racial group (in this case, black people in the U.K.) should be getting arrested more on average than other racial groups, if they engage in anti-social behaviour more frequently. We should be happy to see anyone get arrested and punished for committing crimes, particularly serious ones, regardless of their race. Cult members don't obviously.

In summary, this is all just part of the crazy, civilisation-destroying effect of the enforcement of artificial equality, in addition to the breakdown of law and order that the ideology creates.

The *gov.co.uk* website's figures for "Arrests" published in October 2023 showed that "the arrest rate for black people was 2.4 times higher than for white people—there were 21.2 arrests for every 1,000 black people, and 9.0 arrests for every 1,000 white people" (April 2020—March 2022 period). The "By ethnicity" heading shows the "arrest rate" (number of arrests for every 1,000 people), by ethnicity" (for Apr 2021—Mar 2022): first place is "Any Other Black Background" at 53.5, then "Black Caribbean" at 24.4, then "Black" at 21.2, then "Mixed White and Black Caribbean" at 17.5 in

---

[92] Baroness Casey of Blackstock, "An independent review into the standards of behaviour and internal culture of the Metropolitan Police Service", March 2023.

https://www.met.police.uk/SysSiteAssets/media/downloads/met/about-us/baroness-casey- review/update-march-2023/baroness-casey-review-march-2023a.pdf

[93] Dodd, V. "Met police found to be institutionally racist, misogynistic and homophobic", 21 March 2023. https://www.theguardian.com/uk-news/2023/mar/21/metropolitan-police-institutionally-racist-misogynistic-homophobic-louise-casey-report

fourth place.[94]

Chicago riots 2023

In April 2023, gangs of overwhelmingly non-white youths rioted in the highly contaminated city of Chicago, Illinois. They engaged in assault, property damage, jumping on vehicles and general degenerate behaviour in the downtown and Lakefront areas. One teenager was shot in the thigh.[95] It's obvious that this is the result of the ideology's presence.

The black Mayor of Chicago is cult member and Democrat Brandon Johnson, who has a history of involvement with 'progressive' causes and groups.[96] After the riots he refused to outright condemn the criminality, displaying text-book symptoms of Marxist indoctrination. He was in Springfield to speak to the Illinois general assembly and spoke to the media outside: "demonising children is wrong…we have to keep them safe as well…they're young…sometimes they make silly decisions.", suggesting that the solution was to invest in young people (!).[97]

What a weird response! He was really showing his expertise here, as he received a Marxian 'education' in 'youth development' at Aurora University, Illinois. At least he stopped short of saying they were oppressed victims somehow when they were jumping on the roofs of people's cars.

His advocacy of 'caring' for 'the community' etc. is part of the legacy of Marxist agitator Saul Alinsky. During the BLM unrest, Johnson authored the "Justice for Black Lives" resolution which passed in July 2022. In it he suggested that the county should "redirect funds from policing and incarceration to public services not administered by law enforcement".[98] Obviously, "public services" are Marxism-infected 'services'. I wonder if

---

[94] "Arrests", 24 October 2023. https://www.ethnicity-facts-figures.service.gov.uk/crime-justice-and-the-law/policing/number-of-arrests/latest/

[95] Nguyen and Stefanski, "Chicago Police Respond to Large Groups of Teenagers Downtown for 2nd Night in a Row", 15 April 2023. https://www.nbcchicago.com/news/local/chicago-police-millennium-park-crowds-31st-street-beach/3119992/

[96] https://en.wikipedia.org/wiki/Brandon_Johnson

[97] Fox 32 Chicago, "Chicago mayor-elect says 'demonizing children is wrong' after downtown chaos", 19 April 2023. https://www.YouTube.com/watch?v=TBOL1Au4tQ8

[98] Yin, A., "Brandon Johnson once said it was a 'political goal' to defund police. He's been less precise running for mayor", 23 February 2023. https://www.chicagotribune.com/politics/elections/ct-brandon-johnson-defund-police-justice-for-black-lives-20230223-lrapyjp5xzcilfmvkys3bajcki-story.html

such re-direction of funding sentiment explains why, during the April 2023 riots, the police did not appear to have riot gear?

In a press conference in August 2023, he spoke of his administration being based on "care" and that certain "trends" were happening in the city. When a reporter asked him to provide examples of some of these trends, he referred to the riots as "large gatherings". Another reporter asked if he was referring to the "mob actions", he said: "No, that's not appropriate, we're not talking about mob actions..". He silenced the reporters several times, and again referred to them as "large gatherings" continuing: "it's important we talk about these dynamics in an appropriate way...this is not to obfuscate what is taking place, but we have to be very careful when we use language to describe certain behaviours".[99] What an audacious attitude! Who does this guy think he is?! An insult to Chicago!

Obviously, the term "large gatherings" is a 'nice', non-judgemental term (as compared to "mob", "gang" etc.). Judgement of those poor, 'oppressed' minority group youths is obviously not permitted, right? The underlined sentence exemplifies the cult's insistence on controlling language—and therefore the narrative—as outlined elsewhere. In addition, mentioning obfuscation while engaging in obfuscation is also typical Marxist con speak. Sneaky snaky behaviour.

No doubt sane Chicagoans would have been outraged at the riots and are entitled to describe the perpetrators however they wish! Even the most abusive language imaginable is too good for them, and anyone sane would agree they should've been swifty punished. Once warned to desist and disperse, any ignoring youths should've been immediately surrounded, compressed, roughed-up, then carted-off in police vans to spend the night locked-up. This sets a standard, dissuading further behaviour in future; a weak reaction from the authorities only encourages more of the same. Otherwise, you can imagine what kind of fucked-up 'adults' these spoilt brat teenagers will turn out to be.

A young mixed-race couple were assaulted by the teenage mob, in what they stated to be a random, unprovoked attack. Another cult member—state Senator Robert Peters—was quoted as saying "I would look at the behaviour of young people as a political act and statement. It's a mass protest against poverty and segregation". [100] No condemnation and

---

[99] NBC Chicago, "Chicago Mayor Brandon Johnson's full remark on teen violence on Wednesday's press conference", 3 Aug 2023.
https://www.YouTube.com/watch?v=aYILmiuH_BE

[100] Potter, W. "They said they were trying to kill us!' Chicago couple who were battered by violent mob say it was a 'completely random' attack", 19 April 2023.

attempted justification of this criminal behaviour exposes him as a Marxist. What he really wanted to say was "oppression and apartheid segregation of the proletariat".

Friday 4 August 2023 saw a riot at New York City's Union Square Park, featuring the usual property damage, hurling missiles at police, traffic disruption, climbing up structures like monkeys, and the terrorising of locals. Good samaritan and social media star Kai Cenat had the bright idea of organising a giveaway of gaming items, announcing it on a live stream.[101] Video footage shows mostly non-white participants.[102] Cenat was charged with inciting a riot. Obviously Cenat and the Playstations are irrelevant here; he was just a noisy, stupid kid. What is of significance is the anti-establishment sentiment oozing from non-whites, bubbling under the surface, and their willingness to participate in the destruction of civilisation at the drop of a hat (or Playstation). This mentality is mostly due to Marxist brainwashing.

Feminism

"We can no longer ignore that voice within women that says: 'I want something more than my husband and my children and my home"[103]

Betty Friedan, *The Feminine Mystique*, 1963

"We must not be like some Christians who sin for six days and go to church on the seventh, but we must speak for the cause daily, and make the men, and especially the women that we meet, come into the ranks to help us"[104]

Eleanor Marx, Speech on the First May Day, 1890

"In the radical feminist view, the new feminism is not just the revival of a serious political movement for social equality. It is the second wave of most important revolution in history. Its aim: overthrow of the oldest, most rigid class/caste system in existence, the class system based

---

https://www.dailymail.co.uk/news/article-11988761/Chicago-couple-battered-violent-mob-condemn-random-attack-state-senator-DEFENDS-rioters.html

[101] https://en.wikipedia.org/wiki/Kai_Cenat_Union_Square_giveaway

[102] Eyewitness News, "LIVE | Twitch streamer's giveaway sparks mayhem in Union Square", 4 August 2023. https://www.YouTube.com/watch?v=b9Hvl7k2SRk

[103] Friedan, B., *The Feminine Mystique* (1963). https://libquotes.com/betty-friedan/quote/lbo3h2k

[104] Marx, E., Speech on the First May Day, 1890. https://www.marxists.org/archive/eleanor-marx/works/mayday.htm

on sex—a system consolidated over thousands of years.. (it is) the dawn of a long struggle to break free from the oppressive power structures set up by nature and reinforced by man"[105]

Shulamith "Firestone" Feuerstein, *The Dialectic of Sex,* 1970

Commie checklist

This sub-agenda/sub-cult is perhaps the most problematic of them all. It uses the opp. v opp. principle in the usual diabolical way, driving a wedge between heterosexual males and females. It's arguably the key to the global impact of the cult/ideology at this time.

When attacking a people/nation with the intention to weaken, it's the ultimate divide-and-conquer tactic, since there is no social divide more universal than that of male/female. Naturally, this opportunity for creating division has not been overlooked by the cult/ideology.

This sub-agenda is an attack on several key components that provide strength, unity and defence to a nation, including the family unit, and the role of men as the builders and defenders of civilisations (and the inter-linked masculinity). It helps to neutralise men in their traditional, millennia-old roles as protectors of a society, by portraying them as 'oppressors' (inversion again). It encourages females to have a negative, cynical/suspicious, distorted attitude towards males by default, which in turn weakens men collectively (and therefore their ability to be protectors). It has conjured-up propaganda terms like 'Toxic Masculinity' and 'Rape Culture'.

On a societal level, it not only encourages a lack of appreciation for men (and the irreplaceable contributions they make every day), but a palpable disdain for them. On a personal level, it often distorts a female's perception of the males she interacts with, particularly males who are genuinely strong of character ('dominant'). A strong, healthy society/nation is one in which males and females compliment and support each other; they are viewed as being complimentary, not 'equal'. This becomes impossible in a Marxism-contaminated society, to the detriment of all. The popularisation of the notion of 'equality' of the sexes itself is a result of the infection.

The new class system, double standards/hypocrisy are evident in how heterosexual males are being systematically neglected, marginalised, or discriminated against (in education, divorce courts, positions of authority

---

[105] Feuerstein, S., *The Dialectic of Sex* (1970), P. 15.

https://teoriaevolutiva.files.wordpress.com/2013/10/firestone-shulamith-dialectic-sex-case-feminist-revolution.pdf etc). The ideology prioritises females and attempts to put them in the (formerly 'oppressed', now) superior class, thereby manifesting female privilege on a societal level, and the resultant inflation of the ego on an individual level. The results of this ego-inflation in indoctrinated females are there to see, are plainly obvious, and are catastrophic for society.

It's a Trojan Horse because it's marketed as something beneficial for a just, thriving society—a requirement even. It starts out as seemingly benevolent, championing certain apparently harmless causes like the woman's right to work or vote etc.; then, in a matter of a few generations, they are out on the street protesting that abortion is not widely available enough (participating in the genocide of their own people). It's a great example of how the Trojan Horse principle works. The different so-called 'waves' or interpretations of feminism were merely stages.

Feminism is founded on a distorted Marxian perception of history that women have historically suffered more than men, due to the oppression of males/the patriarchy—and must now be given preferential treatment (aka privilege). The distortion is applied to the present too, insinuating that females still suffer more than males (more inversion, since females are now being prioritised over males). Feminism is also clearly promoted/supported by the 'progressive' system.

Does it attack the pillars of western civilisation? Since Christianity (particularly the Catholic Church) has generally been an opponent of the cult/ideology, it's not surprising that feminism has been in conflict with it, helping to erode its influence on issues such as abortion, contraception, marriage etc. It's clearly an assault on the traditional heterosexual nuclear family unit, by successfully indoctrinating many females away from motherhood. Finally, this sub-agenda quite obviously attempts to enforce 'equality' and uses virtue-signalling.

In addition to all of that, feminism also compliments the ideology's anti-white sub-agenda since it has mostly proliferated in western countries. Feminism, combined with its product of abortion contributes towards anti-white eugenics arguably more than the other sub-agendas.

Its effects and what it really is

Feminism produces the following effects, some of which are expanded further along: helps to imbalance society in terms of the yin/yang masculine/feminine dynamic; increases psychotic behaviour in females psychologically thorough egocentric hedonistic indoctrination, and chemically through the contraceptive pill (progesterone); demoralizes the warrior class (i.e. males); reduces the birthrates in an affected population (reduction in creation of life), plus increases and normalizes abortion (anti-life); places an increasing number of women and gay men in positions of authority or influence (in the name of 'diversity' and 'equality'), which helps the ideology to proliferate further due to the feminisation of society and politics.

Some might argue that it apparently makes some women happy, or that women enjoy describing themselves as being feminist, or they like feminism etc. These things mean nothing. Just because someone likes something, doesn't mean it's good. A rapist enjoys the act of rape, I'm sure. Anyone who enjoys being feminist is participating in a crime worse than the rape of any single female—the Marxian rape of the female psych, of true femininity, and of the integrity of women as a collective (not to mention the Marxian rape of civilisation).

Besides, what about over the long term? It's easy for a teenage female or a twenty-something female to say they like feminism, but what about later in life? When she leaves it too late to start having meaningful relationships and start a family, will she defend her beliefs then, after it dawns on her that she missed her opportunity? I doubt there are many out there with the guts to admit that they had the wrong attitude all along…a lifetime of being delusional and hiding from 'negative' emotions will see to that; but there are some exceptions.

In December 2023, Fox News featured a 38-year-old woman who made a tearful video, showing she had finally 'woken-up' from the indoctrination.[106] Melissa Persling had previously written an article for Business Insider expressing her fear that she had "missed the opportunity" to start a family etc. She said: "It's such a me-focused culture right now…and I think some of us are missing out", adding "I feel unbelievably betrayed by feminism". On her upbringing she said "I was constantly fed this idea that.. "women can do everything, we don't really need men" (but) women can't do it all". Though Persling apparently received some abuse from the public after the article was published (for bringing this on herself, essentially), she did a positive thing, similarly for the video. She should be commended, not abused.

Again, Marxist brainwashing uses hedonism as the carrot—it gives you short term pleasure, in exchange for long-term unfulfillment, delusion etc. Many females have fallen in to this trap, due to naivety and gullibility,

---

[106] Grossman, H., "Woman in her 30s cries describing finally wanting kids after swearing off marriage: 'Betrayed by feminism'", 11 December 2023.

https://www.foxnews.com/media/woman-30s-cries-describing-finally-wanting-kids-after-swearing-off-marriage-betrayed-feminism which is not surprising. Unfortunately, the consequences of their poor choices are not just confined to their lives, since the decisions of females to refuse the traditional responsibility of having children (or delaying until later in life) impacts the whole of society. In the pre-Marxism/pre-feminism age, it wasn't socially acceptable for females to refuse this responsibility. In this new post-feminism age, it's more than acceptable, and too many women are making bad choices, thanks to the indoctrination.

Feminism is not pro-women, it's pro-Marxism. Supporting this sub-agenda means you are supporting the degeneracy and destruction of women, rather than being humanitarian, 'compassionate' etc. Being a feminist means you're supporting the civilisation-destroying ideology of Marxism (via one of its sub-agendas)—the very same civilisation that you are a part of, that has created you, that allows you to live, experience happiness etc. Essentially, it means you are being anti-civilisation, and anti-human. Conversely, there is no benefit societally in supporting feminism; either for women or for society in general. It's now only being promoted since it's a sub-agenda of the ideology designed to bring about unnatural, reality-distorting uniform equality, which is not good. Again, Marxism doesn't care about people or groups, it just uses them to advance itself. The ideology is good at finding disgruntled people/groups and co-opting their grievances, to its own benefit. Essentially, it encourages them to revolt against their 'oppressors'.

Feminist Commies

The connections between feminism and the greater cult/ideology are endless, with several hundred key figures involved in the last couple of centuries. There are different varieties of feminists, with many believing that in order to stop the 'oppression' of women, capitalism must be overthrown since 'class division' is inherent in a capitalistic society. Some examples of feminist commies include:

Feminists Betty Millard (1911–2010),[107] Mary Inman (1894–1985),[108] and Eleanor Flexner (1908–1995)[109] were all members of the Communist Party USA (CPUSA). During the 1940s, Millard wrote for a Marxist rag called *New Masses*, and wrote "Woman Against Myth"—a twenty-four-page feminist text about male supremacy, amongst other things.

In her 1940 book *In Woman's Defense*, Inman wrote about gender

---

[107] https://en.wikipedia.org/wiki/Betty_Millard

[108] https://en.wikipedia.org/wiki/Mary_Inman

[109] https://en.wikipedia.org/wiki/Eleanor_Flexner

inequality and the oppression of women. Flexner wrote *Century of Struggle: The Women's Rights Movement in the United States* (1959). It wasn't until later in life, after decades of promoting the ideology, that she publicly admitted to being a party member.

Feminist Elizabeth Gurley Flynn (1890–1964) was the Chair of the National Committee of the CPUSA, from 1961 – 1964. She was involved with various cult activities, making a name for herself as an organiser for the *Industrial Workers of the World* (IWW) in the early 20th century. Flynn was contaminated by her parents as a teenager, who were themselves cult members it seems. A lifelong traitor to America, she was given the equivalent of a state funeral in Moscow in 1964.[110]

Angela Davis is a black American feminist activist and former American Communist Party member. She was once on the FBI's Ten Most Wanted Fugitive List, for her involvement in the death of Judge Harold Hely in 1970. Davis was also director of the feminist studies department at the University of California, Santa Cruz until her retirement.[111]

In 1970, Shulamith (Feuerstein) Firestone (1945–2012) wrote *The Dialectic of Sex: The Case for Feminist Revolution*, in which she stated "Feminists have to question, not just all of Western culture, but the organization of culture itself, and further, even the organization of nature".[112]

Firestone is regarded as a 'radical feminist'—an interpretation which calls for the dismantling of the dreaded, sexist, oppressive patriarchy. In her book she suggested that the goal of the feminist revolution was the elimination "of the sex distinction itself", and not merely male privilege (this should resonate due to the tranny society we now live in). Apparently, it was the over-controlling behaviour of her Orthodox Jewish father which inspired her activism.[113] Feuerstein was involved with creating several feminist groups, including the *Redstockings* in 1969.[114] Plagued by schizophrenia for many years, Feuerstein died a social recluse in 2012, at

---

[110] https://www.britannica.com/biography/Elizabeth-Gurley-Flynn

[111] https://www.britannica.com/biography/Angela-Davis

[112] Feuerstein, S., *The Dialectic of Sex: The Case for Feminist Revolution* (1970).

https://teoriaevolutiva.files.wordpress.com/2013/10/firestone-shulamith-dialectic-sex-case-feminist-revolution.pdf

[113] https://en.wikipedia.org/wiki/Shulamith_Firestone#Early_life

[114] https://en.wikipedia.org/wiki/Redstockings

the age of 67. Another life wasted.

In the same year, another piece of classy Marxian feminist trash was written entitled *The Myth of the Vaginal Orgasm*.[115] The author was Anne Koedt, who was involved in creating several feminist activist groups.[116]

The Marxist mystique

Betty Friedan (1921–2006; born Bettye Goldstein) was another cult member active in the U.S. in the 20th century. Regarded as a feminist icon, and a key figure in creating what is called 'Second-Wave' feminism, she authored a much-revered book entitled *The Feminine Mystique* (1963) (amusing ironic title as femininity and feminism don't usually go together).[117]

Friedan gave the impression that she was an oppressed housewife who 'woke-up' from this horrible reality she was living in, and then decided to write a book about it. The truth was however, that it was all a big Marxist conjob: Friedan was attached to the Communist movement in the states, as an activist and propagandist for many years.[118] Unfortunately, for the U.S. (and for other countries subsequently damaged by feminism), the public fell for this con hook-line-and-sinker. The book sold millions of copies. It's because of shit like that..

In the book, she described her suburban family life in dramatic terms, referring to the household as "a comfortable concentration camp" (back to Nazis again!). It turns out, according to her husband Carl, that they had a full-time maid and Betty was too busy being an activist outside the home to be a functioning wife and mother! The blood boils… She was the epitome of what 'revolutionary' indoctrination can do to a woman's mind—too busy trying to 'save' the world to do-right by those around her. Friedan's commie past was highlighted in *Betty Friedan and the Making of the Feminine Mystique: The American Left, the Cold War and Modern*

---

[115] Koedt, A., "The Myth of the Vaginal Orgasm", 1970.

https://web.archive.org/web/20130106211856/http://www.uic.edu/orgs/cwluherstory/CWLUArchive/vaginalmyth.html ; https://en.wikipedia.org/wiki/Anne_Koedt

[116] https://en.wikipedia.org/wiki/Anne_Koedt

[117] https://www.britannica.com/biography/Betty-Friedan

[118] Horowitz, D.,"Betty Friedan's secret Communist past", 18 January 1999.

http://www.writing.upenn.edu/~afilreis/50s/friedan-per-horowitz.html

Feminism (1999), by Professor David Horowitz.[119]

Feminist professor Alison Jagger once called the nuclear family "a cornerstone of women's oppression: it enforces women's dependence on men, it enforces heterosexuality and it imposes the prevailing masculine and feminine character structures on the next generation".[120] Jagger's overall contribution to the spread of the ideology was to fuse feminism with philosophical studies. She has has been involved with Universities across the U.S, in New Zealand, and Norway.[121]

The above listed books and text written by cult members are, in a sense, contain examples of the ideological 'payloads' that Kent Clizbe talked about in his book *Willing Accomplices,* mentioned earlier. For example, the notion that a woman being a traditional housewife is a form of 'oppression' and will make her miserable.

Feminist groups

In Ireland, the most prominent feminist group is *National Women's Council.* From the "About us" page: "Our purpose is to lead action for the achievement of women's and girls' equality through mobilising, influencing, and building solidarity.", and "feminism is a core and essential value of our organisation. This means we consistently act to achieve true equality for all women and girls".[122]

Another is *Radicailín.* This name is another Marxian portmanteau combining "radical" with "cailín" (the Gaelic Irish language word for "girl"); another typical attempt to feign Irishness. From their website's homepage (underline for emphasis): "We are a women's liberation group made up of Irish and migrant women who recognise that women's oppression is based on the material reality of our biological sex. This group was created to counter the misogynistic narratives and practices in our

---

[119] Horowitz, D. *Betty Friedan and the Making of "The Feminine Mystique": The American Left, the Cold War, and Modern Feminism* (1999).

https://www.umasspress.com/9781558492769/betty-friedan-and-the-making-of-the-feminine-mystique/

[120] Jaggar, A., *Feminist Politics and Human Nature* (1983).

https://archive.org/details/FeministPoliticsAndHumanNature/page/n23/mode/2up?view=theater

[121] Jaggar, A., "Encyclopedia, Science News & Research Reviews".

https://academic-accelerator.com/encyclopedia/alison-jaggar

[122] https://www.nwci.ie/discover/about_us

culture. We are secular and we hold an abolitionist position on all forms of violence against women and girls. Our group provides advocacy and community to women interested in campaigning for women's liberation".[123] Free those enslaved women, mo chailiní! ("my girls!")

In the UK, we have *The Fawcett Society*, named after the 19th century suffragette activist Millicent Fawcett (1847–1929). From the "Our History" page (underlined for emphasis): "We've been fighting for gender equality for over 150 years and continue to do that now, in 2022. We work to close the gender pay gap, get more women into roles of political power.. Right now, we're campaigning to make misogyny a hate crime, so that women who are targeted get the same protection as other groups".[124] On women in political roles, the "Who we are" section states the organisation campaigns to "secure equal power", stating "Just 34% of MPs and 35% of councillors are women. We're campaigning to get more women in all our diversity into politics at every level".[125] As mentioned, injecting more 'empowered' females in to politics will only accelerate the decline of civilisation. It's the ideology using brainwashed females to further proliferate itself, via their egos. As for 'misogyny'—if cult members have their way, male non-cult members (including yours truly) will be treated as criminals for highlighting any degenerate indoctrinated behaviour in females.

In Australia, there is the *One Woman Project* (OWP)—a splendid example of how much Marxism a single group can spout. From the "Values and Beliefs" page of their website, on "Anti-Colonialism" it states that the OWP is "based on stolen Indigenous land, and all feminist work from this place must act against the ongoing structures of settler colonialism. Globally, the feminist movement must be anti-colonialist, and must not participate in, or promote, white saviourism".[126] So this is admitting it's essentially an anti-Australian Australian organisation, in Australia.

On anti-racism: "feminism must be anti-racist and actively fighting against white supremacy. It must always prioritise the voices and needs of women and folk of colour, particularly First Nations people, who are founders of feminism and continue to be leaders in our movement.". A women's rights group? No, we can see that mask slipping. It also promotes the climate change con, LGBTQ, abortion, and the decriminalisation of "sex work"

---

[123] https://radicailin.com/

[124] https://www.fawcettsociety.org.uk/our-history

[125] https://www.fawcettsociety.org.uk/about

[126] https://www.onewomanproject.org/about-us

(aka promotion of degeneracy).

How feminism can affect the mind

This sub-agenda—and the various interpretations it inspires—are toxic for the minds of females particularly young females, who will obviously compose the female population in the future. Here are some of the possible impacts on their minds:

Disempowers, not empowers

Feminist dogma puts the toxic idea in female's minds that they are from this special, protected group—the oppressed/victim mentality. This distorted perspective only encourages females to blame external sources/people for any difficulties or failures in life (e.g. the 'patriarchy', males etc.). This has a rotten effect on the mind! It weakens a person, giving them a convenient outlet for their negative emotions when they have to face adversity in their life. Instead of "take responsibility yourself for your own successes or failures" it's "you poor thing must be because you're a girl/woman!".

Instead, females should be told "just live your life. Be a genuine individual, not merely the member of a group (including a Marxist cult member). Nobody is going to hold you back unjustly. Don't use your gender as an excuse for not making something of your life. You can either be a victim or a victor; it's one or the other". A person can't be both 'oppressed' (weak) and 'empowered' (strong) at the same time!

Only weak-minded, non-empowered females 'need' feminism; truly empowered females don't. True empowerment comes from within, towards oneself from oneself. Certainly, a person—female or not—does not have the right to support a destructive ideology (or one of its tentacles, such as feminism) because they have self-esteem issues! Essentially, seeking 'empowerment' can no longer be used by females as an excuse to support feminism.

My advice to any females who want to be strong, complete individuals is to stay away from feminist thinking as much as possible. Feminism and feminists are the enemy. If you want to feel 'empowered' (whatever that means to you) and have a great, rewarding, successful life of meaning, do it, provided you still fulfil your responsibilities to society and your nation. Nothing or nobody is holding you back except yourself.

Remember, that nothing—no career, no fleeting pleasures, no frivolities, nor travelling—is going to give you more satisfaction than having a great family of your own. That will be your greatest, most important achievement. Anything suggesting the contrary stems from feminist propaganda. Keep in mind that a female's worst enemy is not males or the patriarchy, it's indoctrinated females who will happily drag you down with them (in 'solidarity').

In addition, if you really want to test your metal and wisdom as a woman, how about being an anti-feminism female, as other women have done? This would be, ironically, doing females a great service—you would literally be saving women's lives! An anti-Marxism 'feminist'.

Being above criticism = ego inflation

The presence of feminism can make females feel above criticism, as its apparently immoral to further 'oppress' an already 'oppressed' group. They may also feel—consciously or unconsciously—that they deserve to be prioritised at the expense of men. Aside from being sexist (and therefore hypocritical), this is bad, because the ego becomes inflated, and they become devoid of humility.

Feminism, combined with the current social media/ego/popularity-driven culture we have, is a very toxic mix for the minds of young women. This is because the combination further amplifies the ego inflation. The result of this ego inflation on such a large scale is an epidemic of insufferable brats! Imagine giving essentially half the population the message that they are perfect just the way they are and should never accept criticism?!

This is the impact feminism can have if it's left unchecked. The result, to put it bluntly, is that they are being indoctrinated to become self-orientated bitches, particularly where the oppressor—white heterosexual males—are concerned (which is sexist). Again, this is destructive to all parties involved, including society itself (note: It's not 'PC' to call a female a "bitch", especially publicly, is it? Wonder where that comes from...?).

Oppressed or spoilt?

In today's world, young females indoctrinated to a sufficient degree may walk around complaining about living under an oppressive patriarchy (giggles), whereas what is more likely the case for these females is the exact opposite—they are treated too-well relative to their behaviour (see "spoilt")! It's an inversion, as not only is their attitude not reflective of their reality, it can suggest the exact opposite. This is because, considering the Marxist culture they are growing up in, and the effects of the indoctrination on them/those around them (feminism or otherwise), they are more likely to be: narcissistic, superficial, and spoilt, not 'oppressed'! Besides, spouting sexist, evil Marxist feminist propaganda deserves some sort of chastisement in and of itself. Naivety doesn't make it any less evil. Ironically, being in that state of mind and being spoilt makes someone miserable, since they are in a degenerate mental state. In this case, a female in this state of mind has a convenient outlet for her misery—feminism—which allows the misery to be expressed as this 'intellectual' dogmatic garbage. Essentially, being a degenerate is not noble and is no way to live, which is what this is all about really.

Over-compensating, due to being indoctrinated

This group victim mentality creates weakness, not strength. Some females actually over-compensate by becoming dominant and aggressive. In their gullibility, they genuinely believe the feminist propaganda and think "Well that's not gonna happen to me! I'm not a victim!" and they then become the oppressor/dominator themselves; which is a form of ironic hypocrisy is it not? The "I will attack them before they can attack me!" mentality, when in reality they are not going to be attacked at all. The result is aggressive, weak, repulsive/unattractive, severely imbalanced minds/personalities. Interestingly, feminist indoctrination transforms females to the point where any semblance of femininity is amputated from the personality. The indoctrination convinces them that femininity is the opposite to 'empowerment' and is therefore weakness, so they should suppress it. They are convinced that this previously-sacred positive thing which can bring balance to life, and which should be part of their identity—their femininity—should be denied and suppressed at all costs. The result is that feminism is anti-femininity, and these indoctrinated females are not fully functioning females. This is sad. Female femininity is a beautiful, sacred thing, unique to (authentic) females. Humanity would be a bleaker collective if it were to disappear completely.

'Bitch Culture' and Misandry

Another consequence of feminism is Bitch Culture ™—a society where it's socially acceptable for women to act like bitches. Since they belong to an 'oppressed' class, it now means they don't have to act like decent human beings, and can now engage in 'oppressive', negative behaviour themselves (as this is somehow fair and justifiable). They have carte blanche to act however they choose in this environment, including becoming Marxist activists, without being held accountable for their actions.

Misandry—hostility towards men—is the opposite to misogyny. You will notice that this behaviour is mostly directed towards heterosexual white males, which is apparently totally acceptable (as these are the worst oppressors, right?). It's a mentality not directed at males in 'oppressed' groups as often (e.g. gay men or migrant men). However, you will notice that women who are inclined to engage in bitch culture behaviour, will act like this towards anyone regardless of whether they belong to a designated 'oppressor' group or not. The difference is that the bitchiness that's directed towards straight white males is seen as justified, noble, even revolutionary(!).

In this case the whole 'men are the oppressors' concept just gives them an excuse to be bitches. They don't genuinely care about 'women's rights' or anything 'noble', or anything but themselves really. The cult/ideology accommodates all sorts of degenerate behaviour and personalities. So, it's true—the ideology empowers females alright; it empowers them to act like degenerate, socially-parasitic bitches.

'Beta' males

> "Hard times create strong men. Strong men create good times. Good times create weak men. And weak men create hard times"[127]

G. Michael Hopf, *Those Who Remain*, 2016

A 'Beta Male' is essentially a masculinity-free male. It benefits the ideology/cult greatly that feminism helps to create more of these males in society. It knows the power that young females can have over young males. The males will want to impress the females, who want them to be attracted to them, have sex with them etc.—which is only natural and has been an enduring feature of humanity!

When feminist indoctrination enters the picture, it tips us all over in the wrong direction, drawing-out the worst characteristics in women. We can see the effects of this when looking at how collectives of (somewhat indoctrinated) females treat men who don't conform to their attitudes. The males are forced to then either submit to the indoctrinated behaviour, or they will be ostracised. This is a very powerful form of psychological blackmail, that females can use on males, which is virtually non-existent when we reverse the sexes involved.

The males are then forced to choose between keeping their masculinity intact and steering clear of the contaminated females, or capitulating and interacting with them despite the draining effect it has on them. For the young men of today (who will likely not understand what is happening) choosing the former is just too difficult of course. In choosing the latter, they are going with their desire to be accepted, along with their biological urges; but they pay a heavy price… This is happening to young males all across the world at this very moment, conditioning them to comply with

---

[127] Hopf, G., *Those Who Remain* (2016).

these brats.

The madness of all this is that the indoctrinated females may then complain about the lack of (superficial) masculinity in males! It may be overtly expressed or else it can form part of their disdainful attitudes towards males in the undercurrent. The indoctrinated females, being perplexed, will have this mindset while being blissfully unaware of the masculinity-draining effects of the indoctrination, emanating from themselves!

Interestingly, all this can produce the opposite effect of the 'survival of the fittest' (eugenics again). The higher-intelligence/higher-integrity males will struggle to have relationships with the indoctrinated females. The weaker, compliant, lower-quality males will fare much better overall. The effects on society are obviously degenerative, and the negative influence of the ideology (via feminism) will ensure this situation persists. This will lead to newer generations of males not growing up with positive male role models (i.e. ball-less men), and may themselves have problems developing masculinity; and on and on it goes in its downward spiral...

As stated, a society full of males like this cannot defend itself either from ideological subversion, or direct conquest. It also can't deal with the problem of how to get control of these indoctrinated females (!), who will continuously drag society down with them. Being virtually masculinity-free, a society like this literally doesn't have the balls to do what is required... In summary, feminism destroys both femininity and masculinity.

The rape 'pandemic'

Rape is not as big an issue as feminists would have us believe. Since deception is a central part of the Marxist playbook, it shouldn't surprise us to learn that the frequency of rape has been much exaggerated. Leaving that aside, I offer this following analysis based on actual rape cases. The feminist movement is not going to stop women from being raped! The fact that feminist cult members think their efforts are going to achieve this, shows us they don't understand what rape is.

Rape is an abuse of power. It's someone who puts what they want, above the well-being of someone else. This is psychopathic/sociopathic behaviour, and the kind of person who engages in that behaviour will be unaffected by anything that the feminist movement does; all those NGO's/non-profits/charities, marches, initiatives, catch-phrases, books, TV shows, articles mean nothing to a predator like that. They achieve nothing and serve no purpose, other than to promote feminist propaganda. Is anybody stupid enough to believe otherwise?

The tragedy in all this, is that innocent males are constantly caught in the cross hairs, including young boys. The simple-minded 'logic' of the indoctrination means that their solutions will always be based on punishing the whole collective of men (as Marxism doesn't do individuals, or ethics; it does groups though!). The actions of a man who rapes are then explained like this—he is a man, and this is what men do. The truth is, the only thing a rapist has in common with a real man is they are both male, and that's all. Other than that, they are completely different.

It was reported in the Irish Independent newspaper in December 2021 that 'consent' was going to be emphasised in sex education in schools.[128] Does anyone really think that this won't be directed primarily at young males? So, students across the country will sooner or later be confronted with a 'teacher' describing the art of giving a good blowjob and mimicking how best to shove a dildo up the arse/ass, while simultaneously talking about the objectification of women and 'consent' (and that's just the male teachers). Much of this crap is filtering down from the United Nations (expanded elsewhere).

In the UK, consent was part of the "Relationships and Sex Education" being taught in English schools in 2020.[129] In April 2022, the Australian media reported that consent education was set to be mandated in schools there.[130]

Abortion

> "No woman should be told she can't make decisions about her own body. When women's rights are under attack, we fight back"[131]
>
> Tweet by cult member and first female U.S.
> Vice-President Kamala Harris, February 2017

---

[128] Gataveckaite, G., "Consent to be taught in schools as part of new relationship and sexuality education", 31 Dec 2021. https://www.independent.ie/irish-news/education/consent-to-be-taught-in-schools-as-part-of-new-relationship-and-sexuality-education-41196300.html

[129] Long, R., "Relationships and Sex Education in Schools (England)", 22 December 2023.

https://commonslibrary.parliament.uk/research-briefings/sn06103/

[130] Meacham, S., "What mandatory consent education will look like in Australian schools", 16 April 2022. https://www.9news.com.au/national/mandatory-consent-education-rolled-out-in-all-australian-schools-history-of-sex-education-explainer/6655e9d2-3dd5-400d-9b6a-67b89debb853

[131] *Harris, K., Twitter, February 2017.*
https://twitter.com/kamalaharris/status/831613559297736705?lang=en

"Human child birth is an act which transforms the woman into an almost lifeless, bloodstained heap of flesh, tortured, tormented and driven frantic by pain"[132]

Vladimir "Feminist" Lenin, "Prophetic Words", 1918

Abortion as it exists in the world today is an extension of feminism; it would not exist on such a large scale without it. It certainly wouldn't be called 'healthcare' or be regarded as socially acceptable behaviour to the extent it is now. Indeed, the brainwashing has managed to convince many that a pregnant woman is somehow 'oppressed' by being pregnant; she is giving in to the patriarchy by being this way basically! This is evil, degenerate, anti-humanity rubbish!

Of course, this sub-agenda also connects to the eugenics being pushed by the system. It greatly assists the 'replacement level migration' sub-agenda being pushed by the UN and other Marxism-riddled entities; the goal being to reduce the amount of 'indigenous' people in a target country. The formula when it comes to birthrates is very simple—increase the number of migrants/migrant births and reduce the number of indigenous births. You will then see a reduction in the numbers of indigenous people; this is how you would do it (of course there are many other connected elements, such as demographic-specific 'vaccines', diet, the trans/gender 'non-binary' sub-agenda etc.).

The Feminist movements have been crucial in increasing the number of abortions in the world, in their respective countries, through normalisation etc. Ireland's recent constitutional changes on abortion would not have happened without the cult's activities. These changes, planned long in advance by resident cult members, were unfortunately inevitable due to the level of infection in the country.

It was almost amusing to see the bewilderment of (casually) 'pro-choice' people, when confronted with the idea that these constitutional changes would increase the rate of abortions in Ireland. When you make abortion more convenient, fully legal, and more socially acceptable (by systematically removing any stigma attached to the act), you will see an increase in the number of aborted Irish babies. It doesn't take a bullshit Marxian sociology degree to figure that out!

The bewilderment was also evident when the term "pro-choice" was broken down for them—if you are "pro-choice" you are pro-abortion; the term was carefully engineered to absolve the person from any sort of moral

---

[132] Lenin, V.I., "Prophetic Words", 2 July 1918.
https://www.marxists.org/archive/lenin/works/1918/jun/29b.htm

consciousness in their support of this evil act. In the case of abortion, just because another person is actually committing the act doesn't absolve you of all responsibility.

Abortion figures

Abort73.com is an American website. From their homepage: "abortion is an act of violence that kills an innocent human being" and "kills the smallest and weakest members of the community". The U.S. Abortion statistics page provides estimates, citing two sources "privately from the *Guttmacher Institute* (AGI) and publicly from the *Centers for Disease Control* (CDC)".

It states that, based on state-level data "approximately 961,000 abortions took place in the United States in 2021". The Guttmacher institute figures used, which go back a few decades, show the annual figures ranging from 1.3 million in 2000 to 930,000 in 2020. There were an estimated 60 million abortions since 1973, showing a correlation with the increasing influence of feminism (and therefore feminist brainwashing).[133]

The site also gives estimates by country, including the Republic of Ireland. The constitutional amendment election in 2018 marked a turning point in the accessibility—and social acceptability—of abortion. Up to this point in history, it was only permitted in certain circumstances in the Republic (i.e. medical danger to the pregnant mother), so often females travelled to the UK to get the procedure done.

(As an aside—in the run-up to the abortion referendum, we again saw the Marxian cultish behaviour in action. People came back home to Ireland to vote in it, particularly Irish women, in a bizarre and infuriating display of traitorous behaviour.[134] These idiot females were literally going out of their own way to destroy their own homeland, and then fucking-off back to where they came from, no doubt satisfied and blissfully unaware they had participated in a horrific cult ritual!

The author was present at Dublin Castle to witness the election result celebrations, and witnessed a few hundred ecstatic, cheering, singing cult members).

The Abort73 article uses information gathered from Ireland's Department

---

[133] "U.S. Abortion Statistics".
https://abort73.com/abortion_facts/us_abortion_statistics/

[134] Amnesty International, "Why Ireland's emigrants are coming home to fight for safe abortion", 21 May 2018. https://www.amnesty.org/en/latest/news/2018/05/irish-expats-come-home-to-vote-for-abortion/

of Health and the UK's *www.gov.uk* website (underline for emphasis): "In 2019, a reported 6,666 abortions took place in the Republic of Ireland.". It states that there were 59,796 births recorded that year, and that an almost negligible percentage of those abortions were for health reasons or fetal abnormalities (0.5% and 2% respectively). The figures for 2018 showing abortions executed in the UK are at 2,879.

Since Ireland's new abortion laws came in to effect on 1 January 2019, these figures show the obvious—the cult's 'democratic' referendum 'victory' resulted in an upsurge in aborted Irish babies. This was enabled by the activated network of GP surgeries, 'family planning' clinics, and participating hospitals across the country. (I'm sure the reader has noticed the number of the beast… Interestingly, the cult won the referendum with just over 66.4% of the vote, with 33.6% being against (the 33rd degree is the officially highest level in Scottish Rite Freemasonry).[135]

The underlined highlights the obvious—the majority of abortions were for 'social' reasons (i.e. the females just didn't want the child). One of the pieces of feminist propaganda circulating in Ireland before the referendum, as spouted by many, was that a change in the law would allow abortion for health reasons (including fatal foetal anomalies), and rape pregnancy, of course. As outlined elsewhere, this tactic is typical of the cult—find something that occurs in relatively few instances, exaggerate it as an issue, and use that as a propaganda tool to justify the whole transformation of society! Countless morons in Ireland fell for that one, and repeated that propaganda like parrots.

The cult wants more babies' blood…

Post referendum, on 20 December 2018, Irish President and cult member Michael D. Higgins signed The Health (Regulation of Termination of Pregnancy) Act 2018 into law. The *ifpa.ie* website states this essentially means that: "So long as a 3-day waiting period has elapsed, abortion care is lawful on request up to 12 weeks of pregnancy. Abortion is also lawful for reasons of risk to a woman's life or of serious harm to her health and in cases of fatal foetal anomaly. Abortion remains criminalised in all other cases".[136]

Obviously, this isn't good enough for Irish cult members, who claim that the law as it stands is too restrictive (!). For these degenerates, abortions

---

[135] https://en.wikipedia.org/wiki/Thirty-sixth_Amendment_of_the_Constitution_of_Ireland

[136] "History of Abortion in Ireland". https://www.ifpa.ie/advocacy/abortion-in-ireland-legal-timeline/

are simply not happening with enough frequency around the country, and it's too much hassle to get one, basically. Naturally, they want abortions to be available after 12 weeks, to remove the three-day waiting period, and to remove criminalisation (we could guess these things; it's the same pattern in other western countries). Due to these restrictive factors, according to feminist groups, women in Ireland are still travelling abroad to get abortions. They want to make it as convenient as possible for females to have that 'patriarchal oppression' ripped from their wombs.

In January 2022, it was reported by *Irish Legal* that Barrister Marie O' Shea would "lead the second phase of the independent review of Ireland's abortion laws", and that "Section 7 of the Health (Regulation of Termination of Pregnancy) Act 2018 provides for a review of the legislation no later than three years".[137] Of course, the cult knew this opportunity for 'progress' would arise, being planned all along.

In April 2022, cult feminist group the *National Women's Council of Ireland* (NWCI) stated on its website that it "warmly welcomed Marie O'Shea's review of the abortion system", and "particularly welcome recommendations on increasing geographical coverage, on making the three-day wait optional, on decriminalisation, and on reviewing arbitrary restrictions on care in cases of fatal foetal anomaly". In April 2023, Irish Minister for Health Stephen Donnelly published the report.[138]

Interestingly, a 22 November 2023 post on the NWCI website very cultishly refers to the United Nations, stating: "Since the 2018 vote, the World Health Organisation has published its guidelines for abortion care, with explicit guidelines that any barriers to care, such as mandatory waiting periods, gestational age limits and criminalisation should be removed".[139]

Oh, well then in that case, if the UN says so, I guess it's the right thing to do.. This is basically one cult group referring to another, that's all. "Barriers

---

[137] "NWC Abortion Working Group", 26 Jan 2022.

https://www.irishlegal.com/articles/marie-oshea-to-lead-second-phase-of-abortion-law-review

[138] "O'Shea Abortion Review must be catalyst for system change: NWC", 26 April 2023.

https://www.nwci.ie/learn/article/oshea_abortion_review_must_be_catalyst_for_system_change_nwc

[139]

https://www.nwci.ie/learn/article/nwc_strongly_welcomes_oireachtas_committee_proposals_to_change_abortion_law to care", my god, aren't these 'people' fucking despicable?

Your body, your choice?!

Why is it that, when it comes to abortion, cult members were insisting on the mantra of "My body, my choice!", but when it comes to Covid it was "Do what you're told with your body!". The retort is "It's not the same thing! Covid is dangerous and is killing other people It affects us all!". Even if Covid was this deadly, Spanish-Flu-esque pandemic, let's examine their logic here:

"Covid is dangerous…": abortion is dangerous too. Dangerous for a society. Dangerous for the mental health of women. Dangerous for their future prospects of reproducing.

"…and is killing other people!". Killing is anti-life (obviously), and abortion is the same. It doesn't matter if we are talking about a deadly pathogen that kills, or a woman who decides to have the foetus inside her killed. They are both anti-life.

"It affects us all!". And abortion doesn't?! It's not just about what a woman wants! Giving birth (to life) is a very serious responsibility (and privilege!) that women have, which men don't have. If too many women in any particular country/ethnic group decide they don't want to have kids (or put it off until very late in life!), this group is in danger of disappearing. There is also the possibility of this group becoming bred-out of their own countries, which particularly applies if this country is importing large amounts of migrants. These things are more important than any individual female's personal feelings and desires! Obviously, this level of self-examination and selflessness is beyond the comprehension of cult members.

To summarise—women do not have the right, en-masse, to put their own (often irrelevant, egotistical, or frivolous) desires above the survival of their own ethnic groups! This is the case regardless of the fact that, in recent decades, birthrates in western countries have fallen below replacement level. The irresponsible, self-centred, short-sighted attitudes of certain females is a massive contributory factor here. When the tables turn on the cult, we will start replacing the current generations of feminism-contaminated females with more traditional-minded females, by progressively detoxifying society of feminism. This must be done for existential reasons, at least.

The Porn Industry: Her body, her choice

Another monstrosity linked to 'women's liberation' is the porn industry. It would not exist without feminism, and the programmed association between sex and hedonism. A large subject unto itself but deserving of a mention here. Of course, men are responsible for its proliferation too, but in a more traditional, feminism-free society there would be virtually no participating women! No women willing to objectify themselves means no porn industry. This is because (feminist propaganda aside) in the overwhelming majority of instances in the world, women decide what they do with their bodies and sexuality, particularly in Western countries.

The degenerate porn industry helps to break down the normal relationships between males and females, distorts perceptions of the human body, sex, relationships, and is extremely harmful for the dopamine, serotonin reward system in the brain in males (psychological/emotional degeneracy). The early days of the porn industry was all about film; the 'adult movie' era.

Nowadays, it has evolved with the technology to being online porn. As an extension of this, the lines between the 'porn star' and every day female are being blurred, with websites such as *Onlyfans.com* and *Sex.com* etc allowing pretty much any female with an internet connection to participate in this degeneracy. These things have a eugenics effect on society, helping to further detach sexuality from reproduction by moving sexuality into a virtual realm (nobody is going to get pregnant over the internet!). Of course, females are the ones deciding to prostitute themselves online like this and are now shining examples of female self-objectification. Indeed, it's virtual prostitution—women choosing to perform sexual acts for money—while being filmed for the whole world to see. It's the epitome of being devoid of talent. In an even more disturbing emerging development, there is now the use of Artificial Intelligence and "Deep Fakes" in online porn to further distort the user's perception of reality. Marxism really is the slippery slope of degeneracy.

Climate Change

> "The green movement is on to something with the environment with our planet, but it has this hideous red interior which keeps exposing itself as desiring not a better relationship between ourselves and our environment but the end of capitalism"[140]

> British author and journalist Douglas Murray, May 2022

> "A lot of it's a hoax, it's a hoax, it's a money-making industry"[141]

---

[140] John Anderson, "Douglas Murray | 'The Incoherence of LGBTQI+", 24 May 2022.

https://www.YouTube.com/watch?v=ntX0xWvjGrI

[141] MSNBC YouTube, "Donald Trump Believes Climate Change Is A Hoax", 3 June 2017.

President Donald Trump on climate change, June 2017

Commie checklist

In this sub-agenda, in the opp. v. opp. principle, humans are the oppressors, and the planet is the oppressed victim (naaaawww, the poor planet!). This also ties-in with the barely hidden, anti-human notion woven into the ideology that human beings are just evil, and it's in their nature to be destructive/self-destructive.. Obviously, this is the biggest load of crap in this context.

It creates a new class system between those who support the 'green' movement and 'go green' and those who don't (individuals and nations). Those who don't are "climate sceptics" or "climate change deniers". It also endeavours to create a new class system in economics in terms of (Marxian) 'ethics', as businesses and industries that don't 'go green' will be treated as ethically inferior. This allows for discrimination of them by cult members. This sub-agenda also uses the Trojan Horse principle since 'going green' is promoted as something beneficial for nations, individuals, economies, agriculture, and nature, but in fact it's detrimental for them.

It's based on a distorted perception of history and the present. It's pseudo-science, based on scientific theory, apparently supported by the whole of recorded history and the climate today. Yet climate records don't go back that far in history, and conclusive evidence that human activity makes the climate 'change' has not been produced (we didn't have the means to start accurately taking global temperatures until the late 19th century).

Of course, many great minds contemplated climate issues in history, and others contributed useful scientific inventions: in around 340BC the great Greek intellect Aristotle, for example, wrote *Meteorologica,* a philosophical treatise on the subject of atmospheric phenomena.[142] Another outstanding intellect Galileo Galilei invented the thermometer in 1592.[143] But the technology hasn't existed throughout history to accurately measure climate activity and gather reliable data. The cult, as usual, however, have found ways to cherry-pick information from the past to suit their narrative. An example of this is how the ice core data is used—data which shows fluctuations in atmospheric Carbon Dioxide levels and temperatures going

---

https://www.YouTube.com/watch?v=yqgMECkW3Ak

[142] https://www.britannica.com/biography/Aristotle

[143] https://www.britannica.com/biography/Galileo-Galilei

back thousands of years.[144]

This sub-agenda is supported by the system to a massive degree on the global stage. Most of the world's big organisations are pushing this including the United Nations (UN), and *The Club of Rome* (COR). Tellingly, the *World Meterological Organisation* (WMO) is a tentacle of the Marxist UN. The Secretary-General in some recent periods was Jukka Petteri Taalas. Taalas was appointed by the UN's Commie-in-chief and Portuguese cult member Antonio Guterres.[145] (We look at the UN and the COR later).

It attacks the pillars of western civilisation. It attacks capitalism by impacting on agriculture and industry through governmental restrictions, taxation etc., forcing these sectors to 'go green' even if doing so negatively impacts—or destroys—them. The 'green' movement also insidiously allows the cult to gain control of a nation's resource management, which is central in gaining control of that nation's economy (itself a stepping stone towards implementing a socialist system).

The cult just loves to blame any issue/situation they can on capitalism, using any means at its disposal—including twisting the established facts, or fabrication of new concepts entirely. Their pseudo-scientific climate con-job is a prime example of that. Any problems with pollution that are related to business or industry in any form, will be blamed on capitalism—the unethical pursuits of profits, and the bourgeois oppression of the workers etc! They will attribute any sort of environmental issues on it, as it hits two birds with one stone: it promotes the climate deception sub-agenda (and all the benefits for the ideology contained therein) and attacks their old foe.

Conversely, just look at the behaviour (environmentally) of a country fully under the control of cult members—the "People's" Republic of China. It has always been resistant to any sort of multi-national attempts to control its behaviour on this issue. In other words, while the rest of the world gets its gullible knickers in a twist over 'saving the planet', China will do as it pleases, because the climate deception sub-agenda doesn't need to be applied in that country (since Marxism is already sufficiently in the driving seat). This climate sub-agenda is about making the planet more Marxist, not about caring for it or 'saving' it.

It attempts to enforce equality between (selected) countries in terms of

---

[144] Bauska, T.,"Ice cores and climate change", 3 June 2022.

https://www.bas.ac.uk/data/our-data/publication/ice-cores-and-climate-change/

[145] https://en.wikipedia.org/wiki/World_Meteorological_Organization

energy production efficiency (i.e. having limited ability to produce energy, as they are forced to go 'green'). It forces compliance with internationalist climate initiatives, creating equality on an international level (aka uniformity).

Finally, there is perhaps no bigger expression of Marxian virtue-signalling than stating you are going to save an entire planet! Very funny. Gargantuan egos.

Marxism doesn't do economics; they're not compatible at all. As mentioned, wherever and whenever 'socialist' regimes have taken hold, the economies have been run into the ground. So, it's not surprising that many cult members are on-board with the 'green' movement, as they are oblivious to the economy-destroying implications (for the more fanatical types, perhaps, they are aware).

It's interesting too that the 'save the planet' agenda is resulting in the desecration of the natural landscape. These unnatural-looking, inefficient windfarms and solar panels are now appearing everywhere they can be accommodated, as obviously large amounts are needed. To get around this space problem, windfarms are being placed offshore, which is even more expensive. Wherever they are placed they'll take up a lot of room, chewing up the environment in the process. The 'Save the Planet' agenda is actually destroying the planet (inversion again), while wasting time, money, and natural resources. All that makes this sub-agenda anti-nature.

Of course, the climate sub-agenda is part of the cult's ambitions for global control, which it can achieve via internationalist organisations like the UN.

Climate 'Change' or Pollution?

Why do cult members push the climate change scam sub-agenda? Why are we seeing all these Marxist "watermelon" (red on inside) ' green' activist groups telling us that there's a climate emergency? Why the climate 'alarmism'?

It was once called "global warming", but then it was changed to "climate change", because the overall fluctuation of global temperatures did not support the original name over time. To state (what should be) the obvious before we proceed: there is no major issue to be fixed here, and the planet does not need saving (nor is it being 'oppressed')! The climate changes— that's what it does! It changes, going through different phases, primarily because of solar activity—the Earth's relationship to the Sun—and that's been the case for millennia. It has nothing to do with human behaviour or carbon dioxide emissions. It's an alarmist narrative, backed-up by 'science' and 'experts', which is emotionally manipulative just like the other

Marxian sub-agendas.

Pollution, on the other hand, is a separate issue which tends to get tangled-up in the mix, but it does not create changes in the climate! It can affect the air, land, or water quality (amongst other things) and absolutely we could make improvements in these areas, but this still doesn't justify the existence of the Marxist 'green' movement! Again, the ideology is not needed here. Recycling, too, is a positive thing: conserving resources is efficient, which is always good, but recyclable tin cans, cardboard, and plastic have fuck-all to do with weather patterns and certainly don't save any planets!

This sub-agenda is not about 'the planet', it's about control. It's about: aiding the destruction of the capitalist system (in developed countries) and attempting to prevent its development (in under-developed countries); stealing (carbon tax); getting control of land and resources; trying to enforce 'equality' in the business world; and about creating a Marxist One World Government. In practice, as we've seen during 20th century's 'Communist' regimes, socialist systems/initiatives don't benefit the environment at all (economic basket-case countries are usually badly organised, corrupt, inefficient, and often neglectful, dirty, polluting etc).

Remember, the success of the ideology's/cult's big 'revolution' depends upon their control of the public narrative. The 'experts' who peddle climate change theory operate within the same system as other 'experts' who propelled the Covid fiasco, 'multiculturalism', socialism, gender non-binary crap etc. The credibility of the system, at this stage of the game, should be a well-deserved nil.

'Renewables' or Nuclear

So-called 'renewable' energy sources—such as wind, solar, hydroelectric power etc.—are inefficient and insufficient for our energy needs; and perhaps never will be. Forcing their usage now will only waste time, money, and resources. Besides, nuclear power is by far the superior, cleaner choice, with newer reactors able to use spent fuel from older reactors. Nuclear fission reactors, compared to solar and wind: produce vast amounts of power, take up much less space, are much more reliable (able to run twenty-four seven, all year round, whatever the weather), and also produce very little CO_2 (not that this matters really). [146] Obviously, best of luck convincing your average 'environmentalist' cult member of all that! They

---

[146] "5 Fast Facts about Spent Nuclear Fuel", 3 October 2022.

https://www.energy.gov/ne/articles/5-fast-facts-about-spent-nuclear-fuel

will mention the entirely circumstantial incidents of Three-Mile Island (1979; some believe this was sabotage), Chernobyl (1986) and Fukishima (2011). The internet is awash with cultish counter-propaganda articles attempting to minimise nuclear power in favour of renewables, dismissing the advantages listed above.

France powers approximately seventy percent of its grid with nuclear. In addition, it "is the world's largest net exporter of electricity due to its very low cost of generation, and gains over €3 billion per year from this".[147] A Feb 2023 article on *energydigital.com* ranked the "Top 10 Nuclear Energy-Producing Countries". The U.S., France, and China occupy the top three spots, with 93, 56, and 51 reactors respectively. While France and the U.S. don't seem to have enthusiastic plans to expand their grid, China "is planning to grow its power system, with 18 reactors to open soon. Collectively, this would generate 17.2GW for China's power systems. The country is also planning to build an additional 39 nuclear reactors with a combined gross capacity of 43GW".[148] This corroborates with (the Chinese Communist Party-led) China's present strategy on all other fronts—expand, expand, expand.

A noticeable absentee from that list is Germany, despite the country's tradition of excellence in engineering. Not surprisingly, under commie former Chancellor Angela Merkel, their nuclear power infrastructure was increasingly dismantled and replaced with 'renewables'. The Fukushima incident in Japan in 2011 provided German cult members with a great opportunity to further this sub-agenda, by holding massive co-ordinated anti-nuclear demonstrations in concerns over safety;[149] despite the fact that an underwater earthquake—and subsequent fifteen-foot tsunami—caused the Fukushima incident.[150] I can't remember the last time Germany had a

---

[147] "Nuclear Power in France", August 2023.

https://world-nuclear.org/information-library/country-profiles/countries-a-f/france.aspx

[148] Ahmad, M., "Top 10: Nuclear Energy-Producing Countries", 8 Feb 2023.

https://energydigital.com/top10/top-10-nuclear-energy-producing-countries

[149] Appunn, K., "The history behind Germany's nuclear phase-out", 9 March 2021.

https://www.cleanenergywire.org/factsheets/history-behind-germanys-nuclear-phase-out

[150] "Fukushima Daiichi Accident", August 2023.

https://world-nuclear.org/information-library/safety-and-security/safety-of-plants/fukushima-daiichi-accident.aspx

9.0 earthquake followed by an enormous tsunami, can you? Yet another example of the cult capitalising on something and creating alarmism to further the revolution.

Marxist groups such as *Friends of the Earth* and *Greenpeace* have a track record of opposing nuclear power and, by extension, nuclear weapons. Most of this 'noble' protesting was done in primarily Western (non-Communist) countries during the Cold War years. No comment needed.

Going 'green' stunts economic growth

The Marxist 'green' movements in western countries are constantly pressuring governments to invest money on renewable tech and infrastructure. Third world and developing countries will be forced to get on-board with this sub-agenda, if the climate movement continues unopposed. Due to being pressured in to 'going green' by the cult internationally (via the UN and a host of activist organisations), these countries will not be using conventional fossil fuels for energy. This means they won't have access to cheap power, which could allow their economies to grow. Instead, they will be 'encouraged' (coerced) to use expensive 'green' renewable energy sources while they are developing. This retards their growth economically (attack on capitalism). Since Marxism has always taken hold in third world countries quite easily anyway, this may be another way of making sure that these countries continue to choose Marxism as a (doomed) 'way out' of their situation. The pressure to 'go green' from the big orgs ensures that the option to enthusiastically choose capitalism is not open to them.

And then there's the infamous carbon tax scam. When companies (or even countries) are coerced in to paying it they are essentially punished for their industrial output. The higher their output, the more they are taxed for it (attack on capitalism). Therefore, this tax also makes this sub-agenda a financial scam. Those involved will be able to get filthy rich. It's a form of stealing (as per plank two of the Communist Manifesto). The cult/ideology will take any opportunity to destroy the capitalist system—including privately-owned non-government-controlled industry—via taxation. With the carbon tax, they have found a way of charging people tax (aka stealing their profits) for literally nothing. Additionally, this taxation makes 'renewables' seem more competitive cost-wise. Former U.S. Vice President Al Gore, perhaps the prominent political climate alarmist voice, raked-in the cash while on his noble quest to save us all. A January 2023 article in the Daily Mail stated "the former VP has been at the forefront of green technology investment that has seen his wealth balloon to an estimated \$330 million.". It also stated that he receives a salary of \$2 million-a-month at Generation Investment Management. He also spent years flying around in CO2 producing aircraft and owns several properties.[151] He's the epitome of a hypocritical cult member.

Watermelon groups

Just Stop Oil began saving humanity in 2022. From their website's homepage: "Just Stop Oil is a non-violent civil resistance group demanding the UK Government stop licensing all new oil, gas and coal projects". Amusingly, their chosen branding colour is orange (website, t-shirts etc.), which is a decent attempt at originality in all fairness (again, commie red would be too obvious). Their logo is very interesting and has multiple meanings—it's a human skull in a light-bulb shape, yet also contains a sad person and has a drop of oil for a tear drop.[152] I approve—Marxist revolutionary activism is a miserable idea, that leads to human extinction.

This group has received attention for its glorious revolutionary actions in the media and online. In 2023, protestors were seen throwing orange powder around the place, including at high-profile sporting events in April and July—the World Snooker Championship in Sheffield, and the British Open golf tournament in Liverpool. In Formula One, they also disrupted the 2022 British Grand Prix by sitting down on the track. If I came around the bend and saw those pricks on the track, I'd turn on the window-wipers, beep the horn, shift-up a gear and floor it…

Another tactic is their disruption of (amateur driver) traffic, particularly in central London, UK.[153] These idiots were sitting on the road infuriating everyday Londoners, who were often forced to just sit in the vehicles while the 'police' looked on. Some brilliant members of the public tore their banners, dragged them off the road and otherwise harassed them, but obviously, with the police threatening to arrest them and not the protestors(!), the protests continued. Often protestors, once dragged off the road, would infuriatingly then crawl back on. Some people tried lecturing the activists, a complete waste of time—trying to reason with brainwashed cult members. Remember, these are great revolutionary heroes of humanity,

---

[151] Farrell, P., "How Al Gore has made $330m with climate alarmism: Former VP made a fortune after losing to George W when he set up a green investment firm now worth $36BN that pays him $2m a month… as he warns about 'rain bombs' and 'boiling oceans'", 19 January 2023. https://www.dailymail.co.uk/news/article-11653723/How-Al-Gore-300m-climate-alarmism-Former-VP-fortune-losing-George-W.html

[152] https://juststopoil.org/

[153] "Just Stop Oil: What is it and what are its goals?", 8 November 2023. https://www.bbc.com/news/uk-63543307

levitating above the rest of us, who know better.[154]

Absolutely ludicrous that this was allowed to happen! The UK establishment is riddled with cult members, so no hope of making Marxist protests illegal for now. In a saner society, they would be packed in to police vans and forced to work in a coal mine or on an oil rig somewhere for the rest of their lives. As the ideal solution to protestors sitting on the road, here's a word from the late American comedian Bill Hicks (1961–1994) who said this about the L.A. riots of 1992: "Step on the fuckin gas man! They're on foot you're in a truck... I think I see a way out of this...".[155]

Many online commenters noted how these activists are mostly students, retirees, and may be unemployed (and therefore not currently contributing to the economy), while simultaneously stopping workers/commuters from doing the same. While this much was acknowledged and understood, it's less obvious that their action of stopping traffic is symbolic of the ideology's anti-capitalism, anti-civilisation stance.

Interestingly, the everyday workers who the activists were inconveniencing included the 'proletariat' worker class, not to mention that the longer you hold someone up in traffic, extending their journey time, the more fuel used, and the more pollution the vehicle produces overall via its tailpipe. Even more overtly anti-capitalistic actions were seen in April 2022, when they attempted blockades of several oil facilities, infrastructure and terminals.[156]

Another connected predecessor UK group, albeit on a higher level of Kamikaze-esque craziness, is *Insulate Britain*. From the homepage of their website *insulatebritain.com* (underline for emphasis): "We need the government to insulate Britain's homes to save thousands of lives and prevent economic and social collapse. Each year in the UK, hundreds of thousands of families are forced to choose between heating or eating, cold children or hungry children, and many 1000s die because they are too cold. Insulating the homes of Britain will save lives and provide warm homes while pound for pound making the most effective contribution to reducing

---

[154] "'Just Stop Oil' Protestors Getting Wrecked", 3 July 2023.
https://www.YouTube.com/watch?v=s7XPNM_Om9Q

[155] "Bill Hicks: Revelations (1992/ 93)".
https://www.YouTube.com/watch?v=6wG0wZD3Kh8

[156] "Just Stop Oil: What is it and what are its goals?", 8 November 2023.https://www.bbc.com/news/uk-63543307

carbon and providing meaningful jobs".[157]

Thank Satan we have these wonderful people to save us from this collapse, while they save the poor proletarians. These nuts were seen obstructing traffic at several junctions of the M25 motorway near London in late 2021.[158]

A related cult group is *Extinction Rebellion* (ER. This name is another contender for the "how to shove as much Marxism as you can in to one title" title). In fact, Just Stop Oil and Insulate Britain are offshoots, as ER is slightly higher up the totem pole of the cult's international structure. From the "Why Rebel?" section of their site, under "Non-Violent Civil Disobedience": "We follow in the footsteps of many who have come before us. From India's Independence Movement to Women's Suffrage, the Civil Rights Movement to the Arab Spring, history has shown us time and time again that non-violent protest does work as a powerful means to bring about change. And yet, there are no guarantees. As rebels, we know that tomorrow's reality is today's concern".[159] Following in footsteps indeed.

Letzte Generation (Last Generation) are a German group also active in Italy and Austria. Their logo is a heart surrounded by a reddish circle (Marxism = love!). They are known for similar tactics—dousing public monuments in paint, glueing themselves to the road, using fire extinguishers to spray orange paint on shop fronts and restaurants. They even defaced a Claude Monet painting once with mashed potatoes, and a Van Gogh painting got the soup treatment.[160] Weirdos. From the "Who we are" page of their website (underline for emphasis): "We are the last generation that can stop the collapse of our society. Facing this reality, we fearlessly accept high fees, criminal charges and imprisonment".[161]

Gargantuan egos evident here, again, also a stark reminder that these are fanatics, and therefore no amount of coercion or punishment will dissuade them. The only way to deal with fundamentalist ideologues is with physical force. Amusingly, two of the members were berated in the media in Feb 2023 for flying to Asia on vacation, spewing CO_2 galore.[162] Again, in a

---

[157] https://insulatebritain.com/

[158] https://en.wikipedia.org/wiki/Insulate_Britain_protests

[159] https://rebellion.global/why-rebel/

[160] https://en.wikipedia.org/wiki/Last_Generation_(climate_movement)

[161] https://letztegeneration.org/en/wer-wir-sind/

[162] Scally, D., "German climate activists swap court date for Bali holiday", 3 Feb 2023.

sane society, any identified cult members won't be permitted to leave or enter a country at will. If all goes well and goes to plan, this will be the 'last generation' of Marxist cult members.

Note also how these groups talk about this inevitable societal collapse. The genesis of this was Karl Marx's assumption that capitalism contained within it the seeds of its own destruction. The cult uses this tool a lot, to try to trigger an emotional sense of urgency, which may produce a reaction favourable to the cult/ideology.

Another is the Australian *Stop Fossil Fuel Subsidies* activist group (SFFS, or "Stop for fuck's sake!"; which is super Aussie). Their homepage, featuring the colour red again, states they are "a new politically non-affiliated group of ordinary citizens taking action to force governments to cease their support for the fossil fuel industry".[163] Impartial cult members? Tell me more! In addition, "we have been forced to embark on a path of non-violent civil resistance in order to stop this obscenity". Nope, nobody's forcing you to do anything.

They also state "Decades of dangerous, greed-fuelled inaction have accelerated human-caused global heating to the point where civilization will not be viable, unless urgent steps are taken to rapidly reduce greenhouse gas emissions. Now is the time for stronger demands and civil resistance proportional to the existential threat we all face". These two sentences include (in order): anti-capitalism/anti-profits, pseudo-science, alarmism, revolution, more alarmism.

David and Joanne

Dr. David Evans and his wife Joanne Nova are two notable 'climate skeptics' in Australia. They have both spoken-out on this issue for many years. Very interesting characters since both were involved as somewhat advocates of this sub-agenda earlier in their careers.

An engineer and mathematician, Evans has no less than six university degrees including a PhD in electrical engineering which he acquired at Stanford University, California. He worked as a consultant for the Australian Greenhouse Office—renamed "Department of climate change"—from 1999 to 2005, and 2008 to 2010. He was involved with the development of Fullcam—a system for measuring carbon levels in the

---

https://www.irishtimes.com/world/europe/2023/02/03/german-climate-activists-swap-court-date-for-bali-holiday/

[163] https://www.stopffs.org/about

environment.[164] [165] Evans became somewhat of a pariah when he started to question the narrative, citing the ice core data as a major turning point for him personally. A great man, he had the conscience and bravery to speak out.

On 23 March 2011, he made a speech at a "No Carbon Tax" protest on the steps of Western Australia's parliament house (full speech available from his website *www.sciencespeak.com*).[166] He began: "The debate about global warming has reached ridiculous proportions. It is full of micro-thin half-truths, misunderstandings, and exaggerations. I am a scientist. I was on the carbon gravy train, I understand the evidence, I was once an alarmist, but now am a skeptic".

Evans continued: "The idea that carbon dioxide is the main cause of the recent global warming is based on a guess that was proved false by empirical evidence during the 1990s. But the gravy train was too big, with too many jobs, industries, trading profits, political careers, and the possibility of world government and total control riding on the outcome. So rather than admit they were wrong, the governments, and their climate scientists, now outrageously maintain the fiction that carbon dioxide is a dangerous pollutant.".

He also stated that CO2 does help warm the planet, but that "the climate models are fundamentally flawed", and that they "greatly overestimate the temperature increases due to carbon dioxide". He referred to evidence that contradicted the official narrative, such as weather balloon data, and that it was essentially ignored.

Other 'alternative' sources of knowledge in the world say that the Earth, like our star—the Sun—is in fact an organism, in a sense, that ebbs and flows and goes through different stage of development; it can also react to changes in its environment/conditions (as living things tend to do) and can also impact on its surroundings. Evans alluded to this concept in his speech, from a scientific point of view: "There are now several independent pieces of evidence showing that the earth responds to the warming due to extra carbon dioxide by dampening that warming. Every long-lived natural system behaves this way, counteracting any disturbance, otherwise the system would be unstable. The climate system is no exception, and now we can prove it.".

---

[164] https://sciencespeak.com/about.html

[165] https://en.wikipedia.org/wiki/David_Evans_(mathematician_and_engineer)

[166] https://sciencespeak.com/rally.pdf

Essentially, to zoom out here for a moment, the climate "alarmists" (cult members) are erroneously suggesting that the planet can't handle what humans are doing (in terms of our emissions etc.) and that this creates several environmental imbalances, but Evans correctly suggested that the planet can—and does—adapt. The cult's argument to the contrary, central to their movement, is false.

To say that the climate sub-cult is exaggerating and distorting information in a biased fashion is an understatement; it's propaganda. The use of thermometers and their physical placement is obviously central to claims that the planet is heating up. Evans explained: "Global warming is measured in tenths of a degree, so any extra heating nudge is important. In the United States, in a survey by volunteers, nearly 90% of official thermometers violate official siting requirements that they not be too close to an artificial heating source.". He added: "The misrepresentation is that they use selected thermometers in artificially warming locations and call the results "global" warming.".

Satellites provide an accurate, global measurement of temperatures, Evans highlighted, and do so in an unbiased way. Their data indicates "the hottest recent year was 1998, and that since 2001 the global temperature has levelled off.", adding "why does the western climate establishment present only the surface thermometer results and not mention the satellite results?".

These are typical examples of the cult/ideology cherry-picking information to promote a certain narrative, by distorting reality. He concluded his speech with "Yes carbon dioxide is a cause of global warming, but it's so minor it's not worth doing much about.". On another occasion, Evans singled-out solar activity as being the primary influence on the Earth's climate.

Joanne

David's wife Joanne Nova, also with a scientific background, is a well-respected voice for climate truth. Her excellent website *joannenova.com.au* is one of the biggest climate sceptic sites in the world. The blog posts cover several related topics, and she writes with great insight and attitude. She also published "The Skeptic's Handbook" in 2009. Amongst other things, her work has highlighted the extreme energy inefficiency, high-cost and general unfeasibility of 'renewable' energy sources as compared to conventional sources.[167] [168]

---

[167] https://en.wikipedia.org/wiki/Joanne_Nova

[168] https://joannenova.com.au/

In July 2023, Nova did a YouTube interview with host Topher Field on *The Aussie Wire*. She spoke about 'green energy' products and that essentially slave labour was being used to produce them. The conversation highlighted the hypocrisy of the 'green' movement who are ostensibly about human rights.[169]

An organisation drawing attention to this issue is *Walk Free*—a Perth-based "international human rights group focused on the eradication of modern slavery, in all its forms, in our lifetime." Interestingly, their website— *walkfree.org*—has a distinctly Marxian tone (since the cult often reminds us that slavery is a form of oppression) yet they somewhat inadvertently have drawn attention to Marxist slavery.[170]

Uyghurs can't 'Walk Free'

On Wed 24 May 2023, an article on the *abc.net.au* website stated: "Xinjiang, a province in China's north-west, is home to ethnic groups including the Uyghurs, who have reportedly been subject to persecution by authorities from Beijing. There have also been reports suggesting the widespread use of coerced Uyghur labour in camps to produce polysilicon—the key ingredient for solar panels".[171]

The founding director of Walk Free, Grace Forrest, was quoted as saying: "The risk with solar panels, as with many parts of the green economy, is the fact that they are transnational supply chains lacking severely in transparency and accountability. The fact is that by default right now a green economy will be built on modern slavery. And we have an opportunity, a very strong responsibility to say you cannot harm people in the name of saving the planet.". The article also stated "Almost 90 per cent of the global supply for polysilicon comes from China, with Walk Free noting that about half of that came from Xinjiang".

Again, the ideology doesn't care about people, it just feigns it to proliferate itself. Since the cult's fanaticism progresses in ever-increasing waves, even if most cult members in the world are against this form of slavery, as Yuri Besmenov taught us, that won't stop the Chinese communists (who would be happy to enslave them too, for dissident against the 'revolution').

---

[169] The Aussie Wire, "The Truth About Coal and Power in Australia: Joanne Nova Explains", 26 July 2023. https://www.YouTube.com/watch?v=GwFDlsTSwNI

[170] https://www.walkfree.org/

[171] Mercer and Dole, "Forrest group Walk Free warns of slavery threat in Australia's solar panel supply chains", 24 May 2023. https://www.abc.net.au/news/2023-05-24/forrest-group-walk-free-warns-slavery-threat-solar-panels/102383470

As for the Xinjiang internment camps, in typical cult fashion, they are officially designated "vocational education and training centres" by the country's ruling Chinese Communist Party (CCP).[172] The epitome of racism and oppression, these camps are the regional incarnation of the country wide Laogai prison network. The Xinjiang camps, in particular, were created to oppress/eliminate ethnic and religious minorities— including the Uyghurs, who are Muslim—while preventing any real separation from China.

Cobalt Commie Cars

In a blog post on Tuesday 8 August 2023, Nova highlighted that the Chinese are now the chief exporters of electric vehicles (EV's): "As long as the West forces EV's on its own population, and then taxes them to subsidize all the charging stations and extra generation required, the put-upon and suffering customers will choose the cheapest car they can find. And without cheap electricity from coal or slave labor in the factories, how could the Western car industry ever compete?".[173] Considering the modus operandi and ambitions of the CCP, this situation must surely be by design! Nova also noted the potential threats that Chinese electric cars pose to Western countries (surveillance etc.).

The key ingredient used to produce EV batteries is the elemental metal Cobalt. An article appeared on the *E&E News* website on 15 March 2022, entitled "Cobalt poses human rights test for Biden on clean energy".[174]

It stated the Democratic Republic of Congo (DRC) is a major source of this metal: "The DRC, sometimes called the "the Saudi Arabia of the electric vehicle age," produces about 70 percent of the world's cobalt. About 80 percent of cobalt processing occurs in China before being incorporated into lithium-ion batteries".

It added: "Allegations of forced labor in Chinese polysilicon factories prompted Congress last year to pass a blanket ban on solar imports tied to one region of that country. Customs officials impounded huge shipments

---

[172] Maizland, L., "China's Repression of Uyghurs in Xinjiang", 22 September 2022.

https://www.cfr.org/backgrounder/china-xinjiang-uyghurs-muslims-repression-genocide-human-rights

[173] Nova, J., "How to paralyze a city with one easy EV "update"", 8 August 2023.

https://joannenova.com.au/2023/08/how-to-paralyze-a-city-with-one-easy-ev-update/

[174] Holzman, J., "Cobalt poses human rights test for Biden on clean energy", 15 March 2022. https://www.eenews.net/articles/cobalt-poses-human-rights-test-for-biden-on-clean-energy/

from at least three companies and blacklisted one major Chinese supplier. Polysilicon is a key input for most types of solar panels. Products using Congolese cobalt, like the lithium-ion batteries used in EVs and energy storage, have escaped those kinds of enforcement actions".

Eco economic warfare

Zooming away from the climate con sub-agenda momentarily, these issues are extremely significant in terms of the ideology's global presence. It seems the Chinese, who are obviously not playing along with the 'green agenda', are basically using slave labour to produce and sell these inefficient, useless products. This is a win-win for them, since, as they continue to build up their economic infrastructure using coal-fired plants and nuclear power plants, they will eventually outperform western countries who are busy crippling themselves by going 'green'. As China knocks up more conventional power plants, western countries will be knocking up more wind farms. If global economics is a race—they are pressing the gas pedal (pun), and the west is coming off it. In addition, the carbon tax helps Chinese industry to easily out-compete its western counterparts, since they won't be paying these taxes.

This all connects in with the CCP's *Belt and Road Initiative* (BRI)—using economics to build their global empire through various means including territorial and resource acquisition, thereby furthering international Marxism[175] (an important subject covered sufficiently by other authors). The name "Belt and Road" was formerly "One Belt, One Road". CCP Premier Xi Jinping apparently suggested the name, and it's a reference to China's plans for overland (an economic 'belt') and maritime trade and shipping routes ('road').[176]

Considering Xi is considered by some as the new Mao, it crossed this author's mind that "One Belt, One Road" had a deeper significance: it may be a reference to a historical military souvenir from the *Long March* of 1934 (a two-year period of retreat for Communist forces from their nationalist enemies). The souvenir was half a belt—a symbol of their struggle to survive despite having nothing left. In January 2016, during a museum visit where he saw the artefact, Xi said it represented "the power

---

[175] Jie and Wallace, "What is China's Belt and Road Initiative (BRI)?", 13 September 2021.https://www.chathamhouse.org/2021/09/what-chinas-belt-and-road-initiative-bri

[176] Kuo and Kommenda, "What is China's *Belt and Road* Initiative?".

https://web.archive.org/web/20180905062336/https://www.theguardian.com/cities/ng-interactive/2018/jul/30/what-china-belt-road-initiative-silk-road-explainer of belief". It was donated to the National Museum of China in 1975.[177]).

In November 2018, Joanne Nova spoke at the twelfth *EIKE Climate and Energy Conference* in Munich, Germany. This excellent and comprehensive presentation was entitled "How to destroy a power grid in three simple steps".[178]

Nova stated that Australia has the world's fourth largest coal resource, is the world's largest exporter, and that it has enough of it to last "300 years at our current rate of using it as our main electricity source". She also highlighted that the country has the world's largest uranium reserves (second biggest producer), and that "there are 450 nuclear reactors around the world and in Australia, we have none of them".[179] These things are testament to how much the cult has stifled progress in that country.

Cov(a)id(s) 19(84)—the 'People's' virus

> "Power don't come from a badge or a gun power comes from lying, lying big and gettin' the whole damn world to play along with ye. Once you got everybody agreeing with what they know in their hearts ain't true, you've got 'em by the balls"[180]

> Senator Ethan Roark (Powers Booth), *Sin City*, 2005

> "Of all the things that are out there, what could cause an excess in a single year of ten million deaths? Now clearly a big war could, and a pandemic—natural or created by bio terror"[181]

> A rich computer nerd weirdo obsessed with pandemics, vaccines, population levels, and bioterror called William Gates, April 2018

Commie checklist

---

[177] "Party history shared by Xi: Half a belt reminds people of the power of belief", 23 April 2021. http://en.moj.gov.cn/2021-04/23/c_613668.htm

[178] EIKE, "Joanne Nova - How to destroy a power grid in three simple steps", 18 Feb 2022.

[179] "Uranium Production By Country".

https://wisevoter.com/country-rankings/uranium-production-by-country/#uranium-production-by-country

[180] "Sin City - Senator Roark's Speech (hardsub)", 14 March 2012.

https://www.YouTube.com/watch?v=Os9TU3e0kMo

[181] Bill Gates: 'What could cause, in a single year, an excess of 10 million deaths?', 30 April 2018. https://www.YouTube.com/watch?v=5ToWY_BYb00

The whole Covid fiasco had the fingerprints of the cult all over it. This sub-agenda created division between those who were too dumb to see what was happening and those who were not. It created an obedient class and a non-obedient class, while simultaneously encouraging mistreatment of the non-obedient. It put the 'victims' of Covid in the 'oppressed' class and insinuated that those who refused vaccines were essentially the 'oppressor', as a form of emotional blackmail to force people to comply. It created a new class system by treating those who did not get vaccinated as second-class citizens, through denial or attempted denial of certain 'rights' (travel, entry to establishments, right to work etc.). Obviously 'non-vaxxers' are stupid and a danger to society, right? To the simple-minded, therefore, they should be treated as such.

The Covid 19(84) plandemic was clearly an attempt by the globalists to consolidate their control over the masses. Not surprisingly, overall, the Marxist elements all over the west supported this totalitarian agenda. Predictably, they brought in a system for tracking those who were 'vaccinated', and those who were not. Cult members were insinuating that those who refused the injections should be effectively treated like second-class citizens since they were not complying with the system. Essentially, this meant they would be denied rights, which is the very definition of second-class citizenship; no rights to freely travel and socialise etc.

Taking a mysterious 'vaccine' (or vaccines) that you just don't need is the perfect symbol of the Trojan Horse principle. Once people start down this road, they are willing to take all sorts of injections. This sub-agenda is also based on a distorted perception of reality because it's not a genuine pandemic. Of course, to say that Covid was emphatically supported by the system is an understatement.

Most tellingly, the plandemic also qualified as a blatant attack on capitalism. During the forced governmental lockdowns, society—and therefore the economy—was essentially ground to a halt (albeit temporary in some sectors). It forced many small business owners to endure months of agonising waiting and worrying over their re-opening, while forcing many others to fold entirely. A horrific government crime against business owners!

It was infuriating to witness this madness, and the despicable traitorous police forces who enforced it! A November 2022 Irish Times article referred to Central Statistics Office findings, stating "some 24 per cent of the companies responding to its surveys in April and May 2020 temporarily or permanently ceasing trading" (though actual figures were likely much higher).[182]

In many countries during this period, Covid payments were issued—by cult members in government—to those unable to work in their jobs to 'compensate' them for a situation which they had created! So essentially the colluding cult members worldwide caused the Covid situation in the first place (Communist China, our contaminated governments, open borders, cult members in the MSM across the world etc.), then starts doing things like: denying people the right to work and earn money by denying them travel to/from work unless they are "essential" workers; denying them the right to open their businesses, leading to their bankruptcy; forcing them to accept the state Covid payments to survive; calling those who resist government pressure to get vaccines "conspiracy theorists"; saying that any protests/riots about all this are fuelled by misguided 'far-right' thinking individuals etc. This provocation should infuriate people!

What audacious 'charity' to issue these Covid payments! Yet another instance of the cult dishing out free money, which drains finances from the economy (anti-capitalism). The lockdowns essentially forced many to lose their jobs and livelihoods, in addition to getting them on the dole/benefits/social security, and therefore dependent on the state. Taking financial independence away from the proletariat is just typical of the cult. Obviously, they wouldn't give a damn about any wealthy 'bourgeois' business owners who were impacted.

Denying people the right to go to work, or run their own business, or coercing them to take Covid payments are all attacks on capitalism and on an individual's financial independence from the state.

It was the enforcement of equality in that everyone was being coerced to comply with the state through propaganda and social collective pressure to get vaccinated; equality of conformity. It contained virtue-signalling in that getting the vaccine was the morally responsible thing to do, for the 'safety' of others; for the good of the 'collective'.

Cult members' attitudes and vaccine promotion

Very revealing that the cult in general encouraged people to obey the state/system at all costs. Are they not supposed to be 'rebels'? This is one of the symptoms of a highly infected society—there's not enough scepticism, too much complying with state control. Perhaps the masses

---

[182] Slattery, L. "'Dramatic effect' of pandemic on Irish businesses still being felt", 2 November 2022. https://www.irishtimes.com/business/2022/11/02/dramatic-effect-of-pandemic-on-irish-businesses-still-being-felt/

would not be so willing to go along with the Covid con if our countries were not previously injected with Marxism. Many cult members did not object when the highly capitalistic Bill Gates and Big Pharma stepped-in to offer their vaccine 'cures'.

Plus, there was the vaccine promotion. As we saw in the media, those who refused them, should—according to cult members—be punished for not complying. The virtuous ones advocated these measures in their droves for the benefit of society, naturally. Australian Labour Senator Raff Ciccone had this to say to 'anti-vaxxers' in *The Age* on 16 June 2020: "Our tolerance for your wilful ignorance is over. We cannot afford, morally or economically, to give any ground to those who choose not to be vaccinated...I'm not advocating that we vaccinate people against their will. That would be wrong. We must ensure that the safety of our community is the number one priority. That means that participation in everyday life cannot put others at risk. If you do not want to be vaccinated against COVID-19, you ought to bear the consequences of that decision".[183]

He continues the article by advocating this new class system via the refusal of employment, childcare, and entry to premises to those opposed to the vaccine, referring to them as "conspiracy theorists". Just another cult member pushing totalitarianism, while trying to convince us they are benevolent by virtue-signalling.

Former UK PM, Labour Party Leader and Fabian Tony Blair was an avid supporter of Covid passports during the 'pandemic', as was the *Tony Blair Institute for Global Change*. They advocated for a "robust Covid pass" in the UK, which would include essentially giving more freedoms to those who were fully-vaccinated.[184] In an article on the Sky News website on 6 June 2021, he was quoted as saying: "It is time to distinguish for the purposes of freedom from restriction between the vaccinated and unvaccinated, both for citizens here for domestic purposes; but also for our citizens and those from other countries in respect of travel on the basis that

---

[183] Ciccone, R., "New COVID-19 restrictions will be needed for anti-vaxxers", June 2020.

https://www.theage.com.au/national/victoria/new-covid-19-restrictions-will-be-needed-for-anti-vaxxers-20200616-p55330.html

[184] Beacon and Innis, "Covid Passes: Evidence and Models for Future Use", 6 April 2022.

https://institute.global/policy/covid-passes-evidence-and-models-future-use

being vaccinated substantially reduces risk".[185]

In November 2020, as part of the desperate effort to pre-emptively control the narrative, the British Labour Party called for the swift suppression of any 'anti-vax' content circulating online. They "called on the Government to urgently bring forward legislation that would include financial and criminal penalties for companies that fail to act to "stamp out dangerous anti-vaccine content".[186]

In February 2022, as the Irish government's mandatory mask-wearing mandate was about to be lifted, another prominent cult member was in opposition. In an interview on the Newstalk radio station, People Before Profit TD Paul Murphy stated "I think it's a mistake to abandon the mask mandate at this point".[187] He expressed concern for the well-being of workers (rolls eyes) and the vulnerable (aka the oppressed), but not the bourgeoisie of course(!), adding "Some people will lose their lives as a consequence of this decision". He also advertised Covid injection clinics on his Facebook page, and proudly announced his first vaccine in a 12 July 2021 post entitled "First vaccine working its way in to my system now!#vaccinationdone".[188] Stupid, irresponsible bastard.

Murphy was not only keen to vaccinate Ireland, but also the world, post-haste. Here's a post from his Facebook page on 7 Dec 2021: "The greed of big pharma is delaying the global roll-out of vaccines, particularly to Africa and other countries in the global south. These big pharmaceutical companies are artificially restricting supply of vaccines, and driving up the prices, by enforcing so-called 'intellectual property' and patents. We can't

---

[185] Sephton, C., "COVID-19: 'Time to distinguish' between those who have and have not had a vaccine, Tony Blair says", 6 June 2021.

https://news.sky.com/story/covid-19-time-to-distinguish-between-those-who-have-and-have-not-had-a-vaccine-tony-blair-says-12325869

[186] "Labour calls for emergency legislation to "stamp out dangerous anti-vax content"", 14 November 2020.
https://www.laboureast.org.uk/news/2020/11/14/labour-calls-for-emergency-legislation-to-stamp-out-dangerous-anti-vax-content/

[187] McNeice, S., "I think it's a mistake to abandon the mask mandate at this point" - Murphy", 17 February 2022. https://www.newstalk.com/news/paul-murphy-i-think-its-a-mistake-to-abandon-the-mask-mandate-at-this-point-1312908

[188] Paul Murphy TD, "First vaccine working its way in to my system now!#vaccinationdone", 12 July 2021.
https://www.facebook.com/719890584766018/posts/4194734213948287/?paipv=0&e av=AfYIU7NhUi45-lTfq6BSSUj7A2mIEsyWpASXzBbouG3reNn_ynery5G-pwuJFkUkiXY&_rdr

fight Covid in the EU alone—it must be beaten worldwide to stop new variants. That means scrapping Big Pharma's patents and sharing the vaccine recipes and tech to allow countries to produce vaccines locally and speed up the vaccination roll-out".

Typically, he was suggesting racist, capitalistic discrimination of third-world countries (sigh). Putting this in context—this is a Marxist cult member, in the middle of a manufactured Marxist 'pandemic', attempting to divert contempt towards that eternal oppressor of humanity—capitalism. On another occasion in the Dail (Irish parliament) during a speech, he expressed his desire that "the whole world can be vaccinated as soon as possible".[189] It should go without saying that none of this shit is rebellious or 'radical'!

The "Chinese virus"

Since the ~~bio-weapon~~ virus originated in Wuhan, China, President Trump called it the "Chinese Virus". Obviously Trump knows what President Xi Jinping and the Communist Party of China (CCP) are all about, and he held their 'government' responsible for the situation, directing blame there on several occasions. He was one hundred percent correct. Weijia Jiang is a Chinese American reporter and the senior White House correspondent for CBS News. She's an example of a member of the Chinese diaspora serving CCP interests in the western media, wittingly or unwittingly, by deflecting attention away from their activities. During Covid, she had several high-profile jousts with the U.S. president. During a press conference in March 2020, she once asked him "why do you keep calling this "the Chinese Virus?", insinuating that he was being racist, accusing him of not having "concerns for Chinese Americans in this country". Trump replied: "It's not racist at all, no, not at all, it comes from China, that's why. I want to be accurate".[190]

On another occasion in April 2020, this disrespectful brat blamed Trump for an inadequate response to the pandemic, again accusing him of unjustifiable discrimination against "Chinese nationals".[191]

---

[189] Paul Murphy TD, "Roll out vaccines worldwide - scrap Big Pharma's patents" (video), 7 December 2021. https://www.facebook.com/watch/?v=6441599159243350

[190] CNBC, "President Donald Trump: Calling it the 'Chinese virus' is not racist at all, it comes from China", 18 March 2020. https://www.YouTube.com/watch?v=dl78PQGJpiI

[191] Guardian News, "'Keep your voice down': Trump berates female reporter when questioned over Covid-19 response", 20 April 2020. https://www.YouTube.com/watch?v=5c3wWNsmLA0

At another press conference, this time on the White House lawn, Jiang referred to Trump's previous statements when he suggested America's Covid testing rate was better than that of other countries. She asked him "why is this a global competition to you, if every day Americans are still losing their lives?", basically accusing him of putting his ego before the well-being of those people. (Keep in mind that in an above example, she was accusing him of not responding quickly or adequately enough, and in this example, she was essentially accusing him of responding too vigorously (!). Obviously the accusatory 'questions' were too stupid to be answerable, so Trump replied "Well they're losing their lives everywhere in the world, and maybe that's a question you should ask China…Don't ask me, ask China that question ok?". And once again, Jiang tried to make it a race issue: "Sir, why are you saying that to me, specifically?".[192] Not suggesting Jiang is in direct employ of the CCP per se, but this is textbook disruptive, deflective behaviour typical of Marxist subversion. Either way, 'journalists' like that should be barred from interacting with legitimate heads of state. Imagine trying to run a country and having to deal with unprofessional time wasters like that.

Wuhan

Covid should indeed have been universally labelled the Chinese virus since the Wuhan Institute of Virology (WIV) was universally named as the source of the outbreak. This means, by extension, that the totalitarian CCP was involved too; nothing happens in China that they are not in control of. It was sad to see so many, who were smart enough to acknowledge that the Covid drama was a manufactured situation, blame the 'elites', the 'new world order', and big pharma etc. It should've been obvious who was behind it, given the origin. We could've named it the "People's Virus" instead. Covid highlighted the level of ignorance about international Marxism and its manipulative, conspiratorial nature.

On 15 January 2021, a factsheet appeared on the U.S. Department of State website entitled "Activity at the Wuhan Institute of Virology".[193] It opened with "For more than a year, the Chinese Communist Party (CCP) has systematically prevented a transparent and thorough investigation of the COVID-19 pandemic's origin, choosing instead to devote enormous

---

[192] CBS News, "Trump tells CBS News reporter to "ask China" about deaths and abruptly end briefing", 11 May 2020.
https://www.YouTube.com/watch?v=hF_LvrUvozQ

[193] U.S. Dept. of State, "Fact Sheet: Activity at the Wuhan Institute of Virology", 15 January 2021. https://2017-2021.state.gov/fact-sheet-activity-at-the-wuhan-institute-of-virology/

resources to deceit and disinformation". It stated that the U.S. government didn't know exactly how or where it originated and focused on the behaviour of the Chinese government on the issue, suggesting that improper practices at the WIV "increased the risk for accidental and potentially unwitting exposure". The webpage also noted the CCP's "deadly obsession with secrecy and control" and highlighted the pre-pandemic staff illnesses at the WIV; also, its research and "secret military activity" there, referring to China's "past biological weapons work". The CCP prevented anyone—journalists and health authorities included—from interviewing the ill WIV personnel before the outbreak. Though the WIV is officially a "civilian institution", the article stated how it "engaged in classified research, including laboratory animal experiments, on behalf of the Chinese military since at least 2017".

In June 2020, a documentary was released entitled *The Cover-up of the Century*. Hosted by Chinese American investigative journalist Simone Gao, it provides great insight into the circumstances surrounding the outbreak.[194] It revealed how a doctor at Wuhan Central Hospital named Dr. Li Wienlang, who warned his fellow staff about Covid, was summarily reprimanded by his employer and publicly shamed by the media. The state broadcaster—CCTV (China Central Television)—is under the direct control of the CCP's propaganda department, has 50 channels, and broadcasts to over a billion viewers in six languages. It was the brainchild of Mao Zedong, first going on air in 1958.[195] The documentary stated "starting from January second (2020), the Party's mouthpiece CCTV continuously aired a series of programmes condemning so-called "rumour mongers"" (yet another commie propaganda term, like "conspiracy theorist"). It continued "anyone who had shared information about the virus fell into this category, including Dr. Li". Obviously, considering how the Chinese establishment operates, the order to give Li the harsh treatment came from the very top, to make an example of him, to suppress further discussion. Commie police state stuff.

The documentary also highlighted how, according to internal documents, that the Chinese military knew as early as December 2019 how contagious the virus was, adding: "The CCP kept the 1.4 billion people of China

---

[194] Zooming in with Simone Gao, "(中文字幕) The Coverup of the Century | Zooming In's one-hour documentary movie | zooming in special", 29 June 2020. https://www.YouTube.com/watch?v=MZ74NhEUY-w

[195] CCTV, "ABOUT CCTV".
https://www.cctv.com/special/guanyunew/gongsijianjie/index.shtml?spm=C96370.PP
DB2vhvSivD.E0NoLLx8hyIZ.3#cctvpage1

unaware of the danger of this virus for at least 20 days". Revealingly, the documentary showed that the WHO (World Health Organisation) played-down the transmissibility in mid-January 2020, essentially repeating CCP propaganda. The CCP acted in such a way not to contain the outbreak, but to facilitate its spread. They allowed millions to depart on international flights during this period. They knew what was happening yet did nothing. If we couple this with China's global ambitions, and their subversion and infiltration tactics, it's likely this whole Covid fiasco was a manufactured 'crisis'; a biological, economic attack on the West.

Veganism: the vegetable-minded revolution

"Veganism is not just a diet. It is not just a "lifestyle". It is a nonviolent act of defiance. It is a refusal to participate in the oppression of the innocent and the vulnerable. Join the revolution of the heart. Go Vegan."[196]

Vegan activist Gary L. Francione, Facebook, May 2013

In 2019, it was reported that the Fabian Socialist Mayor of London Sadiq Khan was promoting the Planetary Health Diet. The goal being for the city's almost nine million residents to be eating 'eco-friendly' diets by 2030. The *dailyskeptic.org* website noted that this diet "was one of the first to suggest that individual calories should be cut to Second World War levels and meat rationed to just 44 grams a day". [197] (Here we go again.. Communism historically equates to rationing and starvation..).

An organisation that promotes this Planetary Health Diet is the *Lancet Group*, and their "EAT-Lancet Commission on Food, Planet, Health". Other 'expert' and 'scientific' recommendations include drastically reducing or eliminating saturated and animal fats (the significance of which is outlined further along).[198]

There's clearly a historical connection between veganism and the cult/ideology since it's a form of 'revolution'. We can go as far back as the 19th century to find socialistic characters who advocated animal rights

---

[196] Francione, G., Facebook, 20 May 2013.https://www.facebook.com/abolitionistapproach/posts/veganism-is-not-just-a-diet-it-is-not-just-a-lifestyle-it-is-a-nonviolent-act-of/598432076843217/

[197] Morrison, C., "Sadiq Khan Signs Up Londoners for the 'Planetary Health Diet' by 2030 With Meat Cut to WW2 Levels of 44g a Day", 17 October 2023. https://dailysceptic.org/2023/10/17/sadiq-khan-signs-up-londoners-for-the-planetary-health-diet-by-2030-with-meat-cut-to-ww2-levels-of-44g-a-day/

[198] "The EAT-Lancet Commission on Food, Planet, Health". https://eatforum.org/eat-lancet-commission/

diets such as James Pierrepont Greaves (1777–1842) and Amon Bronson Alcott (1799–1888).[199] [200] Of course, Veganism would not have the level of popularity it does now if not for the cult/ideology.

Now, people believe that their food choices make them revolutionaries, destined to save all life on Earth! Heroic eating! Wow! In the past, when you were eating a piece of cucumber, you were simply eating cucumber; nowadays, when you're eating cucumber, you are literally saving humanity from itself, in addition to saving the poor oppressed animals of course. Let's not dwell on how veganism is the hypocritical, uncompassionate, racist/species-ist murder of innocent, defenceless plants...

Interestingly, many 'leftist' Vegans will get hysterical over animals and think it's wrong to kill and eat them; yet also happily support abortion! Abortion is racism against the human race. So basically, animal lives may not be taken, but human lives may be? Not equality! Perhaps they feel this way because their 'moral' standpoint is based on what gives them pleasure: animals give them pleasure, while human babies—and the responsibility of being a parent—does not (back to hedonism and the ego again).

There's more to this sub-agenda than just 'sustainability' and pushing Marxist 'environmentalism'. Veganism is a form of popularised malnutrition that assists many objectives of the cult/ideology. If this degenerate, unnatural diet [201]—which lacks 'animal fats', cholesterol, saturated fat, and complete bioavailable proteins—is adopted by a population en masse, it leads to several severe degenerative consequences. In fact, veganism helps to damage the human organism primarily on three levels, all of which help the cult/ideology and the internationalists agenda: it accelerates the ageing process (cholesterol is a crucial component of most cells in the body; sufficient, bioavailable (usable), quality protein is an issue too); it deprives the endocrine system of the raw materials (cholesterol) to make hormones and thereby helps blurs the lines between male and female; and it deprives the brain of raw materials (cholesterol and saturated fat) which helps to generate crazy, emotionally-unstable

[199] https://en.wikipedia.org/wiki/James_Pierrepont_Greaves

[200] https://en.wikipedia.org/wiki/Amos_Bronson_Alcott

[201] Bramante, S., "What would happen in a vegan world?", 23 May 2023.

https://www.carnisostenibili.it/en/what-would-happen-if-the-world-went-completely-vegan/

individuals, complimenting Marxian indoctrination nicely.[202][203][204] In fact, veganism is Marxism—it's anti-human virtue-signalling and pathological altruism in diet form.

Naturally the diet weakens a society through the destruction of masculinity, via the reduction of testosterone levels (testosterone is 95% cholesterol, and a vegan diet is virtually cholesterol-free). One of the consequences of this is the breakdown of normal male-to-female relationships, reduction of birthrates, increased demoralisation of males, and the inability to resist takeover by the cult due to the resultant absence of resistance. Of course, veganism doesn't result in all of that on its own, but it's an important contributory factor; it works with the other Marxist sub-agendas to produce these effects.

Commie checklist

It uses the oppr. v oppr. principle because it labels humans—those who produce/consume animal products—as being the oppressor, and animals as the oppressed victims. This ties-in to the whole 'humans are evil' mentality mentioned earlier, which the cult/ideology pushes via several sub-agendas.

A new class system is created, a division, between those who are participating in this great, planet-saving revolution and those who are not. Those who are not belong to the oppressor class obviously, and are therefore the immoral, uncompassionate class. This is hypocritical and insane as it places the welfare of virtually mindless, soul-less agricultural animals above the welfare of humans (because veganism results in the degeneration of human beings, due to malnutrition). The judgement emanating from vegans towards these backwards, neanderthal 'oppressors' results in considerable social pressure to join the sub-cult.

Veganism features a typical use of the Trojan Horse principle. Apparently, it's good for humans, animals, and the planet itself; but results in the destruction/damage of all three in the long run. It aids in the degeneracy of humanity, which can only have a negative impact on other parties involved. If humans are destroyed through degeneracy, so will everything else.

---

[202] Ede. G, "The Brain Needs Animal Fat", 31 March 2019. https://www.psychologytoday.com/us/blog/diagnosis-diet/201903/the-brain-needs-animal-fat

[203] MacAuliffe, L., "Is Animal Fat Good for You? The Science on Why it's The Optimal Food for Humans", 18 December 2023. https://www.doctorkiltz.com/is-animal-fat-good-for-you/

[204] National Library of Medicine (several authors), "Biochemistry, Cholesterol", 8 August 2023. https://www.ncbi.nlm.nih.gov/books/NBK513326/

Basically, when you fuck around with the natural order of things (as the cult/ideology tends to do), everything collapses.

It's based on a distorted perception of history/reality because it suggests that humans don't have the right to use animals for food (a grandiose claim); it also suggests that humans can be healthy (physically and mentally) without consuming animal products, which is a distortion of reality. Cult propaganda has suggested that veganism has existed in the past without catastrophic effects (expanded later), which is a distortion of history (see *Game Changers* documentary below; it spoke of Roman gladiators being vegan).

It's heavily promoted by the system, and clearly supported by the many Marxism-riddled facets of it—the 'transmission belts of culture', online and social media—in addition to governments, the United Nations, NGO/non-profit complex etc. It ties-in with the climate change sub-agenda and 'sustainability' etc., as adopting this diet will 'save the planet' etc.

As an example, a 2018 Netflix 'documentary' called The *Game Changers* involved some big Hollywood names, including James Cameron, Arnold Schwarzenegger, and Jackie Chan. This piece of Marxian trash propaganda peddled veganism to gullible athletes and the general public. We wouldn't be talking about Arnie today if not for animal products (and steroids etc). Lettuce, Tofu and beans was never the Terminator's snack of choice.[205]

Another Netflix 'documentary' called *Cowspiracy: The Sustainability Secret* was released in 2014. It's tagline was "Learn how factory farming is decimating the planet's natural resources—and why this crisis has been largely ignored by major environmental groups".[206] Amusingly titled, this propaganda piece linked veganism with the climate change sub-agenda, asserting that the agricultural industry is dangerously contributing to global CO2 levels. And let's not speak of the evil methane 'emissions' from those poor oppressed cows...

The mentality expressed here is the reason why the traditional farming infrastructure across western countries—including the livelihoods of so many cattle farmers—is now under attack by the cult. In Ireland in recent years, there were several high-profile protests by farmers on related issues.

In July 2023 they protested government plans to reduce methane emissions

---

[205] https://gamechangersmovie.com/

[206] https://en.wikipedia.org/wiki/Cowspiracy

by having a mass-cull of the cattle population.[207] So the cult wants to kill in order to make things better eh? Typical.

In January 2024, the famous, much-liked tech billionaire Elon Musk made an appearance on the Irish non-MSM outlet *Gript*. The host Ben Scanlon raised this issue with Musk, who said: "there's absolutely no need to do anything to farming... changing (it) will have no effect on the environment...stop attacking the farmers". He added that the intended culling would have zero beneficial impact.[208] Musk champions renewable energy sources but doesn't support everything associated with the 'green' movement. (At time of editing, Jan 2024, there are large-scale anti-government farmers' protests in France and Germany over similar issues).[209]

It's an attack on western civilisation as it attempts to change dietary habits; habits which are part of western culture, and which led to the creation of Western civilisation itself (it wasn't built by men drinking soy or oat milk, or eating avocado, salad etc., I can guaran-f*cking-tee you that). It's an attack on agricultural industries, themselves a part of what allows capitalistic economies to function. It's an attack on the natural order and religion, as it defies what some call 'God's plan'—the idea that humans are supposed to have dominion over the animal kingdom, and that we are supposed to use them for agricultural purposes. On this note—it is true that we should endeavour to minimise/eliminate needless suffering in our agriculture.

Veganism also attempts to enforce equality/uniformity by reducing the general population (males in particular) to over-emotional, mentally unstable weaklings, more likely to support the various sub-agendas of the cult/ideology. It encourages the general populace as a collective to eat the same way, as if they are agricultural animals themselves (the whole anti-human theme again—that we, the lowly masses, are as low as animals). It would be equality in that the general public would have a degenerate low-nutrition diet, while the 'champagne socialist' (elitist) types eat as normal.

---

[207] Barker, E., "Irish farmers protest plans to cull 200,000 cows, Elon Musk weighs in", 21 July 2023. https://www.beefcentral.com/news/irish-farmers-protest-plans-to-cull-200000-cows-elon-musk-weighs-in/

[208] Gript Media, "Elon Musk hits out at Irish climate plan to cut 200k cattle", 25 January 2024. https://www.YouTube.com/watch?v=9cwNFpmu7B0

[209] Tanno And Liakos, "Farmers' protests have erupted across Europe. Here's why", 10 February 2024. https://edition.cnn.com/2024/02/03/europe/europe-farmers-protests-explainer-intl/index.html

Lest we forget: the history of Marxism features an obsession with controlling agriculture to control the food supply, which usually results in starvation (aka malnutrition, which veganism essentially is). In this context concepts like scarcity and rationing will be familiar to the reader. Of course, this is not about the welfare of animals; it's about control of human behaviour.

The personal desires, motivations, justifications of cult members who support veganism are irrelevant—once the cult/ideology is in the driving seat and controls the food supply, it inevitably leads to the same results—wide-spread starvation, illness, and death.

Veganism and Socialism

Here is an excerpt from the Marxist website *morningstaronline.co.uk* (this title is another reference to Lucifer, the light bringer, the 'morning star').[210] The piece of spiel is entitled "Veganism and Socialism go hand in hand" (underlined for emphasis):

"Vegan activists are tirelessly exposing the internal flaws that capitalism is renowned for. The movement is entirely compatible and indeed moulded on the principles of socialism. Campaigning to take control of a corrupt industry which maximises profit over ordinary lives is a fundamental ethos". And "by directly challenging the integrated custom that some lives are more important than others, veganism aligns itself with radical campaigns throughout history. The most well-known aspect of veganism is the rejection of meat and other animal products. This in itself is a revolutionary act in more ways than is often realised. Most obviously, it highlights that animals are treated as commodities raised and slaughtered for cash". Capitalism, profits are evil, ok gotcha.

It continues: "In short, veganism is not only compatible with the left but also firmly rooted in socialist principles", and "far from a campaign of privileged ideologues, this radical, ever-accelerating movement is continually striking at the heart of capitalism. The emancipation of humankind and the battle for socialism remains unfinished business, but the radical left can find a trusty ally and companion in the vegan community.". There you go—oppression, capitalism, revolution, saving humanity etc. etc. Obviously, the writer, being a cult member themselves, uses the erroneous terms "compatible" and "ally", as if it isn't all just essentially one single ideology—Marxism. (we acknowledged this

---

[210] Swanson, D., "Veganism and socialism go hand in hand", 1 November 2018.

https://morningstaronline.co.uk/article/veganism-and-socialism-go-hand-hand

problematic compartmentalisation early on).

It concludes: "Through education, agitation and organisation we can create a better world in which everyone, human or otherwise, has equal opportunity to flourish". Cows, pigs, chickens, and sheep can "flourish" can they? Career-wise? Or perhaps, if free to do as they please, they would choose not to work, and be 'free-spirits'—do yoga, do charity work abroad, look after other animals etc? Or even better, they could become Marxist activists of some kind, right? "Cows against racism" or "Gender non-binary Tranny Chickens?". How splendid! I get it now!

In all seriousness, cows/sheep/chickens have no other purpose in this world but to be used as agricultural animals by humans, as has been the case since the dawn of man. End of f*cking discussion.

I once had a highly animated 'conversation' with a brainwashed, overweight, university student who had recently become vegan. She spoke about the oppression of chickens, and that we are taking the eggs without their 'consent' (a popular Marxian buzzword, to attack the 'oppressors'). What an insult to the animal kingdom—projecting a lunatic Marxist mindset on to it. She was suggesting that, when the chickens realise the eggs are gone, they think this is "Brutal, shameless, naked exploitation of our feathered proletariat comrades! Chickens of the world, unite!".

Anti-Americanism

"America will always choose independence and co-operation over global governance, control and domination...We reject the ideology of globalism. And we embrace the doctrine of patriotism"211

President Donald Trump's excellent
UN General Assembly address, September 2018

"The United States will eventually fly the Communist Red Flag... the American people will hoist it themselves"212

Soviet Premier Nikita Khruschev, Bucharest, June 1962

"The menace of communism in this country will remain a menace until the American people make themselves aware of the techniques of communism.. the individual is handicapped by coming face to face with a conspiracy so monstrous he cannot believe it exists. The American mind

---

211 C-SPAN, "President Trump addresses U.N. General Assembly - FULL SPEECH (C-SPAN)", 25 September 2018.
https://www.YouTube.com/watch?v=KfVdIKaQzW8

212 Stormer, John A., *None Dare Call it Treason* (1964), P. 9.

simply has not come to a realization of the evil which has been intro-duced into our midst. It rejects even the assumption that human crea-tures could espouse a philosophy which must ultimately destroy all that is good and decent"

J. Edgar Hoover, *The Elks Magazine* (August 1956)213

Another sign of infection in your society is when there are anti-American sentiments being expressed. The cult/ideology has traditionally encouraged the perception that the U.S. is the most powerful, evil, and dominant militaristic force in the world; that they have a quasi-empire of sorts. On a geopolitical scale, its propaganda has been effective at convincing many of the imperialistic tendencies of such a capitalist juggernaut. It's the U.S. military-economic-corporate-media dominance of the world, right? In addition, they've tried to equate this 'imperialism' with American patriotism, which is another Marxian trick. But is this actually true? While it may seem to some that the U.S. has been this globe-trotting domineering force in some ways, we must ask—where does this perception come from? And who or what promotes it? Not surprisingly, many indoctrinated university students are fed (and spew!) such ideas. Predictably, the cult/ideology is happy for us to believe that being a warmonger is part of being American and for us to talk of this 'American Empire' etc.; while their own involvement is intentionally ignored/suppressed.

There is another major benefit for the cult if people believe this propaganda that the U.S. in an oppressive, imperialistic monster—they can use this to justify the destruction of America. In mass immigration for example, since 'warmongers' like the U.S. are apparently responsible for all these 'refugees', they now 'owe' the rest of the world. It's the same formula that's used on European countries with colonial pasts. In addition, the 'foreign policy' of the U.S. is sometimes explained with the notion that Americans are just violent and dominant by nature; that these things are part of the American heritage almost. We hear things like "look what they did to the native American Indians!", that they are gung-ho gun-toting fanatics, or that militant imperialism is just a natural consequence of having a big evil capitalist consumer-ridden country (thank you V.I. Lenin)!

Makes sense, right? (rolls eyes). Interesting that some might argue that 'U.S. dominance' outside its borders is not merely geo-political and military, but also 'cultural'—which includes the influence of American media, entertainment, Hollywood, music industry etc.

---

213 Hoover, J., *The Elks Magazine, August 1956.* https://libquotes.com/j-edgar-hoover/quote/lbj3c3u

The disdain for the U.S. in your society, you'll notice, is not merely directed at U.S. foreign policy/military 'interventionism' but directed at Americans/American culture in general. Non-Americans may have heard the negative stereotypes that people in that country are crazy, stupid, arrogant, obnoxious, gun-toting, culture-less, warmongers etc. The last in particular — "warmongers"—is very interesting, and classic Marxist defamation; it's also easily dis-proven. Warmongers compared to who/what? Naturally, any anti-Communist military action taken by U.S. forces is 'wrong' according to cult members; therefore, behaviour like this must be labelled as "war mongering". Interesting to note that most of the military actions by U.S. forces in the 20th century post WW2 (overt or covert) involved dealing with the forces of communism: South America, Grenada, Cuba, Korea, Vietnam, and of course, the Cold War including Afghanistan. (The actions since then—the Gulf War (1991), the Iraq War (2003–2011), and the invasion and occupation of Afghanistan (2001–2021)—were conducted for other reasons, but still—the American people should not be stereotyped because of the decision makers in those cases).

Leaving "warmongers" aside for a moment—we have people with the above negative attributes all over the world, so why should the U.S. be regarded as exceptionally bad? And what do we mean by "the U.S." exactly anyway? Are we talking about a few Americans? Or a few hundred, or thousand, or million? It's a big place! With a population over 334 million, labelling the whole country negatively like that is itself just stupid, crazy, arrogant etc. In addition, there are degenerate brainwashed cult members all over the world, so a person's nationality doesn't matter. The vast majority of nationalities around the world don't have the luxury of pointing fingers on this issue! There are plenty of fantastic human beings in the U.S.; great patriots and thinkers of all kinds. Despite any anti-American bias that may be present, we should be able to see that. We should not regard patriots in Ireland or the UK or Germany or Italy or anywhere else to be superior to American patriots; a patriot is a patriot—you are either pro-freedom/anti-internationalism/anti-Marxism or you're not.

U.S. right to self-defence

"The communist movement in the Unites States began to manifest itself in 1919. Since then it has changed its name and its party line whenever expedient and tactical.. it stands for the destruction of our American form of government; it stands for the destruction of American Democracy; it stands for the destruction of free enterprise; and it stands for the creation of a 'Soviet of the United States' and ultimate world revolution"[214]

FBI Director J. Edgar Hoover, House Committee
On Un-American Activities speech, 1947

It's part of the Marxist DNA to hate America, and they have historically sought to destroy it, not primarily through outright military conquest, but via subversion, propaganda etc. The U.S. has been an example of a generally prosperous, economically powerful country (due to having a capitalistic economy). This is why countless cult members since Lenin's time considered it a prime target. In addition, in post-colonial times, the U.S. establishment has been predominantly white and Christian.

Once patriotic Americans became aware of the cult's intentions to attack the U.S., it gave them permission to defend themselves. This is the first point to justify U.S. actions against it—self-defence. Secondly, since the cult is global, dealing with it becomes an international matter; being defensive in this case requires going on the attack abroad. U.S. actions to stop the Marxist rot from gathering strength near its borders in Latin America were totally justified.

The idea that the U.S. could just sit back and allow the rot to fully take South America, the rest of the Caribbean, and Central American countries is ludicrous; such thinking is the result of not understanding the aggressive fanaticism of the cult! Marxism, remember, is a form of internationalist imperialism—it will always keep pushing to control more territory. If it wasn't for the military opposition that the U.S. has historically presented it with, the cult/ideology might have already achieved complete dominance... To summarise—the ideology never forgets and stays bitter.

Opposing the cult globally

It must be noted too that despite the apparent efforts of the U.S. to combat the cult directly worldwide, they hardly had much success in some major engagements (as listed earlier)—they had to withdraw from Vietnam, didn't do enough to help Cambodia, and couldn't prevent the loss of North Korea. They also failed to take Cuba in the ill-fated Bay of Pigs invasion (again, due to only committing half-heartedly). They were successful in taking little Grenada, however.

Those were direct engagements with the cult, but there's also the proxy-war engagements during the Cold War era including the Soviet Afghan war

---

[214] FBI Director J. Edgar Hoover, speech before the House Committee On Un-American Activities, 26 March 1947.

when the U.S.-backed the Mujahideen against the Soviet-backed Marxist government of the 'Democratic' Republic of Afghanistan, or the U.S.-backed Contras active against the Marxist Sandinistas running Nicaragua.

And then, most pertinently, there's another area of opposition to the cult—the ideological battleground, which was waged against the U.S. primarily on U.S. soil by cult members (American traitors or foreign Marxist operatives).

Of course, things are not always black and white, and it seems that the U.S. administration (or some elements of it, at least) has not always been clearly opposed to the spread of communism (e.g. its condemnation and economic sanctions of the minority white anti-Communist South African government in the Apartheid years).[215] Regardless of such contradictions, in general, the U.S. has been a military opponent to communism during the second half of the 20th century.

A matter of responsibility

And this leads us to the next point. The cult just loves to argue that the U.S. is an imperial force and this is why it engaged in military actions in Vietnam, Korea etc. (which essentially were anti-Marxist military actions). U.S. actions in the Middle East in recent decades are also viewed as imperialistic by the cult since if the U.S. controls territory there, the cult cannot (i.e. the ambitions of Russia and China).

What is overlooked here is that military forces around the world have the responsibility to oppose military actions by the cult, by deterrence or direct opposition! This particularly applies to highly capable nations and military forces like those of the United States. Contemporary examples of this process in action include President Trump's stances towards the nuclear weapons posturing of North Korea, and China's territorial ambitions.

As evidence that the U.S. is imperial, the cult has often raised the point that there are U.S. bases all over the world. These bases existed to prevent the spread of communism and we should be supportive of this. Military actions against the cult are not merely for the purpose of retaining political or geographical control to maintain interests in a certain region (i.e. in the case of the U.S.), but for the good of humankind. Using military force anywhere in the world to stop the spread of 'communism' is a noble act. If you have the power to do so, you have a responsibility to do so. In addition, as Yuri Besmenov said, at a certain point of infection military intervention is the

---

[215] "The End of Apartheid", 20 January 2001. https://2001-2009.state.gov/r/pa/ho/time/pcw/98678.htm

only option available; therefore, this is sometimes inevitable.

Since 2002, in preparation for its Middle Eastern operations, the U.S. military has been using Shannon Airport, County Clare, Ireland as a stopover. Various Marxian political groups, including an activist group called *Shannonwatch* have protested this use of the airport.

An Irish Times article on Sunday 19 November 2023 revisited the issue due to the current Israel-Palestine conflict.[216] It mentions a "motion from People Before Profit (PBP) which calls for Ireland to unilaterally impose sanctions on Israeli politicians due to the bombardment of Gaza and for Shannon Airport to be closed to the US military". PBP are one of the overtly Marxist groups in Ireland. The cult members, in this motion, suspected that the airport is being used to transport weapons to Israel. Shannonwatch held a 'peace' vigil there on Sunday 12 November, symbolically blocking the entrance road. They also read out the names of children killed in the conflict.[217]

As usual, this is nothing to do with humanitarianism, whatever the cult members involved think (activist, politician, or journalist); the brainwashing compels them to take these stances, it's that simple. This is about their engrained ideological opposition to the U.S.'s international operations since they have traditionally hindered the ideology's spread. In addition, any perceived pro-Israel activity by the U.S. will be opposed by cult members by proxy since they are pro-Palestine.

Capable nations are the immune system

Opposing the cult—militarily or otherwise—is a dirty job, but someone has to do it. It's an act of cleansing. To come back to the theme of Marxism being an ideological pandemic: countries that oppose Marxist expansionism represent the immune system of mankind, attacking the pathogen wherever it's found. Some will retort "well, why is it necessary for the U.S. or anyone else to maintain a global militarily presence?". It's because, to continue the analogy, an effective immune system needs to always remain on guard across the whole organism, this is how it should function. This isn't a fight that you fight once and then it's done; there must

---

[216] McQuinn, C., "Shannon Airport not being used by US to supply military equipment to Israel – Varadkar", 19 November 2023.
https://www.irishtimes.com/politics/2023/11/19/shannon-airport-not-being-used-by-us-to-supply-military-equipment-to-israel-varadkar/

[217] Shannonwatch, "Shannon Peace Rally Remembers those Killed in Gaza and Other Wars", 12 November 2023. https://www.shannonwatch.org/content/shannon-peace-rally-remembers-those-killed-gaza-and-other-wars

be a commitment to fight as many times that are necessary to suppress the infection if it should appear again. Eternal military vigilance is indispensable.

Some may struggle to accept this concept (of having an aggressive, suppressive stance), but it's necessary in this case; the history of the struggle against the ideology shows that it will always keep re-emerging, and perhaps always will. The only question is, can we at least keep it sufficiently suppressed? There's also the naive perception that "well, why should the U.S. or any other group dominate, and 'Communist' countries are not allowed to…why isn't it more equal??". This perception comes from the ideology! "Naawww, look at the poor Communist regimes being oppressed and annihilated!". I-n-s-a-n-e. Communist Countries Matter? No, countries driven by the ideology don't deserve to have an equal footing with those who are not! History proves that often infected nations—despite not being able to manage their own countries efficiently—always seem to be more pre-occupied with forcing other countries to be like theirs (instead of focusing on managing their own affairs efficiently). Of course, we shouldn't endeavour to have any single country being in a position of global control, but if we have a choice between a highly infected country or a much less-infected country dominating affairs, we should choose the latter.

Summary

Marxist propaganda highlighting 'U.S. imperialism' distracts us from the global threat posed by the cult/ideology (in addition to having a destabilising effect on the U.S. itself). Is the cult's anti-U.S. propaganda simply a case of them throwing their toys out of the pram? Interesting isn't it that the Soviet counter propaganda of its era actually convinced (some) people that the U.S. created the Communist threat in Vietnam as a deception to justify its imperialism! I'm sure the tens of millions of unfortunate souls/skeletons under the ground in Asia would debate the idea that the spread of communism was simply U.S. propaganda.

Of course, the author is not excusing any actual crimes committed by the U.S. forces in any conflict, but simply pointing-out that the idea that U.S. armed forces have been the chief belligerents of the 20th century is a massive distortion of the facts. We must also look at the Middle East with fresh eyes. Not all intervention in those regions is simply a case of U.S. 'imperialist' action (as the cult would have us believe). We must always examine for signs of Marxist infection in countries first before we decide if a military action is justified.

As a final point, we must consider the hypocrisy on show here: when it comes to crimes against humanity, totalitarianism, and imperial ambitions, there is no contest when it comes to casualties and body count (civilian or otherwise) if we compare U.S. activity and the actions of the cult.

At time of editing, U.S. patriots are trying to impeach the Marxist President Joe Biden due to his decidedly anti-American activities; cult members desperately try to protect him by keeping his traitorous foreign business dealings under wraps. In congress, predictably, they used the 'conspiracy theory' defence.[218] The cult is also desperately fighting to keep the influx of illegal immigrants going, amongst other things. The fight for control of America continues..

In addition, at this time (February 2024), there are strong signs that the decidedly non-Western alliance of China, North Korea, Russia (and their allies) are preparing for large scale conflict. If a Communist alliance has ambitions to attack the currently weakened West, they are choosing a good time…

---

[218] Yerushalmy, J., "Biden impeachment inquiry explained: what is happening and could the president be convicted?", 14 Dec 2023. https://www.theguardian.com/us-news/2023/dec/14/biden-impeachment-inquiry-explained-what-is-happening-and-could-the-president-be-convicted

Section X—Other Signs & Symptoms

"The revolution will move forward until its consolidation is total. The time is still far off when there can be a period of relative calm. And life is always revolution"[1]

Antonio Gramsci, *The Russian Maximalists* (1916)

Introduction

To what degree is your country infected? How can we 'test' for this? Are there visual signs we can see such as symbols, logos etc? Are there things we can hear in the media or in the way people speak? How about in politics or education? Sexuality? Relationships? Religion and spirituality? Should we look for subtle attitudes, easy-to-spot catchphrases, or both? How can we spot these (commie) red flags when they present themselves? Here are some other signs and symptoms of infection within a society:

Marxists/Marxism itself

Here are some signs that are directly related to the ideology/cult:

Overtly Marxist groups, such as Antifa, are allowed to operate in public, making a mockery of law and order. There may also be collusion between them and the police/state (at an official or unofficial level).

Individuals get offended when you criticize Marxism/socialism/communism, cult members or anyone who supports these ideas, and leap to its/their defence. Any public criticism of the cult/ideology or Marxist groups/initiatives is countered by collectivist, pack-like attacks of anyone who dispenses it.

There is a noticeable perception that the ideology/cult represents genuine, constructive rebellion/revolution. Though they are indoctrinated/infected, many actually think they are a 'rebel' opposed to totalitarianism; they may also insinuate they are immune to any ideological indoctrination coming from the system(!). You may hear "How can you talk about the Globalist elites and the New World Order and also criticize socialism?!? Don't you

---

[1] Gramsci, A., "The Russian Maximalists", 1916.
https://www.marxists.org/subject/quotes/miscellaneous.htm

realise we're all on the same team?!?"

There is palpable social pressure to be a cult member and conform with the ideology. If not, you must be an unethical extremist (Nazi, fascist etc). It's not permitted that you can just disagree with their ideology, certainly not without repercussions.

People seem to be slightly infected with Marxism, by default. Obviously, you can't be sure until someone gives you a clear sign—like when they express their 'opinions'—but these types may be everywhere and anywhere in society (I say 'opinions' because they're just repeating Marxist rhetoric). A person may be already primed to be politically, psychologically, and sociologically aligned to the ideology without being fully indoctrinated. The person in question may not even think that they have any political opinions/stances in their minds, yet when they express some, they are undoubtedly Marxist stances.

This can be something as simple as: 'Left-wing' or 'Progressive' is good, and 'Right-wing' is bad; or the idea that "countries shouldn't exist", as this is "an old, uncool idea" etc.; or that "there shouldn't be a gender pay gap" in the workplace.

Even if it's just a casual, pro-Marxist bias, this goes a long way. If you give Marxism an inch, it will take a mile. Every single pro-Marxist thought in the population all adds-up, it produces an overall quantum effect.

A cultish 'protest culture'

> "Our task is to utilise every manifestation of discontent, and to gather and turn to the best account every protest, however small"[2]

> V.I. Lenin, "What is to be done?", 1902

Another sign is that there are protests constantly which over-saturates and dominates the protest environment to the point where they are both unnoticed and ineffective. This prevents any sort of real, constructive, impactful incarnations (i.e. non-Marxist ones).

Being a highly significant traditional element of the cult/ideology, protest culture gets these would-be 'revolutionaries' out on the streets, marking their territory. It gives them confidence, makes them feel empowered; that they can change things; that they are special (not simply whores of the ideology). On all the important issues, they serve internationalist

---

[2] Lenin, V.I., "What is to be done?", 1902, P. 54.

https://www.marxists.org/archive/lenin/works/1901/witbd/

totalitarianism by doing its bidding, while simultaneously giving the illusion that democracy works in a sense and 'people power' is real.

Strategically, Marxist protest culture is important for the system, since it creates an army of activists who can be rolled-out on command to do its bidding—such as when they oppose nationalistic or 'right-wing' pushback at every turn, or push the various Marxian sub-agendas etc.

Protest culture also gives those involved their collectivist high from it. It's part of their social life and gives their lives meaning. In their naivety, they feel they're doing a good thing, plus they get to have some fun surrounded by people who encourage them and agree with them. How lovely! This is the psychological trap of Marxism in action. It's the red nectar. The Marxism-riddled universities are especially to blame for this, as they encourage this protest culture.

You might hear such chants as: "One race, human race!" (insinuates 'equality' and uniformity between racial groups), or "Power to the people!" (should be "power to the proletariat"), or the highly imaginative "Nazi scum off our streets!". Another is "No justice, No peace"—another nod to 'Continuous Revolution', in chant form. 'Justice' to them is a Communist utopia. Until that is achieved, they will continue to make noise (unless they are prevented from doing so, obviously).

Interestingly, this chant is what the ideology/cult is telling us, via the useful idiots. It's telling us that there will be no justice or no peace while the ideology/ cult is present. Obviously, the irony is lost on the useful idiots who shout it.

Symbols and images

We may see classic Marxist symbols such as the Communist hammer and sickle, or the Red Star openly used in public (e.g. on banners at protests), or Marxist iconography seen on clothing. For example: Che Guevara t-shirts (a student favourite), or other items emblazoned with images of Marx, Lenin, Mao, Castro. We may even see some of these prophets featured on stamps! In 2017, a red Irish postage stamp was issued which celebrated the 50th anniversary of the death of the Marxist terrorist Che Guevara.[3] Surely that would be noticeably odd, even to someone complimentary ignorant of the cult/ideology (even if Guevera had some Irish ancestry)! Another

---

[3] Fox News, "Che Guevara stamp in Ireland outrages Cuban-Americans", 10 October 2017.

https://www.foxnews.com/world/che-guevara-stamp-in-ireland-outrages-cuban-americans

blatant insult to Irishness and an example of the cult marking its territory.

The Raised Fist of Marxism

> "Socialists cry 'power to the people!' and raise their clenched fist as they say it. We all know what they really mean, power over the people, power to the state"[4]

> The "Iron Lady" Margaret Thatcher on socialism

Another sign of infection is that the clenched fist, or variations of it, are visible throughout society; they may be attached to various activist groups, NGO's/non-profits, and even governmental organisations etc. Examples: a pink clenched fist for feminism; a black one for Black Lives Matter or other 'Black Power' groups; a multi-coloured one for an LGBTQ "Pride" event; a green one for the climate change Scam; one holding a medical syringe to promote Vaccinations; one crushing a foetus to promote abortion; one punching a nun in the face (because she's Christian); and one fisting a (commie) red asshole (because that's what they are there for, right?). The clenched fist represents strength, solidarity, combativeness and rebellion. It sums-up the situation in the world now that many people recoil in horror to see the fascist Roman salute, but don't have the same reaction when they see the clenched fist of Marxism.

The colour Red

Though not an invention of the cult, it is their favourite colour. When we start seeing too much of it everywhere we look in society, it's another sign of infection. We may see it dominating in promotional materials, websites, magazines, logos, architectural/interior design, corporate etc. In particular, we may notice it in areas involving politics, NGO's/non-profits, or public/social affairs groups who may, or may not, be openly 'left wing'. Though its use may not always necessarily be subversive in nature, due to the ideology's presence in society and high levels of indoctrination, the colour is regarded as being the colour of revolution, progress, evolution etc. From a marketing psychology point of view, red suggests action, passion etc.

As for why they use red: some say it has its origins in the French Revolution; that it symbolised the blood of the oppressed working classes who've sacrificed their lives under the yoke of capitalism, or the blood of martyrs to the cause in times gone by.

The Red Flag is the anthem song of several Labour parties in Ireland and

---

[4] Thatcher, M., Speech to Conservative Central Council, 15 March 1986 (second term as Prime Minister). https://libquotes.com/margaret-thatcher/quote/lbr1a0w

the UK. The first verse is "The People's flag is deepest red, It shrouded oft our martyred dead, And ere their limbs grew stiff and cold, Their hearts' blood dyed its ev'ry fold".[5]

The LGBTQ 'Rainbow'-Coloured Flag

We have all noticed this one, due to it being shoved in our faces all year round. While not a part of traditional Marxism (overtly), seeing this all over the place in your country is another clear sign of infection. It was flown above the Irish government buildings of Leinster House in June 2019 to mark Pride month.[6]

Although these symbolic 'rainbow' colours are usually associated with the LGBTQ Pride marches, organisations, initiatives etc., there is a much deeper significance to them. Though outside the immediate scope of this particular book, for clarity, the reader may research in to the *Noahide Laws* (it's also the flag of the Jewish Autonomous Oblast near the Russia/China border).[7] [8] The use of this flag is occult psychological manipulation ("revelation of the method"), as it suggests a eugenics-based genocidal intent not understood by the average symbology-illiterate person. This flag essentially signifies that an anti-white eugenics operation is under way, which the LGBTQ movement (and Marxism in general) serves. The thought of low-intelligence, brainwashed cult members trying to grasp this is amusing—to them it's just a pretty flag of rainbow-coloured gayness— "maybe each colour represents a different gender" etc.

Society In General

Here are some signs that are not often associated with the ideology's presence, but that are either linked to it or caused by it. They also may be more difficult to spot, initially.

There is a general increase of crazy people/signs of mental illness: Of course, when I say 'mental illness' I am not referring to the technical, state-approved, academia-corroborated definition. I'm taking about everyday looney behaviour.

---

[5] Connell, J., "The Red Flag", 1889.
https://www.marxists.org/subject/art/music/lyrics/en/red-flag.htm

[6] "Rainbow flag flying at Leinster House to mark Pride", 29 June 2019.

https://www.irishtimes.com/news/politics/rainbow-flag-flying-at-leinster-house-to-mark-pride-1.3941776

[7] https://en.wikipedia.org/wiki/Noahidism

[8] https://www.britannica.com/place/Jewish-Autonomous-Region

People become duller and more predictable: If everyone is programmed according to the Marxist formula, then their behaviour becomes predictable. Plus, their negative influence over the rest of us (who are sane) means we are pressured to be dull and 'PC', as they are; either that, or we will be ostracised once they realise we're not like them (the horror!). Of course, we have the option to just ostracise ourselves, and avoid them. If "Variety's the very spice of life, that gives it all its flavour" (quote by William Cowper), then uniformity is the stench that sticks to life, and gives it all its stink.

Everybody must be manically 'positive' and 'nice': This is connected to the previous point. It's important for the cult/ideology to cultivate a uniformly dumb, manically—'positive' environment in society. This is because it will be easier to spot any 'crazy' person like you and me a mile away when we start expressing other 'negative' states of mind (frustration, anger etc.). A happy, 'positive', uniform cult-like environment is more beneficial for the ideology to spread; it pre-emptively discourages opposition in society. This is linked to degeneracy, hedonism, and docility too of course, expanded on elsewhere.

There is an overall feminisation of a society (briefly covered earlier): You may notice an excessive amount of overly feminine attitudes towards things. Not only are they more noticeable, they actually start to dominate. This is an aspect of 'feminisation'/destruction of the masculine (emasculation), in order to weaken a society. Example—you will hear more people saying 'naaaaaw' at everything as if it were a cute puppy or a baby. I suppose we could call this pampering or babying or mollycoddling. This obnoxious 'naaaawww" sound will be used in conversation, by 'adults', towards other adults (!).

Women and gay men in particular will be the main culprits here, but less-masculine heterosexual men will engage in it too. Of all the types of person who might be on the receiving end, it's most potentially destructive/draining where masculine males are concerned. In essence, it's disempowering and demoralising as it encourages sensitivity and weakness where there may be none. This idiocy seems like something quite trivial, but it's actually very serious; it's a symptom of an excessive compassionate/excess feminine mentality, which is a form of degeneration that feeds into the cult's sub-agendas. Again, it helps create a psychological environment beneficial to the cult/ideology.

The idea that being white is bad: You may hear talk to this effect, or phrases like "whiteness is a disease". Since whites are the 'oppressor' race (according to the Marxist version of history), they deserve to be treated as the oppressor class in the present, a scourge of humanity.

Actual things become make-believe things and vice-versa: Due to the influences of Marxian post-modernism, you hear concepts that try to distort people's perceptions of reality. Some new terms/concepts are created, others are dismissed or 'deconstructed'. Things which were previously believed to be real, are now considered non-existent. Therefore, you hear things like "gender is a social construct!" or "race is a social construct!". Conversely, fabricated (by the cult) terms/concepts such as "heteronormativity" and "non-cis gender" become real things. Marxism doesn't do nature or science.

In politics and geo-politics

There is no legitimate opposition to the government or internationalism: The parties call themselves "centre-right" or "centre-left" etc., but it's all misleading nonsense. They are all essentially Marxist to one degree or another. When it comes to bigger-picture issues, they are all generally in favour of internationalism/globalism.

There is no "right", only "far-right!": You won't hear the term "right wing" being used; you will hear "far-right". This is done because it immediately labels anyone who doesn't support internationalism as being extremist, dangerous etc. It's dramatic and derogatory. The cult/ideology cannot allow the term "right wing" to be used too often (when describing anyone with a nationalistic stance) because this would allow a non-Marxist opposing group to exist without being sufficiently abused. Essentially, they can't afford to let anyone describe 'right-wing' politics without attaching it to extremism.

Internationalism = good, Nationalism = bad

The idea is present that we should have a 'world without borders', and that borders are immoral or downright evil; even that nations shouldn't exist at all (as the world should be in 'solidarity'). Any sort of genuinely patriotic or nationalistic thought is viewed as being Nazi/fascist/far-right and being old, backward, uncool, out of touch with the modern world etc.

According to the cult, anyone who believes these types of things are benevolent obviously wants their country to be the best/dominant and to take over the world etc. (which links to the WW2 period and distorted perceptions of the events and groups involved).

You will hear political figures stating that the country needs to be more integrated with the international community, that we need to think 'more openly', that the country is 'part of a global community'…that it isn't an independent sovereign country anymore basically; that it's a 'member state' of the world. There may be suggestions that your country needs to be 'global', or it won't survive ("communism or death"). So, they are basically promoting Marxian internationalism (a borderless world), saying that it's 'inevitable' (to demoralise nationalists) and saying national sovereignty is bad, evil etc.

In May 2017, during a Dáil & Seanad session, the Irish politician and Fianna Fáil party leader Micheal Martin gave a speech on the Brexit referendum: "Let there be no doubt about where Ireland stands. We want nothing to do with a backward-looking idea of sovereignty. We remain absolutely committed to the ideals of the European Union. We see the Union for what it is—the most successful international organisation in world history".[9] Obviously, where he said "Ireland", he is only speaking on behalf of other traitorous indoctrinated cult members who think just like him. Indeed, the EU is a successful Marxist international organisation as is the UN ('successful' for the ideology). It would be amusing at this point (Dec 2023) to call the EU "successful" as it's starting to collapse, thanks in part to people like Martin.

Martin continued: "We have no nostalgia for a lost empire and no wish to assert superiority over others. We have never sought to stand apart from the world, jealously guarding the right to say no to everything.". This is high-level Marxian con speak. Red snake (serpent) language. As always, the use of the word "empire" by cult members is amusing, classic deflection. The "assert superiority over others" is an obvious nod to oppression, and links to the point (made elsewhere) that cult members erroneously believe that nationalism equates to a nation having dominant, imperialistic tendencies towards other countries (ref WW2). This is simply Marxian virtue-signalling hypocrisy since the cult/ideology is all about dominance over others.

Unsurprisingly, your politicians dutifully insist that you remain part of internationalist organisations (i.e. EU). They insist that your country does this, even to its own detriment (which they will not emphasise obviously). In early 2019, during discussions on Brexit, Irish Taoiseach (PM) Leo Varadkar stated in an interview: "I am the European Union when it comes to these matters. The Irish government and the European Union are all one when it comes to Brexit...If they (the people) haven't realised that for the

---

[9] The National Party, "Micheál Martin rejects a "backward-looking idea of sovereignty" for no sovereignty at all", 18 May 2017.
https://www.YouTube.com/watch?v=akkPu-FJyiA

past two years, they are coming to realise it". [10] All one? Uh oh.. solidarity…

Other 'Irish' cult members don't even want the Republic of Ireland/Northern Ireland border to exist. Indeed, it's been a long tradition within the Irish Republican movement to call for a 'united Ireland'—a thirty-two county Socialist Republic. The pseudo-nationalist Marxist party Sinn Fein wants a united Ireland for this reason.

Even more 'fringe' cult members do, such as People Before Profit Chief Commissar Richard Boyd Barrett. A March 2021 RTE News article quoted him as saying that his party wanted to see the end of this partition, and that "uniting people for a different type of Ireland north and south is seriously on the agenda".[11] (A note on this point, for my fellow Irish patriots—forget about a united Ireland! Let's not talk like cult members, and then play in to their hands by helping them to dissolve more borders! Besides, we have more pressing concerns right now, wouldn't you agree?).

An increase of governmental power and regulation: A sign that the cult/ideology is consolidating control over a country, is when the government pushes for more and more regulations (centralisation of power). These can be across the board but are particularly evident on economic issues. There is an increase in the size of government and government departments, including government—associated or contracted departments, organisations, and employees (putting massive strain on the public finances yet serving no useful purpose).

Increasing numbers of public representatives from 'oppressed' groups: You see that politicians/authority figures will be increasingly appointed not due to their merits, but due to their group (sex, race, sexual orientation, religion etc. or combinations of same). The more 'diverse' they are, the better. In 2007, Nigerian immigrant Rotimi Adebari became the mayor of Portlaoise, County Laois, and Ireland's first black mayor. The Guardian reported that he "recently gained a master's degree in intercultural studies at Dublin City University, (and) now works for the county council on an integration project for new immigrants".[12] In 2020, Hazel Chu was made Lord Mayor

---

[10] Irish News, ""I Am The European Union" Says Arrogant Puffed Up EU Rent Boy, Leo Varadkar", 10 February 2019.
https://www.YouTube.com/watch?v=9bbT_A5T6qg

[11] Meskill, T., "Dublin South-West TD Paul Murphy joins People Before Profit", 1 March 2021. https://www.rte.ie/news/politics/2021/0301/1200161-paul-murphy-pbp/

[12] Bowcott, O., "From asylum seeker to Ireland's first black mayor in seven years", 29 June 2007. https://www.theguardian.com/world/2007/jun/29/ireland

of Dublin, becoming "the first person of Chinese ethnicity to be mayor of a European capital".[13] In June 2023, a Fianna Fáil councillor Abul Kalam Azad Talukder was elected chairman of the Metropolitan District in Limerick.[14] Talukder is a Muslim from Bangladesh. After the 23 Nov 2023 Dublin riots (mentioned earlier) following the stabbing of children outside a school in Dublin city, Talukder commented about the rioters: "I'd like to see them shot in the head".[15]

Diversity, fashion and the media

You will see more and more TV shows, movies etc. with a 'diverse' line-up of actors/hosts/guests etc. The same in print media, magazines, shop windows etc. In Ireland, the *Life Style Sports* retail chain amusingly adorned its stores with images featuring several mixed-race faces (even in towns where the population is upwards of 90–95% white Irish). Whenever you see a family on TV (i.e. advertisements), you won't see a white couple with kids. At least one of them will be mixed race. Or we may see unusual combinations of people presented to us in couples, in TV shows, for example: a small downs syndrome midget black female in a relationship with a tall yet wheelchair bound Lenin-goatee-sporting albino white male. This is all done in the name of 'equality', and to combat the evil of 'heteronormativity'.

'Ugly' is beautiful

Thanks to the cult's/ideology's gleeful promotion of 'diversity' and degeneracy, and its tendency to invert things, we are now being told essentially that ugly is the new beautiful.

We see this in advertising when, for example, a very overweight woman is presented as being beautiful. This is a terrible influence on females in general and is even dangerous for someone already in that state of ill-health. An irresponsible society is one where anyone who is extremely unhealthy—and needs (and usually wants!) to change for their own sake—is being told that they are perfect just the way they are. A famous American "plus size" model is Tess Holliday, who is also known for being a "body

[13] https://en.wikipedia.org/wiki/Lord_Mayor_of_Dublin

[14] Jacques, A., "Historic moment as Cllr Talukder voted Limerick's first Muslim Metropolitan Cathaoirleach", 20 June 2023.
https://www.limerickpost.ie/2023/06/20/historic-moment-as-cllr-talukder-voted-limericks-first-muslim-metropolitan-cathaoirleach/

[15] Jacques, A., "'I'd like to see them shot in the head': Councillor's hard line on Dublin riots", 29 November 2023. https://www.limerickpost.ie/2023/11/29/id-like-to-see-them-shot-in-the-head-councillors-hard-line-on-dublin-riots/

positive activist".[16] The term "body positivity" in this context convinces females that it's ok to be a physical degenerate.

Being "positive" in this context means hiding from uncomfortable emotions that may arise during self-criticism and facing-up to the truth about oneself (aka delusion). Bizarrely, such overweight models are held aloft by some as being symbols of female 'empowerment' etc, despite the fact they are a negative, disempowering influence on females. If you can't even control your food cravings you are not 'empowered'.

Other examples are disfigured or disabled people. The British ex-model Katie Piper—who suffered a facial sulphuric acid attack in 2008—was featured in an advert for Pantene shampoo in 2010 (even though she lost much of her hair in the attack).[17] Sofia Jirau, a Puerto Rican model with down's syndrome, was hired by Victoria's Secret in 2022.[18] Obviously, we are not attacking these females here, rather the virtue-signalling, degenerative principle at play behind the facade; the ideology promoting the 'diversity' of such things. It's true that not all attraction centres around superficial beauty and conventional perceptions of same, but that's not the issue here.

There are Babylonian undertones here—the ideology paves the way for a type of hell-world, where all types of perversions of aesthetic beauty, sexuality and behaviour will become normalised; just like in the ill-fated 'diverse' ancient Mesopotamian city.[19] The examples above (combined with the sexual perversion/gender perversion that the cult/ideology promotes elsewhere) are just the beginning of what is to come... Unless the cult is stopped.

Virtue Signalling faces

There will be a prevalence of virtue-signalling in these industries, from anyone who has a public platform. Watch out for that stupid virtue-signalling expression on the faces of media personalities and celebrities the

---

[16] https://en.wikipedia.org/wiki/Tess_Holliday

[17] Pearson-Jones, B., "Katie Piper shares surprise at being asked to model for a hair care brand a decade after losing her locks - and admits she relies on her tresses for giving her confidence", 5 January 2020. https://www.dailymail.co.uk/femail/article-7525749/Katie-Piper-reveals-joy-asked-model-hair-care-brand-10-years-losing-locks.html

[18] Blance, E., "Who is Sofia Jirau, the first model with Down syndrome to pose for Victoria's Secret?", 23 February 2022. https://www.vogue.fr/fashion/article/sofia-jirau-model

[19] https://www.britannica.com/place/Babylon-ancient-city-Mesopotamia-Asia

world over! It's an "I am sad" face, usually pulled when listening to someone (i.e. guest/interviewee) explaining how "oppressed" they are. It's a face that tells us "this is sad, and you should feel sad about this". Chat show presenters, for example. The now-shamed former Irish Late Late Show host Ryan Tubridy was a master at this expression.

The politicians too, via the media. After the Christchurch mosque shooting incident in New Zealand in March 2019, then PM Jacinda Arden donned a hijab in (Marxian) solidarity for the victims. She had a pathetic-looking virtue-signalling expression on her face, as if in some horrific OTT pantomime. Amusingly, she was given world-wide praise by other cult members for showing so much 'solidarity' and 'compassion'. [20] A committed cult member guilty of many crimes against her country, Arden was leader of the New Zealand Labour Party and Prime Minister from 2017 to 2023.

Policing, security, and warfare

> "The word "peace" as given by the communist means the victory of socialism"[21]
>
> > Communist whistleblower Bella Dodd,
> > lecture at Fordham University, 1953

Present may be the attitude we need 'peace' at all costs; that wars, violence and armies are bad. In fact, it may manifest as the notion that all forceful resistance is bad (unless it's 'revolutionary', of course). This is another hypocritical, virtue-signalling notion present in society due to the infection. What the ideology is really suggesting is that any forceful resistance to the cult/ideology (and globalism/internationalism) is bad; particularly the most potent kind—large-scale military resistance and all-out warfare.

This kind of naive, hippy, 'positive' mindset is exactly the attitude your enemy wants you to have, so you will drop your guard. If a hostile force/ideology plans to destroy your nation, they want you to have this mentality, because they won't. There's a big difference between using physical force to attack another group/country for unjustifiable reasons (conquest, oppression, territorial or resource acquisition etc.) and defensive force (i.e. using it to cleanse your country of the cult/ideology). The latter

---

[20] McConnell, G., "Face of empathy: Jacinda Ardern photo resonates worldwide after attack", 18 March 2019. https://www.smh.com.au/world/oceania/face-of-empathy-jacinda-ardern-photo-resonates-worldwide-after-attack-20190318-p5152g.html

[21] *"Bella Dodd Explains Communism Ducks"*, *Fordham University Lecture, 1953.*

https://www.YouTube.com/watch?v=VLHNz2YMnRY

is absolutely justifiable! Of course, your enemies don't want you making this discernment—they want you to think that all use of force is bad. This "we must be peaceful!" attitude, of course, is another form of virtue-signalling.

Soldiers and armies are bad

Many (indoctrinated) people look at soldiers and armies as being inherently bad; that they are all murderers, as if every soldier/warrior in the history of mankind have all been the same. What total crap! It's amusing to hear the brain-less, virtue-signalling opinions of someone in our relatively comfortable, modern society who has little or no respect for a soldier almost by default; particularly if they can't even handle a little bit of stress, discomfort or criticism (never mind physical conflict or actual to-the-death combat).

This is the residue from years of 'PC' brainwashing, which can come from a variety of sources (education, entertainment, "new age" beliefs, drugs use and/or being a hippie etc.). Obviously, if this opinion is coming from a Marxist-indoctrinated person, this condemnation of soldiers/violence does not apply to all those wondrous Marxist 'revolutionaries' such as Trotsky, Che Guevera, Castro, the many African Marxists, cult terrorist groups etc.

It does however apply to any sort of armed force that has been/is an opponent of Marxism, or an Imperial armed force: U.S. forces; French and British Imperial forces; Germany's National Socialist army in WW2; Franco's nationalist army in the Spanish Civil War, White Boer armies in South Africa or Rhodesia etc. These are all fascist, capitalist, racist evil oppressor soldiers. Now I am not condoning any crimes committed by any armed force in the world, past or present, but the key word here is "crime". No doubt many soldiers/armed forces have committed crimes, but that doesn't make them all equally ethical or unethical.

What we are emphasising here is the effect of 'peace' programming on the masses. Of course, when they are programming us to hate militarism or any kind of physical strength, it's to soften us up and make us defenceless; they are not promoting these ideas for benevolent reasons! As we are finding out in the world right now—without the ability to use physical force to defend yourself, your country, your people (or if you refuse to use force); sooner or later, force will be used on you.

At time of editing (Jan 2024), there is talk in the UK of a war with Russia. Many commentators have noted how the will to fight for the UK is not what it was historically (this is due to the erosion of British patriotism by the cult/ideology). On 12 February 2024, a video appeared on the YouTube channel of former British Brexiteer politician and GB News presenter

Nigel Farage. The subject was the condition of the UK armed forces against the backdrop of potential global conflict. He spoke of "woke diversity targets", the recent trend of retroactive prosecutions for former soldiers, and relaxed security screening for admittance to the UK services. Obviously, this relaxation of security screening allows the enemies of the West to infiltrate, including Islamic extremists, or Marxist elements.

The outcome of all this is that the UK army would "not be fit for purpose to defend this country if indeed we do head in to global conflict". [22] Certainly these factors compound the problem of low recruitment numbers in recent times. 'Wokeness' is the death of a nation.

A GB news video on 12 February 2024 showed the UK army's new 'woke' recruitment advertisement. It featured a Muslim solider praying in the middle of the battlefield on his prayer in front of his non-Muslim comrades. The tagline was "keeping my faith".[23] Farage pointed-out that there were suggestions from some quarters to remove Christianity from the annual armed forces Remembrance Day service.

In December 2023, it was reported in the U.S. that Democratic Senator Dick Durbin spoke on similar issues involving the U.S. military. He suggested that migrants could be recruited to the services in exchange for American citizenship, and he spoke of a new bill to this effect. Speaking in the U.S. Senate, he mentioned the military recruitment issues, that the services are not reaching their quotas. On migrants being allowed to sign-up, he said "Should we give them the chance? I think we should".[24] He was pushing similar ideas in May/June 2023.[25]

This is highly irresponsible, borderline treasonous rhetoric. Clumsy at the absolute minimum. Firstly, migrants world-wide don't need any more encouragement to enter Western countries. Secondly, again, this encourages infiltration by America's enemies. The impact of the cult/ideology on America and American patriotism over the decades has

---

[22] Nigel Farage, "The British Army is being Destroyed!", 12 Feb 2024.

https://www.YouTube.com/watch?v=qPN2ahYC6W4

[23] GB News, "'British soldiers Praying to Allah': Nigel Farage Rages at Banishing of Christianity from army", 12 February 2024.
https://www.YouTube.com/watch?v=T5U3XbMvau4

[24] "Durbin proposes U.S. citizenship for illegal immigrants through military service".
https://www.YouTube.com/watch?v=B-XmAs5xGTs

[25] Forbes Breaking News, "Dick Durbin Pushes For 'Pathway To Citizenship' For DACA Recipients Who Serve", 3 June 2023.
https://www.YouTube.com/watch?v=N8PBmVyBPoE

been primarily responsible for reducing the recruitment levels. Now, there are suggestions to risk recruiting anti-American cult members from abroad!

Here is another connected, disturbing element. On 2 February 2024 the *Tucker Carlson* YouTube channel featured an interview with biologist Bert Weinstein. Weinstein had recently witnessed occurrences at the Darien gap in Panama, Central America—a focal point for migrants travelling to the U.S. from South America. Weinstein spoke of how there were increasing numbers of Chinese migrants—primarily males of military age—who were a little bit cagey about why they were migrating...[26] Combined with the above listed factors, and the cult's historical military clashes with the U.S., it should be obvious what's afoot here...

"Guns are bad and the general public shouldn't have them"

In a society fully controlled by the cult/ideology, only the state should have weapons. The cult will always push for disarmament of the general public in the name of 'peace' and virtue etc. We have seen this one play out constantly in the U.S., where cult members of all stripes at all levels have promoted this notion. The Socialist-in-Chief Barack Obama was constantly attempting to change the gun culture during his tenure and was backed-up by cult members working in the media all across the west.

The notion that Americans are gun-toting nuts is part of the anti-Americanism pushed by the cult and is obviously linked to its attempts to disarm the American public. Having guns in a relatively civilised society is a good thing, because it allows citizens to protect themselves. Not just from criminals, but from tyrannical governments; particularly if those governments have cult members at the helm.. Many believe that without the second amendment of the U.S. constitution and the general public's access to arms, the traitorous (Marxist) elements in the establishment would already have initiated militaristic control on U.S. soil. I would also add that a well-armed general public is another layer of deterrent to America's foreign enemies.

A "Cops and Soldiers" gay disco

Another sign of infection is when members of the Police and armed forces—who should be symbols of strength, masculinity, and national defence—are dancing in the streets, or engaging in sexually suggestive behaviour (particularly the homo-erotic variety); or may have their vehicles covered in LGBTQ colours etc. And not on their nights off, or on private

---

[26] Tucker Carlson, "How China and the UN are Fueling the Invasion of America", 2 February 2024. https://www.YouTube.com/watch?v=wOxksFHAHRU

property somewhere, or in the car park behind the police station, but out in public, in full view of countless bemused eyes and trained smartphones. In Ireland in June 2018, the Irish Defence Forces participated in an LGBTQ Pride march through Dublin City; some of the top brass participated.[27]

In late 2021, Irish police danced like idiots wearing Covid masks in a produced, choreographed video, to the song "Jersusalema".[28] Police in Sweden, the U.K., and elsewhere were also seen dancing at Pride events in the period from 2015.[29] [30] (It did cross the author's mind that actors were being used in some cases (particularly those wearing Covid masks), in an act designed to publicly demoralise the police forces. Still, even the impersonation should not be permitted; it's criminal). In Ireland's South-West, in June 2023, the Garda Siochana (Irish police) unveiled a new patrol car—draped in the 'rainbow' colours—in 'solidarity' with LGBTQ Pride marches and groups in the area (there were other instances elsewhere).[31]

Conversely, look at the public military parades in North Korea and China, and how they flex those masculine muscles. Tanks, missile launchers, APCs, artillery pieces, you name it, along with thousands of infantry personnel. Look in to the eyes of the service personnel—they are desperate to prove themselves to the Party! Desperate to show their willingness to kill for the great global revolution! Not a hint of dancing, pelvic thrusting, gayness, gender dysphoria, gimp masks, or ass-less pants anywhere.

Con-jobs and infiltrators

Another obvious sign of infection is the presence of con jobs, infiltrators, and pseudo-patriots. In the history of Marxist subversion and propaganda, there's already been many forms of operative/deceiver/apologist, either

---

[27] Murtage, P., "Head of Defence Forces to walk in Dublin Pride Parade", 30 June 2018. https://www.irishtimes.com/news/ireland/irish-news/head-of-defence-forces-to-walk-in-dublin-pride-parade-1.3548434

[28] All things Ireland, "Gardaí Irish Police In Ireland Dancing on the Jerusalema Song", 14 Dec 2021. https://www.YouTube.com/watch?v=NGkzgqisiBU

[29] Haigh, E., "Fury at 'woke' Lincoln Police after officers are filmed dancing the Macarena at Pride festival while number of unsolved crimes across the UK remains high", 21 August 2022. https://www.dailymail.co.uk/news/article-11132029/Fury-woke-Lincoln-Police-officers-filmed-dancing-Macarena-Pride-festival.html

[30] "Swedish Police dancing for Pride", May 2020. https://www.YouTube.com/watch?v=apE9vH-pcow

[31] O'Shea, J., "Gardai unveil new rainbow 'Pride' patrol car for West Cork in shout out to LGBTQ community", 30 June 2023. https://www.corkbeo.ie/news/local-news/gardai-unveil-new-rainbow-pride-27229628

witting or unwitting. Marxism has a history of subverting nationalist movements, in ever more creative ways. The cult has historically used the tactic of Entryism—infiltrating opposing groups and rising up the ranks within them—to essentially derail them, particularly in the political sphere.

In this internet era, we see a similar contamination by cult members, particularly on YouTube. Their roles can include trying to confuse people or dissuade them from nationalistic or patriotic points of view; to convince them that they don't want or need sovereignty. They can also assist in de-railing the 'anti-globalist' movement by distraction from (or outright dismissal of) any concerns about Marxism. We must also watch out for anyone who is blatantly or subtly promoting Marxist concepts, as an apologist or a proponent. Sometimes this can be difficult to spot. The fact that many are still not aware of what Marxism is (and the threat it poses) makes this process all the more difficult.

Red-tubers

Cult members will attract and con the masses in different ways. They may come in the form of 'philosophers', political analysts, online media personalities, fake Christians etc. Some may pretend to be nationalist or patriots (or at least sympathetic) in order to de-rail this movement. Others are 'spiritual' gurus, analysts, speakers, authors etc. These types come in all shapes and sizes.

They may convince those who will listen that "aggression is wrong" or "We are all one, so we shouldn't have countries.." or "All religions are the same and primitive...Christianity is just as bad as Talmudism or Islam.."; or those promoting any sort of pro-Marxian degeneracy, post-modernism, 'spirituality', any sort of damaging head-in-the-clouds stuff.

Think of a Russell Brand type. A sometimes comedian, actor, radio host, author, actor, and now a YouTuber and 'spiritual' voice, with a massive fanbase. I have heard him regurgitate pseudo-spiritual crap, sure, but the more significant stuff is his overtly Marxist leanings. He was once involved with The New Statesman—a famous socialist magazine created by the Fabian Society. He's also quite clearly a 'leftie' activist. Tellingly, he published a book called *Revolution* (2014), with the letters e,v,o,l coloured Marxist red on the book cover; trying to equate the ideology/Marxist revolution with love.[32] At times he has presented himself as more of a 'neutral', yet has a distinctly Marxian attitude to world affairs. He also

---

[32] https://en.wikipedia.org/wiki/Revolution_(book)

quotes from sources such as the *World Socialist Web Site* (WSWS).[33] [34] Brand opens his videos with "Hello there you awakening wonders! Thanks for joining us on our voyage to truth and freedom that we are undertaking together".[35] "Awakening" in a Marxian sense? In a 'woke' sense?

Another example is British YouTuber Tom Nicholas. His channel presently has almost 500,000 subscribers. One of his videos is entitled "How to spot a (potential) Fascist".[36] We could just stop here.

Another is the unambiguously named "Marxism Today" channel.[37] It's hosted by Irish cult member Paul Connolly who 'educates' the audience about the virtues of socialism and communism, by dazzling them with partisan information. The streamlined video production style shows how the cult always tries to re-package Marxism as being cool and benevolent, to attract the youth in particular. The red snake shedding its skin again.

In his "Why Communism? Socialism 101" video, Connolly states with a proud smile: "Welcome to Socialism 101—a series designed to help educate people with no prior knowledge on the basics of socialism and communism from an explicitly Marxist-Leninist and Marxist-Leninist-Maoist perspective with short and easily digestible videos".[38] Yikes. I would rather paint a huge wall, then pull up a stool and put on my watching glasses. Imagine endorsing three of the worst human beings of all time with a smile on your face, for the whole world to see. With 71k subs at time of editing, it's awash with images of Communist idols and the colour red.

Another is British YouTuber Harris "hbomberguy" Brewis with 1.6 million subs at time of editing. Another smiling, brainwashed, deranged, manipulative red snake promoting/defending various sub-agendas including climate change, mass vaccinations, and feminism; while also denying that the anti-Christianity sub-agenda or "Cultural Marxism" exists.

---

[33] Russel Brand, "It's Full-Scale War!" - No One Is Ready For What's Coming!", 18 January 2024. https://www.YouTube.com/watch?v=_w8psH6NKNw

[34] https://www.wsws.org/en

[35] https://www.YouTube.com/@RussellBrand

[36] Tom Nicholas, "How to Spot a (Potential) Fascist", 19 July 2020. https://www.YouTube.com/watch?v=vymeTZkiKD0

[37] https://www.YouTube.com/@Marxism_Today

[38] Marxism Today, "Why Communism? | Socialism 101", 2 April 2021.

https://www.YouTube.com/watch?v=N52bJRe0Gg8&list=PL0J754r0IteXABJntjBg1YuNsn6jItWXQ

One video is called "Climate Denial: A measured Response". The videos are a mixture of PC (Marxian) 'comedy' and the usual mockery/bitchiness towards anyone who disagrees with the cult/ideology. Some of them feature his commentary on videos made by non-Marxist voices ('Nazis' and 'Racists'), allowing him to 'debunk' these opposing views.[39] I'm sure to other cult members he comes across as articulate, witty, perceptive, charming etc. Interestingly, he uses the term 'true believers' about nationalist/non-Marxian voices or their followers, almost insinuating that these people are part of a cult. Inversion, again.

Brewis 'identifies' as bisexual, and once described himself as "a very far left Socialist type with a reverence for the actual philosophers of the communist movement and their writings". So under all the silly faces and predictable 'gags', he's just another fanatic pedalling the ideology online.[40]

These are just a few of the numerous examples. YouTube will obviously support these channels, allowing them to exist and grow. Conversely and simultaneously, channels that do not conform to Marxism will be suppressed. Any serious criticism of the cult/ideology, explaining that it's a massive, insane, global cult will not be permitted. You will, however, be allowed to spread the glorious revolution, or criticise the cult's opponents as much as you want.

Such propaganda listed above must be purged from the net, and those involved contained. Indoctrinated people cannot be permitted to infect others, especially not on such a scale. Maybe we should invent and implement "Marx-speech" laws?

---

[39] Hbomberguy YouTube channel.
https://www.YouTube.com/channel/UClt01z1wHHT7c5lKcU8pxRQ

[40] https://rationalwiki.org/wiki/Hbomberguy

Section XI— The Divided Nations

"There is no salvation for civilization, or even the human race, other than the creation of a world government"[1]

Famous 'genius' scientist and cult member Albert Einstein

"Humanity is in pain... Humanity is strongest when we stand together"[2]

UN Secretary-General António Guterres,
Dec 2023 New Year message

Introduction

Is the United Nations a Marxist entity? Does it promote and support the ideology in any way? Is this an internationalist organisation that centralises power at the expense of the sovereignty of member countries? The UN is an intriguing and large beast, deserving a book of its own, but here are some relevant pieces of info:

Overview

The UN is headquartered in New York City, on international territory. As a global, intergovernmental organisation it has main offices in Nairobi, Vienna, and Geneva, and six official languages. Formed in 1945 and composed of 193 member states at present, the ostensible purpose of the UN is 'peace' and 'security'. In addition to upholding international law, it performs humanitarian and peacekeeping roles, as well as a variety of seemingly benevolent functions.[3]

The structure of the UN or United Nations System includes six groups: the General Assembly, the Security Council, the Economic and Social Council, the Trusteeship Council, International Court of Justice, and the UN Secretariat. Other high-profile sub-organisations connected with the UN

---

[1] Albert Einstein as quoted by Charles Kegley, *World Politics: Trend and Transformation* (2008), P. 537. https://en.wikiquote.org/wiki/World_government

[2] United Nations, "UN Chief's 2024 New Year's Message | United Nations", 28 Dec 2023.

https://www.YouTube.com/watch?v=cxFvUbhVz50

[3] https://www.britannica.com/topic/United-Nations

include: ILO (International Labour Organisation); WTO (World Trade Organisation); WHO (World Health Organisation); UNESCO (United Nations Educational, Scientific and Cultural Organisation); and the IMF (International Money Fund). (Plus the WMO (World Meteorological Organisation) mentioned earlier).[4]

Some other notable entities spawned from the UN: UNHCR (United Nations High Commissioner for Refugees); UNIFEM (United Nations Development Fund for Women) and UN WOMEN (United Nations Entity for Gender Equality and the Empowerment of Women), both merged together in to UN WOMEN in 2011; UNRWA (United Nations Relief and Works Agency for Palestine Refugees in the Near East).

Clearly these are a sub-group of organisations that facilitate the mass migration, feminism, and Palestinian rights Marxian sub-agendas of the cult/ideology.

The "UN System" page of the *un.org* website shows some other "Funds and Programmes" including: UNICEF (United Nations Children's Fund) which works "to save children's lives, to defend their rights, and to help them fulfil their potential, from early childhood through adolescence.". This obviously must be referring to parent-less children, or clearly unfit parents, right? The United Nations Development Programme (UNDP) helps "to eradicate poverty, reduce inequalities". The UNFPA (United Nations Population Fund aims to deliver "a world where every pregnancy is wanted, every birth is safe, and every young person's potential is fulfilled"; this has a eugenics tone, and means they advocate abortion.[5]

Founding

The UN was ostensibly created to play the role the League of Nations was intended to play in 'world peace', but in a post-WW2 world to "save succeeding generations from the scourge of war, which twice in our life-time has brought untold sorrow to mankind"; in addition to promoting "social progress".[6] On the establishment of the UN, the acting Secretary General was Alger Hiss—a commie spy active in the U.S. Hiss was Secretary-General of the *United Nations Conference on International Organisation* in 1945. This group was responsible for creating the UN charter, with Hiss in his central role. (He was later convicted for two counts

---

[4] https://en.wikipedia.org/wiki/United_Nations_System#United_Nations

[5] "UN System". https://www.un.org/en/about-us/un-system

[6] "Charter Of The United Nations And Statute Of The International Court Of Justice", 1945, P. 2. https://treaties.un.org/doc/publication/ctc/uncharter.pdf

of perjury in 1950, after being exposed by several cult member defectors).[7]

Interestingly, the infamous ComIntern (Communist International or Third International) was dissolved in May 1943, the same time the UN started to form. The UN insignia on the light blue flag of the United Nations—the Earth flanked by two Olive leaves—is very similar to the emblem of the Soviet Union. Again, I think the colour blue throws you off a bit...[8][9][10]

Leaders past and present

There was an undeniably Marxist presence in the early leadership of this new international 'peace' organisation. The first official Secretary General of the UN (1946–1952) was Trygve Lie (1896–1968); a most apt surname. [11] Lie was a high-ranking member of Norway's Social Democratic party. The second (1953–1961) was a Swedish Socialist named Dag Hammarskjold (1905–1961), who openly pushed the cult's 'Communist' policies.[12] The third (1961–1971) was U Thant (1909–1974), a Burmese Marxist.[13] I'm detecting a pattern here...

Annan

Kofi Annan (1938–2018) was the seventh Secretary-General (1997–2006). He received his 'education' studying economics at the *Kwame Nkrumah University of Science and Technology of Ghana,* and *Macalester College* in Minnesota in the U.S.[14]

(The former is named after the avid Pan-Africanist cult member mentioned earlier, in the Africa section, and the latter is openly pro-internationalism and multiculturalism).[15][16] Here's some of his quotes:

This first one sums-up the UN nicely. In 2004, in his message to celebrate

---

[7] Federal Bureau of Investigation, "Alger Hiss".https://www.fbi.gov/history/famous-cases/alger-hiss

[8] https://en.wikipedia.org/wiki/Communist_International

[9] https://www.britannica.com/topic/flag-of-the-United-Nations

[10] https://en.wikipedia.org/wiki/State_Emblem_of_the_Soviet_Union

[11] https://www.britannica.com/biography/Trygve-Lie

[12] https://www.britannica.com/biography/Dag-Hammarskjold

[13] https://www.britannica.com/biography/U-Thant

[14] https://www.britannica.com/biography/Kofi-Annan

[15] https://www.knust.edu.gh

[16] "A force for positive change". https://www.macalester.edu/about/

the International Day of Peace, he stated "Nothing can be more dangerous to our efforts to build peace and development than a world divided along religious, ethnic or cultural lines. In each nation, and among all nations, we must work to promote unity based on our shared humanity".[17] Since people tend to naturally divide along those lines, this is insinuating that the UN needs to change how the world naturally functions—to try to remove religion, race, and culture from people's consciousness (which is exactly what its been doing). Otherwise, they won't be able to achieve 'peace'.

In September 2002 in Johannesburg at the World Summit on Sustainable Development, he spoke on climate change stating "but let us not be deceived, when looking at a clear blue sky, into thinking that all is well. All is not well. Science tells us that if we do not take the right action now, climate change will bring havoc, even within our lifetime".[18] So basically don't trust your own senses; the end of the world is upon us (rolls eyes).

In June 2000, in his statement to the General Assembly special session "Women 2000: Gender Equality, Development and Peace for the Twenty-first Century", he stated "There is no development strategy more beneficial to society as a whole—women and men alike—than the one which involves women as central players".[19] As mentioned elsewhere, it's in the interests of the cult/ideology to increasingly put women in positions of authority at this time, as this strengthens its grip. On racism, in September 2016 he stated "We may have different religions, different languages, different colored skin, but we all belong to one human race".[20]

On International Women's Day March 1999, he stated "Violence against women is perhaps the most shameful human rights violation, and it is perhaps the most pervasive. It knows no boundaries of geography, culture or wealth. As long as it continues, we cannot claim to be making real progress towards equality, development, and peace". [21] What virtue-

---

[17] "Kofi Annan Quotes". https://www.kofiannanfoundation.org/kofi-annan/kofi-annan-quotes/

[18] "Kofi Annan Quotes". https://www.kofiannanfoundation.org/kofi-annan/kofi-annan-quotes/

[19] UN Press Release, "Secretary-General, In Address To Women 2000 Special Session, Says Future Of Planet Depends Upon Women", 5 June 2000. https://press.un.org/en/2000/20000605.sgsm7430.doc.html

[20] https://www.kofiannanfoundation.org/kofi-annan/kofi-annan-quotes/

[21] UN Press Release, "Violence Against Women 'MOST Shameful', Pervasive Human Rights Violation, Says Secretary-General In Remarks On International Women's Day", 8 March 1999. https://press.un.org/en/1999/19990308.sgsm6919.html

signalling rubbish! Abortion is the most shameful human rights violation! Interestingly, Annan was also involved with a group of New World Order nuts called The Elders.

Moon

Fanatical cult member Ban Ki Moon was the South Korean eighth Secretary-General of the UN (2007–2016). In January 2011, at Davos, Switzerland, in a speech at the World Economic Forum (WEF), Moon went-full Marxist: "We are running out of time. Time to tackle climate change. Time to ensure sustainable, climate-resilient green growth. Time to generate a clean energy revolution", claiming the world's current economic model was essentially "a suicide pact".

He added "Here at Davos—this meeting of the mighty and the powerful, represented by some key countries—it may sound strange to speak of revolution, but that is what we need at this time. We need a revolution. Revolutionary thinking. Revolutionary action".[22]

In February 2014, for the World Day of Social Justice, he stated that this day "is observed to highlight the power of global solidarity to advance opportunity for all", and "We must do more to empower individuals through decent work, support people through social protection, and ensure the voices of the poor and marginalised are heard…let us make social justice central to achieving equitable and sustainable growth for all".[23] Impressive! This guy is fluent in Marxism.

At the COP22 event in November 2016 he said "I will never cease, even after my retirement, to work with the United Nations and my colleagues, and world leaders to make sure that this climate change agreement is in full implementation".[24] Drama, anyone? Moon was also a key player in the UN's Agenda 2030, and it's "sustainable development" goals.

In addition to being a planetary saviour, Moon was outspoken on several other sub-agendas. For Women's Equality Day in August 2016, he said: "Countries with more gender equality have better economic growth.

---

[22] UN Press Release, "Warning of 'global suicide,' Ban calls for revolution to ensure sustainable development", January 2011. https://news.un.org/en/story/2011/01/365432

[23] Ki-Moon, B., "World Day of Social Justice", 20 February 2014.

https://www.cepal.org/en/articles/2014-world-day-social-justice

[24] COP 22, "Secretary-General's remarks to the press at COP2", 15 November 2016.

https://www.un.org/sustainabledevelopment/blog/2016/11/secretary-generals-remarks-to-the-press-at-cop22/

Companies with more women leaders perform better…The evidence is clear: equality for women means progress for all".[25] (similar to what Kofi Annan said, above).

He spoke in defence of the LGBTQ sub-agenda when he said this in his "The Time Has Come" speech in March 2012 : ""It is an outrage that in our modern world, so many countries continue to criminalize people simply for loving another human being of the same sex".[26] Very clever using the word "loving" (as opposed to saying "being attracted to"), to steer away from the notion of (potentially) superficial attraction and suggesting potentially casual or meaningless relationships.

Guterres

The current and ninth secretary-general is Antonio Guterres, who was PM of Portugal for a time and a member of the Portuguese Socialist Party. Significantly, he was President of the Socialist International from 1999 – 2005.[27] He made these remarks on climate change on September 2018, describing it as "the defining issue of our time and we are at a defining moment. We face a direct existential threat". He stated "We need to shift away from our dependence on fossil fuels to replace them with clean energy from water, wind and sun… We must change the way we farm.". He also spouted anti-capitalist bullshit: "The world's richest nations are the most responsible for the climate crisis, yet the effects are being felt first by the poorest nations and the most vulnerable peoples and communities".[28] Back to those damn rich bourgeoisie oppressing the vulnerable proletarians again…

Some more gems from Guterres. A Tweet on 25 March 2020: "The transatlantic slave trade is one of the biggest crimes in the history of humankind. And we continue to live in its shadow. We can only move forward by confronting the racist legacy of slavery together".[29] The head of the UN—a world government, pro-mass migration organisation—

[25] Tavares, C., "This #WomensEqualityDay, Remember What Your Vote Means", 26 August 2016. https://www.huffpost.com/entry/this-womensequalityday-re_b_11705836

[26] UN Human Rights, "UN Secretary-General message at Human Rights Council", 7 March 2012. https://www.YouTube.com/watch?v=qtxU9iOx348

[27] "Secretary-General, Biography". https://www.un.org/sg/en/content/sg/biography

[28] New York Speech, "Secretary-General's remarks on Climate Change [as delivered]", 10 September 2018. https://www.un.org/sg/en/content/sg/statement/2018-09-10/secretary-generals-remarks-climate-change-delivered

[29] https://en.wikiquote.org/wiki/Antonio_Guterres

peddling anti-white European, racist, white guilt tripping.

Another on April 2020, pushing the UN's Covid narrative: "As the world fights #COVID19, we are also fighting an epidemic of harmful falsehoods & lies. I'm announcing a new @UN Communications Response initiative to spread facts & science, countering the scourge of misinformation—a poison putting more lives at risk".[29] Thank you Comrade Guterres!

In a July 2020 Tweet, he pushes several Marxian sub-agendas at the same time: "@COVID19 has deepened existing inequalities & vulnerabilities for women & girls. On Saturday's #WorldPopulationDay and every day, we must protect the rights of women and girls, end gender-based violence and safeguard sexual and reproductive health care".[29] This one is amusing— from social inequality ('class struggle') to eugenics to feminism, to wife-beating to contraception/eugenics, all in one Tweet!

Let's keep in mind that even though these men were/are at the helm of arguably the largest, most powerful global intergovernmental entity, their attitudes are similar to the average everyday Marxist cult members. Same thoughts and words. Same ideology.

The WHO?

Formed in 1948, the World Health Organisation (WHO) is the 'medical' arm (or tentacle) of the UN. It's an organisation that ""connects nations, partners and people to promote health, keep the world safe and serve the vulnerable—so everyone, everywhere can attain the highest level of health".[30] That sounds very nice. "Keep the world safe" is boss-level virtue-signalling. "Vulnerable" equates to "oppressed".

This sub-organisation, along with the Club of Rome, was instrumental in generating and implementing the Covid 19 agenda. The UN, via the WHO, was key in ensuring the global lockdowns. This organisation was founded on the Fabian principle of intending to use every available avenue to push the Marxian world-without-borders One World Government agenda; including 'medical' avenues. Obviously, this world 'health' organisation wasn't created to benefit anyone's health! It was created to further the one world agenda, via another structure.

So, let's upgrade our definition of the WHO—it's the medical arm of a global Marxist organisation. The current Director General of the WHO is Tedros Ghebreyesus—a Somalian cult member, and an alleged former member of the Tigray People's Liberation Front (another Marxist terror

---

[30] "About WHO". https://www.who.int/about

group).[31]

The first Director-General of the WHO was a Canadian psychiatrist, WW1 veteran and fanatical cult member by the name of George Brock Chisholm.[32] He was a champion of Marxian 'mental health' and sought to use psychiatric means to destroy traditional moral values.

On page five of *The Psychiatry of Enduring Peace and Social Progress* (1946), he said: "The re-interpretation and eventually eradication of the concept of right and wrong which has been the basis of child training, the substitution of intelligent and rational thinking for faith in the certainties of the old people, these are the belated objectives of practically all effective psychotherapy".[33] Hmm, 'therapy' to change a person's perception of morality?

He ostensibly desired a world of 'peace', and believed that in to order to achieve this, human behaviour needed to be "modified very extensively". He believed that the psychologists, psychiatrists, sociologists, and politicians needed to be responsible "for charting the necessary changes".[34]

He also barely conceals his hatred for any notion of religious morality describing it as the "concept of right and wrong, the poison long ago described and warned against as 'the fruit of the tree of the knowledge of good and evil'".[35] He made many statements like this revealing his moral relativist (Satanic) mentality—the idea that we can make-up our idea of 'right and wrong'. We can consider him the psychotic psychiatric godfather of the UN's 'conscience'. Note the reference to the Garden of Eden (and by extension Lucifer/Satan, again).

Significantly, Chisholm also co-founded the *World Federation of Mental Health* (WFMH) in 1948 in London. I'm sure western readers will have noticed all the talk about 'mental health' in the last few decades. According to the WFMH website, Chisholm "envisaged the WFMH as an

---

[31] Reuters, "Ethiopia says WHO chief has links to rebellious Tigrayan forces", 15 January 2022. https://www.reuters.com/world/africa/ethiopia-accuses-who-chief-links-rebellious-tigrayan-forces-2022-01-14/

[32] https://www.britannica.com/topic/World-Health-Organization

[33] Chisholm, G., "The Psychiatry of Enduring Peace and Social Progress", 1946, P. 5.

https://mikemcclaughry.files.wordpress.com/2012/12/psychiatry-of-enduring-peace-and-social-progress-chisholm-and-sullivan-1946.pdf

[34] Ibid. P. 7.

[35] Ibid. P. 9.

international, non-governmental body to provide a link to 'grassroots' mental health organizations and United Nations agencies".[36] Huh? Linking peoples' mental health (minds) to a Marxist internationalist one-world-government entity?

Alluded to earlier is the fact that many of the personnel populating mental health services today have come through the Marxism-riddled education system, and therefore will be, at the very least, sympathetic to the cult/ideology, blissfully unaware of the irony of their position.

Earth Summits and Agendas 21 and 30

> "The United Nations is nothing but a trapdoor to the Red World's immense concentration camp. We pretty much control the U.N."[37]

> Harold Rosenthal, "The Hidden Tyranny", 1978

The Marxist one-world-government monstrosity (the UN) has pulled many manoeuvres to push the climate change sub-agenda. There was its "Framework Convention on Climate Change" (UNFCCC) at its Earth Summit in Rio De Janeiro in June 1992; then the Kyoto Protocol in 1997 and the Copenhagen Accord, followed by the Paris Agreement in 2016. These resulted in the "Agenda for Environment and Development" or Agenda 21.

In September 2015, the UN's "Sustainable Development Summit" resulted in the creation of Agenda 2030. [38] [39] [40]

An omnipresent propaganda word here is "sustainability"—it comes from the minds of cult members who presume that capitalist societies are doomed to fail (as the Marxist prophets predicted). It suggests civilisation cannot survive unless we have global communism. Naturally, the Agenda

---

[36] "Who we are – History". https://wfmh.global/who-we-are/history

[37] Rosenthal, H., "The Hidden Tyranny", 1978.
https://ia803207.us.archive.org/9/items/rosenthal-document-hidden-tyranny-1983/Rosenthal%20Document-HiddenTyranny%281983%29.pdf

[38] United Nations, "United Nations Framework Convention On Climate Change", 1992.

https://unfccc.int/files/essential_background/background_publications_htmlpdf/applic ation/pdf/conveng.pdf

[39] "What is the Kyoto Protocol?". https://unfccc.int/kyoto_protocol

[40] United Nations, "Copenhagen Accord", 18 December 2009.
https://unfccc.int/resource/docs/2009/cop15/eng/l07.pdf

2030 document has the usual virtue-signalling Marxian tone.

After paragraph 59, on page 18 of the Agenda 2030 document (91 paragraphs total), there are 17 sustainable development goals listed (notes in brackets): "end poverty in all its forms everywhere (socialist fantasy); end hunger, achieve food security and improved nutrition and promote sustainable agriculture (no more animal farming); ensure healthy lives and promote well-being for all at all ages (note: no free will to do otherwise?); ensure inclusive & equitable quality education & promote lifelong learning opportunities for all (more control of education systems); achieve gender equality and empower all women and girls. (Note: how childish does this sound? Not to mention sexist); ensure availability & sustainable management of water & sanitation for all (including control of drinking water supply); ensure access to affordable, reliable, sustainable and modern energy for all (make the whole world go 'green'); promote sustained, inclusive and sustainable economic growth, full and productive employment and decent work for all (save the workers); build resilient infrastructure, promote inclusive and sustainable industrialization and foster innovation; reduce inequality within and among countries (trying to enforce equality within countries and between countries! Suppress national prosperity); make cities and human settlements inclusive, safe, resilient & sustainable (so lots of diversity, 'pandemic' compliance, and no dangerous 'far-right' thinking etc); ensure sustainable consumption and production patterns (e.g. control how people eat, how they live etc.); take urgent action to combat climate change and its impacts (sigh); conserve and sustainably use the oceans, seas and marine resources for sustainable development (further attack on fisheries industries of nations); protect, restore and promote sustainable use of terrestrial ecosystems, sustainably manage forests, combat desertification, and halt and reverse land degradation and halt biodiversity loss; promote peaceful and inclusive societies for sustainable development, provide access to justice for all and build effective, accountable and inclusive institutions at all levels (make countries go full-Marxist); strengthen the means of implementation and revitalize the global partnership for sustainable development (the UN will force the world to comply)".[41]

The Club of Rome

Another group of control freak nutjobs closely connected with the UN is

---

[41] United Nations, "Transforming our world: the 2030 Agenda for Sustainable Development", P. 18.
https://sustainabledevelopment.un.org/content/documents/21252030AgendaforSustainableDevelopmentweb.pdf

the Club of Rome (COR).[42] Some have commented that the COR has a 'think tank' relationship with the UN; that it 'suggests' things which the UN then puts in to practice globally (I concur with this assessment). Established in 1968, the Club of Rome is regarded by many as one of the "Big 6" Round Table 'world government' groups who apparently exert a lot of control over world affairs.

(The other five are the: Royal Institute of International Affairs (established in 1920); Council on Foreign Relations (1921); United Nations (1945); Bilderberg Group (1954); Trilateral Commission (1973). Note how they emerged in the era after the Russian Revolution of 1917, when the ideology was starting to gain significant global momentum).

The COR website's "About Us" page and their info PDF page contains the usual Marxian rhetoric: "Decades of exponential consumption and population growth have come to imperil the earth's climate and life-supporting systems, while reinforcing social and economic inequalities and impoverishing billions globally". Apparently "the limits of the Earth's biosphere" were being reached, "destabilising the foundations of life as we know it". The COR wants us to act now to save the Earth basically, and that we needed to "move towards more equitable economic, finance and socio-political models" (code for "let's have a socialist planet").[43][44] To simplify its role, the COR is a scientific, biological, environmental, and technological department of the internationalist 'globalist' system. When you hear initiatives related to vaccines/diseases, climate, tracking technologies, Genetically Modified Organisms being pushed by the system, you know this group is involved. In short, it's opposed to nature/God and human freedom. The COR represents a modern approach to achieving One World Government—the creation of supposed crises, and solutions (suggested by them) which benefit their overall agenda (Hegelian dynamics). It's run by an executive committee, but its sponsors include many power elites—royals to politicians to business types etc.

Limits or Revolution

The COR's associated publications include the anti-capitalism entitled *Limits to Growth* (1972), and the more overtly Marxist publication *The*

---

[42] "Organization:Club of Rome".
https://handwiki.org/wiki/Organization:Club_of_Rome

[43] "About us". https://www.clubofrome.org/about-us/

[44] "The Club of Rome".https://www.clubofrome.org/wp-content/uploads/2023/11/CoR_Flyer_A4_Oct2023-digital.pdf

First Global Revolution (1991). [45][46] These works and other materials endorsed by the COR include themes such as: the notion of overpopulation and that human beings are problematic for the world; the idea that we have overindulged living in capitalistic societies (anti-capitalism); the idea that we need an international 'revolution' (Trotskyite rhetoric), that all countries should be united (solidarity) to deal with these apparent environmental/biological/demographical problems (the one-world-government agenda).

Limits to Growth is a piece of Marxian propaganda that has its origins in a 1970 study at the Massachusetts Institute of Technology (MIT). The focus of the study was "the implications of continued worldwide growth". It was conducted by a team of international researchers who "examined the five basic factors that determine and, in their interactions, ultimately limit growth on this planet—population increase, agricultural production, non-renewable resource depletion, industrial output, and pollution generation. The MIT team fed data on these five factors into a global computer model and then tested the behavior of the model under several sets of assumptions to determine alternative patterns for mankind's future. The Limits to Growth is the nontechnical report of their findings".[45]

Wow! Mapping mankind's future using computer models?!? Star Trek level shit! Borderline wizardry even! Let's keep in mind here—even the supercomputers of 1970 were about as powerful as the popular Commodore Amiga 500 home PC, which was released in 1987.[47] I could probably make one from the bits and piece in my desk drawers here...

The cover of The First Global Revolution book shows the globe with all the countries coloured (commie) red. Considering it was published just after the collapse of the U.S.S.R., this is nothing if not blatant. In addition, the first pages contain the same quatrain by Omar Khayyam mentioned earlier in the Fabian Society section, immortalised in the Fabian window at the London School of Economics: ".. would not we shatter it to bits and then, remould it nearer to the heart's desire." (the plan to destroy/re-build the world).[48]

---

[45] Several authors, *The Limits to Growth* (1972).
https://www.clubofrome.org/publication/the-limits-to-growth/

[46] King and Schneider, *The First Global Revolution* (1991).

https://www.clubofrome.org/publication/the-first-global-revolution-1991/

[47] https://en.wikipedia.org/wiki/Amiga_500

[48] Khayyam, O., "[73] Ah Love! Could thou and I with Fate conspire", 11th century.

This book suggested that humanity itself is the problem on the Earth (anti-humanity/anti-God message). On page 115, there is a sub-heading "The Common Enemy of Humanity is Man", which states: "In searching for a new enemy to unite us, we came up with the idea that pollution, the threat of global warming, water shortages, famine and the like would fit the bill these phenomena do constitute a common threat which demands the solidarity of all peoples...All these dangers are caused by human intervention and it is only through changed attitudes and behaviour that they can be overcome. The real enemy, then, is humanity itself".[49] Oh I see, humanity is the problem. The Devil smiles. In a sane world, anyone caught writing or spouting this inflammatory nonsense would be immediately arrested and taken in for psyche evaluation. More treason against humanity.

From the COR website, a 2020 'article' entitled "A Green Reboot After the Pandemic" states: "The coronavirus pandemic is a wake-up call to stop exceeding the planet's limits. After all, deforestation, biodiversity loss, and climate change all make pandemics more likely. Deforestation drives wild animals closer to human populations, increasing the likelihood that zoonotic viruses like SARS-CoV-2 will make the cross-species leap. Likewise, the Intergovernmental Panel on Climate Change warns that global warming will likely accelerate the emergence of new viruses".[50] What utter rubbish! This sounds like it was written by a brainwashed uni student doing temp work for the Chinese Communist Party! This should make the blood boil—these nutjobs create these situations, then blame it on capitalism! It could be entitled "A Marxist Reboot After the Pandemic".

The article was correct: the pandemic was a wake-up call alright—a wake-up call that the Earth is infested with brainwashed activist control freaks.

---

https://www.poetry-chaikhana.com/Poets/K/KhayyamOmar/73AhLovecoul/index.html

[49] King and Schneider, *The First Global Revolution* (1991). P. 115.

https://www.clubofrome.org/publication/the-first-global-revolution-1991/

[50] COR, "A Green Reboot After the Pandemic" (2020).

https://www.clubofrome.org/impact-hubs/climate-emergency/a-green-reboot-after-the-pandemic/

Section XII—Marxism V Freedom

"Freedom is never more than one generation away from extinction. We didn't pass it to our children in the bloodstream. It must be fought for, protected, and handed on for them to do the same"[1]

U.S. President Ronald Reagan

"The conflict between communism and freedom is the problem of our time. It overshadows all other problems. This conflict mirrors our age, its toils, its tensions, its troubles, and its tasks. On the outcome of this conflict depends the future of all mankind"[2]

Prominent American labour union leader
and AFL-CIO President George Meany (1894–1980)

Introduction

We all know that whenever we express any sort of patriotic, nationalist, or anti-'PC' opinions, or are critical of internationalism/globalism, you can be sure that sooner or later, a Marxist (or three) will materialise to dissuade, debate, mock, slander, or threaten. Yes, this is nauseatingly predictable (often amusing), and we know it's because they're programmed to do so. The Marxist saint Lev Bronstein (aka Leon Trotsky) once wrote in "Their Morals and Ours" (1938) "He who slanders the victim aids the executioner"[3] (we could swap "executioner" for "oppressor"; in modern parlance, it's 'victim-blaming'). Is it not telling that cult members—particularly the more fanatical ones—aggressively 'attack' those of us who are on the receiving end of this internationalist tyranny? In this equation, by acting as above, the cult sides with the 'oppressor'.

As irritating and frustrating this behaviour can be, we need not view the

---

[1] Reagan, R., "*A Time for Choosing: The Speeches of Ronald Reagan, 1961–1982*" (1983).

https://www.azquotes.com/quote/241175

[2] Skousen, W., *The Naked Communist* (1958), preface.

https://ia601509.us.archive.org/13/items/B-001-002-046/B-001-002-046.pdf

[3] Trotsky, L., "Their Moral and Ours", 1938.
https://www.marxists.org/archive/trotsky/1938/morals/morals.htm

situation as negative. On the contrary, it's evidence that we're displaying the right attitudes (ones that the internationalist 'elites' don't want us having). In fact, a quick way to judge how much desire there is for freedom within a society, is how much Marxist suppression there is. This is because there's a very clear correlation between the intensity level of traitorous (globalist/internationalist) Marxist activity in a society, and the level of anti-globalist/internationalist sentiment that exists.

Whenever anyone starts expressing opposing ideas/ideologies (including objecting to globalism/internationalism), there will be an immediate reaction from the cult once these sentiments are detected. The reaction is proportionate to the level of prevalence and frequency of these ideas, as they appear in the discourse of a society.

All the vitriol cult members spew is a measure of how much of a threat they deem these 'dangerous, far-right' ideas to be. Hence the much referred-to phrase "If you're not catching flak, you're not over the target". Therefore, the level of anti-patriotic vitriol coming from the traitorous cult in any given country is an indicator of how much a society is waking-up to the internationalist globalist's plans; of how much they are refusing to comply.

To put it another way—if a whole nation is full of zombified, pro-internationalism, brainwashed people without a hint of 'evil' right-wing attitudes or any love for their country, you would not hear a single bitchy bark from the Marxist doggies. The whole country would be full of fucked-up degenerates just like them—everyone would be a part of the big cult!—and the brats wouldn't have anyone to disagree with them. There would be no resistance to the globalist flow—all would swim towards the light of the totalitarian One World Government with soy-induced emotion, rainbow—coloured tears, and manic, wide-eyed smiles, saying (robot voice) "We are one".

Another apt phrase is "It's always darkest before the dawn": the system—and the Marxist cult who serves it—is going to complain with ever increasing intensity as a society wakes-up, refuses to comply, and clashes with it. Inevitably, things are going to get nasty, and as the age of Marxism goes through its death throes, a retaliatory tantrum of gigantic proportions awaits us (e.g. WW3). In the meantime, we should take all the cult's vitriol and actions as a compliment—it shows we are being perceived as a threat. In fact, let's hope for more! For them, it's tantamount to digging one's own grave by vocation. All their criminal actions are duly noted by us, and each of them will be judged and pay the price for their treason.

The AIDS of nations

"Communism is like an autoimmune disorder; it doesn't do the killing itself, but it weakens the system so much that the victim is left helpless and unable to fight off anything else"[4]

Chess legend and political activist
Garry Kasparov, *Winter is Coming*, 2015

Marxism does to nations what the HIV virus does to the human body. It's not the actual virus that kills a person. However, it may neutralise the immune system, rendering it ineffective. When this weakened immuno state is reached, a HIV+ person may be diagnosed with Acquired Immuno Deficiency Syndrome (AIDS). A person can then die of multiple causes that would, under normal circumstances, be dealt with by the immune system. Essentially, an ineffective immune system leads to a weakened, vulnerable organism.[5] If a country is an organism, then its immune system is its sense of uniqueness, traditions, patriotism, religiosity, culture etc. As we've seen, the cult/ideology erodes and eventually neutralizes these aspects. Once this immune system is removed from the equation, the organism/nation is then wide-open to attack. Not only does Marxism break down the wall that protects the nation, it invites in dangerous pathogens— the various Marxian sub-agendas (feminism, mass immigration, LGBTQ, economy-destroying climate change activism etc.) and their effects. Its obsession with destroying nations is evident in its own stances on these issues. The cult/ideology, in a sense, is a diseased wrecking ball for a nation's perimeter wall (both symbolically and literally if we include a country's international border).

Trying to get a patriotic, anti-internationalist/globalist movement going in a country while there is too much Marxism present, would be like trying to fill up a bath with water while there is no plug in the sinkhole. There is a problem under the surface which you must deal with first. You may be wondering "Why is the bath not filling up? The taps are at full blast here!".

Perhaps you can't see the plug, because your view is obscured by all the progressive LGBTQIXY+ Rainbow-coloured Chairman Mao-flavoured bubbles in the way? The bubbles are symbolic of the countless in-your-face distractions that a Marxism-infected culture is constantly throws at us. Let's not be distracted. Let's deal with the problem that is holding us back the most. Let's plug that leak with a big, masculine, patriotically coloured,

---

[4] Kasparov, G., *Winter is Coming* (2015), P. 33.

[5] Scaccia, A., "Facts About HIV: Life Expectancy and Long-Term Outlook", 23 Jan 2023.

https://www.healthline.com/health/hiv-aids/life-expectancy

anti-Marxism angry-as-Hitler dildo.

Marxism sabotages patriotism

Marxism is where the globalist structure meets the masses, in a sense. The ideology allows the globalist system to control a significant portion of the population in each country psychologically, to keep that population sufficiently divided so that it will not be able to mount a resistance. This Marxist element serves the globalist system by suppressing the patriotic/pro-freedom/non-Marxist section of the population. Basically, Marxism sabotages nationalism, at the ground level; that's its role. The minute this patriotic nationalism appears, they are right there, to derail it.

Marxism not only turns people into traitors, it also amputates their nationality from them, as compared to those who are not infected. For example, an Irish person isn't fully Irish if they are infected. They may look, sound, seem Irish, and be ethnically Irish, but their mind, heart and soul is not. On an ideological level, they are anti-Irish. This is the brutal reality of the situation we are in (and that goes for other nationalities too). Once indoctrinated, a person goes against their own nationality/ethnic group, wittingly or unwittingly. If they are part of a nation, they become an enemy of that nation, often while being within it.

What's called 'nationalism' is a rational response to the monster of internationalist totalitarianism. The role of the cult/ideology is to deflect or diffuse that energy; to stamp-out that flame; to drown out those cries; to block the light (e.g. the light emanating from that 'Nazi' lightbulb).

This worldwide natural movement towards freedom (coming from the non-infected portion of the population in each country) would be able to grow and gather some momentum and would eventually turn this whole ship around. Indeed, we've all seen this movement develop in recent times as a genuine reaction to 'globalism'. The obstacle which stands in the way is the cult/ideology. It's the weight which drags us down. This is why directly addressing it must be a top priority. If you had to run up a very steep and long hill, or indeed had a mountain to climb, and then realised you had a heavy bag of rocks on your back, is it not wise to first put this down? You could give it a try regardless, but don't be surprised when you start popping disks and blowing ligaments left, right and centre as you inevitably fail (and fall) over and over.

Prisoners blaming the prison officers

Considering the global state of affairs at present, we need to view ignorance as a crime. Ignorance of the globalist monster and its ideological methods of control is a crime. It's a crime that Marxism happily takes advantage of.

It's a crime we have all collectively served enough time for. I raise this point because, even today, you'll often hear people blaming whatever political party/parties is/are currently in power. Or they'll blame some political front man/woman. It could be Leo Varadkar as the Taoiseach (PM) of Ireland, or U.S. President Joe Biden, or Sadiq Khan as the Major of London, or Justin Trudeau as the PM in Canada, or it might be Emmanuel "Micro" Macron in France, or UK PM Rishi Sunak etc.

With regards to the level of Marxist infection in our countries—and the anti-freedom internationalist chaos that it brings—the responsibility of this must rest with the population themselves. It's so easy to project blame on a certain figure, group etc. Unfortunately, this is not constructive at all, and merely provides an emotional target for our frustrations; they're an out-of-reach celebrity-esque political punching bag we can pop that verbal jab in to. This is a bad habit that stops real progress and understanding.

It's also incredibly juvenile. As if a single political figure (like the ones listed) are in control of this massive, complex, co-ordinated worldwide agenda, or are driving the ideology/cult on their town? There are going to be countless more where they came from! To me they are meaningless nothings. Merely mouthpieces that we can study the mouth noises of, for clues as to what's in store for us next… That attitude—of thinking these types actually run the show or make the big decisions—just shows naivety of the bigger-picture, that we are controlled by a 'globalist' Marxist machine and the ideology/cult allows it to function. The same goes for political parties too, in general. Their ideological leanings are often a reflection of the ideological leanings of the general public (or a significant section of it, at least).

It's also very Marxian for a people to cry victim and claim to be oppressed! There is always someone outside themselves to blame! National empowerment, or freedom in any other sense, can never come this way! The (non-indoctrinated) general public in affected countries need to accept responsibility for not detecting the Marxist infection sooner (and in some cases, unwittingly supporting it). Leaving the past behind us (and our excuses with it), we can now take responsibility ourselves and start to turn the tide ideologically in our societies, by choosing patriotic nationalism.

Instead of blaming political frontmen/frontwomen we can focus our energy on fixing this big problem all around us. We have more power than these leaders do, because if we refuse to acquiesce anymore, and actively resist internationalist control/ideologies, then it does not matter who the official leaders are. Any internationalist 'leader' types like Biden, Trudeau, Varadkar, Macron etc. are not the problem—they are symptoms of the problem.

The sane become less 'progressive' with age

Have you noticed that many will go from being 'progressive'/'PC' when they were younger, to being more 'conservative'/'non-PC' when they're older, but not the other way around? (you might find some apparent examples of the latter, but I would check those for sincerity; likely Marxist deceivers). Why is that? I'm talking about the difference between someone who is younger (late teens and 20s, even 30s for some people), and more mature ages. Why this general trend?

It's because people don't get dumber/more ignorant as they get older but being dumb/ignorant due to immaturity is not only common, it's par for the course. This applies to every single human being, to one degree or another. People don't de-evolve as time goes by!

However, they may 'wake-up' to things with the progression of time. I say 'may' because, obviously, there are plenty who don't ever wake-up to things. Some people manage to stay detached from reality their whole lives! Rejoice as you are not one of these people (unless a cult member is reading these lines, with that brain-dead, smug look on their face).

For those of us with more potential than that, we tend to advance more with the passage of time. This can be only slightly or more pronounced, depending on our constitution emotionally (ego/fear/self-esteem), attitude towards learning/improvement, skill, curiosity/enthusiasm, our psychological/physiological health status, and the strength of will etc.

For some of us, we can evaluate and re-evaluate our belief-systems as time goes by. This gives us the opportunity to 'upgrade' our attitudes so to speak. It gives us a greater chance of realising that we may have absorbed some ideas from indoctrination (i.e. Marxist 'progressive' programming). Once we realise this is the case, we can then choose to stop having those older, inferior perspectives, essentially detoxifying of them, and to choose new, superior ones.

Essentially, transitioning from 'progressive' beliefs/perspectives to non-progressive ones means that you develop a conscience—you now understand the difference between right and wrong. A true conscience! You can develop this true conscience more as you make progress throughout your life. But it does not go the other way around: it's not possible to find someone who went from being an intelligent person with a well-developed conscience in their 20s, to being a full-retard morally degenerate person with no conscience in their 30s (unless there was some extreme brain-damage/trauma, psychotropic drug use and brainwashing to essentially change who they are etc.). This process should be explained to children by parents and ingrained in them.

Of course, those who are in the 'progressive' category have a more limited level of consciousness. This is the crux of the matter. They are failing to join the dots; missing some screws (including knowledge) and possess an inferior conscience. Those with a higher level of consciousness, will (sooner or later in life) end up being more traditionalist/'conservative' and anti-globalist/internationalist, as they realise that this is the correct attitude to have.

The left and right wings of a bird

> "In today's world, if you are neutral, you are already an enemy"[6]
>
> Soviet defector Yuri Besmenov, Summit
> University Forum interview in Los Angeles, 1983

Are 'left' and 'right' really the same, on a bigger-picture level? Are they both just the two wings of one big internationalist, globalist 'New World Order' bird? Some people think that this is a stupid debate, since both wings must obviously be controlled by some shadowy, Illuminati-esque globalist 'elites' (the proverbial nefarious men behind the curtain). We have seen this belief become almost fashionable in some circles, in others—an axiom. But is the debate stupid? Is this belief correct?

If it's true that we have a 'globalist' control system directing world affairs (and many believe this to be the case), does this not mean that we, the lowly voting masses, and government/politics, democracy and voting etc.—are all irrelevant and the whole left/right dichotomy is just a big distraction? Is it all just one big circus show to distract us from the truth—that we have no power? There are many who feel this way. In addition, many of those people feel that anyone who thinks otherwise (i.e. someone who 'believe' in left v right politics) is unintelligent, uninformed, or a person of 'low consciousness' etc.

We clearly see this perception in the so-called New Age movement, and in what we can call the 'conspiracy theory' culture. Of course, having a cynical, hopeless attitude about politics is understandable, so it exists elsewhere in society too.

However, this is an infuriating, unacceptable situation! The perception— that left v right politics is all the same and meaningless—is extremely unhelpful, irresponsible, and disempowering for the cause of genuine freedom! Additionally, it empowers internationalist totalitarianism (which

---

[6] Yuri Bezmenov 1983 Interview and Lecture (1080p HD).

https://youtu.be/Z0j181tR5WM?feature=shared&t=6231

Marxism is/serves). It's a distorted perception of how the world actually operates, and what's actually happening to it right now. So, it's a contradictory behaviour engaged-in by those who assume they have it all figured out already! Let's be direct about this—you are either for international totalitarianism, or you are against it, to one degree or another. Unless you enjoy the idea of your fellow humans living as submissive miserable slaves in a future dystopian degenerate hell-world, it's recommended we collectively (and enthusiastically!) choose the latter option.

Being 'right' right now, is right

> "The heart of the wise inclines to the right, but the heart of the fool to the left"[7]

> New International Bible, Ecclesiastes 10:2

Given the condition of the world right now, and the circumstances we are in, it's clear that being a 'nationalist' is a wise stance to take. (Don't be uncomfortable with this label, but if you insist, then choose another that means the same thing). If 'nationalist' means having a separate, sovereign country, then logically this allows for a degree of separation from the internationalist globalist control structure. This is actually a good idea (!). Considering that civilisation is literally collapsing all around us due to internationalism, it's probably the best idea humanity has ever had.

If this all falls into the category of 'right-wing', and being 'left-wing' doesn't (and does the opposite, in fact), then the choice is clear, isn't it? In this equation, being 'right-wing' is objectively superior to being 'left-wing', as the former potentially results in freedom for the country in question, while the latter results in the opposite (no true sovereignty, destruction of our countries, peoples, cultures, ultra-degenerate societies etc).

What's called 'left-wing'/'leftism' or anything associated with Marxism—regardless of what it started out as, what the 'left' is or isn't now, what it was 'supposed' to be originally, whether it's labelled 'liberal' or not etc.—is generally the problem. Therefore, anything that is generally opposed to that is part of the solution. We cannot emphasise this enough! This is one of the big fundamental undiscussed truths about life in this world for the past couple of centuries, particularly since the beginning of the 20th century. This should be a tactical axiom going forward for the world patriotic movement.

---

[7] New International Bible, Ecclesiastes 10:2. https://biblehub.com/ecclesiastes/10-2.htm

The idea that 'left' and 'right' are both equal in terms of value to humanity in our present situation is false. It's a distortion of the facts. For those 'new age/spiritual' types or those with a primarily conspiratorial word-view to insist that they are, just shows us how detached from reality someone can be. The mere fact that an ordinary everyday person might feel embarrassed, fearful, or paranoid in even associating themselves with anything 'right-wing' is a clear indicator of which end of the political spectrum is the major influence on society.

The idea that 'right' and 'left' are faux alternatives controlled by a shadowy bourgeois elite, and that there is no difference between them, has a demoralising effect. It results in many believing we have no control over the situation—that globalist internationalism is inevitable—while preventing nations from choosing the liberating 'right' path.

Essentially, whatever label(s) we choose to use, there is a 'political' solution to all this, and dismissing politics entirely is extremely unwise. In addition, it would be extremely helpful for more of us to vigorously engage with the political sphere, provided it's done the right way.

Left V Right = Oppressed V Oppressor

The left v right dichotomy also contains the oppressor vs oppressed formula, with the usual inversion/distortion of the truth. The Marxian narrative says: left = good, and right = bad. It says those on the right are siding with the oppressors (capitalist bourgeois imperialist oligarchs etc.), whereas those on the left are on the side of the 'oppressed' (minorities, the non-wealthy/proletariat etc.).

In reality those on the 'left', in general, support the aforementioned Marxian sub-agendas which claim to help the 'oppressed', but also serve these bourgeois totalitarian globalists (who are the real oppressors!). So, even here, the red formula is being used once again on the most fundamentally basic descriptive terms of the political spectrum; and flipping reality on its head in the process.

This distortion of reality, this inversion (that those on the 'right' are allied with the oppressors) is emphasised constantly to reinforce brainwashing and stop any opposition to the internationalist Marxist globalist agenda. Hence the clearly evident and bizarre upside-down mentality emanating from cult members in today's word which says: if you are genuinely against the control system (as 'right-wingers'/nationalists are), surely you are supporting the evil oppressive capitalistic bourgeois system! This is backwards!

In this recent, severely Marxism-infected era of world history, the terms 'right' and 'left' have been used to divide the opinions of people and categorise them based on whether or not they will conform to being ruled within a 'globalist' one-world government system. It's also used to denote who is opposed to the cult/ideology.

As outlined, "right wing" and "fascist" are used as derogatory/suppressive terms, while conversely terms such as "progressive'" are used as complimentary/commendatory terms, and this is constantly emphasised. It has been an effective brainwashing tactic that encourages the sheep to police other sheep.

In terms of how a modern cult member uses these terms, it's all connected to what transpired during the WW1-WW2 period. Though the traitorous activism and subversion of cult members is much older, it's centrally important with regards to how they behave today. Cult members all over the world—who assist the internationalist globalist agenda—are traitors who label their countrymen 'fascists' etc, in an attempt to equate their actions in the present with evil acts apparently committed in the past by other groups. I'm referring of course to acts committed by the various non-Marxist/'fascist' regimes in the 20th century—such as having imperial ambitions and wanting to take over the world; of being authoritarian and violent; of suppressing (Marxist) free speech etc.

Fascism vs Marxism

Here is a monumental piece of truth that the relatively sane, non-indoctrinated portion of the world's populace needs to fully understand. The cult/ideology and what's broadly termed 'fascism' are mortal enemies because they are ideological opponents/rivals. In addition, considering the cult's predictable tendency to slander anything that opposes it, this means that fascism will constantly be upheld as the epitome of injustice and evil in a society sufficiently contaminated with Marxism. The cult obviously does this while hypocritically destroying everything, claiming it itself is the epitome of justice, benevolence, 'progressivism' etc. Hopefully some pennies will drop for the reader in this section...

Post-WW1, the ideology was rapidly gaining popularity around Europe; and there were many attempted Marxist takeovers, with varying levels of success. Inspired by the murderous Bolsheviks in Russia, various cult groups made their move. It's important to understand the overall historical significance of events in the ideological battlegrounds of Italy, Germany, and Spain, and how the cult was dealt with in those instances. The hatred emanating from the cult towards anything they regard as being 'fascist' stems from these historical conflicts; particularly the ones where they were beaten down or defeated entirely by their ideological opponents. This is why the cult hates fascists! Mortal enemies! The 'fascists' in Germany and Italy in the inter-war period treated cult members as such. First, Benito Mussolini (1883–1945) and his fascist 'black shirts' dealt with them in Italy, setting the precedent for the struggle other patriots would have in their respective countries.

Before we continue, we must address an important question, as it often causes confusion; this confusion may limit our understanding of the cult's hatred of fascism (and we must fully understand the cult). Some think fascism is just another form of Marxism. Though a somewhat complex, large subject, the short answer is no—they were not the same thing (we will expand on this after we look at some historical events).

The birth of Fascism

> "We declare war against socialism, not because it is socialism, but because it has opposed nationalism"[8]

Benito Mussolini, speech in Milan, March 23, 1919

> "We have no compassion and we ask no compassion from you. When our turn comes, we shall not make excuses for the terror"[9]

Karl Marx, *Suppression of the Neue Rheinische Zeitung* (1849)

The ideological struggle for control of the (then) Kingdom of Italy lasted from the latter stages of WW1 until roughly 1926, when the cult was relatively neutralised. The cult used typical tactics to gain control during this period—worker's strikes, occupying factories and properties, violence, and assassinations etc.

Since the cult, spear-headed by the *Partito Socialista Italiano* (Italian Socialist Party) was trying to 'revolt' against land and business owners, these owners naturally had an ally in Mussolini's fascists who were not Marxist (in fact, this was one of the many reasons why Mussolini gained popular support—he didn't seek to divide the nation along class/economic lines, as the cult does). It was this support which allowed the anti-Marxist fascists to prevail in the end, along with the support of the Royal Italian Army.[10]

---

[8] Pugliese, S., *Fascism, Anti-fascism, and the Resistance in Italy: 1919 to the Present*, (2004) p. 43. (Mussolini's speech in Milan, March 23, 1919).
https://libquotes.com/benito-mussolini/quote/lbw9x1q

[9] Marx, K., "Suppression of the *Neue Rheinische Zeitung*", 1849.
https://www.marxists.org/archive/marx/works/1849/05/19c.htm

[10] https://www.britannica.com/biography/Benito-Mussolini

Mussolini's March on Rome in Oct 1922, saw the beginning of fascist rule when King Victor Emmanuel III (1869–1947) appointed him Prime Minister.[11] What led to this situation—and this is the crucial bit—was the use of brutal force by Mussolini's supporters and allies against the cult. It had been somewhat of a back-and-forth affair, with assassinations on both sides; even later attempts made on the Duce ("leader) himself. His 'black shirts' assaulted and eliminated cult members, essentially suppressing the cult for the duration of his reign (roughly two decades). Those perished included a Marxist prophet—Antonio Gramsci. [12] Obviously, cult members—then and now—view this as 'oppression' and 'authoritarianism'. Two decades is a long time for a group of crazy brats not to get their own way! They would get their revenge on Mussolini at the end of WW2.

Mussolini was once a socialist and identified as such, but he created a new type of nationalist ideology, separate from Marxian socialism, as an opponent to it. He and his Fascist Party got Italy back on track, and not only that, but it was also a more stable, prosperous and (relatively) Marxism-free and Mafia-free Italy. Essentially, the inter-war period in Italy was the first major conflict that the cult lost, and the cult never forgets. Being bitterly anti-fascist is written in the DNA of the indoctrination, and Mussolini was the man mostly responsible.

The German revolution

In Germany, the Weimar Republic (1919–1933) was formed, under the pro-Marxism *Social Democrat Party*. This period saw a Germany in dire straits.[13] In January 1919, the *Spartacus League* led uprisings throughout Germany.

This group was founded by the likes of Rosa Luxemburg and Karl Liebknecht (1871–1919), and was a forerunner of the *Kommunistiche Partei Deutschlands* (KPD) (Communist Party of Germany). [14] Soviet republics sprang-up in Leipzig, Bavaria (aka Munich Soviet Republic), Hamburg and Bremen. There was open fighting on the streets between

---

[11] https://www.britannica.com/event/March-on-Rome

[12] https://military-history.fandom.com/wiki/Italian_Civil_War

[13] "The Weimar Republic (1918 – 1933)".

https://www.bundestag.de/en/parliament/history/parliamentarism/weimar/weimar-200326

[14] Cavendish, R., "The Spartacist Uprising in Berlin", 1 January 2009.

https://www.historytoday.com/archive/spartacist-uprising-berlin

these cult groups and state forces.

As in Italy, this movement was suppressed by force, albeit not as immediately or as consistently (over the years). As the German army was in disarray at this point, the government hired a WW1 veteran mercenary group called the *Freikorps Oberland* to support the troops.[15] Of course, it was understandable that veterans did not appreciate this anti-Germany, Bolshevik-backed movement taking over, especially so recently after their sacrifices in WW1.

Eventually, Luxemburg and Liebknecht were again captured, but were executed this time, with Luxemburg's body being unceremoniously dumped into the Landwehr canal. Her funeral procession saw thousands in the streets (full of witting and unwitting cult members no doubt).[16] The uber-fanatical Luxemburg in particular is regarded as a Marxist prophet, who was still spewing revolutionary bile up until the end.

On 14 January 1919, on the evening of her execution, she wrote: "future victories will spring from this "defeat". "Order prevails in Berlin!" You foolish lackeys! Your "order" is built on sand. Tomorrow the revolution will "rise up again, clashing its weapons," and to your horror it will proclaim with trumpets blazing: I was, I am, I shall be!".[17] The nutcase was right—the cult/ideology didn't die with her, unfortunately. As mentioned, even at the point of death, there is no backward step, or no realisation of what they are.

As for Liebknecht, Marx and Engels were his godparents, which is all we need to know about who he was (I wonder which one wore the tranny skirt?).[18] Their 'murders' are still commemorated and in January 2019, cult members in Germany marked the centenary.[19] So this occasion showed brainwashed anti-German cult members in modern day Germany honouring anti-German cult members who were shot for being cult members a century ago. Crazy! Unacceptable that this is permitted.

---

[15] "Freikorps".https://www.studysmarter.co.uk/explanations/history/democracy-and-dictatorship-in-germany/freikorps/

[16] https://www.britannica.com/biography/Rosa-Luxemburg

[17] Luxemburg, R. "Order Prevails in Berlin", January 1919. https://www.marxists.org/archive/luxemburg/1919/01/14.htm

[18] https://www.britannica.com/biography/Karl-Liebknecht

[19] Connolly and LeBlond, "Germany remembers Rosa Luxemburg 100 years after her murder", 15 January 2019. https://www.theguardian.com/world/2019/jan/15/germans-take-to-the-streets-to-celebrate-rosa-luxemburg-karl-liebknecht-berlin

Despite the efforts of the Freikorps, the Marxist infection would eventually take hold of Germany, helping to create a divided, chaotic place. This situation prevailed until this guy called "Adolf Hitler" and the NSDAP party took control of the country, who were (despite misguided arguments to the contrary) staunchly and brutally anti-Marxist.

They too used organised groups and violent suppression to deny the cult power, handing them their second major defeat of the period. As in Italy, they were prevented taking control of a country by a rival group.

The 'Spanish' Civil War

> "One thing that I am sure of, and which I can answer truthfully, is that whatever the contingencies that may arise here, wherever I am there will be no Communism"[20]

Generalissimo Francisco Franco, in discussion
with Niceto Alcalá-Zamora (1938)

Here's a very important lesson on the subject of national infection, providing an early and dramatic example. Unlike the infections in Italy and Germany, what happened in Spain shows us the catastrophic consequences of allowing the cult to establish a comfortable foothold in the political establishment. This is why you need to get on top of them earlier, or they will dig right in, and you may not get them out without a bloody struggle.

The cult gathered political momentum via the newly created democratic situation there during the years of instability in the 1920s; the culmination of which was the establishment of the Second Spanish Republic in 1931. This period was essentially a struggle between nationalism and Marxism, during which the cult committed crimes against their 'fascist' enemies (including the clergy and the non-Marxist proletarians); they also predictably attempted to run the country into the ground any way they could when they weren't in control (protests, strike action etc). Obviously, the nationalistic, religious, non-indoctrinated Spanish wanted them out. With more elections and the ensuing nationalist pushback, the events that followed created a horrific conflict.[21] [22]

These events of course culminated in the brutal, bloody Spanish Civil War

---

[20] Franco, F., In discussion with Niceto Alcalá-Zamora, as quoted in Francisco Franco: The Times and the Man (1938) by Joaquin Arraras, P. 159. https://libquotes.com/francisco-franco/quote/lbi7y5y

[21] https://www.britannica.com/place/Spain/Primo-de-Rivera-1923-30-and-the-Second-Republic-1931-36

[22] "Red Terror Spain". https://academic-accelerator.com/encyclopedia/red-terror-spain

(1936–1939). Cult members ('volunteers') came from all over the world to help the 'revolution', with significant support from Stalin's regime in Russia. This war included the murder of thousands of Catholic priests and nuns, who were forced to take up arms. With the victory of nationalist Spain by the end of the conflict (thanks in part to logistical support from Hitler's Germany), General Francisco Franco (1892–1975) emerged as dictator.[23]

I like to call this the 'Spanish' Civil War, because calling it the "Spanish Civil War" is a distortion of the truth. It was a conflict between sane Spanish people and insane/brainwashed Marxist traitors and invaders. Only one side in that conflict was genuinely Spanish, so it was not a civil war. This is the nature of all conflicts of this kind—it divides populations of infected countries between those who are indoctrinated and those who are not.

General Franco blamed communism and freemasonry for what happened to Spain (and both are linked, as mentioned). In a December 1946 article in *Arriba* he wrote "The whole secret of the campaigns unleashed against Spain can be explained in two words: Masonry and Communism… we have to extirpate these two evils from our land".[24]

In September 1945 in a speech to a Falangist group in Madrid, he said "We have torn up Marxist materialism and we have disorientated Masonry. We have thwarted the Satanic machinations of the clandestine Masonic superstate. Despite its control of the world's press and numerous international politicians. Spain's struggle is a Crusade; as soldiers of God we carry with us the evangelism of the world!".[25] Should we call him "General 'conspiracy theorist' Franco"? Or "Franky Conspiracy Theory"?

Franco's Spain was avidly anti-Communist, and he gave the cult no quarter until his death in 1975, suppressing it using arrest, interrogation, torture, and executions. We can see how such regimes attract the eternal wrath of the cult. The generalissimo gave them their third big loss of the era, this time on the world stage, despite the fact he faced the weight of the internationalist Marxist community. In 1977, two years after Franco's

---

[23] https://www.britannica.com/event/Spanish-Civil-War

[24] Franco, F., Writing under the alias Jakin Boor in the journal *Arriba* in an article, "Masonry and Communism" (14 December 1946), as quoted in *Franco: A Biography* by Juan Pablo Fusi Aizpurú?, P. 71. https://libquotes.com/francisco-franco/quote/lbs2d0t

[25] Franco, F., Speech to the women's section of the Falange in Madrid (11 September 1945). https://libquotes.com/francisco-franco/quote/lbp4a9v

death, the ban on the Communist Party of Spain was lifted.

'Fascism' as another form of Marxism

To take up the point made earlier—no, what's called 'fascism' (and the various regimes given this name), were not variations of Marxism. Generally, the 'fascist' regimes were collectivist, of course, but not the same as the cult on an ideological level. Besides, there were several variations of what are termed 'fascist' movements, and the regimes of Mussolini, Hitler, Franco, Salazar (Portugal), Pinochet (Chile) etc. were different to each other.

In fact, to use the term "fascist" in all cases is somewhat of a misnomer. All had alliances with the Roman Catholic Church—the cult's main organisational enemy throughout history—and they were predominantly Christian. They were all focused on keeping their countries intact, and not being part of an internationalist collective that erodes national identity (as the cult is). And most pertinently, they were all anti-Marxist.

Italy

The fascist movement in Italy was about the upliftment of the whole nation not just specifically the working class/proletariat (like in Marxian socialism). Unlike the cult, it was not anti-capitalistic, but sought to bring it under control in service of the nation. Workers strikes were not permitted by the regime (since these are used as a form of anti-capitalistic economic blackmail). We've already examined the downright stupidity of demonising and attacking wealth/the wealthy as the cult does, so these stances were much more rational, and didn't create class-division.

Mussolini gave the definitive definition of fascism in *The Doctrine of Fascism* (1932). It rejected classical liberalism—which placed more emphasis on the individual: "Anti-individualistic, the Fascist conception of life stresses the importance of the State and accepts the individual only in so far as his interests coincide with those of the State. It is opposed to classical liberalism... Liberalism denied the State in the name of the individual; Fascism reasserts".

Obviously, this would only be sensible if the state was ethical; something that those of us in modern western society may struggle to imagine.[26] Fascism was intended as a compromise of strong state power and individual sovereignty, to bring things back in to balance essentially, since

---

[26] Mussolini, B., The Doctrine of Fascism Benito Mussolini (1932), P. 3.

https://ia600800.us.archive.org/14/items/TheDoctrineOfFascismByBenitoMussolini/The Doctrine of Fascism by Benito Mussolini.pdf classical liberalism obviously did/ does nothing to stop Marxism (unlike fascism, which was created to stop it).

As Mussolini wrote, fascism "sees not only the individual but the nation and the country; individuals and generations bound together by a moral law".[27] It also acknowledged superficial hedonism, talking of "suppressing the instinct for life closed in a brief circle of pleasure".[28]

It was opposed to "all Jacobinistic utopias and innovations… it therefore rejects the notion that at some future time the human family will secure a final settlement of all its difficulties".[29] Fascism didn't believe in the Marxian utopia idea, where we all get to hold hands and sing "Kumbaya" together in solidarity across the world, which is another pretty big difference.

It also didn't agree with socialism (underline for emphasis): "No individuals or groups (political parties, cultural associations, economic unions, social classes) (exist) outside the State. Fascism is therefore opposed to socialism to which unity within the State (which amalgamates classes into a single economic and ethical reality) is unknown, and which sees in history nothing but the class struggle. Fascism is likewise opposed to trade unionism as a class weapon. But when brought within the orbit of the State, Fascism recognizes the real needs which gave rise to socialism and trade unionism, giving them due weight in the guild or corporative system in which divergent interests are coordinated and harmonized in the unity of the State".[30]

So not only is Fascism different from the cult/ideology, it aimed to beat it at its own game of improving society (which cult members falsely believe is its raison d'etre). This is another big reason why the cult/ideology is historically hostile towards fascism and considers it a bitter rival.

As a final point on Italian fascism, even at this point, it's easy to see where the cult's/ideology's hatred for its rival comes from, since fascism either opposed or upstaged Marxism. And brats don't like it when they don't get their own way (or don't get the attention they crave).

Germany

"Communism is not socialism. Marxism is not socialism. The Marxians

---

[27] Ibid. P. 2.

[28] Ibid. P. 2.

[29] Ibid. P. 3.

[30] Ibid. P. 3.

have stolen the term and confused its meaning. I shall take socialism away from the socialists.. Marxism has no right to disguise itself as socialism. Unlike Marxism, it involves no negation of personality, and unlike Marxism, it is patriotic. We chose to call ourselves the National Socialists. We are not internationalists. Our socialism is national"[31]

Adolf Hitler, interview with George Sylvester Viereck, Munich, 1923

Of course, some also think that the National Socialism of Germany was just another form of Marxism too; no doubt in part due to the word "Socialist" in their chosen name.

Hitler's Germany—the 'Third Reich'—was an authoritarian state, of course. Yes, there was virtual state control of the means of production in many cases across industry (with strong oversight in others), but their method of doing so was extremely successful (unlike the cult); Germany transformed into an economic powerhouse. It's true that the regime was perhaps the most anti-capitalistic in its rhetoric (compared to other 'fascist' regimes) but not in the way that the Marxist cult is; this was partly because the internationalist 'capitalist' system had not been kind to them (i.e. their nation-crippling WW1 debts imposed by the Treaty of Versailles in 1919).[32] Essentially, they were not stupid enough to destroy their own economic potential/power (as the cult does with their socialism), especially since Germany had been bankrupt post-WW1. Since they placed a strong emphasis on Germany being ethnically German, they have been termed 'ultra-nationalists'—another difference between them and the cult. (considering how the cult fanatically pushes open-borders and mass immigration nowadays, it makes sense they would view them as racist ultra-nationalists, white supremacists etc).

In addition, the National Socialist regime was also a staunch promoter and defender of German culture, in retaliation somewhat to the cult's contamination/desecration of it during the Weimar Republic (the 'pre-Nazi' years). The list (of differences) goes on…

Mr. Hitler

Let's get some words from the horse's mouth for clarification on these issues shall we. Perhaps you've heard of this guy? Widely regarded as the evilest man in history, especially by cult members, Adolf Hitler (1889–1945) was the leader of National Socialist Germany from 1933 until his

---

[31] Hitler, A., interview by George Sylvester Viereck *The American Monthly* (1923).

https://famous-trials.com/hitler/2529-1923-interview-with-adolf-hitler

[32] "Treaty of Versailles". https://www.britannica.com/event/Treaty-of-Versailles-1919

death at the end of WW2.[33] Here's an excerpt from an excellent book by American author Benton L. Bradberry entitled *The Myth of Germany Villany* (2008):

"Hitler had this to say about the meaning of "Socialism" for Germany, as printed in an article in the UK's "Guardian, Sunday Express," December 28, 1938: "'Socialist' I define from the word 'social' meaning in the main 'social equity'. A Socialist is one who serves the common good without giving up his individuality or personality or the product of his personal efficiency. Our adopted term 'Socialist' has nothing to do with Marxian socialism. Marxism is anti-property; true socialism is not. Marxism places no value on the individual, or individual effort, or efficiency; true socialism values the individual and encourages him in individual efficiency, at the same time holding that his interests as an individual must be in consonance with those of the community...It is charged against me that I am against property, that I am an atheist. Both charges are false".[34] I'm sure the reader can see the similarities with the fascist regime in Italy. Indeed, Hitler was inspired by the successes of Mussolini.

"... the Marxist world pest..."

Here's Hitler's prophetic words on democracy and Marxism from his 1925 book *Mein Kampf:* "Democracy, as practised in Western Europe to-day, is the forerunner of Marxism. In fact, the latter would not be conceivable without the former. Democracy is the breeding-ground in which the bacilli of the Marxist world pest can grow and spread".[35] (A quick word search in a PDF reader confirms that book was full of vitriol towards the cult/ideology; an important truth not emphasised in official, politically-correct/Marxist narratives).

If you ever wondered why some peoples in history were 'crazy' enough to support nationalistic dictators, this is why—a democratic system allows the cult to gain political power. Of course, the cult only talks about 'democracy' when they are not in the driving seat, then it's totalitarian Marxism all the way (which non-indoctrinated people across the West are currently finding out).

On 10 February 1933, during his first speech as German chancellor at the Sportpalast, Berlin, Hitler stated "At that time, the fight against Marxism,

---

[33] "Adolf Hitler – dictator of Germany".
https://www.britannica.com/biography/Adolf-Hitler/Rise-to-power

[34] Bradberry. B., *The Myth of Germany Villainy* (2008), P. 148.

[35] Hitler, A., *Mein Kampf* (1925), P. 71.

was, for the first time, declared a battle objective. That was when I first made the vow as an unknown individual, to begin this war and not to rest until this phenomenon is finally eradicated from German life". [36] Revealingly, Nazi banners at this event said "Mach deutschland uom marxismus frei" ("make germany marxism-free"), and "Der marxismus mub sterben domit die nation wieder oufer" ("marxism must die and the nation will rise again").[37] The speech is available on Bitchute ("Adolf Hitler's First Speech"), and excerpts from it have been featured in several Netflix documentaries.

From page 149 of The Myth of German Villainy (edited slightly):"In an article in the Nazi newspaper, "Volkischer Beobachter," May 11, 1933— soon after becoming Chancellor—Hitler wrote: "For fourteen or fifteen years I have continually proclaimed to the German nation that I regard it as my task before posterity to destroy Marxism, and that is a solemn oath which I shall follow as long as I live…We see in Marxism the enemy of our people which we will root out and destroy without mercy… Communism is the forerunner of death, of national destruction, and extinction. We have joined battle with it and will fight it to the death".[38] Hitler delivered on his promise in June 1941, when the Germany military executed Operation Barbarossa—the failed attempt to annihilate the Soviet Union.[39] That attempt to destroy the home of international communism would be the beginning of the end for the Third Reich, as they never held the advantage again in WW2. The result, unfortunately, was that the Soviet Union would survive as the world's main infection point for the cult/ideology (another important fact that's not widely understood).

The successes that Italy and Germany enjoyed under these 'fascist' regimes, and how both countries' leaders were highly respected before WW2 (combined with their brutal suppression of cult members), were certainly major factors to evoke eternal hatred from the cult. The famous WW2 concentration camps were full of cult members, which is often overlooked. This is why they were constructed initially—to house any perceived enemies of the state.

---

[36] Hitler, A., "Proclamation to the German Nation", Sportpalast, Berlin, 10 February 1933.

http://www.emersonkent.com/speeches/proclamation_to_the_german_nation.htm

[37] "Adolf Hitler's First Speech As Reich Chancellor".
https://www.bitchute.com/video/IKpfU2NBnoWc/

[38] Bradberry. B., The Myth of Germany Villainy (2008), P. 149.

[39] https://www.britannica.com/event/Operation-Barbarossa

The hatred these 'fascist' regimes had for the cult/ideology also helps us to understand the scale of the problem we are dealing with today, as it shows us how troublesome and infuriating it was even back in those times. The world has been dealing with these troublemakers largely since the end of WW1, yet today—a quarter way through the 21st century—many are not even fully-aware of the problem, never mind understand its significance! This is beyond disturbing!!

In addition, the confused opinions which conflate the 'fascist' regimes with the cult has helped hide the fact they were bitter enemies, that the cult/ideology was problematic and hated back then too, and that this conflict with Marxism has been raging constantly since the Russian Revolution of 1917.

Pinochet

A notable anti-Marxist in South America, Augusto Pinochet (1915–2006) was a military man who took control of Chile after it became severely infected. His reign began via a military coup against the Marxist establishment in 1973. In a press conference on 11 September of that year he stated: "The armed forces have acted today solely from the patriotic inspiration of saving the country from the tremendous chaos into which it was being plunged by the Marxist government of Salvador Allende".[40]

His seventeen-year reign was particularly brutal, reminiscent of Franco's Spain. He engaged in widespread systematic violence, torture, and execution of cult members. At one point, during Operation Condor (the continent-wide cross-border CIA-backed purge of cult members, mentioned earlier), Pinochet and 'right-wing' allies used 'death flights': cult members were taken up in aircraft and dumped—still alive in some cases—in to a body of water, or over the Andes mountains.[41]

He made several statements on the purge including "We practically wiped this nation clean of Marxists", and "Rome cut off the heads of Christians and they continued to reappear one way or another. Something similar happens with Marxists".[42][43] In a statement on 8 November 1998 he said:

---

[40] Pinochet, A., Press conference (11 September 1973, YouTube.com).

https://libquotes.com/augusto-pinochet/quote/lbs2j2o

[41] "Death Flights". https://academic-accelerator.com/encyclopedia/death-flights

[42] Pinochet, A., Speech (February 23, 1988), quoted in "Las frases para el bronce de Pinochet". https://libquotes.com/augusto-pinochet/quote/lbu2d0v

[43] Pinochet, A., Speech (10 November 1995), quoted in "Las frases para el bronce de Pinochet." https://libquotes.com/augusto-pinochet/quote/lbg5e9a

"I am clear in my mind that the return to Chile of true democracy, and from that the true freedom to which all individual people are entitled, could not have been achieved without the removal of the Marxist government".[44]

Predictably, the perception that Pinochet was a monster has been cultivated by the cult during and since his reign.[45] This is done for the cult's very survival. It's necessary for them to constantly spew hatred for their historical enemies, to prevent the rest of us from ever eventually taking similar brutal action against them.

So henceforth whenever we hear them talking about "suppression of free speech", "human rights", "fascism", "authoritarianism", and "dictatorships" etc. this is why they are doing it (consciously or unconsciously)—for their own survival. They want to continue with being insane cult members, and therefore destroying humanity unopposed, with no punishment of any kind.

The World Wars as a propaganda tool

The WW2 period has been turned in to a highly effective propaganda tool which greatly assists the cult/ideology. The constant emphasis/re-emphasis on that period—and Hitler's Germany in particular—serves a few purposes: it hides the crimes of the cult throughout the 20th century by deflecting attention away from it, and it helps to associate any ideas of genuine national sovereignty, nationalism or patriotism with evil acts. It re-enforces the idea that "if you are not Marxist, you are evil!" (hence them labelling anti-globalist nationalists "Nazi scum").

Is it possible that the globalist internationalists don't want the general public knowing the hidden anti-Marxist truth about the 'fascist' regimes of the 20th century, because it could potentially be a tremendous morale boost for nationalistic patriots all around the world today?

Also, it would create tremendous anger towards the liars and pseudo-intellectuals who have not informed the general public about this truth, either due to ignorance, narrow-mindedness, indoctrination, or outright deception.

---

[44] Pinochet, A., Statement, November 08, 1998.
https://www.azquotes.com/quote/1096354

[45] https://en.wikipedia.org/wiki/Augusto_Pinochet

Section XIII—Epilogue: A Zombie Apocalypse

"Zombies of the world unite! We have nothing to eat but your brains!"

Marl Karx

"You've got red on you"[1]

Shaun of the Dead, 2004

A red zombie world war

Zombie movies are a great analogy for our current global predicament, and there have been many over the decades. I see them as being prophetic, apocalyptic foreshadowing. In today's world, we have some who are infected, and others who are not, just like in those movies. Zombies are not truly alive, but they are kind of alive—there are signs of life—just like cult members. They are not equal to those who are not infected, of course, in terms of consciousness (as outlined earlier; how truly present/aware/intelligent someone is). Zombies can infect others, by 'turning' them when they make contact (via touch, bite etc. depending on the film); similar to how the brainwashed 'infected' cult members influence/contaminate their 'victims'—the naive, and as yet uninfected. They may use violence against their enemies, or instigate others to violence; but most of the time, is it not psychological? They will try to drain your mental energy, enthusiasm, and morale. Eating away at your mind essentially.

We are all in an ideological, psychological, spiritual World War against a global army of zombie-like brainwashed 'people'. The image of the infected eating the brains of the uninfected is symbolic—it's the 'devouring' of human consciousness by zombie-like behaviour. When seeing the world in terms of indoctrination and lack of consciousness, these movies take on a whole new meaning. Zombies are dumb and are essentially missing something, this is why they eat brains—they need yours because they don't

---

[1] "You've Got Red on You", *Shaun of the Dead* (2004)

https://www.YouTube.com/watch?v=T1GYsCMCLpo

have any.

Call them Marxist cult members

It's time for us all to acknowledge and speak the truth, en masse. Generally, as a society, we are not being honest and direct enough with them about their cult membership. This is an issue we all personally need to address in our lives if we have the constitution to do so. We may have to be direct, even brutally honest. This is not the time to worry about being 'polite' and sparing people's feelings! There's nothing noble about being 'nice' if doing so hastens the collapse of the world around you; you have no right to claim such a status in this instance.

We all need to start confronting the indoctrination/indoctrinated head-on, telling them what they are doing is wrong, and why they are doing it. They need to be told that they are hypocrites too, since they often 'oppress' the rest of us while they're being glorious revolutionaries (while assuming they are acting in an anti-oppression manner). In many cases, we shouldn't do this and then expect positive results in the person we are dealing with. Not to necessarily convince or 'de-brainwash', no, since this is futile in many cases.

Rather, we should just confront on principle. Those who are capable of 'snapping out of it' will; those who can't show us they are beyond redemption, which helps us to draw that line in the sand (it also often repels them from you to your benefit). We'll also do it to create social pressure, to suppress and humiliate, and to make it socially uncomfortable to openly be a cult member, to starve the movement of its cultish social oxygen. This will be the great challenge of the modern age; nay, the greatest challenge humanity has ever faced...

Advice to parents: keeping children immune

> "If your heart remains pure and beats in a purely human way, and no demonic spirit is capable of estranging your heart from finer feelings— only then would I find the happiness that for many years past I have dreamed of finding through you; otherwise I would see the finest aim of my life in ruins"[2]

> An 1837 letter from Heinrich Marx to his demon-possessed son, who was already too far gone...

This advice only applies to parents who are not themselves contaminated,

---

[2] Marxists.org, "Letter from Heinrich Marx to son Karl", 1837

https://marxists.architexturez.net/archive/marx/letters/papa/1837-fl2.htm

of course. Beware of anyone working with, or on behalf of, the state! Especially watch out for those in an 'educational' or influential capacity. The odds are high that they've received a contaminated Marxist education, and they will then pass this on to your children. Parents also need, unfortunately, to keep an eye on anyone else who could influence their child. This can come from friends, relations, co-workers, team-mates at sports etc., and let's not forget media, entertainment, and social media influences! Your work is cut out for you...

It's a tragedy when a parent loses their child to Marxist brainwashing (unless they themselves are already indoctrinated). The scummy ideology even causes division within families. So, parents need to be vigilant and protect their children from the cult/ideology, in addition to all the usual, basic responsibilities of parenting such as: providing food, shelter, clothing, protection, and the other responsibilities (not delivered in many cases) such as teaching them about love, health, discipline, confidence, patience, humility etc. This really is a shitty environment to raise a child in for so many reasons, but nevertheless we must be vigilant, and these things must be done. The landscape is much more toxic and arguably more complex than ever, but keeping children immune is essential or the future is lost...

Any rational, sane parent would protect their children from an attacker, a paedophile, or someone else who would cause them harm. Responsible parents must now start to view Marxist cult members in this way, or anyone they may suspect of being one, including: teachers and professors at all levels; government employees; community organisers; social workers etc. Suspicion, in this case is, very useful. Everyone must be vetted for Marxist indoctrination before they are allowed contact with the young.

Of course, as mentioned throughout, a person (parent or not) needs to understand the ideology/cult sufficiently in order to identify who is a cult member and who isn't! So, in addition to all the other responsibilities of the parent mentioned above, they must devote some time to studying and understanding this subject.

A book such as this is an ideal starting point. It's my wish that parents arm themselves with this knowledge, in order to make good judgement calls on who their children interact with, and what information they are exposed to. Consider this knowledge/training a wise investment; an 'upgrade' to your personality for the sake of our children.

In an old documentary (name I can't recall) about what happened in Cambodia with Pol Pot and his fellow Khmer Rouge cult members, a woman said that she raised her son well, but yet he still went to work for Pol Pot; they still managed to indoctrinate him. This raises a point—many parents before may not have been able to prepare for this, as they were not aware of the Marxist threat. Of course, there are plenty of parents out there who've raised their kids 'well', but without being aware of the ideology and the risk of indoctrination, their kids may still fall victim to it. This is the tragedy of the situation, unfortunately. Therefore, we can't be too vigilant.

There is a predator out there in the world—a hidden, complex, psychological predator, that can pray on anyone, but the young are especially at risk. We must forgive the well-intentioned parents of the past for not being able to see this coming down the tracks. It's difficult for the everyday person to even see that this monster exists in our world, never mind galvanise their children against it. Having said that, it's important for this message to reach as many parents as possible, so no-one can claim they simply weren't informed. We all need to ensure that this is not an acceptable excuse.

The zombie reviews

Of course, some will acknowledge the value of this work. Many will either not do so or will in fact actively try to tarnish it, thereby protecting the cult/ideology (wittingly or unwittingly). In this way, the impact of the book may be suppressed. The more fervent the anticipated impact, the greater the suppressive attack by cult members. Of course, they will use the usual bitchy criticism, and there will be predictable reviews on various Marxist platforms (websites, papers, shows, podcasts etc.). They will highlight any sort of perceived weaknesses in it and exaggerate them, in addition to being petty by finding any errors/perceived errors or engage in general mocking. They will futilely try to fabricate, dig-up, exaggerate and repeat anything they can use about the author.

If this book is being discussed via certain media (or wherever you can see a collective response), you will notice the following comments that are the usual 'criticisms' used by the offended zombies; some being more overtly Marxist and some apparently 'neutral' ones: "that's not what Marxism is! He doesn't even know what it means!"; "well, I agree with him on certain points, but not on others"; "He's blaming everything on Marxism!"; "He's confusing Marxism/socialism with communism/Stalinism/Marxism-Leninism!"; "Written like a true fascist. 2 stars"; "He repeats things!"; "Has he actually read Marx and Engels?!?"; Words to the effect of "Many experts disagree with (this or that point) so how can you take this book seriously"; the book is "hyperbolic" or "conspiracy theory nonsense!, or "I stopped reading after page (X) because of a mistake about (Y)" etc. etc.

They will do all this because, deep down, they are upset. They are upset that they—and their (erroneous) worldview—are being criticised. This kind of petty venom can only emanate from one with no semblance of a spine, deep-down. The childish element is a mixture of being upset, arrogance, pseudo-intellectualism etc. We witness this manifesting in the vitriol—there is no ability to control the emotions. These kinds of reactions to the book prove that it is correct, in addition to proving that it's important and needed.

If these types of reactions are attempts to suppress the book, then they could not be more self-sabotaging. Every time the indoctrinated types try this, they only expose themselves more for what they are. They also encourage people like us to expose them more. The burial tomb of Karl Marx features the grandiose statement ""Philosophers have only interpreted the world, in various ways; the point, however, is to change it".[3] Sure, only if you can do so in a positive way. In this respect, Marx and the Marxist cult are the eternal failures.

As for those who are not necessarily indoctrinated but who hinder the book's impact, they are a problem too. There is a lack of ability in society to acknowledge the truth. Often ego and/or excessive intellectualism can get in the way, as a person puts their own personal gratification above what's best for the group. This is a tendency that the cult/ideology can take full advantage of, as it wants this reaction from/to its foes. It loves the idea that the reactions to this book may be divergent; the more divergent they are, the less of a threat the book's ideas are to the cult/ideology.

Put it this way—when we are living in a society where what is true and beneficial is treated with a collective acknowledgement/support, and given the respect it deserves, we are living in a society where you will see positive change. It really is up to the individuals involved in public discourse on this issue to have the required maturity, intelligence, and courage, to put themselves in service to the truth. They must put everything else aside—including egotistical intellectualisms—and propel the message of this book forward any way they can, for the sake of all.

---

[3] https://en.wikipedia.org/wiki/Tomb_of_Karl_Marx

Index

Korean War, 32, 78, 79, 157

Labour Party, 107, 113, 114, 116, 117, 118, 125, 126, 127, 128, 129, 133, 134, 145, 146, 148, 149, 152, 154, 161, 164, 165, 168, 245, 249, 250, 251, 256, 258, 268, 343, 378, 436, 529, 530, 559

League of Nations, 251, 568

Lenin, V.I., 24, 32, 43, 48, 62, 64, 68, 71, 98, 106, 232, 323

LGBTQ, 1, 40, 46, 47, 216, 228, 231, 236, 238, 292, 330, 332, 343, 363, 365, 383, 400, 411, 436, 441, 443, 444, 445, 446, 452, 466, 469, 471, 472, 474, 475, 481, 498, 551, 552, 562, 563, 572, 582

Liberal, 22, 60, 70, 102, 111, 139, 165, 255, 258

Liberalism, 39, 40, 41, 42, 43, 249, 323, 595

Liebknecht, Karl, 591, 592

Little Red Book, 31, 77

London, 6, 16, 133, 144, 169, 229, 230, 231, 245, 249, 250, 251, 253, 257, 259, 309, 328, 329, 330, 353, 473, 478, 487, 517, 519, 534, 574, 578, 584

London School of Economics, 253, 257

Los Angeles, 6, 283, 289, 419, 479, 586

Lucifer, 215, 223, 306, 539, 574

Lukacs, Gyorgy, 33, 209, 261

Luxemburg, Rosa, 98, 221, 369, 591, 592

Luxemburgism, 24

Lyotard, Jean-Francois, 270, 272, 276

Mandela, Nelson, 136, 137, 138, 231, 259, 342

Maoism, 24, 25, 77, 98, 169, 374, 473

Marcuse, Herbert, 50, 221, 259, 260, 262, 263, 264, 266, 267, 268, 269, 270, 272, 282, 473

Martin, Michael, 462

Marx, Eleanor, 246, 348

Marx, Karl, 8, 12, 24, 28, 48, 63, 66, 98, 183, 184, 198, 209, 210, 246, 250, 263, 371, 520, 590

Marxism-Leninism, 24, 32, 82, 98, 169, 290, 406, 605

Mass Immigration, 14, 177, 187, 199, 204, 218, 238, 317, 352, 359, 366, 386, 394, 395, 400, 409, 410, 424, 427, 429, 438, 444, 445, 447, 448, 449, 451, 452, 454, 455, 457, 458, 465, 466, 541, 582, 597

Matrix, 312

Other titles

OMNIA VERITAS

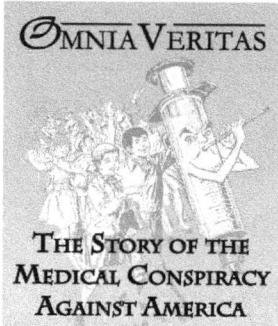

Omnia Veritas Ltd presents:

MURDER BY INJECTION

THE STORY OF THE MEDICAL CONSPIRACY AGAINST AMERICA

by

EUSTACE MULLINS

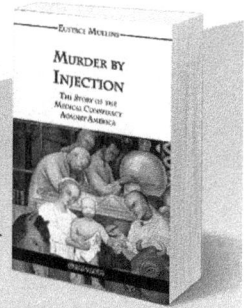

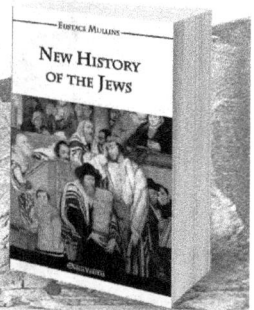

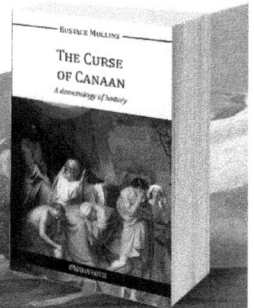

MURDER BY INJECTION
The Story of the Medical Conspiracy Against America

The cynicism and malice of these conspirators is something beyond the imagination of most Americans.

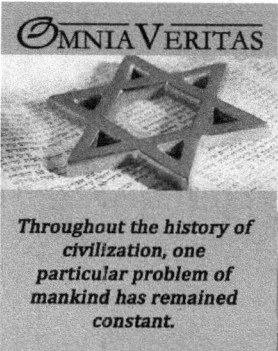

OMNIA VERITAS

Omnia Veritas Ltd presents:

NEW HISTORY OF THE JEWS

Throughout the history of civilization, one particular problem of mankind has remained constant.

by

EUSTACE MULLINS

NEW HISTORY OF THE JEWS

Only one people has irritated its host nations in every part of the civilized world

OMNIA VERITAS

Omnia Veritas Ltd presents:

THE CURSE OF CANAAN

A demonology of history

Liberalism, more popularly known as secular humanism, can be traced in an unbroken line all the way back to the Biblical "Curse of Canaan."

by

EUSTACE MULLINS

THE CURSE OF CANAAN
A demonology of history

Humanism is the logical result of the demonology of history

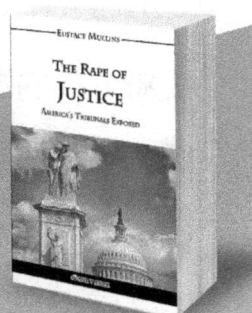

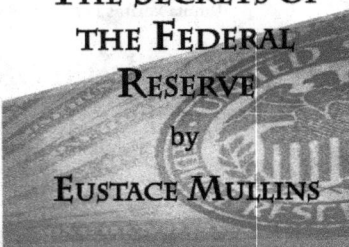

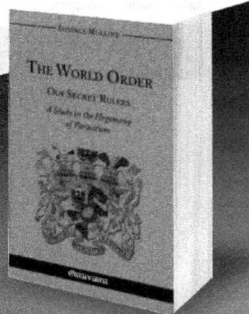

OMNIA VERITAS
OMNIA VERITAS LTD PRESENTS:
DRUG WAR against AMERICA
The drug trade cannot be eradicated because its directors will not allow the world's most lucrative market to be taken away from them...
BY JOHN COLEMAN
JOHN COLEMAN
DRUG WAR against AMERICA
The real promoters of this cursed trade are the "elites" of this world.

OMNIA VERITAS
OMNIA VERITAS LTD PRESENTS:
FREEMASONRY
from A to Z
by John Coleman
In the 21st century, Freemasonry has become less a secret society than a "society of secrets".
JOHN COLEMAN
FREEMASONRY from A to Z
This book explains what masonry is

OMNIA VERITAS
OMNIA VERITAS LTD PRESENTS:
THE ROTHSCHILD DYNASTY
by John Coleman
JOHN COLEMAN
THE ROTHSCHILD DYNASTY
Historical events are often caused by a "hidden hand"...

OMNIA VERITAS LTD PRESENTS:

ONE WORLD ORDER
SOCIALIST
DICTATORSHIP

BY JOHN COLEMAN

All these years, while our attention was focused on the evils of communism in Moscow, the socialists in Washington were busy stealing from America!

"The enemy in Washington is more to be feared than the enemy in Moscow."

OMNIA VERITAS LTD PRESENTS :

WE FIGHT FOR OIL

BY JOHN COLEMAN

The story of the oil industry takes us into the twists and turns of "diplomacy".

The struggle to monopolize the resource coveted by all nations

OMNIA VERITAS LTD PRESENTS:

THE HIDDEN AUTHORS
of the
FRENCH REVOLUTION

by HENRI POGGET DE SAINT-ANDRÉ

It seems," Robespierre once said to Amar, "that we are being carried away by an invisible hand beyond our control..."

The more we study the history of the French Revolution, the more we come up against enigmas....

OMNIA VERITAS
OMNIA VERITAS LTD PRESENTS
THE DISPOSSESSED MAJORITY
THE DISPOSSESSED MAJORITY
THE TRAGIC AND HUMILIATING FATE OF THE AMERICAN MAJORITY

OMNIA VERITAS
OMNIA VERITAS LTD PRESENTS:
SCARLET AND THE BEAST
My research has revealed that there are two separate and opposing powers in Freemasonry...
SCARLET AND THE BEAST
One is Scarlet. The other, the Beast.
A HISTORY OF THE WAR BETWEEN ENGLISH AND FRENCH FREEMASONRY

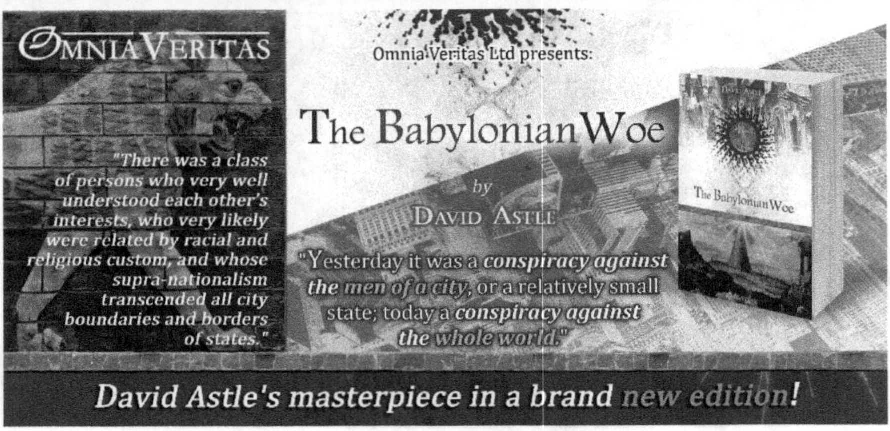
OMNIA VERITAS
Omnia Veritas Ltd presents:
The Babylonian Woe
by
DAVID ASTLE
"There was a class of persons who very well understood each other's interests, who very likely were related by racial and religious custom, and whose supra-nationalism transcended all city boundaries and borders of states."
"Yesterday it was a conspiracy against the men of a city, or a relatively small state; today a conspiracy against the whole world."
The Babylonian Woe
David Astle's masterpiece in a brand new edition!

OMNIA VERITAS

Omnia Veritas Ltd presents:

FREDERICK SODDY

THE ROLE OF MONEY

WHAT IT SHOULD BE CONTRASTED WITH WHAT IT HAS BECOME

This book attempts to clear up the mystery of money in its social aspect

This, surely, is what the public really wants to know about money

OMNIA VERITAS

Omnia Veritas Ltd presents:

FREDERICK SODDY

WEALTH, VIRTUAL WEALTH AND DEBT

The most powerful tyranny and the most universal conspiracy against the economic freedom of individuals and the autonomy of nations the world has yet known.

THE SOLUTION OF THE ECONOMIC PARADOX

The public are most carefully shielded from any real knowledge...

OMNIA VERITAS

Omnia Veritas Ltd presents:

It is no wonder that Wahhabis are now the backbone of terrorism, authorising, financing and planning the shedding of the blood of Muslims and other innocents.

British enmity against Islam

Confessions of a **BRITISH SPY**

This document reveals the true context of the Wahhabi movement

* 9 7 8 1 8 0 5 4 0 1 6 6 7 *